October 27–31, 2012
Sanibel Island, Florida

I0060956

**Association for
Computing Machinery**

Advancing Computing as a Science & Profession

GROUP'12

Proceedings of the ACM 2012 International Conference on
Support Group Work

Sponsored by:
ACM SIGCHI

Supported by:
Microsoft Research & National Science Foundation

**Association for
Computing Machinery**

Advancing Computing as a Science & Profession

The Association for Computing Machinery
2 Penn Plaza, Suite 701
New York, New York 10121-0701

Notice to Past Authors of ACM-Published Articles
ACM intends to create a complete electronic archive of all articles and/or other material previously published by ACM. If you have written a work that has been previously published by ACM in any journal or conference proceedings prior to 1978, or any SIG Newsletter at any time, and you do NOT want this work to appear in the ACM Digital Library, please inform permissions@acm.org, stating the title of the work, the author(s), and where and when published.

ISBN: 978-1-4503-1486-2 (Digital)

ISBN: 978-1-4503-1928-7 (Print)

Additional copies may be ordered prepaid from:

ACM Order Department
PO Box 30777
New York, NY 10087-0777, USA

Phone: 1-800-342-6626 (USA and Canada)
+1-212-626-0500 (Global)
Fax: +1-212-944-1318
E-mail: acmhelp@acm.org
Hours of Operation: 8:30 am – 4:30 pm ET

Printed in the USA

GROUP 2012 Welcome Message from the Conference Co-Chairs

It is our great pleasure to welcome you to the *2012 ACM International Conference on Supporting Group Work – GROUP'12*. This is the 17th gathering in this influential international conference series which despite sporadic name changes – from Organizational Information Systems, to Organizational Computing Systems, to Group – remains focused on the challenges of evaluating and developing socio-technical systems to support collaborative work among individuals, within and across groups, organizations, and geo-political boundaries. We find ourselves again on lovely Sanibel Island, Florida. We are very pleased with the commitment to GROUP by our colleagues who have generously contributed their time and effort to organize the conference, review papers, lead the Doctoral Colloquium, convene workshops, chair sessions, and be student volunteers. The conference would not be possible without their efforts.

The GROUP'12 call for papers attracted 94 submissions (64 papers and 30 notes) from Asia, Latin America, Europe, and North America. The program committee accepted 24 papers and 11 notes covering a wide variety of topics including: awareness and avatars – visualizing speech, workflow and identity; understanding collaboration in organizations; citizen science and healthcare – real world communities; collaborative systems and group editing; cross-cultural chat, file sync and real-time dating; behavior patterns in online communities; understanding information in social media; and methods for understanding and supporting online communities. In addition to two pre-conference workshops, we are able to host our fourth Doctoral Colloquium. Generous funding from the National Science Foundation allows us to bring together advanced Ph.D. students from around the world for a full-day program of interaction with leading researchers in our field. During the poster session you will be able to see what these students are working on, and you will also find posters from other researchers in academia and industry.

Organizing GROUP'12 has been a truly international collaborative effort. First of all, we would like to deeply thank our technical program team led by Kori Inkpen (Microsoft Research) and Tom Gross (University of Bamburg) as program co-chairs; Volker Wulf (University of Siegen) and Jennifer Thom-Santelli (IBM TJ Watson Research) as panel co-chairs; Libby Hemphill (Illinois Institute of Technology) and Stephan Lukosch (Delft University of Technology) as poster co-chairs; Luigina Ciolfi (Limerick University) and Gregorio Convertino (Xerox Research Center Europe, Grenoble) as workshop co-chairs. We are also grateful to Dan Cosley (Cornell University), Aleksandra Sarcevic (Drexel University), Dave Randall (Manchester Metropolitan University) and Pernille Bjørn (IT University Copenhagen) for chairing the Doctoral Colloquium. We acknowledge the hard work of David Gurzick (Hood College) as webmaster, Sean Goggins (Drexel University) and Isa Janke (Umeâ University) as our publicity co-chairs and indefatigable masters of all social media. We also thank Stephen Hayne (Colorado State University) who as the treasurer, once again kept a watchful eye on our finances, Stephanie Teasley (University of Michigan) who took care of local arrangements, and Norman Su (University College Dublin) who was in charge of organizing the production of the proceedings. Xiaomu Zhou (Rutgers University) recruited and organized the important cadre of student volunteers. We appreciate the work of Lisa Tolles and her team at Sheridan Printing Company for assembling our proceedings on a tight timetable. We would like to express our gratitude to the 35-member international program committee and additional external reviewers who expertly critiqued our submissions in order to provide constructive feedback to all authors.

Finally, we would like to thank our sponsors for their continued support of these successful conferences. We hope that you will find this program interesting and thought provoking, and that you will be able to take advantage of this wonderful opportunity to be inspired as you share and discuss ideas with colleagues from around the world on the beautiful Gulf Coast.

Hilda Tellioğlu
GROUP'12 General Chair
Vienna University of Technology, Austria

Thomas A. Finholt
GROUP'12 General Chair
University of Michigan, USA

Table of Contents

Session 1: Awareness & Avatars - Visualizing Speech, Workflow & Identity
Session Chair: Volker Wulf *(University of Siegen)*

Session 2: Understanding Collaboration in Organizations
Session Chair: Sasa Junuzovic *(Microsoft Research)*

Session 3: Citizen Science & Healthcare - Real World Communities
Session Chair: Madhu Reddy *(Penn State University)*

Session 4: Collaborative Systems & Group Editing
Session Chair: Marcos R. S. Borges *(Federal University of Rio de Janeiro)*

Session 5: *Best of Group* Backchannels, Cross-Cultural Chat, File Sync & Real-Time Dating
Session Chair: Stephanie Teasley *(University of Michigan)*

Session 6: Behaviour Patterns in Online Communities
Session Chair: Sean Goggins *(Drexel University)*

Session 7: Understanding Information in Social Media
Session Chair: Isa Jahnke *(Umeå University)*

Session 8: Methods for Understanding & Supporting Online Communities
Session Chair: Louise Barkhuus *(Stockholm University)*

Doctoral Colloquium

Posters

Workshops

GROUP 2012 Conference Organization

General Chairs: Thomas A. Finholt *(University of Michigan, USA)*
Hilda Tellioğlu *(Vienna University of Technology, Austria)*

Program Chairs: Kori Inkpen *(Microsoft Research, USA)*
Tom Gross *(University of Bamburg, Germany)*

Panels Chairs: Volker Wulf *(University of Siegen, Germany)*
Jennifer Thom-Santelli *(IBM TJ Watson Research, USA)*

Poster Chairs: Libby Hemphill *(Illinois Institute of Technology, USA)*
Stephan Lukosch *(Delft University of Technology, Nederlands)*

Workshop Chairs: Luigina Ciolfi *(University of Limerick, Ireland)*
Gregorio Convertino *(Xerox Research Center Europe (XRCE), France)*

Doctoral Colloquium Chairs: Dan Cosley *(Cornell University, USA)*
Dave Randall *(Manchester Metropolitan University, UK)*
Aleksandra Sarcevic *(Drexel University, USA)*
Pernille Bjorn *(IT University Copenhagen, Denmark)*

Proceedings Chair: Norman Su *(University College Dublin, Ireland)*

Local Arrangements Chair: Stephanie Teasley *(University of Michigan, USA)*

Publicity Chairs: Sean P. Goggins *(Drexel University, USA)*
Isa Jahnke *(Umeâ University, Sweden)*

Treasurer & Registration Chair: Stephen C. Hayne *(Colorado State University, USA)*

Webmaster: David Gurzick *(Hood College, USA)*

Student Volunteer: Xiaomu Zhou *(Rutgers University, USA)*

GROUP 2012 Sponsor & Supporters

Sponsor:  SIGCHI

Supporters:

Can a Table Regulate Participation in Top Level Managers' Meetings?

Flaviu Roman
Ecole Polytechnique Fédérale
de Lausanne (EPFL)
Lausanne, Switzerland
flaviu.roman@epfl.ch

Stefano Mastrogiacomo
Université de Lausanne
(UNIL),
Lausanne, Switzerland
smastrog@unil.ch

Dyna Mlotkowski
Banque Priveé Edmond de
Rothschild
Geneva, Switzerland
dmlotkowski@bper.ch

Frédéric Kaplan
Ecole Polytechnique Fédérale
de Lausanne (EPFL)
Lausanne, Switzerland
frederic.kaplan@epfl.ch

Pierre Dillenbourg
Ecole Polytechnique Fédérale
de Lausanne (EPFL)
Lausanne, Switzerland
pierre.dillenbourg@epfl.ch

ABSTRACT

We present a longitudinal study on the participation regulation effects in the presence of a speech aware interactive table. This study focuses on training meetings of groups of top level managers, whose compositions do not change, in a corporate organization. We show that an effect of balancing participation develops over time. We also report other emerging group-specific features such as interaction patterns and signatures, leadership effects, and behavioral changes between meetings. Finally we collect feedback from the participants and analyze qualitatively the human and social aspects of the participants interaction mediated by the technology.

Categories and Subject Descriptors

D.5.3 [**Group and Organization Interfaces**]: Collaborative computing, Computer supported cooperative work, Synchronous interaction; H.5.2 [**User Interfaces**]: Graphical User Interfaces

General Terms

Experimentation, Human Factors

Keywords

Meetings, Visualization, Group Evolution, Human Computer Interaction

1. INTRODUCTION

A large amount of effort has been devoted lately to meetings techniques and tools, to improve their effectiveness in light of the increase of costs and decrease of productivity visible in many meetings. In this study, we evaluate the use of a previously developed technology called the Reflect Table [1] bundled with a new meeting analysis software (ReflectVisualizations), which we use as awareness and support tools for groups of top level managers in training sessions. We present new results of the influence of this technology and some insights about group dynamics over time. The outcomes of this new "real world" study are also checked against the outcomes of previous studies of the Reflect Table in controlled environments of undergraduate students' face to face encounters. We measure speech participation awareness and analyze its effects on balancing, by making this information available to the participants during the meeting, in the form of ratios of speech times. This is done without suggesting any form of regulation. Rather, the group members, when presented with this type of evidence, are responsible for applying self-regulation if and how they see fit, while meeting researchers can observe and analyze if the presence of this extended knowledge about their habits did trigger behavioral changes or not. Therefore, the group is responsible for its own regulation criteria.

1.1 Motivation. Balanced Participation.

In all organizations, face to face meetings are ubiquitous events. However, many of them fall short of their intended goals, and when it comes to collaborative learning, unbalanced participation leads to poor outcome for some attendants. A comprehensive analysis by Romano and Nunamaker [18] quantitatively breaks down the meetings problems and outcomes, with the goal of identifying and classifying practices and causes that lead to the sub-optimality of the meetings outcomes with respect to their goals. Among these are participation imbalance, overdue lengths due to poor time management, impaired agenda management, suboptimal preparation or lack of appropriate participants skills in conducting efficient meetings.

Balanced participation is thus one of the factors that lead to poor performance of meetings, and it is the chosen topic of interest for this study. Papers by Salomon [19], and Webster [22] discuss about socio-psychological causes that risk prevent team members from engaging equally into collaborative activities. In terms of learning, Cohen [9] investigates productivity and outcomes, concluding that collaborative exchanges are necessary for conceptual learning effectiveness, and that the more individuals participate, the more they learn. Hoyles [13] shows that verbalization is important in formation and fixation of concepts in the context of learning, therefore reduced participation can negatively impact the learning gain. Also, Huber [14] claims that both in the context of trainings and of problem solving, adequate information sharing plays an essential role because existing participants holding critical information or expertise but not sharing it will yield substandard aftereffects of those meetings.

Bettenhausen [7] studied the development of norms in newly formed groups, and found that members use their past experiences in similar social settings as scripts for choosing behaviors in their current situation. Another important contribution in what regards the way individuals in groups influence each other is done by Hackman [12] who concludes that ambient stimuli, discretionary stimuli and structure of group norms represent types of influences on individuals.

1.2 Related Work

Various academic researchers have devoted themselves to creating technological tools to assist the meeting process, both online (during the meeting) and offline (as post-meeting visualization of meeting data). The Meeting Mediator [16], which requires users to wear a sociometric badge, and the Agent Augmented Meeting [11], which creates virtual participants are such tools, and while researchers have proved their utility, we consider these methods to be too intrusive and interrupt the natural flow of the interaction in a meeting. We intend to follow a less-intrusive direction, of soft computing, latent technology and background or peripheral vision displays. In these lines, a metaphoric group mirror system was developed by Streng [21] that uses image metaphores to present insights from discussions. Similar work has been done by Bergstrom and Karahalios [5], whose time visualization patterns have the advantage of showing time evolution, but whose sizes are difficult to assess and matching a color with its corresponding participants is a challenge. In a similar manner, they also designed a contribution value voting system [6]. Skog, Ljungblad and Holmquist [20] produced a visualization system, where the data visualized contains, among other information, reports about speech time in meetings; they project these images on on a vertical space or wall. DiMicco [10] created various types of information displays and evaluated their impact on the participants, finding that introduction to the display and no feedback redundancies were the most valued properties.

Among offline meetings support and analysis or data retrieval tools we can mention Nijholt's Meeting Information Visualization [17], and Hunter's MemTable [15]. Some of these solutions are still constrained by the portability of the technology, i.e. data can only be obtained from meetings held in a special room.

Most of these works suffer from one shortcoming present in our previous works as well: the lack of a real world study. This paper capitalizes on this by studying and evaluating our technology for the first time in the wild.

1.3 Paper Structure

The remainder of the paper is structured as follows: Section 2 describes the technology we used to support this user study of meetings, including the new modules and increments from previous versions (a new graphical visualization tool for post-meeting support and analysis), previous results in controlled environments of graduate students, and the methodology used in this study. Section 3 dissects the results and goes in-depth into analyzing the observations, while sections 4 and 5 discuss future development directions and conclusions of this research.

2. TECHNOLOGY AND METHODOLOGY

The Reflect Table [1] (Fig. 1) was created to be a *background*, *unobtrusive* and *normative-neutral* tool for in meetings *participation awareness*. The aim is to only be a mirror of the group interaction, presenting objective data, and remaining completely neutral in terms of judging the quality of discussions or group cooperation.

Figure 1: Reflect Table (from [1])

Unobtrusiveness is a key factor of the design aimed at keeping the communication flow as natural as possible. As opposed to private displays, the shared semi-ambient display was preferred for its capacity of integration into the table surface, and to relieve the participants from actively seeking information. This way, a breakdown of the speech times is presented in background of the active view area. The shared display reinforces the group mirror characteristic of the table. Participants have access to the values of speech time relative to each other, as well as to the link between the identity of each speaker and its relative speech time. The identity recall proves to be an important element in the qualitative assessment of the study.

2.1 Reflect Table: Technical Description

The technology relies on a physical 6-persons shaped table. Inside it contains a computer with input for speech capturing by means of a triangle array of microphones, and two special led panels with a total of 16x8 LEDs for output display (Fig. 1).

The LEDs use a technology that allows them to light up in different colors, based on a command sent through a device driver. The LED panels are used for dis-playing real-time meeting information. Each user has his/her corresponding color based in front of his position. The panels are smaller than the area of the table, so participants can still make use of paper documents or physical objects without disrupting the visibility of the LEDs. This display has several selectable modes, and in our current study we are using two of them: a hidden mode (nothing displayed while engine still running), and a territorial mode (Fig. 1). In this mode the LEDs display a territory in front of each participant, which accounts for the total speech ratio of his/her speech time with respect to the total detected speech. The participants can switch modes by gently touching the microphones on the top, which generates a recognizable waveform interpreted as a command.

The microphone array uses a triangulation algorithm that detects the speaker's direction based on comparing the time shifts of speech detected by the three microphones, and using this information to reconstruct the direction. The central placement of the microphones ensures that the space in front of the participants is freed from technical elements, thus they can use it for their natural interaction [4]. Another advantage of this design is that the time consistency of detection is guaranteed by the detection of a unique speaker from multiple sources.

The microphones acquire the signal, retain the speech duration from each direction (identifying each participant), and pass the waveforms to a speech features detection module [8] which computes some voice features (like pitch and its variance, intensity, speech rate, etc.). An average of the normalization of these 4 features is then used to compute the instant voice arousal or engagement. Apart from displaying a synthesis using the LEDs, the table is also a logger, by saving information to data files which are only kept internally, therefore offering no online connectivity.

2.2 Reflect Visualizations: Meetings Analysis Software

There are some inherent limitations that arise from the Reflect Table's creation as intelligent furniture, and from its design which targets a very specific setting. Also the previous studies did not benefit from support for complex offline analysis of data (which was done manually). The table itself cannot act as a comprehensive post-meeting display surface because it only has a few output LEDs, which do not offer the appropriate resolution required by such displays. Also, currently there is no study in an uncontrolled environment use of the Reflect Table, which is covered by this paper for the first time.

We came to the creation of a software that we called ReflectVisualizations to address the offline visualization limitations of the Reflect Table. We acknowledged the need for a more automated analysis tool (as opposed to manually using Excel or other software able to produce visualizations), as a module that can automatically process the table's specific logs to help distinguish characteristics that are easier to observe from visualizing data in a graphical form. The purpose of this tool is to be bundled with the Reflect Table to enable more in-depth analysis of meetings, and capacitate group evolution studies, by integrating data from several meetings with the same attendance composition.

2.2.1 Concept

We designed the software as a leverage for the meetings analysis we perform, but also to be distributed to different categories of people involved in the process, namely the facilitators (if any) and the participants themselves, taking into account the need for interoperability, scalability, and dissemination requirements. The tool was created using C#

on .net platform, using several custom made controls along with other open source libraries, including the complex Zed-Graph library for evolution plots. Other plots are made by an engine drawing directly on the canvas.

We chose to split the available frame into three sectors, according to the type of visualization we wanted to display. The following types were created: *table replay*, which aims to reproduce the display on the table, *table syntheses*, which shows in a graphical way some interaction features, and *evolution graphs*, which show the evolution of interaction on several scopes.

2.2.2 Table Replay and Syntheses

The upper left part of the ReflectVisualization screen shows a reconstruction of the table display in time. Here one can review the display of the table at any chosen moment, which we implemented as a video replay tool, as shown in Figure 2. This mode is typically useful for group support within debriefing sessions that may be organized to discuss their meeting practices.

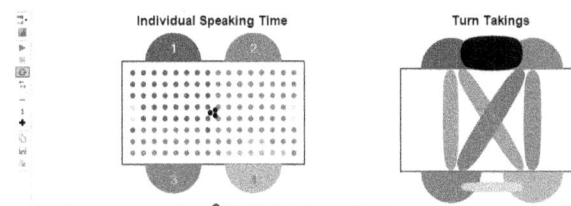

Figure 2: Table Replay and Synthesis Display

The upper right part is the summary display which computes other synthetic meeting features. They are created to overcome the limitation of the table display restricted to LEDs, and can show new syntheses that are available from the recorded data. Here we display the Turn Takings (Fig. 2) to show who spoke more after who (which we view as an indication of pair speech and dual interactivity). The drawing consists of pairwise lines whose gradient point out the number of speech acts transfers from one person to another, and where the darker color suggests a higher number of transfers.

2.2.3 Evolution Graphic and Report

The most important part of the visualization tool is the graphical evolutionary form of presenting the data (Fig. 3). This is the main added value of the tool, to make available information in a graphical, evolutionary representation. The participants colors are the same as the ones used on the Reflect Table display. The X coordinate represents each minute of the meeting (either relative to the beginning or absolute time of day), while the Y coordinate represents the fraction of a minute that the participant was recorded to produce speech chunks.

The plots use evolution curves for each participant, and they can be smoothened by moving-averaging values over more minutes. A scattered plot is also available, a total speech histogram can be created, and a dashed line can be displayed to correlate the moment chosen on the Replay sector with the time in this graphic.

We acknowledge that often managers do not have the time to look deeper into the analysis provided by the tool, and debriefing sessions may not be organized after each session.

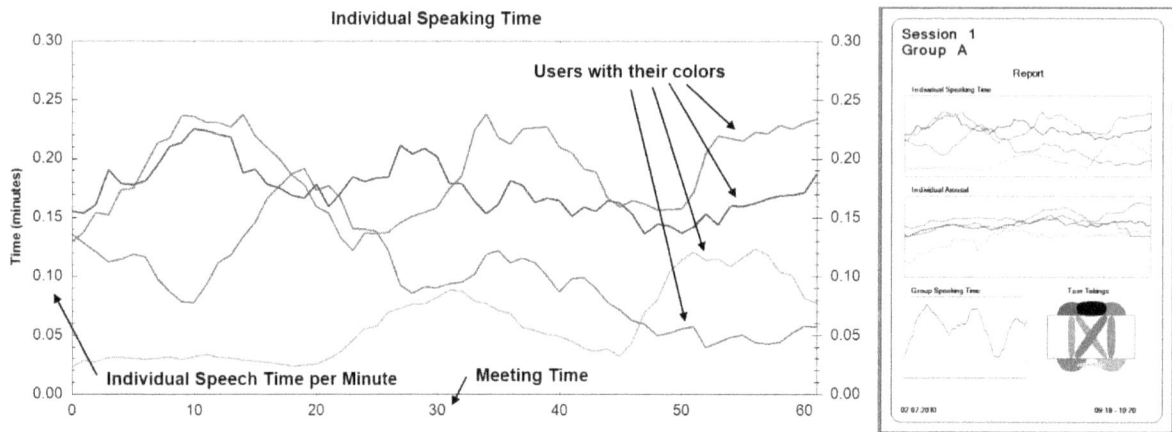

Figure 3: Reflect Visualizations: Evolution Graphic and Report

Therefore we conceived a one-snapshot summary in the form of a group PDF Report (Fig. 3) which shows the evolution of individual and group measures, as well as turn takings, and represents, for the participant, a first glimpse at their meeting dynamics. The report is aimed to be distributed to each group after each session. We maintain the principle of objectively presenting data only, and do not include any comments about the developments in the meeting.

2.3 Previous Experiments: Results and Limitations of the studies

The Reflect Table has been previously used only in controlled environments [2, 3], producing encouraging results. Scenarios for studies included analyzing groups with the Reflect Table versus control groups without a Reflect Table, comparisons of displays such as the type of display used (hidden or territories), or displays of speech times of individuals versus speech times per topics (a Wizard-of-Oz technique was employed where a scientist would silently and inadvertently attend the meeting and mark the changes in the topics).

The participants were undergraduate IT students that were paid for the experiment, and asked to solve a murder mystery given as a hidden profile task, where pieces of information were either shared among booklets or available only in one of the booklets. The students were constrained to read only from their copy and not allowed to physically exchange the booklets. This type of task inherently requires the participants to collaborate to share the information, for the correct identification of a perpetrator. The students were not informed of and there was no mentioning of any theoretical benefit from balanced participation. The measurements included participation time and discussion time per topics, and a questionnaire at the end of the meeting was aimed at collecting qualitative data about the participants' perspectives.

The results showed that in the absence of participation information, the participants were not able to correctly identify ratios of participation. More than 95% of the participants reported looking at the table for information, with only less than 25% claiming to be distracted by it, which ensures the design is appropriate. Further findings show that for extreme over participators (dominants or floor-monopolizers),

the availability of the speech time information had an effect of determining them to reduce their speaking time and free the floor. However, no significant results were obtained for under-participators, except that all extreme under participators reported in the questionnaire that they did not consider equal or balanced participation to be important in any meeting.

A certain difference between previous studies and the current one rests in the fact that all previous studies were done on groups that were meeting a single time, whereas in the current study, we have the opportunity to observe teams meeting several times and evaluate the evolution of their behavior. Also, previous studies did not benefit from the availability of Reflect Visualizations or from debriefings.

2.4 Methodology: A Real World approach

The main research goal of this paper is to expand the study of this speech awareness tool in meetings to verify whether there is an added value and benefit in real world as well, after the incipient studies brought promising results. We want to see whether teams of top level managers undergoing training reunions, with the purpose of enlarging their expertise by sharing knowledge, experience the same behavioral changes (e.g. floor monopolizers release it and end their turn when becoming aware of over-participating) as students in a laboratory-organized experiment. The degree of success and the experience

This effort is the first assessment of a Reflect Table in an uncontrolled, real world situation. The setup is a training activity that involves 6 teams or groups, labeled from A to F, each one composed of 5 or 6 people, undergoing multiple meetings with the Reflect Table, and having access to the ReflectVisualizations and to the report page after every meeting. There are a total of 10 meetings for each group (taking place roughly every month for a total period of one year), and the participants plan and schedule the sessions themselves at this frequency. The groups are composed of peer top level managers, but are heterogeneous in the sense that they manage distinct divisions in a large corporate organization. The teams were built in such a way that the attendants did not know each other before the start of the trainings. The members of the groups never change throughout the unfolding of the sessions. The collected speech time

4

and features data is completely content-free and text confidential, the table can only log the speech time based on the direction of the sound. The overall content of their discussions is unknown, but the target of the training framework is to improve their mutual knowledge by exchanging individual work experiences about given topics (which are also unknown).

We only require each participant to use the same position at the table during all their planned group meetings, therefore ensuring consistency in the relationship between the color on the table and identity of each participant. We label the participants with numbers (1-6) and corresponding colors based on the table position (Blue, Red, Fuchsia, Green, Yellow, White). The groups have a coordinator who is managing the sessions, without participating herself in the meetings, and which ensures that the participants receive and read at least the reports of the sessions.

A short first encounter (Session 1) was organized without the Reflect Table with the goal to briefly introduce the participants to the purpose of the training and to each other. From the second session, the groups started using the Reflect Table in a specially designed room. Before the beginning of this session, they were given an introduction to the table, its features, and how to change the display mode. Besides touching the microphones to select this display mode, there is no other physical interaction of the participants with the table. From there, the teams are left alone and completely autonomous to devise their styles of interaction. Regarding the display mode, we advised them to use a hidden mode for the first two sessions, and a territory mode for the rest (the two values of display modes are one independent variable of the experiment). Post-meeting questionnaires were created for some meetings and distributed by the facilitator, but the response rate to any such questionnaires was out of our control. Overall we considered that this user study is done in an uncontrolled environment because we had no access to any other types of measurements, or control parameters.

3. RESULTS

To date, we have collected and analyzed data from meetings spanning over 6 sessions (sessions 2 to 7). We did not receive data from all the sessions, due to participants forgetting to turn the table on in some instances, schedule conflicts that forced some sessions to be held in a different room without the Reflect Table, and, in one case, a software problem that prevented meaningful data to be gathered during that session. In total, we procured data from 27 meetings, with a per-group collection of data from 4 to 6 sessions, depending on the group. We have confirmation that the first two meetings were held using the hidden mode, while the rest used the territories, as we recommended. At the end of each session held in hidden mode, they switched to the territories mode and discussed for about one minute about whether the result was expected or was a surprise.

3.1 Quantitative Data Analysis

We analyze the data gathered from the groups using the ReflectVisualization tool. We used a per-group data merging to put together all data from these sessions for each group.

3.1.1 A metric for participation imbalance: When visual instant feedback is present, there is regulation over time

We defined and computed a measure of imbalance of the participation. In the process of defining this notion we considered a certain number of properties that should build up the definition, and also some issues required for keeping the measurement consistent throughout different sessions and different groups:

1. The measure is inversed-scale, meaning that the lower the value is (towards zero), the better. A value of zero indicates equal speech time among all participants

2. The sessions have a random duration, therefore the influence of number of minutes of each session should be avoided

3. The group (overall) speech time per minute varies among sessions, therefore it should not influence the result

Thus we defined the imbalance as the *Session-averaged sum of absolute deviations of per-minute speech time of each participant*, or more formally given N as the participants number, M as session time in minutes, and X_{ij} as the speech time of participant i in the minute j of the session, the average session imbalance over all groups is defined as

$$I = \frac{1}{M} \sum_{j=1}^{M} \sum_{i=1}^{N} AbsDev(X_{ij})$$

where

$$AbsDev(x_i) = |x_i - \frac{1}{N} \sum_{k=1}^{N} X_k|$$

therefore giving the final formula of

$$I = \frac{1}{M} \sum_{j=1}^{M} \sum_{i=1}^{N} |X_{ij} - \frac{1}{N} \sum_{k=1}^{N} X_{kj}| \qquad (1)$$

We used the averaging over the total duration of the meeting to overcome the random times of the sessions. We applied the formula to all meetings, and then averaged the results of each group on the same meeting number. When we had missing data (no sessions), the missing value was just discarded from the average.

By plotting the values obtained for each meeting (averaged over all groups), we notice the evolution of Imbalance, as shown in Fig. 4. The immediate visible result is that there is no effect in the hidden mode, however a balancing effect becomes visible in time with the use of the territories mode. It is difficult to decipher why the imbalance actually grew from the first hidden session to the second, but a tentative explanation could take into account the presence of the instructor to introduce the table at the beginning of the second session, revealing the ideas of participation equilibration, or the need to share more equally in the early context of getting to know each other better.

The effect of balancing of participation over time new and encouraging, and although the number of groups ($G = 6$) and number of meetings ($M = 6$) are insufficient for a sound statistical analysis of the phenomenon, we are optimistic to believe that possessing such a speech time awareness tool does help groups balance their participation over time.

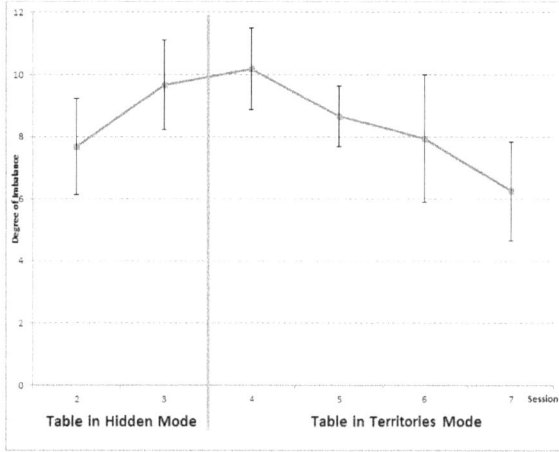

Figure 4: Evolution of Degree of Imbalance. A lower value means more balanced participation.

3.1.2 Speech Time and Leadership: No leader vs. One leader

Information on leadership is useful to shape the internals of the groups. We define and use the notion of leader based on a combination between their duration of speech and interactivity. We consider the assumption that those who want to share more could have more knowledge and hence become a higher authority for the group. What we observed by analyzing speech is that there are different types of leaderships. For example, in group D, there is no consistent leader throughout the sessions (Fig. 5).

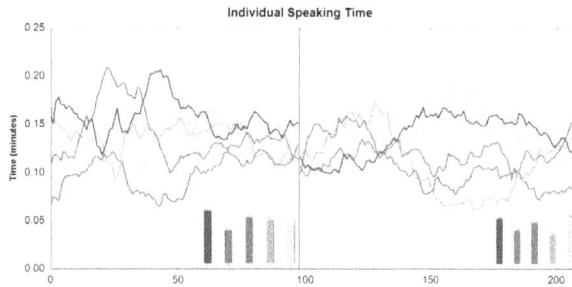

Figure 5: Balanced Participation and No Leadership in Group D

On the contrary, group C (Fig. 6) is representative for having a single, distinguishable leader (the red participant). The plot clearly shows that the leader was not only speaking the most, but he was also speaking the most at all times during the session. Also, the other participants rarely regulated their contributions, and the count of changes or adjustments in the amount of speech throughout the meeting is the least among all groups.

The behavior of group D persisted throughout all the sessions, be it hidden mode or territory. We take particular interest in this group, for having certain specific characteristics: they were the only group to schedule and attend all the meetings with the table, never losing data and giving more feedback than other groups. We suspect that a high commitment and a very professional organization between

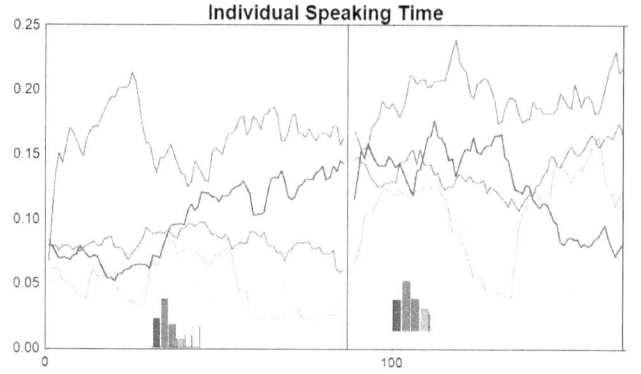

Figure 6: Red participant is the Leader in Group C

the members exists within this group. Also, the behavior of group C repeated throughout all the sessions, therefore prompting us to assert that the functional aspect of the group relied on that leader (red participant).

3.1.3 Meeting Phases: a form of regulation

After analyzing data from meetings in territories mode, we present in Fig. 7 a graph of one meeting with an evident pattern of in-meeting floor turns of four participants, in Group E, occurring during session number 4 (the first one with the territory display). The picture clearly shows a pattern of participants sharing the floor in turns, which could have come as an effect of the territories displayed during the meeting. The longer floor captures leads to assumptions of existence of phases in meetings, which if enforced by the participants, are still a form of participation regulation.

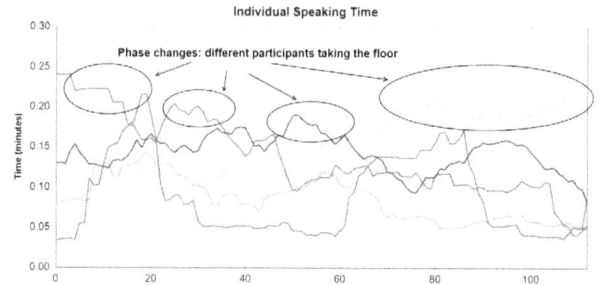

Figure 7: Speech turns within one meetings

This might suggest that since the participants are required to share individual experiences, this group might have defined a strategy to allocate time intervals for each member to share his story and later to discuss about it.

3.1.4 Turn Takings: more interactivity when territories are visible

We compared the graphical plots of turn takings in the hidden mode and in the territories mode, observing that typically there is less interactivity in the hidden mode. pairwise lines whose colors point out the number of speech acts transfers from one person to another and where the darker gradient suggests a higher number of transfers.

For group F, This is visible with the larger number of darker lines than in Figure 8. This pattern is less strong for the other groups, but a slight improvement in interactivity

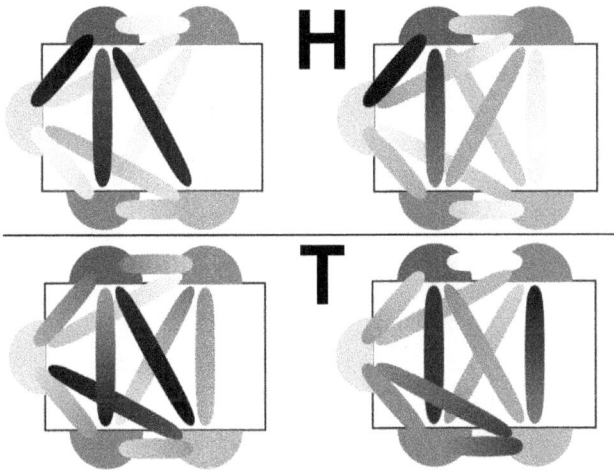

Figure 8: Turn Takings: Hidden vs. Territories

is seen in most of them. An assessment of the effect of interactivity on the quality of interaction would be useful, especially to judge the quantity of speech overlapping (which occurs more in the case of increased interactivity) and its possible detrimental effect. However our technology does not support a reliable enough measurement capacity for such overlappings.

3.1.5 Effects of the distribution of the Report: there is regulation between meetings as well

Regarding the availability of the report, by looking at the first sessions, it is our contention that there is an effect from its very first distribution on some people. Data from groups A and B shows that the two most and least speaking persons during the first session practically exchanged these roles during the second meeting (Fig. 9). Group A continued this exchange within the 3rd meeting as well, where the red participant came back to speaking more.

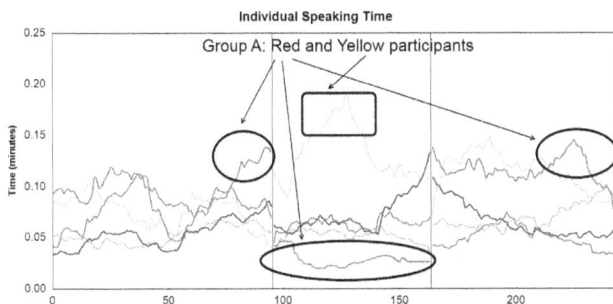

Figure 9: Behavioral Change in Group A

Another type of regulation that we observed and which could come as an effect of distributing the reports, was an in-meeting pair domination in group B throughout all sessions, but with a different pair of participants dominating each meeting (Fig. 10). This result is new and suggests that a distributed pair leadership pattern emerges for this group, probably as a means of structuration of interaction.

Figure 10: Pair dominance group B

3.1.6 Group Speaking Time: groups have meetings trademarks and reproducible behavior

We moved on to analyze the in-meeting group interaction in terms of evolution of total group speaking time (per minute). By analyzing all the available meetings, we concluded that there are 3 patterns of speech in a meeting: a *double hill*, an *increasing* interaction, and a *decreasing* interaction. The patterns observed are completely new and could be used to predict meeting phases, or even meeting signatures for some groups. In the case of groups D, E, and F (Fig. 11), the same pattern was present throughout all their encounters therefore suggesting some internal fingerprint of the group.

The other groups did not have such consistency between meetings, but still they had an evolution combining meetings with one of these these three patterns. Group A had a prevalence for the two hills, Group B a majority of sessions in slightly downtrend, and group C mixed two hills with uptrend.

3.2 Qualitative Assessment

Among the questionnaires we sent, some of them were concerned with the use of the table and its perceived impact in the hidden mode (after 3rd sessions), others were about the territories mode (after 5th sessions), and some were concerned with the quality and utility of the report (around 4th sessions). Open feedback was gathered by the coordinator in a general debriefing reunion around the time of the 7th sessions. A first observation about the questionnaires is that we received a rather low overall response rate (between 32% and 58%), probably due to the participants not taking the time to fill them in.

3.2.1 Individual sessions Impressions

The questionnaire for the hidden mode evaluated the reaction at the end of the meeting, when switching to the territories. We received a low number of replies. In all cases there was a debriefing discussion of at least one minute about the participation, interaction, and the table display. Half the respondents were surprised by the result, the other half foresaw the territories to look like they did.

In the territories questionnaire, we asked how often they looked at the table during the session, what they saw, and if that prompted them change their behavior. We received a much higher number of replies for this questionnaire, 77% of the respondents reporting looking at the table display during the session, and of these, 40% identified themselves as speaking more than others, all of them claiming to give the floor away from that moment on. When asked to evaluate if the changes in the behavior of the others were perceivable (adjusting to speak more or speak less), half of the replies were positive. However, among those who identified themselves as speaking less, almost no one reported taking any immediate initiative of balancing by speaking more.

The reports questionnaire was distributed online, decoupled from the meetings dates, with a rather medium re-

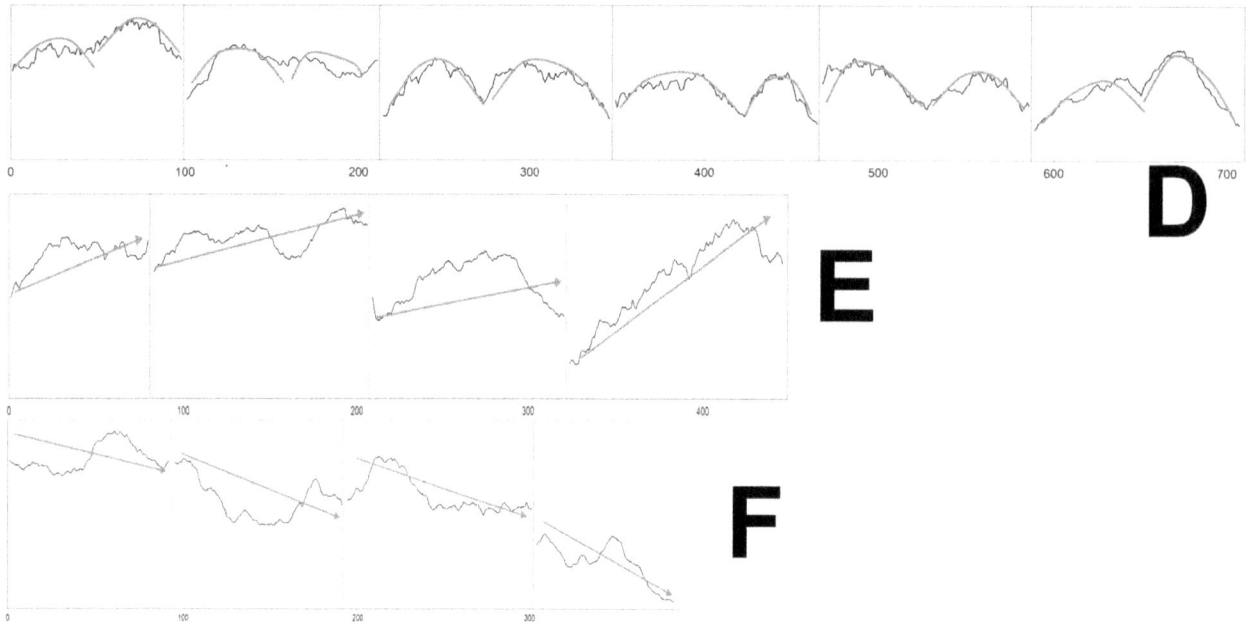

Figure 11: Three Group Speech Patterns emerge across sessions: Double Hill, Increasing, Decreasing

sponse rate compared to the other questionnaires. Many participants were interested to get more in-depth on the analysis and explanations of graphics, which suggests that the idea of distributing a report was well received. 83% of the replies qualified the report as useful or extremely useful, and they stated they do use it to reflect on their behavior as a guide for the next meetings. There were demands for group evolution measures as well. We interpret that continuing to offer reports and expanding or improving the information in them can have a positive effect on individual adaptation towards group cohesion and performance.

3.2.2 System Feedback from Users: new findings

We received the highest degree of responses in the open feedback, and we classified the remarks into 3 categories: positive (39%), neutral or observing no effects (44%) and negative (16%), with respect to the perceived value of the Reflect Table and meeting analysis.

Among the positive feedback, we read statements commending the utility of the system for its designed purpose, users reporting adjusting their behaviors when their territories were too large, as well as the system itself being labeled as a reference for scheduling meetings by one of the teams (the constraint of a specific room made it easier for them to schedule the meetings), while others viewed it as an objective technology promoting participation from all sides.

The sum of the neutral feedback was filled by reports that attendants did not perceive the table to be necessarily the cause of in-meeting regulation, but rather relied on self-designed group norms for that. We can think that most of these replies were from people who did not find themselves speaking a lot more than others. Participants did mention however that they took note of their evolution of behavior throughout the meetings by looking at the reports.

We classified the negative feedback as the comments that were against having the technology or using it. We collected remarks of people who were not convinced that the tech-

nology works, especially because of the existing wider side in the table, and considered that showing this data (which they perceived as inaccurate) was counterproductive for the group. One person complained that we don't count *active listening* as participation, another one expressed concern that the territories sizes are never surprising and thus the value of having them is discounted by the group. Another one complained that the link between the color and his identity (due to the construction of the territories, which originate in front of each user) affected his reputation when he intentionally did not want to contribute to a part of the discussion (he perceived that his intention of non-participating was actually revealed by the table to the others, whereas he would have liked to conceal it). The aspects revealed will be deeply considered in our future work.

By corroborating these findings with the other feedback and the quantitative analysis, we can well believe that even if there was average enthusiasm expressed by the participants in the questionnaires, the system did well in fulfilling the goal of regulating participation over time and helping the teams become cohesive and productive.

3.3 Limitations and Discussion

The uncontrolled nature of the study brings about limitations and discussions regarding the results obtained. Since we had no access to content and measurements of process variables, or clues about the unfolding of social rapports between individuals within groups, and also there is only scarce assessment of sociocognitive aspects of interactions (that might have an impact on the speech time behavior), it is difficult to strongly claim that our system and technology was all that it took to balance participation.

We are convinced that the principles used for the design of such support systems are adequate and the support the tools bring to the social cognition and interactions of groups in meetings are helpful, however we cannot rule out that

8

certain characteristics of the context of the study did not carry effects into the results. For example:

- *Specific characteristics of the groups composition*: not knowing each other prior to the creation of the groups can be a factor of increased mutual respect and predisposition for speech time sharing;

- *Type of meetings*: trainings based on sharing experiences may be more prone to balanced participation than other types of meetings, such as information or decision making where imbalanced participation may be natural. We restate that our technology is not normative, hence it only provides knowledge that the participants are free to use the way they feel appropriate;

- *Type of attendance*: having peers in an organizational context is certainly a distinct situation with respect to the outcome, when compared to groups that are composed of people with different hierarchical authorities.

We would therefore limit our claims to the context of these particular aspects of the study. However, within this framework, we do believe that the cognizance provided by our system has a positive effect even for top level managers.

4. FUTURE

The added value brought by the Reflect Table and ReflectVisualizations system is encouraging us to continue to pursue research in the field of our interest, using these tools or similar ones, in several directions.

One of them is to upgrade the technology above the Reflect Table's principles by optimizing the parameters measured and creating other tools that mitigate some of the existing limitations. We are creating a *dematerialized version* of the Reflect Table, in the form of software running on mobile devices aiming to retain similar features. With the emergence and omniscience of the iPhones, iPads, Android and similar technologies, we can leverage their adoption to port our work on them, therefore eliminating the drawback of location-dependency on a heavy table, enabling parallel meetings support, centralized data processing, and better analysis and reporting. We can change Reflect Visualizations to be an even more integrated module. The pursuit can follow either of two directions: using a single iPad and detecting who is speaking (based on a calibration and fingerprinting of the voices of the participants), or using one iPad per participant, and synchronizing the data generated. The main challenges are, in both cases, the correct detection of the speaker, with an additional requirement for consistency of generated data timestamps in the second scenario.

The added support for in-depth post-meeting analysis of the encounter provides insight on group evolution and evolution of individual behavior throughout multiple meetings in the same group. We expect more group evolution to unfold in time, and further research on future sessions will help us better see the effects of technologies in these meetings. The next step is to perform more thorough analysis of group evolution, by evaluating more precise leadership traits, and also emerging norms and types of self-organization within these groups.

5. CONCLUSIONS

We presented a meeting toolkit rooted in the Reflect Table and extended with new functionalities of the ReflectVisualizations software for meetings analysis. We devised a study in an uncontrolled environment of top level managers, in the context of training meetings that were designed to achieve a good level of mutual knowledge between participants by exchanging individual past experiences, where they used the Reflect Table and the reports generated by the ReflectVisualizations software. Previous studies of the Reflect Table done with students showed that awareness about speech time has an effect of equilibrating participation within a meeting, and we wanted to evaluate whether the same effect would be obtained in a real life setting, rather than a laboratory experiment, either as in-meeting or over multiple meetings. The results of the current study are light for in-meeting balancing effect, but are very positive in terms of balancing over time after more meetings, showing that the top level managers do use self-regulation when becoming aware of their speech, with a more pronounced effect observed after several meetings.

The main contribution of this work is that it extends the study of awareness tools in meetings, to show their positive results in real world as well. With the creation of the new tools that expand the existing Reflect Table for meetings analysis, we make available a complete system that is robust enough to be used in measuring and assessing long term groups evolution, in any given organizational habitat where a team, task force or contingent performs a collaborative face to face activity, and where contribution from individual members is valued.

6. ACKNOWLEDGMENT

We are strongly indebted to Banque Privée Edmond de Rothschild, Geneva, Switzerland, member of the Edmond de Rothschild Group, for the sponsorship and support of our research.

7. REFERENCES

[1] K. Bachour. *Augmenting Face-to-Face Collaboration with Low-Resolution Semi-Ambient Feedback*. PhD thesis, EPFL, Lausanne, 2010.

[2] K. Bachour, F. Kaplan, and P. Dillenbourg. Reflect : An interactive table for regulating face-to-face collaborative learning. In *Lecture Notes in Computer Science*. Springer, Berlin / Heidelberg, 2008.

[3] K. Bachour, F. Kaplan, and P. Dillenbourg. An interactive table for supporting participation balance in face-to-face collaborative learning. *IEEE Transactions on Learning Technologies*, 3:203–213, 2010.

[4] K. Bachour, H. Seiied Alavi, F. Kaplan, and P. Dillenbourg. Low-resolution ambient awareness tools for educational support. In *The Future of HCI And Education*, 2010. CHI 2010 Workshop: The Future of HCI And Education, Atlanta, Georgia, USA, April 11, 2010.

[5] T. Bergstrom and K. Karahalios. Conversation clock: Visualizing audio patterns in co-located groups. In *Proceedings of the 40th Annual Hawaii International Conference on System Sciences*, HICSS '07, pages 78–, Washington, DC, USA, 2007. IEEE Computer Society.

[6] T. Bergstrom and K. Karahalios. Visualizing colocated conversation feedback. *IEEE Tabletop*, 1:165–178, 2007.

[7] K. Bettenhausen and J. K. Murnighan. The emergence of norms in competitive decision-making groups. *Administrative Science Quarterly*, 30(3):pp. 350–372, 1985.

[8] P. Boersma and D. Weenink. Praat: doing phonetics by computer (version 5). *Glot International*, 5:341–345, 2001.

[9] E. G. Cohen. Restructuring the classroom: Conditions for productive small groups. *Review of Educational Research*, 64(1):1–35, 1994.

[10] J. DiMicco and W. Bender. Group reactions to visual feedback tools. In Y. de Kort, W. IJsselsteijn, C. Midden, B. Eggen, and B. Fogg, editors, *Persuasive Technology*, volume 4744 of *Lecture Notes in Computer Science*, pages 132–143. Springer Berlin / Heidelberg, 2007.

[11] C. Ellis, P. Barthelmess, B. Quan, and J. Wainer. Neem: An agent based meeting augmentation system, 2001.

[12] J. R. Hackman. Group influences on individuals in organizations. *Handbook of industrial and organizational psychology*, 3:199–267, 1992.

[13] C. Hoyles. What is the point of group discussion in mathematics? *Educational Studies in Mathematics*, 16:205–214, 1985. 10.1007/BF02400938.

[14] G. P. Huber. A theory of the effects of advanced information technologies on organizational design, intelligence, and decision making. *The Academy of Management Review*, 15(1):pp. 47–71, 1990.

[15] S. Hunter, P. Maes, S. Scott, and H. Kaufman. Memtable: an integrated system for capture and recall of shared histories in group workspaces. In *Proceedings of the 2011 annual conference on Human factors in computing systems*, CHI '11, pages 3305–3314, New York, NY, USA, 2011. ACM.

[16] T. Kim, A. Chang, L. Holl, and A. Pentland. Meeting mediator: Enhancing group collaboration using sociometric feedback. In *Proceedings of the 2008 ACM conference on Computer supported cooperative work*, 2008.

[17] A. Nijholt, R. Rienks, and D. Reidsma. Online and off-line visualization of meeting information and meeting support. *The Visual Computer*, 1:965–976, 2006.

[18] N. Romano Jr and J. Nunamaker Jr. Meeting analysis: Findings from research and practice. In *Proceedings of the 34th Annual Hawaii International Conference on System Sciences (HICSS-34)-Volume 1 - Volume 1*, HICSS '01, pages 1072–, Washington, DC, USA, 2001. IEEE Computer Society.

[19] G. Salomon and T. Globerson. When teams do not function the way they ought to. *International Journal of Educational Research*, 13:89–99, 1989.

[20] T. Skog, S. Ljungblad, and L. E. Holmquist. Between aesthetics and utility: designing ambient information visualizations. In *Proceedings of the Ninth annual IEEE conference on Information visualization*, INFOVIS'03, pages 233–240, Washington, DC, USA, 2003. IEEE Computer Society.

[21] S. Streng, K. Stegmann, H. Hussmann, and F. Fischer. Metaphor or diagram?: comparing different representations for group mirrors. In *Proceedings of the 21st Annual Conference of the Australian Computer-Human Interaction Special Interest Group: Design: Open 24/7*, OZCHI '09, pages 249–256, New York, NY, USA, 2009. ACM.

[22] J. Webster, Murray and J. Driskell, James E. Beauty as status. *American Journal of Sociology*, 89(1):pp. 140–165, 1983.

Visualizing History to Improve Users' Location and Comprehension of Collaborative Work

DoHyoung Kim and Frank M. Shipman III
Department of Computer Science and Engineering
Texas A&M University
College Station, TX 77843-3112
1-979-862-3216

shipman@cs.tamu.edu

ABSTRACT

Many applications place users into collaborations with unknown and distant partners. Collaboration between participants in such environments is more efficient if individuals can identify and understand the contributions of others. A traditional approach to supporting such understanding within the CSCW community is to record user activity for later access. Issues with this approach include difficulties in locating activity of interest in large tasks and that history is often recorded at a system-activity level instead of at a human-activity level. To address these issues, this paper introduces CoActIVE, a history mechanism that clusters records of user activity and extracts keywords from manipulated content in an attempt to provide a human-level representation of history. Multiple visualization techniques' based on this processing were compared in their ability to improve users' location and comprehension of the activity of others. The results show the combination of clustering low level history events into activity segments and new visualizations summarizing activity within a segment result in a significant improvement over prior interfaces.

Categories and Subject Descriptors

H.5.3 [**Information Interfaces and Presentation (e.g., HCI)**]: Group and Organization Interfaces – Asynchronous interaction, Computer-supported cooperative work

General Terms

Design, Experimentation, Human Factors.

Keywords

User history, history clustering, history visualization, history navigation, long-term indirect collaboration.

1. INTRODUCTION

With the increase in server-based and cloud-based computing, there has been a corresponding increase in applications supporting remote collaborative work. This is resulting in a growth in what

Fischer and colleagues call **long-term indirect collaboration** [4]. In long-term indirect collaboration, people working on the same project or activity collaborate without ever communicating or knowing each other. For example, engineers on a multi-year project in industry may work on the same design but not ever work for the engineering firm simultaneously. Wikis and other web-based shared authoring or design environments create similar situations often supporting particular communities of practice [13][14].

This form of collaboration cannot rely on real-time communication or coordination support that assumes collaborators know one another. Instead, these collaborations are characterized by collaborators with potentially little shared understanding. However, without sufficient understanding between collaborators, such remote collaboration will be less efficient and productive. For example, individuals may make duplicate work already done by others or may unknowingly delete others' work while instantiating their work.

A traditional approach to improving understanding between collaborators is to record user activity for later access [4]. Through access to history of activities, the participant can not only understand the intentions of their collaborators, but also increase the value of their contribution based on an improved understanding of the past work history [20][21].

Despite the benefits of preserving records of user activity [11][20], there are challenges for its presentation and use in a system. First, locating activity of interest in large tasks becomes a potentially time-consuming activity. Second, users can have problems comprehending automatically-recorded history, which is represented at a system-activity level instead of at a human-activity level.

This paper introduces CoActIVE, a history mechanism designed to improve users' ability to locate and comprehend activity within large recorded histories. The mechanism clusters history records and extracts keywords in an attempt to provide a more human-level representation of history. Based on this processing, it provides multiple visualizations of collaboration history. CoActIVE is developed as a Java library, which can be integrated in Java applications.

Evaluation of CoActIVE occurred by integrating it in the Visual Knowledge Builder (VKB), a publicly-available Java application that includes history recording [24]. The evaluation compared the traditional history interface of VKB with three new interfaces provided via CoActIVE. Those interfaces were compared in their ability to improve users' ability to locate and comprehend the activity of others.

The next section discusses issues in the presentation and use of activity history. This is followed by related work, an overview of our approach, a description of CoActIVE, its integration with VKB, and the evaluation of CoActIVE. We conclude with a results and directions for future work.

2. ISSUES IN SUPPORTING HISTORY

A variety of systems collect records of user activity as history. Such systems often enable users to navigate through the history to see previous work by going back and forth between the current and prior state [21]. For a single-person task, this acts as a reminder of prior activity and decisions, while in collaborative applications it provides a source of awareness and understanding of the work of others. For group projects with changing group membership, navigating the efforts of collaborators can give a new participant hints to understand group work more quickly and provide insight into the decisions of those no longer participating in the project [20].

2.1 Understanding of System-Level History

The typical method for representing user history is to record edit events to the underlying data structures involved in an application as user activity occurs in the interface. The resulting record includes low-level properties such as event type and timestamp.

However, the fine-grained representation of events can create problems for user interaction with history due to the potential for a mismatch with the user's understanding of their activity. For example, in a document editing application, an operation of inserting a figure in the middle of a page would be recognized as single activity to human users. But, at the low-level of the application, this activity is accomplished by applying a series of system-level events such as "import a figure", "move a figure", "resize a figure", and so on. The history interface needs to assist in the mapping between a potentially long series of edits recorded by the system to the user's mental model of their activity. This need becomes more severe in collaborative settings since users are often left to interpret collaborators' intention by recognizing coherent activities from recorded history.

2.2 Navigation and Orientation Difficulties

As collaborative work continues, the recorded history can quickly become very large increasing orientation and navigation difficulties. Most history interfaces, e.g. controls for playing forward and backward, lists and even scrubbing sliders, increase the time and effort required for locating a particular activity in the history as the history increases in size. Once found, users can be disoriented when they navigate between different points in a history without an indication of how far in time and effort they have traveled.

In general, there is often a trade-off between the effort required to locate an activity and the orientation provided by the interface (e.g. through animation). Interfaces that provide more direct access to prior activities often provide less feedback on the intermediate activities being skipped. Consequently, techniques are necessary to facilitate users' understanding of where they are in a recorded history and where particular sub-activities occur within that history.

3. RELATED WORK

History information has been employed for various purposes such as reuse, navigation, reminding, error recovery, user modeling, user interface adaptation, and inter-referential I/O [11]. While some of these uses are for single-user systems, history information has great potential to facilitate collaborative work by increasing awareness and understanding between users.

Reeves' collaborative design system, INDY, enabled users to replay and trace collaboration history as well as return to specific events in history. Through the improved support of history, the users could resolve ambiguities in understanding the progress and meaning of collaborative work [20]. The spatial hypertext system VKB includes a history mechanism similar to that in INDY, including a variety of methods for navigating the history. VKB includes an interface where users can group system-level history events into higher-level activities manually [24].

Automatically grouping events was explored in SmartBack, which identified important states in a history of web navigation to provide more direct access to the most valuable pages in a history [15]. For grouping edit events, applications have included a simple time gap approach to define sessions or noted application start times to generate checkpoints in the history of an artifact. Shirai and colleagues [25] developed a time-slicing method to group events for history summarization.

Numerous studies visualize aggregated history information to enhance user comprehension of collaborative work. Hill and Hollan's edit wear and read wear visualize the history of author and reader interaction with documents onto document scrollbars [8]. Plaisant et al. propose LifeLines that visualizes summaries of personal history. It provides an overview of a personal history with visual cues, such as line color and thickness. Users can also filter the history to focus on part of the record in detail [18]. This technique was also employed in education [19]. Similarly, Begole et al. visualize the history of user activity when using a computer and accessing e-mails to extract meaningful patterns of common activity between individuals and within individuals [1]. Viégas et al. introduces a history flow tool that visualizes relationships between multiple document versions in the Wikipedia corpus. From the visualization it revealed the patterns of cooperation and conflict among those versions [28]. These systems aid in understanding general trends in activity rather than supporting the location and comprehension of specific portions of an activity.

Closest to our work, Nakamura et al. employs a comic strip metaphor to visualize user activity which occurred in Java GUI applications. To summarize the history visually, they provide visual cues, such as word balloons for keyboard operations as annotations on each snapshot [16].

Visualization and awareness techniques are employed in asynchronous collaborative work settings as well. Based on Gutwin's workspace awareness in real-time groupware [7], Tam and Greenberg develop a framework that categorizes question types (e.g. where, who, what, how, when, and why) for tracking change awareness during asynchronous collaboration. The framework provides those changes via an artifact-based view, a person-based view, and a workspace-based view to meet the needs of users [27]. To help developers in distributed development teams analyze code and relevant activities around it, Froehlich and Dourish introduce a visualization tool, Augur. This tool extends SeeSoft [3] by visualizing the combined information of artifacts and activities [5]. Neuwirth et al. claims that basically participants forget what is going on in asynchronous collaboration so that they depend more on external representation than in synchronous collaboration. Through an observational study, they found that a hypertextual task-tailored representation can significantly improve performance [17].

Long-term indirect collaboration [4] involves the addition of new collaborations, or latecomers. Manohar and Prakash suggest a replay mechanism for latecomers in asynchronous collaboration. They propose a session object which consists of multiple stream objects (e.g. audio stream and window events), and users annotate, modify, and exchange it during collaboration. This object is used to replay collaborative activity by dispatching the stream objects to an application [12]. On the other hand, Gutwin et al. treat latecomers as a user who has been disconnected from the beginning of a session. Their Disco framework identifies disconnection, determines what to do during the disconnection, and handles accumulated data after re-connection [6].

In general, our approach to event aggregation and feature extraction significantly expands on prior work. Also, to our knowledge, the comparison of visualizations for locating and comprehending the work of others is unique.

4. APPROACH

To address the issues previously described, our approach is to develop a history mechanism that aggregates the system-level record of history into higher-level and hopefully more meaningful activities and visualizes salient characteristics of these activities to increase users' ability to locate and comprehend prior work.

4.1 Meaningful Aggregations of System-Level History

Human activities are often described, whether retrospectively explaining ones actions or in planning for future action, via a vocabulary of tasks and sub-tasks [26]. The goal of aggregating the system-level activity is to form a hierarchic representation of the recorded system-level events that roughly corresponds to the tasks and sub-tasks people would use to describe the activity.

Such an aggregation would help users more quickly comprehend the relationship between the history and their memory/understanding of the activity. A multi-level representation would benefit larger tasks if the levels correspond to the participants' mental model of the tasks and sub-tasks of their activity.

To generate such a representation, CoActIVE employs Hierarchical Agglomerative Clustering (HAC). This algorithm repeatedly clusters history events until a list of low-level events is organized as a tree representing a hierarchic structure of human activity. HAC relies on a distance function in order to determine which low-level events and previously-generated groupings to merge next. While others have explored purely time-based clustering [25], i.e. merge the next pair of subclusters with the smallest gap, such a function will not work in a synchronous CSCW environment where there are expected to be activities corresponding to separate simultaneous sequences of edits. While simply using time-based clustering for each individual user solves most of such problems, it will misrepresent the rapid transition between activities. As a result, CoActIVE enables an application-specific distance model that can be used to include numerous features of the system-level record of activity (e.g. time, user, content, location, etc.).

4.2 Navigation Interfaces and Visualizations

In our work, the recorded history's value lies in its ability to provide insight to users. Such insight requires that users are able to locate and comprehend periods of activity relevant to their current work. Thus, navigation interfaces and visualizations are central to such a process.

History interfaces need to facilitate users' understanding of specific states of the history. The history states are characterized by their point in time and by the representation of the domain-specific artifact at that time. By displaying lists of times and an indication of the associated artifact states, users get a sense for the flow of activity. Expanding from a list to a tree visualization facilitates a hierarchical structure that indicates the relation between states via sequence of tree nodes, levels of the tree, etc. but requires user interaction to open/close branches of the tree to show/hide details.

Another goal of these interfaces is to help users understand the process of work that led to particular states. Processes are composed of series of actions. While static visualizations, especially filmstrip visualizations of artifacts, provide some sense of process, animations that play back user activity provide a natural view of process.

When history becomes large, visualizations that represent the whole structure of the history in detail are not possible. Instead, the visualization and interface must select specific points in the history to present or they must determine abstract characteristics of the history states or event sequences which provide adequate information to the user.

Our approach is to provide navigation interfaces that visualize the aggregated history. Through the interfaces users will be aware of their current location in the history and be able to navigate to other locations in the history. We employ techniques to generate visual/textual hints to better represent the history segments resulting from aggregation. Simultaneously, the visualizations provide opportunities for users to access event-level information when needed.

4.3 Application-Independent History Mechanism

Many applications would benefit from support for activity location and comprehension and already include basic undo/redo capabilities. By relying on such existing features of applications, CoActIVE can be incorporated in a number of existing JAVA applications. CoActIVE only requires temporal and action information but allows developers to include application-specific features (e.g. an application-specific distance function for clustering events) as desired.

5. COACTIVE

CoActIVE, the Collaborative Activity Interpretation and Visualization Engine, is a Java library that can be integrated into Java applications that already have an undo/redo capability. Here, we describe its integration use in VKB.

5.1 The Visual Knowledge Builder

The Visual Knowledge Builder (VKB) is a spatial hypertext system developed to support collaborative knowledge building [24]. The system provides two-dimensional workspace where users author and collect information, and share this workspace with their collaborators. In the workspace, information is represented as information objects which can contain text, attributes and values, links to files or URLs, and images. Users can assign visual characteristics (e.g. border/background color and border width) to objects and place objects in a hierarchy of two-dimensional spaces called collections. Through the placement of the objects with visual attributes, users can categorize the objects and interpret collaborators' representation of information [22]. VKB was chosen as the first application to be modified to use CoActIVE because it already contained a history mechanism [21] and an interface that could be compared to CoActIVE.

5.2 CoActIVE Architecture and Components

Figure 1 shows the CoActIVE architecture, consisting of five main parts: a history manager, a history interpretation module, visualization components, I/O interfaces, and a database.

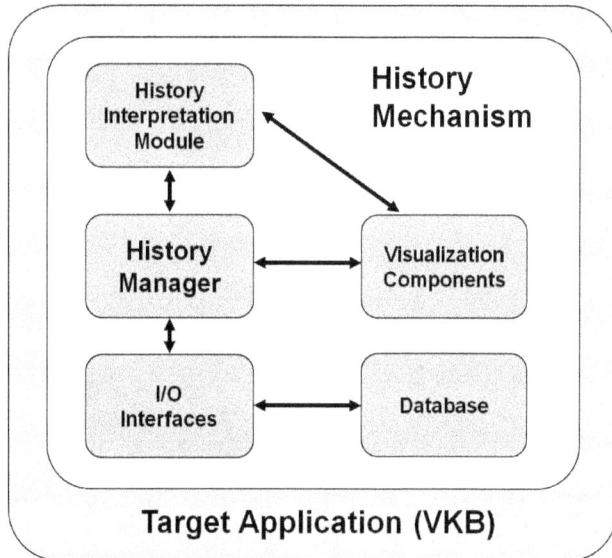

Figure 1. CoActIVE Architecture

The history manager is the central component of CoActIVE. It creates a history event when a user activity occurs, manages it in an underlying data structure, and provides history information to the other parts.

User activity in an application is represented as a system-level event or a series of events by the history manager. When those events occur, the manager stores them in a database through I/O interfaces. The recorded history is provided to the history interpretation module and visualization components for additional processing.

System-level event structures include the information required by the history mechanism. The information stored for each event includes an event id, an event type, a task description, a username, and a timestamp. The event id is unique and assigned by the history manager.

Each application will have its own set of event types – these generally correspond to the alternative actions found in the application's existing undo/redo software. Information specific to the event type can be attached to the event. For VKB events, this includes information about the content, visual properties and locations of objects being manipulated.

5.3 History Interpretation Module

CoActIVE's History Interpretation Module generates a higher level representation of the history in order to aid the user. It clusters the individual history events into (hopefully) meaningful groups and generates summaries for these clusters.

5.3.1 History Clustering

Conceptually, the goal of history clustering is for the tree to represent a form of hierarchic task decomposition of the effort that is recorded in the history. The interpretation module uses Hierarchical Agglomerative Clustering (HAC) to group similar events together into an initially unknown number of higher-level activities in a two-step process.

First, the interpretation module computes the distances between each pair of consecutive events. In the module, each history event is initially regarded as a single leaf node, and similar nodes will be grouped until the remaining nodes are too far apart to be viewed as part of the same activity. Therefore, it is important to define a distance function that determines what it means for events to be similar.

The distance function can take into account both application-independent (e.g. a timestamp) and application-dependent characteristics of events. By default, the time gap between events is used as the distance function. However, the distance function can be redefined based on the characteristics of a target application.

CoActIVE's integration in VKB provides an example of an application-specific distance function. Here, a spatio-temporal distance metric is used that defines the distance as a weighted sum of the spatial distance and the temporal distance between consecutive events. The temporal distance is simply the time between events. Determining the spatial distance between events is complicated as the hierarchy of collections does not provide a single Euclidean space and events may have two areas of effect that can span collections (e.g. moving muliptle objects from one collection to another has an area of effect that includes portions of each collection.) The spatial distance is computed to be the minimum distance between the areas of effect of subsequent events. When two areas of effect do not share a collection in common, a large constant is added for each collection traversal between the two areas of effect.

The second step in clustering events is to select the distance thresholds used to group events. The more thresholds selected, the deeper the resulting tree of events. CoActIVE dynamically selects the thresholds based on an analysis of the distribution of pairwise distances between consecutive history events. The pairwise distances are sorted in ascending order and the dramatically increasing values in the distance curve are selected as thresholds. Once the thresholds are selected the events are grouped into the final event tree that will be used to generate visualizations.

5.3.2 Summary Generation and Keyword Extraction

Once a history is clustered, CoActIVE generates a textual summary to represent each cluster. When no other information is available, the time period for the history acts as the summary. CoActIVE includes an optional textual content field for each event that can be populated by an application-dependent function added during integration. For VKB, this is filled in by aggregating the text in the objects affected by an event.

When CoActIVE has content field data, the interpretation module extracts keywords for each cluster by employing the Java

Figure 2. History Session Viewer

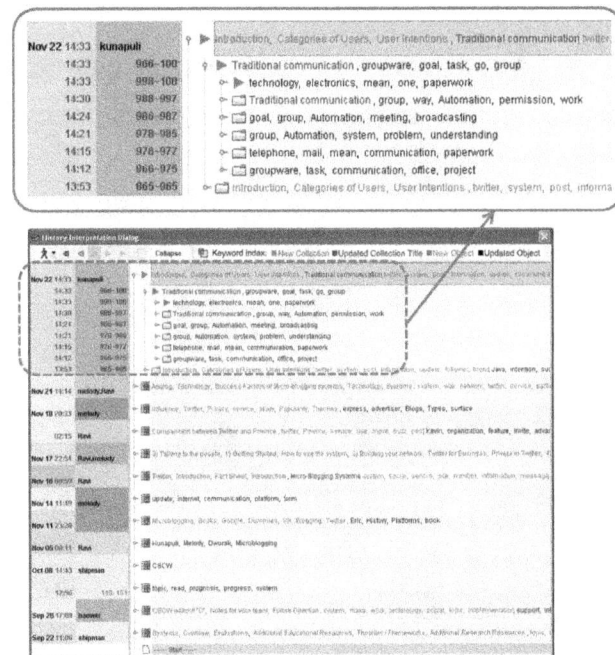

Figure 3. History Interpretation Viewer

WordNet Library (JWNL) [9]. Only nouns are considered after removing stop words from the content. With the selected nouns, their TF-IDF (Term Frequency – Inverse Document Frequency) weights are calculated to suggest significant keywords for groups at each level of the cluster tree. The keywords are then added to the time period to be the summary of an event cluster.

5.4 Visualization Components

CoActIVE employs multiple visualization techniques to assist users in locating particular activity and understanding the history of collaborative work. By providing both high-level and low-level navigation components, users can navigate history via overview and detailed views simultaneously. These views are tightly-coupled to help the users orient themselves during history navigation. The focus of this paper is on novel detailed visualizations enabled by the History Interpretation Module. We now describe the four visualizations compared in the evaluation: the History Session Viewer, the History Interpretation Viewer, and Filmstrips with textual and visual summaries.

5.4.1 History Session Viewer

The first, and most basic, detailed visualization is the history session viewer. It is almost same as the history interface found in VKB 2. The viewer shows a list of recorded events via a history tree component (see Figure 2). The history tree presents those events via a two-level tree where leaf nodes represent system-level events and their parent node is a grouping of those events into sessions based on a predefined time gap. Each tree node displays an event type (e.g. "MoveSymbol"), operation details (e.g. "move from L1[17, 72] to L2[19,166]"), and content from which the event was applied. In the tree, recent events are shown at the top, while earlier ones are at the bottom.

5.4.2 History Interpretation Viewer

The History Interpretation Viewer presents the results of History Interpretation Module in an augmented version of the History Session Viewer's tree view. As shown in Figure 3, top-level

nodes of the history tree represent the highest level clusters identified. Instead of the two-level tree of the session viewer, users investigate more detailed activity by unfolding the nodes and their descendants. Also, keywords are provided for each group of events in the tree. To the left of the tree view is information about the time/date of the activity and the user(s) involved in the activity.

Color coding of terms provides cues for the role of keywords in the activity represented by a cluster. Red indicates the term comes from the title of a collection created during the activity. Blue indicates a term from a collection title that was modified. Similarly, green and black indicate terms from information objects that were either created or modified.

5.4.3 Filmstrip Visualization

Filmstrip visualizations of history are a natural way to present change to a visual artifact over time. The cluster tree from the History Interpretation Module is used to decide which images to include in the filmstrip. In order to limit the amount of scrolling required of users, the visualization includes a maximum on the number of segments presented (current default is 16). Figure 4 shows the filmstrip with thumbnails of a VKB workspace for each history segment along with associated time, keyword, and user information.

Visual cues are also provided to indicate the user's current location in the history. In Figure 4, the yellow background of the time range field shows that the user is currently viewing a state within the sixth group, and the red vertical line with an event id indicates that particular location is right after the 202nd event was performed.

When a user places a mouse pointer over the thumbnail of the selected group, a small window pops up on it and shows a list of collection titles. The window employs a blue-colored "Updated" label to specify an updated title and a red-colored "New" label for

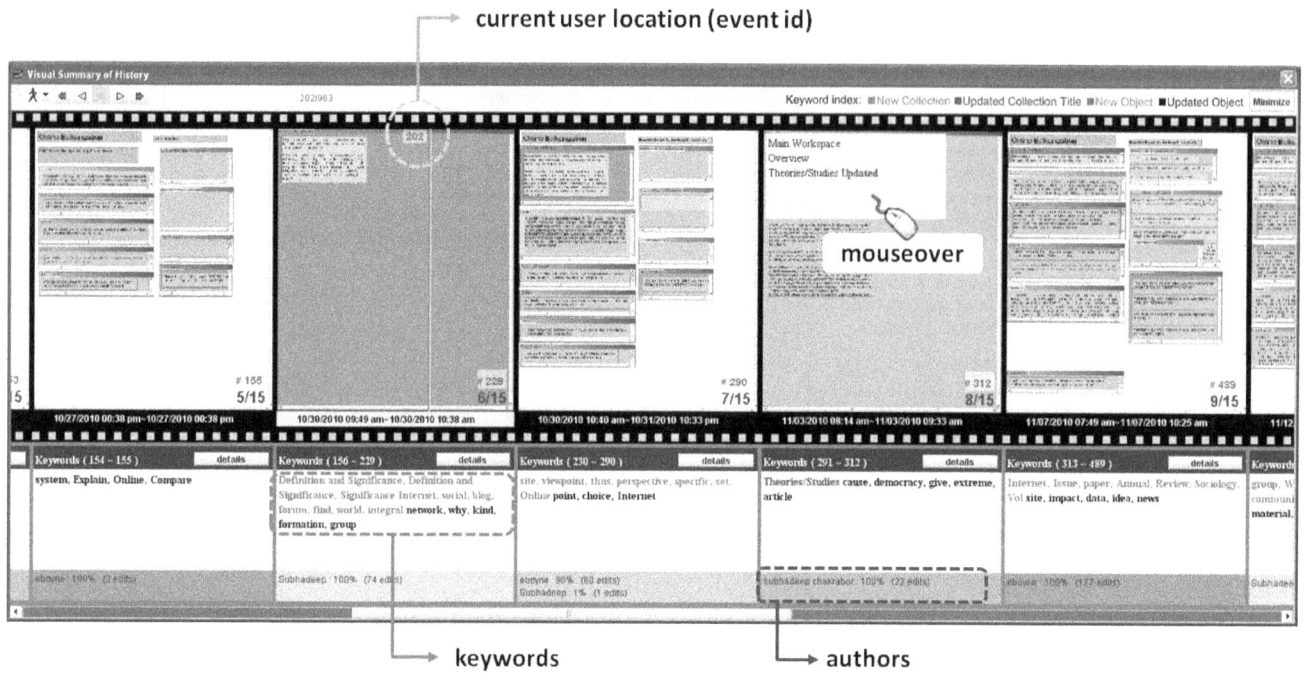

Figure 5. Filmstrip visualization includes thumbnails of states selected to represent segments of activity above and text related to the activity in the segment of activity below.

a new one. The title with no label means that the user was active in the collection.

Under each image is a "details" button for accessing more information about a particular history segment. In the following study, we compared two alternative details views: a textual summary and a visual summary.

5.4.4 Textual Summary

The textual summary aggregates and presents the textual content of objects and collections modified during a history segment. This provides detail beyond that found in the filmstrip to determine if particular content was involved in a segment and to identify themes involved in the segment. Figure 5 shows an example of a textual summary. As with the mouseover in the thumbnail image in the filmstrip, a label indicates if a piece of text was created or deleted is provided.

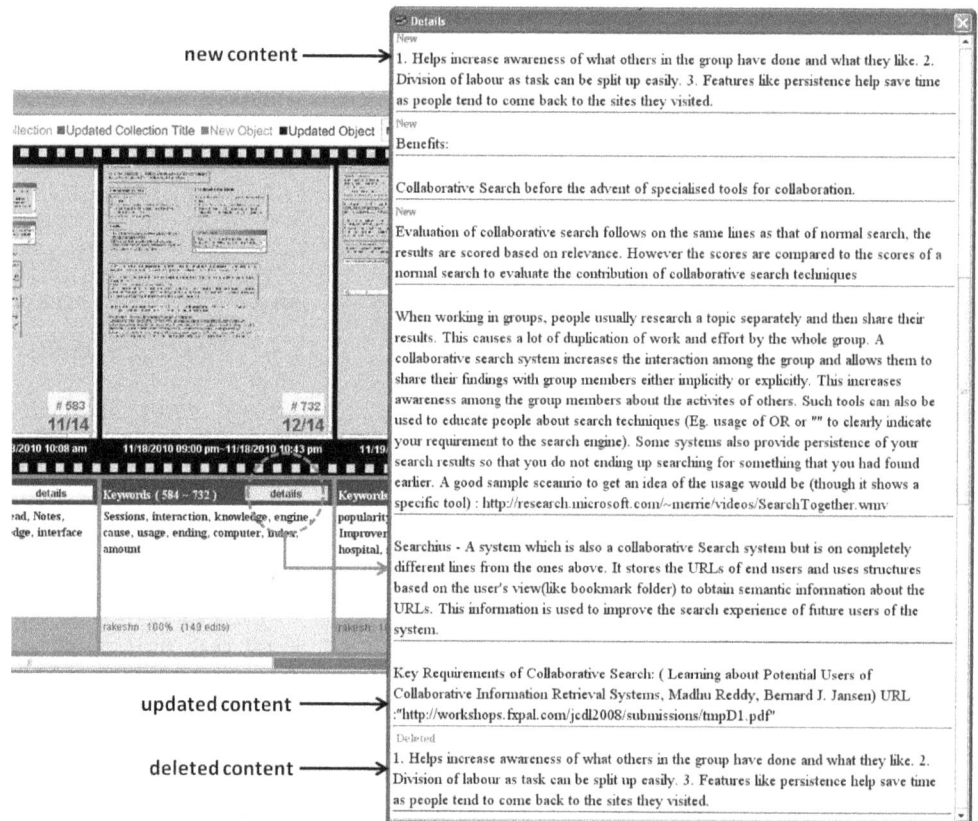

Figure 4. Textual summary of activity appears when user selects the details button for an activity segment.

16

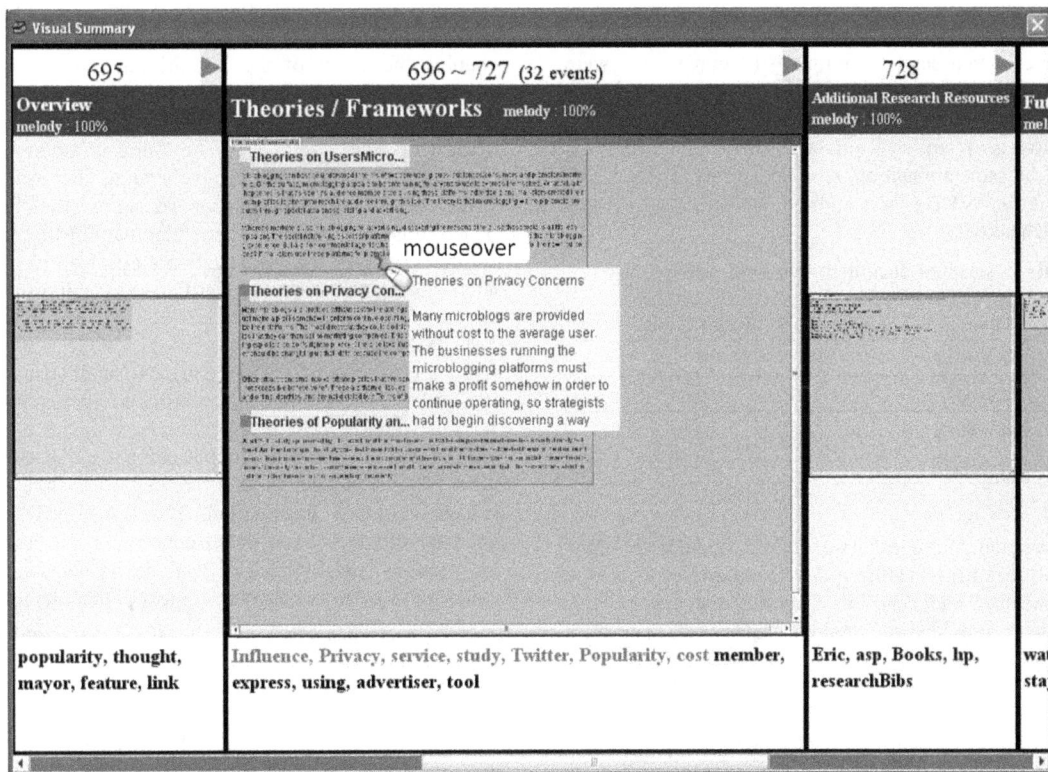

Figure 6. The visual summary provides filmstrip visualization of shorter segments of activity.

5.4.5 Visual Summary

Where the filmstrip component provides an overview of the users' work process, the visual summary provides more detailed visual cues regarding specific user activities via a series of thumbnails that can be thought of as a more detailed filmstrip.

The main advantage of the visual summary is that each user action will be visible in an element in the visual summary. When multiple subsequent actions take place in the same region, a single thumbnail is included (e.g. the middle of Figure 6). When a user action cannot be part of the same thumbnail as the previous user action, a new thumbnail is created.

Each thumbnail includes visual cues indicating user activities that happened during the period. In the figure, the thumbnail representing the group from the 696th event to the 727th includes a dot on the left-top side of each three objects and one popup window on the middle object. The dot is yellow when the object or collection was updated and red when it was created. Next to the dot, a brief text field provides a snippet of the object's or collection's textual content. Placing the mouse pointer over the text results in popup window showing more of the text. A smaller thumbnail without dots is provided for individual events.

6. EVALUATION

At the core of the CoActIVE design is the goal to improve users' ability to locate and comprehend the work of others. A study was performed to determine the effect of the alternate visualizations towards achieving these goals. The study used the recorded history from previous collaborative activities in VKB where the study participants would have no prior knowledge of the activity or the people involved in the activity. This is the same situation as

someone just beginning to participate in an existing on-line collaboration, such as suggesting edits to a wiki page.

6.1 Participants

24 graduate students were recruited via email and in-person contact. 75% of the participants had an engineering background and the others were from diverse areas (architecture, natural science, social science, and education).

All participants reported using a computer daily and have used computers for more than four years. All participants also answered that they had experience with history tools, and have used undo/redo in document or picture editing applications. Other uses of history reported by participants included revisiting web pages, version control, and history support in an Integrated Development Environment. Overall, most participants felt they needed history tools for undo/redo and tended to be satisfied with the existing tools (25% were neutral and 67% were satisfied).

15 of the 24 participants (62.5%) had experience working with other people via collaboration applications. Only two participants reported using history information to find particular activity or to understand work progress in such a collaboration. Most participants mentioned that they had a hard time recognizing the work of collaborators, and some reported not trying to understand the work of others due to such difficulties. Some participants reported browsing the modified parts of a work (e.g. document, design) relying on their memory of previous work to locate changes.

6.2 Experimental Design

Participants were placed in the role of a teaching assistant examining collaboratively authored VKB documents to determine which students did what. Each participant was asked to answer an equivalent series of questions about four different recorded activities. The recorded activities (documents) were collaboratively authored by two students spread across two classes at different universities. The four documents used were selected based on having relatively similar work practices and approximately the same amount of recorded activity. Table 1 lists the topics of the four VKB spaces and the number of user events recorded for each activity.

Table 1. Selected documents for evaluation

Topic	Event count
Online Balkanization	963
Blogging	981
Online Voting	945
Microblogging	1003

As a teaching assistant, participants were asked to understand how the given VKB documents had been developed and in what way each project member had contributed to the documents. Four visualizations were provided to answer the questions; they were the history session viewer, the history interpretation viewer, the filmstrip visualization with textual summaries, and the filmstrip visualization with visual summaries.

Each participant used a different visualization to answer the questions for each recorded activity. The assignment of recorded activity to visualization type was balanced (6 for each pair). Due to the potential for learning effects, the order of the visualizations was balanced across subjects; each of the 24 participants had a unique visualization order. Participants could also use the VKB's embedded history playback capabilities in all conditions.

A tutorial session was given before beginning the first task. The session covered the use of both VKB and the history mechanism. After the task, participants answered a short questionnaire that asked about their satisfaction with history support and visualization settings. A brief interview followed after the survey.

Table 2. Five types of questions

Type	Question
1	Find the event ID where **Jill** created the information object contained below.
2	What is the previous title of the "**How to Start a Blog**" collection?
3	Which one of **X** and **Y** was created earlier in the document?
4	Find the event ID where the collection, "**CSCW without C**" is displayed on a screen as shown below.
5	Find as many places as **Jack** worked on the "**Current research**" collection as possible in 3 minutes.

6.2.1 Task

Each task included five questions, one of each type shown in Table 2. Questions of type one though four were assessed based on both the time required to answer the question and the correctness of the answer. The last question was measured based on the number of correct and incorrect answers provided in the time provided (3 minutes).

The five types of questions represent five different history location and comprehension activities. The first question is to examine the effect of the visualization on locating a specific activity by a certain user. The second question determines the visualization's effect on recovering the prior state of a specified element in the document. The third question examines the visualization's effect on comprehending the order of specific activities. The forth question explores the effect of the visualization on locating a particular state of the document. The last question tests the visualization's effect on identifying all the activity of a particular user regarding specific information.

6.3 Results

While we expected the clustering and summarization would aid the location and comprehension tasks, we were not sure which of the augmented views would be of most aid to participants and which would be preferred. In particular, the History Interpretation Viewer provided a simple interface that is easy to use but does not provide as much information. The filmstrip with the textual summary provides more detail concerning the content modified and requires less interaction than the visual summary but the visual summary provides more context of the interactions.

Here we present results indicating the effect of the visualization on time required for tasks, error rate for tasks, and user satisfaction.

6.3.1 Time Spent on Each Visualization Setting

The mean time which 24 participants spent on the four tasks was 58.52 minutes. The total time for the evaluation was around two hours including demographic and domain surveys, tutorial session, questionnaire, and interview.

Table 3. Overall time spent on each setting

	VS1	VS2	VS3	VS4
Mean (min)	17.04	13.43	8.62	7.44
Std Dev	5.99	4.01	2.71	2.81

VS1 : History session viewer   **VS3** : Filmstrip + Textual summary
VS2 : History interpretation viewer   **VS4** : Filmstrip + Visual summary

Table 3 shows the mean and standard deviation of total time the participants spent on the first four questions with each visualization. Participants took the most time when using the history session viewer (VS1: Visual Setting #1) and the least time when using the filmstrip visualization+visual summary (VS4). The difference between VS4 and VS1 is significant (Kruskal-Wallis, p<.001). A post-hoc Tukey's test showed significant differences between all permutations of the pair VS3 and VS4 with the pair VS1 and VS2 with p<.001, The difference between VS3 and VS4 was not significant (p=.62) nor was the difference between VS1 and VS2 (p=.13).

6.3.2 Time Spent on Each Type of Question

Table 4 shows the mean and the standard deviation of time taken to perform each of the first four types of questions under four visualization settings. The results found in the overall time continue for each of the four question types. VS4 has the shortest mean time to complete each type of question, with VS3 taking slightly longer and VS2 being somewhat faster than VS1. The notable exception was that for Type 2 questions, VS2 was only slightly slower than VS3 and took less than half the time of VS1. The Kruskal-Wallis test shows that, for each question type, VS4 and VS1 results are significantly different (p<.001). Tukey's test shows a similar pattern as the overall results – that VS1 is significantly different from VS3 and VS4 for all question types (p<.003 for closest) and that VS3 and VS4 are not significantly different from each other for any question type.

Table 4. Time spent on each question type

	Means (min)				Standard Deviation			
	VS1	VS2	VS3	VS4	VS1	VS2	VS3	VS4
Type 1	4.16	3.70	2.55	2.02	1.44	2.34	1.31	0.96
Type 2	3.56	1.62	1.49	1.25	2.41	0.83	0.88	0.48
Type 3	5.23	4.21	2.59	2.46	3.19	2.24	2.05	1.65
Type 4	4.09	3.90	1.98	1.70	2.69	2.04	1.10	0.94

6.3.3 Correctness of Answers

Answers provided by participants were not always correct. Table 5 shows the number of incorrect answers for each visualization setting for each of the first four question types. Among the settings, 11 errors (55% of the total errors across all conditions) were during use of the history session viewer. From this result, it seems that working with low-level history yields a higher error rate. Particularly, participants seemed to have difficulty in understanding the order of specific activities (type 3) and locating a particular state of the document in the history (type 4). The History Interpretation Viewer also resulted in a number of errors when locating a particular state of the document.

Table 5. Number of incorrect answers

	VS1	VS2	VS3	VS4	Total
Type 1	1	0	2	0	3
Type 2	0	0	0	0	0
Type 3	4	1	0	0	5
Type 4	6	5	0	1	12
Total	11	6	2	1	20

The fifth question in each task was designed to assess the efficiency of each interface for finding all the activity of a particular type. Table 6 presents the average number of correct answers and their standard deviation in the three minutes provided. Here again the filmstrip with visual summaries performed the best. This time the difference between this interface and all other interfaces is significant.

Table 6. Number of correct answers for type 5 question

	VS1	VS2	VS3	VS4
Mean	1.83	1.58	2.38	4.42
Std Dev	1.37	1.47	0.92	1.25

6.3.4 Questionnaire Results

After the completion of the task, participants responded to a set of questions regarding their satisfaction. The questions employed a Likert scale where a value of 1 indicated strong disagreement, and 7 indicated strong agreement.

Overall, participants' reported preference matched the performance results: VS4, VS3, VS2, and VS1. VS4 was the most preferred (21 strongly agrees, 2 agrees) while VS1, which is

similar to the history interface found in VKB 2, was least preferred (18 strongly disagrees, 3 disagrees).

While being preferred overall, a few participants reported being confused when navigating the filmstrip visualization. One issue was that the thumbnail for a segment showed the final state of that segment so when users go the segment and move forward in time they immediately see work that is part of the next segment.

When asked about the value of particular features, participants responded positively to the automatically-generated hierarchic interpretation of history, and the presentation of keywords and author information associated with the segments of activity.

7. CONCLUSIONS

The increase in server-based and cloud-based applications has brought a corresponding increase in long-term collaborations among people who may never know one another. Records of user activity support can be used to provide an understanding of prior effort in such situations but locating and comprehending particular activity within large history records can be difficult for users.

CoActIVE is a history mechanism that clusters system-level activity into higher-level episodes, generates textual and visual summaries of these episodes, and provides a variety of history visualizations based on the inferred episodes. CoActIVE can be adapted for use with most Java applications that already support undo/redo.

An evaluation compared performance and satisfaction for participants answering questions that required them to locate particular events or states in a recorded history and to comprehend who performed different activities and the order of activity. Two list/tree views of the history record and two filmstrip views of the history record were compared. The list views included a traditional event-list view as found in current applications and an augmented tree view of the hierarchically-clustered activity. The two filmstrip views differed in that one provided textual summaries of changes and one provided visual summaries.

The results of the study showed improvements for all three new interfaces over the traditional event view but the two filmstrip views significantly outperformed the two list/tree views. Participants were able to perform the tasks most efficiently with the fewest errors with the film strip view with visual summaries. This view was also their favored view in post-task surveys and interviews.

Future work can build on these results. The evaluation performed did not specifically examine the quality of the clustering results. Comparing alternative event-clustering algorithms has the potential to improve the overall support of such interfaces. Similarly, the four visualizations compared are examples from a large design space for history visualization. The results show visual presentations of history and state were the most valuable but that may differ depending on the application being supported. Finally, while we have integrated CoActIVE in a second Java application, it is future work to determine if the results seen here will transfer to that application.

8. ACKNOWLEDGMENTS

This material is based upon work supported in part by the National Science Foundation under grants DUE-0938074 and IIS-1049217.

9. REFERENCES

[1] Begole, J., Tang, J.C., Smith, R.B., and Yankelovich, N. Work rhythms: analyzing visualizations of awareness histories of distributed groups. In *Proc. CSCW 2002*, ACM Press (2002), 334-343.

[2] Derthick, M. and Roth, S.F. Data exploration across temporal contexts. In *Proc. IUI 2000*, ACM Press (2000), 60-67.

[3] Eick, S., Steffen, J., and Sumner, E. Seesoft-a tool for visualizing line oriented software statistics. In *IEEE Trans. Softw. Eng.* 18, 11 (1992), 957-968.

[4] Fischer, G., Grudin, J., McCall, R., Ostwald, J., Redmiles, D., Reeves, B., and Shipman, F. Seeding, Evolutionary Growth and Reseeding: The Incremental Development of Collaborative Design Environments, in *Coordination Theory and Collaboration Technology*, Lawrence Erlbaum Associates, 2001, 447-472.

[5] Froehlich, J. and Dourish, P. Unifying artifacts and activities in a visual tool for distributed software development teams. In *Proc. ICSE 2004*, IEEE Computer Society (2004), 387-396.

[6] Gutwin, C., Graham, N., Wolfe, C., Wong, N., and Alwis, B. Gone but not forgotten: designing for disconnection in synchronous groupware. In *Proc. CSCW 2010*, ACM Press (2010), 179-188.

[7] Gutwin, C. and Greenberg, S. The effects of workspace awareness support on the usability of real-time distributed groupware. In *ACM Trans. Comput.-Hum. Interact.* 6, 3 (1999), 243-281.

[8] Hill, W.C., Hollan, J.D., Wroblewski, D., and McCandless, T. Edit wear and read wear. In *Proc. CHI 1992*, ACM Press (1992), 3-9.

[9] Java WordNet Library, http://jwordnet.sourceforge.net.

[10] Klemmer, S.R., Thomsen, M., Phelps-Goodman, E., Lee, R. and Landay, J.A. Where do web sites come from? Capturing and interacting with design history. In *Proc. CHI 2002*, ACM Press (2002), 1-8.

[11] Lee, A. *Investigations into History Tools for User Support*. Technical Report CSRI-271, University of Toronto, 1992.

[12] Manohar, N. and Prakash, A. The session capture and replay paradigm for asynchronous collaboration. In *Proc. ECSCW 1995*, Kluwer Academic Publishers (1995), 149-164.

[13] Marshall, C.C., Shipman, F.M., and McCall, R.J. "Putting digital libraries to work: issues and experience with community memories", *Proceedings of Digital Libraries '94*, Texas A&M University, 1994.

[14] Marshall, C.C., Shipman, F.M., and McCall, R.J. "Making large-scale information resources serve communities of practice" *Journal of Management Information Systems*, 11 (4) (1995), 65-86.

[15] Milic-Frayling, N., Jones, R., Rodden, K., Smyth, G., Blackwell, A., and Sommerer, R. Smartback: supporting users in back navigation. In *Proc. WWW 2004*, ACM Press (2004), 63-71.

[16] Nakamura, T., Igarashi, T. An application-independent system for visualizing user operation history, In *Proc. UIST 2008*, ACM Press (2008), 23-31.

[17] Neuwirth, C., James H. Morris, J., Regli, S., Chandhok, R., and Wenger, G. Envisioning communication: task-tailorable representations of communication in asynchronous work. In *Proc. CSCW 1998*, ACM Press (1998), 265-274.

[18] Plaisant, C., Milash, B., Rose, A., Widoff, S., and Shneiderman, B. LifeLines: visualizing personal histories. In *Proc. CHI 1996*, ACM Press (1996), 221-227.

[19] Plaisant, C., Rose, A., Rubloff, G., Salter, R., and Shneiderman, B. The design of history mechanisms and their use in collaborative educational simulations. In *Proc. CSCL 1999*, International Society of the Learning Sciences (1999), 348-359.

[20] Reeves, B. *Supporting Collaborative Design by Embedded Communication and History in Design Artifacts*. Ph.D. Dissertation, Department of Computer Science, University of Colorado, 1993.

[21] Reeves, B.N., and Shipman, F.M. "Supporting Communication between Designers with Artifact-Centered Evolving Information Spaces". *Proc. CSCW `92*, ACM Press (1992), 394-401.

[22] Shipman, F., Airhart, R., Hsieh, H., Maloor, P., Moore, J.M., and Shah, D. "Visual and spatial communication and task organization in the Visual Knowledge Builder". In *Proc. of GROUP '01*, ACM Press, (2001), 260-269.

[23] Shipman, F. and Hsieh, H. Navigable History: A Reader's View of Writer's Time. *New Review of Hypermedia and Multimedia*, 6 (2000), 147-167.

[24] Shipman, F.M., Hsieh, H., Maloor, P., and Moore, J. M. The visual knowledge builder: a second generation spatial hypertext. *Proc. Hypertext 2001*, ACM Press (2001), 113-122.

[25] Shirai, Y., Yamamoto, Y., and Nakakoji, K. Time-Based Authoring Tools for Informal Information Management, *Symposium on Interactive Visual Information Collections and Activity (IVICA2009)*, 2009.

[26] Suchman, L.A., *Plans and situated actions: The problem of human-machine communication*. Cambridge University Press, New York, NY, 1987.

[27] Tam, J. and Greenberg, S. A framework for asynchronous change awareness in collaborative documents and workspaces. *Int. J. Hum.-Comput. Stud.* 64, 7 (July 2006), 583-598.

[28] Viégas, F.B., Wattenberg, M., and Dave, K. Studying cooperation and conflict between authors with history flow visualizations. In *Proc. CHI 2004*, ACM Press (2004), 575-582.

Controlling an Avatar's Pointing Gestures in Desktop Collaborative Virtual Environments

Nelson Wong and Carl Gutwin
Department of Computer Science, University of Saskatchewan
110 Science Place
Saskatoon, SK, Canada S7N 5C9
nelson.wong, carl.gutwin @usask.ca

ABSTRACT

Collaborative Virtual Environments (CVEs) allow people to interact with each other in virtual worlds through computer-generated avatars. Avatars are much less expressive than real bodies, and one main limitation is their lack of support for non-verbal communication such as pointing gestures. Part of the problem is that these gestures must be created through an input device, but the user is already busy controlling the avatar's location, rotation, and view direction. Pointing gestures are only useful for collaborative communication if they can be controlled simultaneously with all other avatar actions. To determine whether there are input configurations that make pointing gestures feasible, we carried out a study that compared five different widely-available input devices in three non-verbal communication tasks. We found that users were able to successfully incorporate pointing gestures into tasks that already involved moving, turning, and looking, but that there were significant and substantial differences between devices. Two configurations performed best: a mode-switched version of standard mouse-and-keyboard control, and a direct-pointing scheme using a Wii remote. There were also minor effects of gender and video-game experience. Our study suggests that users will be able to successfully create free pointing gestures in CVEs, greatly improving the communicative richness of these environments.

Categories and Subject Descriptors

H.5.3 [**Information Interfaces and Presentation**]: *CSCW*

General Terms

Human Factors, Design, Performance.

Keywords

Gestural communication, deictic pointing, CVEs.

1. INTRODUCTION

Collaborative Virtual Environments (CVEs) are 3D worlds where people can interact with objects and other people through a computer-generated representation of themselves called an avatar. CVEs are common in first-person shooter (FPS) games, massively multiplayer online role-playing games such as World of Warcraft, and social environments such as Second Life.

Interaction in these environments is based on the idea that avatars will manipulate objects and communicate with each other in ways that are similar to what happens in the real world. This suggests that people should be able to communicate both verbally and non-verbally, since both are important in everyday human interaction. Although verbal communication is generally well supported using voice over IP, non-verbal communication in CVEs is much less developed. Human communication in the real world involves many types of non-verbal communication, including facial expressions and body postures [1]; in this work we focus on gestural communication, and on hand-and-arm-based deictic pointing gestures in particular (called *free pointing*).

Support for gestural communication represents an important step forward for interaction in CVEs. These techniques add valuable expressivity to communication, particularly when referencing objects and relationships that are spatially situated in the virtual world. With free pointing, people could make rich statements such as the following instructions: "Go that way <points> and turn past that building <shows direction>, then loop around like this <draws circular path>; I'll be moving like this <draws zigzag path> and we'll meet up there <points>."

However, hand-and-arm gestures are not well supported in CVEs. One reason is that it may be difficult for users to control the additional degrees of freedom needed for pointing. Typical CVEs already ask users to control three aspects of the avatar (location, rotation, and view direction) with their left and right hands, and it is not clear whether people will be able to manipulate and make use of the additional controls needed for free pointing. Adding gestural capabilities to avatars is an example of how improving collaboration support (i.e., better gestural communication) can have substantial ramifications for individual effort (i.e., time and practice to learn and master complex controls). The question of whether people can successfully manipulate these more expressive avatars must be answered before CVEs can truly support natural non-verbal communication.

In this paper we address this question by developing five different input configurations using commonly-available input devices for CVEs that can support a simple kind of free pointing (straight-arm pointing) in addition to controlling moving, turning, and looking. The five configurations are a mode-switched mouse and keyboard, a mouse+trackball device, a game controller, a joystick, and a direct-pointing setup using the Wii Remote, Nunchuk, and Balance Board. We compared these devices in an experiment where participants used the different configurations to carry out three non-verbal communication tasks in a CVE. The tasks also involved different combinations of moving, turning, and looking.

Our main finding is that participants were able to successfully control free pointing, even when the task also required all three other types of movement. This result shows that control over free pointing can be feasibly added to CVEs, and makes progress towards the goal of richer non-verbal communication in these environments. Second, we found that there were significant differences between the different devices. Two configurations stood out: the mode-switched mouse and keyboard, and the Wii-remote configuration. Both of these controllers were easy for participants to learn and to use, and the requirement for a mode switch (to change between turning and pointing) did not cause problems for participants. The game controller and the joystick performed worst in the study, even for people with game experience. In addition, there were only small effects of gender: in one task, women performed slightly better than men with the mode-switched mouse and Wii setup, but slightly worse with the game controller and joystick.

Our work makes three contributions. First, we identify the problem that attempting to make communication more expressive for the group can substantially add to the burden of control for the individual. Second, we show that there are usable configurations for controlling free pointing, and that these can successfully be added to existing avatar controls for CVEs. Third, we present several new input techniques using widely-available input devices for free pointing, and provide empirical evidence about the performance characteristics of, and differences between, these input configurations. Our work suggests that support for gestural communication can and should be added into CVEs, allowing people to communicate in ways that are far richer than what is possible in current environments.

2. BACKGROUND
2.1 Pointing in Real-World Communication
Pointing is ubiquitous in real-world human communication, and is primarily used to indicate objects referred to in speech (called *deictic* reference) [17]. Deixis allows people to greatly simplify communication when it is difficult to rely on verbal descriptions (e.g., indicating objects with hard-to-describe shapes) [13], as long as the observer can see and interpret the pointing gesture.

A deictic pointing gesture can be divided into four stages. First, the producer of the gesture must ensure *mutual orientation* with the observer, such that both parties can see the gesture and the target. Second, the producer may engage in *preparation* actions that indicate to the observer that a pointing gesture is going to be made. *Production of the gesture* occurs next, and the fact that this production is gradual allows people to predict the general direction of the gesture before it is completed [7, 18]. Finally, the producer must continue *holding* the gesture until they are sure that the observer has seen it, and until they are sure that mutual understanding has been reached [18].

2.2 Pointing in CVEs
Although pointing is ubiquitous in the real world, it is not well supported in CVEs. This is part of a general lack of interactional capabilities: as Moore and colleagues state, "despite their ever-increasing visual realism, today's virtual game worlds are much less advanced in terms of their *interactional* sophistication" ([18], p. 267). Researchers have noted several problems that make pointing gestures difficult in CVEs. Mutual orientation is difficult to achieve because of narrow fields of view in CVEs, and pointing at objects that are not close by often leads to frequent misunderstandings [6, 10]. Pointing actions in CVEs are often produced immediately (e.g., with commands such as '/point'), and do not provide the gradual information available from real-world gestures. Pointing in CVEs is also often restricted to objects in the world, greatly reducing the expressiveness of pointing actions.

Object-based pointing has been shown to cause severe communication problems in collaborative work [5].

Various techniques for improving interaction in CVEs have been suggested [6, 11], including wide-angle peripheral lenses to increase a user's field of view; a visible view frustum to better indicate what others can see; elongated arms for improved visibility, object highlighting to enhance awareness of what others are looking at; or the ability to look through another person's view to determine what they can see [11]. In addition, studies have shown that people are almost as accurate in pointing with an avatar (and interpreting avatar pointing) as they are in the real world [25]. However, none of these solutions have addressed the problem of controlling free pointing, which is part of the problem of avatar control more generally.

2.3 Controlling Avatars in Desktop CVEs
Researchers have explored a wide variety of devices and techniques for avatar control, including using the mouse [15], keyboard [21], gamepad [24], data glove [8], head and hand tracker [2], eye tracker [4, 22], hand gestures [14], full body actions [20], and brain activities [16, 23]. Some of these control methods are intended for immersive virtual environments with head-mounted displays; we limit our scope to desktop CVEs, where users look at the virtual world through a computer monitor.

The most common input devices for controlling avatars in these situations are mice, keyboards, and game controllers. Much research has been done to improve the functions and usability of these devices for avatar control. For example, Mackinlay and colleagues [15] used a mouse and on-screen icons to control an avatar's body and gaze locations, and Salem and Earle [21] used different keystrokes to control the facial expressions of avatars. Templeman et al. [24] altered the conventional control mapping of a gamepad to make it more suitable for tactical movement, by separating the control of avatar movement and viewing direction.

There are many avatar control mechanisms, but it is still unclear how to better manipulate simultaneous pointing, moving, looking, and turning using commonly-available input devices. The problem in adding controls is that each new degree of freedom must be learnt by users, and the new manipulation techniques are often overloaded onto the user's hands. We run the risk of forcing CVE users to become skilled puppeteers, having to spend time and effort learning to flex every limb and joint of their avatar.

This issue shifts the problem of controlling avatars to a consideration of what humans can in fact successfully manipulate with their arms and hands. Therefore, we must look at underlying principles that are known from research in human motor control.

2.4 Human Manual Control
The study of human performance with input devices has a long history [3, 9, 12], and several issues have been identified both on the human side and on the device side that affect the design of human-computer control systems.

On the human side, motor control involves a human's capability to manipulate an input device using their limbs and muscles [26]. This capability is governed to some degree by the muscle groups used, with smaller groups (e.g., fingers and wrists as opposed to shoulder and arm muscles) allowing for greater precision and finer-grained control. Feedback about control actions is provided in two ways: first, the human's awareness of the position of their limbs in space (proprioception) which allows input control without system feedback (e.g., for open-loop actions); second, external perception is used to gather feedback from the control action itself (e.g., for closed-loop control).

On the device side, several properties of the input device have been shown to affect human performance [3, 9, 12]. First, different physical properties can be sensed by the device, including position (e.g., the mouse) and force (e.g., isometric or isotonic joysticks). Second, the translation of raw device input to movement of an object is the device's transfer function, and can be zero-order (i.e., position control), first-order (i.e., rate control), or higher-order (e.g., acceleration control). In general, only position and rate control are used in human motor control tasks.

The mapping of the input space to the virtual space can be either absolute, where each point on the input space corresponds to a point in virtual space; or relative, which allows more flexible movement but can require clutching. The directness of the device is also an issue: direct input implies that the input space is the same as the output space (e.g., touch screens or Wii remotes); indirect devices use a separate input space (e.g., the mouse).

3. A DESIGN FRAMEWORK FOR AVATAR CONTROL

To better understand free pointing for CVEs, we identify three factors that affect avatar control: basic actions that can be controlled; the degrees of freedom needed for those actions; and means for providing input for actions.

3.1 Basic Avatar Actions

Most avatars have three basic actions: moving, looking, and turning. To this, we add a fourth action, free pointing.

Moving (body location). Moving an avatar involves translating its position on the surface of the CVE world (as would occur if the avatar walked sideways, forward, or backwards). Avatar movement also alters the avatar's view and pointing gestures, since the eyes and arm are moved along with the body. In many CVEs, avatar movement is accomplished using a four-directional keypad (e.g., the A-S-D-W keys on a keyboard).

Turning (body direction). Turning an avatar means rotating it around its vertical axis. Turning does not change the avatar's location, but does change the view and the direction of pointing. In addition, turning control is often used in concert with keypad-based movement in order to allow precise translation: that is, by turning as the avatar moves forward, better control over movement can be achieved. In many CVEs, turning is the only way to change the avatar's view left or right, as there is no separate control over horizontal view direction.

Looking (head direction). Looking involves changing an avatar's view – that is, the direction of the view frustum originating from the avatar's eye position. Changing the avatar's view also changes what the user can see on the screen if a first-person view is used. Looking does not affect the avatar's location, rotation, or pointing direction. Many CVEs only provide dedicated control over up-down looking, with left-right looking tied to turning.

Pointing (arm direction). Pointing means extending the avatar's arm to indicate a particular direction relative to the avatar. In the system described below, we simplify the pointing action to use a straight arm gesture: the arm is held straight with a finger extended, and can be rotated horizontally and vertically at the avatar's shoulder (Figure 1). Free pointing does not change the avatar's location, rotation, or view. This type of free pointing is not supported in any current CVE.

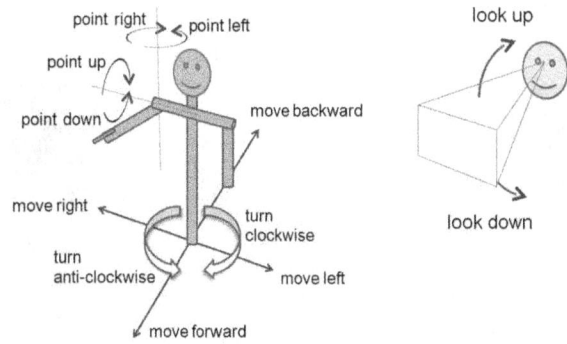

Figure 1. Control dimensions of an avatar.

3.2 Degree-of-Freedom Control Requirements

Moving, looking, and pointing in general involve continuous two-dimensional control, whereas turning involves continuous control over one dimension only. However, few if any CVEs actually provide full control over all of these dimensions. In particular, many game environments simplify control by reducing the expressiveness of movement to simple four-direction control (forward, back, left, right), and by locking horizontal view direction to avatar rotation direction.

Free pointing adds another two-dimensional space in which pointing direction must be specified: that is, vertical and horizontal rotation of the straight arm around the shoulder.

3.3 Input Devices for Controlling Pointing

There are numerous possibilities for matching input devices to the problem of controlling free pointing:

Discrete directions. Keypads or arrow keys can provide discrete n-directional control at a fixed velocity. Although this scheme can work well for 2D control over movement (see above), it is awkward to use without simultaneous control over rotation.

Relative position control. A mouse or trackball provides control over the position of the controlled object. Mice and trackballs are relative (they require clutching).

Rate (velocity) control. Isotonic or isometric joysticks generally provide variable-rate 2D control (although some can also provide position control). The input is usually mapped to velocity of the controlled object (e.g., the cursor or the pointing finger).

Direct pointing. A direct pointing device allows people to simply point towards the representation of the target. Devices such as the Wiimote, the Kinect, or 6DoF trackers allow this type of pointing.

4. SCENARIOS FOR COMMUNICATIVE POINTING IN CVES

Three typical situations in CVEs illustrate the value of being able to control different combinations of pointing, moving, turning, and looking. The situations are oriented around a typical game scenario called a 'collaborative escort mission' (Figure 2). The objective of the mission is for two players to escort an in-game character (the VIP) from one location to another. There are several requirements to an escort mission: the players need to move from the starting location to the destination, must defend against enemies on the way, and must ensure the VIP's safety. The following situations describe episodes where one player must communicate targets to their partner – in current versions of FPS games, this communication must take place through a combination of weapon-based pointing and verbal descriptions, neither of which is likely to be as successful as free pointing.

Figure 2. 1ˢᵗ-person view in an escort mission (Rainbow Six).

Situation 1: Point at different targets in the same view. Multiple enemies are often located at different places on the screen simultaneously. While keeping an eye on the VIP, the player must both point out targets to the partner, and shoot at some of the enemies (Figure 2). It is important to maintain a certain viewing angle to keep all of the targets, the VIP, and the partner in view at the same time. It will be valuable to be able to move the avatar's arm freely and point at different targets within the view. This type of action is not possible with common control schemes where weapon-based pointing is tied to the center of the view.

Situation 2: Point at targets while moving. Sometimes it is dangerous to stop or even slow down during the escort mission. Players must keep moving while at the same time keeping track of the VIP and pointing out enemies. This situation requires that the player be able to point freely with the avatar while also looking, moving, and turning to follow a path or track the VIP.

Situation 3: Point at targets while changing the view. After arriving at a relatively safe location during the mission, the player may need to communicate the locations of multiple enemies that are spread out over a wide area. This situation requires pointing with the avatar while also moving the view (both horizontally and vertically) to cover the entire range where enemies are located.

5. INPUT CONFIGURATIONS TO SUPPORT POINTING

Input devices used in CVEs are not explicitly designed to control pointing together with other actions. To test if free pointing could be successfully controlled, we configured five widely-available input devices to allow control of all four types of avatar action (Figures 3 to 7). These input devices are all commonly available; however, the input mappings are in some cases different from their conventional settings.

In all configurations, we combined looking and turning (as described in Section 3.1) to match the approach of most first-person games. Since turning also changes the view, people can still look at all directions through the avatar's view. The avatar needs to change its orientation to look sideways, but this does not affect our investigation of pointing.

5.1 Mouse and Keyboard

These devices are the most common configuration for controlling avatars on PCs. We retained the conventional mappings of the mouse and keyboard, but added a mode switch to control pointing: when the mouse button is pressed, the mouse controls pointing; when the button is up, the mouse controls rotation and view as normal. When pointing, forward and backward movement of the mouse moves the pointing arm up and down, and left and right mouse movement turns the arm left and right (see Figure 3). This configuration has the restriction that view control and pointing cannot be done at the same time.

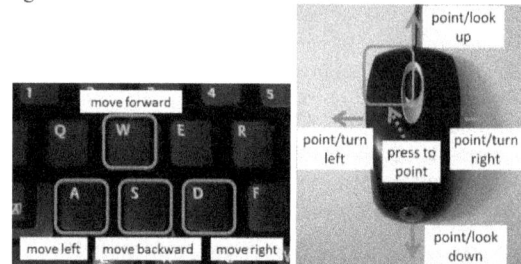

Figure 3. Mouse and keyboard.

5.2 Trackball, Mouse, and Keyboard

This combination is similar to the mouse-and-keyboard configuration, except that in place of a mode switch, an additional 2D input device (a trackball) is added to the top of the mouse in the normal mousewheel location (we used an Apple Mighty Mouse). Pointing is controlled at any time by the trackball: rotating the ball forward, backward, left, or right changes the pointing direction up, down, left, and right (Figure 4). Other input mappings for the mouse and keyboard were as above. This configuration is similar to the mouse but allows simultaneous control of pointing.

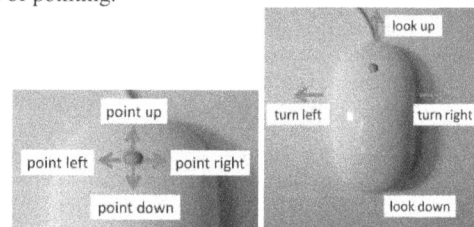

Figure 4. Mouse and trackball.

5.3 Gamepad

A gamepad is the primary input device for CVEs on game console systems. We used an Xbox controller with two rate-based thumbsticks, and a directional control pad (d-pad). We used the right stick to control pointing, the left stick for looking and turning, and the d-pad for fixed-rate moving (Figure 5). We used standard directional mappings of the thumbsticks and d-pad for pointing, looking, turning, and moving. This configuration was chosen to match common console systems, and also to test the effectiveness of rate-based control of pointing.

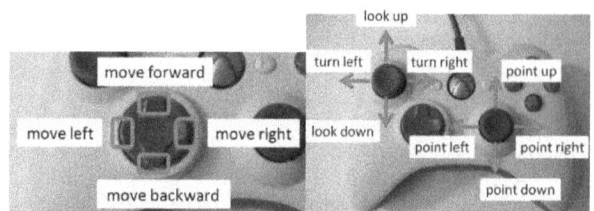

Figure 5. Gamepad: d-pad (left) and thumbstick (right).

5.4 Joystick

Many game joysticks allow control over multiple dimensions with a single device; we used a Microsoft SideWinder Precision 2 joystick to control all avatar actions (see Figure 6). The main stick (forward, back, left, right) is used for pointing, and the 'hat' at the tip of the stick is for fixed-rate looking and turning. We used the four buttons on the base of the joystick (left of the main stick) to control moving. This configuration allows us to test rate-based simultaneous control of multiple dimensions (turning/viewing and pointing) with one hand.

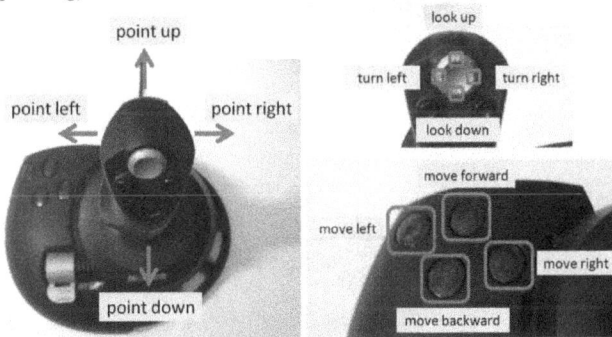

Figure 6. Joystick: main stick (left), hat (top right), and buttons (bottom right).

5.5 Wii Controls

The Nintendo Wiimote allows direct pointing at the screen, allowing us to test one configuration that let people point as they would in the real world. Pointing direction was thus controlled by the user's (real) arm: to point the avatar's arm in certain direction, move the Wiimote in the corresponding direction. The thumbstick on the Nunchuk controller is used to control turning and looking (as with the thumbstick on the gamepad). The Wii Balance Board controls the movement of the avatar. When seated, the user presses on different parts of the board to move forward, back, left, and right (see Figure 7).

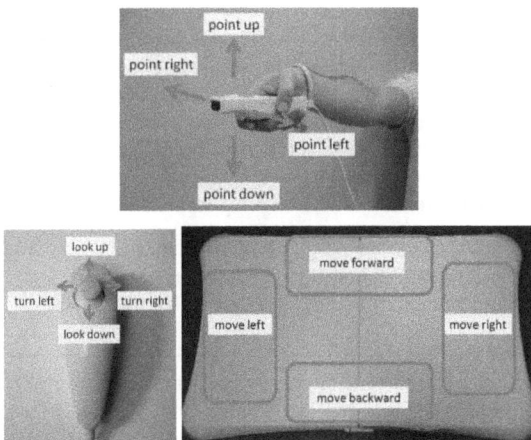

Figure 7. Wiimote, Nunchuk, and Wii Balance Board.

6. USER STUDY: EVALUATING POINTING CONTROL CONFIGURATIONS

We carried out a controlled study to determine which input configurations were best able to support free pointing. We devised three communication tasks that involved deictic pointing; all tasks also involved combinations of other avatar actions (moving, turning, and looking). These tasks were carried out in a custom CVE that allows full communication between multiple people all represented by avatars, and participants were told to point out the required objects to another person who was standing beside them in the CVE. However, in order to find out if people can control free pointing at all, we wanted the participants to focus on pointing control. To do that, we simulated the other person in the task, and did not ask participants to communicate verbally.

Our goal was to find out whether free pointing is feasible with commonly-available real-world devices. While these devices have different characteristics, we used reasonable settings for each device (e.g., rates for the rate-based controls, mouse and trackball C/D ratios) that were determined through a small pilot study.

Table 1. Summary of input configurations.
(R / A: Relative / Absolute. I / D: Indirect / Direct.
P / S: Position / Speed control. F / V: Fixed / Variable rate)

Mouse	Point	Mouse (mode)	R	I	P	
	Move	Keyboard	A	I	S	F
	Look/Turn	Mouse (mode)	R	I	P	
Trackball	Point	Trackball	R	I	P	
	Move	Keyboard	A	I	S	F
	Look/Turn	Mouse	R	I	P	
Gamepad	Point	Right stick	A	I	S	V
	Move	D-pad	A	I	S	F
	Look/Turn	Left stick	A	I	S	V
Joystick	Point	Main stick	A	I	S	V
	Move	Buttons	A	I	S	F
	Look/Turn	Hat	A	I	S	F
Wii	Point	Wiimote	A	D	P	
	Move	Balance board	A	I	S	V
	Look/Turn	Nunchuk	A	I	S	V

6.1 Tasks

6.1.1 Task 1: Move-and-Point (MP)

In the move-and-point (MP) task, objects were located on a wall in front of the avatar (Figure 8), and participants pointed at the objects while moving sideways. This corresponds to many real-world communicative situations (e.g., discussing what items to buy on a grocery store shelf). Avatars were restricted to moving left and right in this task, to prevent participants from simply moving back until they could see all the objects at once.

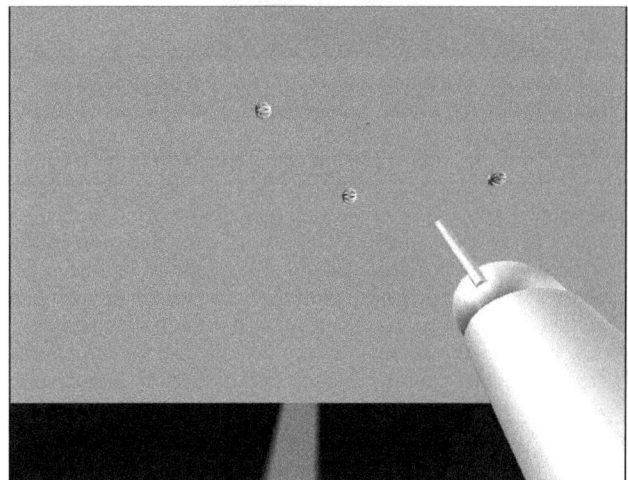

Figure 8. Move-and-Point task. Participant moves left or right, pointing at objects along the way.

Participants moved the avatar's arm (using the input device specified by the experimental condition) to point at the objects. A red dot on the CVE's wall indicated where the avatar was pointing. The object disappeared once it was pointed to, and a trial ended once all ten objects were correctly indicated with deictic pointing (i.e., as if the participants was stating "*this* one and *this* one and *this* one..."). The task involved eight trials of ten objects each, with the first three trials marked as training. The dependent measure was completion time.

6.1.2 Task 2: Turn-Look-and-Point (TLP)

In the turn-look-and-point (TLP) task, objects were placed on the walls of a room in the CVE (Figure 9). The participants were asked to turn all the way around in the room, looking up and down to find the objects, and indicating each object to the simulated listener by pointing at it. This task corresponds to real-world communicative scenarios such as when a realtor indicates various features of a room when showing a house. This task also involved eight trials (first three were for training) of ten objects each, with completion time as the dependent measure.

In the MP and TLP tasks, object locations were pre-set with different locations for each trial. Participants saw the same locations for each configuration, but since there were several different sets of objects, and trials were randomly ordered, participants did not learn the locations. Since some pointing situations in CVEs require high accuracy [25], we designed these tasks to need high accuracy, under the assumption that if people can point precisely, they can clearly also do less-accurate tasks.

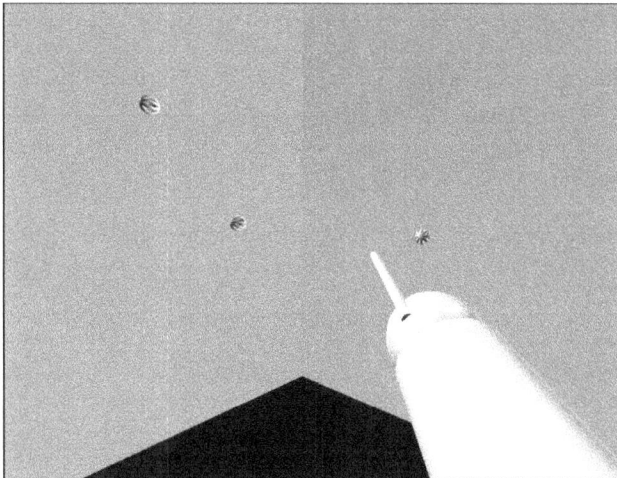

Figure 9. Turn-Look-and-Point task. Participant turns around inside the room, finding objects and pointing to them.

6.1.3 Task 3: Move-Turn-Look-and-Point (MTLP)

In the move-turn-look-and-point (MTLP) task, participants pointed at a green spot on the wall while moving to a particular location in the room (marked with a ball on the floor, see Figure 10). The green spot travelled in a slow circle on the wall, requiring that participants continually adjust their pointing direction. Since the task also required that the avatar turn en route to the destination (to remain facing the green spot), participants were required to control all four avatar actions simultaneously. This task corresponds to situations where people must point out a moving object to another person, while also moving to a particular location (e.g., pointing out the movements of a bird to a friend, while walking towards and through a gate).

In the MTLP task, each trial had only one spot and one destination (there were three spot locations, and three destination locations). Participants carried out 20 trials, with the first two marked as training; the remaining trials covered all spot/destination combinations. To force participants to maintain a certain level of accuracy in their pointing, the trial would re-start if the avatar's arm left the green spot for two seconds. The dependent measure was the percentage of total time that participants' gesture was outside the green spot (i.e., error time).

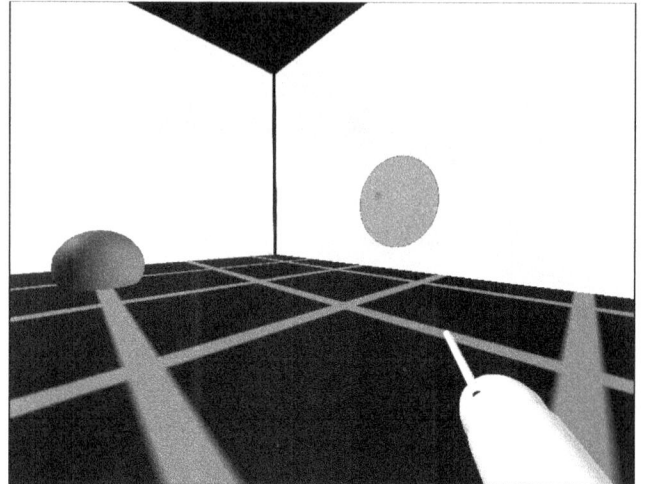

Figure 10. Move-Turn-Look-and-Point task. Participant moves to the ball while continuing to point at the green spot on the wall.

6.2 Study Methods and Design

The study used a custom CVE built in XNA and C#, running on a Windows 7 PC with a 22-inch 1680x1050 LCD monitor. Ten participants (five male) were recruited from a local university; ages were between 20 and 28 (mean 23.7), and five participants were experienced with video games (>3 hrs/week).

The study tested one main factor (input configuration, with five levels as described above) in a within-participants design. Differences between tasks were expected and so tasks were analysed separately. Secondary factors were gender and prior gaming experience (gamer or non-gamer). The first two tasks were presented in balanced order, with the third task always last (for additional training time, since it was the most difficult).

After using each input configuration, participants filled out NASA TLX worksheets [19], and at the end of the study, they stated their preferences and gave comments for the different devices.

6.3 Results

The following sections analyse results from the three tasks, look at the effects of gaming experience and gender, and report perception of effort and preference ratings.

6.3.1 Task 1: Move-and-Point (MP)

The mean time to finish a trial was 16.6s. Analysis of variance (ANOVA) showed a significant main effect of device ($F_{4,36} = 31.79$, $p < .001$). A post-hoc Tukey HSD test showed that the mode-switched mouse was significantly faster than the trackball, gamepad, or joystick; and that the Wii setup was faster than the gamepad or the joystick (all $p < .05$). As seen in Figure 11, the differences were substantial: the mouse took half the time of the slower devices.

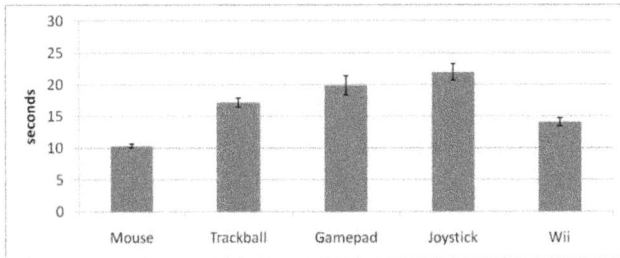

Figure 11. Mean completion time, MP task.

6.3.2 Task 2: Turn-Look-and-Point (TLP)

The mean time to finish a trial was 19.90s. ANOVA again showed a significant main effect of device ($F_{4,36}$ = 36.09, p < .001). A Tukey HSD test showed that the Wii setup was significantly faster than the gamepad and the joystick; and that the mouse and trackball were also significantly faster than the joystick (all p < .05). Again, the differences are large (Figure 12): for example, the Wii was almost 15 seconds faster than the joystick and almost eight seconds faster than the gamepad.

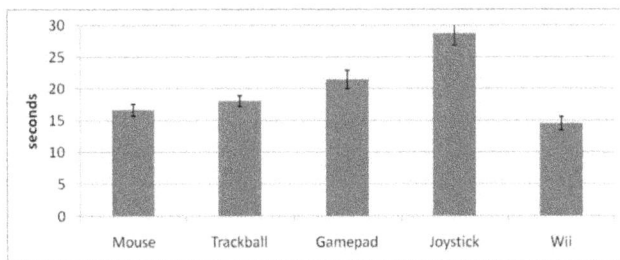

Figure 12. Mean completion time, TLP task.

6.3.3 Task 3: Move-Turn-Look-and-Point (MTLP)

The mean error time (percentage of time the avatar was not pointing at the green spot) was 28.1%. ANOVA again showed a significant main effect of device ($F_{4,36}$ = 18.41, p < .001). A Tukey HSD test showed that the mouse and the trackball were more accurate than the gamepad or joystick, and that the Wii setup was faster than the joystick (p < .05). As seen in Figure 13, accuracy results are similar to the completion-time results above: the better-performing devices are substantially more accurate (less than half the error time in some cases) than the poorer devices.

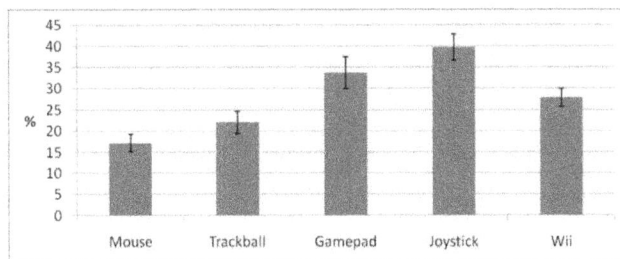

Figure 13. Mean error time, MTLP task.

6.3.4 Effects of Video-Game Experience

ANOVA showed no effect of game experience in either the MP task ($F_{1,8}$ = 3.57, p = .095) or the TLP task ($F_{1,8}$ = 2.85, p = .13), but a significant effect was found in the MTLP task ($F_{1,8}$ = 5.34, p < .05) (see Figure 14). In this task, gamers were slightly better able to continue pointing at the green spot as they moved (8% less error time) than non-gamers. There were no interactions between device and game experience for any task: MP ($F_{4,32}$ = 0.63, p = .65); TLP ($F_{4,32}$ = 1.19, p = .34); MTLP($F_{4,32}$ = 0.27, p = .90).

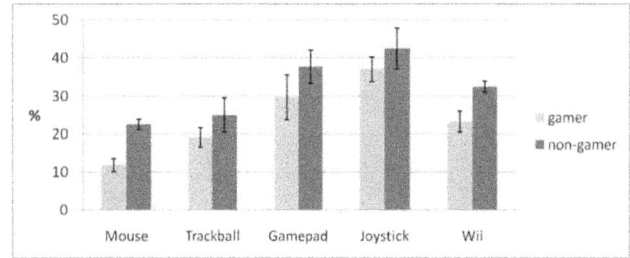

Figure 14. Mean error time, by game experience.

6.3.5 Effects of Gender

ANOVA showed no main effect on gender in any of the three tasks: MP ($F_{1,8}$ = 0.17, p = .69), TLP ($F_{1,8}$ = 0.00, p = .99), and MTLP ($F_{1,8}$ = 0.00, p = .99). No significant interaction was found between the devices and gender in the MP ($F_{4,32}$ = 0.88, p = .49) or TLP tasks ($F_{4,32}$ = 0.96, p = .44), but there was a device by gender interaction in MTLP ($F_{4,32}$ = 2.72, p < .05). As shown in Figure 15, the interaction likely arises from the fact that women were better with the mouse and Wii setup than men, but worse with the gamepad and the joystick.

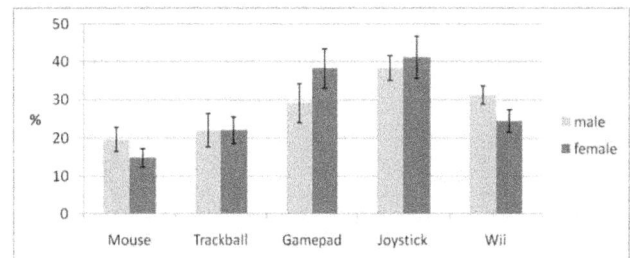

Figure 15. Mean error time, by gender.

6.3.6 Perception of Effort and Preferences

The TLX workload questionnaires (taken after each device condition) showed results that are fairly consistent with the performance data (Figure 16). In general, people felt that the mouse required the least workload (considering all three tasks), and that the joystick and gamepad required the most. Exceptions did appear, however: for example, the trackball and the gamepad were seen as requiring low physical effort but high mental load.

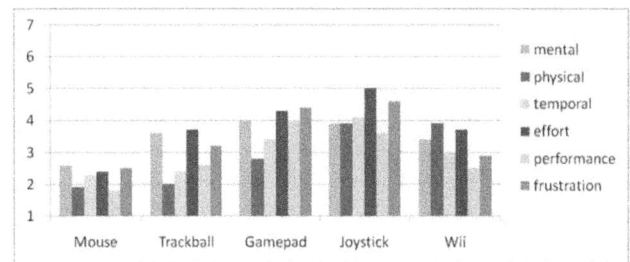

Figure 16. Mean scores (1-best, 7-worst) for workload assessment across all devices.

Figure 17 shows participants' overall ratings of the devices (1 = best, 10 = worst). There were substantial differences in these ratings: most participants preferred either the Wii configuration or the mouse; the trackball and gamepad were generally next, and the joystick was rated worst.

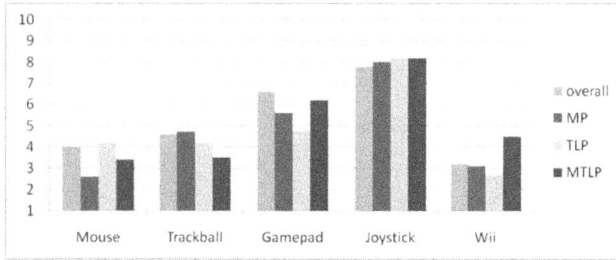

Figure 17. Mean rating by control and task (1-best, 10-worst).

6.4 General Observations

Several participants found the simultaneous control tasks difficult at first, but they became more comfortable using the devices as the study progressed. Some participants tried to avoid using different controls at the same time in the MP and TLP tasks: for example, they moved (in MP) or turned (in TLP) the avatar, stopped, and pointed at all the objects showing on the screen; then repeated the same action sequence until all objects were indicated. However, in MTLP – where it was easier to complete the task with all actions used together – the participants tried to use multiple controls simultaneously. They manipulated all the controls with the trackball, joystick, and Wii configurations (it was possible to manipulate all controls at the same time with these devices, but not with the mouse or gamepad).

Participants also used a variety of motions to point to objects: in addition to the pointing controls, they also utilized the avatar's movement and rotation. In the process of pointing to an object, people sometimes adjusted the arm to the correct horizontal level (where the object was), and then either moved or turned the avatar so that the arm direction gradually approached the object. This behavior happened with all input devices except the Wii controls; but most often with the trackball setting. This appeared to be because the Wiimote was easier to control for pointing, whereas the trackball was harder for left-right manipulation (see below).

6.5 Observations by Configuration

6.5.1 Mouse

Participants were very comfortable using the mouse and keyboard. They were able to switch between modes (pointing and looking/turning) with ease. The mouse's familiarity and simplicity are likely reasons for its top performance.

The mouse was slower in TLP than in MP, and this may have occurred for two reasons. First, the requirement for mode switching may have slowed participants (pointing and viewing controls were both required, but were in different modes). Although participants found the mode switch easy to do, it is impossible to carry out the two actions simultaneously. Second, turning required clutching, whereas there is no clutching when using the keyboard keys to move in the MP task.

6.5.2 Trackball

The trackball showed reasonable performance. While this configuration allows simultaneous control of all actions, horizontal ball manipulation was difficult. Most participants only used the trackball to move the arm vertically – we saw very few horizontal movements with this configuration. It appeared that left-right manipulation of a mouse-mounted trackball was a somewhat unnatural motion. A typical trackball is controlled with the combination of wrist movement (for left and right) and finger movement (for up and down). However, the trackball in the

Mighty Mouse must be manipulated by the finger in both directions, which participants felt was unnatural.

6.5.3 Gamepad

Some participants commented that they wanted to simultaneously manipulate all the avatar's actions with the gamepad but it was impossible to do so in normal use (the left thumb can only control either the left thumbstick or the d-pad). Others said that they would have liked to use the thumbstick (a variable-rate input) to change the view, which explains why the gamepad's preference ranking was the best with the TLP task.

6.5.4 Joystick

The joystick was the worst configuration on all measures (performance, preference, and workload). It caused considerable frustration across all participants, and one main reason is that participants often unintentionally changed their pointing and viewing directions. This happened more often in the MTLP task where the participant tried to use all the actions at the same time. They had substantial difficulty controlling pointing and looking/turning on the same device with one hand. Most participants experienced problems of simultaneous control with the joystick: for example, losing track of the avatar's arm by looking up while pointing down. This occurred because there are two 2D-velocity-based inputs (the main stick and the hat) assigned to one hand. In addition, the two inputs are physically stacked (the hat is built on top of the main stick). Pointing (with the stick) and turning/looking (with the hat) often affect each other – this also appears to be why participants spent more time in the TLP task than the MP task.

6.5.5 Wii controls

Participants liked the Wii configuration, and were enthusiastic about using it. They liked the naturalness of pointing with the Wiimote, and were all able to point easily and comfortably. Participants' comments and preference rankings suggest that they liked using the Wiimote to point and the Nunchuk (thumbstick) to look and turn, but did not like the Balance Board for movement as much. Some participants experienced difficulty with using the Balance Board – for example, moving the avatar past the desired destination in the MTLP task. Some participants also commented that they preferred not to use a foot-control device as it was physically demanding. This difficulty could be improved with different thresholds, or by changing the setup to allow the use of keyboard keys for movement (described below). Despite problems with the Balance Board, the Wii controls were very good in both performance and preference. The main advantage of this configuration is the ability to point directly at objects, which enables natural motor control and proprioception (since people carry out pointing the same way that they do in the real world).

7. DISCUSSION

Our study provides four main findings:
- People can successfully control free pointing in tasks that already involve moving, turning, and looking;
- There were significant and substantial differences between the input devices for all three tasks;
- The mouse and Wii configurations were consistently better, and the game controller and joystick were consistently worse;
- There were minor effects of game experience and gender.

Overall the most important conclusion from these results is that there are avatar control configurations in which adding communicative expressiveness (free pointing) does not unduly burden the individual's control abilities.

28

7.1 Lessons and Design Issues from the Study

Adding free pointing to CVEs is feasible. Our study clearly shows that people can handle the addition of free pointing to existing avatar controls. In all of our tasks, participants were able to complete the tasks successfully and without undue difficulty (although the device matters). This main result suggests that designers can feasibly incorporate this additional capability into CVEs.

A mode-switch mouse is a usable option. The mouse configuration made it impossible to turn and point simultaneously, yet the mouse had the best overall performance and was second best in preference. Even with mode switching, people were able to perform very well with the device. This configuration also represents the simplest extension of standard controls, and could easily be implemented in CVEs. (We note that the left button is often already used in many games, but a different mode switch could also be equally successful).

Direct input is good for pointing. The Wii controls had strong performance (best in the TLP task, second best in the MP task, and third in the MTLP task) and the best overall preference. Even though the participants did not have much experience with the controls, they got used to this configuration very quickly. Also, the Wii was the only condition where participants did not offload aiming to the avatar's movement and rotation (that is, they always used the pointing controls to move the arm towards the object). Direct-pointing configurations appear to be a useful new direction for avatar control systems. An additional benefit of direct pointing is that it can easily be extended to more complex gestures – which is the goal that initially motivated this work.

Effects of previous experience. People have more experience with the mouse and less with the Wii, yet these devices both showed better results than others. Also, gamers – surprisingly – did not perform significantly better with game controllers. These results suggest that the differences between devices are not solely due to people's experience – and that although people can learn to control almost any device, there are configurations that are more natural and simpler for controlling free pointing.

Controlling two 2D inputs with one hand is difficult. The joystick was the worst configuration overall. It required people to control two actions (pointing and turning/ looking) with one hand, and was disliked and seen as difficult. Comments and observations also showed that people simply had more difficulty controlling the avatar in these configurations: for example, trying to turn one way and point in the opposite direction was problematic. The trackball configuration also had two 2D inputs on one hand, and although it performed well in the MTLP task, people commented that the combined actions were difficult.

Variable-rate control is good for panning the view. For the gamepad and Wii controls, the TLP task had the best preference ranking compared to overall, MP, and MTLP. This is mainly because of the variable-rate controls that were used for look and turn. With the variable-rate control, the participants were able to control the turning rate by holding the thumbstick at a certain angle, allowing them to focus on other actions. This is interesting because many current CVEs put turning control on the mouse, which is a position-based device.

Physiological constraints affect device use. Participants felt that the Mighty Mouse trackball was unnatural for controlling arm movement because the trackball cannot be used normally (where the wrist is used for left and right control). These results reinforce earlier cautions about designing input configurations with an understanding of ergonomic factors such as the range of motion of different limbs.

Input sensitivity should be adjustable. Different participants had very different preferences in terms of input sensitivity (most obviously seen on the Wii Balance Board). While having default sensitivity is important, it should be adjustable. Although adjustable settings are common in desktop applications, it is not always common in CVEs to allow full specification of parameters.

7.2 Generalization to Other Communication Tasks

Our results are likely to translate to more realistic collaborative task situations and other collaborative virtual environments. First, real communication situations will involve the additional task of producing verbal communication along with the avatar's gestures. This is not likely to create problems for free pointing since the control situations that we studied likely require more simultaneous activity than what is needed in many collaborative situations, and since people in real tasks will have far more experience with the controls than our participants. In addition, using natural actions such as direct pointing can greatly simplify the task of producing these gestures. We believe our results can also be useful in non-CVE systems where pointing gestures are important, e.g., rescue operations and equipment maintenance supported by remote experts.

Second, pointing control worked for a broad range of participants: gamers and non-gamers, and men and women. Although further evaluations will be carried out, it seems clear that the ability to control free pointing is not limited to only a small group of users. Finally, the devices that we tested are all readily available and do not require specialized hardware or software – this means that pointing control could be easily added to a wide range of CVEs.

Recently, we have tested the mode-switched mouse and the Wiimote devices in real two-person collaboration in the CVE; people carried out a variety of shared activities involving pointing and deictic reference, in a real distributed setting. Initial results are consistent with the study described above – people were successfully able to use the input configurations for free pointing, in addition to controlling other aspects of the avatar as well as engaging in verbal communication.

7.3 Directions for Future Work

There are several ways that our research can be extended. First, we will explore variations on the configurations described above. We will combine the direct-pointing capabilities of the Wiimote with the simple movement control of the keyboard. In this configuration, users will hold the Nunchuk and the Wiimote (tied together) with one hand: free pointing would thus be controlled by the arm and hand, and view would be controlled by the thumb – leaving the other hand free to use keys for movement (avoiding the problems seen with the Balance Board). In addition, we will explore the possibility of using Kinect for controlling free pointing. Another novel configuration will involve a wide-screen display, in which horizontal looking is controlled simply by allowing the user to turn their head and look at different parts of the display. Also, we plan to add additional degrees of freedom to direct pointing, allowing users to bend their avatar's elbow and thus create more complex gestures. Finally, we will continue to explore the use of these techniques in real CVE activities, and will integrate our controls into broader support for all the phases of non-verbal communication–orientation, preparation, production, and holding.

8. CONCLUSION

Avatars in CVEs are far less expressive than real bodies, and in particular lack the ability to carry out gestural communication. One main problem is how gestures can be controlled in a desktop CVE. We looked at the control of one type of gesture called free pointing; we presented a design framework for avatar control, and five example input configurations that can support free pointing. An evaluation showed that people are able to control pointing in addition to other avatar actions for non-verbal communication tasks, and that some of the devices worked significantly better than others. Our work shows that support for free pointing can be feasibly added into CVEs and establishes a foundation for more expressive gestural communication in CVEs, allowing people to carry out interaction and communication that is richer than what is possible in current environments.

9. ACKNOWLEDGMENTS

We would like to thank our colleagues in the Interaction Lab at the University of Saskatchewan who provided invaluable feedback to our work. We would also like to thank NSERC and GRAND NCE for funding.

10. REFERENCES

[1] Argyle, M. 1975. *Bodily Communication*, London.

[2] Benford, S., Greenhalgh, C., Snowdon, D., and Bullock, A. 1997. Staging a Public Poetry Performance in a Collaborative Virtual Environment. In *Proceedings of the fifth conference on European Conference on Computer-Supported Cooperative Work,* 125-140.

[3] Buxton, W. 1983. Lexical and Pragmatic Considerations of Input Structures. *ACM SIGGRAPH Computer Graphics*, 17, 1, 31-37.

[4] Duchowski, A., Cournia, N., Cumming, B., McCallum, D., Gramopadhye, A., Greenstein, J., Sadasivan, S., and Tyrrell, R. 2004. Visual Deictic Reference a Collaborative Virtual Environment. In *Proceedings of the Symposium on Eye Tracking Research & Applications*, 35-40.

[5] Fraser, M., and Benford, S. 2002. Interaction Effects of Virtual Structures. In *Proceedings of the 4th international conference on Collaborative virtual environments*, 128-134.

[6] Fraser, M., Benford, S., Hindmarsh, J., and Heath, C. 1999. Supporting Awareness and Interaction through Collaborative Virtual Interfaces. In *Proceedings of the Symposium on User Interface Software and Technology*, 27-36.

[7] Gutwin, C., and Penner, R. 2002. Improving Interpretation of Remote Gestures with Telepointer Traces. In *Proceedings of the Conference on Computer Supported Cooperative Work,* 49-57.

[8] Hagsand, O. 1996. Interactive Multiuser VEs in the DIVE System. *Multimedia, IEEE, 3*(1), 30-39.

[9] Hinckley, K. 2002. Input Technologies and Techniques. *The HCI Handbook,* 151-168.

[10] Hindmarsh, J., Fraser, M., Heath, C., Benford, S., and Greenhalgh, C. 1998. Fragmented Interaction: Establishing Mutual Orientation Virtual Environments. In *Proceedings of the conference on Computer supported cooperative work*, 217-226.

[11] Hindmarsh, J., Fraser, M., Heath, C., Benford, S., and Greenhalgh, C. 2000. Object-Focused Interaction in Collaborative Virtual Environments, *Transactions on Computer-Human Interaction, 7*, 4, 477-509.

[12] Jacob, R. 1996. Human-Computer Interaction: Input Devices. *ACM Computing Surveys (CSUR), 28*, 1, 177-179.

[13] Krauss, R., and Fussell, S. 1990. Mutual Knowledge and Communicative Effectiveness. In, J. Galegher, R. Kraut & C. Egido (Eds.), *Intellectual Teamwork*. Hillsdale, NJ: Erlbaum. 111-145.

[14] Lee, C., Ghyme, S., Park, C. J., and Wohn, K. Y. 1998. The Control of Avatar Motion Using Hand Gesture. In *Proceedings of the Symposium on Virtual Reality Software and Technology,* 59-65.

[15] Mackinlay, J., Card, S. K., and Robertson, G. G. 1990. A Semantic Analysis of the Design Space of Input Devices. *Human-Computer Interaction, 5*(2), 145-190.

[16] Mason, S. G., Bohringer, R., Borisoff, J. F., and Birch, G. E. 2004. Real-Time Control of a Video Game with a Direct Brain-Computer Interface. *Journal of Clinical Neurophysiology, 21*, 6, 404-408.

[17] McNeill, D. 1996. *Hand and Mind. What Gestures Reveal about Thought*. Chicago: Univ. Chicago Press.

[18] Moore, R., Ducheneaut, N., and Nickell, E. Doing Virtually Nothing: Awareness and Accountability in Massively Multiplayer Online Worlds, *Computer Supported Cooperative Work*, 16, 3, 265-305.

[19] NASA *TLX: Task Load Index*. humansystems.arc.nasa. gov/groups/TLX

[20] Peinado, M., Maupu, D., Raunhardt, D., Meziat, D., Thalmann, D., and Boulic, R. 2009. Full-Body Avatar Control with Environment Awareness. *Computer Graphics and Applications*, 62-75.

[21] Salem, B., and Earle, N. 2000. Designing a Non-Verbal Language for Expressive Avatars, In *Proceedings of the 3rd International Conference on Collaborative Virtual Environments,* 93-101.

[22] Steptoe, W., Oyekoya, O., Murgia, A., Wolff, R., Rae, J., Guimaraes, E., Roberts, D., and Steed, A. 2009. Eye Tracking for Avatar Eye Gaze Control During Object-Focused Multiparty Interaction in Immersive Collaborative Virtual Environments, In *Proceedings of Virtual Reality Conference,* 83-90.

[23] Soraghan, C. J., Matthews, F., Kelly, D., Ward, T., Markham, C., Pearlmutter, B., and O'Neill, R. 2006. A Dual-Channel Optical Brain-Computer Interface in a Gaming Environment. In *Proceedings of Computer Games*, 35-39.

[24] Templeman, J., Sibert, L., Page, R., and Denbrook, P., 2007. Pointman – A Device-Based Control for Realistic Tactical Movement, In *Proceedings of the Symposium on 3D User Interfaces*, 163-166.

[25] Wong, N., and Gutwin, C. 2010. Where Are You Pointing? The Accuracy of Deictic Pointing in CVEs, In *Proceedings of the 28th International Conference on Human Factors in Computing Systems*, 1029-1038.

[26] Zhai, S. Human Performance. In *Human Input to Computer Systems*, unpublished manuscript at: billbuxton.com/inputManuscript.html (August. 2012).

To See or Not to See: A Study Comparing Four-way Avatar, Video, and Audio Conferencing for Work

Sasa Junuzovic, Kori Inkpen, John Tang
Microsoft Research
Redmond, WA
{sasajun,kori,johntang}@microsoft.com

Mara Sedlins
Dept. of Psychology, UW
Seattle, WA
sedlins@uw.edu

Kristie Fisher
Microsoft
Redmond, WA
kfisher@microsoft.com

Figure 1. Four-way Microsoft Avatar Kinect (left) and Skype Group Video (right) conference

ABSTRACT

We conducted a study comparing avatar conferencing with video and audio conferencing for work scenarios. We studied nine four-person teams using a within-subjects design that measured users' perceptions and preferences across the conferencing conditions. Video was rated highest in all measures. Avatar and Audio were rated similarly, except for sociability, where Avatar was rated higher than Audio, and realism, where Avatar was rated lower than Audio. While users appreciated how avatar conferencing brought them together in a common virtual space, they found the cartoon avatars to be inappropriate for a professional discussion. As a result, participants preferred Video the most and Avatar the least for a business meeting. Lower ratings for the avatar condition were partly due to users' frustrations when the avatar system did not track them perfectly. When assuming a "perfect" system, preference for Avatar increased significantly while preference for Audio and Video remained unchanged.

Categories and Subject Descriptors

H5.3. Group and Organization Interfaces (CSCW).

Keywords

Conferencing; audio; video; avatar; distributed teams.

1. INTRODUCTION

Recently available commercial technologies have enabled new forms of synchronous conferencing using video and avatars.

Desktop video services enable n-way video conferences where each participant can be seen at all times. Meanwhile, avatar representations in a virtual world, popularized by online gaming, afford meeting and interacting together in a virtually constructed setting. As these technologies gain popularity in consumer markets, we expect they will also be used in workplace meetings. However, the visual representation of meeting participants may affect the interactions that occur in these mediated environments, and we explore their impact in this study.

We were interested to see how avatar conferencing compared with more traditional audio and video conferencing in the workplace. Avatar conferencing enables users to collaborate together through virtual avatars that represent each person's bodily movements in both gaming [6] and commercial applications [3]. Until recently, embodying these avatars required users to make manual keyboard and mouse commands that translated into basic avatar actions (e.g., walk forward, wave). More recent systems, such as Microsoft's Avatar Kinect, capture users' motions through depth cameras and use the depth information to animate 3D cartoon avatars to reflect users' body movements. This natural user interface can automatically convey non-verbal cues.

Compared to video conferencing, avatar conferencing has many potential user experience advantages. Virtual avatars abstract away the users' real environments, which can mitigate privacy concerns that video evokes [2] and also enable users to manage their appearance (for example, looking professional when joining from home). Furthermore, virtual worlds can create a common meeting space for distributed team members connecting from diverse settings. Virtual avatars can even synthesize non-verbal cues, such as turning toward the current speaker, which could strengthen the sense of presence (defined as the feeling of being socially present with people at a remote location [8]).

The goal of our study was to compare multi-party avatar conferencing to video and audio conferencing for workplace collaboration. Several prior studies have already compared video and audio conferencing and documented advantages of the visual channel [10], [11]. In particular, social presence increased with the bandwidth of the communication medium (e.g., social presence was higher for video than audio) [9]. We were interested in how avatar conferencing would compare with audio and video.

Previous work by Bente et al. [1] compared avatar conferencing with audio, video, and text conferencing in two-way conferences between strangers. They found that avatar and video conferencing were similar with respect to user satisfaction, trust, and social presence. However, it is unclear how these results generalize to multi-party groups, where the fidelity of visual cues, such as facial expressions and gaze awareness, become more important. Prior work [7], [10] has shown that using video to provide these visual cues can help reduce potential interaction ambiguities that can occur with more than two people in a conference. Thus, it is important to re-evaluate avatar, audio, and video conferencing in multi-party scenarios. We chose to examine four-way conferencing as a large enough group to exercise both gaze awareness and non-verbal communication cues.

By studying avatar, video, and audio conferencing, we could see how adding different representations of visual cues to the shared audio communication (which was common across all conditions) affected the collaboration. Intuitively, adding avatar visual cues should improve the experience over audio alone. However, avatars are not as high fidelity as video. Moreover, cartoon aspects of avatars may conflict with users' expectations of how remote people should be presented visually. Thus, it is interesting to explore how the avatar experience compares to video.

2. METHODOLOGY

Our user study compared audio-only (*Audio*) and audio-video (*Video*) conferencing with 3D-avatar conferencing (*Avatar*) using existing commercial tools. In all three conditions, Skype group audio conferencing provided the audio channel. For Video conferencing, we used Skype Group Video Calling, configured to show all of the remote participants aligned horizontally, as shown in Figure 1 (right panel).

For Avatar conferencing, we used a beta version of Microsoft Avatar Kinect, an XBOX 360 avatar chat application. Avatar Kinect animates a cartoon avatar in a virtual world based on a user's movements in the real world. The Kinect sensor tracks the user's upper body motion, including torso and arm positions, as well as some facial features, namely, mouth and eyebrows. Based on the tracking data, the avatar mimics posture changes, hand waves, head turns, lip movements, and facial expressions in real time. However, unlike video, these visual cues are presented by animating a computer-generated, cartoon avatar. We chose a virtual world where avatars sat in a circle (see Figure 1, left panel). Each participant had a third-person view of the world as if standing behind their own avatar. This view most closely matched the view of others in Skype, although Skype's preview of oneself is frontal and not over-the-shoulder. In Figure 1, the local user, whose avatar is at the bottom of the screen, can see that all avatars are looking at the avatar at the top of the screen, thus conveying a shared sense of gaze awareness.

2.1 Participants and Procedure

We recruited 36 participants (16 females, 20 males), in 9 groups with 4 participants per group, from within Microsoft, a large software company. As prior work has demonstrated, participants' familiarity with each other affects their conferencing experience

[4], and since participants in a business meeting are usually familiar with each other, we recruited participants who already knew each other. Our participants will be referred to as ($P_{x,y}$) where x is the group number and y is the participant number within that group.

Each group of participants used all three conferencing technologies and worked through three brainstorming meetings that were equivalent in structure but involved different, although related, topics. We chose a brainstorming task since it is a common business practice that requires participation from everyone and may involve persuasion and negotiation, for which visual cues are important. We selected discussion topics (features of next generation mobile devices) that are important to our participants' company to provide some inherent motivation for the task. One discussion focused on smartphones, another on tablet devices, and the remaining discussion focused on mobile search. For each condition, the participants brainstormed for about 10 minutes. The study administrators then interrupted them and asked them to agree on the top four features discussed during the brainstorming and their priority order.

Each of the four conference participants was placed in a different room that had a 40" LCD 1080p TV, a headset, an XBOX 360, and a computer. For the Avatar condition, participants spent 5-10 minutes creating avatars that looked like them by tailoring avatar attributes, such as hair style, and facial features. For all three conferencing technologies, the participants used a headset to hear and talk to each other. In the Audio condition, the TV showed a blank computer desktop. In the Video condition, participants saw video windows of remote participants on the TV through Skype Group Video Calling, as shown in Figure 1 (right). In the Avatar condition, participants saw their avatars in a virtual location together with the avatars of the remote participants through Microsoft Avatar Kinect, as shown in Figure 1 (left).

2.2 Experimental Design

We used a within-subjects study design with condition order counterbalanced using a Partial Latin Square design. All groups performed the brainstorming tasks in the same order, starting with smartphone features, followed by tablet features, and finishing with mobile search features on smartphone and tablet devices. We chose a within-subjects design to reduce the impact of individual differences and enable users to compare across conditions.

At the start of a study session, all participants completed an initial questionnaire that asked for their demographic information and prior experience with smartphones, tablets, and avatars. The participants also completed a questionnaire after each brainstorming task. Finally, all participants completed a questionnaire at the end of the session that compared across conditions and took part in a group debriefing session.

The post-task questionnaires consisted of different groups of questions: *social presence*; *conversation mechanics and non-verbal communication cues*; and *realism*. The social presence questions used anchored seven-point scales, while the remainder of the questions utilized seven-point Likert-type scales from 1 (strongly disagree) to 7 (strongly agree).

The *social presence* questions focused on how the users perceived the various conferencing technologies from a social perspective. These questions probed four dimensions that have been shown to differentiate social presence in telecommunications [9]: *impersonal-personal, cold-warm, insensitive-sensitive,* and

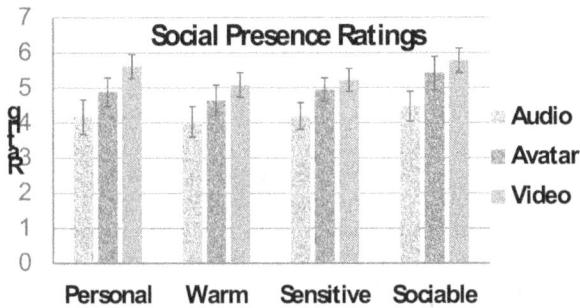

Figure 2. Average ratings for each social presence factor.

unsociable-sociable. The questions regarding *conversation mechanics* and *non-verbal cues* probed for the impact of the conferencing technologies on the conversation flow and non-verbal cue awareness. Sample questions included: "I could easily tell who was speaking" and "I could speak up in the discussion without interrupting someone else." The questions focusing on *realism* were included to help us understand how cartoon avatars compared to audio and video for communication purposes. Sample questions included: "It was just as though we were all in the same room", "The other people seemed real". Participants were also invited to provide free-form comments, reactions, likes, and dislikes about each system.

After completing all three tasks, participants were asked to rate each condition on a scale from 1 to 10, where 1 was "not useful at all" and 10 was "extremely useful." This question was repeated after asking the participants to assume perfect system performance, looking past current system flaws, such as poor motion tracking or audio lag.

3. RESULTS
Analyses were performed using Aligned Rank Transform, a new technique to enable use of parametric statistics on non-parametric data [12]. There were no significant effects of gender.

3.1 Social Presence
Significant main effects of condition were found for each of the social presence factors: impersonal-personal ($F_{2,70}$=16.33 p<.001), cold-warm ($F_{2,70}$=6.88 p<.005), insensitive-sensitive ($F_{2,70}$=19.07 p<.001), and unsociable-sociable ($F_{2,70}$=16.33 p<.001). Figure 2 shows the mean rating for each factor. Bonferroni corrected post-hoc pairwise comparison revealed that for all of the factors, the Video condition was rated significantly higher than Audio (p<.005). The Video condition was also rated significantly higher than the Avatar condition for the *personal* and *sensitive* dimensions (p<.005). However, no significant differences were found between Video and Avatar for *warm* (p=.19) and *sociable* (p=.47). The Avatar condition was rated significantly higher than Audio for being *sociable* (p<.005) but was not significantly different from Audio for the other three factors (p>.09). Participants' comments supported these results: "*Audio was the least personal and hardest to use in the realm of an unstructured meeting. Video was the most personal and the easiest to use. Kinect was easy to use and slightly more personal than audio* (P$_{4,3}$)". "*I liked the video the best because you can see how people react; get to know their personalities + it is like being in the same room as people. The avatar was a cool way at looking at conferences but I think it could be distracting if the discussion is business related. Audio is good, just very impersonal* (P$_{6,1}$)."

Table 1. Results for non-verbal cues and realism. Significant differences were found for all questions (p<.001).

Non-Verbal Cues	
I could perceive and respond to non-verbal cues of people in the discussion	$F_{2,70}$=66.77
I could speak up in the discussion without interrupting someone else	$F_{2,70}$=26.76
I could speak up in the discussion without being interrupted by someone else	$F_{2,70}$=13.86
I got a good idea of how the other people were reacting	$F_{2,70}$=64.79
I got a real impression of personal contact with the other people	$F_{2,70}$=16.30
I could easily access the other people's reactions to what had been said	$F_{2,70}$=40.01
I could easily tell whom other people are directing their comments toward	$F_{2,70}$=16.39
Realism	
The discussion environment had a great sense of realism.	$F_{2,70}$=24.30
It was like having a face-to-face discussion.	$F_{2,70}$=35.70
It was just as though we were all in the same room.	$F_{2,70}$=23.82
The other people seemed "real."	$F_{2,70}$=34.80

3.2 Non-verbal Cues
The questionnaire also probed participants' impressions of non-verbal cues in the conferencing conditions, the seamlessness of the conversation, and whether people felt they could speak up without being interrupted (see Table 1). A significant main effect of condition was found for each question and Bonferroni corrected post-hoc pairwise comparison revealed Video was rated significantly higher than Avatar and Audio (p<.005), with no significant differences between the Avatar and Audio conditions (p>.07). Commenting on Video, one participant said: "*Much more able to glean subtle reactions* (P$_{10,1}$)."

3.3 Realism
Four questions probed the realism of the conferencing environments and how close it was to "having a face-to-face discussion" (see Table 1). Significant main effects of condition were found for each question. Bonferroni corrected post-hoc pairwise comparison revealed that for all of these questions Video was rated significantly higher than Avatar and Audio (p<.001) and no significant differences were found between Avatar and Audio (p>.05). When asked whether "it was just as though we were all in the same room," the Video condition was rated significantly higher than Avatar and Audio (p<.05), and the Avatar condition was rated significantly higher than the Audio condition (p<.005). As one participant commented, "*The people sitting in the one virtual room in the avatar space is a really important factor – makes you feel you are all at the same table and on equal footing* (P$_{5,4}$)".

3.4 Overall Preference
Consistent with the above ratings (on a scale from 1-10), a significant main effect of condition was found for overall preference ($F_{2,70}$=15.66 p<.001). Bonferroni corrected post-hoc pairwise comparison revealed that Video (m=8.9) was rated as significantly more useful for distributed meetings than Audio (m=6.9) and Avatar (m=5.1) (p<.005), with 78% of participants rating Video highest. While the Avatar condition was rated similarly to (and sometimes higher than) Audio on all of the individual dimensions examined, it was rated significantly lower than Audio in terms of overall usefulness (p<.05).

Consistent with results from previous studies of video communication, participants preferred the Video condition mostly because of the presence and fidelity of non-verbal cues. For example, "*I could see people's expressions* (P$_{10,4}$)"; "*allows for non-verbal cues + really lets you communicate effectively* (P$_{7,5}$)"; and "*helpful to gauge body language* (P$_{9,2}$)." Video was also considered to be the "*most personal and professional* (P$_{6,4}$)" and the "*most real* (P$_{8,4}$)."

Users liked the Audio condition for its comfort and familiarity. For example, "*Audio is next best + is readily available worldwide* (P$_{7,5}$)"; "*Audio=Not great, but not terrible. Something that we are all used to.* (P$_{6,4}$)"; and "*I'm used to it—it's comfortable* (P$_{7,3}$)." Other benefits included the fact that it was "*easy to use* (P$_{4,2}$)" and "*least distracting* (P$_{7,3}$)." However, they found that in the Audio condition, it was sometimes "*difficult to interject and add thoughts and concerns* (P$_{4,3}$)"; "*was hard to stay focused* (P$_{8,4}$)"; and was "*hard to manage conversation mechanics* (P$_{5,1}$)."

While many of the participants found the Avatar condition to be "*fun*," their main reservations were that it was not professional or serious enough for a business meeting. For example, "*I can't see it being used in a professional setting. I would have a hard time taking a Kinect meeting seriously* (P$_{4,3}$)" and "*Kinect is fun but not for business. The exception would be if you needed to communicate as effectively as possible but had to remain anonymous* (P$_{7,5}$)."

Participants also found the Avatar condition distracting because of "*erratic arm movements and not always picking up who was talking* (P$_{6,5}$)." Users also wanted "*a clearer way to see who is speaking* (P$_{5,4}$)" and more realistic avatars. However, when participants re-evaluated the three conferencing conditions assuming they were "perfect", the ratings for Video (m=9.1) and Audio (m=7.0) did not change significantly ($p>.2$) whereas the ratings for the Avatar condition (m=6.8) increased significantly (Wilcoxon Z=-4.4, $p<.001$). As a result, the difference between Avatar and Audio was no longer significant, ($p>.9$). Besides illustrating the future potential of avatar conferencing as the technology progresses, these responses also suggest a perception that audio and video have "topped out," with little expectation for improved user experiences in video or audio.

4. DISCUSSION AND CONCLUSION

Overall, we found that Video was significantly better in almost all measures of social presence, non-verbal cues and conversational mechanics, and realism than the Audio and Avatar conditions. This result contrasts with Bente et al. [1], who did not find a difference in video compared to other conferencing technologies. We hypothesize that our groups of four who were familiar with each other presented higher interaction demands compared to the dyads of strangers used in their study.

We were surprised that users preferred Audio over the Avatar condition despite ranking Avatar similarly and sometimes higher on the dimensions studied. Survey responses indicated that the workplace context was not a good fit with the cartoon avatars currently offered in Avatar Kinect. This reaction extends prior work [5] which found certain static cartoon avatar icons to be unsuitable for work. It was also interesting to see that users rated the Avatar condition lower on realism (m=4.0) compared to Audio (m=4.7). We surmise that since the participants knew each other, they were able to project a realistic conference experience even in the Audio condition, but that the cartoon avatars actually interfered with their

sense of realism. More research is needed to find avatars that are realistic enough to appear professional but avoid negative reactions around the uncanny valley.

Furthermore, some users found the Avatar system distracting because of flaws in the motion tracking. Nevertheless, users did recognize the benefit of a common setting and opportunity for anonymity in avatar conferencing. Also, their ratings for a perfected system show that avatar conferencing has future potential. As this technology matures with more accurate tracking and more professional avatar representations, there is an opportunity for more widespread use of it in workplace settings.

Although we focused on participant perceptions in audio, video, and avatar conferencing, it would also be useful to evaluate the task outcomes with each technology. A comparison of the brainstorming results among the conditions in a future study could offer further insights into the use of avatar conferencing in stimulating creative work.

5. REFERENCES

[1] Bente, G., Rüggenberg, S., Krämer, N.C, Eschenburg, F. Avatar-mediated networking: Increasing social presence and interpersonal trust in net-based collaborations, *Human Communications Research*, 34 (2008), 287-318.

[2] Boyle, M. and Greenberg, S. The Language of Privacy: Learning from Video Media Space Analysis and Design, *ACM TOCHI*, 12(2), June 2005, 328-368.

[3] Erickson, T., Shami, N.S., Kellogg, W.A., Levine, D. Synchronous interaction among hundreds: An evaluation of a conference in an avatar-based virtual environment. *ACM CHI 2011*, 503-512.

[4] Espinosa, J.A., Slaughter, S.A., Kraut, R.E., Herbsleb, J.D. Familiarity, complexity, and team performance in geographically distributed software development. *Organization Science*, 2007, 18(4), 613-630.

[5] Inkpen, K. and Sedlins, M. Me and my avatar: Exploring users' comfort with avatars for workplace communication. *ACM CSCW 2011*, 383-386.

[6] Nardi, B. and Harris, J. Strangers and friends: Collaborative play in World of Warcraft. *ACM CSCW 2006*, 149-158.

[7] Nguyen, David and Canny, John, "Multiview: improving trust in group video conferencing through spatial faithfulness", *ACM CHI 2007*, 1465-1747.

[8] Sallnas, E., Rassmus-grohn, K., and Sjöström, C. Supporting presence in collaborative environments by haptic force feedback. *ACM TOCHI*, 7, 2000, 461-476.

[9] Short, J., Williams, E., and Christie, B. *The social psychology of telecommunications*. London: John Wiley & Sons, 1976.

[10] Tang, J.C. and Isaacs, E.A. Why Do Users Like Video? Studies of Multimedia-Supported Collaboration. *CSCW: An International Journal*, 1(3), 1993, 163-196.

[11] Whittaker, S. and O'Conaill, B. The role of vision in face-to-face and mediated communication. In *Video-mediated Communication*, 1997.

[12] Wobbrock, J.O., Findlater, L., Gergle, D., Higgins, J.J. The aligned rank transform for nonparametric factorial analyses using only anova procedures. *ACM CHI 2011*.

The Sociality of Fieldwork: Designing for Social Science Research Practice and Collaboration

Louise Barkhuus
Department of Computer and Systems Sciences
Stockholm University
164 40 Kista, Sweden
barkhuus@dsv.su.se

Barry Brown
Mobile Life Centre
Stockholm University
164 40 Kista, Sweden
barry@mobilelifecentre.org

ABSTRACT

Supporting scientific practice has been a longstanding goal of CSCW research. This paper explores how we might design for social science research practices and collaboration. Drawing on sixteen interviews with fieldwork-based social scientists we document the importance of small-scale long-term collaborative arrangements for research and intellectual work - pairs of researchers who work together in-depth over their careers, developing a common yet distinctive view of their research field. This contrasts with the large-scale short-lived collaborations that have classically been the target of cyber-infrastructure work. We describe technology practices among social scientists and how these can inform technology design for fieldwork practices.

Categories and Subject Descriptors

H.4.0 [Information Systems]: Information Systems Applications: General

General Terms

Human Factors.

Keywords

Cyber-infrastructure, e-social science, fieldwork

1. INTRODUCTION

One of the major uses of group technologies is collaborative science and research; the emerging programs of cyber-infrastructure and e-social science are testament to an increasing use of these technologies for science [13, 20]. But where much research within these programs looks at large collaboration structures, less attention has been paid to the smaller tight-knit collaborations that are part of particularly social science research. This lack of attention by researchers might be explained by most social science research being undertaken by small groups of individuals, even single individuals, who perform work that is conducted using generic ad-hoc technologies (such as email, internet information search and word processing), using well-established methods. The reflection of this process has so far been expressed through literature analyses, co-authorship evaluation [17] and quantitative project evaluations with clear success criteria [22, 31]. Particularly small-scale field-work research has received little attention, possibly due to its perceived utilization of generic technology use ("office technologies") but also its

diversity in approach. How is it even possible to group social science fieldworkers as one type of technology users? In this paper we take a first step towards analyzing social science fieldwork from an inclusive but detailed perspective. We look at the detailed collaborations and collaboration technologies for the tight-knit social scientists that conduct fieldwork; although this group seem broadly defined, we find that these researchers have much in common and that addressing technology utilization is a productive step in the direction of designing and implementing future technologies for e-social science. Small-scale fieldwork is just as important to explore as the large-scale cyberinfrastructure research.

We present interview data with a set of sixteen social scientists, describing how these social scientists collaborate, collect data, conduct analysis and work together on publications. While the social sciences span a huge diversity of different approaches and methods, we focus here on scientists who use field methods of one shape or form – collecting empirical data in the home environments of those being studied. The researchers we studied span sociology, criminology, drug policy, education and social psychology, draw on quantitative and qualitative methods, as well as spanning a range of distinct theoretical and disciplinary commitments.

Focusing on the researchers' fieldwork practices and their technology use, it was reaffirmed how the close-knit collaborations were of essence. This contrasts with those who have argued for an increase in the scale of social science; for example, Atkins et al. [2] argue that "social science research is on the verge of being transformed through distributed global collaborations, the use of very large data collections, tera-scale computing resources, and high performance visualization". To the social scientists we studied these "tera-scale computing resources" were on the whole irrelevant. The collaborations that were most important to them were much smaller groups of two or three researchers working together over long periods of time - career-long in many cases. These collaborations were often conducted over a distance, yet researchers still formed a distinctive joint worldview and analytic approach. What is key to the collaborative practices is how social science researchers become tied together with distinct theoretical commitments and worldviews.

2. LITERATURE

The Internet has greatly increased the possibilities for collaboration between scientists, witnessed by an increase of co-authorship in many disciplines [38]. Research shows that the increasing use of computer-mediated communication can lead to higher scientific productivity [37, 42] and 'cyber-infrastructures' more generally have been shown to facilitate geographically dispersed research. However, much current research on cyber-infrastructure has been dominated by the natural sciences [36]. While grid computing, shared access to computational models, or very large data sets, do have major applications to some parts of the social sciences, much social science research tackles quite distinct research problems that render these systems inappropriate [10]. The emerging program of e-social science, or 'e-research' has developed to address the distinctive problems of social science research [3]. While acknowledging the great diversity within the social sciences, social science research frequently deals with relatively small sets of data, theoretical explorations, activist engagements, and a long term commitment to investigating from interpretivist, or at least non-positivist, traditions [16, 26, 41]. For these social scientists their work problems and potential use of cyber-infrastructure are distinctly different from the concerns of 'big science'. The study of many complex activities - such as learning or language socialization - involves collaboration that is seldom reducible to sharing raw data, but rather a complex process of 'coming to see' the world in common [6, 18, 19]. These practices demand distinctive collaborative tools, tools built from an understanding of the intellectual and collaborative processes involved.

Indeed, a number of recent critiques have argued that current cyber-infrastructure work has been dominated by technology [3], and that there has been insufficient consideration of the nature of scientific work [22], conditions of technology use [23], and system usability [35, 36]. As David [10] pointed out: "engineering breakthroughs alone will not be enough to achieve the outcomes envisaged for these undertakings. Success in realizing the potential of 'e-research' and 'cyber-infrastructure' will more likely be the resultant of a nexus of interrelated social, legal and technical transformations". These issues come particularly to the fore when considering the social sciences.

Studies of scientific practice are most strongly exemplified by work in science and technology studies. However only recently has attention been paid to studying the work of the social sciences. Notable here is Porter's work on statistics and discussions of reflexivity and social science practice [15, 32, 36]. Recently studies of economics, and the relationships between its intellectual concepts and the behavior of markets [7, 27, 28] have gained prominence, alongside studies of interaction in interviews and survey settings, and the related questions of standardization in social science survey research [29, 30].

Within CSCW there has been growing interest in examining and designing for the work of scientists [5, 9, 13, 25]. Our field has a particularly powerful position here, drawing on the tradition of studying the practice of difficult to understand, complex work situations, and using those studies to produce rich design interventions. This has motivated work on how cyber-infrastructure can support new data collection techniques, such as instant messaging [39], phone based experience sampling [8], or electronic laboratory notebooks. One system of note is Butterflynet [42], which allowed field biologists to share and augment paper-based field-notes.

In Europe a number of researchers have also taken the lead in developing 'e-Infrastructure' research, drawing on ethnographic approaches to cyber-infrastructure [20, 33]. One example of this research is the eDiaMoND project that studied the development of new practices in mamography and the key importance of skill and trust between scientists [21, 23]. More recently, Brown et al. explored how wikis could be appropriated to support collaboration amongst ethnographers [6] and Fraser et al. examined how tools could support practices of remote joint video analysis sessions [14]. This work has been part of the move away from notions of 'eScience' into the concept of 'eResearch'.

Lastly, a growing body of literature has documented experiences with the use of cyber-infrastructure in science practice [4]. A key focus of this work has been on data sharing - several initiatives support the practice of data sharing and modeling for the purpose of collaborating on social science projects, for example the Virtual Data Center, an open-source, digital library system designed to assist researchers in sharing and disseminating data [1]. Other researchers have used 'Grid technologies' to explore and model spatial distribution of crime using analytical frameworks from science and technology studies [40]. Here, studies emphasize that data sharing should fit into communities of practice and that the social role of data within science is important to consider when designing data sharing systems [5, 14]. One of the greater challenges is that these communities of practices are fluid and constantly renegotiated [5].

3. METHOD

Our research interests were broadly in the collaborative practices of social science research, and how this collaboration extended to the practice of fieldwork and field based research. We interviewed sixteen researchers attempting an open-ended way to understand their collaborative practices, how they initiate and manage connections with colleagues, and how they manage and conduct their fieldwork. Initial inquiry emphasized general practices but further questions asked directly to technology use in relation to collaborations. We included researchers who published work that involved direct interactions with those who were being studied, with data collected from the field in the actual places where those being studied worked, lived or visited - broadly research that involved 'field work'.

This encompassed work that would be recognizable as traditional ethnography, research that involved the use of structured questionnaires, video analysis of settings, life histories collected from in-depth interviews, and even observations and video analysis of congressional debates. This fieldwork spanned a large variety of different materials and our participants in turn brought a range of analytic approaches and orientations, in part tied to the very different topics that they researched. We recruited participants through snowball sampling using personal contacts at three universities, one in the US, one in Denmark and one in Sweden as well as a criminal policy research institute, and one health institute, both in the US.

While the concept of fieldwork is familiar in CSCW, it is important to recognize that not all fieldwork is the same. Our interviewees differed in their use of methods noticeably - four made use of computer assisted survey systems alongside paper questionnaires in their fieldwork, one used life histories, others used focus groups. In particular our researchers used much more structured methods ('instruments') with larger sample sizes than traditional open-ended ethnographic-led methods that characterize for example HCI fieldwork. A broader range of settings also constituted 'the field' - e.g. prisons, street corners, remote South American villages or the alcohol sections in supermarkets.

Few of the researchers we spoke to only used fieldwork - most supplemented their materials with others' data, archive records, and of course with the writings of other researchers. Six researchers identified themselves as sociologists, three as education researchers, two researched substance abuse, and one each for cognitive science, science and technology studies, economics, ethnology and criminology. The participants ranged from graduate students and research assistants to full professors with over 20 years of research experience. Eight of them were researchers in Sweden and Denmark, four were at large public US universities, and four worked in non-profit research organizations in the US. None of the researchers worked directly in the CSCW or the HCI field, although technology was of interest for four of our researchers.

4. COLLABORATION STRUCTURES

Collaboration was key to the scientific practices we studied, but not simply based around data sharing - as Ellis et al. argue that data sharing is only a small part of most of the interactions that take place in both science and social science [12], despite the attention it has been given in the current generation of cyber-infrastructure systems. For the social scientists of our study, their social relationships were much more important than any notion of 'data sharing'. Collaboration with other scientists was not only common to our participants but a characteristic of virtually all their research. Some of the senior professors mused that this had changed from when they had conducted their thesis work some 20-30 years ago and argued that with the increased pressure to publish, it was now necessary to collaborate in order to keep up publication count. They simply did not have enough time to work on solo projects any longer.

4.1 Four Types of Collaborative Setups

Amongst our social scientists we broadly identified four types of collaborations: long term small group, local opportunistic, apprenticeship, and large scale collaborations. To an extent these categories are fluid, yet they each characterize distinct types of collaboration:

4.1.1 Long-term small group collaborations

One of the most important forms of collaboration that our social scientists described involved close-knit collaboration between themselves and one or two other peers. All except two interviewees (who were relatively junior) had these types of collaborators. In some cases they were from the same department or a local institution, but usually due to the high mobility of social scientists these collaborations took place over a distance. Our academics co-authored repeatedly within this group, and the relationships often represented the single most important collaboration of that researcher in his or her career. Some researchers were polygamous, in that they would be a member of more than one close collaboration, with each group featuring a different research topic or interest, but many kept to one close collaboration, sometimes for their whole career to-date.

These collaborations often emerged early on in the researcher's career - in one case it had started as an advisory relationship, but in other cases they had started serendipitously between researchers when they were in the same institution. They were maintained highly regular contact (multiple emails or face to face meetings per week) and a collective set of views and opinions in relation to 'other' researchers. For example, one collaboration started between three researchers who had watched a documentary film together, approached the creators of the documentary, wrote up a funding proposal with their assistance and after receiving the grant began a long-term collaboration together. Another example was a reoccurring collaboration between a Swedish researcher and two US researchers (a husband and wife) who had spent the last ten or so summers in Sweden working with him. This collaboration was surprisingly close-knit considering the distance, particularly during the summer when they were co-located. Most other researchers' collaborations did not involve regular visits, but rather opportunistic meetings and a large amount of communication through email and phone. Two of our researchers

had actually moved institution to be closer to those they collaborated with.

4.1.2 Local group collaborations

A distinct set of collaborations took place between colleagues who were at the same institution. These were not valued as the long-term small group collaborations, but instead took place opportunistic around shared resources, funding or interests. In many cases our researchers would collaborate with a local colleague despite differences in approach because their locality removed the costs of working at a distance. Alternatively, often a local fieldwork sites would provide an impetus for working with local colleagues. Potentially these collaborations could grow into longer term collaborations, but in most cases they acted more like low-commitment 'trial relationships'. These collaborations also helped to expand researchers interests and knowledge - exposing them to new ideas and literatures.

Alongside these local group collaborations, our participants also often worked in local research groups, and other groups that were mandated (or at least inspired) by organizational commitments. Usually these groups did not feature intense co-authorship, but rather acted more as intellectual spaces where ideas could be presented, visitors could be hosted etc. This is not to say that co-authorships were rare- they often came about through collaborations between students and faculty where the students brought together the faculty through co-writing projects.

4.1.3 Apprenticeships

An interesting difference between the Scandinavian researchers and the US based researchers was their approach and collaboration with students, both graduate and undergraduate students. The Scandinavian researchers rarely talked about their students and when they mentioned them, they did not view their relationship as a collaborative one but instead an advisory one. We found two exceptions out of the eight Scandinavian researchers, one researcher who hired Masters students as research assistants each year for one of her research projects and another who maintained a strong small-group collaboration with a PhD student. The US based researchers on the other hand all mentioned students as collaborative relationships. Their rhetoric about students also differed; one professor for example, repeatedly talked about students "working for him" collecting data and performing analysis on several of his research projects. The differentiation in approach to student collaboration obviously reflects not only cultural differences but also differences in student infrastructure between the countries. Where PhD students in Scandinavia tend to be older than their US counterparts they also often have only 3 years to complete their PhD, leading to a more condensed period where the student is allowed to focus solely on their own project. In the US, where PhDs generally take 6-8 years, it is not uncommon for new graduate students to work on projects dictated by their advisors for the first few years in order to 'tune in' to the world of research.

4.1.4 Large scale collaborations

Eight of our interviewees had worked or currently worked on large-scale cross-country collaborations. These included cross-Nordic collaborations, EU projects, NSF projects and national institute of health funded US-wide projects. The interviewees who had not had cross-country collaborations were mainly young researchers. The cross-country collaborations were often described as problematic; factors such as differing research approaches and lack of coordination were often cited. Other factors were the rather bureaucratic nature of particularly EU projects that the researchers often faced. One participant described how a Nordic project on alcohol consumption in restaurants had ended up rather differently than he had intended when he started as director:

[The researchers' different research approaches] caused quite disparate papers [ha ha]... they do different things. [...] I think the ambition in the beginning was to do [the research project] more comparatively, to use the same research questions, the same methodologies. Ehm, different traditions, histories, lack of resource, I would say, led to situations where people... Okay 'do your thing', instead of trying to raise funding, coordinate it, [...] I don't know if it quite failed, it changed and in the process you have ambitions... meeting reality... that thing happens.

The concept of 'meeting reality' was a reoccurring obstacle noted in relation to these larger projects. While initial plans (often described in a funding proposal) would involve deep collaborations, these came to be discarded as projects 'met reality'. Collaborations took place around loose-coupled work, with research mostly in isolation and only one document (often the funding proposal) and an initial meeting as basis for the research. Although these collaborations did generate face-to-face workshops, one interviewee reported about a project that even though "we met all the time", the research practices and perhaps cultural differences contributed to a diversity that prevented close-nit coherent work.

We now continue by outlining a few core concepts that emerged as being valuable for the collaborations that were described positively and that most often ended up with results not just publishable, but results considered significant for the individual researcher and his/her career.

5. RESEARCH COLLABORATION PRACTICES

Conceptually one can divide up fieldwork in terms of its distinct phases - from formulating and planning research (and obtaining funding), through participant or setting recruitment, the interviews and observations themselves, data entry and transformation of data, analytic revision, revision and extraction of arguments, to writing and revision. Each of these phases not only involves different jobs and work processes, but also features differences in terms of how easily or essential collaboration was to the task.

While it is tempting to characterize certain phases as loosely or highly coupled, each stage features characteristics of both. Fieldwork, for example, is something that can be easily conducted in parallel more or less independently. Yet there are aspects of fieldwork that need to be coupled - in particular the emerging interest and insight of those carrying out the fieldwork. Without this then different fieldworkers could end up with radically divergent views of a particular setting, and viewpoints that are not necessarily in conflict but are instead irrelevant to each other. For this reason if fieldworkers regularly communicate then the later analysis stages can be much more successful. Indeed through many of the phases of a research project there is the challenge of keeping the independent paths engaged with each other, such that when it came to writing the report or paper at the end the different materials could be brought together.

This is what often went wrong in large-scale projects. Individual researchers focused on different branches of the overall theme or project and despite workshops that should have brought the fieldwork together, participants reported that these workshops were often failures in other than very general idea exchange. When it came to the final report, it often consisted of separate

distinct research pieces rather than connected parts of a whole. Research groups working together at a distance often found difficulty in calibrating expectations on what was going to be done where. For example, one of our researchers worked on an autobiography study of alcohol consumption, aiming to be a comparison between people's perception of alcohol in Sweden and Finland. The Swedish researchers created a website where participants could provide their biography, yet the Finish researchers only put up flyers in public forums with no corresponding Finish website. This resulted in a large difference between the number of entries received and the length of the entries between Sweden and Finland.

One of the key aspects to collaboration then is to find the right times to work together, and the right times to work apart. For researchers that are physically close this could entail simply working from the same office - such as when a senior fieldworker and a more junior fieldworker worked together, supporting a fluidity in moving between tight and loose coupled work throughout the fieldwork. In particular, we highlight two core issues that contribute to successful collaborations.

5.1 Routines

One way of dealing with complexities of collaboration is to make use of routines - such as weekly phone calls or meetings. For those working together at a distance these sort of temporal structures were important - as has been confirmed in much earlier CSCW work [24]. For the long-term small group collaborations that we discussed above the flexibility of the academic calendar proved to be essential to support their work. Researchers would use visits (such as the summer or sabbaticals) to spend intense time working together, packing the 'tightly coupled' work into the time they were together. Others would travel together on fieldwork trips, for example one researcher travelled to the north of Sweden with two of his collaborators for a month to gather data and produce a documentary film. Fieldwork time together was important not just for conducting fieldwork but also for understanding better other researchers.

Meetings also took place over video conferencing systems and simply telephone conferences, popularly over Skype. One researcher who worked within smaller but geographically widely spread groups (for example Japan, the US, Sweden) used it extensively: "Yep, I use Skype, but we also use something called Marratech, which is a videoconference system, basically that you have it on your laptop or computer [...] we use it a lot and it's very, very good." Other researchers relied mostly on the phone, particularly if their small core collaborations were couple based. All in all seniority or experience had little connection with level of meeting technology used, instead it seemed to be used if one of the collaborators were a 'driver' of new technology and had introduced it to the rest of the group.

Interestingly, the approach to these meetings were mixed; some were considered important and essential, other meetings were simply considered mandatory and possibly time wasting, depending on the level of autonomy the researcher had over them.

We have a weekly conference call. On Mondays. [...] we talk about our field experiences. We'll write a short note on who we interviewed this week [...] You are asking the same questions, [but] you might get a more colorful story. "She was a college student she was using Xanex 30 times in the last month. And --- 60 times in the last months. And she had a friend that died, and she had used heroin but had stopped when her friend had died." It's really a debrief, I don't think it does anything, it might generate the odd idea every now and then but it's more about being a team. (US based health researcher)

As the example above show, the meetings were not just in place for the sake of communication, but as much as a complement to team building. For the rare collaborations where the researcher had not met in person, they expressed that it was nice to be able 'to put a face to the name' through video conferencing. Viewing regular meetings as part of the routines that contribute to successful collaborations might seem obvious; however, the important point here is that it was not only the communication conveyed at the meetings that made collaborations; instead it was establishment of the meetings as routine and the routine around the meeting technology, that meant these meetings contributed to the successful collaboration.

5.2 Collaborators Learning to See Together

Earlier research into the practices of ethnographers emphasized the importance of 'seeing together' amongst fieldworkers [6], a sense that researchers share a developing view of what they are studying together, and that over the course of a project they can come to a consensus on what are the important aspects of the setting they are studying.

This was as much the case in quantitative work as much as qualitative. Broadly in quantitative work there is a desire that the results from different participants are comparable. Yet this depends upon considerable work by the researchers [29]. Questions might be phrased in a particular - standardized - way, yet participants might simply not understand the question and require some explanation before they can answer. This presents a challenge in terms of making sure that different participants are answering the same question. Or alternatively, participants might have their answers codified and it can be necessary to make considerable judgment about what answer fits into what category. This creates a need to work out a common approach across fieldworkers, but also there is a need for those analyzing the data to be aware of these contingencies further down the process.

Moving beyond the individual study there was a similar sense of seeing together for our long-term small group collaborators, but something that acted on a different scale than an individual study. For these groups what was key was not necessarily that those involved agreed as such, but that they came to define their research field in similar ways - that they identified similar problems, found similar aspects interesting, and that they characterized the research field in similar ways. Behind this there would of course be a certain level of agreement (researchers might come form the same intellectual school or tradition, or might have similar views on others work) but this base acted to set a scene where productive work could be done, often through disagreements, and the resolving of those disagreements.

This common viewpoint came in part from working together over a long period of time - not only reading the same pieces, or discussing them together, but also reflecting on others' positions - particularly how this came out in writing together. For example, one academic met his close collaborator during his PhD through a shared advisor, and they now worked together on nearly all their research projects.

So even academic relationships that might be characterized by disagreement - at least to a practical level, still depended on a large amount of agreement - agreement in the sense of seeing together the academic field. For students of our researchers, frequently their 'job' as such was to try and understand and come to see the worldview of their advisor. Indeed, most of our researchers considered themselves still 'attached' in some way to their advisor in that they had inherited their view of the field. This might not be something that they would agree with, or even that they might share, but to understand the subtly and complexity of a particular viewpoint on a research field proves to be valuable training for future academic work.

Seeing together also constituted a common view of collaboration technologies, what was appropriate to use and what was working well for their specific collaboration practices. Obviously Internet based information search and email were the major players in terms of research collaboration technologies, but data collection and data analysis technologies helped this process of learning to see together. One professor explains about a colleague who enjoys programming, even though he potentially could hire people to do that work:

He programs the statistical techniques, and so he uses this [...], which is a programming language. Our cooperation is quite interesting because I like to write the first ideas, and so on, and he loves programming, so he jokes in a self-ironic way, he says it's wonderful to be a research assistant. That's when I'm most productive, you see? [...] So, when he and I work together, I push the project and he does the program. He loves that. So, he said yesterday when we went to lunch, "My favorite programs are when I'm the research assistant." He is a leading researcher.

The creation of the statistical equations and programming measures contribute to the researchers common understanding of the data and helps them view their data from specific perspectives. We now continue describing some of the challenges that the researchers encountered in their research practices in relation to research coordination.

6. CHALLENGES TO RESEARCH COLLABORATION

Fieldwork practices relied heavily not only on the researchers' own individual previous and established practices but also on the practices and influences of collaborators. This often posed challenges at different stages in the projects from the initiation to the writing up of results. We found it valuable for the analysis to explore our data in terms of structural challenges. We have themed the challenges into five themes: initial phrasing of projects, the collection of information and data from electronic sources, access to fieldwork sites, fieldwork practices affecting the results and sharing data.

6.1 Initial Phrasing of Projects

As with any research project one initial job is the formulation of the project, gaining funding and institutional approval. Fieldwork based projects present a particular challenge here in that the nature of the work prevents the exact formulation of the study prior to the study being conducted. Yet the requirements of funders for a clear overview and plan for the work - can conflict with the emergent nature of the findings of fieldwork. This can be problematic even in the most structured and quantitative of studies where applications for funding might require an outline of all the questions that will be asked - even though it might be desirable for these questions to emerge from preliminary work. This can also be the case for ethics approval where for the study to be 'signed off' before the start of empirical work.

The challenges herein were particularly profound among the Scandinavian researchers who had been involved in EU projects. These often require a specific variety of partners in different countries and areas of Europe; such requirement resulted in having to 'cold-call' research colleagues unfamiliar to the participants or being involved in projects mainly because of their geographical position. One of the Swedish professors explained a situation:

I'm very skeptical and prejudice to the process, 'cause they [the EU] are forcing a structure upon you [...] What happens is that someone somehow now ... this was in Barcelona, got an idea. Here we have a possibility to get a lot of EU money, [...] so this is an opportunity for us to do some research around the subjects focused around the strategy in some kind of form. [...] What they do then is 'yeah, we should apply, but we need partners'. So then they sent out, often just by email 'hi this is [name] from England'.

Interviewer: People you don't necessarily know?

Well, no, I know him, but not the others down there. So they describe the idea ... then they try to describe there is a lot of money in it for you and it is no hard work [laugh], and then it continues like that. But then the EU forces you to formulate your research in a particular, certain way, which really is, it is very strange I think. People don't think. It is just formalities. It is superficial...

These projects were not based on long-term collaborations or tight-knit colleagues and were more likely to encounter problems, as also described above. The challenges were particularly profound in the initial phase of a project, where partners attempted to gauge one another in terms of motivations and planned effort. Communication between partners was key, but it was rare to see actual workshop based meetings in the initial phase of projects. Instead the researchers communicated almost solely via email until the funding was acquired and then they met at so-called 'kick-off meetings'.

6.2 Collecting Electronically Available Data

A profoundly technological challenge to fieldwork research was an activity also often taking place initially in a project. Even though all of our participants conducted fieldwork with human subjects, all project included phases of collection of electronic information, including searching for related literature, source material in libraries and picture material through electronic of analog networks. A few of the researchers based the majority of their research on mainly electronically available data.

Unsurprisingly all of the researchers used Internet based information search, but some needed more structured data than others. Here, limitations introduced themselves as problems accessing the right data through library websites and the data sometimes being constrained to access from within the actual libraries, making it necessary to work together either in the library or make sure enough notes was in order for a collaborator to understand the original data. A US based researcher for example, had to travel or have his research assistants travel to Washington DC to collect archived law material from the 19th century. These documents were not online and only available at the Library of Congress; the travel to Washington DC always meant a cross-country flight adding significantly to his research expenses.

Although the information collection was at times problematic, the researchers showed a significant ability to 'work around the systems', to find a way to get the information they needed. This is in many ways of course the essence of fieldwork research, but we found that it was a characteristic of activities connected to the long-term small group collaborations; researchers relied to a large extent on their close colleagues to do this type of work with/for them and help out in complicated cases.

6.3 Access to Field-Sites

A third set of problems emerged around access to particular settings and enrolling participants in the study. While access can be arranged in advance it is always contingent on changes in personnel, or simply the changing conditions of the field-site. One of our social scientists, for example, was studying shopping habits in supermarkets. She relied on the particular supermarket manager's cooperation each time she went out in the field to interview shoppers, even though she had a general permission from the greater company who were partners in the project. She found it frustrating that some times they were allowed to video-record customers (after customers' permission of course) but other times had to rely on paper notes. A similar but more pronounced problem of access was encountered by another researcher who was doing fieldwork in hospitals and hospital-attached accommodation for outpatients who lived too far away to commute. Not only was she continuously denied access to the hospital ward that the project had originally negotiated collaboration with when submitting a funding proposal, she also felt she was approached with hostility from nurses and staff when she finally gained access to the hospital accommodation house ('the patient hotel'). She did report that the patients themselves that agreed to talk to her were very welcoming and approachable and she was able to collect data through interviews and observations with them. These examples illustrate how collaboration between researchers is not the only issue of importance; also the collaboration between researchers and people at the field site is of essence, particularly in environments where people of power to grant access can readily change their policy.

Four of our researchers worked with vulnerable populations, making use of public places (homeless, transexuals, drug addicts) for 'street' recruitment. This involved walking up to 'likely' individuals in settings where the groups of interest were known to inhabit. To get around problems of commitment in these settings these researchers made use of screener interviews - shorter interviews that, if the right candidates were found, resulted in an invitation for the main interview. While this at least increased the proportion of potential interviewees, screening interviewees on the street presented practical problems of climate and environment. Interviewing only those available and willing 'on the street' to take a small renumeration for their time was also lamented as skewing the sample of informants.

This set of challenges is characteristic of a great deal of fieldwork but among our social scientists, it sometimes defined the organization of the fieldwork to a further extent than planned and desired. So although the researchers managed to work around obstacles of recruitment and access, the fact that such settings are problematic to navigate in the first place meant that collaborating with other researchers on these projects was not contributing to the main challenges within the project, except conflicts internally about what kind of access had originally been negotiated. Two researchers expressed frustration about this 'lack of communication' that occasionally influenced their access to the field sites.

6.4 Fieldwork practices affecting the results

As with any form of fieldwork a key issue is that the conditions where it is conducted are not under the control of the researcher. This is the very advantage of fieldwork - that the researcher can find out the unexpected and work is embedded in the settings it investigates, but it also presents 'everyday fieldwork problems' that need be resolved.

The actual collection itself often presented its own challenges and trade-offs. For example, one of our social scientists was video recording the interactions of children in a museum - she knew she got more useful data from using a head mounted camera on her child participants alongside filming the learning activity, but she worried that the actions of the child with the camera were to a certain extent affected by the presence of the camera. This researcher explained in length how small the camera was, but admitted that the children constantly commented on the fact that they were being recorded when interacting with the camera-mounted child.

For our researchers who had more structured projects an ongoing challenge was in managing how questions were asked, and how the answers that were given were translated into results. Behind the use of survey data there is the desire for comparability, that the survey can be used to say that a set number of individual had a certain behavior or opinion. Yet this rests on making comparable the natural variability of individuals. Moreover, the concepts that lie behind the survey questions must in some way connect with the behaviors that are being surveyed.

One technology that had received widespread use was digital audio recorders - the different fieldworkers we interviewed all collected large corpuses of audio data from their fieldwork. Yet this audio data was seldom used as part of the analytic process, but more as a safeguard should data be lost from the other ways in which it was collected. The key problem with audio was that it was difficult to index and access - in particular there was no way of comparing audio data by (say) question asked. Moreover, since transcribing audio data was expensive and difficult to arrange audio data usually remained an under exploited resource. For our researchers who used video data they shared the data through online repositories or simply by viewing it together with others or sending a selected snippet to a collaborator. As with audio, video also was a frustrating material to work with in that it was extremely time consuming to review and to analyze. As one researcher expressed: "Often [our] qualitative data isn't used because they end up with hundreds of hours of tape and no reference or start point." Instead the researchers relied solely on the quantitative survey data they had recorded within their system.

Perhaps the key problem for research though turned on how questions were asked, understood and answered. Key to good survey research is asking the same question the same way across all the different participants who are being interviewed. Yet different participants might understand questions in very different ways, or simply not understand the question. This requires the researcher to explain what the question means. While this might seem unproblematic, it can lead to slightly different questions being asked. For example, a term such as 'sexual partner' might mean very different things for different people both in terms of interviewer and interviewee. The order that a question is asked might also lead to different interpretations - if a question about number of sexual partners follows a set of questions about oral sex, transgender, casual sexual encounters and the like, then it is likely to get a higher answer than if it is asked individually.

Questions are also answered in different ways. Most surveys are designed with a small set of answers to each question so as to support the comparability of answers between those interviewed. Yet the answers that are given often do not clearly fit with these different coded answers - one of the jobs of the interviewer is to convert the answers given to standardized answers. Yet if there is more than one fieldworker, or if interviews are being done in different places, it can be difficult to ensure any sort of regularity between interviews.

I worked on a survey last year where they changed the instrument all the time. And it was such a mess. It just ended up, you couldn't use 10% of the questions. It's a really difficult. People talk about quant data as if it's the guiding light, of real and true. Whatever. And it's just not at all if you've got people asking people. People ask the questions differently.

To address this survey researchers would tape record their interviews with the goal of being able to 'back track' should there be any problems with the questions being asked. Yet this was rarely done because of the difficulty of sharing and accessing audio files. More open ended or qualitative work was not immune from these problems either - most ethnographic work relies upon comparability between different settings that might in many ways be quite distinct. While there is not the strong commitment to straightforward simple comparability, ethnographers who worked together resorted instead to sharing fieldnotes and summaries of interviews as a way of making sure that the other researchers shared a similar viewpoint on the field [6].

6.5 Sharing Data

A final challenge emerged when the researchers were ready to share (empirical) data with their collaborators for discussion and analysis. Their physical and digitally mediated meetings were augmented by the constant sharing of electronic data of different sorts. Fieldworkers often upload data in different forms, such as field-notes that are sharable with a team, or data that had been input from questionnaires in the field. We were struck by the reliance of the different researchers we studied on the uploading and downloading of data to servers. Participants used a multitude of tools - FTP, Sharepoint, Entryware, emailing files around and uploading video files. While there were shortcomings in all these mechanisms, and the mechanisms used were relatively crude, data sharing was not identified as a problem for research as such. Indeed, current technologies successfully supported a background expectation amongst those working together that their data was shared as it was collected. Yet, the lack of structure and generally accepted data sharing formats introduced problems for the collaborations, particularly the large-scale ones. In a cross-country project for example, the data had been collected on paper in one country and electronically in the other. The researchers we talked to were unable to get an overview of the paper-based material before actually visiting the other country's research team. Their electronic data entry practices did not afford a direct comparison without actually meeting in person and get a mutual understanding of the two different data sets. In essence a characteristic was that the shared data did not exist in itself - it acted as a background to other interactions around the fieldwork project - data was important but could not be understood if shared without further interactions.

While many of these practices described will be familiar to readers, our broader sample presents some interesting insights. It is important to point out that by describing these collective practices we are addressing a more diverse set of fieldwork researchers than what one individual could describe in terms of own experiences. These practices are important to trace and analyze in order to provide insights into broader research collaboration technology design.

This brings on the subject of how, more specifically, technologies can be used to support the different fieldwork and collaboration practices that we have outlined so far.

7. DESIGNING TECHNOLOGIES FOR COLLABORATIVE RESEARCH

The examples above illustrate some of the constraints and common challenges that the researchers had in their fieldwork collection and analysis. It was evident that they adjusted their practices to the technologies as much as they chose technologies appropriate for the tasks at hand. Their choices were often made together with their close collaborators and similar to previous research on collaborative software for information workers, this choice often helped establish a group identity and form intra-group bonding [34]. Challenges to collaboration were often reflected in technology challenges, either as conflicting utilization of specific applications or simply as a lack of utilization of a wider set of communication technologies. The large-scale, more complicated collaborative relationships were often solely based on email contact alongside sporadic or regular face-to-face workshops despite the availability of both video conferencing and simple phone conversations. These 'richer' communication technologies required an intimacy that was rarely present in broader collaborations, or they required a considerable effort from the partners initially in the project.

A relevant implication is the potential for the use of more 'in-between' technologies such as text-chat and the blending of informal and formal communication tools. The ability to talk more informally, yet regularly about projects is likely to promote better collaborations within the long-distance large-scale projects and text-chat has many characteristics of informality. In the corporate world, companies have had success with social media specific to the company, meaning that social relations with work colleagues promotes closer work relations [11]; it is likely that social media relationships between larger groups of collaborators can also cultivate better communication and increased collaboration.

An emerging characteristic of the technology use among our set of social scientists was that although each technology tool affected the collaboration 'moments' and even the overall projects, technologies as such were not responsible for successful or less successful projects. Instead they reflected the quality of the collaboration by being diversely used within successfully described collaborations and limitedly used in less successful projects. The optimal situation was when the social scientist worked around the technologies and picked the ones that worked for them in their particular situation. They developed a common vocabulary within their tight-knit collaboration, something characteristic of the smaller scale collaborations.

7.1 TagPad

We were able to address two issues with a technology prototype for fieldwork interviews. The first issue relates to how our participants often found it difficult to structure interviews in a way so colleagues could replicate them or at least conduct them similarly enough for an appropriate analysis. The second issue was one of more ongoing analysis during or right after actual data collection. We developed TagPad, an application that runs on an iPad, and which records interviews and let the user structure the audio according the interview schedule. On a conceptual level TagPad can be divided into three different parts: the TagPad application itself, the platform it is running on – a tablet computer, specifically an iPad, and the integration with a cloud storage service, in this case the service Dropbox. This combination is what makes up and defines TagPad. The TagPad application has two different views: the interview view and the analysis view, the interview view being the main view (See Figure 1). As input data TagPad can record audio, save short text entries and use multiple-

choice items. The researcher decides how to combine the input. For example, TagPad can be used to record audio only, it can be used for only short text entries and/or multiple-choice questions (or a combination) or a combination of text and audio. Because of this flexibility TagPad can be considered a multi purpose interview tool suitable for a wide selection of qualitative and quantitative studies.

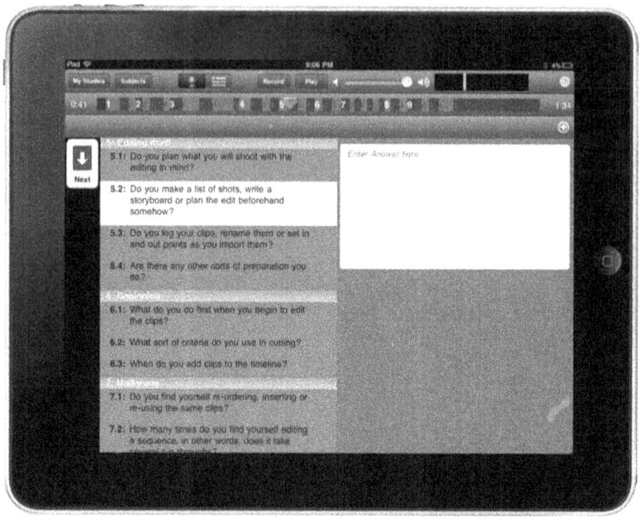

Figure 1. The interview view: An interview guide loaded into TagPad and question 5.2 is selected.

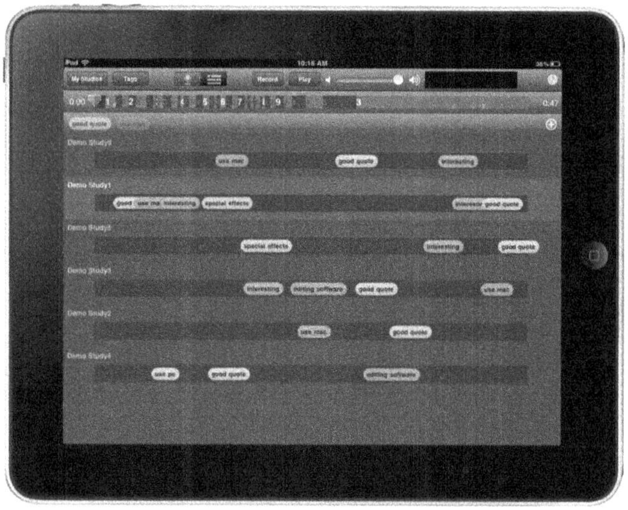

Figure 2: The analysis view of TagPad. Custom tags can be added to each interview for pre-analysis.

TagPad has a simple analysis view for quick analysis to support selective transcription (See Figure 2). Besides having playback capabilities tags are automatically added to the audio timeline for each question so it is possible to locate where in the audio a specific question was asked. Custom tags can be added making it possible to navigate, locate and share specific audio segments. Tags can be added both during and after an interview.

The portability of the iPad addresses the vital aspect: mobility. Additionally mobility is supported because the iPad agilely can be prepared for an interview and operates fairly long on battery without the need for an external power source. Mobility is essential because data collections in the form of interviews often will take place in the field requiring flexibility of the researcher.

The use of cloud storage is also a defining feature. Advantages are effective and simple data maintaining, distribution, and support for collaboration. With cloud storage the service provider handles most of the technical aspects such as backup of data and there is no need for manual management of the storage and configuration of the system. Disadvantages include potential issues with bandwidth, performance, reliability and availability and that some projects may have very specific records-keeping requirements.

TagPad is designed to address only a subset of the reported findings from our study and we are not expecting it to influence the larger collaboration structures at place among social science researchers. However, we do believe that a tool like TagPad has potential in terms of improving some research activities that have been discussed here.

8. CONCLUSION

Drawing on interviews this paper has documented different collaborative aspects of science research practice. We focused on the sociality of social science fieldwork practice - how is that social science collaboration depends upon small group long term collaborations, alongside local and larger scale research collaboration. The paper went on to document how collaboration practices were arranged - the amount of coupling of different parts of the work process, spatial and temporal routines and the importance of 'seeing together' of researchers being able to share a viewpoint on what was important in their research field. From this we documented specific challenges in terms of research practices and how technologies are involved in the fieldwork.

It is important to highlight how our results add to a growing field of cyberinfrastructures and group technologies but by addressing a more qualitative research space. Much other relevant research focuses on information workers and their collaboration tools but the profound characteristics of social science researchers have rarely been addressed. Our results are a first step in the direction of exploring the fieldwork research technology space and while many of our findings overlap with the findings from those two other spaces, we find it important to point them out in an aim to suggest designs for technology for small-scale fieldwork. TagPad, which we briefly presented here, is a tool that we are developing for empirical data collection and initial analysis, particularly focused on small-scale close collaborations. It is designed to support collaborative social science fieldwork practice - in particular collaborative interview based fieldwork projects. We are currently studying TagPad amongst a number of different research groups who are using it in their fieldwork practice, and are planning to provide further insight into the use of it in future publications.

Beyond the implications of this work for cyber-infrastructure it is worth considering how different models of research practice inform funding decisions and the organization of funding councils, as well as more broadly support for academic and intellectual work. If the key relationships for the social sciences are smaller and more longer term than science, this would suggest quite different arrangements to how we currently organize much of the support for collaborative scientific practice.

9. ACKNOWLEDGMENTS

Thanks to the social scientists that participated in our interviews. Thanks to Malcolm Hall and Nis Bornø for their efforts on design and development of TagPad. This research was funded by NSF Grant #0838330.

10. REFERENCES

[1] Altman, M., et al. A Digital Library for the Dissemination and Replication of Quantitative Social Science Research: The Virtual Data Center. *Social Science Computer Review,* 19, 4 (2001), 458-470.

[2] Atkins, D. Building a UK foundation for the transformative enhancement of research and innovation. *Report of the international panel for the 2009 review of the UK research councils e-science programme* (2010).

[3] Beaulieu, A. and Walters, P. Imagining e-science beyond computation. In *New infrastructures for knowledge production: Understanding e-science* (2006), 48-70.

[4] Berman, F. and Brady, H. *Final Report: NSF SBE-CISE Workshop on Cyberinfrastructure and the Social Sciences.* NSF Report, 2005.

[5] Birnholtz, J. P. and Bietz, M. J. Data at work: supporting sharing in science and engineering. In *GROUP 2003,* ACM (2003), 339-348.

[6] Brown, B., Lundin, J., Rost, M. Lymer, G. and Holmquist, L.E. Seeing Ethnographically: Teaching ethnography as part of CSCW. In *ECSCW 2007* (2007), 411-430.

[7] Callon, M. *The Laws of the Markets.* Blackwell Publishing Limited, 1998.

[8] Carter, S. and Mankoff, J. When participants do the capturing: the role of media in diary studies. In *Proceedings of CHI 2005,* ACM Press (2005), 899-908.

[9] Cragin, M. H. and Shankar, K. Scientific Data Collections and Distributed Collective Practice. *Comput. Supported Coop. Work,* 15, 2-3 (2006), 185-204.

[10] David, P. A. Towards a cyberinfrastructure for enhanced scientific collaboration. In *Advancing Knowledge and the Knowledge Economy,* MIT Press (2005).

[11] DiMicco, J., Millen, D. R., Geyer, W., Dugan, C., Brownholtz, B. and Muller, M. 2008. Motivations for social networking at work. In *Proceedings of the 2008 ACM conference on Computer supported cooperative work* (CSCW '08). ACM, New York, NY, USA, 711-720.

[12] Ellis, D., Oldridge, R. and Vasconcelos, A. Community and virtual community. In *Annual review of information science and technology* (2004), 145-188.

[13] Flor, G. d. l., Luff, P., Jirotka, M., Pybus, J., Kirkham, R. and Carusi, A. The Case of the Disappearing Ox: Seeing Through Digital Images to an Analysis of Ancient Texts. In *Proceedings of the 28th international conference on Human factors in computing systems* (2010),473-482 ACM.

[14] Fraser, M., Hindmarsh, J., Best, K., Heath, C., Biegel, G., Greenhalgh, G. and Reeves, S. Remote Collaboration Over Video Data: Towards Real-Time e-Social Science. *Computer Supported Cooperative Work (CSCW),* 15, 4 (2006), 257-279.

[15] Fry, J. Coordination and control of research practice across scientific fields: Implications for a differentiated e-science. In *New infrastructures for knowledge production: Understanding e-science* (2006), 48-70.

[16] Geertz, C. *The Interpretation Of Cultures.* Basic Books, 1977.

[17] Glänzel, W. and Schubert, A. Analysing Scientific Networks Through Co-Authorship. In Handbook of Quantitative Science and Technology Research, Springer (2005), 257-276.

[18] Goodwin, C. Seeing in depth. *Social Studies of Science,* 25(1995), 237-274.

[19] Goodwin, C. Practices of Seeing: Visual Analysis - An Ethnomethodological Approach. In *Handbook of Visual Analysis,* Sage (2000), 157-182.

[20] Halfpenny, P. and Procter, R. The e-Social Science research agenda. *Phil. Trans. R. Soc.,* 368, 1925 (2010), 3761-3778.

[21] Hartswood, M., Procter, R., Rouncefield, M., Slack, R., Soutter, J. and Voss, A. 'Repairing' the machine: a case study of the evaluation of computer-aided detection tools in breast screening. In *Proceedings of ECSCW 2003,* Kluwer Academic Publishers (2003), 375-394.

[22] Hine, C. Databases as Scientific Instruments and Their Role in the Ordering of Scientific Work. *Social Studies of Science,* 36, 2 (2006), 269-298.

[23] Jirotka, M., Procter, R., Hartswood, M., Slack, R., Simpson, A., Coopmans, C., Hinds, C. and Voss, A. Collaboration and Trust in Healthcare Innovation: The eDiaMoND Case Study. *Computer Supported Cooperation Work,* 14, 4 (2005), 369-398.

[24] Kraut, R., Galegher, J. and Egido, C. Relationships and tasks in scientific research collaboration. *Human-Computer Interaction,* 3, 1 (1987), 31-58.

[25] Lee, C. P., Dourish, P. and Mark, G. The human infrastructure of cyberinfrastructure. In *Proceedings of the 2006 20th conference on Computer supported cooperative work,* ACM (2006), 483-492.

[26] Lynch, M. A new disease of the intellect? Some reflections on the therapeutic value of Peter Winch's philosophy for and cultural studies of science. *History of the Human Sciences,* 13, 1 (2000), 140-156.

[27] Mackenzie, D. An Equation and its Worlds: Bricolage, Exemplars, Disunity and Performativity in Financial Economics. *Social Studies of Science,* 33, 6 (2003), 831-868.

[28] MacKenzie, D. *An Engine, Not a Camera: How Financial Models Shape Markets.* The MIT Press, 2006.

[29] Maynard, D. and Schaeffer, N. Standardization and its discontents. In *Standardization and tacit knowledge: Interaction and practice in the survey interview,* Wiley (2002), 3-46.

[30] Moore, R. Managing troubles in answering survey questions: respondents' uses of projective reporting. *Social Psychology Quarterly,* 67, 1 (2004), 50.

[31] Olson, G. M., Zimmerman, A. and Bos, N. 2008. *Scientific Collaboration on the Internet.* The MIT Press.

[32] Porter, T. M. *The Rise of Statistical Thinking, 1820-1900.* Princeton University Press, 1988.

[33] Procter, R., Borgman, C., Bowker, G., Jirotka, M., Olson, G., Pancake, C., Rodden, T. and schraefel, m.c. Usability research challenges for cyberinfrastructure and tools. In *CHI '06 extended abstracts on Human factors in computing systems,* ACM (2006), 1675-1678.

[34] Redmiles, D., Wilensky, H., Kosaka, K. and de Paula, R. 2005. What ideal end users teach us about collaborative software. In *Proceedings of the 2005 international ACM SIGGROUP conference on Supporting group work (GROUP '05).* ACM, New York, NY, USA, 260-263.

[35] Schroeder, R. e-Sciences as research technologies: reconfiguring disciplines, globalizing knowledge. *Social Science Information,* 47, 2 (2008), 131-157.

[36] Schroeder, R. and Fry, J. Social Science Approaches to e-Science: Framing an Agenda. *Journal of Computer-Mediated Communication,* 12(2007), 563-582.

[37] Sonnenwald, D. H. *Expectations for a scientific collaboratory: a case study.* ACM, City, 2003.

[38] Sonnenwald, D. H. Scientific Collaboration: A Synthesis of Collaborations and Strategies. In *Annual Review of Information Science and Technology, vol. 4,* Information Today (2007).

[39] Voida, A., Mynatt, E.D., Erickson, T. and Kellogg, W. Interviewing over instant messaging. In *CHI '04 extended abstracts on Human factors in computing systems,* ACM (2004), 1344-1347.

[40] Wessels, B. and Craglia, M. Situated Innovation of e-Social Science: Integrating Infrastructure, Collaboration, and

Knowledge in Developing e-Social Science. *Journal of Computer-Mediated Communication,* 12(2007), 692-711.

[41] Winch, P. *The Idea of a social science and its relation to philosophy.* Routledge and Kegan Paul, London, 1958.

[42] Wulf, W. A. The collaboratory opportunity. *Science (New York, N.Y.),* 261, 5123 (1993), 854-855.

[43] Yeh, R., Liao, C., Klemmer, S. Guimbretière, F., Lee, B., Kakaradov, B., Stamberger, J. and Paepcke, A 2006. ButterflyNet: a mobile capture and access system for field biology research. In *Proceedings of the SIGCHI conference on Human Factors in computing systems (CHI '06),* ACM, New York, NY, USA, 571-580.

Human Infrastructure as Process and Effect: Its Impact on Individual Scientists' Participation in International Collaboration

Airong Luo
University of Michigan Medical School
4101 Medical Science I 5624,
Ann Arbor, MI 48109
Tel: 1-734-9987766
Email: airongl@umich.edu

Margaret Ann Murphy
University of Michigan Medical School
4101 Medical Science I 5624,
Ann Arbor, MI 48109
Tel: 1-734-9987757
Email: margm@umich.edu

Ted Hanss
University of Michigan Medical School
4101 Medical Science I 5624,
Ann Arbor, MI 48109
Tel:1-734-3302575
Email: ted@umich.edu

ABSTRACT

We adopt the concept of human infrastructure as our analytic lens to examine two high energy physics collaborations. Our analysis goes beyond the macro level of virtual organizations to include the human infrastructures in scientists' home institutions and personal networks. While previous literature tends to focus on the macro level of analysis of management and coordination within virtual organizations, our study concentrates on individual scientists, especially junior scientists' gains and challenges when participating in international collaboration. We compare the experiences of scientists from lesser-resourced and well-resourced nations to examine how specific components of basic social structures enable or impede individual scientists' participation in international collaboration. Identifying the social mechanisms that constrain scientists will enable us to better understand how to build human infrastructure to facilitate individual scientists' participation in collaboration.

Categories and Subject Descriptors

K.4.3 [**Organizational Impacts**]: Computer-Supported Collaborative Work; K.6.1 [Project and People Management]: Systems Analysis and Design

General Terms

Design, Human Factors

Keywords

Human infrastructure, International collaboration, Collaboration between differently resourced nations, High energy physics

1. INTRODUCTION

The advancement of science, technology, and education depend increasingly on internationally distributed scientific collaboration facilitated by virtual organizations [8]. International collaboration allows researchers to tackle complex research problems by

harnessing the creativity of distributed investigators and applying locally-based scientific resources [14].Virtual organizations bring about rich opportunities, but previous research has identified many challenges in distributed collaboration, including difficulty in establishing and maintaining common ground [6], trust among collaborators [28], poorly designed incentive systems [12,25], and differing organizational structures and governance systems [13].

Lee et al. [17] assert that most prior research on distributed scientific collaboration focuses on management and social coordination within virtual organizations. They argue that virtual organizations are "not so virtual" because participants in virtual organizations are enabled or constrained by their home institutions. Researchers of distributed collaboration contend that the unit of analysis should extend beyond the boundary of virtual teams. More research is needed to understand how resources, policies, and administrative and management structures in individual researchers' home institutions shape their participation in collaborative projects. We also need to understand how individuals' personal networks, existing outside or along with traditional and virtual organizations, enable them to overcome organizational constraints and access information and resources [17,22].

We studied human infrastructure in two large international high energy physics (HEP) collaborations with a focus on the social processes that shape and are affected by dynamic relations among participants from differently resourced nations. Human infrastructure is defined as "the arrangements of organizations and actors that must be brought into alignment for work to be done" ([17], p491). Infrastructure mediates between "local" and "global." The theoretical framework of human infrastructure allows us to examine not only the dynamics within virtual organizations, but also the impact of local organizations and personal networks on the effectiveness and productivity of individuals. In this paper, we seek to understand how different components of human infrastructure facilitate or impede individual scientists' participation in international collaboration and how we can improve human infrastructure to facilitate scientists' participation in international collaboration.

Our research makes two contributions to the literature of distributed scientific collaboration: (1) Previous literature on the social practices of distributed collaboration tends to focus on macro analysis of coordination and management within virtual organizations. In our study, through examining multilayered human infrastructure, we intend to connect individuals with the administrative and management infrastructure in which they are embedded and to reveal how human infrastructures constrain and enable individual participants in collaborations; (2) Prior literature often considers all participants within the same rank as uniform, and directs little attention to the impact of scientists' position in the social structure of science. Scientists' national, institutional, and research cultures, their home institutions' policies and resources, and their personal networks define their position in the social structure of science. In our study, by comparing scientists from both well resourced and lesser resourced nations and institutions, we reveal the impact of human infrastructure on participation in international collaboration by scientists with various backgrounds.

2. RELATED LITERATURE

A large body of research on distributed collaboration has been performed in scientific research settings. Sonnenwald's [29] review paper synthesizes factors that have an impact on scientific collaboration. Political factors affecting scientific collaboration include the leadership and organizational structure of participating institutions and participants' learning from each other. Socio-economic factors include adoption and implementation of information and communications technology. Resource accessibility, individuals' social networks, and personal factors can also affect scientific collaboration.

Much of our knowledge of distributed collaboration also comes from studies of corporate settings, where virtual teams collaborate at a distance, adopt information technologies and social practices to help them coordinate and collaborate to accomplish their work (for review, see [26]). A large component of "Computer Supported Cooperative Work" (CSCW) examines distributed collaboration and technologies and social practices that facilitate its success (e.g., [23]). CSCW research focuses primarily on the situational components, such as technology used, habits of use, and so on. Studies in organizational behavior and management concentrate on virtual team members' inherent characteristics (such as expertise, motivation to collaboration, leadership, etc.) and the collaboration structure that help maximize the integration of individual efforts (e.g., [3]).

Some research leads toward a more comprehensive understanding of factors that contribute to the success of distributed collaboration. Olson and colleagues [24] develop the Theory of Remote Scientific Collaboration (TORSC) based on their own research on collaboratories and previous studies of distributed collaboration. The TORSC first defines a broader range of success measures, including effects on science itself, science careers, learning and science education, inspiration for other collaborations, funding and public perception of collaboration, and tool use. The TORSC then asserts that there are five clusters of factors that are critical to success in distributed collaboration, including the nature of work, management, planning and decision-making, common ground, collaboration readiness and technology readiness.

Other researchers note that literature on distributed collaboration tends to focus on coordination and management within virtual teams, but fails to reveal the dynamics of interaction between the virtual organizations and the local organizations from which participants in distributed collaboration come. Lee et al. [17] point out that virtual organizations are actually "not so virtual." Through the conceptual lens of human infrastructure, Lee et al. examine multiple layers of the local organizations that support distributed collaboration in virtual organizations. Researchers involved in distributed collaboration rely on their local organizations for resources such as research equipment, computing services for data storage and analysis, subject recruitment, etc. Lee et al. also discuss how researchers' personal networks shape and are shaped by their participation in distributed collaboration. Lee et al. recommend considering the variations in researchers' personal networks and local institutions. However, they did not address how differences in researchers' personal networks and institutional backgrounds may result in different corresponding locations in the social structure of science, which will ultimately affect participation in collaboration. In CSCW and team science literature, discussion of researchers' differential locations in the social structure of science has been limited to rank (i.e., senior vs. junior) and disciplinary differences [31].

Previous studies in the sociology of science have shown that scientists' productivity is affected by their working environments [1,18,19]. Prestigious institutions promote scholarly productivity, while non-prestigious institutions often fail to do so. However, this line of literature does not specify which environmental factors lead to the productivity differences between scientists from prestigious and non-prestigious institutions. Nor does the literature discuss how institutional affiliation affects scientists' participation in collaboration.

Some researchers hypothesize that distributed collaboration facilitated by virtual organization has the potential to enable scientists from lesser resourced institutions to overcome the limits of their local institutions and access resources and highly productive researchers from other institutions their local institutions cannot afford [10]. A large portion of the literature on collaboration between developing and developed countries focuses on how collaboration changes the structure of science and how this change may affect scientific outcomes. For example, Duque et al. [9] study the relationship between collaboration and scientists' self-reported productivity in developing areas. They find that, in general, collaboration is not associated with an increase in scientific productivity. They also find that although access to email helps attenuate research problems, difficulties in research are defined more by national and regional contexts than by the collaboration process itself. They suggest that benefits brought about by information technology might be attenuated by the local conditions, which confounds the relationship between collaboration and scientific productivity. They did not explain how the national and local contexts interact with information technology, which in turn affects the collaboration process and ultimately affects scientific productivity.

3. RESEARCH SITES

We studied two experiments in high energy physics—HEP1 and HEP2, which are two virtual organizations that share similar goals and management structures. The enormous size of the HEP1 and HEP2 collaborations is unprecedented. Both require great amounts of funding and human resources. HEP1 consists of 3000 scientists from 38 countries, while HEP2 consists of 3200 scientists from about 41 countries. In order to join either collaboration, participating institutions typically obtain support from funding agencies in their home countries. The main instruments of HEP1 and HEP2 are placed in Institute X, which is located on the border of Switzerland and France. Institute X is also the physical center of HEP1 and HEP2. Institute X is comprised of 20 European member states. Funding from the member states is allocated or controlled by Institute X and experiment leadership. Other funds are controlled by participating institutes in accordance with the experiments' Memoranda of Understanding. The HEP collaborations aim to accomplish two major tasks: to build and maintain detectors (which are used to measure properties of particles passing through them), and to perform physics analysis. Scientists work in different workgroups and subgroups, which are aligned with different parts of the detector and the different particles their physics analyses target.

4. METHODS

We adopt qualitative research methods to analyze complex relationships such as research collaborations. Our research is informed by, but not limited to Lee et al.'s [17] conceptual framework of human infrastructure. We sift evidence about how physicists' home institutions exert systematic influence on participants in the HEP collaborations. We compare individuals and research groups coming from resource rich and resource poor institutions along three dimensions: culture, which includes language, interpersonal styles and research cultures associated with nations and institutes; personal networks within and outside the collaborations; and organization structure, the management and policies within the virtual organizations and participating institutions that support the HEP collaborations. These three dimensions largely determine the position of countries and individuals in the social structure of science and within scientific collaboration groups.

Infrastructure is invisible until it breaks [30]. In the HEP Collaborations studied, some collaboration participants' concerns come up again and again, and we examine those concerns because we agree with Ribes and Finholt [27] that tensions "reveal[s] conflicting goals, purposes, and motivations of participants." Understanding the causes for these tensions enables us to understand how human infrastructures facilitate individuals' participation in international collaboration in some ways and imped it in other ways.

Our data collection includes 24 semi-structured interviews complemented by field observations and document analysis. We focus on sub-projects of HEP1 and HEP2 that involve close collaboration among Chinese, Korean, and Japanese scientists and their partners in the U.S. and Europe. The lead author of this paper interviewed five Japanese, seven Chinese, four Korean, one German, one French, and six U.S. scientists. She conducted field observation in Institute X for three weeks. She also visited three home institutions for Chinese participants and stayed at each institution for a week. Except that one interview was conducted via Skype, all the others were face-to-face. She interviewed junior and senior scientists to reveal different perspectives.

Analysis of interview data and field notes was performed using NVivo 9.0 software on transcripts of the interviews and field notes, which were coded by speaker, topic, and themes and then codes were cross checked with one of the other authors. Main themes were coded and analyzed by the constant comparative method [21]. We compared social and technological processes involved in international collaboration formation and how collaboration members relate to one another, especially regarding similarities and differences in work process.

5. FINDINGS

5.1 Virtual Organization Enables Simultaneous Competition and Collaboration

The HEP collaborations involve many countries, and the management of these virtual organizations does not have power over individual countries. Yet, thousands of international participants work together towards the same scientific goal. We find that the human infrastructure of the HEP collaborations interfaces with a communitarian, competitive, and reputation culture, which motivates physicists to contribute their very best efforts.

The epistemic culture in high energy physics is characterized by a "communitarian structure" that emphasizes "collective ways of working" and "[erases] the individual as an epistemic subject" [15]. Within an experiment, researchers align themselves with different workgroups and work tasks. The division of labor in HEP collaborations is based on work tasks, which then provide the loci for the formation of work groups [4]. When building detectors, workgroups were formed based on the components of the detector such as inner detector, muon, trigger/data acquisition, etc. There are also different work groups for physics analysis, including Higgs, B physics, top physics, Heavy Higgs, SUSY, etc. The Higgs group includes subgroups such as gluton-gluton fusion, Vector Boson fusion, and WH/ZH Higgs.

The communitarian culture of HEP collaborations is highlighted by "hyperauthorship."[2,7] Publications from HEP experiments include thousands of authors. The rationale behind the "hyperauthorship" is that all the scientists and engineers that contribute to detector building and physics analysis should be credited. A high energy physicist's name may appear on hundreds of papers, some of which they have never read. The hyperauthorship system distinguishes HEP from other fields, such as biomedical science, because it is difficult to use publications to evaluate individual high energy physicists during the hiring and promotion process.

However, the communitarian culture does not extend to crediting high energy physicists collectively when it comes to hiring and promotion. Hiring and promotion evaluations are still based on individual achievements, which are measured by a person's reputation in the work community and word-of-mouth recommendations. Competitiveness also thrives in the high energy physics community. The reputation system encourages participants in HEP collaborations to strive hard to "get noticed" and obtain a favorable reputation. Participants' contributions in daily work are the basis for evaluation. Even though a researcher's name may appear on hundreds of papers, a researcher knows which papers are "my papers" and the community would also know in which papers the researcher made a major contribution. The fierce competition in the HEP community and the pressure individual researchers feel every day is represented by this Korean postdoctoral fellow, Dr. Kim's [1]statement:

> I have to work hard every day. If I don't, if I can't show my results more quickly, other people will. Then their results will be used. There are so many postdocs in the collaboration. If this happens a few times, I may be forgotten.

---

[1] All scientists' names appearing in this paper are pseudonyms.

Participation in research group meetings, contribution to data analysis, presentations at conferences, and writing internal notes are all opportunities for participants to increase their visibility as well as chances for them to be evaluated. This motivates researchers to contribute their best efforts to build up their reputation.

In addition to making intellectual contributions, researchers also strive to build their reputations through service work. In the HEP collaborations, service work includes maintenance of the detector's hardware, data generation, and other activities that do not directly produce physics results. Performing service work well means others will seek out their help and their skills will be valued. Researchers said that through service work, they can become known as a "reliable" person. For example, a U.S. doctoral student working in a highly competitive physics analysis group commented that U.S. and European scientists dominated his group. However, a Japanese postdoctoral fellow became noticed amid the fierce competition within the group because he was in charge of the data production task and people became very reliant on him.

Displaying leadership is another way for researchers to "get noticed." Senior researchers mentioned that they hoped to give junior researchers opportunities to increase their visibility. Thus, they try to offer opportunities for junior researchers to take leadership roles, such as serving as conveners for different workgroups, as sub-workgroup team leaders, and as editors for major papers. When asked about their career development plan, many junior researchers mentioned that they would next endeavor to be a team leader and then a convener. A postdoctoral fellow from Germany, Dr. Haufmann mentioned:

> And then [the hiring committee] look [for] that [the candidate] has already shown some kind of leadership or qualities---that they can manage a team. So I believe in my case it was maybe where I think I have shown management qualities. That I was leading a very big analysis for this conference that was in May and I was leading all of the students and postdocs together to get this result to do the analysis, to publish this result ... for this conference.

Leadership is related to service work because it is time consuming to manage people from different cultures and with different working styles. Dr. Haufmann who was leading a research team mentioned that he needed to spend time guiding doctoral students and considering how to best make appropriate work assignments for the doctoral students. He believed that working as a team leader enhanced his management skills, but he had to sacrifice time that could have been used for physics analysis. He commented:

> And now for me it's that I do less analysis and more like coordinating and seeing that is there a topic that could be interesting but that nobody is doing. Is there a student that doesn't have a topic but would want to work on it? Then I can try to say, "Hey, why don't you look into this?"

The organization of the HEP collaborations creates ample opportunities for physicists to display their intellectual capability, service contribution, and leadership. Workgroups and subgroups in the HEP collaborations are interdependent. People who focus on physics analysis may want to know the hardware and operation of a detector. A subgroup's physics analysis may depend on another subgroup's results. The interdependency between workgroups and subgroups creates the need and the occasion for individual physicists to display their contributions in different roles: that of a researcher, a service person, or a team leader in daily work. Thus, the high energy physicists tend to value opportunities for sharing valuable information and for service to the group because this work will contribute to building up their reputation. This contrasts sharply with other fields, where scientists are motivated by producing first-authored papers. When researchers focus on first-authored papers, they tend to keep the important information to themselves so that they can retain their competitive edge [5] and are not motivated to contribute service work to the group.

The lack of hierarchical management structure in HEP collaborations allows individuals to choose the workgroups where they believe they can make their best contributions. It is not uncommon at research group meetings or big conferences to hear presenters say that they need help in certain areas and invite anybody interested to join. Creativity and love for the work are also accommodated in the HEP collaboration. For example, a researcher working for a U.S. institution devoted part of his research time to creating 3D animation materials for the HEP1 outreach programs, mainly out of his own interest. He enjoyed this work enough to continue it in his spare time and became known for it.

Another strength of the interplay among the reward structure, communitarian culture, and flat management style lies in that it creates potentials for an egalitarian evaluation process. When physicists are evaluated based on their contributions in daily work, this means that everybody has an equal opportunity to show their talents, regardless of their seniority or their institutional affiliation. A U.S. postdoctoral fellow, Dr. Peterson, described how Chinese students are different from other students:

> So they work many, many hours without holidays, without weekends. Also in the weekends, also during the night if it's needed. So it's a very high motivation—and how to say it?— eager to complete something and to distinguish himself ...

She also described how one Chinese student she worked with became visible in one of the highly competitive work groups:

> Lin is very good and he works very hard .... So in his case, I think that he really is visible in S group and people recognize his work and he is sent to a very important conference last summer in Germany 2010. So he is very well known and he is visible.

Thus, even though they are from less resourced institutions, the Chinese students got noticed because of their hard work and their contribution to the collaboration.

Despite opportunities that exist for researchers to display their talents, the degree to which researchers can seize these opportunities is affected by the researchers' positions in the social structure of science, which is influenced by researchers' organizational affiliation and their formal training.

When physicists first enter the large-scale HEP collaborations we studied, they face information overload. They need to decide which groups to join, what analytical tools they should use, and where and how they can learn about those tools. They must also understand how to efficiently locate people to get the information they need as well as learn how to navigate the immense labyrinth of collaboration web pages. Researchers who are provided a better orientation to the experiment, and are not just dropped into a collaboration, are able to start their work more quickly. Different institutions offer new researchers different levels of orientation, which will be discussed in our next section.

Scientists that succeed are separated from those that are lost by their abilities to communicate their ideas, demonstrate useful skills, and show their scientific prowess. Junior researchers experience hardship and delays in their professional involvement in work groups when they do not have enough English to express themselves and understand what others are saying and doing. People with very different cultural origins, especially those from strict hierarchical societies, may have trouble asserting themselves and being aggressive enough to promote their own ideas in such a competitive environment. A Korean postdoctoral fellow, Dr. Lee commented:

> *Normally in Korea we have to listen and we don't have to—you are not supposed to—I mean now it's changing. Because we are not supposed to talk back like to an older person and things like that. ... At the beginning actually I think I am a little bit afraid to say what I am really thinking. But I think I am getting better*

Power struggles in the collaboration also lead to some researcher's ideas being neglected, which will be discussed in our next section.

5.2 Impact of Researchers' Home Institutions

Lee et al. [17] contend that collaboration participants' home institutions "set the context" for an individual researcher's participation in large collaborations. Our study finds that researchers are both enabled and constrained by their home institution's incentive structure, funding limitations, and research culture.

5.2.1 Group effect

The large-scale experiments HEP1 and HEP2 are challenging for junior scientists who must digest mountains of rapidly changing knowledge and information. One Chinese doctoral student, Mr. Ping, gave an example of the challenges he faced:

> *In physics analysis, there are experts writing and recommending to us what software package we should use, what definitions we should adopt during the computing process, etc. There is a lot of information there. It is very easy to make mistakes. It is hard for the beginners. I need to always keep in touch with experienced people to talk and discuss with them.*

Researchers mentioned that staying at Institute X and belonging to a work group is the most efficient way to access information and experts. If a home institution can afford to fund researchers with different levels of expertise to stay at Institute X, it helps to increase individual researcher's competitiveness and nurture junior scientists' development.

The lead researcher of this study used a U.S. university, University M's office at Institute X as a temporary office when she worked there for three weeks during June and July of 2011. While there, she observed how researchers from University M worked together. For example, two doctoral students and a senior faculty member from University M collaborated in a very competitive physics analysis group. The University M group tried to obtain results faster than other members. Group members sat in the same cubical area and discussed ideas and issues among themselves whenever they needed to do so. Sometimes they divided their work. Once Mr. Lian, a doctoral student, commented, "In these days, I mainly focus on analysis. My adviser works like an information processor. He reads all the email messages related to analysis, filters and digests all the messages. He gave me advice on the direction of our analysis based on the information."

University M's group efforts enhance team and individual competitiveness. However, not every university can afford to have many members stay in Institute X. Senior Chinese researchers and Korean researchers reported that they could only make short visits to Institute X once or twice a year because of their heavy teaching load and their home institution's funding limitations. By contrast, American and Japanese researchers could obtain much more travel funding. Senior researchers from the U.S. and Japan said that they could manage to stay at Institute X for about two weeks every month. Even though senior researchers from the U.S. and Japan had administrative responsibilities at their home institutions, their research focuses mainly on the large HEP experiment in which they are participating. In contrast, senior Korean and Chinese researchers reported that they were constantly under pressure to apply for different grants for their own career and to support their doctoral students. It was not uncommon for senior Korean and Chinese researchers to work on several projects at the same time.

Also, due to their limited funds, Chinese institutions could not hire postdoctoral fellows to stay at Institute X. It is widely acknowledged in the HEP community that postdoctoral fellows play an important role in physics analysis and training doctoral students because senior researchers tend to spend more time on administrative tasks and doctoral students are not sufficiently experienced. Without postdoctoral fellows and without a research group's presence, Chinese doctoral students cannot enjoy the benefits of the in-house expertise that drive advantageous group effects.

The Korean junior researchers also wished they could obtain guidance from experienced Korean researchers. There are several Korean postdoctoral fellows working at Institute X, most new to the large HEP experiments. Some of these postdoctoral fellows previously worked in a smaller scale experiment in Japan. One postdoctoral fellow, Dr. Park's comment showed the Korean researchers' need for within-group guidance:

> *If there is some Korean group, that group has the same kind of interest like me, then I can join that group, that Korean group, and then we know each other, so some of them can guide me.*

When asked how her adviser back at her home institution helped her, a Korean doctoral student stated:

> *I talked to my adviser once every two weeks and we had group meetings every week. At the meetings, we mainly talked about my progress and my focus on my dissertation. Because my adviser does not know much about what is happening here, it is difficult for him to give me some concrete suggestions on my analysis.*

The strength of group effects also comes from "the history" of researchers' home institutions' participation in the HEP collaborations. A long history of presence in the collaboration results in a better group knowledge of the detector, more experience with the software package for data analysis, more political power, and stronger personal networks. Dr. Park further explained:

> *I guess everyone in here, if he belongs to some good ... group, then everything is just easier. And she belongs to some institute, that institute belongs to some physics group for quite a long time, so she is instructed, have lots of history, a lot of experience and lots of materials such as a [software] program for [analysis] and some reserved in their computer that it's easier to follow.*

5.2.2 Power Struggles

Researchers' home institutions also affect researchers' position in power struggles. The epistemic process in HEP involves "convoluted tangles" of different possibilities of "calculating mathematical functions of simulating events that are neither easily calculable nor measurable, and making measurements experimentally"([15], p77). The process involves many somewhat subjective decisions, for example, when deciding where to cut a plot. Researchers complained that even though decisions in research should be objective, they felt there were power differentials at work in the decision making process. They felt that some institutions which were involved in the HEP collaborations since the very beginning, contributed more funds, and worked on important components of a detector, seemed to be more powerful. Dr. Suzuki, a postdoctoral fellow from Japan, talked about his frustrations with the political struggles. He complained that some of the decisions were "not scientific." He compared his experience of working in an experiment based in the U.S. with his experience with the HEP1 based in Europe:

> *... the difference is I think the culture of the United States and Europe. So I think United States people are very open for the newcomer or some doing the same ... newly started work and so on. So they can collaborate [with] such people also. However, in Europe, it's not the case. [Europeans] always have ... their territories. So and if some newcomer or some new student enters, they at first don't want such kind of new people... My feeling is they want to keep their position or some territories so... There are political things. So it's not scientific.*

Similarly, a junior faculty member from a Chinese institution, Dr. An commented:

> *People in the workgroups sometimes presented different approaches to the same problem. We needed to make decision on which approach to adopt. Then you can see the difference. I may be the only member from China. But other people from an institution which has a big team in the HEP collaboration as a whole or a few people in our team are more powerful than I am. I mean they may adopt the approach proposed by their colleagues from their own institutions even though I do not think their approach is necessarily better than mine.*

Dr. An went on to explain that there seemed to be prejudice against people from institutions which have a shorter history in the collaborations and that favored colleagues from groups that had been part of Institute X for a longer time. It is also because they have been working together for a long time and their thinking is influenced by each other.

5.2.3 Incentivizing Contributions to the Scientific Community vs. Individual Productivity

Home institution policy and incentive structures affect individual researchers' contributions to their collaborations. As discussed in the previous section, the HEP collaborations require constant service from different institutions to maintain the normal operation of the detector. Offering service work can also increase individual researchers' visibility. U.S. and Chinese researchers reported how they appreciate Japanese researchers' service. One Chinese doctoral student told a story of how a Japanese postdoctoral fellow offered to work on a database to clearly record data and the status of data generation. He said that the database had been a mess until the Japanese postdoctoral fellow offered to rebuild the database.

Chinese researchers explained that it was difficult for Chinese doctoral students to offer service work because of the stringent time requirements for their degree and the incentive structure in Chinese institutions. Chinese doctoral students on average have three years to finish their dissertations, which is two years shorter than U.S. doctoral programs. The Chinese institutions also ask their doctoral students to display their individual contributions in their dissertations. For example, one Chinese institution required that their doctoral students have a first-authored note and at least a presentation at a significant international conference. These kinds of requirements motivate junior researchers to focus more on physics analysis rather than service work because publications and presentations require results from physics analysis. The senior Chinese scientists reported that one of the biggest challenges they faced is having to battle with their home institutions, urging those institutions to consider recognizing professional contributions to the collaborative HEP projects when they design incentive structures. The senior Chinese scientists pointed out that their junior faculty members were frequently behind in the promotion process because they could not show as many first-authored papers as their colleagues in other sub-fields in physics.

5.3 Personal Networks

Personal networks affect how individual researchers participate in collaboration; in an iterative process, collaboration then enables researchers to build and expand their personal networks.

Senior researchers' networks influence which work groups junior researchers will join and how they will be oriented to the experiment. Dr. Suzuki, a Japanese postdoctoral fellow, described how he entered the HEP1 Collaboration:

> *My institute has one assistant professor. When I was joining the group, he is a sub-convenor of that group. But he is the only person from Japan. ... That's why I can enter the group very smoothly.*

Dr. Suzuki's experience is typical for junior researchers. In such large collaborations as HEP1 and HEP2, it is challenging for junior researchers to identify their research focus and select workgroups when they first come to the project. They rely heavily on their senior researchers' personal networks to introduce them to workgroups. They were introduced into a workgroup because their advisers or some professors from their home institutions were associated with or are participating in that workgroup.

For institutions that are comparatively new to the HEP1 and HEP2 collaborations and that do not have their own institutional research focus, senior researchers' personal networks are especially important. Earlier in their careers, some now senior Chinese researchers worked at U.S. and European labs and represented those U.S. or European labs as participants in the HEP collaborations, which enabled them to build their personal networks in the HEP community. The senior researchers' personal networks then became social capital for the Chinese institutions. For example, Professor Tian worked at HEP1 and as a researcher at University M in the US for many years, and came to know Professor Anderson from another US university. Later, after Professor Tian returned to China, he was able to introduce his doctoral student Mr. Yu to Professor Anderson. Mr. Yu then worked with a group led by Professor Anderson from a U.S. university. Guided by Professor Anderson, Mr. Yu could gradually identify his own research focus. Professor Tian also introduced Mr. Lin, who was able to work in the University M's group.

Even though Chinese institutions could not afford to have their own postdoctoral fellows present at Institute X, some Chinese doctoral graduates found postdoctoral training in the U.S. or in Europe. Their former professors in China then introduced current Chinese doctoral students into the US. or European labs through the Chinese postdoctoral scholars working in those labs. For example, Chinese doctoral student Mr. Ping first worked in a French institute to obtain a joint doctoral degree, but because of the language problem, he could not adjust to the French institute. His adviser introduced him to work in a U.S. lab, to which a Chinese postdoctoral, Dr. Hong, is affiliated. When this study was conducted, Mr. Ping and Dr. Hong worked together at Institute X. Mr. Ping mentioned that after working with Dr. Hong and his group, he felt that his research was raised to a much higher level.

Junior researchers also build their own networks through participation in different workgroups. As discussed in previous sections, interdependence among workgroups and individuals creates the necessity for physicists to communicate in order to exchange information. In the process of communicating and helping each other, they get to know each other. When asked how physicists obtained helpful information, Dr. Haufmann, a postdoctoral fellow from Germany, commented:

> So usually it starts with your officemate. Institute X does not have a single office with one person. So you usually have three-four other people or you have the open space where maybe it's just one table next to the other. And usually you just start asking your officemate and say, "Hey, do you know—have you ever done this?" Most likely he doesn't know because he is usually doing something completely different. But he might have heard about it or he might have an idea. And then the other thing is that in HEP2, it's a very big effort of documenting things, so we have the wiki pages with the workbook that we give the students in the beginning and it goes through with hands-on exercises about everything. Then every chapter has links to more detailed pages. So you can try to search those pages and find something. .... If it doesn't have an answer you just contact the [page author] or a mailing list that you should ask questions to.

In this comment, Dr. Haufmann emphasized that the layout of the office in Institute X enables junior physicists from various institutions to sit close to each other and to communicate with each other easily. The impact of office layout on physicists' network building was also reflected by the Japanese physicists working for HEP1. The Japanese scientists' office building was comparatively far from the main administration offices where most of the meetings were held. The Japanese physicists were clustered together in their building and there are not many physicists from other countries working there. When interviewed, the Japanese physicists admitted that they felt somewhat isolated and they did not have much chance to talk to people from other countries to improve their English and communication skills.

Dr. Hauffman's comments also illustrate that physicists have various channels to communicate with each other: wiki pages, face-to-face meetings, email, etc. Dr. Lee from Korea described his strategy of communicating with people:

> I have a strategy like this. First, I read the document, the relevant document. So in that way, I know what is the problem ... and what is the thing which is difficult to learn just from the document. And then I take part in the meeting and see some presentation and then I find the one which I like to learn. Then after meeting, I contact the [author or presenter]

Communication is not easy for everybody. Traweek [32] described how difficult it is for some American junior physicists to understand how they could "establish, express, and manipulate relationships in networks" through communication. The language barrier and the hierarchical culture of some physicists' home countries may create additional barriers for them to participate in large-scale collaborations. A junior faculty member from a Japanese institution, Dr. Yamata remembered his experiences when he first joined the collaboration:

> So jumping into such a collaboration itself, it was a challenge first of all. And try to know more persons around myself. So every day I have to meet—if I want to do something, I have to meet somebody and talk with somebody. That [is] something like a challenge to me and just the—yeah, I was feeling it very difficult thing, especially for the first half a year or so.

Realizing the importance of communication skills and developing personal networks, senior Chinese physicists commented that it is important to train their students in good communication technique and "how to work with people." The lead researcher of the current study observed that in some Chinese institutions, senior physicists started to require their students present and discuss their work in English at local research meetings even when there was no foreigner present. One senior physicist told the researcher that she also encouraged her students to participate in student association activities to develop their interpersonal abilities.

6. CONCLUSION AND DISCUSSION

Large-scale international collaborations benefit from heterogeneous efforts by many scientists from all over the world. However, scientific collaboration cannot reap its full benefit if individual scientists are constrained by non-scientific social parameters such as institutional and funding policies, power struggles, and scientists' lack of communication and collaboration skills. In this paper, we adopt the concept of human infrastructure as our analytic lens to examine two high energy physics collaborations. Concentrating on human infrastructure allows us to see how specific components of basic social structures facilitate or impede individual scientists' participation in international collaboration.

While previous literature tends to focus on the macro level of analysis, the management and coordination within virtual organizations, our study concentrates on individual scientists, especially junior scientists' gains and challenges when participating in international collaboration. Scientists have multiple affiliations, which means we must analyze the impact of and interaction between different components of human infrastructure. Our human infrastructure analysis goes beyond the virtual organizations and includes scientists' home institutions and personal networks. In this way, we gain a more comprehensive understanding of what enhances or impedes scientists' participation in international collaboration. Identifying the mechanisms that constrain scientists enables us to build human infrastructure that facilitates individual scientists' participation in collaboration.

In order to ensure the best outcomes from international collaboration, it is important for individual participants to produce their best efforts [2]. The best efforts aim to both maximize individual productivity to help scientists gain professional credit for hiring and promotion, and to augment individual's contribution to collaborations. The HEP community's reward structure, along with its communitarian epistemic culture and effective non-hierarchical management, enable individual participants to be productive, collaborative, and contributive. However, individuals' positions in the social structure affect their participation in collaboration. Our study reveals that scientists from lesser-resourced institutions are placed in a disadvantageous position in collaboration, which is counter to the hypothesis that distributed scientific collaboration will result in more equal participation in science [10]. Even though the HEP community values individuals' reputation over of publications and citations, some researchers' home institutions' reward structure does not match the HEP reward structure. Thus, scientists from institutions whose reward structures do not match HEP's must still struggle for individual productivity and are reluctant to do service work, which the HEP community values. Lesser resourced institutions cannot afford strong home institutions' team presence at the physical center of the virtual organization, which hinders junior scientists from gaining better and more timely guidance; lesser resourced institutions cannot provide the home institution's teamwork, which decreases individuals' competitiveness. In long-term collaborations like the two HEP collaborations we studied, having an historic institutional presence enhances individual scientists' political power. Lesser resourced institutions usually do not have long history of presence.

Thus, in order to ensure that scientists can be both productive and contributive, scientists' home institutions should set up incentive policy that values essential contributions to collaborative work, even if that work might not result in individual products. Home institutions must appreciate the importance of establishing a home team presence in virtual collaborations and work to create their own teams or establish team relationships with other institutions. Funding agencies should provide sufficient funds for scientists and trainees to travel and be present at the physical center for collaboration. Funding agencies should also allow scientists to concentrate their efforts on fewer projects, avoiding the dilution of effort into less effective fractions. This trend has begun in U.S.

institutions, some of which have now allotted an extra year for collaborative researchers to build their research and publication resources when applying for tenure [33]. There are also discussions in U.S. institutions of assigning proper credit to tenure candidates whose scholarship yields multiple collaborative authorships; alternative measures of academic achievement are being explored [11]. It will also be helpful for individual institutions to provide researchers systematic training on specific collaboration skills.

Joint institutes between lesser resourced and well resourced institutions allow scientists to overcome their home institutions' limitations. Joint institutes enable junior scientists to develop their personal networks early in their careers. Joint institutes provide junior researchers from less resourced countries more guidance and also offer them a home base at the physical center of the virtual organization.

Administrative and management efforts from virtual organizations that facilitate large-scale collaborations can help scientists overcome their home institutions' constraints. We found that the management structure that lacks hierarchical control enables scientists to choose their workgroups, manage and organize their own time and effort, volunteer to work in the area they are interested in, and provides ample opportunities for junior researchers to learn from other HEP community members. However, we also found that junior researchers felt overwhelmed and disoriented when they first came to the collaboration. Thus, virtual organizations should provide basic but systematic orientation for the junior researchers in order to save their precious time and effort and allow them to be productive more quickly. For example, virtual organizations like the HEP1 and HEP2 Experiments could provide face-to-face training, distance education or online materials regarding the organizational structure of different workgroups as well as providing in-person workshops on communication and interpersonal skills. Virtual organizations could also produce a repository of digital stories [20], where scientists talk about their own experiences of working in a large collaboration and how they met the challenges they faced when they first arrived.

7. Acknowledgment

This paper is based in part upon work supported by the National Science Foundation under Grant Number 1025618. Any opinions, findings, and conclusions or recommendations expressed in this material are those of the author(s) and do not necessarily reflect the views of the National Science Foundation.

8. REFERENCES

1. Allison, P.D. and Stewart, J.A. Productivity differences among scientists: evidence for accumulative advantage. *American Sociological Review 39*, 4 (1974), 596–606.

2. Birnholtz, J. What does it mean to be an author? The intersection of credit, contribution, and collaboration in science. *Journal of the American Society for Information Science and Technology 57*, 13 (2006), 1758–1770.

3. Boh, W.F., Kiesler, S., and Bussjaeger, R. Expertise and collaboration in the geographically dispersed organization. *Organization Science 18*, 4 (2007), 595–612.

4. Bressan, B. and Boisot, M. The Individual in the ATLAS Collaboration: A Learning Perspective. In *Collisions and Collaboration: The Organization of Learning in the ATLAS*

Experiment at the LHC. Oxford University Press. 2011, 201–225.

5. Campbell, E.G., Clarridge, B.R., Gokhale, M., Higartner, S., Holtzman, N.A., and Blumenthal, D. Data withholding in academic genetics: Evidence from a national survey. *JAMA*, (2002), 473–480.

6. Cramton, C.D. The mutual knowledge problem and its consequences. *Organization Science 12*, 3 (2001), 346–371.

7. Cronin, B. *The hand of science: Academic writing and its rewards*. Scarecrow Press, 2005.

8. Cummings, J., Finholt, T., Foster, I., and Kesselman, C. *Beyond Being There: A Blueprint for Advancing the Design, Development and Evaluation of Virtual Organizations. The Final Report from the Workshops on Building Effective Virtual Organizations*. National Science Foundation, 2008.

9. Duque, R.B., Ynalves, M., Sooryamoorthy, R., Mbatia, P., Dzorgbo, D.-B., and Shrum, W. The collaboration Paradox: Scientific productivity, the Internet, and problems of research in developing areas. *Social Studies of Science 35*, 5 (2005), 755–785.

10. Finholt, T.A. From laboratories to collaboratories: A new organizational form for scientific collaboration. *psychological science 8*, 1 (1997), 28–36.

11. Garcia-Perez, A., Wyatt, R.G., and Gottesman, M.M. Changes in NIH criteria for tenure to reward clinical/translational teams. *Clinical and Translational Science 3*, 1 (2010), 4–5.

12. Grudin, J. Why CSCW applications fail: problems in the design and evaluation of organizational interfaces. *Proceedings of the ACM Conference on Computer-supported Cooperative Work*, (1988), 85–93.

13. Hesse, B.W., Sproull, L.S., Keisler, S.B., and Walsh, J.P. Returns to science: Computer networks in oceanography. *Communications of the ACM 36*, 8 (1993), 90–101.

14. Holmgren, M. and Schnitzer, S.A. Science on the rise in developing countries. *PLoS Biology 2*, 1 (2004), 11–13.

15. Knorr-Cetina, K. *Epistemic cultures: how the sciences make knowledge*. Harvard University Press, 1999.

16. Lee, C.P., Dourish, P., and Mark, G. The human infrastructure of Cyberinfrastructure. *Poceedings of Computer Supported Cooperative Work*, (2006), 483–492.

17. Lee, C.P., Dourish, P., and Mark, G. The human infrastructure of cyberinfrastructure. *Computer Supported Collaborative Work*, (2006), 483–492.

18. Long, J.S. and Fox, M.F. Scientific careers: universalism and particularism. *Annual Review of Sociology 21*, (1995), 45–71.

19. Long, J.S. and McGinnis, R. Organizational context and scientific productivity. *American Sociological Review 46*, 4 (1981).

20. Lowenthal, P. and Professor, P.L.A. Digital Storytelling in Education. In *Story Circle*. Wiley⬛Blackwell, 252–259.

21. Miles, M.B. and Huberman, A.M. *Qualitative Data Analysis*. Sage Publication, Thousand Oaks, California, 1994.

22. Nardi, B.A., Whittaker, S., and Schwarz, H. NetWORkers and their activity in intentional networks. *Computer Supported Cooperative Work 11*, 2 (2002), 205–242.

23. Olson, G.M. and Olson, J.S. Distance matters. *Human-Computer Interaction 15*, (2000), 139–178.

24. Olson, J.S., Hofer, E., Bos, N., et al. A theory of remote scientific collaboration (TORSC). In G.M. Olson, A. Zimmerman and N. Bos, eds., *Science on the Internet*. MIT Press, Cambridge, Massachusetts, 2008.

25. Orlikowski, W.J. Learning from notes: Organizational issues in groupware implementation. *The Information Society 9*, 3 (1993), 237–250.

26. Powell, A., Gabriele, P., and Blake, I. Virtual teams: a review of current literature and directions for future research. *SIGMIS Database 35*, 1 (2004), 6–36.

27. Ribes, D. and Finholt. The long now of technology infrastructure: Articulating tensions in development. *Journal of the Association for Information Systems 10*, (2009), 375–398.

28. Shrum, W., Chomalov, I., and Genuth, J. Trust, conflict and Performance in Scientific Collaborations. *Social Studies of Science 31*, 5 (2001), 681–730.

29. Sonnenwald, D. Scientific Collaboration. *Annual Review of Information Science and Technology 41*, 1 (2007), 643–681.

30. Star, S.L. and Ruhleder, K. Steps towards an ecology of infrastructure: complex problems in design and access for large-scale collaborative systems. *Proceedings of the 1994 ACM conference on Computer supported cooperative work*, ACM (1994), 253–264.

31. Stokols, D., Misra, S., Moser, R.P., Hall, K.L., and Taylor, B.K. The Ecology of Team Science: Understanding Contextual Influences on Transdisciplinary Collaboration. *American Journal of Preventive Medicine 35*, 2, Supplement 1 (2008), S96–S115.

32. Traweek, S. *Beamtimes and Life Times: the World of High Energy Physicists*. Harvard University Press, Cambridge, 1992.

33. Woolliscroft, J.O. Creating the Future of Health Care. Internal document. University of Michigan Medical School. 2011.

Collaborative Reflection at Work: Supporting Informal Learning at a Healthcare Workplace

Michael Prilla, Marin Degeling, Thomas Herrmann

Information and Technology Management, Institute for Applied Work Science, University of Bochum

Universitaetsstr. 150

44780 Bochum, Germany

+49 231 3222735

{michael.prilla,martin.degeling,thomas.herrmann}@rub.de

ABSTRACT

Reflection is a common means to improve work: Every day, people think back to past work and – oftentimes in a group – try to find out whether they can improve it or whether they can derive better practices from it. However, especially collaborative reflection is neglected in research and design and consequently, there are hardly any insights on how it takes place in the practice of daily work and how tools can support it. To shed light on these questions, this paper presents a case that has been analyzed in a hospital as part of a series of studies on collaborative reflection in practice. Focusing this case and backing it with the other studies, the paper presents peculiarities and needs of collaborative reflection in healthcare workplaces as well as a more general formalization of collaborative reflection characteristics. Based on these results, an application to support physicians in their reflection was prototyped and tested. The presented results primarily apply to healthcare workplaces, but also cover general findings for the support of collaborative reflection.

Categories and Subject Descriptors

H.5.3 [**Group and Organization Interfaces**]: Computer-supported cooperative work

General Terms

Design, Human Factors

Keywords

Reflection, collaboration, workplace, learning, healthcare

1. INTRODUCTION

Reflection is a frequent and ubiquitous task performed explicitly and (more often) implicitly during and after everyday work: People think about whether they acted appropriately in a certain situation, whether their cooperation with others runs smoothly and how things can be improved. This process includes going back to past experiences, reassessing them and deriving consequences for future behavior [2] and is typical for most of nowadays' workers.

Reflection has been recognized earlier on as an integral task for (cooperative) work and learning [14, 20]. This holds especially true for workplaces with a strong emotional influence on workers such as in healthcare, where emotional stress needs to be reflected

in order to learn for the future instead of affecting employees on the long run [9, 23]. Accordingly, reflection has been found to be a well-established task among healthcare workers [24].

The ubiquity of reflection in daily work and life does not mean that it is always applied successfully or supported sufficiently. One striking issue of reflection is that – without further support – it is mainly based in memories of past situations, which may have become hazy and, in terms of describing the situation reflected about, can be incomplete. Subsequently, this can lead to improper conclusions drawn from reflection. While this can be diminished by using existing documentation of work, such material is often not at hand immediately or it is insufficient to support reflection. In addition, the majority of work on reflection support regards reflection as an *individual* and *cognitive* process (see section 2 for an elaboration on this). This leaves out reflection as a *communicative* process happening in *collaboration* – e.g. meetings in which a team reflects on its practice, or discussions in which workers mutually reflect on stressful situations. Thus, important and potentially fruitful occurrences of reflection lack proper support.

As a result of the shortcomings addressed above, there is hardly any tool support for collaborative reflection. Such support needs to provide users with data complementing their memories of certain situations, help them structure this data and make sense of it for reflection, including both subjective perspectives and objective data on what has happened. With respect to *collaborative* reflection, it needs to support groups reflecting together to mutually make sense of their experiences and learn from each other. However, little is known about the process of collaborative reflection and how to support it with tools.

This paper reports on research done to investigate and support collaborative reflection. It presents a case study eliciting the characteristics and needs of collaborative reflection in practice and follow-up work in developing and evaluating a tool for its support. The paper mainly draws on work done in cooperation with a German hospital and is backed up by similar studies conducted in parallel[1]. The initial study in the hospital covers an exploration of collaborative reflection in practice and its results have been checked against the other studies. The tool developed according to the resulting insights into collaborative reflection was evaluated formatively in workshops with physicians from the same hospital. This paper describes the whole cycle of exploring collaborative reflection, operationalizing results from this exploration as well as developing and initially evaluating a tool based on these results.

---

[1] This work is part of the MIRROR project funded by the European Commission in FP 7. The MIRROR projects aims at supporting reflection in various settings, stages and levels. More information can be found at http://www.mirror-project.eu/.

In the remainder of this paper, we first discuss existing work on (collaborative) reflection, IT support for it and its specific characteristics and constraints at the healthcare workplace (section 2). After that, we describe our case study at the hospital and observations stemming from that (section 3), which – in accordance to results of the other studies done in parallel – will be analyzed in section 4. Based on this analysis, which form an initial framework to support collaborative reflection, we describe the design and evaluation of a prototype to support reflection in healthcare contexts (section 5). The paper concludes with remarks on our work and plans for the continuation of its underlying research.

2. REFLECTION AT THE WORKPLACE

2.1 Characteristics of reflection

Reflection is a common activity at workplaces. It occurs frequently and more or less implicitly, as there is not always a conscious decision to reflect. It can be described as "those intellectual and affective activities in which individuals engage to explore their experiences in order to lead to new understandings and appreciations" [2]. Reflection consists of three steps: going back to past experiences, re-evaluating it and deriving insights for future behavior from this reassessment (Figure 1, [2]).

Figure 1: Phases of reflection, based on [2].

As Figure 1 shows, experience consists of past behavior, ideas and feelings towards past events. Reflection means to mentally return to these elements of experience and to re-evaluate them. Outcomes of this process include new perspectives on own experience, changes in behavior or at least knowledge on or readiness for changing behavior. The model shown in Figure 1 also indicates that reflecting and going back to experiences do not necessarily lead to outcomes in a linear fashion, but make reflection an iterative with loopbacks. With respect to reflection support, it has to be emphasized that reflection is not limited to resolving problematic situations, but can (and should) also be applied to identify and sustain good practice. Reflection in this sense means learning from experiences and has been identified as a decisive mechanism in modern workplaces [1, 2, 14]. Schön [20] added that there is a differentiation between reflection "in action", which is happening during the conduction of an action, and reflection "on action", which covers reflection happening after the action is finished. Although Schön originally focused on individual reflection in this distinction, it also applies to collaborative reflection. It is obvious that both modes pose different needs and constraints for support.

Reflection needs to be differentiated from other forms of thinking about past or current issues. What differentiates it, for example, from rumination is that reflection needs to have an outcome, meaning that new insights on past behavior are derived from a reflection process. Reflection is also close to problem-based learning [20], which requires reflection on experiences past with problem solving, particularly in those cases where problems may be solved by reflecting on their past occurrences in practice. However, it can be differentiated from problem solving by the premise that reflection is based on past behavior. Reflection and sense-

making [25] also have a lot in common, but again the strong orientation of reflection towards reassessing past events does not account in general for sensemaking. The triad of past experience, reassessment and learning for the future thus makes reflection a unique process of learning and knowledge construction.

2.2 Collaborative reflection

The majority of research on reflection is done with a focus on individual reflection. Therefore, most models of reflection have a strong individual focus (e.g. [2, 14, 20]). Collaborative reflection, in contrast, is far less covered by current literature [13].

Collaborative reflection can be described as a social process in which "people engage in finding common meanings in making sense of the collective work they do" [11] or as "tool(s) for explicating and making implicit knowledge embedded in contexts" [12]. The main difference between collaborative and individual reflection is the process taking place: for individual reflection, it is mainly made up by individual cognitive activity, whereas collaborative reflection is based on communication and coordination: engagement in dialogical interaction as well as sharing and processing of mutual experiences have to be seen as core elements of collaborative reflection [4, 21].

For collaborative reflection, people must share their experiences and communicate about them, ideally leading to shared sense making [3, 9, 21]. Collaborative reflection then occurs if an individual links her knowledge to the experience of others [3] or when a group combines experiences of its members to reflect on them collaboratively [11]. Thus, collaborative reflection may be about individual *or* collaborative work and requires support for the communicative interaction of people reflecting together. Compared to individual reflection, collaborative reflection has the advantage to learn from each other and to craft new knowledge from shared experiences. However, it is also more complex in terms of structuring communication and experiences exchange.

Existing work on collaborative reflection is often restricted to specific and static situations such as debriefing sessions and project review meetings [2], or regards reflection mainly as an activity triggered by an individual seeking assistance in individual reflection [27]. Therefore, most insights on processes of reflection and on tool support (see section 2.3) deal solely with such situations. There are contributions emphasizing that collaborative reflection also happens in more dynamic situations [3, 4], but little is known on collaborative reflection support in such situations. Therefore, further research on characteristics of collaborative reflection in practice is needed.

However, it is hard to determine whether collaborative reflection actually occurs: not each discursive interaction about past events is collaborative reflection. A key to recognizing it can be found in the work of van Woerkom and Croon [26], who describe indicators for reflection such as "critical opinion sharing" during discourse, "challenging groupthink" as opposed to sticking to norms, "asking for feedback" on own actions and "experimenting with alternatives" [26]. In the work described here, these indicators were used to identify collaborative reflection.

2.3 IT support for reflection

Returning to own experiences is central to reflection, but human memory is limited: memories fade and thus, returning to past experiences is hard. Therefore, reflection can be supported with data describing past experiences, ranging from simple heart ratios indicating stress to written notes describing experiences (cf. [13]). While this data may be captured and shared among collaborators with generic tools like databases and notebooks, there are only little insights on specific tool support for collaborative reflection.

Among the scarce literature on reflection support, the usage of personal journals for individual reflection is mentioned often (e.g. [15]). In such journals, people can note experiences as in diaries or collect other artifacts such as pictures. Later, they can return to this data for reflection. Other authors propose digital portfolios for learners, including learning material and personal notes to reflect about the success of learning processes ([21]). While these tools can be beneficial when returning to the data contained in them, they need the user to write down all experiences that could possibly be valuable for later reflection.

Among tools for more special purpose reflection support, the Microsoft SenseCam, which takes pictures when the scenery in front of it changes, has been reported to support reflection well, even in reflection groups [7, 8]. Individuals and groups use the resulting pictures to recreate the events in which they wore the SenseCam and to point to certain experiences during these events. To the knowledge of the authors, besides this and very few other special purpose tools, there is no proper tool support for collaborative reflection available. What can be seen from these few examples is that all kind of IT-support has to be flexibly integrated into the context of work practice, acting as a socio-technical solution [6].

2.4 Reflection at the healthcare workplace

At healthcare workplaces such as hospitals, reflection has been found to be well established [9, 17, 24]. The majority of existing literature points to applications of reflection in two areas: medical issues such as diagnosis [17, 24] and training for work [9, 17].

Concerning *medical aspects*, literature assumes that reflection is mostly triggered by medical problems such as difficult diagnoses. Its conduction depends on personal inclinations and preferences [17]: For example it was found that the tendency for physicians to reflect on their daily work decreases in parallel with an increase of years of practice [16]. Concerning support for reflective practice, literature mentions guidance and supervision. Typical applications of reflection involve evaluating previous assumptions on a patient's health development, comparing difficult situations with past experiences and challenging own diagnoses [16]. While this is primarily done individually, it is also common in healthcare environments that staff (especially physicians) holds meetings and discusses patients and their states.

Reflection is considered to be an important practice of nurses and caretakers in *training* before and on the job, as these groups need to develop a habit of critical thinking and to gradually adopt good practice by learning from others [9, 10, 24]. In such situations, using a journal to write down experiences and learn from them for later practice is common, although it has been shown to reduce face to face communication and reflection [9].

Research on the reflection of nurses also points to the *collaborative* dimension of reflection in healthcare workplaces. Collaborative reflection has been observed when nurses developed ideas and solutions for care problems together [10] or to improve their behavior in certain situations [24] – both situations transcend medical or training issues and show the need to collaboratively create better work practice at such workplaces. Thus, aspects such as work organization and social issues also need to be regarded in reflective practice of healthcare workers. However, besides describing reflection in supervision or meetings, literature does not provide details on reflection processes or needs in such cases.

3. COLLABORATIVE REFLECTION IN HEALTHCARE: A CASE STUDY

There are hardly any insights into collaborative processes of reflection. To gain such insights for the development of proper tool support and as part of a series of workplace studies on collaborative reflection[2], we conducted an exploratory study at a German hospital ward dealing with stroke patients.

3.1 Methodology

The study was conducted as an exploration of collaborative reflection practice and needs – the state of the art in research on collaborative reflection and tool support for it did not allow us to build sufficient assumptions prior to this study. Therefore, we conducted explorative interviews and observations in the stroke ward of the hospital, which included physicians and nurses. In total, we observed two workers and conducted interviews with four people, which we consider sufficient for an exploration.

During the work observations, two researchers followed a nurse and a physician during their whole shift for two days, documenting all situations of their work with a special focus on reflection. The purpose of these observations was to understand the work done in healthcare environments as a basis for tool development, including habits of communication and cooperation, constraints imposed by the workplace and actual practice of reflection as opposed to literature. For this, the observers oriented their notes towards an observation scheme containing aspects of reflection such as interaction with colleagues (participants, place, time etc.), occurrences of reflection (participants, topic, data used etc.) and technology used (purpose, relation to work etc.). The resulting notes were transcribed and coded with the categories from the observation scheme.

The interviews were conducted with the observed workers and additional staff of the ward with the main purpose to clarify rationales, needs and wishes of healthcare staff with respect to (collaborative) reflection. The interviews lasted 45 to 60 minutes each and contained questions about the interviewees' workplace, special characteristics of learning and motivation, communication and collaboration during the day as well as existing and envisioned practice of individual and collaborative reflection – some of these were omitted for the persons who had already been observed for two days. Sample questions from the inventory are *"When and how do you communicate with others about your work?"* or *"Please give an example of when a colleague talked to you about his work-related experience"*. Each interview was audiotaped, transcribed literally and coded in a process aligned to Grounded Theory [22]. This was complemented with preset codes representing the indicators for collaborative reflection described in section 2.2 (cf. [26]). This approach was taken to be open for the identification of characteristics and needs of collaborative reflection on one hand and to be sure to detect situations of collaborative reflection completely and correctly on the other hand. For example, we coded a situation in which nurses asked each other to assess and validate the treatment given to a patient during the day to be collaborative reflection as it is an example of asking for feedback (see sections 2.1 and 2.2).

In the analysis, interviews and observation complemented each other: while in interviews outcomes can be based on particular episodes and thus not represent daily work, observations allow for

---

[2] Additional studies were conducted at e.g. British care homes and, to broaden the view on collaborative reflection, at a German IT consulting company.

insights into daily routines. Likewise, interviewees might not sufficiently describe their practice of reflection since it often happens implicitly. On the other hand, observations cannot result in an overview of all aspects relevant for collaborative reflection. Therefore, for the staff both observed and interviewed, we intertwined the resulting material in our analysis.

3.2 Background: Work in the hospital ward

The target group we interviewed and observed consisted of physicians and nurses working in the stroke ward of a German hospital. Before we present observations from this study, we briefly describe work on this ward to give a context of the study.

Staff on the stroke ward is highly trained. Nurses, for example, need special skills to be allowed to work with acute stroke patients. Their primary motivation to work on the ward could be found in the desire to help people. Providing good care, saving lives and improving the quality of patients' lives are examples for this we found in the material. Work is organized in shifts for both nurses and physicians: physicians work in a two shift system covering days and nights, nurses work in shifts for the morning, the afternoon and the night. Between shifts, handovers are done within and between these two professional groups. Work at the ward highly depends on communication and cooperation: while physicians are responsible for monitoring patients, diagnoses and decisions about medical treatment, nurses do the daily tasks of assistance, care, and drug application based on physicians' prescriptions. Nurses do most of their work in the patients' rooms and help each other in difficult or exhausting tasks. Physicians partly spend their day in patients' rooms, e.g. during the ward round and daily check ups, in their offices, e.g. doing documentation and research and around the ward, e.g. talking to relatives of their patients.

Work in the ward is constrained by time pressure. Physicians have a highly packed day consisting of ward rounds, daily meetings with colleagues to discuss patients' cases, examinations, documentation and emergencies. Nurses are taking care of one or two patient rooms per day, giving them treatment and care. In parallel, they need to do the documentation of treatment given, physiological data such as blood pressure, medications given and incidents happening during the day. We were told that because of the resulting time pressure staff often completes mandatory documentation tasks after their shift has finished to guarantee that patients are being cared for properly in the first place.

In order to coordinate work under these circumstances, physicians and nurses use a chart placed at the bed of each patient, which they call "the curve" and in which each change in the status of patients or in treatment as well as results from examinations are written down in a protocol and serve as a basis of the work of nurses. In addition, some documentation such as patients leaving or joining the station is done in a hospital information system.

The work of physicians and nurses is emotionally stressful. Nurses need to work closely with patients who may not be able to articulate what they need or get worse every day. Physicians need to make decisions, which might affect patients' lives or at least their quality of life. Moreover, they need to talk to relatives of patients, which oftentimes include telling bad news. In an example, we observed a physician deliberately looking for other tasks to do in order to avoid holding a potentially different conversation with relatives. Therefore, supervision is considered to be an important mechanism by both nurses and physicians and the solidarity among all members of the ward is very high – mutual help in stressful and sad situations is a matter of course in the ward. The other way around, we observed collective happiness when patients recovered quickly from a stroke.

This solidarity is also mirrored in the regular meetings of ward staff. Besides the daily meetings and handovers, once in a month there is a meeting for all staff members. We even observed staff from the night shift joining this meeting, although they had finished their shift a couple of hours ago. The meeting is announced with a bulletin in the break room, and everybody can add topics to this bulletin. We observed the discussion culture to be very open, as everybody is taken for serious and may pose a problem or comment on certain issues.

The usage of information technology differs much between nurses and physicians. While nurses have access to shared computers, they may not access the Internet but only the hospital information system and a digital quality management handbook on the intranet. Physicians, in contrast, can use computers connected to the Internet in their offices for research purposes.

3.3 Reflection practice in the hospital

Our analysis of the hospital study also contains detailed insights into the structures and constraints influencing collaborative reflection at this workplace. This contains different reflection settings, barriers and opportunities for reflection as well as insights into the collaboration of reflection participants.

One insight in reflection practice is that reflection happens both in (scheduled) meetings and spontaneously during the day. It is prominent among staff if topics concern interaction with patients and incidents of them and occurred mostly when an individual lacked understanding of a patient's situation or treatment and asked others to reflect on this situation together.

As for **reflection in meetings**, we found the daily meetings of physicians, the handovers between shifts and the ward meetings to be most important. In handover sessions, which are usually run by one of the nurses summarizing the shift for her colleagues and informing them about the most relevant issues to be taken care of, staff often collaboratively reflect for short periods of time, e.g. by asking each other for feedback based on experiences with the patients or similar cases. In the daily meeting of physicians, reflection may occur due to one of the physicians presenting a case and others stepping in on aspects such as diagnosis or treatment based on their experiences with similar cases. In the ward meetings, we observed reflection to be more structured, but also more difficult with respect to creating a shared context. Such meetings, as explained above, are prepared with a public agenda, which all members of staff may edit. As a typical example, we observed a meeting in which a nurse proposed to change the way breaks are taken in the morning. As some participants of the meeting did not understand why this was proposed, she gave examples how slight deviations of break times interfered with the daily ward round. After that, others reported on their experiences with this issue and the participants decided to change the break times. In another example, the head nurse complained that physicians to often enter rooms without talking enough to patients. As physicians did not understand the problem immediately, she explained that this often results in patients asking the nurses afterwards about what happened and if there was something new. Some physicians explained that they could not always start a conversation with the patient because this would take too much time. After a discussion they agreed that both groups should make it more clear to the patients in which situations (e.g. ward rounds) they can ask questions and when not. They also agreed that during handover meetings between physicians that take place at the bedside, they would do short conversations with patients, as these are the first contacts between them on each day.

Reflection outside meetings is more informal and significantly shorter than reflection in meetings. Although these reflection situations are oftentimes implicit and embedded into other communication, which makes them harder to recognize both for interviewees and observers, our analysis shows that there are plenty of such situations and that they have more relevance for the support of collaborative reflection than literature represents. Typical examples of such occasions are breaks, in which nurses and physicians sit together, working together on the same task and reflecting on it, and spontaneous encounters on the hallway, during which staff briefly reflects on (mostly) small issues. Such reflection occurs when staff talks about problems in daily work, such as supply with equipment, or as a result of implicit routines, such as asking each other for help or reassurance during the day. For example, we observed nurses reflecting frequently on how supply with specific medical gloves could be organized more efficiently.

Looking at **constraints and challenges** for supporting collaborative reflection, we observed that many small outcomes from spontaneous reflection were not sustained. Taking the example of break times described in section 3.2, we observed how nurses briefly reflected a couple of times during one day on how to deal with this issue (e.g. on the hallway) and then turned back to work with patients. However, follow up actions were never planned in such situations and the nurses never took notes. This shows that outcomes and topics of spontaneous reflection are less persistent. Such behavior may then result in situations such as described for the meeting above (section 3.2), in which some people cannot remember problems or are not consciously aware of them.

Moreover, we also found that in terms of **documenting experiences**, physicians and nurses do not take notes unless they see an immediate or at least mid-term personal benefit or if it is inevitable to e.g. legal restrictions. This is not a new insight, as personal benefit is a critical precondition for knowledge exchange in general [5]. However, in healthcare settings documentation is even more critical in terms of time and priorities: given the highly packed work day of staff, they are cautious to take unnecessary efforts, which may then result in less time for patients. Therefore, solutions supporting reflection at such workplaces need to show the potential benefit. Nevertheless, we found that *existing* documentation was often used as a trigger or guide for reflection: Documents like the abovementioned curve at patients' beds often guided the reflection of nurses and physicians, for example when two or more nurses gathering around this documentation and reflecting on treatment given to a patient. This suggests that documented experiences can be valuable guides for collaborative reflection in healthcare.

3.4 Discussion: New insights into reflection at healthcare workplaces

The study shows that staff in healthcare is faced with scarcity of time and emotionally demanding, responsible tasks. In addition, the teamwork aspect is very present in such workplaces: nurses and physicians formed a collective and help each other in stressful situations. This underpins the insight that reflection is a common practice at healthcare workplaces.

There are two novel foci of support to take away from our studies with respect to reflection specific for healthcare workplaces. First, reflection in healthcare is not limited to medical and training aspects, but is also common on team coordination, communication and similar aspects. Therefore, in addition to literature (see sec-

tion 2.4), a focus of reflection support should also be set to these issues, as these are crucial for good care. The topic of communication with patients described above is a typical example for this, as it is a matter of ward organization but directly affects the quality of care. Second, tools to support the documentation and reflection of experiences need to be flexible in space and time: Staff did not have much time to explicitly step back and reflect – in contrast, we observed nurses and physicians to reflect often during and between tasks or after their shift. The challenge thus is to fit support into these constraints.

Our study indicates that support for collaborative reflection is both underdeveloped and needed in such workplaces. Means to deal with e.g. stressful situations such as supervision are too infrequent. Thus, we observed many situations in which colleagues started to reflect in place of this external support – one example is nurses asking each other for reassurance on treatment given to a patient. In addition, we noticed situations in which the opportunity to reflect in a task would have been needed but was not there, e.g. when the physician tried to avoid talking to relatives and giving them bad news.

4. ANALYSIS: MODES, TOPICS AND THE PROCESS OF COLLABORATIVE REFLECTION

Analyzing the observations from the study described above and combining them with insights from other studies run in parallel allows for an operationalization of collaborative reflection (see [18, 19] for details of the analysis of all studies). This includes modes of collaborative reflection, the relation between topic contextualization and aggregation as well as process characteristics of collaborative reflection. In what follows, we will describe the resulting constructs with a focus on their occurrence in healthcare workplaces like the hospital ward.

4.1 Context: Modes of reflection

There are different settings of collaborative reflection and necessary documentation of experiences: Sometimes, reflection happens in a **planned** meeting, whereas in other occasions it is **spontaneous**. In addition, it may happen **during** the task reflected on or **after** it – this is closely related to Schön's distinction between reflection in and on action (section 2.1). Based on this distinction, we developed a two-dimensional scheme describing **modes of reflection** along an axis between planned and spontaneous reflection and another axis representing reflection on past work events and reflection occurring during work.

Table 1 shows the resulting matrix and examples for **reflection sessions** from the healthcare study. Looking at the examples shown in Table 1, it is obvious that these modes need to be sup-

Occurrence / Relation to reflected work	planned	spontaneous
Reflection on past work events, "on action"	Scheduled meetings in which reflection is part of the agenda	Breaks, talks on the hallway, before / after work
Reflection on current task, "in action"	Daily handover sessions, meeting of physicians	Reflection on a patient while caring for her

Table 1: Occurrences of reflection (planned, spontaneous) and relation to work reflected about (on action, in action [20]) with examples from the healthcare study.

ported in different ways. For example, reflection in scheduled meetings can be prepared by an **agenda** (e.g. announcing topics) and may benefit from e.g. **facilitation**, whereas spontaneous reflection needs to be done without these aids. In addition, both spontaneous reflection and reflection on action restrict the **time** for reflection. Our observation of staff making mandatory documentation in their free time shows that support for the non-mandatory task of documenting experience needs to be very flexible with respect to time. Moreover, all modes have a different timeframe for **following up** on earlier and planning later reflection: In meetings this may be done systematically by minutes, but in other modes existing topics have to be at hand spontaneously.

Although done in different modes, different sessions of collaborative reflection might be about the **same topic** or at least share a **common context**. Results from e.g. a reflection session during a break might be needed or at least be interesting for a regular meeting but forgotten due lacking documentation. Support for collaborative reflection therefore also needs to provide means for transitions between outcomes stemming from different modes and to establish a shared context between reflection actors.

4.2 Topics: Context and aggregation

Besides different modes of collaborative reflection, the topical level – whether a concrete situation or a more abstract problem is discussed – is important for reflection support. The description of collaborative reflection practice in section 3.3 already indicates corresponding problems of starting and successfully practicing collaborative reflection on different topic levels: For example, in handovers, nurses do not have much time to reflect and mostly stay on an **instance** (i.e. an **episode** happening during the day) or **case** (i.e. a patient) level, but only rarely relate episodes or cases to more comprehensive topics such as general care practice. Thus, problems are discussed redundantly and existing resolutions are not (re-) applied. The example of nurses discussing about medical gloves underpins this, as it happened frequently on the hallway but, according to our interviewees, had never been discussed in a meeting. The other way around, reflection in meetings tends to be about more **comprehensive** topics (i.e. organizational issues) that can be announced on an agenda. This may lead to situations in which participants lack the context of such a topic: Like the examples of changes in the break structure and of communicating with patients show, this context often has to be reconstructed by communicating episodes in which the problem have occurred.

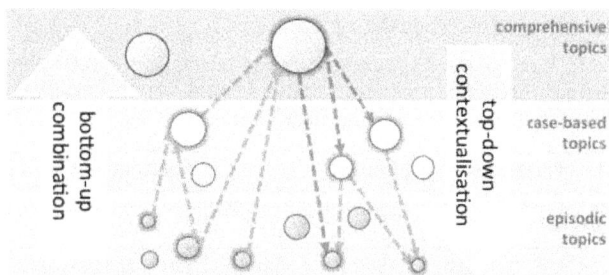

Figure 2: Topical levels in collaborative reflection.

Figure 2 describes the relations between the levels of episodes, cases and comprehensive topics in collaborative reflection and the corresponding bottom-up and top-down processes. In the healthcare study (and in parallel studies) we found that collaborative reflection in practice oftentimes is made up by multiple bottom-up and top-down cycles. This can be seen in the example of medical gloves and break times. Therefore, collaborative reflection support must relate these topical levels to each other, com-

plementing comprehensive topics with context from episodes and cases and enabling workers to derive (aggregate) comprehensive topics from episodes and cases.

4.3 Process: A blueprint for collaborative reflection support

As another result, our observations show that there are five ingredients of collaborative reflection support. First, there is need to support the **documentation** of experiences and the **capturing of data** contextualizing experiences in order to form a thorough base for returning to experiences. Second, workers need to **individually reflect** on experiences in order to understand them better and to develop ideas for resolutions. It should be noted that these phases might also happen in parallel as the documentation of experience may trigger individual reflection of it. Third, **collaborative reflection** takes place, which includes sharing experiences, communicating about them and negotiating resolutions. After that, **sustaining outcomes** is done to not let results go but document them properly. These phases include and are connected by **articulation**, which serves different purposes such as explicating and explaining experiences or writing down outcomes. Figure 3 shows the resulting blueprint for the implementation of tool support for collaborative reflection.

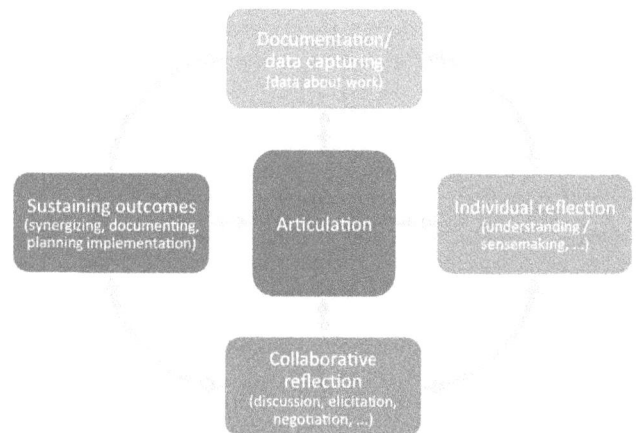

Figure 3: A blueprint for collaborative reflection support.

This blueprint can be illustrated by the example of physicians' communication with patients. Nurses had documented this issue for the head nurse, who had started to reflect on her experiences with this issue. Then, she had prepared the topic for reflection in the ward meeting and nurses and physicians present in the meeting reflected on it collaboratively. After that, they agreed on outcomes and the head nurse wrote down their resolution.

The blueprint is not meant to prescribe a **linear sequence** for collaborative reflection, but explicitly allows going back to other steps. Examples such as the break time discussion at the ward, in which staff went back to individual reflection of episodes in the meeting, shows that this is necessary. Likewise, the blueprint also allows **loops** within single steps like in the example of short-term, iterative collaborative reflection on the hallway. It also emphasizes the need for articulation and the need to support people in sustaining outcomes. However, steps of the process may also be left out if e.g. collaborative reflection on a new topic emerges spontaneously from a talk between workers, omitting phases of individual reflection.

5. SUPPORTING COLLABORATIVE REFLECTION

Based on the insights on collaborative reflection in general and for healthcare workplaces in particular, we developed the "Talk Reflection App" for its support. It is designed for the reflection of different topics. For first field tests, we tailored it to support the collaborative reflection of physicians' talks to patient relatives, (see section 5.2). Its concept was also tested for the collaborative reflection of nursing work by using a paper prototype.

5.1 Pre-Testing the Process Blueprint

Before we designed the app, we conducted a workshop to pre-test our blueprint described in 4.3 to find out whether the process was applicable in practice. For this workshop, we gathered five employees of the ward (four nurses and a physician). In the workshop, we asked them to reflect on scenes taken from their daily work such as a patient complaining and a patient missing her valuables. The scenes were illustrated by a picture (see Figure 4). For reflection, we asked the participants to follow a scripted process, which asked them to first **write down** similar scenes they had experienced (documentation, see section 4.3) on paper cards and briefly **reflect on them individually**. After that, they were asked to share their experiences by pinning the cards to a board (Figure 4) and explain them to the others. In a third step, they were asked to **discuss** different experiences of a respective scene (collaborative reflection) and to write down **resolutions** for the scene (sustaining outcomes). Articulation was present in many ways, e.g. to explain experiences to others and discuss them.

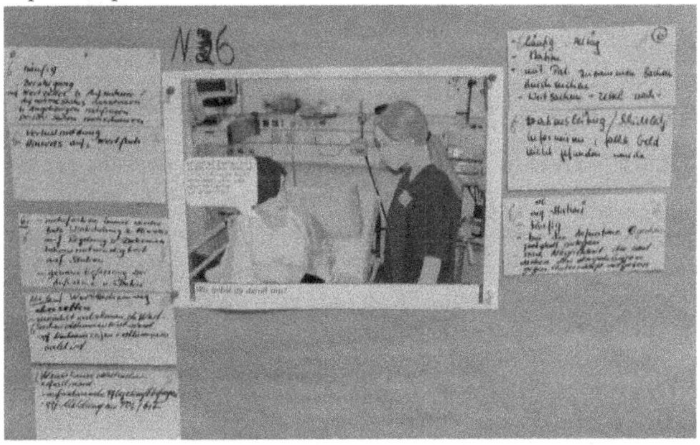

Figure 4: Results of the pre-Test of the process blueprint for collaborative reflection support.

The workshop produced rich results and the participants reported that had achieved new insights on their work. In particular, the participants wrote 41 paper cards, among which we found 13 stories of experiences and 17 resolutions for problems identified in the scenes. This indicates that documenting stories of experiences is a proper means to support reflection – it took only a short time and was expressive enough to support later reflection. The number of resolutions suggests that the process we scripted for the participants in combination with the paper prototype was adequate and helpful to derive insights on how to change future behavior. In addition, for some resolutions the participants agreed on further actions such as proposing a different way of handling patients' valuables for as a new standard of the hospital.

The participants referred to each other in the way we had planned: They documented their experiences regarding the respective scene and added personal reflection results such as potential resolutions. They easily articulated their experiences to explain them to others and derived many insights from the different experiences dis-

cussed. This suggests that our blueprint can be used as a basis to create tools supporting collaborative reflection. In an informal talk after the workshop, three participants reported that they had reached a level of certainty and agreement among colleagues that would not have been possible without the collaborative reflection of their different experiences.

5.2 The Talk Reflection App: A prototypical tool for reflection support of relative talks

Based on the evaluation of the paper prototype, we implemented a mobile application to support collaborative reflection. As a pilot area for evaluation of this application, we chose physicians' talks to relatives, which is an area in which physicians are usually not trained during their education. Talking to relatives is a frequent and very important task for physicians, as physicians are obliged to inform and emotionally assist relatives and need information from relatives to better judge the case of the patient.

As described above, physicians were unsure about this task, as they perceive it as stressful, and even tried to avoid it (see section 3.2). They told us that they were interested in improving their skills for this task and agreed to support each other in this process. As they told us, there is a relation between how good one manages talking to relatives and whether relatives complain about the treatment of patients – better conversations apparently lower the complaint rate. Because of this, supporting relative talks was found to be more pressuring than other tasks such as supporting the reflection of nursing work as described in the paper prototype evaluation. However, as can be seen from the description below, the prototype can also be used for this task with minor changes.

The Talk Reflection App is aligned to the blueprint of collaborative reflection presented in 4.3: Aiming at supporting physicians in the articulation and collaborative reflection of relative talks, it consists of four basic elements representing the phases of the blueprint: a form for **adding documentation** (Figure 5), a private space for **individual reflection** (Figure 6), group spaces for **collaborative reflection** and a space to **sustain outcomes** of the reflection process (**Figure 7**). It also supports articulation in the self-assessments for documented cases (see Figure 5) or comments on own and shared documents (e.g. Figure 6, number 4).

Implementing the need to be used flexibly and to fit into the work of physicians, the Talk Reflection App runs on mobile devices such as tablets (iPads), and it is connected to a server enabling the exchange of data among users and enable cooperation by exchange of comments (see below). This way, physicians can carry it around with them and use the same interface and device in different modes of reflection. Considering the form factor, we had proposed smaller devices, as these are better to carry around than iPads, but the physicians preferred display size to mobility.

For the **documentation of conversations**, the app allows physicians to describe conversation content and, being prompted by questions, assess their own emotions as well the reaction of relatives during the talk. Given that a physician had a difficult conversation with relatives, she can document the talk, using the soft keyboard built into tablet devices to create title and description of the conversation and chose a (medical) topic[3] for it (no. 1 in Figure 5). After she has described what happened, she is prompted to assess her and the relative's feeling (**self-assessments**, e.g. "How

---

[3] To sustain the confidentiality of real documentation made with the app in the hospital, all entries in the figures have been created by the authors (but resemble real entries).

did your conversation partner presumably feel", second question in Figure 5, no. 2). To remember the talk later in collaborative reflection, she can mark it (3). As physicians already have to document these talks as part of their work, e.g. to prove that relatives have been informed properly, the app fits into their work and provides direct benefit for documentation work.

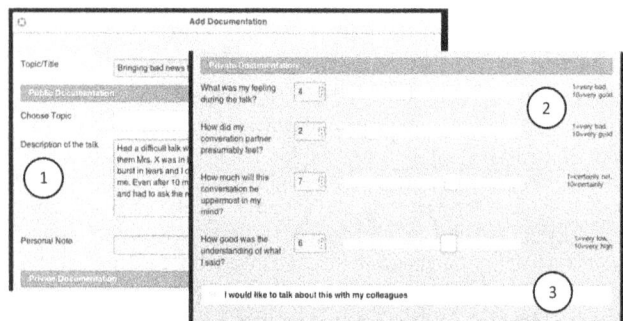

Figure 5: Interface for documenting conversations (left) and self-assessments (right).

After this input, the documentation is available only for the physician who has created it and can be shared with others. Physicians can add comments to their own content (**individual reflection**) and to the content shared with them (**collaborative reflection**). Figure 6 shows the respective interface, which enables the navigation to own (1a) and shared (1b) content spaces. It also shows that a user can share her documents easily while inspecting them (2). The document itself is shown in full length to enable physicians to remember own and understand others' conversation descriptions. In addition, Figure 6 shows traces of individual and collaborative reflection: In the comments below the documentation (yellow boxes in no. 4 of Figure 6), the upper comment ("I did not know that …") stems from the author of the document, who has realized that she was missing information, and the lower comment ("I had a similar case…") shows how a colleague has thought about the case and reflects on it based on his experiences. Using comments in the latter way enables collaborative reflection and communication asynchronously. Sharing the resulting set of information on experiences can then help others to better understand the situation and makes it available for collaborative reflection.

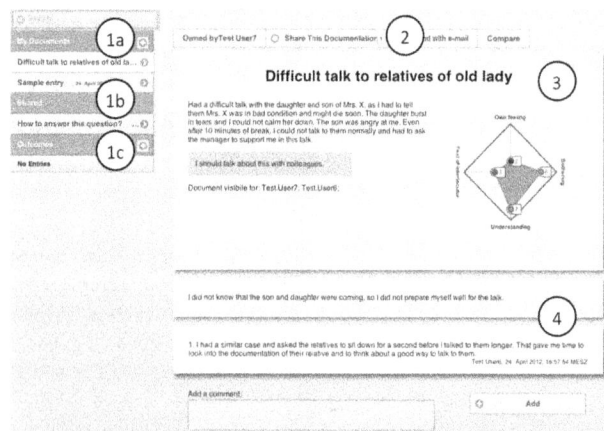

Figure 6: Individual and collaborative reflection spaces: Each documentation can be viewed, shared and discussed. Assessments displayed in spider graphs for a quick overview.

Activities such as reading own and shared conversation documentation as well as commenting and discussing them should lead to **outcomes** – the physicians should **learn from collaborative re-**

flection of the conversations. **Figure 7** shows how such outcomes can be documented and sustained within the Talk Reflection App: Once reflection participants have agreed on a certain outcome (e.g. "Calm down relatives in stressful situations" in no.1 of **Figure 7**), they may open the outcome documentation view (1c in Figure 6) and add both a title and a description of the outcome (1 and 2 in **Figure 7**). To contextualize these comprehensive outcomes with concrete examples, the app displays recently used documentations and enables the users to link them to the outcome documentation (no. 3) – this supports the **top-down linking of comprehensive topics to their episodic and case-based context** (see the topical levels described above).

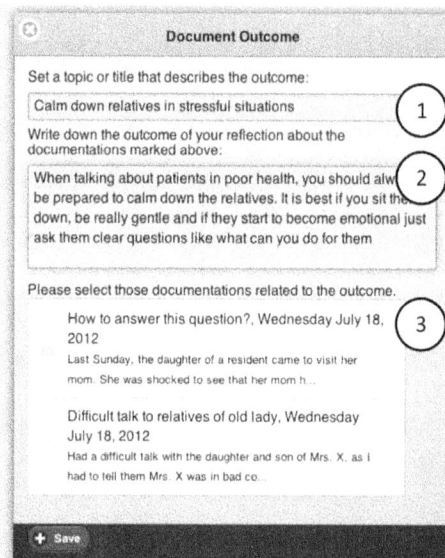

Figure 7: Outcomes of collaborative reflection sessions can be saved and related to cases.

The app covers all steps of the process blueprint presented above and integrates them into the daily work of physicians, fitting constraints of time and space by running on mobile devices. This also makes it applicable in all **modes of collaborative reflection** – be it meetings as described above or spontaneous reflection in breaks, as physicians can take the mobile devices with them. Likewise, the app supports the aggregation and contextualization of topics by using talk documentation to identify comprehensive topics (bottom-up outcome generation) and relating them back to documentation (top-down contextualization).

The app also supports the **bottom-up and top-down relations between the topical levels** described in section 4.2, as it enables physicians to **collect episodic or case based documentation** and **derive comprehensive topics** from them during collaborative reflection. The outcome shown in **Figure 7** (numbers 2 and 3) is an example of this, showing the comprehensive topic of coordinating relatives derived from two episodic documentations (checked cases in **Figure 7**, number 1). The other way around, the app can also be used for the reflection of comprehensive topics, e.g. when there is a need to understand the background of topics or find examples in meetings.

5.3 Evaluation and Discussion

An initial evaluation of the app was done in two workshops, which were meant to provide formative information for further development. First, we conducted a workshop with three physicians, who used an early prototype of the app and were asked to give feedback on its applicability and potential utility. In a second step, we conducted two workshop sessions with two physicians each. In these sessions, the physicians used an improved prototype in order to test-drive its rollout in the ward.

In the **first evaluation workshop**, we combined the elicitation of further requirements with an evaluation of an initial prototype of the app. In this workshop, three physicians took part, among which there was one young assistant physician, one experienced physician and the head physician of the ward. We asked these physicians about aspects such as motivation, topics and goals for collaborative reflection and gave them the opportunity to use the app. For the latter, we asked them to tell us about their impression on utility and applicability, missing or unnecessary features, proposals for improvement and situations in which they would like to use it. As one result, the participants told us that they liked the idea of using this app to document and reflect on relative talks – one physicians even said he and his colleagues might like the app because they can take it with them and use it during small leaks in their daily schedule (as opposed to doing all documentation at one after work). As a result of the workshop, the physicians also came up with proposals for organizational support of using the app for reflection. One of these proposals was to establish a regular meeting in which documented talks should be reflected on – according to one physician, this would also motivate colleagues to use the app, as they would know that there is an event in which they get feedback on their talks from others. This does not only show the fit of the app into physicians' work but also indicates acceptance of the tool. Overall, the participating physicians stated that they liked the app and volunteered to take part in follow up workshops and a field test.

In the **second workshop**, in which three physicians took part (two form the first workshop and a different assistant physician, while the other assistant the workshop because of an emergency case), we asked the physicians to work through a script, using an improved version of the app. This script included the different phases of the collaborative reflection process blueprint (Figure 3) and linked them to the respective functionality of the Talk Reflection App. In particular, we seated the participants on the same table and asked them to enter one or more recent experiences, to *individually* reflect on them and articulate outcomes of this reflection by adding comments to the documentation. Switching to *collaborative* reflection, we asked them to share their material with others, to annotate others' material and discuss the documented cases verbally by referring to the documentation shared in the app. To conclude this collaborative reflection, they were asked to create an outcome as shown in Figure 7 by writing it down in the app and linking relevant material to it. This approach was meant to simulate app usage in the real context of the physicians. In addition, we asked them to focus on whether the app could foster their discussion and reflection.

After the workshop, we interviewed the physicians about their experiences with the app and about how it could be integrated in their daily work routines. In general they were satisfied with the improved app and were looking forward to using it as part of their daily work. Discussing situations in which they could use the app, they developed a schedule for meetings in which documented cases could be reflected collaboratively. Besides this plan, which shows that the app fits the needs of the physicians, they asked for stronger scaffolding of articulation and a more differentiated input form including selection options for categories of the talks (e.g. "Information", "Report about diagnostics", "Discussion about therapy options") in order to produce more structured documentation and better refer to it in later reflection. Moreover, they asked for a function to mark up certain parts of longer documentations

separately, e.g. as good practice, and share these with others, differentiating between different groups to share content with. This again shows the adoption of the app and the importance of articulation in collaborative reflection.

Figure 8: A physician using the Talk Reflection App on a tablet device during the second evaluation workshop.

While both of the evaluation workshops were conducted in a formative approach, they already show that the tool and the process it is based on can support collaborative reflection in healthcare workplaces: The physicians envisioned scenarios in which they wanted to use the app, they asked for adaptations to fit it even more to their needs and they liked the flexibility of taking the mobile app with them and documenting or reflecting in a time chose by them. This suggests that the intentions of the app as described in section 5.2 can be fulfilled in the hospital.

6. CONCLUSION AND FURTHER WORK

In this paper, we presented an approach in supporting collaborative reflection at the workplace as a means to improve work practice and create knowledge in organizations. Regarding the lack of insights into the practice of collaborative reflection and tool support for it, we used an exploratory approach to shed light on this topic. In order to show concrete options of support, we focused the description on a study done with a German hospital and complemented this with other studies done in parallel.

As we found, collaborative reflection in healthcare (and other workplaces) is characterized by a mixture of scheduled settings such as meetings and unscheduled occurrences of reflection such as spontaneous conversations on the hallway. We also found that in healthcare work, a special focus has to be set to unscheduled occurrences, as these happen more frequently than e.g. meetings. From the study, we derived a taxonomy for different modes of collaborative reflection, a model of topical levels in collaborative reflection covering episodic, case-based experiences and comprehensive topics and a blueprint describing the steps and course of collaborative reflection in practice. Most important, we emphasized the need to support articulation for collaborative reflection. We also showed how tools can support this task in healthcare workplace by describing a prototype for the reflection of physicians. As the feedback of users shows, the tool suits the various needs of this workplace well and was embraced by the physicians. Given the similarity of different modes of reflection and other aspects between healthcare and other workplaces we found in our studies [18, 19], our results also suggest that the tool – with slight adaptations – can be used as general support to reflect conversations in daily work and improve them. Examples of such conversations could be talks with clients or suppliers.

The results presented here show how tools can support collaborative reflection in different contexts. At the time of completing this paper, we prepare a field test of the app in the hospital, including an evaluation of app usage in different contexts such as spontaneous collaborative reflection or meetings. In further work, we will also evaluate it in different domains. Currently, additional evaluations are planned for domains such as care for the elderly, telecommunications and IT consulting.

7. ACKNOWLEDGMENTS

We thank the whole MIRROR consortium for talks and other support for this work. Special thanks go to Dominik and Volker, who made our work in the hospital work and still support it.

8. REFERENCES

[1] Argyris, C. and Schön, D.A. 1996. *Organizational learning II: Theory, method, and practice.* Addison-Wesley.

[2] Boud, D., Keogh, R. and Walker, D. 1985. *Reflection: turning experience into learning.* Routledge.

[3] Daudelin, W. 1996. Learning from experience through reflection. *Organizational Dynamics.* 24, 3 (1996), 36–48.

[4] Dyke, M. 2006. The role of the "Other" in reflection, knowledge formation and action in a late modernity. *International Journal of Lifelong Education.* 25, (Mar. 2006), 105–123.

[5] Efimova, L. 2004. Discovering the iceberg of knowledge work: A weblog case. *Proceedings of The Fifth European Conference on Organisational Knowledge, Learning and Capabilities (OKLC 2004), April 2-3, 2004* (Apr. 2004).

[6] Fischer, G. and Herrmann, T. 2011. Socio-Technical Systems: A Meta-Design Perspective. *International Journal for Sociotechnology and Knowledge Development.* 3, 1 (2011), 1–33.

[7] Fleck, R. and Fitzpatrick, G. Supporting Collaborative Reflection with Passive Image Capture. *IN SUPPLEMENTARY PROCEEDINGS OF COOP'06.* 41–48.

[8] Fleck, R. and Fitzpatrick, G. 2009. Teachers' and tutors' social reflection around SenseCam images. *International Journal of Human-Computer Studies.* 67, 12 (2009), 1024–1036.

[9] Forneris, S.G. and Peden-McAlpine, C.J. 2006. Contextual Learning: A Reflective Learning Intervention for Nursing Education. *International Journal of Nursing Education Scholarship.* 3, 1 (2006).

[10] Gustafsson, C. and Fagerberg, I. 2004. Reflection, the way to professional development? *Journal of Clinical Nursing.* 13, 3 (2004), 271–280.

[11] Høyrup, S. 2004. Reflection as a core process in organisational learning. *Journal of Workplace Learning.* 16, 8 (Dec. 2004), 442–454.

[12] Järvinen, A. and Poikela, E. 2001. Modelling reflective and contextual learning at work. *Journal of Workplace Learning.* 13, 7/8 (Dec. 2001), 282–290.

[13] Knipfer, K., Prilla, M., Cress, U. and Herrmann, T. 2011. Computer Support for Collaborative Reflection on Captured Teamwork Data. *Proceedings of the 9th International Conference on Computer Supported Collaborative Learning* (2011), 938–939.

[14] Kolb, D. 1984. *Experiential learning□: experience as the source of learning and development.* Prentice-Hall.

[15] Loo, R. and Thorpe, K. 2002. Using reflective learning journals to improve individual and team performance. *Team Performance Management.* 8, 5 (2002), 134.

[16] Mamede, S. and Schmidt, H.G. 2005. Correlates of reflective practice in medicine. *Advances in health sciences education.* 10, 4 (2005), 327–337.

[17] Mann, K., Gordon, J. and MacLeod, A. 2009. Reflection and reflective practice in health professions education: a systematic review. *Advances in Health Sciences Education.* 14, 4 (2009), 595–621.

[18] Prilla, M., Herrmann, T. and Degeling, M. 2012. Collaborative Reflection for Learning at the Healthcare Workplace. *CSCL@Work: Case Studies of Collaborative Learning at Work.* S. Goggins, I. Jahnke, and V. Wulf, eds. Springer.

[19] Prilla, M., Knipfer, K., Degeling, M., Cress, U. and Herrmann, T. 2011. Computer Support for Collaborative Reflection on Captured Teamwork Data. *Proceedings of 1st European Workshop on Awareness and Reflection in Learning Networks (ARNets11) at EC-TEL 2011* (2011).

[20] Schön, D.A. 1983. *The reflective practitioner.* Basic books New York.

[21] Scott, S.G. 2010. Enhancing Reflection Skills Through Learning Portfolios: An Empirical Test. *Journal of Management Education.* 34, 3 (Jun. 2010), 430–457.

[22] Strauss, A.L. and Corbin, J.M. 1998. *Basics of qualitative research: Techniques and procedures for developing grounded theory.* Sage Publications.

[23] Tang, C. and Carpendale, S. 2009. Supporting nurses' information flow by integrating paper and digital charting. *Proceedings of the 11th European Conference on Computer Supported Cooperative Work (ECSCW 09)* (2009).

[24] Teekman, B. 2000. Exploring reflective thinking in nursing practice. *Journal of Advanced Nursing.* 31, 5 (2000), 1125–1135.

[25] Weick, K.E. 1995. *Sensemaking in organizations.* Sage Publications, Inc.

[26] Woerkom, M. van and Croon, M. 2008. Operationalising critically reflective work behaviour. *Personnel Review.* 37, 3 (2008), 317–331.

[27] Yip, K. 2006. Self-reflection in reflective practice: A note of caution. *British Journal of Social Work.* (2006), 777–788.

Newcomer Integration and Learning in Technical Support Communities for Open Source Software

Vandana Singh
School of Information Sciences
University of Tennessee, Knoxville
1345 Circle Park Drive,
Knoxville, TN, 37996
Tel: 865-974-2785
vandana@utk.edu

ABSTRACT

In this paper we present results of an NSF funded project on exploring and understanding cyber learning that happens in online open source software (OSS) communities for technical support. We look across multiple OSS support communities (Firefox, Java, and Koha) to understand the behavior of newcomers in these communities, the role that the community response plays in their continued participation and newcomer best practices. We found that newcomers are not a homogenous group and majority of them display "model" behavior. We also found out that community response is critical for continued participation of newcomers. In our dataset, almost all non returning newcomers can be attributed to receiving no reply or a condescending reply from the community. We found that one third of newcomers' transition into a role of help givers in the community and demonstrate evidence of learning. We also highlight best practices for newcomers to be successful in these online communities.

Categories and Subject Descriptors

H5.m. Information interfaces and presentation (e.g., HCI): Miscellaneous.

Keywords

Open source software, newcomer integrations, online communities, virtual communities, learning, cyber learning, distance education.

1. INTRODUCTION

Online communities are an important part of everyday life for an ever growing number of people globally. One domain in which online communities have significant impact is online learning. Online learning communities have seen a dramatic increase through their adoption by for-profit as well as non-profit educational institutions. Research firm Ambient predicts that by 2014 the number of students taking all of their classes online will increase to 3.55 million, while the number of students taking all of their courses in on-campus classrooms will drop to 5.14 million. The Sloan Consortium found that 66 percent of postsecondary institutions were seeing an increased demand for new distance education course offerings and 73 percent were seeing an increased demand in their existing distance education coursework.

Research in online classrooms has shown that the learning in these environments is influenced by a multitude of factors including the learning environment, the resources provided to the students, and the tools and technology used to deliver content [7]. One important factor that determines student success is their use of learning resources [7]. A learning resource is information or a tool that can be used to assist learners in the process of locating, recording, and processing the learning materials. In this study we investigate one such learning community – online forums of multiple open source software communities for technical support that specifically serve newcomers. Learning has emerged as a key motivational factor for participation in open source software development along with other factors such as element of reciprocity and reputation in the community [15]. In this research, we connect these very distant research streams – learning and open source – as they can shed light on many issues of interest to CSCW scholars. In particular, we investigate characteristics of newcomers who join open source software technical support communities and how their characteristics shape their participation and the response from the community.

The growth and benefit of any cyber learning environment such as an online forum community depends on newcomer entry and sustained participation. Participation is essential for learning to occur and successful participation is itself a valuable learning experience. It is critical for online communities to ensure new members involve in the communities initially as lurkers or peripheral members and progress towards becoming core members.

We conducted an exploratory study on online technical support forums for Mozilla Firefox, Java, and Koha to understand and classify practices and tools used to facilitate newcomer entry and continued participation, as well as the building of a learning community. We examined how newcomers seek help, how community guides them, and how a successful newcomer integrates and learns in a community. Such a study will contribute to fundamental theory on newcomer participation in cyber learning environments as well as theory on how tools successfully mediate learner-teacher or novice-expert relationships.

2. BACKGROUND LITERATURE
Shared Interests

Online communities are built around shared interests, which Zhang et al (2007) [19] define as "advice on medical treatment, programming, software, building a computer from scratch to repairing the kitchen sink." Such communities are of interest to many researchers as they "blur the dichotomy between experts and seekers…such systems allow everyone to contribute as they can". Communities of various topics and implementations are of interest to researchers, whether it is a community centered on questions and answers, social support, or discussion. One of the findings from Zhang et al is that the reason that a user replies to a topic is usually because of an interest in the content of the topic rather than *who* started the thread, this indirectly reflects a particular shared interest between the original poster and the repliers.

A crucial aspect of our research is the integration; acclimatization and involvement of newcomers into online communities. Several scholars have studied this in the context of both offline and online communities. Choi et al [5] studied the impact of socialization tactics in online communities on newcomer commitment, which was measured by the length of the stay in the communities. Commitment to online groups is often lower than to offline groups as it is often easier for members to leave online groups [8]. Choi et al found that standardized tactics were negatively associated with newcomers' contributions, whereas personalized tactics were positively associated with their contribution. With regards to open source communities, Ducheneaut [6] looks at socialization in OSS developer communities. The success of OS projects depends on the ability to attract newcomers. Projects that fail to attract and retain new contributors cannot get beyond a few lines of code. Furthermore, as OSS projects progress, the few people who have been actively involved are the only ones to understand the complex nature of the project. This makes socializing new members essential to the long-term survival of OSS projects. Ducheneaut also found that the successful contribution to an OS project is less about technical expertise and more about construction of identities. Rather than "anyone" being able to contribute, only those who can present themselves as "software craftsmen" could reach developer status on a project. All participants are highly skilled developers, but the newcomers who could play the part well could progress to higher strata on the project.

Informational Behaviors

Burke, Kraut and Joyce [4] researched ways in which newcomers execute proactive socialization tactics within online communities and found that when users mention their presence on the forum in past, express their similarity to the groups by using same vernacular, and request information and received responses to their request, then the group was willing to integrate them in the community. This in return, meant that the newcomers will continue participating in the group. [16] von Krogh et al (2003) differentiated between "joiners and newcomers" and how the role changed once a user was given access to the developer community in the open source community Freenet. They analyzed the use of a "joining script" which is the type of activity a joiner must demonstrate to become a member of the developer community. In this study we build on these studies findings and try to add to the domain knowledge by developing a better understanding in the different types of newcomers and their characteristics.

In terms of motivation of participation, Yang et al (2008) [18] analyzed "witkeys," websites which offer monetary rewards for participation, found that surprisingly money does not provide an incentive for people to participate. Rather, other incentives such as prestige motivate users to participate. The nature of the question also matters. Adamic et al [1] found that questions posed in Yahoo Answers that were more factual in nature had shorter activity levels and less differentiation between helper and asker role. Questions that were more open in nature had "longer threads, broader distribution of activity levels, and their users tended to participate by both posing and replying to questions" (673).

In [2] authors found newcomers exhibited primarily information seeking behavior while established members exhibited information-providing behavior. Most of these studies do not explicitly distinguish the differences among the newcomers and then the

impact that those differences might have on the integration of newcomers into the community. Welser et al (2007) [17] used visualization strategies in order to deduce the various social roles in Usenet communities. Such a strategy allowed viewing all the "signatures" of a social role within an online community, such as the author originations of answer and discussion people. "Answer people" are particularly important to analyze since their contributions are the direct contribution to creating "valuable online resources. Welser et al (2007) found that answer people tend to reply to discussion threads initiated by others and typically only contribute one or two messages per thread". Whether an individual eventually becomes committed to the group is likely to depend on the type of contributions the individual makes to the group and the responses the person gets after contributing. Prior studies have shown the importance and similarities of lurkers with the other social roles in online communities. [11] shows that the three major social roles of uploaders, contributors and lurkers engage in similar behavior and use similar tools in the communities and therefore lurkers should be seen as an important part of the discussion and design of online communities. In their research focusing on lurkers Mueller found that contribution and lurking are partially dependent on a person's overall engagement and also modified by their disposition towards a particular topic, work task or a social group. They did not find any evidence of social learning theory as well as individual trait theory. [12]. Preece [14] provides a "reader to leader' framework for understanding the life cycle and participation of users in online communities and the progression of their participation. According to their model the different social roles present in communities do not make a linear progression from one stage to the next but the social roles can change from one stage to another by skipping stages in the middle.

Analytical Methods

Researchers in this field have used a wide diversity of strategies to analyze the help-seeking behaviors of various users within online communities. Zhang et al (2007) quantitatively analyzed the Java forums to understand the help-seeking behaviors and levels of expertise of various users. They found that algorithms could be produced to analyze expertise levels within the Java community. Such findings [21] could help to match users with a question list that matches their specific expertise level, which would presumably increase their participation. Such research originated when it was found that the Java online community has unequal participation where a few advanced users answer most questions. Yuan et al (2009) [19] also focus on how tools that can motivate participation in an online community. They suggest the implementation of an intelligent recommendation system to increase contribution to online communities.

Nam et al [13] find altruism, learning, and competency are frequent motivations for top answerers to participate, but that participation is often highly intermittent. Using a simple measure of user performance, we find that higher levels of participation correlate with better performance.

3. RESEARCH DESIGN

The main research objective of this study is to find out what makes newcomers stay in an online community and if and how newcomers learn in these communities. We wanted to see the behavior of the newcomers as they enter these communities as well as the behavior of the community members towards these newcomers. This research followed a grounded theory approach because it is exploratory in nature and we wanted to develop an understanding of behaviors and underlying process in these communities. In this study data collection was done in phases and went hand in hand with data analysis. Based on the results of first phase of data analysis, further data collection and analysis was conducted. This type of data collection is called theoretical sampling and is a key

Forum	URL
Mozilla Firefox	http://www.mozilla.org/support/; http://www.mozillazine.org/
Koha	http://koha.1045719.n5.nabble.com/
Java	http://www.oracle.com/technetwork/topics/newtojava/overview/index.html

Table 1 : Data Collection Sources

step in grounded theory based research. It is concept driven it helps researcher to discover the concepts that are relevant to the problem and population and allows researchers to explore the concepts in depth. This process is cumulative; the data collection depends on data analysis and contributes to the next data collection and analysis. We first identified and collected threads with newcomers and then we identified the newcomers in the threads and analyzed their behavior. Then we analyzed the responses that these newcomers received from the community and how that impacted their future participation on the forum. We also wanted to establish the characteristics of a successful newcomer. For this, we identified few successful newcomers from our data set and collected 50 threads corresponding to each successful newcomer. From these 50 threads we developed a profile of a successful newcomer. More details about the particulars of data collection and analysis are given in relevant sections.

3.1 Research questions

Four main research questions were formulated as follows:

RQ1: What is the overall behavior of newcomers when they enter an OSS online community?

1. What is the tone of the newcomer in their messages and thread?
2. Does the newcomer exhibit any prior knowledge about the software in question?
3. Does the newcomer respond to the responder and/or acknowledge help when received?
4. Do the newcomers use comprehendible language when describing their problems?
5. Do the newcomers demonstrate an initiative to learn?

RQ2: What helps newcomers integrate into an OSS online community?

For this question integration means newcomers stayed in the community beyond their first message and came back and posted more messages. We wanted to see what impact the community response has on the continued participation or longevity of these newcomers. So for this question we looked at the behavior of community members, referred to as respondents from here on, and the impact it had on the continued participation/integration of newcomers.

1. What happens to newcomers continued participation when they are not replied to?
2. What happens to newcomers participation when the responders are
   a. Encouraging
   b. Neutral
   c. Condescending

RQ3: Do newcomers learn in these communities, and if so, how does the learning occur? What helps newcomers learn and contribute to the community?

We hypothesize that demonstration of learning occurred will be evident in the messages that the newcomers post overtime. Also, we believe that the ultimate demonstration of learning is when the newcomers feel confident enough to start giving help to others and in this way they contribute back to the community. So, for this question we looked at two things:

1. What are the changes in the content of the messages posted by newcomers over a period of time?
2. How many newcomers change roles and become help givers?

RQ4 – What are best practices of successful newcomers?

The answer to this question was a composite from all the previous analysis about newcomer behavior and responses and additional parameters such as informative subject line, resilience, persistence, etc. were added.

3.2 Data Collection

Data was collected in multiple stages from three different open source online technical support communities. Table 1 below provides a summary of the forums used to collect data.

Mozilla Firefox is an open-source web browser. Two technical support forums for Mozilla Firefox were selected for data collection. One is a part of the official Mozilla support page and the second is an unofficial Mozilla site named Mozillazine. Firefox is a web browser and the support community does not expect technical expertise from its users.

Java is open-source software and the forum used for data collection was the Oracle forum hosted at forums.oracle.com. From all the forums available on this website, New to Java forum was chosen because it is meant to welcome/integrate people who are new to learning java as a programming language. The technical level of expertise needed in Java forums is higher that Firefox and some basic programming skills are expected from the users.

Finally, Koha is an open-source integrated library system (ILS) and data was collected and analyzed from their technical support forum at oldnabble.com. The users of Koha forums are librarians, developers and technical support representatives from commercial vendors who provide technical support for Koha. The expectations of the newcomers are awareness of Koha, its modules and functionalities, so in our opinion this is the intermediate forum to Java and Firefox.

All three forums provided different contexts in which to analyze newcomer and responder behavior, with different and various levels of expertise in different user populations. These communities were chosen so as to learn about the newcomers and how they learn. Such results would not be generalized to developer and developer communities, but rather how new users learn about software and demonstrate this learning in online communities.

For first phase of data collection, each of the four forums was searched using multiple keywords such as new, newbie, newcomer, noob, noobie, etc. Data Collection was done in June 2010 and the forums were searched up to January 2009, so in total 18 months of messages were browsed to collect the threads with the identified keywords in them. A newcomer thread was determined by reading the opening post and seeing if a user declared being new to a specific facet of a particular forum topic. A total of 60 threads were collected for Firefox technical support community (43 from MozillaZine and 15 from official Mozilla support site. Twenty four threads were collected New to Java forum and 47 threads were collected from Koha forum.

For second phase, for the successful newcomer question, the top five posters from our Mozillazine dataset were identified and for

	Model	IM	CI
Tone	Yes for Any four or five	Yes for any 3	Yes for only 2, 1 or 0
Prior Knowledge			
Responsiveness/...			
Comprehendible			
Initiative to Learn			

Table 2: Newcomer Behavior Analysis

each one of them 50 additional threads were collected. This type of data collection is called theoretical sampling and is a key step in grounded theory based research. In this case, based on our analysis of threads collected in phase one, we decided to dig deeper about individual characteristics of most prolific posters. These threads were coded and analyzed on both individual message level as well as overall thread level. These threads were used to get an understanding of the behavior of prolific newcomers. Furthermore, the responses from the responders were also coded to get an overall picture of the participation of these top 5 newcomers experience in the forum. Responders were any users of the site who attempted to answer the question or help the newcomer in any way within the same thread.

3.3 Data analysis

Grounded Theory was used as a basis for data analysis, an approach that has been used in other OSS and online content analysis [14]. In the process of grounded theory development, theory generation and development is done inductively by studying the phenomenon it represents. Concepts are discovered, developed, and provisionally verified through systematic data collection and analysis. One does not begin with a theory, and then prove it. Rather, one begins with an area of study and what is relevant to that area is allowed to emerge. Following this methodology we started with the general research questions as mentioned in the previous section, the sub-research questions were developed during the process of data collection and data analysis. Data Collection guided data analysis and data analysis guided subsequent data collection, which is a characteristic of grounded theory research. Each thread was individually read and coded on various dimensions for newcomer and responder behavior. All the threads were collected and coded iteratively to develop some basic concepts, producing a list of categories for types of discussions, types of questions and types of responses. Once the first round of *open coding* was done and these base categories were obtained, a second round of coding was done to ensure that all the representative categories were accounted for. And also, to verify and count occurrences for each of the categories, the iterative process of *interpretive coding* was done. The best practices of successful newcomer were obtained by *selective coding* for these practices among the data that was already coded for newcomer behavior and responder behavior. Data was coded iteratively and weekly meeting among the two coders were part of the process. In these meetings, coders compared notes/memos and discussed and resolved any confusing categories/concepts. Multiple types of categories and concepts were discovered during the process of this iterative coding and in this paper we focus specifically on newcomer behavior and socialization in online discussion forums for technical support.

Newcomer Behavior

This section provides an overview of how newcomer behavior was categorized and analyzed.

Newcomers were coded based on five dimensions, tone, prior knowledge, acknowledgement of help, comprehendible use of language and an initiative to learn. These five dimensions helped to determine whether a newcomer was a model, intermediate, or can improve newcomer (Table 2 explains further).

For research question 1, model, intermediate, and can improve newcomers were categorized based on coding the messages for five dimensions. The five dimensions are explained below with examples and the multiple categories that were used for each category. Table 2 explains how the newcomers were categorized into model, intermediate (IM) and can improve (NI).

For each thread, each behavior from each dimension was calculated on a rubric of five. If a newcomer used positive tones, exhibited prior knowledge on the subject, responded to the support and acknowledged help received, used clear and comprehendible language, and showed an initiative to learn and fix their problem, then they were assigned a five out of five. A specific breakdown is as follows: a best newcomer exhibits four to five of these characteristics in their particular thread; an intermediate newcomer exhibits three of these characteristics in their particular thread; the worst newcomer exhibits zero to two of these characteristics in their particular thread.

1-Tone is the style of language a newcomer uses when they first post a message and how it is maintained throughout the thread. These were determined based on a positive, neutral, and negative scale. Newcomers that used more positive-oriented tones such as humble, friendly, and polite were considered to act as "better" newcomers than one's that posted something in a desperate or annoyed manner. Neutral and straightforward tones were also considered better than negative tones. A negative tone was labeled as desperate, annoyed, confused, or critical.

*Example of positive tone: "*Howdy folks-This seems like a common newbie question but..."

*Example of neutral tone: "*i close it & then open firefox, but why does this happen? i run windows 7"

Example of negative tone: Critical - "Firefox is strictly for those who wish to cut their teeth on YOUR email programs and all other features. This browser has completely ruined my email program, causing me to have to move to IE and start all over again."

2- Prior efforts and knowledge is how much experience a newcomer has with the specific issue they are facing. A newcomer displays prior knowledge through the use of jargon surrounding the software used, as well as steps already attempted to solve problem. Such display exhibits a familiarity with the software in question.

*Example of prior knowledge: "*Eeverytime I hit the homepage icon a tab is added <Search for web Help> which leads to the help page of Google Web Search. Very annoying. This problem is not present when using IE." *(Newcomer is exhibiting that they've attempted same issue in IE without experiencing problem)*

3- Responsiveness / Acknowledgement of help was measured on whether or not the newcomer returned to the thread after posting the first message. Such an occurrence shows that the newcomer is committed to participating in thread interactions and is acknowledging the help they receive from responders on the forum.

Example of acknowledgment of help: "It works now. Thanks for helping a newbie in Igoogle."

4- Comprehendible use of language was measured on the basis of grammatical and spelling usage. If there were a high number of spelling errors, abbreviated speak, or the conveyance of unclear thoughts, then the newcomer was counted as not using comprehendible language.

Example of non-comprehendible language: "About bookmarks it's all ok but about Sessions? I done a lot of searches to find out something but without seccess. : ("

5- Initiative to learn was displayed through the use of how the newcomer framed their question. If a newcomer seemed uninterested in actually learning how to solve the problem, but rather concerned with how someone else could solve the problem, then this was measured as a low initiative to learn. If a question was framed in the context of, "I've tried everything, please tell me the steps I can take to resolve this issue" then the newcomer was exhibiting a high initiative to learn as they were interested in solving the problem themselves based on the potential advice given.

Example of strong initiative to learn: "I ADORE FF, but can we have a more accurate warning message in cases of non-EV certs, as you know as well as I do, that any lack of padlock could scare a newbie off joining my site and providing account signup info etc".

For research question 2, responder behavior was also analyzed. The messages from responders were coded for three types of responses: encouraging, neutral and condescending. Once all the messages from respondent were coded by this rubric, the newcomers were divided into these three categories: newcomers who were encouraged, newcomers who were condescended to and newcomers who received neutral responses. These newcomers were then followed for their participation after receiving a particular type of response. Also, newcomers who did not receive responses were followed to see if they come back and participate in the forum. Coming back to the forum is important to ensure longevity of the newcomer which in turn is the backbone of any community. When members stay in communities it is then that communities are formed.

For research question 3, we wanted to see if the newcomers who continued to contribute to the community exhibited any evidence of learning. For this we looked at the content of messages from newcomers and coded them for change in help seeking skills overtime. We also looked at the role that the newcomer is playing in the community, so if a newcomer is taking a help giving role than they are demonstrating that they have either learned something while being on the forum or have prior knowledge that they are willing to share with the community members. We believe that this transition to help-givers is very critical to understand a community member life-cycle. We wanted to see if all newcomers who choose to stay on the forum go through this transition or not, and those who do, what is unique about them. Based on these analyses, in the fourth research question we collect and highlight the best practices of a successful newcomer.

4. RESULTS
4.1 Total Newcomers

A total of 129 threads were collected from four forums. In these 129 threads there were a total of 115 unique newcomers. Some newcomers were in more than one thread and therefore the number of newcomers is smaller than the number of threads. The number of threads is not standard across forums because we collected threads in a specified time period and all the messages that were identified as newcomer messages were collected. For that reason, we will be using percentages to talk about the results, so that we get a standard measure across the forums. Table 3 provided the number of threads collected and the number of newcomers identified from each forum.

	Firefox	Java	Koha
Threads	58	24	47
Newcomers	58	23	34
Total Newcomers	115		

Table 3: Total Number of Newcomers

4.2 Newcomers Behavior

This section presents the findings of newcomer behavior for model, intermediate, and can improve. Table 4 presents how the newcomers ranked in these three categories across the three forums. Our results show that the majority of newcomers fall into the model category and equal numbers of newcomers fall into intermediate and can improve categories.

The characteristics of the majority (63%) of newcomers are:

- Messages are positively framed
- Demonstrate prior knowledge
- Use comprehendible language
- Show effort / initiative to learn
- Responsiveness of newcomers
  - Respond back
  - Respond quickly
  - Acknowledge help that they receive

One of the issues that are encountered multiple times in studying any online community participation is the lack of response from the newcomers. That is why we looked at responsiveness of the newcomers by looking at three things. First, if they respond at all, second, if they do respond then how long do they take to respond? Finally when responding do they acknowledge help that they have received by being thankful or do they ignore the previous help and keep asking for more help. We found that overall 63% of the newcomers fall into the *model* category. Overall 18% of newcomers fall into *intermediate* category and 19% fall into *can improve* category.

	Firefox	Java	Koha	Overall
Model	60	48	76	63
Intermediate	26	22	3	18
Can Improve	14	30	21	19

Table 4: Newcomer Behavior Categorization (%)

4.3 Impact of Responder Behavior on Newcomer Integration

This section presents the findings on the impact of responder behavior on newcomer's continued participation and integration. Table 5 presents the findings on newcomers who only posted one time or those who did not return once they were condescended to. Table 6 compares the number of newcomers who did not return once they were not replied to with the newcomers who did not return once they were condescended to. Finally, we analyzed the future participation of newcomers who received encouraging responses, neutral responses, and condescending responses. The key findings are first summarized and then details follow:

- According to our dataset, almost all non returning newcomers can be attributed to not receiving a response or receiving a condescending response.
- A condescending response will lead an active member to cease participation

- Not all newcomers who do not receive a response to their first message stop participating
- Encouraging messages from responders are not any better than neutral messages when it comes to ensuring future participation of newcomers.

For this question the responder messages were coded as following:
No Response is when responders do not respond
Encouraging responses were coded by any form of positive affirmation exhibited by the responder.
Example of encouraging response: "Yes just tried it myself. I had the same results. The import list was blank. So it's nothing you are doing wrong."
Neutral responses were coded by using no positive or negative tone words, but rather a straightforward solution to the situation at hand.
Example of neutral response: "You need to change the folder name to the name of an existing folder or remove the entire label section to make it apply to all folder and change the name of the icon to the one that you have created."
Condescending responses were coded by use of sarcasm or patronizing language towards the newcomers. Such a response would presumably lead the newcomer to feel humbled or less likely to feel comfortable continue posting to the forum.
Example of condescending response: " 'it's not <fill in product name here>'s fault, we made it perfect. Our <insert name product here> is flawless... ish.' In other words, always assume it's your PC's fault, because you are such a newbie if you think you can outsmart someone from <fill in company here>"

	Firefox	Java	Koha
Not Replied To	7	42	41
Did Not Return	3	42	21
Condescended To	17	22	6
Did Not Return	12	13	3

Table 5: Impact of Responder Behavior %

Impact of No Response: We first looked at newcomer behavior after nobody responds to them when they post their first question. We counted the newcomers who were not replied to in their first message and then looked at their continued participation on the forum. (Table 5) If the newcomer does not receive any reply from the community and does not come back to post in the community, we categorize that as did not return after no reply. In our dataset we found that in Firefox and Koha, fifty percent of the newcomers who did not receive replies did not return to the forum. In Java, we saw that *hundred percent* of the newcomers who did not receive a reply did not come back showing a much higher negative impact on the newcomers in Java community.

Firefox had very few (4) messages that were not responded to, showing that it is a very active community and also that it is very responsive to newcomers. Koha had fifty percent of newcomers return to the forums. Java had the highest percentage of no reply messages and the highest percentage of non-returning newcomers. This indicates that the Java forums, because they are more technical in nature (programmer's forums) are more difficult for newcomers to integrate in because community is not responsive to newcomer messages. These numbers give us an insight into how integration/longevity of newcomers is dependent on the

environment of the forum. Some forums are more conducive to newcomers while some are not.

The finding that the no reply messages lead to not returning newcomers is not new. Previous research (as mentioned in literature review section) has shown that, receiving a reply is one of the critical factors to ensure newcomers return to a community. But, that cannot be the only factor responsible for non-returning newcomers and hence we also calculated, out of the total non-returning newcomers (one time posters) how many did not return because of responder behavior. These percentages of "did not return because of responder behavior" in Table 6 is the total of newcomers who did not return after not being replied to and after being condescended to. In Firefox 26 percent of newcomers are one time posters and 16 percent of them did not return back due to responder behavior. In Java, 43 percent of newcomers were one time posters, but there were a larger number of newcomers with multiple messages who did not come back because they received condescending messages from the responder.

Impact of Condescending Responses: Then we looked at newcomers who received condescending responses and analyzed their future participation. Even if they were condescended to/ insulted by the community did they come back? What happens if they were not necessarily condescended to in their first message, but at any time during their participation? In our dataset overall 15% newcomers were condescended to and 10% of them did not return back after being condescended to. Now looking at numbers from each of the forums (Table 5), we can say that again the maximum percentage of newcomers was condescended to in the Java forum – 22 percent. Almost half of the newcomers who were condescended to did not return to Java forums, even if they had posted more than once in the forum. Similarly, in Firefox most of the newcomers who were condescended to did not return to the forum. Firefox has the highest number of non-returning newcomers due to condescending messages. This shows that the newcomers in Firefox are more prone to turn away if they do not receive a welcoming environment, possibly because of the less technical nature of the newcomers. Koha was the forum that had least number of condescending messages by responders and half of these lead to non-returning newcomers. This shows that Koha had most welcoming group of responders and were rarely condescending to the newcomers.

	Firefox	Java	Koha
One Time Poster	29	43	26
Did not return because of responder behavior	15	55	24

Table 6: No Return vs No Return due to Responder Behavior %

Neutral and Encouraging Responses: Almost 75% of the messages that were posted by responders were coded neutral. Neutral messages provided guidance/advice, tips to the newcomers. A few messages were coded encouraging. Encouraging messages have comments such as, "you have done nothing wrong," "you are doing pretty good for a newbie," "good job!," etc. These messages not only did provide the help that was needed but also provided encouragement to the newcomer to try things and post more messages.

In our dataset, almost all the non-returning newcomers can be attributed to either no response or condescending response from responders. Newcomers do not necessarily need encouraging messages to come back to the forum and participate, as neutral messages had the same impact on the newcomers continued participation.

Not related to responders: Also important is the number of newcomers who only posted one message and then never came back, not necessarily because they were not replied to or were condescended to. The one time help seekers joined the forum and only posted one message (Table 6). In our dataset 31 percent of the total newcomers did not return back to the forums. Out of this 31% some were replied to and were given positive or neutral response by the community. In this study we do not have any information on this group of newcomers who do not come back. A larger percentage of these non-returning newcomers can actually be attributed to a discouraging response from the community. Either they were condescended to or were not replied to hence they stopped participating.

Multiple studies in past have shown that one time posters are the largest number of people in any community. We are trying to understand why they don't return, so that we can ensure their participation and integration. Fifty percent of newcomers post even after their first message was not replied to. Some of these in our dataset eventually fall in the model/intermediate user category showing that resilience or persistence is also another quality that works for newcomers when they enter a community.

4.4 Evidence of learning by Newcomers

Evidence of learning from research question 3 was coded by seeking change in help seeking skills overtime. We also looked at the role that the newcomer is playing in the community; if a newcomer is taking a help giving role than they are demonstrating that they have either learned something while being on the forum or have prior knowledge that they are willing to share with the community members.

We observed the following changes in the help seeking skills of the newcomers during their time on the forum:

- The later messages from newcomers were more polite and humble and individuals became very expressive of their gratitude when receiving help.
- In the later messages, most of the newcomers start with a direct, to the point question (as compared to statements like "I am stuck" in their first message) and give suitable details of what they have tried before asking the question.
- The number of clarification questions that they ask also reduces significantly as they post more and stay longer on the forum. For example one newcomer asked 11 clarification questions in their first thread and only one in their last thread.
- The approach to asking questions is not just to get a quick fix for the current problem but more conceptual understanding of why and how things work.
- Few of the newcomers, after posting for some time, starting adding their name and profession information to the message, showing more confidence in their abilities, as well as interest in creating an identity in the community.

We observed the following changes in the technical skills of newcomers after they have been actively participating on forum:

- The language that the newcomers were using to define their problems definitely underwent an obvious change, they start using *acronyms, technical jargon,* and *forum jargon* to express their questions and also give detailed technical explanations of what they have already tried.
- They mention they are using the latest versions of the software and change version during the time in which their messages were analyzed, showing more *confidence with newer versions of software.*

- In Java, people commonly post some code in questions, but in Firefox newcomers seldom post codes for scripting or programming. As they stay longer newcomers in Firefox ask help by *providing code* in their questions.
- The type of questions that the newcomers ask also involve *advanced features of software* and more advanced problem solving skills are needed to help them.

After this, we looked at all the messages from newcomers to see how many newcomers transitioned into the role of help-giver. We believe that this transition to help-givers is very critical to understanding community member life-cycle. Similarly to research question 3, a brief timeline of newcomer's role in each of their threads was created to see when they were help-seekers and when they acted as help-givers. We wanted to see if all newcomers who choose to stay on the forum go through this transition or not, and those who do, what is unique about them.

	Firefox	Java	Koha
One Time Poster	29	43	26
Returning Newcomers	71	57	74
Transitioning to Help Givers (% of returning newcomers)	22	69	68
Overall returning newcomers	69		
Overall newcomers transitioning to help givers	30		

Table 7: Newcomers taking role of Help-Givers %

In Table 7 we see that the percentage of newcomers who return back is highest in Koha, followed closely by Firefox, but the percentage of newcomers who also took the role of help giver is highest in Java. So, the newcomers in Java show the highest percentage of learning in these criteria despite the previous findings Java being a comparatively tough forum for newcomers. This means that the newcomers who stay around in Java forums are more likely to contribute back to the forum what they have learned and demonstrate their learning.

In our dataset overall 69% newcomers return and 30% newcomers become help givers. Showing that about one third of newcomers never come back (31%), about 30% newcomers become help givers, and leaving about 40% newcomers who stay help seekers.

4.5 Best Practices Demonstrated by Successful Newcomers

To develop a complete understanding of successful newcomers we looked at two sets of newcomers: the first set were coded as model newcomers in the first research question and the second set were newcomers who always got their problem solved by the community. So we collected the messages from all these newcomers and analyzed them for some patterns that were obvious across all of them. Some of these patterns are repeated from the previous observations, as expected. For instance all the characteristics that we developed for the first question are part of theme creation, then some of the characteristics that were part of changes in newcomer behavior towards learning were used and some additional common characteristics were identified when the message content was analyzed thoroughly.

Informative Subject Line: The newcomers who used informative subject lines for their first message improved chances of getting responses as well as getting their problems solved by the community. The newcomers who were not using informative subjective lines were sometimes told by a community member that their subject line is not helpful! And some messages with vague subject lines like "I am stuck,,help plz!!!" did not receive any response from the community members.

Tone: Successful newcomers were always positive, humble and grateful in their messages. Positive tone of a message from a newcomer ensured positive responses from responders usually. The newcomers who were friendly and positive usually got good quality responses as compared to the newcomers whose first message was critical of the community or software and who received non friendly remarks from the community.

Resilience/Persistence: As was shown in the results for research question two, the newcomers who were not discouraged by a first no reply or a condescending message eventually became successful contributing members of the community.

Direct, to the point question: This was defined by whether or not a newcomer posed a message that asked a clear, direct question. The newcomers who posted direct to the point questions received very direct and useful help from the community.

Prior efforts and knowledge: It was observed that when newcomers mentioned that they had already tried some options to fix their problem and have put efforts to look for a solution in the forums (usually search) then the responders were quick to respond and were very helpful. Seems like a message of legitimacy from the newcomer along the lines of "I have done my homework, can I get some help now."

Responsiveness This was calculated by looking at the time that the newcomer took to respond to the messages by responders and also if the newcomer responded at all to the messages from responders. Newcomers who engaged in a discussion with the responders by way of asking clarification questions or informing what they had done were more likely to stay longer in the community and contribute.

Acknowledgement of help Acknowledgement was coded in terms of whether or not the newcomer stated "thanks," "thank you" or some variation therein. Also, if the newcomer responded to the advice with, "I tried this" or some similar variation, it was coded as an acknowledgement of help. This is similar to responsiveness by newcomers.

Technical Language/ forum jargon: If the newcomers learn the technical jargon, acronyms of the community and use that to frame questions they get quicker replies. Also, if they form rapport with individuals from community and request for help by name, they get their problems solved.

Comprehendible use of language: This is just a basic requirement for receiving responses, if the newcomer does not post comprehendible messages or uses a language that the forum responders do not understand than their messages are removed from the forum by the moderators.

Initiative to learn: This is demonstrated by newcomers by engaging in a discussion with the community members, by asking conceptual "how" questions, and by showing willingness to learning order to apply this knowledge from the forums. Help givers seem to engage more with future posts from newcomers whom they have helped previously and who have engaged in a rich conversation.

Provides help to other members: Most of the newcomers that we studied as transitioning into help givers had most of the characteristics of model newcomers, showing that successful newcomers learn and share their own knowledge with the community. A successful newcomer contributes to the community by becoming an active member as help seeker as well as help giver whenever possible.

5. DISCUSSION

From the analysis of this data, there were some interesting points raised from newcomer and responder behavior in online communities. Some of our results are in line with previous findings about newcomer integration into online communities, such as community responsiveness in form of a reply is associated with increases in the newcomer's future participation [8], responsiveness to the community [10], and longevity in the group [9]. Replies signal that the group believes the newcomer is a potentially valuable prospective member worth its attention, motivating the newcomer to reciprocate by writing more and replying to others. These conversations help transform newcomers into committed contributors. On the other hand, posters interpret silence as rudeness or unfriendliness which leads to not returning to the forums [3].

Some of our results are completely opposite to previous results. For instance, as opposed to Joyce and Kraut (2006) we found little evidence that the nature of the reply influenced newcomers' commitment to the group. In their study the likelihood of posting again was not associated with the length of the reply, whether it was filled with words indicating agreement or negation or with words indicating positive or negative emotions. In our study we found that no reply as well condescending reply meant that the newcomer will not come back to the forum and is hence adversely impacted by the tone of the message from responder. In our dataset, we could attribute almost all non-returning newcomers to either a condescending reply or no reply from the community.

We also saw that the majority of newcomers exhibit "model" newcomer characteristics. In addition, we saw that newcomers are not a homogenous group of users and their behavior is varied and hence their experience in online communities is varied. We also looked at in-depth evidence of learning in these communities, because ultimately that is what we wanted to identify and measure. We were able to find and highlight evidence of learning the software as well as forum norms by looking at the patterns in the messages posted by newcomers over a period of time. We saw that the messages became more polite, grateful, and technical and to the point direct questions, as the newcomers stayed in the community and participated. So we observed a positive effect on the leaning of newcomers in these communities. And finally, based on all the analysis we were able to develop a set of characteristics of successful newcomers that can be used as a best practices guide for newcomers in such communities.

A key limitation of this research is that it is based on secondary data and not self reported data. As a follow-up to this study we would like to conduct triangulation interviews for the findings from secondary data. We would also like to identify and present self reported evidence of learning in these communities.

In future work, we have started looking at how the behavior of newcomers' impacts the quality of responses that they receive from the community and how can they ensure good quality responses.

6. ACKNOWLEDGMENTS

This material is based in part upon work supported by the National Science Foundation under Grant Number IEEECI #0935156. Any opinions, findings, and conclusions or recommendations expressed in this material are those of the author(s) and do not necessarily reflect the views of the National Science Foundation.

7. REFERENCES

[1] Adamic, L. A., J. Zhang, et al. Knowledge Sharing and Yahoo Answers: Everyone Knows Something. WWW. Beijing, China: (2008). 665-675.

[2] Ahuja, M. K., & Galvin, J. E. Socialization in Virtual Groups. Journal of Management, (2003). 29(2), 161-185.

[3] Arguello, J., Butler, B., Joyce, E., Kraut, R., Ling, K., & Wang, X. (2006). Talk to me: Foundations for successful individual-group interactions in online communities. In *Proceedings of the SIGCHI Conference on Human Factors in Computing Systems* (pp. 959-968). New York: ACM Press.

[4] Burke, M., & Kraut, R. E. Mind your p's and q's: When politeness helps and hurts in online communities. (2008) *Proc. CSCW'08.*

[5] Choi, B., Alexander, A., Kraut, R., Levine, J., Socialization Tactics in Wikipedia and Their Effects. Proc. *CSCW'10.*

[6] Ducheneaut, N. Socialization in an Open Source Software Community: A Socio-Technical Analysis. *Computer Supported Cooperative Work, 14*, (2005) 323-368.

[7] Jeong, H., Hmelo-Silver, A., Productive use of learning resources in an online problem-based learning Environment. *Computers in Human Behavior*, 26 (2010), 84–9

[8] Joyce, E., & Kraut, R. E. (2006). Predicting continued participation in newsgroups. *Journal of Computer-Mediated Communication, 11*(3).

[9] Kraut, R., Wang, X., Butler, B., Joyce, E., and Burke, M. Beyond Information: Developing the Relationship between the Individual and the Group in Online Communities. *Information Systems Research* 2010.

[10] Lampe, C., & Johnston, E. (2005). Follow the (slash) dot: Effects of feedback on new members in an online community. In *Proceedings of the ACM SIGGROUP Conference on Supporting Group Work* (pp. 11-20). New York: ACM Press.

[11] Muller, N. Sadat Shami, David R. Millen, and Jonathan Feinberg. 2010. We are all lurkers: consuming behaviors among authors and readers in an enterprise file-sharing service. In *Proceedings of the 16th ACM international conference on Supporting group work* (GROUP '10). ACM, New York, NY, USA, 201-210. DOI=10.1145/1880071.1880106 http://doi.acm.org/10.1145/1880071.1880106

[12] Muller. 2012. Lurking as personal trait or situational disposition: lurking and contributing in enterprise social media. In *Proceedings of the ACM 2012 conference on Computer Supported Cooperative Work* (CSCW '12). ACM, New York, NY, USA, 253-256. DOI=10.1145/2145204.2145245 http://doi.acm.org/10.1145/2145204.2145245

[13] Nam, K., Ackerman, M.S. and Adamic, L. Questions in, Knowledge iN? A study of Naver's Question Answering Community *ACM Conference on Human Factors in Computing Systems* (CHI'09), p.779-788 (2009)

[14] Preece, Jennifer and Shneiderman, Ben (2009) "The Reader-to-Leader Framework: Motivating Technology-Mediated Social Participation," *AIS Transactions on Human-Computer Interaction* (1) 1, pp. 13-32

[15] Singh, V. and Twidale, M.B. "The Confusion of Crowds: non-dyadic help interactions" *Proc. CSCW (2008).*

[16] von Krogh, G., S. Spaeth, et al. Community, joining, and specialization in open source software innovation: a case study. (2003) Research Policy **32**: 1217-1241.

[17] Welser, H. T., E. Gleave, et al. "Visualizing the Signatures of Social Roles in Online Discussion Groups." (2007). Journal of Social Structure **8** (2): 1-32.

[18] Yang, J., L. A. Adamic, et al. Competing to Share Expertise: the Taskcn Knowledge Sharing Community. (2008). Association for the Advancement of Artificial Intelligence.

[19] Yuan, Y. C., D. Cosley, et al. "The Diffusion of a Task Recommendation System to Facilitate Contributions to an Online Community." (2009). Journal of Computer-Mediated Communication **15**: 32-59.

[20] Zhang, J., M. S. Ackerman, et al. Expertise Networks in Online Communities: Structure and Algorithms. WWW. (2007)..

[21] Zhang, J., M. S. Ackerman, et al. QuME: A Mechanism to Support Expertise Finding In Online Help-seeking Communities. UIST. (2007)

Purposeful Gaming & Socio-Computational Systems: A Citizen Science Design Case

Nathan Prestopnik
Syracuse University
337 Hinds Hall
Syracuse, NY 13244-4100
315-443-2911

napresto@syr.edu

Kevin Crowston
Syracuse University
348 Hinds Hall
Syracuse, NY 13244-4100
315-443-1676

crowston@syr.edu

ABSTRACT

Citizen science is a form of social computation where members of the public are recruited to contribute to scientific investigations. Citizen-science projects often use web-based systems to support collaborative scientific activities, making them a form of computer-supported cooperative work. However, finding ways to attract participants and confirm the veracity of the data they produce are key issues in making such systems successful. We describe a series of web-based tools and games currently under development to support taxonomic classification of organisms in photographs collected by citizen-science projects. In the design science tradition, the systems are purpose-built to test hypotheses about participant motivation and techniques for ensuring data quality. Findings from preliminary evaluation and the design process itself are discussed.

Categories and Subject Descriptors

H.5.3. [**Group and Organization Interfaces**]: Collaborative Computing.

General Terms

Design

Keywords

Citizen-science, socio-computational systems, purposeful gaming motivation, engagement, data quality.

1. INTRODUCTION

Citizen science is a phenomenon where members of the public are recruited to contribute to scientific investigations [1, 2]. Notably successful citizen-science projects include asking participants to help classify astronomical photographs, report bird sightings, count insects in the field, or use spatial reasoning skills to align genomes or fold protein strings. Such activities draw many individuals into a cooperative endeavor toward a common scientific goal. They feature a mix of tasks that can only be performed by people (e.g., making an observation or classifying an image) supported by computational scaffolding to organize these efforts. As such, citizen science often relies on some form of socio-computational system. While citizen science has a long history, such systems are relatively new, providing a variety of open questions of great interest to those who study socio-

computational systems, as well as to scientists who may wish to use citizen science approaches to support their own research.

An interesting and sometimes challenging issue for citizen science is that some scientific topics are highly "charismatic" but many others are not. For example, bird watching, astronomy, and conservation all have existing communities of interest and a certain appeal, even for non-enthusiasts. However, important work is also being conducted in areas that attract much less public interest, such as moth, mold, or lichen classification. While enthusiasts exist for virtually all areas of the natural sciences, socio-computational systems rely on attracting large numbers of participants. As a result, the motivations of citizen science participants are important to understand, to attract new participants and retain old ones.

Furthermore, while some citizen scientists are quite expert, many are not and indeed, many may be novices. Therefore, successful projects must develop scientific tasks that can be performed by novices, while still ensuring the interest of those with more experience. Assuring the quality of data produced by the non-expert citizens using these systems is also of concern. The specific interest of this research, therefore, is to explore the relationships that exist between citizen science, socio-computational system design, attraction and retention of participants, and the impact of these on data quality.

Unfortunately, it is difficult to use current, real-world citizen-science projects as vehicles for exploring motivation, participation, users, technology, and data quality. The challenges are practical: citizen science project developers, researchers, and managers have little time available to devote toward research projects not directly related to their specific object of inquiry. Because currently instantiated citizen-science projects are working production systems, it is difficult to adjust project parameters, conduct experiments, issue surveys, interview participants, or otherwise gather information about the citizen science phenomenon. Invasive data collection efforts are likely to be disruptive and may have deleterious impacts on existing participant enthusiasm and data quality. In short, the potential drawbacks of granting complete access to socio-computational researchers outweigh any benefits that might accrue.

On the other hand, low-impact methods of investigation (e.g., interviewing or surveying staff members or researchers, passively gathering information about project websites and systems, etc.) are less likely to produce data required to address motivational and data-quality questions. Studying citizen science without fine control over the systems of interest creates a different problem: artificiality will infect any knowledge generated by such research, as simulations, mock-ups, and de-contextualized inquiry substitute for realistic exploration of actual systems that are highly situated within complex problem spaces.

We address these challenges by developing socio-computational systems explicitly designed to serve a dual purpose: as vehicles for scientific inquiry and as functional and useful systems built and deployed to solve specific, real-world problems. Building systems is not a new approach to research, but the approach has recently been reconceptualized under the name design science. This approach resides in the familiar territory of system design and evaluation, but wraps these well-known activities around a broader research agenda targeted at natural or social-psychological science. The strength of this approach is that complex phenomenon such as socio-computational systems and/or citizen science can be explored in a very realistic manner, while maintaining a great deal of control over the user experience.

The remainder of this paper is divided into three parts. First, a discussion of design science is presented. Second, an ongoing design science project in the socio-computational and citizen science domains is described. This project involves the creation of several games and tools to support an important science task in the biological sciences: species classification. Finally, results from the design process so far and from preliminary evaluations are reported, including discussions of the design science approach as a vehicle for socio-computational systems scholarship.

2. DESIGN SCIENCE

Design science is an approach to scholarly study that couples traditional research methodologies with the development of an IT artifact to address natural science or social-psychological research questions coupled with design-related problems [3-5]. Design science is practiced (mostly without using the term) in many domains, particularly human-computer interaction (HCI) and computer science (CS) more generally. The term and its formal conceptualization come from the field of information systems (IS), where system design is often viewed as atheoretical and so not research. In this setting, rigorous conceptualizations of design as a research tool are necessary to encourage its broader acceptance. However, even in fields where system design is generally embraced, the reconceptualization can be valuable, as the focus on designing useful artifacts often results in inattention to larger research questions. For example, in [6] many HCI evaluation practices are criticized as "usability evaluations" instead of scientific "evaluations for research", what [7] calls the "I did this and it's cool" form of study.

Design science research has two equally important outcomes: 1) a functional IT artifact that helps address a specific, challenging, and practical design problem within a given context, and 2) meaningful scholarly contributions to a field of inquiry. Compared to typical social-science research approaches, the design science approach requires additional components, including interactions with subject-matter experts (SMEs), a situational focus on the context in which a design will be deployed as well as system building and testing. Compared to typical systems research, the approach requires explicit use of theory to guide design decisions and—importantly—an ability to draw more general conclusions about these theories from the experience of building the system.

The problem spaces addressed by design science inquiry are typically complex, sometimes referred to as "wicked" problems because they defy easy or obvious answers [8-10]. Problems suitable for a design science approach include both those that are unsolved and those which offer opportunities for newer or better solutions [3]. However, to be meaningful to researchers outside of the specific problem space, the IT artifact must also become a vehicle for broader natural science or social-psychological inquiry. Theory, design and evaluation are thus interrelated in design science research, coherent pieces of a whole [11] and conducted iteratively [3, 4].

Theory: The word "theory" is used broadly here [12], encompassing the adoption of existing theory as a lens through which to approach design, as well as consultation with experts and review of non-theoretical, project-specific design literature. This stage may also result in the generation of new theory, produced either from literature or from data, and conceptualized either prior to design of the IT artifact, during its development, or after its evaluation. The theory stage may be seen as both a beginning and an end to design science research: theory adopted early will inform design, and new theory will come from it.

Design: Design science research revolves around the design of an IT artifact, where theoretical and practical underpinnings shape a functional system. The designed artifact may ultimately produce new theory, so artifact design must take future evaluation into account. The design scientist must always keep in mind the research questions to be addressed through research evaluation of the artifact.

Evaluation: The evaluation stage is about more than saying "yes this worked," or, "no, this didn't work." It must address the project's broader research questions by validating adopted theory or leading to the generation of new theory. Evaluation is not always an end point for research; evaluation will often suggest ways to improve the artifact (as a system to address the problem space or as a research tool) in its next design iteration.

3. CITIZEN SCIENCE DESIGN CASE

In this section, we describe our socio-computational system project situated in the citizen science domain, with emphasis on our research goals, the problem space, and design parameters.

3.1 Research Goals

Our study addresses two research questions. First, a critical issue in socio-computational system design generally, and citizen science systems in particular, is attracting and retaining enough participants to make achievement of project goals possible. Systems with too little participation will be unlikely to generate meaningful quantities of scientific data.

To address this question, we draw on psychological theories about motivation [e.g. 13]. In [14], three basic motivations for individuals who are engaged in collective on-line activities are suggested: money, love, and glory. For citizen-science projects, offering payment to participants is rarely an option (project resources are typically too low), and most participants do not expect compensation for their efforts. Instead, participants indicate that inherent interest in the subject of scientific inquiry, the relevance of data collection efforts to particular interests or hobbies, the perception that a project will be fun and engaging, an interest in collaborate with experts, altruistic reasons, and hope for broader recognition as reasons for becoming involved in citizen-science projects [15-19]. These reasons match well with the notions of "love" and "glory" as motivators [14]. There has been less scholarly or practical attention paid to how citizen science systems might be designed to motivate participants who do not hold these predominantly intrinsic motivations. As a result, most citizen-science projects rely heavily on participants who have preexisting enthusiasm for the scientific topic of the project, be it astronomy, bird watching, or classifying insects.

In the broader collective computing domains, several models for attracting participation have been deployed. In systems such as von Ahn's reCAPTCHA [20], which facilitates optical character recognition (OCR) on scanned books, the system is devised as an obstacle between users and their goals; reCAPTCHAs are used to verify that login attempts to web systems are coming from a human user, and to log in, users must use the reCAPTCHA tool. Other systems, such as the ESP game (an image tagging system) [21], Phetch (which produces accessible descriptions of images) [22], or TagATune (where users tag music clips) [23] are designed as games, capitalizing on "love" forms of motivation, and giving people enjoyable activities to undertake while also producing meaningful work almost as a by-product.

Games in particular seem to have great potential as a motivator for participation and as a tool for producing high quality scientific data. However, from a review of citizen science websites [2], it seems that few existing projects use games to motivate participation. Notable exceptions include *Fold It*, which disguises the science of protein string folding as a highly engaging puzzle game, and *Phylo*, where players compare genetic sequences in a colorful and abstract puzzle game. Both capitalize on human spatial reasoning abilities to solve problems that are difficult to automate. The *Fold It* player pages (http://fold.it/portal/players) reveals that more than 300,000 players are contributing to this project; furthermore, *Fold It* recently made headlines for an important AIDS research breakthrough generated by players of the game. Some projects, like *Stardust@Home*, incorporate game-like elements such as leader boards, high scores, or other participation metrics, but do not frame their scientific activities as games per se. Scholarly study of socio-computational games and games for citizen science may produce insights into how different participant groups can be attracted to citizen-science projects and motivated to participate in them.

Our second research question is about techniques for ensuring data quality, a necessary precondition for further scientific use of the data, but difficult for several reasons. First, for many scientific problems there is "ground truth," i.e. correct answers. Participant opinions are not as inherently valid as they might be in systems designed to produce, for example, image tags for search engines. For data to be scientific, valid, and accepted, the right answers must be produced by participants and confirmed by experts. Second, in many areas of science, specialized knowledge is required to provide data, but few citizen science participants are experts. Furthermore, the effect of systems (especially game-like interactions) on data quality is largely unknown. Therefore, finding methods to turn scientific tasks into things that non-scientists can do well, as well as finding techniques to confirm the validity of participant-provided data, are important research goals. To address these questions, we draw on theories from the problem domain, which we describe next.

3.2 Problem Space
The problem space we address in this design research comes from the biological sciences, particularly entomology, botany, and oceanography. In this domain, experts, enthusiasts, and curious members of the general public routinely collect and upload photographs of different living things. A photograph of an insect, plant, or animal, tagged with the date and location where it was taken, can provide valuable scientific data, e.g., on how urban sprawl impacts local ecosystems or evidence of local, regional, or global climactic shifts. However, to be useful, it is necessary to know what the picture is of, expressed in scientific terms, i.e., the scientific name of the species depicted. Some participants have the necessary knowledge (e.g., avid birders can generally identify particular bird species), but many potential participants do not.

To aid in identification of the species of specimens, biologists have developed taxonomic keys, which identify species from their particular combinations of characteristics, known as character-state combinations (i.e., attributes and values). The specific characters and states vary by taxon, but are broadly similar in structure. For example, a moth character might be its "orbicular spot," with states including, "absent," "dark," "light," etc. Given sufficient characters and states, it is possible to identify a photographed specimen to a specific family, genus, species, or even sub-species.

A challenging aspect of this problem is that researchers working within the same biological or ecological disciplines do not necessarily agree upon taxonomic keys. In fact, many researchers develop their own key variations to support their own specific research endeavors. Keys are therefore typically written for expert users, and are often complex, highly variable, and difficult to translate into a form that will be suitable for use in a socio-computational system, where expert understanding of characters, states, and taxonomic identification cannot be assumed.

A second challenge is that even with an established key, some characters and states are beyond the ability of most members of the general public to identify without training (e.g., the previous "orbicular spot" example). Others require true expert knowledge to apply (for example, classifying species by their sex organs). In some cases, especially for sub-species, true identifications cannot be made without access to specialized equipment; for example, some species are distinguishable only through their genetic makeup. This means that an IT artifact designed to support the classification task will be unlikely to effectively support both extremely knowledgeable users and extremely novice users; experts will require advanced tools with great flexibility, while novices may require simplified systems that have expert knowledge pre-built into them. In both cases, a web-based classification system will only be able to support some kinds of characters and states, while others will be impossible.

3.3 Design Parameters
To explore the motivations of citizen science participants and address the challenge of species classification in the biological sciences, a series of IT artifacts were designed and implemented. IT artifacts were designed and developed by a team of 21 professionals and students with varied technical and artistic expertise. Thirteen of the developers were hired on the project as either part- or full-time employees or volunteers. The remaining developers participated through their coursework (i.e. developing systems or components of systems for a class). Because this research is supported by a large and diverse group of developers, an ambitious program of design and development was organized, including five components that address specific aspects of the problem space, enabling exploration of our research questions.

3.3.1 Artifact 1: Citizen Sort

The IT artifacts hosted on the *Citizen Sort* website (http://www.citizensort.org) include both tools and games, organized along a continuum from "tool-like" to "game-like." Arranging the systems in this manner allows for comparative evaluations of participant motivation with regard to tools, games, and IT artifacts that fall somewhere in between. In addition, this arrangement allows researchers to manipulate specific website elements to either direct participants to tools or games or allow participants to self-sort based on their individual interests.

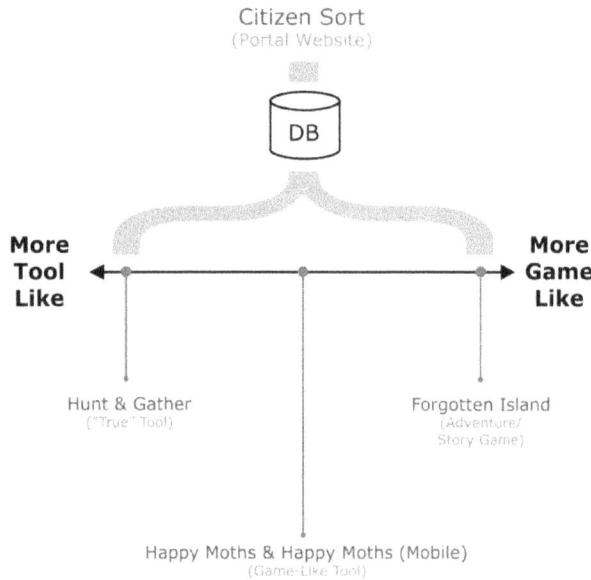

Figure 1. The *Citizen Sort* research design shows a theorized continuum from very tool-like instantiations to very game-like instantiations. Different user groups are hypothesized to be motivated by artifacts in different places on this continuum based on their personal goals, expectations, and interests vis-a-vis citizen science.

Four of the major artifacts of this design effort are organized around a fifth, a portal website (*Citizen Sort*) designed to direct participants to a variety of tools and games for biological classification. The portal website controls global functionality, including features like user-account management, administrative management of tools and games, content management of the website itself, dissemination of project data, and management of subsidiary projects. A centralized database ties all IT artifacts in this project tightly together.

3.3.2 Artifact 2: Hunt & Gather Tool

Hunt & Gather is a "true" tool, designed without additional motivational elements (see [24] for a discussion of motivators vs. satisfiers in web applications). *Hunt & Gather* lets users create characters and states for themselves, tag large numbers of photos with those characters and states, and let other knowledgeable individuals work with the characters, states, and photos on a per project basis.

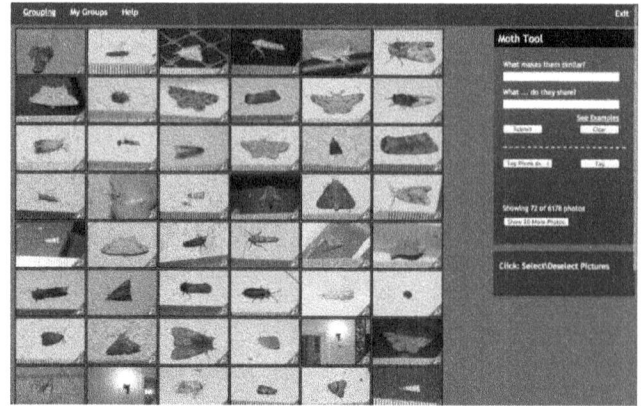

Figure 2. *Hunt & Gather* classification tool. Users can set up a collection of photos and work together to develop a taxonomy of characters and states.

Hunt & Gather will allow socio-computational researchers to explore the motivations of users who are attracted to citizen science tools, rather than games; it is hypothesized that these users will be experts or enthusiasts. Furthermore, characters and states created by novices or enthusiasts can be compared to characters and states generated by professional scientists. *Hunt & Gather* will help explore how good non-expert users are at producing characters and states that might be useful to experts in the biological sciences.

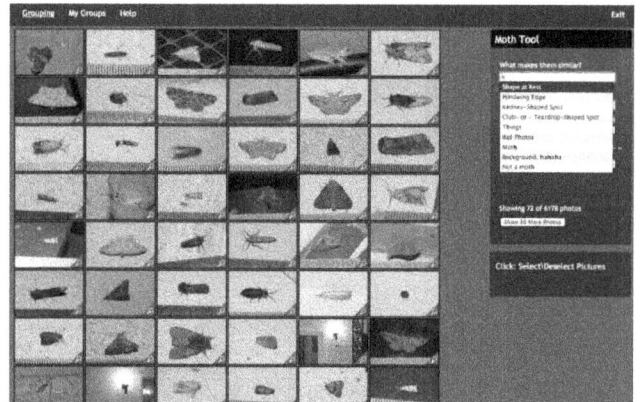

Figure 3. *Hunt & Gather* allows a group of users to collectively develop and refine taxonomies for a given collection of photos. Drop-down suggestions keep users informed about the characters and states that have already been defined. Pre-set choices for bad photos can be used to filter unwanted images from the collection permanently.

3.3.3 Artifact 3: Happy Moths

Happy Moths (designed to be renamed for each new instantiation: *Happy Sharks, Happy Plants, etc.*) is a "game-like tool," in that it offers tool-like functionality but structured as a game. Participants are presented with a set of ten photographs of some organism (in *Happy Moths*, pictures of moths) and then asked to identify the various character-states of each. One difference between *Happy Moths* and *Hunt & Gather* is that the design aims to increase participant motivation by providing a score (per round and overall) giving feedback on performance. *Happy Moths* players are scored based on how well their classification decisions match those of a previously classified-photo that is seeded into the game (the "Happy Moth"). Because players will not know which photo is the Happy Moth until the end of each game, they need to do well on all photos to ensure a high score.

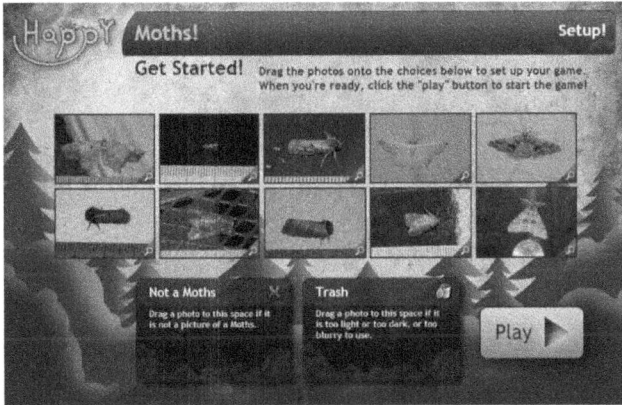

Figure 4. *Happy Moths* **setup screen, where photos can be pre-sorted as bad images or not an example of the specimen of interest.**

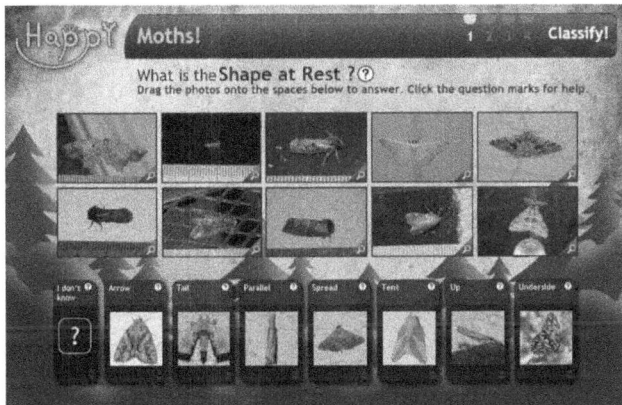

Figure 5. *Happy Moths* **game round, where players are asked to answer a question (character) by dragging a photo to the appropriate answer (states).**

A second difference is that *Happy Moths* is built around characters and states established by professional scientists as a useful taxonomic key. *Happy Moths* is a more controlled experience for users, and may ultimately produce more reliable data when used by novices or enthusiasts with limited classification experience. As well, the quality of a player's performance on the Happy Moth can be taken as evidence of their data quality, and agreement among classifications performed by different users on the same photo can be used as an indicator of data validity.

Happy Moths also includes a mobile version, developed as an HTML5 mobile app and deployable on a variety of mobile devices. The mobile version of the game is very similar to the web-based version of *Happy Moths* (both systems contain the same logic and draw upon the same API and database). *Happy Moths (Mobile)* will introduce mobile technology as a variable in comparative evaluation studies; it will be useful in exploring whether mobile technologies make this game seem more or less game-like to users and whether ubiquitous access will help attract participants. It can also be used to collect data about where, how, and by whom the mobile version of the game might be used, and it will be possible to compare the quality of data produced by players of the two versions of the game.

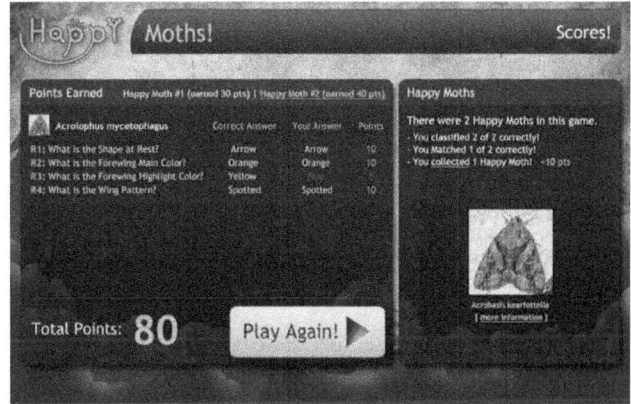

Figure 6. *Happy Moths* **scores page, where players are provided feedback on their performance, and rewarded for correctly classifying the hidden "Happy Moth."**

3.3.4 Artifact 5: Forgotten Island

Finally, an important goal of this research is to explore the full range of the "tool-like" to "game-like" continuum. Few citizen-science projects attempt to leverage the power of storytelling or fantasy in games to motivate users. In [25-27], these elements and others are noted as key motivators in educational games; it is hypothesized that such motivators will hold true in citizen science games as well. To explore this hypothesis, as well as to generate insight into the kinds of users who might be attracted by such a game, the fifth IT artifact in this design-science project is a point-and-click adventure game called *Forgotten Island*.

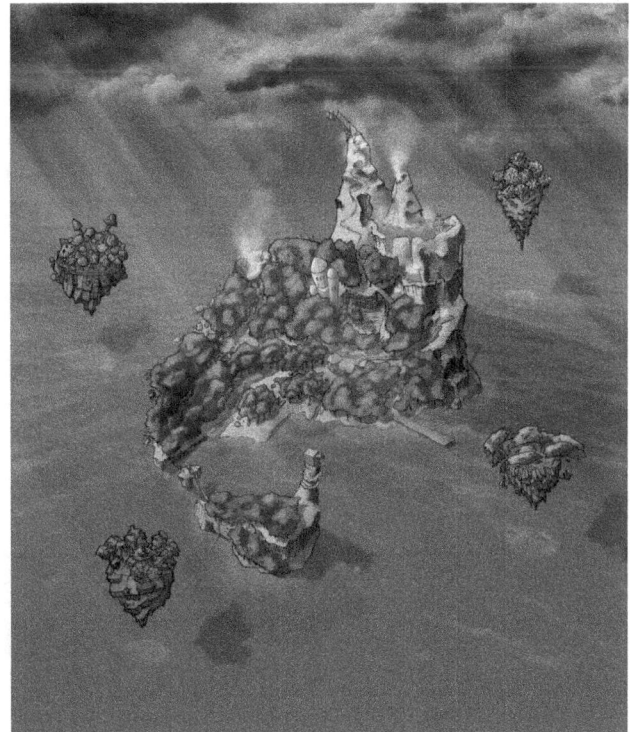

Figure 7. *Forgotten Island's* **game world is a mysterious island that the player explores and rebuilds while undertaking citizen science classification task. The game world was deliberately designed in a hand-drawn style to accentuate that exploring will be a fun, engaging, and whimsical experience for the player.**

Figure 8. The game world is made more mysterious and detailed through immersive, explorable locations. Unlocking these locations and advancing the story requires in-game tools and equipment that can only be acquired by undertaking the classification activity to earn game resources.

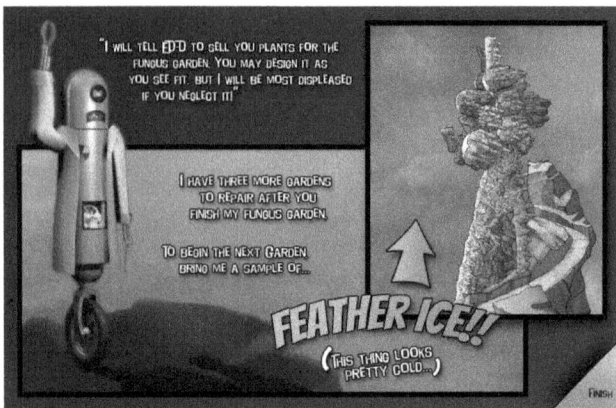

Figure 9. In *Forgotten Island*, the game story motivates the classification task. Story elements are conveyed to players through a comic book style interface.

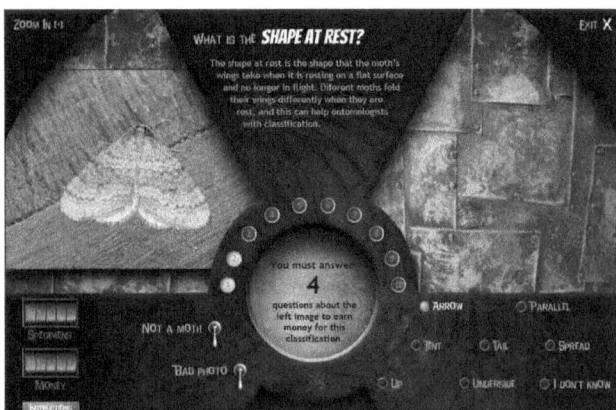

Figure 10. The classification task itself is similar to *Happy Moths*. Key differences include that players in *Forgotten Island* classify one photo at a time to preserve a better balance between game experience and science experience, and that classifications earn the player endogenous rewards (game money) instead of feedback on their scientific contributions and point-based scores in competition with other players.

Forgotten Island is story driven, featuring an island to explore and a mystery to unravel. Players still classify insects, plants, or animals as in *Happy Moths*, but the classification task is motivated by the story and designed to fit into the background texture of the game. Players use classification as a way to earn game money that can be used to purchase equipment or items to progress the fantasy story.

Forgotten Island allows us to explore how endogenous reward systems can motivate players to participate in a scientific collaboration. It will also help explore how established taxonomies of motivational game features for learning [e.g. 25, 26, 27] might apply to non-educational games. Two additional and conflicting hypotheses will be evaluated: 1) that a fantasy adventure game will improve scientific data quality because players will be immersed in the game experience, motivated, and willing to provide high quality data, or 2) that a fantasy adventure game will reduce data quality because players will be more interested in progressing the story than in doing science, and will be willing to "cheat" on the science task to get ahead in the game.

4. EVALUATION METHOD

Prior to starting system development, background research was conducted in the form of literature review, analysis of ongoing citizen science project systems, and SME interviews. Ten SME interviews with nine scientists and developers who are currently undertaking citizen-science projects were conducted. This phase of the project informed research questions and planning for the IT artifacts to be developed, and is reported in more detail elsewhere. As design progressed, additional SMEs were consulted, including naturalists with expertise in classification. Consultation with experts is ongoing, shifting between formal, interview-style consultation and informal participatory-research approaches [28].

This research is in now the design stage, with limited formal evaluation so far. In design science, however, design activities are a central aspect of research and are a vehicle for producing new knowledge. Accordingly, we have developed an evaluation strategy that includes some evaluation activities that take place during design. Individual developers working on the project have been asked to periodically review the games and tools where they have had a central development role, as well as games and tools where they have not been as directly involved. These reviews focus on the artifact itself, rather than individual work practices. Currently, 31 reviews have been collected on three of the five projects (*Happy Moths*, *Hunt & Gather*, and *Forgotten Island*).

In addition, formal focus group evaluation sessions have been conducted, targeted at two different versions of *Happy* Moths. An early focus group session brought four expert entomologists together codify their knowledge of the classification task and to collect their impressions of an early prototype of the *Happy Moths* game. Results from this session resulted in several changes to the game. Participants in a second set of focus groups were students as a large university located in the northeastern United States. Five participants were recruited from an outdoor club and environmental conservation courses, while three were recruited from the university's School of Information Studies. These groups were classified as "nature" and "gamer" participants respectively. Participants were asked to play a new version of *Happy Moths* and provide their opinions on two different visual designs: a "gamer" version designed to look more like a video game, with no naturalistic visual motifs other than the classification photos themselves, and a "nature" version designed to appear more tool-like while showcasing a variety of nature imagery and content.

5. PRELIMINARY RESULTS & DISCUSSION

5.1 Participant Groups

During the first *Happy Moths* focus group session, SMEs helped to define three groups of potential participants who will be important for this research: 1) experts (professional scientists), 2) enthusiasts (individuals with intrinsic interest in science and/or the particular topic of a citizen science project), and 3) gamers (ordinary citizens with no particular interest in citizen science, but at least some interest in online games or entertainment). Because it may be difficult for some projects to attract enough expert and enthusiast users to be viable (especially those lacking "charismatic science" that is inherently interesting to many people), the gamer user group is of particular interest. The gamer group is hypothesized to be much larger than the enthusiast or expert groups, making it a potentially valuable source of participants. However, the gamer group, by definition, is composed of individuals who have virtually no knowledge of scientific classification. Finding ways to make the classification task enjoyable and, critically, understandable to these users will be an important outcome. One way of addressing this challenge, used in *Happy Moths*, is to have SMEs generate character questions and state answers that make sense to laypeople. So, for example, *Happy Moths* asks about simpler character-state combinations such as color or shape, and avoids complex questions about "discal spots," orbicular spots," "reniform spots," etc. In many cases, technical language has also been simplified to help lay users understand characters and states without the need for extensive training. In the *Happy Moths* focus group, SMEs had conflicting opinions about these approaches; some agreed that simplifying the tasks and language would be beneficial and still produce good data, while others felt that more technical nomenclature should be preserved as a learning opportunity for participants.

This disagreement raises another point about the differences between users: systems that motivate gamers may actually be de-motivating to enthusiasts and vice-versa. In the first *Happy Moths* focus group session, researchers suggested that systems designed to appeal to gamers (e.g., *Forgotten Island*) have a high likelihood of alienating enthusiasts. Enthusiasts are seeking opportunities to explore their passions and interests, while gamers are seeking entertainment. Over the course of design and evaluation so far, it has emerged that as a system focuses more on entertainment, it imposes increasing obstacles on enthusiasts who seek rapid access to their hobby of choice. For example, *Forgotten Island* paces the classification task and requires players to explore a variety of locations, collect items, and undertake many other story-driven activities besides classification. For an enthusiast interested in classification, these extra activities may be perceived as annoying wastes of time, rather than as engaging or fun. Similarly, SMEs frequently suggest that players will be more engaged and motivated if they learn something about science, but it is not clear that gamers will be similarly motivated.

5.2 The Role of Iteration

The purpose of taking each project in this design science study through several design iterations is threefold: each iteration 1) improves the IT artifact's ability to address the problem space, 2) produces new research findings, and 3) helps to eliminate poor system design as a confounding factor for research.

In the case of *Citizen Sort*, many specific design decisions have been discussed with the project's SMEs, particularly the decision-making that went into the *Happy Moths* game, which has (because it encapsulates the core classification task) received the most formal evaluation to date. Many design decisions have been upheld, while a few have been questioned (e.g., the visual style of *Happy Moths*, where expert reviewers suggested that a more "natural" or "nature-themed" design would better appeal to enthusiast users). In some cases, design decisions have been rejected outright. In the first iteration of *Happy Moths*, music was included, but focus group SMEs and the developers themselves unanimously rejected the choice to include music after testing it in several different settings. Now finishing its third and final iteration prior to public release, *Happy Moths* has no music and a streamlined game mechanic that is expected to be more fun and less distracting for players.

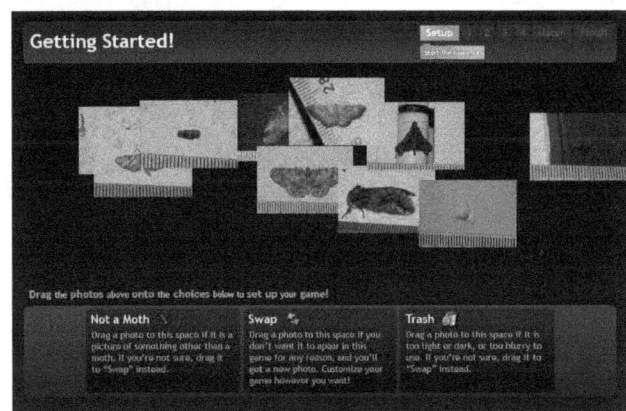

Figure 11. The "gamer" version of *Happy Moths* (version 2).

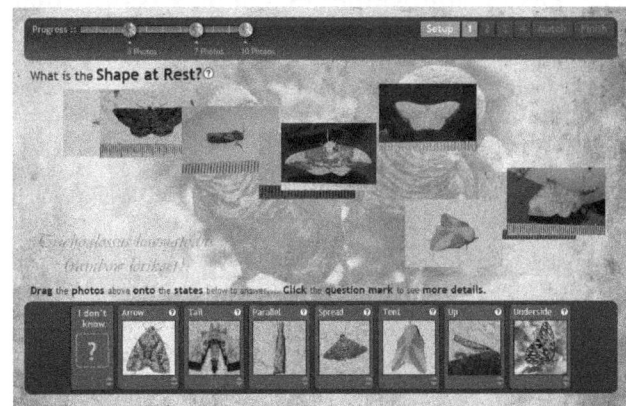

Figure 12. The "nature" version of *Happy Moths* (version 2).

The second round of *Happy Moths* focus groups were specifically designed to test another issue which came out of preliminary evaluation: the visual design of the game. Early visual workups used a contrasting color scheme of dark blue and bright yellow-orange. However, SMEs who are participants in our design partnership, as well as early focus group SMEs, suggested that this "gamer" design "did not emphasize nature enough." Both groups of SMEs were composed of professional naturalists with enthusiasm for science and the outdoors; the blue-orange color scheme didn't speak to them as players. To explore this issue in more detail, second round focus group participants were asked to play one of two versions of the game: a version using the blue-orange color scheme, and a functionally identical version using a nature-themed color scheme and nature imagery.

These focus groups revealed a mix of opinions on visual design. Both gamer and nature participants stated that each design was well conceived and visually attractive. In general, nature participants preferred the nature version of the game, while gamer participants preferred the gamer version. There was agreement that the nature version better supported the science task thematically, while the gamer version's contrasting color scheme made it easier to see and interact with the game space. Participants also agreed that the visual design was a less important issue than usability and how fun and engaging the game's scoring mechanic would be. These findings were very similar to opinions supplied by the development team during individual formal reviews.

We designed the third and final version of *Happy Moths* (see section 3.3.3) drawing extensively upon all of the previously collected evaluation data: focus groups (SME, gamer, and nature), participatory interactions with partner SMEs, developer reviews, and our own prior design experience (for a discussion of design precedent and design as an experience-based activity, see [29, 30]). Great attention was paid to the many perspectives espoused over the course of previous evaluations and design activities, resulting in a greatly polished, more engaging, and more usable game. More extensive evaluation of *Happy Moths* will take place over several months as the game is published online and played by participants as a live citizen science project. This "evaluation for research" [6] will help us to address our deeper research questions on socio-computational system design, motivation, and data quality. The evaluations conducted so far have already helped direct us toward several possible areas of interest.

5.3 Task Gamification vs. Game Taskification

Socio-computational and citizen science games are often developed by "gamifying" an existing task. The *Happy Moths* game adopts this approach, taking a classification task and adding game elements to it: a game-like visual design, scores for doing well, achievements for long-term involvement, leader boards, and high scores to promote competition between players.

The *Citizen Sort* project explores an alternative model, referred to here as "game taskification." In this approach, the typical model of turning tasks into simple games is inverted; rather, the designer starts with the game, rather than the task, designing an interactive entertainment experience and drawing upon well-understood commercial game design principles [e.g. 31]. Rather than simply re-conceptualizing a given task as a game-like activity (i.e. giving players game points for classifying a photo), the game designer must conceptualize the task as just one element or mechanic to be part of a larger (possibly *much* larger) game world. To be effective at generating data, the task must be incorporated in a way that makes it critical to progress through the game, but it need not be the focus of the player experience as it would be in a gamified task. For example, the scientific task might become a way of earning game money, a tool to power up one's character, a lock-picking puzzle, or a host of other possibilities.

The game-taskification approach opens up dramatic possibilities for purposeful games: exploring scientific content through unique themes and stories during play, building unexpected and exciting connections between entertainment and science, or engaging large segments of the population who may not be motivated by gamified tasks alone. However, the game taskification approach is rarely pursued in citizen science or socio-computational system design. Our design and evaluation process for *Forgotten Island* helps to explore one possible reason why not.

Simply put, turning a task into an enjoyable game is a complex endeavor. Developing a fantasy/story game like *Forgotten Island*, which "seduces" players into doing real science [32, 33] without foregrounding the task itself, is an exponentially larger effort than simply implementing the task. By placing the scientific task into the background of a fantasy game, developers are suddenly confronted with a host of new design requirements that are unrelated to the central rationale for designing the game (i.e., in the citizen science domain, collecting scientific data). These include developing a story and writing a script, creating locations, producing concept and final artwork, designing characters, envisioning and producing a compelling sound design, composing a musical score, programming complex functionality such as path finding or AI algorithms, planning and implementing puzzles, and more. In short, the research scientist must take on the role of game director, a role for which few are prepared.

Evaluations of *Forgotten Island*, which includes all of the above elements as design requirements, have underscored these challenges. During individual reviews, developers were asked to make an assessment of how complete they felt an evaluated system was. Developer reviews of *Happy Moths* and *Forgotten Island* conducted at approximately the same time during the development cycle (both in November, 2011) showed significantly different averages for this estimate. *Happy Moths* was evaluated to be 85.9% complete, while *Forgotten Island* was seen as being only 17.5% complete. This contrast in the remaining time to complete each game seems starker with additional information: at the time of review, *Forgotten Island* was still in its first iteration while *Happy Moths* was finishing its second design iteration and moving into its third (i.e., less complete than most developers assessed, but still much more polished than *Forgotten Island*). Currently, *Happy Moths* is nearing completion on its third and final version, while *Forgotten Island* is nearing completion of its first (and due to time and budget constraints, final) iteration.

Given the challenges of development, game taskification may or may not be as realistic an approach for designing citizen science games as better-understood methods of task gamification. A host of extra creative design activities can lead to longer development times and many more required resources. However, these costs may be worthwhile to incur if the end result is a game that is widely popular among the general public and produces a high number of classifications from each player.

The game economy of *Forgotten Island* rewards players with in-game currency for each classification that they complete, but also requires them to spend this money on items that are required to progress the story and finish the game. This makes it possible to balance the game economy by varying the reward amounts and item prices so that players must complete a specified base number of classifications in order to win. In its current balance ($50 reward per classification vs. between $250 and $750 cost for various items), *Forgotten Island* can be completed by a player who undertakes 183 classifications over the course of the game (assuming the player makes no classification mistakes and is also perfectly efficient in their purchases). *Happy Moths*, which adopts the gamified task approach, requires far fewer classifications for each "win" (either 5 or 10 classifications, depending on the number of photos in the game). So a player would need to play between 19 and 37 full games of *Happy Moths* in order to achieve the same number of classifications as one game of *Forgotten*

Island. If the story and fantasy elements of *Forgotten Island* engage more players and engage them for longer than *Happy Moths* (as we expect; experiencing an interactive story should be a more compelling reason for many players to undertake classification than inherent interest in nature or science), then *Forgotten Island* may eventually seem a better investment despite the lengthy development cycle.

Even if *Forgotten Island* itself fails to produce very many classifications, it is valuable as a demonstration of the taskified game approach's potential to produce scientific tools that are also commercial entertainment products. One future possibility is to develop and release games like *Forgotten Island* for profit, supporting scientific research (as well as game development activities) through sales of the game. *Forgotten Island* itself will not follow this commercial model; it is a research prototype, developed without commercialization specifically in mind. However, as a model for the game taskification approach, it will be a useful vehicle for exploring purposeful games as commercial entertainment products, unique methods for developing such games, non-enthusiast motivations for participating in citizen science, and the impact that taskified games have on scientific data quality.

A third approach to purposeful game design is not part of our current *Citizen Sort* project, but bears mentioning because it offers interesting possibilities for future study. This approach is to turn a scientific or socio-computational task into a form of payment for play. Many casual games have successfully adopted a model where micro-payments unlock game items, new content, new game mechanics, or new levels of play. Substituting classification for cash payment could be an effective way to reward users for their help and attract gamers to a project, and this is one possible future direction for our research.

5.4 Friction

One complexity of the design science approach is the friction that generates through competition between problem space, research goals, and feasibility to develop the IT artifact. These factors each require tradeoffs among the others. In the *Citizen Sort* project, SMEs want to take ownership of a suite of games and tools to support a citizen classification effort. Their primary goal is that these should produce large amounts of very high quality data. Virtually all other considerations are secondary. From a socio-computational research perspective, however, the interest is in how different kinds of games or tools can motivate different kinds of users and produce different qualities of data. It matters less that each individual tool or game produce the best quality data or attract the right kind of users, than that each game or tool helps generate useful knowledge about the research questions of interest. This means that games like *Happy Moths* or *Forgotten Island* could produce extremely poor classification data but still be a research success in providing evidence of cheating effects or problems with the fantasy/story approach. This outcome would, of course, be considered a failure by SMEs.

In [11], the need for multi-disciplinary expertise as well as expert developers on a design science project is noted, the better to adequately address both the problem space and research goals. Galison [34] describes how such collaborations can be difficult when friction between the varying goals of different interested parties develops. Galison describes the idea of "trading zones" [34] to accommodate the needs of various collaborators through a negotiating process. *Citizen Sort's* project manager takes a central role in these negotiations, coordinating various groups of SMEs and developers, ensuring that natural science and information science requirements are balanced, and verifying that the project scope is feasible for the development team. Our design efforts have validated "trading zone" efforts on this project, with research goals and the problem space largely complementing rather than conflicting with each other.

6. CONCLUSION

Design science is an approach to scientific inquiry where research goals are pursued through the development of an IT artifact positioned to address a real-world problem. This approach has many strengths, including the ability to tightly control research efforts while still enacting them within realistic use contexts. In addition, evaluation of design science efforts can address numerous research questions.

One constraint of design science is the friction that can develop between research goals, the problem space, and system feasibility. While good project management and careful attention to both researcher and stakeholder needs can mitigate these effects, friction is virtually impossible to eliminate entirely. Nonetheless, as the *Citizen Sort* project demonstrates, design science can be a valuable approach to exploring design issues in citizen science, purposeful gaming, and socio-computational system design.

7. ACKNOWLEDGEMENTS
The authors would like to thank the development team for their efforts on this project: Nathan Brown, Chris Duarte, Susan Furest, Yang Liu, Supriya Mane, Nitin Mule, Gongying Pu, Trupti Rane, Jimit Shah, Sheila Sicilia, Jessica Smith, Dania Souid, Peiyuan Sun, Xueqing Xuan, Shu Zhang, and Zhiruo Zhao. The authors would also like to thank the following for their partnership and assistance in *Citizen Sort's* design and evaluation efforts so far: Anne Bowser, Jennifer Hammock, Nancy Lowe, John Pickering, Jennifer Preece, Dana Rotman, and Andrea Wiggins. This work was partially supported by the US National Science Foundation under grant SOCS 09–68470.

8. REFERENCES

[1] Cohn, J.P., *Citizen Science: Can Volunteers Do Real Research?* BioScience, 2008. **58**(3): p. 192-107.

[2] Wiggins, A. and K. Crowston. *From Conservation to Crowdsourcing: A Typology of Citizen Science.* in *44th Hawaii International Conference on System Sciences.* 2011. Kauai, Hawaii.

[3] Hevner, A.R., S.T. March, J. Park, and S. Ram, *Design Science in Information Systems Research.* MIS Quarterly, 2004. **28**(1): p. 75-105.

[4] March, S.T. and G.F. Smith, *Design and natural science research on information technology.* Decision Support Systems, 1995. **15**(4): p. 251-266.

[5] Peffers, K., T. Tuunanen, M. Rothenberger, and S. Chatterjee, *A Design Science Research Methodology for Information Systems Research.* Journal of Management Information Systems, 2007. **24**(3): p. 45-77.

[6] Dix, A., *Human–computer interaction: A stable discipline, a nascent science, and the growth of the long tail.* Interacting with Computers, 2010. **22**: p. 13-27.

[7] Ellis, G. and A. Dix, *An explorative analysis of user evaluation studies in information visualisation*, in

Proceedings of the 2006 AVI workshop on Beyond time and errors: novel evaluation methods for information visualization. 2006, ACM: Venice, Italy.

[8] Brooks, F.P., Jr., *No Silver Bullet: Essence and Accidents of Software Engineering.* IEEE Computer, 1987. **20**(4): p. 10-19.

[9] Brooks, F.P., Jr., *The Computer Scientist as Toolsmith II.* Communications of the ACM, 1996. **39**(3): p. 61-68.

[10] Rittel, H.J. and M.M. Webber, *Planning Problems Are Wicked Problems*, in *Developments in Design Methodology*, N. Cross, Editor. 1984, John Wiley & Sons: New York.

[11] Prestopnik, N., *Theory, Design and Evaluation – (Don't Just) Pick Any Two.* AIS Transactions on Human-Computer Interaction, 2010. **2**(3): p. 167-177.

[12] Gregor, S., *The Nature of Theory in Information Systems.* MIS Quarterly, 2006. **30**(3).

[13] Crowston, K. and I. Fagnot. *The motivational arc of massive virtual collaboration.* in *IFIP WG 9.5, Working Conference on Virtuality and Society: Massive Virtual Communities.* 2008. Lüneberg, Germany.

[14] Malone, T.W., R. Laubacher, and C.N. Dellarocas, *Harnessing Crowds: Mapping the Genome of Collective Intelligence*, in *MIT Sloan Research Paper No. 4732-09.* 2009.

[15] Bradford, B.M. and G.D. Israel, *Evaluating Volunteer Motivation for Sea Turtle Conservation in Florida.* 2004, University of Florida, Agriculture Education and Communication Department, Institute of Agriculture and Food Sciences: Gainesville, FL. p. 372.

[16] King, K. and C.V. Lynch, *The Motivation of Volunteers in the nature Conservancy - Ohio Chapter, a Non-Profit Environmental Organization.* Journal of Volunteer Administration, 1998. **16**(5).

[17] Raddick, M.J., G. Bracey, K. Carney, G. Gyuk, K. Borne, J. Wallin, et al., *Citizen science: status and research directions for the coming decade*, in *AGB Stars and Related Phenomenastro 2010: The Astronomy and Astrophysics Decadal Survey.* 2009. p. 46P.

[18] Raddick, M.J., G. Bracey, P.L. Gay, C.J. Lintott, P. Murray, K. Schawinski, et al., *Galaxy Zoo: Exploring the Motivations of Citizen Science Volunteers.* Astronomy Education Review, 2010. **9**(1): p. 010103-18.

[19] Wiggins, A. and K. Crowston, *Developing a conceptual model of virtual organizations for citizen science.* International Journal of Organizational Design and Engineering, 2010. **1**(1/2): p. 148-162.

[20] von Ahn, L., *Human computation*, in *Proceedings of the 46th Annual Design Automation Conference.* 2009, ACM: San Francisco, California.

[21] von Ahn, L., *Human computation*, in *Proceedings of the 4th international conference on Knowledge capture.* 2007, ACM: Whistler, BC, Canada.

[22] von Ahn, L., G. Shiry, K. Mihir, L. Ruoran, and B. Manuel, *Improving accessibility of the web with a computer game*, in *Proceedings of the SIGCHI conference on Human Factors in computing systems.* 2006, ACM: Montreal, Quebec, Canada.

[23] Law, E. and L. von Ahn, *Input-agreement: a new mechanism for collecting data using human computation games*, in *Proceedings of the 27th international conference on Human factors in computing systems.* 2009, ACM: Boston, MA, USA.

[24] Zhang, P. and G.M. von Dran, *Satisfiers and dissatisfiers: A two-factor model for Website design and evaluation.* Journal of the American Society for Information Science and Technology, 2000. **51**(14): p. 1253.

[25] Malone, T., W., *What makes things fun to learn? heuristics for designing instructional computer games*, in *Proceedings of the 3rd ACM SIGSMALL symposium and the first SIGPC symposium on Small systems.* 1980, ACM: Palo Alto, California, United States.

[26] Malone, T.W., *Heuristics for designing enjoyable user interfaces: Lessons from computer games*, in *Proceedings of the 1982 conference on Human factors in computing systems.* 1982, ACM: Gaithersburg, Maryland, United States.

[27] Malone, T.W. and M. Lepper, *Making learning fun: A taxonomy of intrinsic motivations for learning.* Aptitude, learning, and instruction: Vol. 3. Cognitive and affective process analyses, ed. R. Snow and M. Fair. 1987, Hills-Dale, NJ: Erlbaum.

[28] DeWalt, K.M. and B.R. DeWalt, *Participant Observation: A Guide for Fieldworkers.* 2002, Walnut Creek, CA: AltaMira Press. 287.

[29] Lawson, B., *Schemata, gambits and precedent: some factors in design expertise.* Design Studies, 2004. **25**(5): p. 443-457.

[30] Lawson, B., *How Designers Think.* 4 ed. 2005, Oxford, UK: Architectural Press.

[31] Schell, J., *The Art of Game Design: A Book of Lenses.* 2008, Burlington, MA: Elsevier, Inc. 483.

[32] Jafarinaimi, N., *Exploring the character of participation in social media: the case of Google Image Labeler*, in *Proceedings of the 2012 iConference.* 2012, ACM: Toronto, Ontario, Canada.

[33] von Ahn, L. and L. Dabbish, *Designing games with a purpose.* Commun. ACM, 2008. **51**(8): p. 58-67.

[34] Galison, P., *Image and Logic: A Material Culture of Microphysics.* 1997, Chicago: The University of Chicago Press.

Location-Based Crowdsourcing of Hyperlocal News – Dimensions of Participation Preferences

Heli Väätäjä
Tampere University of Technology
Korkeakoulunkatu 6
Tampere, Finland
heli.vaataja@tut.fi

Teija Vainio
Tampere University of Technology
Korkeakoulunkatu 6
Tampere, Finland
teija.vainio@tut.fi

Esa Sirkkunen
University of Tampere
Kalevantie 4
Tampere, Finland
esa.sirkkunen@uta.fi

ABSTRACT

We studied the mobile users' preferences and concerns of using location-based assignments (LBA) and geotagging in crowdsourced news making. First, nine readers who had submitted reader's phtos were interviewed about their perceptions of LBA and geotagging scenarios. Second, a quasi-experiment in field conditions was carried out with nineteen participants. After completing four LBA tasks with a mobile phone, participants were interviewed on their perceptions and asked to complete a questionnaire on their preferences for receiving LBA and usage of geotags. Findings indicate that the perceived benefits of LBA and geotagging are greater than the perceived risks. The task type, temporal context, preciseness of location query, proximity to the reporting location, parallel tasks, social context and incentives affected the participation preferences. We propose a framework for participation preferences to support further studies in location-based crowdsourcing and in the development of crowdsourcing processes and systems.

Categories and Subject Descriptors

H.5.3 Computer-supported cooperative work.

Keywords

Crowdsourcing, location, privacy, news, assignment, user-generated content, UGC, reader.

1. INTRODUCTION

Crowdsourcing by using tasks [13] to get readers to contribute news content is one way to collaborate with the audience in news making [43]. It can strengthen the relationship between the participating audience and the newsroom in a new and fruitful way. Using readers' content is a cost-effective way of getting news content, story ideas or new angles to reporting [14][30] and to provide relevant a content for the audience [34][45].

Currently, news industry widely encourages readers to send photos and videos with their mobile phones. For example, a hyperlocal news provider in Helsinki metropolitan area in Finland received 2077 reader's photos in May 2012 and about 20,000 reader's photos in 2011. Majority of these photos were sent as MMS (multimedia) messages from mobile phones.

This article focuses on the process of news content creation collaboratively with readers, who are recruited to collaborate in news making. We concentrate on location-based crowdsourcing, in which the initiator (news organization) sends a task or makes available a task based on the participant's (reader's) mobile phone location (location-based assignment, LBA) for voluntary undertaking using smartphones as an enabler for participation. In addition, we study the attitudes towards geotagging of news content and the use of geotags in news publishing.

In order to succeed in collaborating with the readers in the news making process, it is crucially important to understand what affects readers' willingness to participate and how they understand their position as collaborators in news making with media organisations. Since the role of location information is rapidly increasing in importance in the news media, information that aids in the development of the collaborative news making processes is needed. Furthermore, using everyday technology such as smartphones as tools has great potential especially in the field of hyperlocal journalism where community reporters are recruited for voluntary work. However, location information is considered as private [17][29][40]. Therefore we need to investigate how its use is perceived by readers who participate in news making.

Only a few user studies exist on using a mobile phone's location information in crowdsourcing with tasks [1][43] or on using location-based assignments in news making [42][43], although mobile tools for crowdsourcing have been developed and reported [12],[23],[47]. Especially how readers perceive 1) the usage of their location information for location-based assignments sent by the newsroom and 2) geotagging of the news content they generate as well as 3) what their preferences in these cases are have received little attention.

This paper addresses these issues by presenting results from two user studies. Research questions are: **RQ1.** What affects mobile users' participation preferences in location-based crowdsourcing with LBA that is facilitated by a news organization? **RQ2.** How do users perceive the risks of sharing their location information in the context of news making?

The paper presents the following contributions:
- Framework for the dimensions of readers' preferences to participate in location-based crowdsourcing processes and
- Implications derived from the findings to aid in developing location-based mobile crowdsourcing processes for news.

2. BACKGROUND AND RELATED WORK
2.1 Crowdsourcing in news making
The idea behind the term crowdsourcing has its origins in the notions about the wisdom of the crowds [16],[36] as well as in collaborative creation and production [16],[38]. In addition to using microtasks that can contribute to a larger problem to be

solved [22],[33], crowdsourcing is used in fields requiring specific domain knowledge, expertise or creative skills. Examples include open source software development [38], open innovation [2],[35], eScience [5], and citizen or participatory journalism [34],[45]. In this paper we focus on participatory journalism in which readers or volunteers participate in news making that is facilitated and managed by a news organization [34].

The progress of collaboration with the audience in news journalism has been rather slow despite strong advocates of participatory journalism and collaboration with the audience [4], [11],[14],[30]. There are only few newsrooms in the world that have experimented with opening their whole work process from selecting the news topics to editing and distributing the content to the audience. Usually professional journalists in traditional news organizations are still keeping the decision making power at each stage of the news production to themselves [34].

Most explorative, collaborative and open processes in news making are usually found outside the traditional newsrooms. Typically volunteer contributors are not compensated for their participation in these models. For example, ProPublica[1] has trialed an advanced process for collaboration with volunteers in investigative reporting based on a reporting network which reports on given investigative tasks. ProPublica also taps into the specific domain knowledge of the network members as sources or experts on specific themes under investigation (see also [6]). However, similarly to OhmyNews[2] and Huffington Post[3], which are news sites for citizen journalism, professionals still facilitate and manage to varying extent the participation of the volunteers to news making, even in cases in which volunteers act in the role of content curators [7],[34].

2.2 Types of collaboration in news making

To link the crowdsourcing to different types of collaboration between the participating readers or volunteers and the newsroom, we apply here the categorization of citizen science projects [5]. Bonney et al. [5] describe three categories of co-operation between volunteers and scientists: 1) *contribution*, in which volunteers contribute data, 2) *collaboration*, in which scientists design the project and do the reporting, but volunteers contribute data and may analyze data and 3) *co-creation*, in which both volunteers and scientists are involved in all parts of the project from planning to the interpretation of results. In the context of news making, a similar type of categorization can be used for describing the co-operation types. Crowdsourcing, when defined as tasks to be carried out by the crowd, can be seen to apply to at least the first two types of collaboration.

In journalism, most often readers or volunteers *contribute* content, that is, they send comments, photos and videos to the newsroom and the journalists control the process and publish the news. This type of participation is typically enabled and encouraged by the news organization by providing a possibility to submit content directly from the mobile phone or through online sites. The advantages are clear: new ideas and topics flow from the audience to the newsroom, newsrooms receive cheap content that often interests people in a different way than the usual journalistic content and the process itself strengthens the relationship between citizens and media outlets.

However, volunteers can attain a more equal position when they become reader reporters who create content more independently or help the newsroom with their special information or expertise. Here the news making process resembles more a *collaborative* process. The citizen's role is more of an equal co-worker when the professionals and volunteers join forces to analyze data, such as in open data projects, but where the reporting of the results is still done by professionals. Another example of collaboration are cases where professional journalists use eye-witnesses as informants when reporting breaking news when no professionals are present, or when the eye-witnesses are more informed of the event or possess alternative viewpoints. Professional journalists are transforming into mentors, curators or enablers who are interacting with the users in various ways [7],[25],[45]. The benefits are clear here too - there is often, if not always, more expertise among the audience than in the busy newsroom.

The third stage in the user - newsroom interaction can be called a *co-creative process.* The citizen content creators and professional journalists are working as equals in ideating the news, collecting information and analyzing it, and collaborating even in the reporting jointly. This third stage is a rare model due to the difficulty of opening the journalistic work process into a more democratic one [11],[34]. It is also somewhat unclear as to what kind of economical agreement this kind of co-creation should be based on. When do the volunteers turn into professionals?

2.3 Tools for mobile and location-based news assignments

In order to enable readers to participate in crowdsourcing by carrying out news reporting assignments, one solution is to deliver the assignments to or enable access to them via mobile handheld devices. Solutions vary from using text messages (SMS), social media (Twitter, Facebook) and email to dedicated mobile clients and platforms for news reporting and assignments [15],[43]. CNN is one of the first large news organizations to provide a list of themes to report on in their mobile application for registered reader reporters (iReporters[4]). Readers are asked to share footage and experiences on specific topics, such as the Japanese nuclear catastrophe in spring 2011. A step further is the San Jose State University campus news publication Spartan Daily[5] which provides a mobile client for mobile content creation (Tackable[6]). It geotags captured photos and places them onto a map. It also enables readers to search for assignments based on a map of the campus area. By carrying out tasks readers win points and earn rewards, such as free tacos, i.e., they receive monetary incentives.

Monetary incentives are also used in the case of Scoopshot[7]. It acts as an intermediary, that is, a market place, between the registered citizen photojournalists and the news organizations. It provides a mobile client that enables uploading of photos based on own initiative and pricing them. It also provides a listing of current available tasks to carry out based on the current location of the mobile phone. Tasks can be offered by news organizations to a larger crowd or to a media organization's own recruited community of participants.

---

[1] http://www.propublica.org/ion/reporting-network
[2] http://international.ohmynews.com/join-our-team/
[3] http://www.huffingtonpost.com/

[4] http://ireport.cnn.com/
[5] http://spartandaily.com/
[6] http://www.tackable.com/about/
[7] http://www.scoopshot.com/

As these examples show, the mobile solutions for mobile crowdsourcing with news reporting assignments vary from using simple text messages that are accessible by all who have a mobile phone to sophisticated mobile clients that require smartphones and a data subscription or access to a Wi-Fi network. Furthermore, participation and its compensation vary from voluntary work to semi-professional type of participation with incentives offered for the tasks carried out.

2.4 Preferences in location-based services

In location-based crowdsourcing when using location-based assignments and geotagging, we are dealing with mobile users' location information and the whereabouts of the mobile users. This type of personal information that can reveal for example patterns of daily routines, personal time spending locations and personal spaces, is sensitive for many users [3][9][17][20][21][28][40][41]. Especially in the case of location tracking services (other parties tracking the user's location), the concerns are greater than when using position aware services that rely on the device's knowledge of its own location [3].

Earlier research shows that users' willingness to share their whereabouts varies. To reduce the users' privacy concerns and increase the acceptability of LBS (location-based services), feedback from the service [40] as well as context-aware solutions and adaptation of sharing can be used [29]. Furthermore, factors affecting willingness to disclose location information have been reported as 1) the identity of the requester (who), 2) the reason for requesting (why), and 3) the precision of the request (what) [9].

Recent studies report a number of other factors that affect the willingness to share location information. When looking at sharing location with their social network, users appear more comfortable sharing locations visited by a large and diverse set of people than places visited by fewer people [39]. Users want to protect their home location, obscure their identity and not reveal their precise location or schedule [8]. Approximate and vague levels of location disclosure are reported to be preferred [24],[32]. On the other hand, studies show that if users find that the sharing of location information is useful for them, they are more willing to disclose their location [1], [10]. For example, in the context of news making participants assessed it to be useful that the newsroom could locate professional reporters working in the field as well as reporters in the field could locate each other for organizing the reporting work [42]. To sum up, the willingness to share location based information depends on who wants to know, why the information is needed and what precisely is asked, in addition to the usefulness of sharing, fun and the social context.

Previous studies have presented technical solutions for how users can use LBS without revealing their location information by using a location anonymizer and a privacy-aware query processor [27]. The research has come to discuss technical implications, describing how privacy is related to security and trust [9], how to prevent undesired attacks [37], or the role of push and pull technologies [46]. Furthermore, Kelley et al. [20] found in case of location based advertising that more advanced privacy settings than simple opt-in, opt-out would make participants feel more comfortable with sharing their location with advertisers and lead to sharing more information with them. Being able to control the sharing of information with rules related to the user's time, place and schedule, appears to be the most resistant way to prevent users from mistakenly revealing location information they do not want to disclose [20].

As the aim of our research was to support the development of the future crowdsourcing processes by using location-based assignments, one of the issues to consider is the privacy related preferences of location information. Finding solutions that are acceptable to a wide variety of users is important to ensure not only the contributions but also the democratic representation of the voice of the audience. Privacy related issues are addressed in the findings of our studies and the implications for the development of crowdsourcing processes of news are presented.

3. STUDY 1

The goal of the first study was to support the development of new crowdsourcing processes in hyperlocal news production. One of the Finnish hyperlocal news publishers that publishes online news and two print tabloids in the Helsinki metropolitan area, is developing their reader reporter concept. The contribution of photos from the mobile context is currently enabled by MMS messages. In addition, email and online submission is enabled. Most of the reader's photos are published in an online gallery.

Incoming photos with short descriptive texts of about 200 characters when submitted from the mobile phone are used by the online journalists to spot interesting story ideas and breaking news, such as accidents. When the journalist spots an interesting topic, he/she contacts the reader who submitted the photo as well as other relevant informants such as officials to inquire further information. In case of accidents, the news desk sometimes is ahead of the officials on the facts about the incident. The most interesting story ideas submitted as photos are turned into online news stories by the journalists in 10-15 minutes. Some of these stories are also used in print tabloids. Furthermore, writing, submitting and publishing of reader's stories is supported online. Monetary incentives are paid for the reader's photos published in print tabloids. These incentives usually vary from two movie tickets (value 17 euros) to a maximum of 100 euros. As the news organization was considering the use of locating and location-based assignments, we aimed to explore the readers' perceptions on the use of mobile LBA and automatic geotagging of the news content to gain an initial understanding of the acceptability and related preferences to support the process development.

In the first study in September 2010 [43], one of the themes we explored was how readers who participated in the hyperlocal news creation by contributing news photos perceived future scenarios on location-based assignments (LBA) and geotagging of news photos. We focus here on these results from the interviews (see also [43]). Based on earlier research on privacy concerns, we expected that participants would primarily be concerned with locating and hesitant to disclose their location. This proved to be the case on the personal level for many. On the other hand, participants identified the created value and particularly the perceptions towards geotagging were positive as described next.

3.1 Method

Participants. Nine readers were recruited to participate in an interview on their experiences and future processes by a journalist working in the newsroom of the hyperlocal news publisher. All participants had been rewarded recently for at least one photo, which had been published in a printed news tabloid. The rewards they had received varied from two movie tickets (value 17 euros) to 100 euros. Five participants were 51-60 years old, and four were 16-39 years old. Four participants were female. Two participants had prior experience of using location-based services.

Procedure. Three participants agreed to answer through an online questionnaire, and six were interviewed. The same questions were asked both in the interviews and in the online questionnaire. Questions related to subjective perceptions and views were asked after presenting the scenario. The themes for the questions were created by paying attention to privacy preference related themes from earlier literature [9],[17],[24],[29],[40] on when, where and in what situations they would agree or would not agree to locating in order to receive reporting assignments. We did not mention privacy in the interview questions, following the approach of Kindberg et al. [21]. The interviews were recorded and transcribed. The participants were compensated with two movie tickets (value 17 euros).

Analysis. The data was analyzed by using a qualitative data-driven content analysis for open questions, using open coding for emerging themes. The coding was fixed as the analysis emerged, grouping codes under higher level categories.

3.2 Results

3.2.1 Perceptions on LBA for news reporting

When inquiring about perceptions on locating and location-based news reporting assignments, the following scenario was first described to the participants:

"You have agreed to act as a reader reporter. You have given permission to the newsroom to locate your mobile phone. Based on location, mobile assignments asking to capture multimedia or for reporting can be sent to your mobile phone, for example if there is a fire close to you."

When presented with the scenario, four groups of participants' perceptions emerged: 1) positive (1/9), 2) conditionally positive (3/9), 3) reluctant, i.e. who acknowledged the value of locationing for news reporting but who were not willing to be located themselves (3/9), and 4) negative, i.e. against the idea (2/9). The prerequisites mentioned by the participants for taking part in this type of scenario were related to minimizing disturbance by remaining in control over 1) the availability for receiving assignments, and 2) when and where to be located, as well as 3) the answering to the assignment so that it is not compulsory and one is able to decide whether to take part or not. The preferences mentioned were related to temporal (holiday, workday, not all the time), situational (when occupied with something else, such as with the family), and locational (home, workplace, downtown) issues. Specifically, areas further away from home, for example, when on the move somewhere in the city, downtown or similar, were mentioned as acceptable places to locate for assignments.

Privacy issues and concerns were mentioned spontaneously by the participants (4/9). Three mentioned privacy protection and two mentioned the *"feeling of being watched"* or *"observed"*. One of the participants described how his/her attitude towards locating depends on the consideration of the perceived benefits and risks:
"Then there is the issue of privacy... one need to consider the risks and the benefits, whether the benefits are greater than the risks." P-3.

On the other hand, some participants (3/9) explicitly expressed that they would allow locating for receiving news reporting assignments if they would be compensated for carrying out the task and would remain in control of the locating and availability. One of them did not bring out the privacy related issues during the interview, but rather approached locating and availability to be an issue to be solved with technology: *"It would not bother me if it had been agreed on and you would get compensation for going to the scene based on a request... When I do not want it, when I am in general not*

able to go on a gig, you could perhaps activate it yourself ... If the service could be activated on and off, that would be the best." P-6.

One of the participants described how he/she considers the benefit and cost relationship of privacy on a personal level to depend on the expected incentive: *"If I get paid enough, I can give up my privacy." P-7.* Furthermore, two participants compared the activity to contract work: *"One has to get a reward for contract work." P-8.* The results indicate that people may be willing to give up the privacy of their location in exchange for a monetary benefit. On the other hand, as the nature of the activity that the readers are to be engaged to changes, the expectations of the participants may change towards contracted freelancing work. These issues need to be considered when developing the crowdsourcing based activity further, for example, on how the new way of working is launched and how possible incentives are used in the case of a crowdsourcing type of activity.

3.2.2 Geotagging of content

Geotagged, time-stamped media content submitted by the readers would help the news reporting work at the news desk by 1) giving accurate information of the location and time line of the capture, 2) proving the authenticity of the material and 3) being able to map the content automatically when publishing the news online. Privacy related issues and concerns have in recent years been discussed in the media, like the potential dangers such as stalking and burglaries when users reveal their geolocation in social media. We therefore inquired how the participants view the automatic geotagging of news content. The following scenario was first described to them:

"The location of the scene of capturing media, like photos and videos, can automatically be added to the content based on the location of the mobile phone. Location information is used, for example, so that the photo or video you submitted is geolocated on a map in an online publication."(Scenario 2)

The participants found geotagging to be useful and to create added value in the case of news related content 1) for the news reporting phase as well as 2) for the readers. One participant had used the automatic geotagging of content on a mobile phone. He mentioned that he could control geotagging easily, taking into account privacy issues as well. He found that geotagging helps the journalist to do his/her job more easily, since sometimes there are problems in placing an event to the right location. *"... I feel that especially if I send only a photo [without a description], then the person [journalist] who continues from there [the reporting] can really picture the right location from that information." P-4.*

None of the participants spontaneously mentioned any places or locations that they would not want to geotag. When specifically asked for possible places that they would not like to geotag or disclose, three participants mentioned content created at *"home"*. One participant mentioned as a possible case a situation where the person should have been somewhere else at the time of capturing:
"Maybe someone has a need [not to reveal their location] if one should be somewhere else instead." P-8.

These results on geotagging of media content therefore indicate that the participants may see more benefit than risk in the automatic geotagging of captured content for news reporting purposes. Furthermore, geotagging was perceived to create value in the process of news making by increasing the accuracy of the reporting.

4. STUDY 2

In order to gain a deeper understanding of the perceptions and preferences related to receiving location-based news reporting assignments and the geotagging of captured news photos and videos, we conducted a quasi-experiment in field conditions [18]. We aimed to provide the news publisher with information to further develop their collaboration and news publishing activities.

4.1 Method

In the quasi-experiment we used a simulated mobile crowdsourcing process with location-based assignments (LBA) [43]. The assignments were delivered as SMS messages to the test phone. The experiment was carried out in the mobile context with a within-subjects design. The experiment consisted of 1) four tasks completed with the mobile phone, 2) an interview after completing all the tasks, and 3) filling forms, including a pre- and a post-test questionnaire [43].

4.1.1 Participants

The sample consisted of 19 voluntary participants, who were interested in new mobile services that enable to send reader's content to news organizations [43]. Participants (12 female, 7 male) were recruited through email lists as well as university web pages to participate in a reader reporting experiment with mobile phones. The average age of the participants was 29 years (Md=24). Most participants (16/19) were aged between 20 and 30 years, and the rest were 43, 44 and 61 years old.

Eleven participants were students studying engineering, journalism, visual journalism or media. One participant was a photographer and one a journalist. All participants had prior experience of using mobile phones for photo capture. The majority (10/19) of the participants had experience of using a mobile phone for sending or sharing photos or videos with others. Three participants had prior experience of sending reader's photos or videos to newspapers. Almost half of the participants (8/19) used a navigator or a navigation service on a mobile phone monthly or more frequently. Three participants had prior experience of other location-based services. The participants were compensated with two movie tickets (value 17 euros).

4.1.2 Apparatus

The mobile phone used in the quasi-experiment was HTC Legend. Both the phone's own functionalities (MMS, photo and video capture) and a dedicated mobile service client OKReportteri [43] was used for capturing and uploading mobile media content. SMS messages were used for delivering the LBA. Regarding location information, OKReportteri enabled the uploading of captured photo and video content to a backend service, from which the uploaded content and related metadata including the location of media content capture could be browsed with a standard browser. As the capturing of media content with the client was started, an approximate location was searched with network-based locationing. This search was visible to the user on the mobile client's user interface. After the capturing of a photo or video, the network-based approximate location was always attached, but a GPS based location was attached only if the user agreed to the searching of the precise location.

4.1.3 Location-based assignments

In the experiment we simulated the newsroom locating the mobile users by indicating in the description of the test assignments that the participant's location was known [43]. The location-based assignments were sent to the test phone as text (SMS) messages

prior to each task within the test session that was arranged in a predefined pedestrian area. The assignments indicated an approximate location (central square, pedestrian street, downtown, close to the boulevard), the topic of the assignment and instructions for capturing and sending [43]. Each participant received two photo and two video assignments. The order of the test conditions was pseudo-randomly counterbalanced. The following tasks exemplify photo and video assignments:

"According to the newsroom's information, you are close to the central park. Please take a photo of a typical tree in the cityscape and upload it. Use OKReportteri for capturing and uploading." (a photo task)

"According to the newsroom's information, you are downtown. Please take a video of typical problem to fix in the cityscape. The maximum length of the video is 10 seconds. Send the video as an MMS message to the newsroom number." (a video task)

4.1.4 Procedure

Prior to the test, the participants were asked to fill in a paper-based questionnaire with demographic and other background information. Next, the participants received training for using the mobile phone used in the experiment. After carrying out the four mobile location-based assignments in the mobile context, the participants were interviewed about their experiences. The interview questions covered how the participant perceived 1) the assignments generally, 2) the usage of the location information for assignments, 3) the advantages and disadvantages of using the location information, and 4) the needs related to situational, locational and temporal control in the case of LBA. Privacy issues were addressed only on the participant's spontaneous initiative.

After the post-test interview, the participants were asked to fill in a paper-based questionnaire [31] which addressed 1) their preferences to receive LBA under different context and assignment related characteristics, as well as to 2) geotag their content and 3) the usage of the content's geotag information. By collecting this information at the end of the experiment, we aimed at getting more realistic perceptions than we would have received by asking for assessments without hands-on experience of LBA.

The post-test questionnaire had three components: 1) preferences to share location information in the case of geotagging and location-based assignments with six dimensions for participation preferences (Table 1), adapting the privacy control dimensions by Myles et al. [29] and using prior research findings from sections 2.4 and 4.2, 2) assessment of the level of the participants' privacy concerns, applying the IUIPC scale [26], and 3) the participants' perception of the benefits or risks [40] of precise location sharing for receiving LBA and geotagging of media (Table 1).

To get a general background measure for the participants' privacy concern, we selected six items from the Internet User's Information Privacy Concerns instrument (IUIPC) [24],[40]. We used the following items from the IUIPC scale: 1) Control (nr.2 "Consumer control of personal information lies at the heart of consumer privacy."), 2) Awareness (nr.3 "It is very important to me that I am aware and knowledgeable about how my personal information will be used."), 3) Collection (nr.4 "I'm concerned that online companies are collecting too much personal information about me."), 4) Unauthorized Secondary Use (nr.4, "Online companies should never share personal information with other companies unless it has been authorized by the individuals who provided the information."), 5) Improper Access (nr.3 "Online companies should take more steps to make sure that unauthorized people cannot access personal information in their companies.") and 6) Risk Belief (nr.1, "In general, it would be risky to give the newsroom a permission to locate the mobile phone."). The first five items were used as a scale for the general privacy concern of the participants. The higher the score the more concerned the person is for his/her privacy. The sixth item, Risk Belief, was used separately for the assessment of perceived risk of locating within the context of news reporting. A seven-point Likert scale was used for the assessment of the statements (1=Strongly disagree, 7=Strongly agree).

Table 1. Dimensions of participation preferences and assessment of perceived risk or benefit when using LBA and geotags.

Preference	Themes of items	Nr of items
Organization: share the geotag	Type of news organization (local or national) with which the *geotag is shared*	2
Organization: publish the geotag	Type of the news organization (local or national) that may *use the geotag of content in publishing*	2
Organization: send LBA	Type of the news organization (local or national) *allowed to send LBA*	2
Task type	Type of the *contribution asked for in LBA*: write a news story, conduct an interview, shoot a photo, shoot a video clip	4
Temporal	*When to receive LBA*: anytime, weekdays, weekends, during the day, evenings	5
Location to receive LBA	*Where to receive LBA*: anywhere, downtown, when distance less than 1 km/5 km from the scene	4
Spatial precision of the location query	*Precise* geolocation (i.e., address, place), *approximate* (district, neighborhood), *vague* (city), or *anonymous but precise*	4
Situation	Task context: When having *nothing more important* to do, during *free time*, when *working or studying*. Social context: when *alone*, when *in the company of others*	5
Perceived risk or benefit	Disclosing the *precise location* of the mobile phone, *geotagging* of the content	2

4.1.5 Analysis
The audiorecorded post-test interviews were transcribed and analyzed with data-driven content analysis in NVivo8. As analysis emerged initial open codes were replaced with fixed codes and categorized. Questionnaire data was analyzed with SPSS analysis tool using nonparametric methods, that is, descriptive statistics and with nonparametric correlations (bivariate with Kendall's tau, 2-tailed). The 5-item scale for privacy concern was tested for internal consistency reliability with Cronbach's alpha (α=.73).

4.2 Results

4.2.1 Assessed privacy concern and risk belief
Based on the post-test questionnaire we calculated a general privacy concern score for each participant as the sum of the five IUIPC scale items (1-5). All participants were concerned with their privacy (Privacy concern score: min=5, max=7, Md=6.5, M=6.39, SD=.58). However, based on nonparametric correlations, the privacy concern score did not have statistically significant correlations with any other questionnaire items. This indicates that the general privacy concern score does not give a prediction of participant's perceptions of the privacy concerns in the specific context of crowdsourced news reporting. This is reflected with participants' assessment the IUIPC item on Risk belief: *"In general, it would be risky to give the newsroom a permission to*

locate the mobile phone." Statement was disagreed with (Scale 1="Strongly disagree", 7="Strongly agree": min=2, max=7, Md=3, M=3.68, SD=1.57). Our results therefore indicate that even though participants were concerned for their privacy in general, most of them did not find it especially risky to share their location with the newsroom if acting as reader reporters.

Most of the participants assessed giving permission to locate their mobile phone precisely more beneficial than risky (*"Giving permission to the newsroom to locate my mobile phone precisely is…"* Scale: 1="Much more risky than beneficial", 7="Much more beneficial than risky"; min=2, max=7, Md=5, M=4.74, SD=1.33). This is consistent with the findings on Risk belief. Most participants therefore found benefit in sharing the precise location in the context of mobile news making and assessing the benefits higher than the risks involved.

Geotagging precisely the location of the multimedia capture was assessed as more beneficial than risky by all participants (*"Geotagging the precise location of the place of capture to the multimedia I send to the newsroom is…"* Scale: 1="Much more risky than beneficial", 7="Much more beneficial than risky"; min=5, max=7, Md=6, M=5.95, SD=.78). This finding supports our finding from the first study that in the context of news the participants see value in geotagging and in the use of geotags.

4.2.2 Interview results
The interviews revealed both advantages and disadvantages related to LBA. The mentioned advantages were: getting tip-offs for relevant content that newsroom is interested in, proving the authenticity of the material and therefore increasing the reliability of the reporting, enabling the newsroom to get what they are interested in, and enabling faster news reporting when the newsroom is able to spot someone close-by.

The perceptions on the disadvantages of LBA were related to privacy and disturbance (see Table 2). Three groups of privacy related issues emerged: 1) revealing personal and private time spending locations and patterns 2) the location information ending up in wrong hands or misused for stalking and 3) revealing some location accidentally, which one would like to keep secret from friends or close-ones. One participant exemplified accidental revealing of a secret location that one could be *"caught lying"* and *"end up in trouble"*. This could happen if one is somewhere else where one has told others, like friends, to be at, in case one submits news material based on location information and the identity is revealed. Only three participants specifically mentioned that there would be no disadvantages.

Table 2. Mentioned disadvantages of LBA.

Category	Count	Themes	Count
Privacy	8/19	Personal and private time spending locations revealed	3
		Location information ends up in wrong hands or is misused	2
		A "secret" location is revealed accidentally to friends or similar	3
Disturbance	5/19	Assignment messages received continuously	3
		Private leisure time disturbed	2

The specific locations mentioned by the interviewees that they would not like to disclose or be located at were 1) places described as *"shady"*, *"not acceptable"*, *"embarrassing by their nature"* (4/19), and 2) home or other private places (2/19). By contrast, downtown was mentioned as a specific acceptable place to locate (2/19), similarly to the first study. Some participants said that they would prefer location obfuscation, that is, approximate or vague location disclosure over precise.

Situations in which the participants mentioned a need to control the disclosure of the location were when one wants to be in peace, that is, undisturbed, like on a holiday or at work (3/19), or if doing something illegal (1/19). On the other hand, some participants mentioned that the need for the control of both location disclosure and availability would depend on the agreement made for reporting, and who has access to and is using the location information. One participant spontaneously raised the monetary incentive to change his/her attitude towards being available for assignments, similarly to the first study.

4.2.3 Questionnaire results

The post-test questionnaire focused on the participants' preferences in the case of LBA and geotagging. We used the following type of questionnaire items. For example, in the case of agreement related to location, the item statement for "approximate location" (see Table 1) was the following: *"The newsroom can locate my mobile phone at the precision of the neighborhood because I have given permission to the newsroom to locate my mobile phone".* The scale used for all the items was a seven-point Likert scale (1="Strongly disagree", 7="Strongly agree"). To illustrate the results, we present the assessments in three groups of frequencies by combining disagreements (1-3) to one group ("Disagree"), neutral to one group (4="Neither agree or disagree"), and agreements (5-7) to one group ("Agree").

Organization type. The type of the news organization, whether 1) hyperlocal or 2) national, did not affect the preference to share or publish the geotag nor to receive LBA sent by the newsrooms (Table 3). This seems to indicate that the willingness to collaborate with and trust in both types of organizations is similar.

Table 3. Preferences related to the type of the news organization.

Type of news organization	Disagree	Neutral	Agree
Sharing the geotagged footage with hyperlocal news	0	1	18
Sharing the geotagged footage with national news	0	1	18
Hyperlocal news can geolocate the geotagged footage when published	1	2	16
National news can geolocate the geotagged footage when published	1	1	17
Hyperlocal can send LBA	1	0	18
National can send LBA	1	0	18

Preference for the task type. Shooting photos and video clips was the most preferred task, followed by writing a news article (Table 4). We expected that making an interview would not be preferred by the participants, since it involves being in contact with externals and not being able to carry out the assignment in a very short time. As can be seen from Table 4, making interviews is the least preferred, but still over half of the participants were willing to carry out interview assignments as well. The results indicate that a diversity of contribution types can be asked for and used in the collaboration when using LBA.

Table 4. Preference for the task type.

Type of contribution asked for	Disagree	Neutral	Agree
Write a news article	2	0	17
Conduct an interview	5	2	12
Shoot a photo	1	0	18
Shoot a video clip	1	0	18

Temporal preferences to receive LBA. In general, the participants wanted to control when to receive LBA, but no specific best time can be identified for LBA based on the results (Table 5). This calls for personal control of availability that could be supported by context-aware solutions or with a simple opt-in, opt-out solution.

Table 5. Temporal preference to receive LBA.

Time to receive LBA	Disagree	Neutral	Agree
Any time	9	2	8
Weekdays	5	0	14
Weekends	6	1	12
Daytime	3	0	16
Evenings	4	0	15

Location preferences. The participants assessed their preference to receive LBA in four locations (see Table 6). The proximity to the reporting location seems to be the most important factor for the location related preference to receive LBA. Instead of the push based solution studied here, location-based retrieval (pull) of tasks is a relevant solution to be considered, such as that provided by Tackable or Scoopshot (section 2.3) or proposed by Alt et al. [1].

Table 6. Preferences related to the location of receiving LBA.

Location to receive LBA	Disagree	Neutral	Agree
Anywhere	9	2	8
Downtown	2	4	13
Less than 1 km away from the scene	2	0	17
Less than 5 km away from the scene	5	3	11

Precision of location query. The participants clearly preferred the obfuscation of their location when it comes to locating their mobile phone. Both approximate and vague levels were preferred over precise locating. In addition, anonymous locating in the case of precise locating was preferred, compared with precise locating. Therefore, the obfuscation of the location by lowering the preciseness as well as using anonymity seems to be acceptable and less intrusive. Somewhat surprisingly, over half of the participants were willing to share their precise location with no obfuscation. However, as indicated by the previous results on preferring to receive LBA in the proximity of the reporting location, using either approximate locating or using anonymous but precise locating seem a feasible solution.

Table 7. Preference on the precision of location disclosure.

Preciseness of locating	Disagree	Neutral	Agree
Precise	6	1	12
Approximate (e.g. neighborhood)	1	0	18
Vague (e.g. town)	1	0	18
Anonymous, but precise	2	0	17

Preference for the situation to receive LBA. The participants were the most willing to agree to receive LBA for news content when they have nothing else to do (Table 8). The next most preferred times were in leisure time and alone. Interestingly, about half of the participants were willing to receive LBA when working or studying or when in the company of others. It therefore seems that these participants do not perceive LBA as a disturbance.

Table 8. Preference for the situation to receive LBA.

Context	Disagree	Neutral	Agree
When nothing else to do	1	1	17
In leisure time	4	1	14
When working or studying	7	1	11
When alone	5	1	13
In the company of others	6	3	10

5. DISCUSSION

The goal of our research was to study the preferences to participate in location-based crowdsourcing of news content with location-based assignments (LBA) and attitudes towards geotagging of news content. Our practical aim was to support the development of mobile location-based crowdsourcing processes for hyperlocal news. The presented framework for participation preferences can be applied when studying and implementing mobile crowdsourcing processes. We describe our findings and present implications for designing location-based crowdsourcing processes in the context of news journalism.

RQ1. *What affects mobile users' participation preferences in location-based crowdsourcing with LBA that is facilitated by a news organization?*

Based on earlier research and the results of our first study, we created an initial framework for studying the participation preferences and concerns. It was used in the planning of the second study and in the development of the questionnaire items for users' preferences. We created initially items for six dimensions of preferences (see Table 1):

1) Organization type, 2) Task type, 3) Temporal context, 4) Location to receive LBA, 5) Precision of location query, and 6) Situation (Social and task context).

Organization type. Earlier research shows that *who* is asking for the location disclosure is important for the users [9][29]. In our second study we investigated whether there is a difference if the news organization sending LBA or using geotags is national or hyperlocal. Participants were willing to share their location information independent of the news organization's type for geotagging of news footage and for allowing the use of geolocated content by the news organization when published. No difference between national or hyperlocal news was found for LBA. All except one participant was willing to receive LBA. When using readers' geolocated content in news publishing, the anonymity or pseudonymity of the content creator when publishing may further advance the willingness to add the geotag to reader's content.

These results are promising as they open a variety of possibilities for different types of news organizations to develop their collaboration processes with the audience. Using geotags enables developing new forms of news stories for the audience to consume online and specifically with mobile devices. Geotags enable, for example, pull or push of location-based news. Furthermore, geolocated news could be available through existing social media solutions, such as Foursquare or Facebook or with augmented reality solutions (e.g. Leyar, Junaio or dedicated news clients). These could attract more participants to news making.

Task type. In the second study, we looked at participants' preferences to carry out four types of reporting tasks: Writing a story, carrying out an interview, shooting a photo and shooting a video clip. Shooting news footage (photos, video clips) was the most preferred, along with writing a news story. Conducting an interview was the least preferred, but still over half of the participants were willing to conduct interviews. Requested contribution types of tasks (type of content, activity, needed effort) are therefore relevant aspects to consider when planning the activities as also discussed by Alt et al. [1]. Contribution types or more generally the type of activity that is asked for could also be used in the profiling of the participants, along with special skills, expertise, interests, and the reporters' equipment [41].

Furthermore, the task description should provide the needed information in a compact and easily understandable form [42].

Temporal context. Temporal preferences are related to *when* participants are willing to receive or alternatively retrieve or carry out LBA. In both of the studies, the temporal preferences of the participants to receive LBA varied. This indicates a need to be able to control the receiving of location-based assignments, such as using context-aware solutions that automatically adapt the availability for receiving LBA, like calendar information [29]. However, temporal preferences may also depend on other factors, such as the actual implementation of the LBA process such as: the type and nature of the technological solution or tool that is used for delivering LBA; the use of push or pull solutions; the intrusiveness of the notification; the details of the possible official agreement between the organization and the reader reporter on LBA, such as incentives or a possibility to select and undertake the task to themselves, urgency of the request and whether the LBA is sent to one or a group reporters or generally to anyone involved. These issues are not only related to temporal preferences but also more generally to developing the models, mobile tools and processes of crowdsourcing [1], [35].

Situation. When studying the preferences related to mobile user's situation at the time of receiving the LBA, we looked specifically at the *social* (alone, in the company of others) and *parallel task dimensions* (when nothing else to do, in leisure time, when working or studying) of the context of use [19]. Receiving an assignment was the most preferred when a person had "nothing else to do" followed by "in leisure time" or "when alone". However, over a half of the participants of the second study were willing to receive LBA also "when working or studying" or "in the company of others". Similar issues as presented for temporal context may affect the willingness to receive the assignments. As described for temporal context these aspects can be supported by technology and the developed crowdsourcing processes.

Location. Finally, we studied in both of the studies the perceptions of using location information for LBA and geotagging. The location information was clearly important for participants. In the first study the location related preferences and concerns were primarily related to the publicity of the place or the perceived private nature of the place, the ongoing activity or revealing things about oneself that one would not want to share. These were echoed in the interviews of the second study as well. In the second study, we studied the preferences from the point of view of the place of receiving LBA and the precision of the location query for locating the mobile phone for sending LBA. The proximity to the reporting location was important; the shorter the better. This indicates the importance of receiving relevant and potential tasks to carry out if these are delivered to the phone based on the location of the reader reporter's mobile phone. Alternatively, being able to retrieve LBA based on own location as in [1] or in real-life solutions of Spartan Daily or Scoopshot can be considered. Based on our findings, the effort required due to travelling is an important factor when reporter is considering whether to carry out a task or not. Therefore, solutions for delivering or retrieving LBA that are potentially relevant and feasible to the users to carry out is important.

Obfuscation of location or identity information was clearly preferred over precise locating for LBA. The approximate level of location preciseness (neighbourhood) was preferred in addition to vague level. This seems a reasonable level for news reporting purposes as well. In addition, in combination with the proximity of the reporting scene to the participant, this seems a good option for locating especially when carried out by the news organization and not initiated by the mobile user. Although both locating by the news organization and user initiated retrieval of LBA based on location seem a possible solution, the user initiated retrieval may be more acceptable for a larger number of users, since it potentially decreases the feeling of being monitored or tracked and the intrusiveness of the location request.

Incentive. In addition to the six dimensions of preferences that we defined for the initial framework, findings indicate a seventh dimension, that is, incentives. The interview results from both of the studies indicate that a monetary incentive and possibly an a priori contract for carrying out the task may have an effect on the willingness to share location information when the LBA is sent based on the locating of the reporter's mobile phone by the news organization. However, in practical terms news organizations need to consider as to what kind of effects incentives or contracts have on the activity and on the collaboration in hyperlocal news making. The reader participation to hyperlocal news is currently based primarily on volunteering. In a further study on readers' motivations to contribute to hyperlocal news [44], 39 active readers reported most often fun and the opportunity to get a reward as motivations. Informing others of local issues was the third most often reported motivator. Results indicate that monetary incentives or other ways to get feedback are important [2] when designing crowdsourcing processes.

Further dimensions for preferences. Our findings and previous research suggest also further dimensions to be included in the framework for preference dimensions. These include the anonymity or pseudonymity of the participants. In addition, as discussed earlier, the implementation of the processes and technology, such as use of push or pull of tasks is relevant to consider as a dimension [1]. These issues should therefore be considered when developing the crowdsourcing processes.

RQ2. *How do users perceive the risk of sharing their location information in the context of news making?*

In the first study, most participants were reluctant to share their location information with the newsroom to receive LBA, but they were willing to geotag the created news content. The participants of the second study were concerned for their privacy, when assessed for their general concern for sharing their private information. However, most of them did not find it risky to share their location information with the newsroom. In addition, most participants perceived the benefits of giving permission to locate their mobile phone and geotagging news footage greater than the risks. These findings along with the findings related to the first research question are consistent with findings from earlier studies e.g. [9]. When users identify *who* is requesting the location information and *why* the information is needed, as well as when the sharing is perceived as useful and creating or providing added value, they are more positive towards sharing location related information and privacy concerns are mitigated.

Practical implications. Our results indicate that using location information in reader reporting activity is possible to implement in practice by the news organizations. In case of LBA, this should happen based on an informed consent and agreed terms especially in the case of locating the mobile users based on their mobile location and sending them location-based assignments (push). As discussed earlier, user initiated retrieval of LBA (pull) may be more acceptable than push in terms of considering the privacy related issues. Furthermore, the participants mentioned as benefits

for themselves in location-based crowdsourcing the tip-offs for reporting as well as the usefulness and easiness of automatic geotagging for the activity carried out in mobile context [43]. Geotags were also mentioned to provide value by making it easier to identify and use accurate location information in geolocating. This in turn provides value for the audience when consuming news. Overall, the perceived benefits of using location information seem to be assessed higher than the risks indicating that news organizations may explore this potential and develop their processes as well as reported news stories accordingly.

Relevance, limitations and future work. Overall, only a few user studies exist in the field of journalism that support the development of future location-based assignment processes [42][43]. Results and implications based on our studies can be used as initial guidelines when developing LBA and geotagging related processes and tools from the point of view of readers' preferences. Furthermore, the approach presented to studying and categorizing the relevant preference dimensions provides an initial framework to develop and refine further.

The results from our user studies are not directly generalizable due to the small number of participants, opportunistic sample and the studies not being long-term field trials in real-life journalistic processes. The first study inquiring the perceptions of the users based on scenarios of use and the second study being a quasi-experiment in field conditions provide indicative but not definitive results. In addition, the culture and the country in question may have an effect on the findings as well as the organization type may affect the results in the case of "yellow press", for example.

Future research could address the use of mobile assignments as well as LBA in real-life crowdsourcing settings with news organizations and compare use of intermediaries, such as Scoopshot, with news organizations' own reader reporter communities. Specific issues to address could include the motivations to participate in the activity, incentives, solutions for supporting high quality contributions by the participants, as well as the changes in the work processes, roles of the professionals and in the collaboration between the newsroom and readers, for example.

6. CONCLUSIONS
We presented a framework with seven dimensions for the preferences of readers to participate in location-based crowdsourcing of news content. The seven dimensions are 1) Organization type, 2) Task type, 3) Temporal context, 4) Location to receive LBA, 5) Precision of the location query, 6) Situation (Social and task context), and 7) Incentives. We found that all other dimensions except the organization type affected the willingness to receive LBA. Furthermore, we found that most participants of the second study did not find it risky to share their location information with the newsroom. The benefits and created value of LBA and geotagging were mainly perceived greater than the risks, both on a personal level and for news production. Using location information of the reader reporters therefore seems to offer new possibilities for the news organizations. The presented framework can be used in future studies on location-based crowdsourcing and in informing the development of location-based crowdsourcing processes.

7. ACKNOWLEDGMENTS

We thank Janne Kaijärvi and Santtu Parkkonen at Sanoma Kaupunkilehdet for cooperation. This research was supported by Next Media SHOK programme of TIVIT and by the Finnish Doctoral Program on User-Centered Information Technology (UCIT).

8. REFERENCES

[1] Alt, F., Shirazi, A. S., Schmidt, A., Kramer, U., Nawaz, Z. 2010. Location-based crowdsouring – Extending crowdsourcing to the real world. In *Proc. NordiCHI2010*, 13-22.

[2] Antikainen, M. Väätäjä, H. 2010. Rewarding in open innovation communities – How to motivate members. *Int. J. Entrepreneurship and Innovation Management. (IJEIM), 11*, 4, 440-456.

[3] Barkhuus, L., Dey, A. 2003. Location-based services for mobile telephony: a study of users' privacy concerns. *Proc. Interact 2003*, 709-712.

[4] Beckett, C. 2008. SuperMedia. Blackwell.

[5] Bonney, R., Ballard, H., Jordan, R., McCallie, E., Phillips, T., Shirk, J. And Wilderman, C. C. 2009. *Public Participation in Scientific Research: Defining the Field and Assessing Its Potential for Informal Science Education - a CAISE Inquiry Group Report.*, Center for Advancement of Informal Science Education, Wa, DC.

[6] Bradshaw, P.2011 Crowdsourcing investigative journalism: a case study. http://onlinejournalismblog.com/2011/11/08/crowdsourcing-investigative-journalism-a-case-study-part-1/

[7] Bradshaw, P. And Rohumaa, L. 2011. The online journalism handbook: Skills to survive and thrive in the digital age. Longman.

[8] Brush, A.J., Krumm, J., and Scott, J. Exploring end user preferences for location obfuscation, location-based services, and the value of location. *Proc. Ubicomp 2010*, ACM (2010).

[9] Consolvo, S., Smith, I.E., Matthews, T., LaMarca, A. Tabert, J., Powledge, P. 2005. Location disclosure to social relations: Why, when, & what people want to share. *Proc. CHI 2005*, 81-90.

[10] Cramer, H., Rost, M., Holmquist. L.E. 2011. Performing a check-in: emerging practices, norms and 'conflicts' in location-sharing using foursquare. In *Proc. MobileHCI '11*, ACM, 57-66.

[11] Domingo, D. et al. 2008. Participatory journalism practices in the media and beyond. Journalism Practice 2,3, 326-342.

[12] Eagle, N. 2009. txteagle: Mobile Crowdsourcing. *Proc. HCII2009*, LNCS 5623, Springer, 447-456.

[13] Estelles-Arolas, E., Gonzalez-Ladrod-de-Guevara, F. Towards an integrated crowdsourcing definition. Accepted for publication in Journal of Information Science.

[14] Gillmor, D. 2004. We the media: technology empowers a new grassroots journalism. *Proc. HYPERTEXT '04*. ACM, 270-271.

[15] Greengard, S. 2011. Following the Crowd. Communications of the ACM, 54 (2), 20-22.

[16] Howe, J. 2009. Crowdsourcing: Why the power of the crowd is driving the future of business, Crown business.

[17] Iachello, G., Hong, J. End-user privacy in human-computer interaction. *Found. Trends Hum.-Comp. Int.* 1, 1 (2007), 1-137.

[18] Jumisko-Pyykkö, S., Utriainen, T. 2010. A hybrid method for the context of use: Evaluation of user-centered quality of experience for mobile (3D) television. *Int J of Multimedia Tools and Appl,*, 1-41.

[19] Jumisko-Pyykkö, S., & Vainio, T. (2010). Framing the Context of Use for Mobile HCI. *IJMHCI, 2*(4), 1-28.

[20] Kelley, P., Benisch, M., Cranor, L., Sadeh, N. 2011. When are users comfortable sharing locations with advertisers? *Proc. CHI '11*. ACM, 2449-2452.

[21] Kindberg, T., Sellen, A., Geelhoed E. 2004. Security and Trust in Mobile Interactions: A Study of User's Perceptions and Reasoning. In *Proc. UbiComp 2004*, Springer, 196-213.

[22] Kittur, A., Khamkar, S., André, Pl and Kraut, R. 2012. CrowdWeaver: visually managing complex crowd work. In *Proc. CSCW '12*. ACM, 1033-1036.

[23] Konomi, S., Thepvilojana, N., Suzuki, R., Pirttikangas, S., Sezaki, K., Tobe, Y. 2009. Askus: Amplifying mobile actions. In *Proc. Pervasive 2009*, Springer, 202-219.

[24] Lederer, S., Hong, J.I., Jiang, X., Dey, A.K., Landay, J.A., Mankoff, J.. 2003. Towards everyday privacy for ubiquitous computing. Technical Report UCB-CSD-03-1283, Univ of CA, Berkeley, CA.

[25] Lietsala, K. and Sirkkunen, E. 2008. Social Media. Introduction to the tools and processes of participatory economy. Tampere University Press, Finland.

[26] Malhotra, N., Kim, S., Agarwal, J. 2004. Internet user's information privacy concerns (iuipc): The construct, the scale and a causal model. *Information Systems Research* 15, 4, 336-355.

[27] Mokbel, M. F. Chow, C. and Aref. , W. G. 2006. The new casper: Query processing for location services without compromising privacy. In VLDB, pages 763–774.

[28] Müller, C., Wan, L., and Hrg, D. 2010. Dealing with wandering: a case study on caregivers' attitudes towards privacy and autonomy when reflecting the use of LBS. In *Proc.* GROUP '10, ACM, 75-84.

[29] Myles, G., Friday, A., Davies, N. 2003. Preserving Privacy in Environments with Location-Based Applications. *Pervasive Computing*, 1, IEEE, 56-64.

[30] Outing, S. 2005. The 11 Layers of Citizen Journalism. Poynter org, .http://www.poynter.org/uncategorized/69328/the-11-layers-of-citizen-journalism/

[31] Questionnaire items translated to English available at: https://sites.google.com/site/helivaataja/links

[32] Raento, M. and Oulasvirta, A. 2008. Designing for Privacy and self-presentation in social awareness. *Personal and Ubiquitous Computing*, 12, 7, 527-542.

[33] Savage, N. 2012. Gaining wisdom from the crowds. Communications of the ACM, 53, 3, 13-15.

[34] Singer et. al. 2011. Participatory Journalism: Guarding Open Gates at Online Newspapers, Wiley-Blackwell.

[35] Sloane, P. 2011. A Guide to Open Innovation and Crowdsourcing: Advice From Leading Experts, Kogan Page.

[36] Surowiecki, J. 2005. The Wisdom of Crowds, Abacus.

[37] Talukder, N. and Ahamed, S., I. 2010. Preventing multi-query attack in location-based services. In Proc. WiSec '10. ACM, 25-36.

[38] Tapscott, D. and Williams, A. 2006. Wikinomics: How mass collaboration changes everything, Atlantic Books.

[39] Toch, E., Cranshaw, J., Drielsma, P., Tsai, J., Kelley, P., Springfield, J., Cranor, L., Hong, J., and Sadeh, N.. 2010. Empirical models of privacy in location sharing. *Proc. Ubicomp '10*. ACM, 129-138.

[40] Tsai, J., Kelley, P., Cranor, L., Sadeh, N. 2009. Location-Sharing Technologies: Privacy Risks and Controls. *Proc. TPRC 2009.*

[41] Tsai, J., Kelley, P., Drielsma, P., Cranor, L., Hong, J., and Sadeh N.. 2009. Who's viewed you?: the impact of feedback in a mobile location-sharing application. *Proc. CHI '09*, ACM, 2003-2012.

[42] Väätäjä, H., Egglestone P. 2012. Briefing news reporting with mobile assignments – Perceptions, needs and challenges. *Proc. CSCW2012.* ACM.

[43] Väätäjä, H., Vainio, T., Sirkkunen, E., and Salo, K. 2011. Crowdsourced news reporting: supporting news content creation with mobile phones. In *Proc. MobileHCI '11.* ACM, 435-444.

[44] Väätäjä, H. 2012. Readers' motivations to participate in hyperlocal news content creation. In *Proc. GROUP 2012.* ACM.

[45] Wardle, C. And Williams, A.2008. ugc@thebbc: Understanding its impact upon contributors, non-contributors and BBC News. http://www.bbc.co.uk/blogs/knowledgeexchange/cardiffone.pdf

[46] Xu, H., Teo, H-H., Tan, B. and Agarwal, R. 2009. The Role of Push-Pull Technology in Privacy Calculus: The Case of Location-Based Services. J. Manage. Inf. Syst. 26, 3, 135-174.

[47] Yan, T., Marzilli, M., Holmes, R. Ganesan, D. Corner, M. 2009. mCrowd – A platform for mobile crowdsourcing. *Proc. SenSys '09*, ACM, 347-348.

Designing an Authoring Environment for Community-Created Virtual Heritage Environments: Experiences with the Geografia Platform

Pedro Silva
University of Central Florida
12461 Research Parkway Suite 500, #152
Orlando, FL 32826-3241

pedrosilva@knights.ucf.edu

ABSTRACT
The melding of geographic data and traditional storytelling methods demonstrates great potential for educators across the social sciences. However, despite the drive toward web 2.0 technologies, authoring a location-based narrative for mobile platforms remains a high-barrier proposition difficult to crowd source. Geografia is an authoring tool that gives communities the power to create a virtual heritage environment detailing their town's history. This paper discusses the design of the Geografia platform and the implications raised from its first deployment in which approximately 80 secondary school students collaborated to form a geo-narrative of an event in their community's history.

Categories and Subject Descriptors
K.3.1 Computer Uses in Education --- Collaborative Learning.

General Terms
Design, Human Factors.

Keywords
Mobile storytelling, Geographic narrative, Community history

1. INTRODUCTION
The growing ubiquity of smart phones have created a broad interest in the field of mobile, location-based storytelling, or geo-narratives. Geo-narratives rely on mobile technologies, specifically smart phones' geo-locating services, to give users a sense of narrative agency based on their location. For geo-narratives, the real-world location in which narrative is presented to users is essential. In many cases, geo-narratives transmit story through narration stored via digital audio files. These narrative segments -- narrative nodes for non-linear geo-narratives -- are location-dependant, often triggering only when the user is near the location assigned to the narrative segment. As a result, geo-narratives strive to tell stories about places to users present in those same places.

The melding of geographic data and traditional storytelling methods demonstrates great potential for educators across the social sciences. Geography scholars often cite geo-narratives as an example of an emerging trend toward Neogeography, whose

practitioners use geographic information not for staging claims on scientific standards, but instead "tend towards the intuitive, expressive, personal, absurd, and/or/ artistic" [6].

This increased accessibility has led the "rise of volunteered geographic information, crowd sourcing, Neogeography and citizen science, amongst many other newly emerging terms linked to the geographic profession" [6]. However, despite the drive toward web 2.0 technologies, authoring a geo-narrative for mobile platforms remains a high-barrier proposition difficult to crowd source.

Geografia sought to be an authoring tool for geo-narratives that was powerfully flexible, yet accessible. It strived to allow community curators to (1) crowd source the creation of narrative segments to community members, (2) assign those narrative segments to locations across the community, and (3) easily manipulate those segments into linear and non-linear story structures. In essence, Geografia sought to give communities the power to author a geo-narrative detailing their own history to share with visitors and community members -- ultimately, a community-created virtual heritage environment (VHE).

This paper details the design of the Geografia platform and a walk-through of its final iteration. The paper's final section discusses design and ethical implications raised from its first deployment in which approximately 80 secondary school students collaborated to form a geo-narrative of a controversial event in their community's history.

2. RELATED WORK
Industry and state-funded projects explore location-based applications within the tourism industry, historical site visitations and education across the social sciences [1 - 3]. In addition, several case studies continue to craft narratological frameworks for geo-located storytelling across the arts. Such frameworks include VHEs, virtual spaces in which users may freely navigate and activate non-linear story nodes [4].

Educators argue the benefits of storification when relating history to students, citing its ability to overcome "fragmentation of the knowledge of historical characters and events by relating these with meaningful connections of temporality and sequence" [7].

InStory [1] seeks to incorporate an interactive digital narrative across a historically significant site, Quinta da Regaleira in Sintra, Portugal. Barbas and Correira seek to guide visitors through the heritage site, helping them "map out the vast and intricate geographical area and show the thematic or historical places that could interest [them] among the more than 20 sites" [1]. InStory is driven by a system of fictional threads that repeatedly adjust according to users' location in physical space.

Geo-narratives share many aspects with Hybrid-reality games (HRGs), or alternate-reality games (ARGs), all of which take users' real-world locations as inputs that serve as users' main form of agency [5]. For ARGs and HRGs, these inputs are often translated into a digital, representational space where player interactions and scores are computed according to gameplay rules and presented back to users via mobile phone screens.

3. THE GEOGRAFIA PLATFOM

Geografia takes its title from the Esperanto word for geography, reflecting its hopes for encouraging knowledge convergence across varied communities. Geografia proposes an authoring environment that allows community curators to (1) crowd source the creation of narrative segments to community members, (2) assign those narrative segments to locations across the community, and (3) easily manipulate those segments into linear and non-linear story structures.

Those persons in the role of community curators are tasked with soliciting narrative assets from community members. These assets may take various forms, including digital slideshows, images, text, audio narration, or film clips. Once these assets are collected, community curators upload the assets onto the Geografia server. From here, community curators can assign geographic markers, ties to physical locations across the community, to each asset and edit their behavior. The assignment of assets and editing of geographic markers are the primary building blocks for a geo-narrative authored via the Geografia platform.

Geografia proposes an authoring environment whose workflow is split across three steps: authoring, testing, and presenting. To accommodate these three steps, the Geografia platform consists of three sections: (1) a marker library for storing and editing narrative nodes and their corresponding assets, the primary authoring environment, (2) a website for off-site viewing and testing, entitled the *stage test* and (3) a mobile web-application for on-site viewing, the final product. The three sections are outlined in detail in the sections below.

3.1 The Marker Library

The marker library served as the primary authoring environment for community curators. Within the library, curators are tasked with (1) creating markers that correspond to physical locations across the community, posts on which to tether the community-created assets, (2) linking each community-created asset to a marker, and (3) editing each marker's behavior parameters.

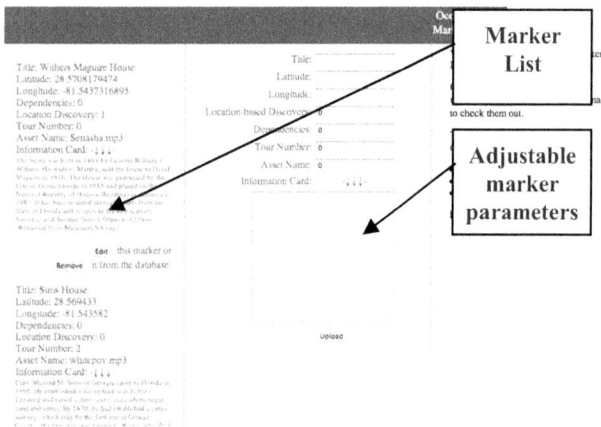

Figure 1. The marker library interface.

To create markers, curators input a new pair of coordinates (longitude and latitude), a name for the marker, and an optional text description. Once created, markers appear in the marker list as shown in figure 1.

To link community-created assets to existing markers, curators select the desired marker from the marker list and enter the desired asset's file name in the corresponding field.

To edit a marker's behavior, curators select the desired marker from the marker list to access a variety of adjustable behavior parameters. These parameters include the following:

☐ *Dependencies*. Curators may form markers whose activation is dependant on the user's visitation of other markers. For this parameter, curators may list a series of markers that must be visited prior to the selected marker. A marker is withheld from the mobile web application's map until all its dependencies are met. For example, if a curator lists *Marker 2* as dependant on *Marker 1*, *Marker 2* will remain inactive until the user visit the location of *Marker 1*.

☐ *Location-based discovery*. Curators have the ability to turn this parameter on or off. When turned on, the selected marker does not appear on a user's mobile web application map until that user is physically near the marker. For example, *Marker 1* is titled *Old Post Office* and corresponds to the location of the town's historical post office. With location-based discovery turned on, the *Old Post Office* marker will not be visible to a user across town; however, a user who is at the historical post office's location is able to interact with the *Old Post Office* marker and view its corresponding assets.

☐ *Path animation*. Curators may animate markers along desired paths at adjustable speeds. For this parameter, curators input destination coordinates (latitude and longitude) and a travel time (in seconds). As soon as a marker appears on the map, the marker animates from its starting position to its destination coordinates, its speed determined by the allotted travel time. Curators have the ability to create a series of these animations in order to form a more complex movement tracks. For example, curators may choose to capture the movement of historical figures, parades, or riots as they passed through town.

These three behavior parameters are mutually compatible, so that curators may design complex behaviors through the myriad combinations of parameters. The curators may, for example, create the following three markers with the corresponding parameters:

☐ (1) *Town Hall*: dependencies: none; location-based discovery: no; path animation: none.

☐ (2) *The Elementary School*: dependencies: *Town Hall*; location-based discovery: no; path animation: none.

☐ (3) *Town Parade:* dependencies: *The Elementary School*; location-based discovery: no; path animation: to *Town Hall* in 10 seconds.

In the above example, a newly arrived user stands near the site of the town's old elementary school and sees the marker *Town Hall* as the only marker on the mobile web application's map. Once the user walks to *Town Hall*'s location and interacts with its corresponding assets, the user may receive a hint to go to where a historical town leader was educated. Upon returning to the site of the old elementary school, the marker *The Elementary School* appears. Once the user views *The Elementary School*'s corresponding assets, the marker *Town Parade* appears on the user's map. Once the user reaches *Town Parade*'s location and activates the marker, the marker immediately begins to trace a path toward town hall.

3.2 The Stage Test
The stage test served as a traditional website on which a curator could see all created markers visualized on a map of the community as seen in figure 2, mirroring the final mobile web application, and access markers' corresponding assets off site.

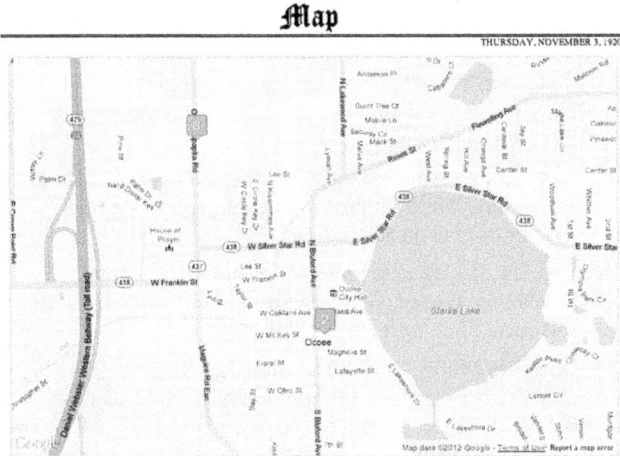

Figure 2. The stage test interface.

The stage test employed an icon to represent a perspective user's location on the map. Curators were free to click and drag this icon to mimic movements in physical space, and in so doing, test complex marker behaviors and use-cases for potential audiences.

The stage test and marker library are designed so that curators can easily switch between them; updates made to the marker library are instantly viewable on the stage test.

3.3 The Final Product
The final product took the form of a mobile web application consisting of two parts: (1) the interactive map, and (2) the marker list.

☐ *Interactive map.* The map allows users to view and interact with markers. Once near a visible marker, users tap on the marker to activate an information card with the marker's name, description and link to its corresponding assets.

☐ *Marker list.* The marker list contains an index of all the community's markers, no matter their visibility according their respective parameters. The marker list allows users an easy access to markers they may have previously discovered or markers tied to assets that the users or users' friends or family may have authored.

4. DEPLOYING GEOGRAFIA
An exploratory study was conducted to evaluate Geografia as a platform for authoring a community-created VHE and identify more focused avenues for future research. Graduate student researchers at the University of Central Florida served as community curators. Graduate students recruited the support of a local community high school whose social science teachers were eager to incorporate Geografia into their current curriculum, the civil rights movement. As a topic, grad students and collaborating teachers chose to establish a VHE that would serve as a memorial for several African-Americans who died during a tumultuous town riot at the turn of the 20th century.

Four social science classes, approximately 80 students, were tasked with interpreting historical documents and secondary sources in order to craft the digital assets that would serve as the building blocks of the town's geo-narrative. Serving as community curators, grad students checked these assets for historical accuracy, assigned them to geographical markers, and arranged the markers into a linear narrative.

4.1 Student Submissions
Although some submissions were displayed intact, many were present in edited form. Most interestingly, these assets serve as creative interpretations, a moment's glimpses into a student's interactions with primary and secondary source materials, as well as their place along cultural boundaries. Student assets depict a decidedly modern ideology of an egalitarian society, oftentimes disassociating themselves from the "racist whites," as they were often labeled. Although perhaps out of place within the confines of the project's historical context, these interpretations allow for interesting insight into student reactions to their community's past and a struggle to define their role within it.

One student, for example, choosing to animate a white family fleeing from the riot, describes a meeting between the white family and Hispanic friends in north Florida. "But why did you guys leave, you're white," says the Hispanic friend. "Yes," they respond. "But we wouldn't want our children to grow up in that kind of society."

In another asset, students recreate a dialogue exchange at a woman's club between white club members and an African-American widow a mere five years after the riot. "I'm so sorry that you lost your husband" says a white club member. "It must have been a very terrible sight to see, looking out your window at all the white protestors."

4.2 Who Interprets Community History
Confrontations regarding the project arose when city council members reacted negatively to students' classification of the riot as a massacre. Meanwhile, collaborating teachers and students felt strongly justified in their classification.

The theme of civil rights and the judgment -- perceived and real -- of a community's past actions strikes particularly contentious and passionate conflicts. However, Geografia gives rise to several ethical implications no matter its target theme. Foremost of them is the matter of who is given the authority to interpret a community's history. It is clear from Geografia's pilot study that this problem needs clear consideration. Most importantly, Geografia must not be positioned as an authentic, non-biased historical retelling on par with museum-curated VHEs. Although it is difficult to measure whether or not community members believed as such, future implementations of Geografia must take further efforts to brief communities on the ethical considerations of community-created history.

However, despite the generated conflict, it is the researcher's conjecture that Geografia serves as a platform for historical interpretations, a snapshot of individuals' intersection with their community's past and their family's place within it. As such a tool, Geografia reflects more closely the methodologies exhibited in Neogeography: the intuitive, the expressive, the personal.

Ethical implications raised through Geografia promote a awareness of author motivation, and as such may serve as an potential tool for media-literacy training. Additionally, these considerations may serve to encourage participating students to engage in an authentic community of practice, navigating issues of interpretation, conflicting primary sources, as well as quandaries of ethics and perspective that closely emulate that of professional historians.

Interactions with collaborating teachers and students hint at an increased level of engagement, many citing the particular draw of creating a tangible narrative that they could walkthrough and showcase. Teachers also cited the benefits of historical storification coupled with the act of creating assets that fit specific town locations. This observed increase in student engagement hints at the potential effects of branding historical events to well-known physical spaces. More focused research to test hypothesises in this area must be conducted in future Geografia implementations.

5. FUTURE RESEARCH AND CONCLUSION

Interactions with collaborating teachers and students hint at the potential of community-created geo-narratives for engaging students in social science classrooms. Future research hopes to explore the potential of coupling historical events to well-known physical locations through focused hypothesis testing and student questionnaires.

Geografia is an authoring tool that gives communities the power to create a virtual heritage environment detailing their town's history. Geografia proposes an authoring environment that allows community curators to (1) crowd source the creation of narrative segments to community members, (2) assign those narrative segments to locations across the community, and (3) easily manipulate those segments into linear and non-linear story structures. Deploying Geografia raises several ethical considerations regarding community-created history that require serious consideration. However, preliminary data hints at the potential of Geografia for encouraging an authentic community of practice that closely simulates the duties of professional historians.

6. REFERENCES

[1] Barbas, H. and N. Correia (2009). "The Making of an Interactive Digital Narrative -- InStory." Euromedia.

[2] Reitmaier, T. and G. Marsden (2009). Bringing Digital Storytelling to the Mobile. Human-Computer Interaction INTERACT, Springer.

[3] Stein, J., S. Ruston, et al. (2009). "Location-Based Mobile Storytelling." International Journal of Technology and Human Interaction 5(1): 41-50.

[4] Tuck, D. and I. Kuksa (2009). Virtual Heritage Tours: Developing Interactive Narrative-Based Environments for Historical Sites, Springer.

[5] De Souza e Silva, A. (2008). "Alien Revolt (2005-2007): A Case Study of the First Location-Based Mobile Game in Brazil." Technology and Society Magazine, IEEE 27(1): 18-28.

[6] Hudson-Smith, A. and A. Crooks (2009). "Neogeography, Gaming and Virtual Environments: Web 2.0, Mapping for the Masses and the Renaissance of Geographic Information."

[7] Akkerman, S., W. Admiraal, et al. (2009). "Storification in History education: A mobile game in and about medieval Amsterdam." Computers & Education 52(2): 449-459.

Decision Making Tasks in Time-Critical Medical Settings

Aleksandra Sarcevic, Zhan Zhang, Diana S. Kusunoki
College of Information Science and Technology, Drexel University
3141 Chestnut Street
Philadelphia, PA 19104

{aleksarc, zhan.zhang, diana.s.kusunoki}@drexel.edu

ABSTRACT

We examine decision-making tasks and information sources during fast-paced, high-risk medical events, such as trauma resuscitation. Interviews with surgical team leaders and ED physicians reveal several environmental aspects that make decision making difficult, including diagnostic tradeoffs, missing and unreliable information, and managing multiple patients simultaneously. We discuss the implications of these findings for the design of wall displays to support decision making in time-critical medical settings.

Categories and Subject Descriptors

H.5.3 [**Group and Organization Interfaces**]: Computer-supported cooperative work.

General Terms

Design; Human Factors.

Keywords

Decision making, information sources, healthcare.

1. INTRODUCTION

The development of clinical decision support systems over the past decades shows continued effort in improving and augmenting a key aspect of high-quality medical care—clinical decision making [5]. Medical researchers have been seeking ways to improve accuracy, efficacy and expediency of decision making by studying how physicians make decisions [3]. Although not directly focusing on decision making, CSCW research has contributed to this body of work through studies of work coordination, awareness, and idea formation [7][8][10]. Yet, little is known about what constitutes decision-making tasks in emergency care and how different information sources support this medical activity. Unlike other areas of medicine, decision density in emergency medicine is extremely high [3]. Understanding the complexity of decision-making process is thus essential to designing and developing computerized support.

This work is part of a larger research effort to examine work processes of trauma teams and elicit design requirements for wall displays to improve situation awareness and decision making. Here we focus on decision-making tasks and information sources used by team leaders. We analyze interviews with ten leaders collected during a six-month field study in a Level I trauma center. This study complements our prior work in which we

observed resuscitation events and performed micro-analysis of video recordings to understand trauma teamwork processes. The contribution of this note lies in empirically identifying major decisions, information sources, and challenges in decision making during a fast-paced, high-risk medical event.

1.1 Trauma Resuscitation Overview

Trauma resuscitation—the initial management and treatment of injured patients in the emergency department—is a fast-paced, information-intensive medical domain, with critical decisions made about once a minute [4]. A team of seven to 15 medical specialists rapidly performs different but complementary tasks that are focused on identifying life-threatening injuries and stabilizing the patient. Patient evaluation follows the Advanced Trauma Life Support (ATLS) protocol that provides an organized approach to management and treatment of an injured patient [1]. Awareness of events that occur during trauma resuscitation is essential for effective decision making.

Trauma teams form dynamically upon patient arrival. Each team has a designated team leader, often a senior surgical resident or a fellow, who supervises patient care, makes major decisions and delegates work to others. The surgical team leader is assisted by a junior surgical resident who performs hands-on evaluation and reports to the team leader. Although directed by surgeons in most U.S. trauma centers, trauma resuscitations at some centers also involve emergency department (ED) physicians.

2. METHODS

Our research site was a Level I trauma center of an urban pediatric teaching hospital in Washington, DC that provides 24-hour emergency and trauma care to over 1,000 patients a year. Trauma patients are treated in one of two designated rooms within the emergency department, called code rooms. The study was approved by the hospital's Institutional Review Board (IRB).

We individually interviewed ten trauma team leaders, including four ED physicians, five senior surgical residents and one surgical fellow. On average, ED physicians reported 20 years of experience in emergency medicine. Senior surgical residents were in their fourth year of residency and on a three-month rotation at our research site during the interviews. The surgical fellow had seven years of surgical training and was board certified in general surgery. Interviews lasted from 30 minutes to an hour, depending on providers' availability. The questions focused on their roles and responsibilities, decisions, and information sources.

The interview transcripts were analyzed using Atlas.ti, a program for organizing, storing, and manipulating qualitative data. All transcripts were read to uncover statements representing key steps in decision making. We then used an open coding technique to identify common themes. This analysis resulted in a set of distinct themes that described major decision-making tasks, information sources, and factors affecting decision making.

3. FINDINGS

We first describe decisions that leaders make from the moment they learn about an incoming trauma patient to the patient's transfer to another hospital unit. We then describe information sources used for decision making. Finally, we discuss factors that increase the difficulty of making decisions.

3.1 Decision Tasks in Trauma Resuscitation

Decision making during trauma resuscitation centers around two goals: (1) address immediate threats to life, and (2) determine multiple treatment plans. Decisions about treatments require observations (evidence), but observations take time and resources. The key is identifying the best tradeoff. The code room is only a temporary stop on a patient's hospitalization path; the patient's stay in the room is kept at a minimum (on average, 20 minutes), until the patient is stable enough to move to a different hospital unit. Because the goal is to treat the greatest threats first, a definitive diagnosis is not a priority. Hence, the very first decisions can be formulated from the triage (routing) perspective. Our interviews revealed three such decisions. First, the leader determines if the patient needs surgery. Making this decision early allows the team to reserve the operating room and notify the surgeon. This initial triage decision is based on patient pre-hospital information. An ED attending explained:

"What was going on in my mind was that he was going to need a very short stay in the code room and was going to quickly need to go to the OR. Especially once I saw him. I thought, he's stable enough, but he needs to go to the OR. Let's just move this along, call the attending, and get him to the place where they can see what's cut, sew it up, fix him up." [ED1]

Second, the leader determines if the patient needs a computer tomography (CT) scan. CT scan decisions are also based on pre-hospital information (e.g., loss of consciousness signals the need for a CT scan) or on physical exam upon patient arrival.

Finally, the leader decides if additional specialists or more experienced providers are needed. Depending on the severity of injury, the patient may need a neurosurgeon, an orthopedic surgeon, or an intensive care unit fellow. Similar to other triage decisions, the decision to call a specialist is made early in the process to allow sufficient time for the specialist to arrive:

"If a patient comes in and it sounds like a pedestrian was struck and is now having a bad airway and is hypotensive, then I know right away I may have to call the anesthesia attending just so there's somebody more experienced there." [SF1]

Once triage decisions are made, the leaders move onto decisions that can be done with people and resources available in the room. These decisions follow the evaluation protocol, and are based on findings from each protocol step. A surgical resident described:

"Does this person need to be intubated? Is their airway clear? Are they awake enough to protect their airway? Do they need fluids? Is their neurological status adequate? Do they need blood? ... So, I have to make those decisions based on what I hear about the physical exam, keeping in mind the mechanism." [SR4]

3.2 A Decision Needs Information

To make decisions, trauma team leaders rely on a diverse set of information sources.

Pre-hospital information: Information about the incoming patient is conveyed by EMS paramedics in a phone call to ED attending physicians receiving the patient. Based on this phone call, a page is sent to the trauma team, giving the first clue about the patient's injuries. Page information includes estimated arrival time, number of patients, mechanism of injury, and patient status. Team leaders use this information to prepare equipment, summon the specialists, and anticipate treatments. An ED attending described the importance of pre-hospital information:

"So [you hear] a child who fell from a tree and landed on their back, breathing 60, oxygen saturation 89%, you are saying to yourself there's a lung contusion or a hemothorax or a pneumothorax. You immediately want to presume that's happening. So you need chest tubes out. And we should think about intubating on arrival. Let's agree upon a weight. Let's get these meds drawn up before the child even arrives..." [ED3]

EMS report: Similar to pre-hospital information, a brief, verbal report provided by the EMS paramedics during patient handover helps guide leaders' decisions about treatments. The most critical information here is the mechanism of injury:

"It's very important because you need to know mechanism of injury, like velocity, whether it's penetrating, whether it's blunt. You need some frame of reference to start. There's a big difference between a restrained passenger in a rear-ended vehicle versus a rollover, unrestrained, with a passenger found outside the car. That's why you listen for 30 seconds or a minute to hear the story, so you know what's going on." [SR5]

Patient: Patients are an important source of information throughout the resuscitation. A quick glance at the patient upon arrival provides valuable context for forming a decision:

"If I hear a three year old fell from the couch, no loss of consciousness, and is now crying, then to me it sounds like not that sick because it's not very significant mechanism and there is no loss of consciousness. I also think, probably does not have to go to the OR because it's stable." [SF1]

Physical exam: Results from exams prescribed by the ATLS protocol (airway, breathing, circulation, and neurological) provide critical information by which leaders maintain awareness about the patient status and make major decisions:

"I typically stand at the foot of the bed, listening to the information from the resident who is on the primary and secondary survey, and making decisions about fluid boluses, medications, x-rays, and blood tests that are required." [ED3]

Sometimes, however, leaders may not be satisfied with the quality of information received from the resident examining the patient. To confirm the findings, leaders evaluate on their own:

"If I don't feel like I'm getting the information that I want from the resident doing the exam then I will do my own exam. If I can't trust what they're doing, it doesn't seem like they know what they're doing, and I need that information to make a decision then yes, you have to jump in there for the patients." [ED4]

Vital signs monitor: The vital signs monitor is a salient source of information. It displays live data such as oxygen saturation, heart rate, respiratory rate, and blood pressure. Vital signs data help leaders monitor patient status and their reactions to treatments:

"A patient is hypotensive, they got a fluid bolus, and then they respond, their blood pressure goes up, and after a while, the blood pressure drops again. The nurse reports 'the pressure is back down, should we give another bolus' and you may say, 'yes, give another bolus." [SF1]

Team members. Trauma resuscitation is a team-based process; each member has a role and a set of responsibilities. Information exchanged during the process is critical to decision making as different team members acquire different information. Although communication breakdowns are common, the collocated nature of work makes information sharing fast and efficient:

"For an individual patient, it's fairly easy to get the information because you have a group of people that are focused on treating the patient, and you have a bunch of nurses and techs there that can draw blood, insert IV, get you the vital signs..." [SR1]

Laboratory tests. Laboratory tests provide additional information but take time to obtain. Most common tests include x-ray imaging, blood, and urine tests. The tests provide reliable evidence, as the results either confirm or refute the initial diagnoses.

3.3 What Makes Decision Making Difficult

Interviews with trauma team leaders revealed several aspects of the resuscitation environment that complicate decision making.

System complexity and diagnostic tradeoffs. Trauma patients are complex systems, each presenting a unique set of symptoms and injury combinations. Although treatment decisions are grounded in evidence from physical exam and laboratory tests, leaders often face situations in which clear indications for an intervention are absent. A surgical resident described:

"There was one patient recently... [where] the mechanism of what actually happened was not clear and then the difficult part was that there was no acute indication to intubate the patient, but the patient ended up intubated, and I don't think it was a wrong or a right decision, but there just was no clear-cut indication to put a definitive airway in the patient." [SR1]

The lack of clear indications for an intervention has significant implications for decision making. Time pressure demands that decisions be made fast. Yet there are associated risks and benefits of proceeding vs. not proceeding with a procedure. Invasive procedures, such as intubation or chest tube insertion may result in further complications (e.g., infections); they also take time and resources. Alternatively, by not proceeding with an intervention, the leader risks overlooking a potential injury that may result in adverse outcomes. The resident continued:

"If a patient doesn't need an invasive intervention, if there's no clear-cut evidence that they need it, then doing that is considered something of—I don't know if faux pas [false step] is the right word—but I guess it's just one of those things where you get into the gray area. There's no definitive reason to do a procedure, there's some subjective, at least hinting at the indication for whatever the procedure is, but it's nothing that's like clear-cut that says I should do this." [SR1]

Similar tradeoffs are made when deciding about CT scans. If the patient moves and is conscious, there is no clear indication to scan the patient' head for a brain injury. Nonetheless, surgical leaders often order head and spinal cord CT scans (exposing patients to unnecessary radiation) to ensure no injury has been missed. To cope with such situations, surgical leaders seek advice from a senior supervisor, such as an attending surgeon or ED attending:

"It's good to let him [attending] know, not only to keep him in the loop but also because sometimes they have stuff to tell, like a feedback. They would say 'I think we should do this too, how about we obtain x-ray, how about we order this.'" [SR3]

If there are no supervisors in the room, leaders make decisions based on their knowledge of past similar cases and medical training. Solo decision making is, in fact, common in trauma resuscitation. Time pressure rarely allows deliberation or brainstorming activities. Because decisions are made individually, surgical leaders often miss the benefits of collaborative reasoning.

Communication breakdowns. Efficient communication helps leaders maintain awareness of patient status and activities in the room. Code rooms are noisy and crowded, with many people moving and talking in parallel. Although ambient factors pose challenges for information sharing, leaders usually manage to get the information they need. A greater challenge, however, is a lack of communication. Leaders rely on others to collect information and report it aloud. Often times this information sharing is absent:

"The worst communication is no communication, like somebody took blood pressure and just didn't tell anybody else..." [SR1]

"It's important to tell things aloud. I like to hear the medications, especially when we're doing CPR or when I'm putting epinephrine in or atropine. I like to hear it because I want to know that it's been given. And second, I want to hear and remember, okay is this the first dose, is this the second dose, because then you know it's been given, as opposed to not knowing, when you wonder, 'okay how many doses did I give?'" [SR3]

Information reliability. Effective decision making depends on an accurate and comprehensive understanding of the patient status. Having reliable information is thus essential. Often, however, information from sources both internal and external to the hospital is unreliable. Interviews with leaders revealed, for example, that pre-hospital information does not always reflect the actual state of the patient. A resident described:

"I try to get the mechanism of injury out of it, and I might try to get a story, but I don't rely heavily on it, even when people come from outside ED, like a physician will tell you something, and it's not necessarily the case. Sometimes what they're saying is true, and sometimes it's not, for whatever reason." [SR2]

Our participants expressed the need for more detailed and timely pre-hospital information. An ED attending elaborated:

"If there was a way to get EMS report to us from the original team on the ground that was more inclusive of the stuff we need to know like vital signs or patient status. There are many intermediary steps they go through to get the information to us, so a text to us directly from the scene might be more useful as far as decision making before the patient arrives." [ED4]

In addition, information from sensors, such as blood pressure cuff, thermometer or pulse oximeter may not always reflect the actual patient status. Here, the leaders have difficulties determining if the problem is caused by equipment malfunction or if something is wrong with the patient. A resident described a case in which the system's malfunction was caused by a patient's condition:

"I think some of the issues were more of a system thing. The patient was cold, so our sensors didn't work as quick as we'd like, so that was a delay in assessment and care." [SR5]

Severely injured or multiple patients: Interviews with trauma leaders showed that managing individual routine trauma patients is feasible. The difficulties with information gathering and retention arise with severely injured or multiple patients, each requiring rapid response and attention. In these situations, decision making is demanding, with margin for error increasing and cognitive resources decreasing for each additional patient:

"If you have two patients you have to start taking notes. Patient A has no loss of consciousness and patient B has loss of consciousness. For many, two patients are still manageable. Let's say you have four! The other night, we had four patients and one is patient L, one is M, one is N, and one is O. So already differentiating between N and M is almost impossible." [SF1]

4. DISCUSSION AND CONCLUSION

Although the experience of team members increases with every resuscitation, currently there are no mechanisms by which patient information is accrued for rapid integration and analysis of patient data. Decision making is now only minimally supported by technology and trauma teams rely mainly on verbal exchanges to gather and share information. Attempts to introduce computer-aided decision support systems so far have shown limited, though encouraging, results [4]. Interviews with trauma leaders revealed several decision-making challenges, including diagnostic tradeoffs, unreliable information, and information overload. These findings suggest three ways in which information technology can facilitate decision making in trauma resuscitation: (1) provide more information about the current patient; (2) engage other team members in the room or remote specialists; and, (3) enable comparison with past similar cases.

CSCW researchers have proposed different solutions to support coordination and awareness in collocated work, including large wall displays. Wall displays and whiteboards provide a shared and focused memory, which helps with engaging team members in collaborative activities [2][11][13]. Visualizing critical patient information could facilitate decision making by enabling shared mental models and providing real-time patient data throughout the resuscitation process. For example, the display could show trends in vital sign data, administered medications and their timing, the amount of fluid received and completed protocol steps. The challenge here is how to effectively capture information from the environment for timely presentation.

Based on our findings, we envision several possibilities for both capturing and providing more information about the patient. First, leaders emphasized the importance of pre-hospital information, yet complained about its reliability and timeliness. Recent advances in ubiquitous computing, such as environment sensors found on roads, in vehicles and buildings could be used for collecting information at the time of the accident (e.g., sensors in vehicles could provide information about the speed or collision impact for motor vehicle accidents). This information could then be fed (in processed and easily accessible form) directly into hospital wall displays in real-time. Moreover, increased citizen participation in gathering and sharing information through social media in times of crisis could also be explored [12]. For example, witnesses and first responders could send pictures or text information from the accident site directly to the hospital. Such information (processed, organized and vetted) could populate wall displays and allow trauma teams to better prepare for the patient.

Second, our data showed that trauma leaders often proceed with unnecessary procedures to ensure that no injury has been missed, preferring to err on the side of caution. To support decision making in such situations, we envision using an evidence-based approach where past cases could be searched and consulted. Given the hands-busy nature of work, leaders could use natural interaction modalities, such as speech (for querying the system) and gesture (for interactive analysis of the visualized data). Recent study on touchless interaction in neurosurgery using Microsoft's motion sensing input device Kinect has shown that such approaches are feasible [6].

Finally, leaders could also engage with remote specialists when confronted with difficult decisions. Our data showed that surgical residents often seek advice from their attending surgeons, if they are available. Currently, leaders use traditional communication channels such as phone to discuss cases with their supervisors. Telepresence technology could be used to sustain this practice and enable richer communication. Soderholm et al. [9] evaluated the potential of such technology for facilitating paramedic-physician collaboration during resuscitation and found fewer harmful procedures when the technology was used.

In conclusion, by examining decision-making tasks and information sources in trauma resuscitation, we have identified factors that complicate decision making during fast-paced, high-risk medical work. This study is a step toward a more comprehensive understanding of complex teamwork processes in safety-critical medical settings; it considers how factors affecting decision making need to be accounted for when designing technology for emergency medical work.

5. Acknowledgments

This work is supported by NSF grant #0915871.

6. REFERENCES

[1] American College of Surgeons. 2008. Advanced Trauma Life Support® (ATLS®). 8th Edition. Chicago, IL.

[2] Bardram, J. E., Hansen, T. R., and Soegaard, M. 2006. AwareMedia: A shared interactive display supporting social, temporal, and spatial awareness in surgery. In *Proc. ACM CSCW 2006*, 109-118.

[3] Croskerry, P. 2002. Achieving quality in clinical decision making: Cognitive strategies and detection of bias. *Acad. Emerg. Med.* 9, 11 (Nov. 2002), 1184-1204.

[4] Fitzgerald, M et al. 2011. Trauma resuscitation errors and computer-assisted decision support. *Arch. Surg.* 146, 2 (Feb. 2011), 218-225.

[5] Garg, A.X. et al. 2005. Effects of computerized clinical decision support systems on practitioner performance and patient outcomes. *JAMA*, 293, 10 (Mar. 2005), 1223-1238.

[6] Mentis, H.M., O'Hara, K., Sellen, A., and Trivedi, R. 2012. Interaction proxemics and image use in neurosurgery. In *Proc. ACM CHI 2012*, 927-936.

[7] Prante, T., Magerkurth, C., and Streitz, N. 2002. Developing CSCW tools for idea finding: Empirical results and implications for design. In *Proc. ACM CSCW 2002*, 106-115.

[8] Schmidt, K., and Simone, C. 1996. Coordination mechanisms: Towards a conceptual foundation of CSCW system design. *CSCW*, 5, 2-3 (June 1996), 155- 200.

[9] Söderholm, H.M., Sonnenwald, D.H., Cairns, B., Manning, J.E., Welch, G.F., and Fuchs, H. 2007. The potential impact of 3D telepresence technology on task performance in emergency trauma care. In *Proc. ACM GROUP 2007*, 79-88.

[10] Stefik, M., Foster, G., Bobrow, D.G., Kahn, K., Lanning, S., and Suchman, L. 1987. Beyond the chalkboard: Computer support for collaboration and problem solving in meetings. *Communications of the ACM*, 30, 1 (Jan 1987), 32-47.

[11] Teasley, S., Covi, L., Krishnan, M. S., and Olsen, J. S. 2000. How does radical collocation help a team succeed? In *Proc. ACM CSCW 2000*, 339-346.

[12] Vieweg, S., Hughes, A., Starbird, K., and Palen. L. 2010. Microblogging during two natural hazards events: What Twitter may contribute to situational awareness. In *Proc. ACM CHI 2010*, 1079-1088.

[13] Xiao, Y., Lasome, C., Moss, J., Mackenzie, C. F., and Faraj, S. 2001. Cognitive properties of a whiteboard: a case study in a trauma centre. In *Proc. ECSCW 2001*, 259-278.

Eating Alone, Together: New Forms of Commensality

Catherine Grevet
School of Interactive Computing &
GVU Center,
Georgia Institute of Technology,
85 Fifth Street NW
Atlanta, GA 30332 USA
cgrevet@gatech.edu

Anthony Tang
University of Calgary
Department of Computer Science,
University of Calgary
2500 University Drive NW, Calgary,
AB, T2N 1N4, Canada
tonyt@ucalgary.ca

Elizabeth Mynatt
School of Interactive Computing &
GVU Center,
Georgia Institute of Technology,
85 Fifth Street NW
Atlanta, GA 30332 USA
mynatt@gatech.edu

ABSTRACT

Eating with others, or commensality, is an enjoyable activity that serves many important social functions; however, many individuals eat meals alone due to life circumstances, meaning that they miss out on these social benefits. We developed and deployed a simple technology probe providing social awareness around mealtimes to explore how social systems might help alleviate the loneliness of solitary dining. Our findings suggest that these systems can convey a sense of connectedness around a meal; further, our analysis revealed three themes relevant to systems of this type: that contextually-located peripheral awareness engenders connectedness; that such tools can foster a feeling of shared social presence, and that they can be a catalyst for other forms of communication around the meal. These findings suggest that "remote commensality" is not only possible, but that it may take on forms entirely different to that which we are accustomed.

Categories and Subject Descriptors

H.5.3 Group and Organization Interfaces

General Terms

Human Factors

Keywords

HCI, Social computing, Awareness, Contextual information, Design, Food, Mealtime

1. INTRODUCTION

Eating with others is an important cultural practice that enables many social functions: a means for identity construction, a time and place for social engagement, and a shared experience for strengthening social ties [5]. In sociology, a meal consumed in the company of others is called a *commensal* meal [5]. While commensal meals traditionally take place within a family unit, life circumstances dictate that for many living away from family (e.g. college students, seniors, hospitalized individuals), eating alone becomes the norm [1]. For these individuals, traditional commensality is a challenge because it now needs to be actively organized and sought out with geographically proximate peers.

What role can social computing play in restoring the benefits of commensality for individuals that eat solitary meals? To explore this question, we developed and deployed a technology probe (Eating Alone Together Probe, or EATProbe) among a group of young adults. The design of the probe was inspired by prior work on simple ambient social awareness displays that support feelings of social connectedness around daily activities. Our probe provided a small group of friends with basic awareness information about their peers' mealtime activities: whether they were eating in or out, or whether they were preparing, eating, or cleaning up a meal. Five participants, all friends who sometimes ate together, used the system over the course of a week.

Our participants' use of and reactions to the probe suggest that mealtimes provide regular, daily opportunities for engaging social interaction, and that even simple awareness tools can provide people with a sense of social connectedness. Further, our analysis reveals several design opportunities for mealtime awareness systems, and new research avenues in this space. The main contribution of this work is an exploration into how technology might support altogether new routines and behaviors and mealtime activities for individuals lacking the setting of traditional commensality.

2. RELATED WORK

We briefly review work most pertinent to our explorations here: intimate awareness systems in domestic computing, and prior work exploring mealtime connectedness.

2.1 Awareness Systems

Awareness systems were first investigated as a means to connect remote work sites. A more recent theme that has emerged in social awareness systems is achieving "connectedness," or the positive feeling associated with ongoing awareness of a social relationship [2]. Pertinent to our interests, we see two important ideas arising from this prior work: (a) that even simple interactions can support rich expressive behavior as embodied by their use [4], and (b) that awareness systems either embrace an automatic or deliberate style of interaction.

Simple interactions can support rich expressive behavior. For example, Kaye et al. explore the use of a simple "one-bit" awareness system where the interface consists of a single button [4]. Clicking the button would trigger a light that slowly fades at the remote site. This work showed that even though the actual piece of useful information consisted of only a single bit of information, the *meaning* of this bit was embodied largely in its use by participants. That is, participants developed their own understanding of what the signal symbolized—gift-giving,

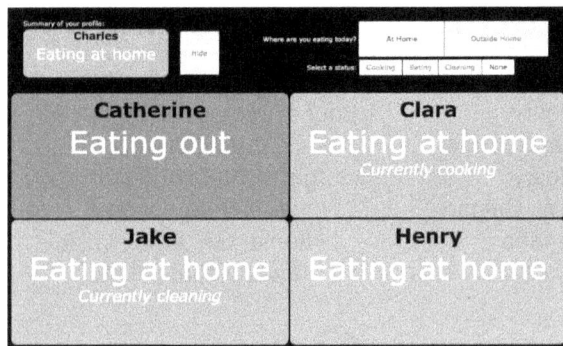

Figure 1. EATProbe interface consisting of a mosaic reflecting the status of each individual

Figure 2. EATProbe installed on the kitchen counter in a participant's house

thoughtfulness, and reciprocity of interaction. The ambiguity inherent in such simple systems seems to afford interpretation and reflection. This reflection formed a core goal of our interest in developing and deploying EATProbe as a means for people to reflect on mealtime interactions with others.

Awareness systems distribute social information either through deliberate user interaction or automatically (e.g. based on sensor information, or reasoning). For example, InPhase fosters a sense of "activity coincidence" when two remote individuals perform similar actions in different homes (e.g. opening a door) by automatically playing a chime when this occurs [6]. Others, such as the one-bit awareness system [4], rely on deliberate user action. The deliberate action of the latter maps closer to the shared experience of a commensal meal, where the social experience is a matter of active, or deliberate participation.

Many of these domestic awareness systems focus on bridging distance between families or intimate partners (e.g. [4]). Our work with EATProbe differs in two fundamental ways: (a) rather than general awareness, we are interested in how awareness systems might be used around what might otherwise be considered a shared social activity (i.e. eating), and (b) we are working with people who do not share the same intimacy as family members (i.e. they are friends). Thus, the basis for understanding what this awareness means is not "grounded in reality" in the same way as with prior domestic awareness systems.

2.2 Mealtime Connectedness

Work focusing on connecting remote individuals around mealtimes has largely explored how to provide an "eating face-to-face" experience. This is generally afforded through a video conferencing system placed near dining areas, or through shared tangible interaction [8]. While this works well for "synchronous meals," where people are eating simultaneously, it works less well for those who live in different time zones. Recent work by Tsujita et al. [7] study how phased recording and playback of "dining videos" can support these individuals. But broadly, these works raise the question of whether video is a necessary medium for this space. For instance, some may not be comfortable with video, as it may draw unnecessary focus on the visual (and aural) experience of the meal (e.g., mastication, or cutlery clinking on dishes). Instead, our work focuses on the unique qualities of this situation that people enjoy experiencing around mealtimes (e.g. company). Our thinking is heavily influenced by the ideas underlying celebratory technologies, where the focus is to support enjoyment and delight, rather than attempting to alleviate deficiencies around an experience [3].

This broadened perspective on commensality is shared in the sociology literature. Commensality is defined by structures: the commensal circle defining the primary social structure [5], and place and time structures facilitate these social organizations [1]. This provides a certain routine to a commensal meal. In contrast, meals eaten alone are usually more flexible and are described as "grazing or snacking" [1]. A system that attempts to support commensality for individuals who live alone should consider these more variant contexts.

3. TECHNOLOGICAL PROBE

At this early stage, it is unclear how the practices of commensal meals carry over when participants are not collocated. The prior work on awareness systems gives us good reason to expect that designs for this space should be fruitful. In this exploratory work, we designed and deployed a simple technological probe to understand this design space.

3.1 Probe Design

Requirements. The design of the Eating Together Alone Probe (EATProbe) was based on three simple requirements: (1) the system should support a group of individuals (e.g. friends)—we were interested in the "modern familial" commensal unit [5]; (2) the system should support only simple awareness signals; (3) the system should employ deliberate interactions. At this early design stage, we focused on simple, deliberate actions, as we were unclear as to the privacy requirements of individuals; further, the simplicity afforded some ambiguity, giving participants latitude in how they interpreted the use of the system.

Description. EATProbe is designed as a simple mosaic presented on a touch-screen tablet interface (Figure 1). Each tile in the mosaic represents the status of an individual in one's social network. A user selects one of six states (no status, eating out, eating in, eating in – cooking, eating in – eating, eating in – cleaning), and can change it whenever he chooses by simply touching the screen.

Probe Deployment. We deployed EATProbe to a small group of five friends, aged 23-28, all male. Each lived either alone, or with roommates with whom he did not typically eat dinner. These friends were technology-savvy, accustomed to using various forms of communication technology on a regular basis, and all lived within the same geographic region. We asked the participants to install EATProbe in their kitchens (e.g. Figure 2), and we logged a week of interaction with the system. We then followed up by interviewing each participant, where we asked him to re-imagine his dinnertime activities given his experiences with the probe. Overall, the participants used the probe every day, except for one day when a participant experienced technical difficulties, around dinnertime. System logs indicate the system was used between about 5:15pm (earliest status change during the week) to 11:45pm (latest status change during the week).

3.2 Lessons Learned and Opportunities
We performed a thematic analysis of the interviews, and arrived at three salient themes that relate to EATProbe: its role as a peripheral, reliable awareness tool; its use in fostering a feeling of shared temporality and social presence, and its use as a catalyst for other forms of communication around the meal. We describe these themes holistically as a set of lessons learned about EATProbe, as well as opportunities for potential future designs.

3.2.1 Peripheral awareness: always-on and fixed
In contrast to social media applications that are opened on-demand, EATProbe was an always-on display, making awareness information available all the time. As an always-on display, users would not have to explicitly *remember* to look for awareness information, nor would it require explicit action to gain access to it. Instead, users would gather this social awareness information unintentionally: "[It's] like a surprise piece of information that you're not actively seeking, but that's present in the environment" [p4]. The act of setting one's status meant that implicitly, they would need to glance at the information on the probe's display—that is, gathering information was done in the same step as setting one's status: awareness was not something to be sought out; instead, it was always available.

This gathering of meal-related social awareness was aided by the fact that the display was fixed in the participants' kitchens, where many mealtime activities occurred. Placing the probe in the kitchen, where meal-related activities would naturally occur, meant that the information would be visible in a contextually relevant location: "When I was cooking, I liked to just look over at it to see what others were up to" [p4]. Placing awareness systems in functionally similar environments at both locations could facilitate the sense of shared experience. Here, users became aware of their peers' activities when they were both in their kitchens during contextually similar activities.

While the probe's kitchen location was well-suited for cooking and cleaning activities, this placement did not suit the solitary eating routines of many of our participants. Many reported that solitary meals were likely to be consumed in the privacy of bedrooms, or in front of the TV. In these locations, our fixed-location probe, and the information it offered was inaccessible. This raises a design tension for mealtime awareness systems: how should we support the same effortless gathering of contextually-appropriate awareness information given the fluid routines of solitary mealtime activities around the home?

3.2.2 Temporal sociability and connectedness
Participants derived a sense of sociability in how they made use of EATProbe's status changes. Plainly, our users enjoyed seeing statuses related to mealtime activities in the home, as they indicated that others were engaging in similar (mealtime) activities in a similar space (kitchen) in their own home. This co-temporality of activity gave users a pleasant feeling of sociability—something akin to the connectedness described by [2]. Beyond just "know[ing] better what's going on around you" [p5], participants reported that it was "cool to feel like there was some indication of company" [p4].

Similarly, the act of *changing a status* took on a social quality. For example, a participant interpreted the use of status changes as a "thinking of you token" [p4] invoked as a simple means of communication (much as in [4]). And, because these status changes were the result of deliberate action on the part of other users, they became a relatively reliable indicator of others' presence—both around the system, and in terms of related mealtime activity. While this may suggest the use of EATProbe as a rich messaging tool, some users were satisfied with these simple tokens of communication (i.e. a status change).

All but one participant reported generally feeling more aware of the group's eating patterns, and were able to articulate what they felt were patterns of others' behaviors, even given only a single week of use: "I got to say I got a better sense of when people eat, how often they go out… There was someone going out every night. Let's see, p2 eats at home quite a bit, um p3 goes out. I guess it's more information, it's like a mental model of what people do" [p5]. Thus, beyond the "in-the-moment sociability" of the status changes themselves, the information itself was helping participants gain an ongoing awareness of others' mealtime routines. This awareness would, in principle, allow participants to easily modify and adapt their own mealtime patterns if they were interested in co-temporal mealtime activity.

To be clear, participants did *not* feel that using the EATProbe was anything like actually eating *with* the other members of the group. However, EATProbe did provide participants with the ability to send and receive basic social signals around mealtime activities, allowing them to engage in additional interaction if they so desired. For example, taking note of the previous evening's statuses, one participant asked another where he had gone to eat out the night before: "I could tease p1 and be like: oh! I saw that you ate out last night" [p4], and another participant imagined that the information could be used to say: "I'm trying this [new recipe] out, who wants to come over and try it and have dinner at my house?" [p2]. This suggests that while the social signals and feelings of social presence may be "enough" in many cases, this type of social awareness around dinnertime activities can also act as a catalyst for additional sociability.

3.2.3 Catalyst for rich interaction
The social awareness afforded by EATProbe sometimes acted as a catalyst for richer forms of interaction, both through the probe, and with other media. For example, one participant reported that given the awareness he had of others' dinner activities, "[he] found [himself] wanting to communicate with them somehow," and toggled between different states as a means to draw the attention of others (unfortunately, our system design did not reflect these changes immediately, meaning his actions were not seen remotely). Consistent with this idea, some users suggested building a chatting module directly into the probe, allowing people to transition from awareness into interaction with the same system such as one participant who would have liked to know more about his friend's plans: "there were several times when p2 was eating out and I was curious where he's eating out" [P2]. Similarly, some participants imagined other potential forms of structured interaction, whereby the probe could be used to expose recipes that were being made, or where people could indicate whether they would be interested in going out for dinner (as a lightweight alternative to calling people explicitly). Thus, participants thought that the EATProbe could potentially act as a "hub" for mealtime communication.

Participants also used the probe as a gateway to richer interaction with other media. In at least one instance, a status change caused a pair of participants to transition to a text messaging interaction about the recipes they were trying that evening. Others envisioned this type of system helping them organize a more traditional commensal meal if they saw their friends eating at home at the same time. This implies that a social awareness system could be enough to nudge people who live alone towards social interactions around mealtime activities.

The conversations and interactions inspired by the awareness system can also extend meal-based conversations beyond mealtime. Participants imagined the status messages to be used for rich, ongoing interactions with one another. Since the people using EATProbe are friends who interact outside of mealtime, talking about the common experience mediated through EATProbe provides more opportunities for social bonding.

3. DISCUSSION

A commensal meal is a shared experience that strengthens the social bond within a family or a group of friends. Prior work has shown that social awareness systems affect feelings of social connectedness [4]. Our goal in deploying this probe was to explore how social systems could mediate remote commensality. We discuss here three research themes arising from this work: supporting a range of social opportunities, personal reflection on meal choices, and peri-synchronous interactions.

Because EATProbe was used by a group of friends, it acted as a catalyst for communication around mealtimes. Many felt the nature of this interaction could also include more explicit, or formal messaging mechanisms such as a chat feature built into the system or through text messaging from a phone. We also saw earlier that some participants were pleased simply with the social presence and "thinking of you token" aspect of the system. This suggests that systems of this type should support commensality among a group of friends in a number of ways: prompting opportunities for people to physically get together; providing transitions into richer forms of interaction (such as messaging); supporting simple social presence as EATProbe did, or giving people solitude if they choose, allowing them to disengage with the system altogether.

Conveying social information also had a direct effect on personal reflections and behaviors. A system like EATProbe can introduce these types of social comparisons, and foster reflection on people's own patterns and behaviours. In the context of food choice, this could lead to systems that might support accountability in a social dieting group (suggested by one of the participants). More broadly, this could have a direct impact on changing daily habits. Mealtime activities are deeply ingrained in routines both in terms of time and space [1]. A system like EATProbe could help people develop new routines such as eating in a fixed place where the awareness system is placed, or perhaps temporally, where people might begin to eat dinner at times to match their friends' meal times. The implications for this work points to possibilities for celebratory technologies to contribute to on-going research in behavior change and persuasive systems.

EATProbe's functionality was focused on dinnertime events, which were relatively stable for our participants (i.e. within six hours of one another). The likelihood of temporal co-occurrence of these activities across people is likely to be relatively high (i.e. two people are likely going to be eating around the same time), adding additional temporal structure around these interactions. This temporality is central to traditional commensality [1], since shared time is central to the shared experience. In EATProbe, the status messages stayed active throughout the night, this was meant to increase this sense of temporal proximity. Since dinnertime can happen at different times for different people, keeping this status available stretched the sense of togetherness by providing some ambiguity about the status change. The activity statuses were real-time, meaning these statuses could highlight activity coincidences, such as resulting in the interaction between the two participants who ended up texting each other. Augmenting the shared temporal experience of dinnertime is a unique design opportunity here.

The work we present here is clearly limited in a number of ways. For instance, our findings are based on a study of a small group of technologically savvy 20-30 year olds males. Yet, our findings already do present a number of interesting new avenues for designers to pursue. The observations reported here suggest that a social system that affords simple interactions around mealtime can support a shared commensal experience. Clearly, these experiences are different than a traditional commensal meal, yet we argue that users still find them meaningful.

4. CONCLUSION

Many individuals often eat alone due to the circumstances in their lives, and consequently, miss out on the social benefits of commensal mealtimes. Danesi argues that these individuals rely on different commensal patterns (e.g. casual BBQs rather than formal sit-down meals), effectively redefining meal-sharing norms [1]. Our findings from the deployment of EATProbe follows this general theme, suggesting that social technology around mealtime can create new opportunities for supporting connectedness and mealtime interactions, allowing these individuals to evolve altogether new forms of commensality.

5. ACKNOWLEDGMENTS
Special thanks to the Everyday Computing Lab for valuable advice on this project.

6. REFERENCES
[1] Danesi, G., Commensality in French and German young adults: An ethnographic study. *Hospitality & Society* 1, 2 (2011), 153–172.

[2] Dey, A., K., De Guzman, E. S., From awareness to connectedness: the design and deployment of presence displays. Proc. CHI (2006), 899-908.

[3] Grimes, A. and Harper, R., Celebratory Technology: New Directions for Food Research in HCI. Proc. CHI (2008), 467-476.

[4] Kaye, J. 'J.', Levitt, M. K., Nevins, J. , Golden, J., Schmidt, V., Communicating intimacy one bit at a time. Proc. CHI 2005 Extended Abstracts (2005), 1529-1532.

[5] Sobal, J. and Nelson, M. K., Commensal eating patterns: A community study. Appetite, 41, 2 (2003), 181–90.

[6] Tsujita, H., Tsukada, K., Itiro, S., InPhase: Evaluation of a Communication System Focused on "Happy Coincidences" of Daily Behaviors. Proc. CHI (2010), 2481-2490.

[7] Tsujita, H., Yarosh, S., Abowd, G., CU-Later: a communication system considering time difference. Proc. Ubicomp (2010), 435-436.

[8] Wei, J., Wang, X., Peiris, R. L., Choi, Y., Martinez, X., R., Tache, R., Koh, J., Halupka, V., Cheok. A.D., CoDine: an interactive multi-sensory system for remote dining. Proc. UbiComp (2011), 21-30.

ATCoPE: Any-Time Collaborative Programming Environment for Seamless Integration of Real-Time and Non-Real-Time Teamwork in Software Development

Hongfei Fan   Chengzheng Sun
School of Computer Engineering
Nanyang Technological University, Singapore
FANH0003@e.ntu.edu.sg   CZSun@ntu.edu.sg

Haifeng Shen
School of Computer Science, Engineering & Mathematics
Flinders University, Australia
haifeng.shen@flinders.edu.au

ABSTRACT

Real-time collaborative programming and non-real-time collaborative programming are two classes of methods and techniques for supporting programmers to jointly conduct complex programming work in software development. They are complementary to each other, and both are useful and effective under different programming circumstances. However, most existing programming tools and environments have been designed for supporting only one of them, and little has been done to provide integrated support for both. In this paper, we contribute a novel *Any-Time Collaborative Programming Environment* (ATCoPE) to seamlessly integrate conventional non-real-time collaborative programming tools and environments with emerging real-time collaborative programming techniques and support collaborating programmers to work in and flexibly switch among different collaboration modes according to their needs. We present the general design objectives for ATCoPE, the system architecture, functional design and specifications, rationales beyond design decisions, and major technical issues and solutions in detail, as well as a proof-of-concept implementation of the *ATCoEclipse* prototype system.

Categories and Subject Descriptors

D.2.2 [**Software Engineering**]: Design Tools and Techniques – *computer-aided software engineering (CASE)*; D.2.6 [**Software Engineering**]: Programming Environments – *interactive environments*; H.5.3 [**Information Interfaces and Presentation**]: Group and Organization Interfaces – *computer-supported cooperative work, collaborative computing, synchronous interaction.*

General Terms

Design, Human Factors.

Keywords

Any-time, non-real-time, real-time, collaborative programming, seamless integration, compatibility, transparency.

1. INTRODUCTION

Software development is a complex process which requires sophisticated coordination and collaboration among software engineers with diverse skills, knowledge and expertise [5]. Programming is one important and critical phase during the software development process, in which multiple programmers work collaboratively to transform software requirements into software solutions. The effectiveness of collaboration in programming work is critical to the productivity of programmers and the quality of software products [3][4][5]. In terms of the interactions among collaborating programmers during the programming work, there are two general classes of collaborative programming: *non-real-time collaborative programming* and *real-time collaborative programming*, which are elaborated below.

1.1 Non-Real-Time Collaborative Programming

Non-real-time collaborative programming supports multiple programmers to access shared programming artifacts (e.g., source code directories and files), complete individual programming tasks (e.g., editing source code directories and files) independently, and merge their changes on the shared programming artifacts at pre-scheduled stages manually. Non-real-time collaborative programming has been widely applied in modern software industry, and commonly supported by software configuration management (SCM) systems. An SCM system is essentially a version control system for managing any collection of directories and files collaboratively edited by distributed users. Sophisticated version control systems include *Subversion*[1] (SVN) [7], *Concurrent Versions System*[2] (CVS) [2], *IBM Rational ClearCase*[3] [1] and *Git*[4] [11], which commonly support the following working process based on a *copy-modify-merge* model [14][20]:

1) The programmer *checks out* a source code tree of the project which is related to the programming tasks assigned to this individual programmer. A copy of the source code tree is then downloaded from the shared version control repository to the programmer's local workspace.

2) The programmer *modifies* the source code copy in the local workspace to complete his/her programming tasks.

---

[1] http://subversion.apache.org

[2] http://www.nongnu.org/cvs

[3] http://www.ibm.com/software/awdtools/clearcase

[4] http://git-scm.com

3) The programmer may *merge* the current source code copy in the local workspace with the latest copy in the version control repository in two ways: (1) by issuing an *update* version control operation, other programmers' changes available at the repository are downloaded to the local workspace and merged with the local source code copy; (2) by issuing a *commit* version control operation, the latest version of the local source code copy (as modified by the local programmer) is uploaded to the version control repository for updating the source code copy in the repository, making this local programmer's changes visible and accessible to others. During the *merge* process, the version control system also detects and reports *conflicts* among *concurrent* changes by multiple programmers (e.g., concurrent changes on the same source code file by two collaborating programmers), and leaves the *conflict resolution* to the programmers if the system is unable to reconcile the conflicting changes automatically [13].

With the support of an SCM system, each programmer can complete the programming work independently without being interrupted by others. Such kind of collaborative programming is regarded as *non-real-time* collaboration because neither local changes performed by an individual programmer are immediately propagated and merged with others' copies, nor changes made by others are immediately propagated and merged with the local copy. The local copy is kept *private* until this programmer manually *commits* the local copy into the *public* repository, and in addition, other programmers also have to explicitly perform *update* operations to incorporate the latest committed changes in the repository into their local copies.

1.2 Real-Time Collaborative Programming

In contrast, real-time collaborative programming supports a group of programmers to work on shared programming artifacts concurrently in a closely-coupled fashion, in which collaborating programmers' changes on the shared source code copy are instantly propagated and merged [12][17]. In addition, such real-time propagation and merging are achieved automatically without requiring programmers to manually issue version control operations (e.g., *update*, *commit*) as they do in non-real-time collaborative programming. Multiple programmers are allowed to access and edit the same source code directory, and even the content of the same source code file at the same time, as follows:

1) One programmer's editing operations performed on source code directories (i.e., adding/deleting/renaming a directory or file) are immediately propagated and executed at all remote sites, as if the programmer is performing the same operations at all collaborating sites. In other words, changes on source code directories performed by any individual programmer are immediately and automatically made visible to all other collaborating programmers.

2) Multiple programmers are also allowed to work jointly on the same source code file at the same time, and their editing operations performed on the content of the shared file are instantly propagated to others for real-time notification and merging. In other words, operations of each individual programmer on the shared file are automatically performed on all remote copies of the same file, as if collaborating programmers are sitting together and jointly editing the same source code file.

Past studies have found that real-time collaborative programming is capable of accelerating the progress of problem-solving, creating better design and shorter code length, making programmers enjoy the work more, and eventually increasing the productivity of programmers and improving the quality of software products [6][12][17][21][22]. Due to these benefits of the emerging method and technique, numerous real-time collaborative programming tools and environments have been built in recent years, including research prototypes such as *RECIPE* [17], *Collabode* [10] and *Saros*[5] [15], as well as commercial products such as *SubEthaEdit*[6], *beWeeVee*[7] and *VS Anywhere*[8].

1.3 Seamless Integration of Real-Time and Non-Real-Time Collaborative Programming

Non-real-time collaborative programming is generally suitable for loosely-coupled, long-duration and pre-scheduled collaboration, which may involve a large number of programmers working on large-size programming modules. In practice, large-scale software projects are commonly decomposed and structured by following well-established design principles (e.g., high modularity, low coupling among modules, separation of concerns), so that each individual programmer is able to work independently on programming modules that are relatively isolated from other programming modules within a large project.

In contrast, real-time collaborative programming is more suitable for a small team of programmers to work on shared and interdependent programming tasks in a closely-coupled fashion. Such kind of work is often unstructured because low-level design, coding and testing activities are mixed within the programming process. It can be started spontaneously and conducted in an ad hoc fashion, and has relatively short durations in a large project.

The main difference between real-time and non-real-time collaborative programming lies on the interactions among programmers. Real-time collaboration enables frequent propagation, notification and merging, while non-real-time collaboration enables infrequent propagation and merging [16]. They are complementary to each other, and both of them are useful and effective under different programming circumstances. However, most existing programming tools and environments have been separately designed for supporting only one of them, with incompatible working processes, user interfaces and working semantics. It is desirable and beneficial to support both of them in one environment, in which programmers can work in any collaboration mode and flexibly switch among different modes according to their needs. In this paper, we propose a novel *Any-Time Collaborative Programming Environment* (ATCoPE) to seamlessly integrate both real-time and non-real-time collaborative programming techniques.

The rest of the paper is organized as follows. In Section 2, general design objectives for ATCoPE are presented as the guidance for system design, functional specifications, and technical implementation. The system architecture and functional design for ATCoPE are presented in Section 3, and major technical issues and solutions of ATCoPE are discussed in Section 4. The implementation of the *ATCoEclipse* prototype system is presented in Section 5, followed by conclusions and future work in Section 6.

---

[5] http://www.saros-project.org

[6] http://www.codingmonkeys.de/subethaedit

[7] http://www.beweevee.com

[8] http://www.vsanywhere.com

2. GENERAL DESIGN OBJECTIVES

In this section, four design objectives for ATCoPE are presented as the general guidance for technical design and implementation.

Design Objective 1: Compatibility and transparency in supporting non-real-time collaborative programming

ATCoPE is compatible with existing non-real-time collaborative programming tools and environments in terms of user interfaces, functionalities and features, working processes, and working semantics. It achieves such compatibility by transparently incorporating existing single-user programming environments and non-real-time collaboration supporting tools, without any change to the source code of existing systems.

For end-users (programmers) of ATCoPE, compatibility means that they can continue to use familiar single-user programming environments (e.g., *Microsoft Visual Studio*[9], *Eclipse*[10]) and non-real-time collaboration supporting tools (e.g., CVS, SVN) with the same skills, knowledge and experience as before, while enjoying emerging real-time collaboration capabilities. For researchers and system builders of ATCoPE, transparency means that they can achieve conventional single-user programming functionalities and non-real-time collaboration supporting capabilities by reusing and incorporating existing tools and environments, without reinventing them from scratch.

Design Objective 2: Capability of supporting advanced real-time collaborative programming

ATCoPE supports multiple programmers to freely and concurrently work in a shared collection of source code directories and files for the same project at the same time. Under the real-time collaboration mode, multiple programmers can create, delete and update any directory and file for the shared project; they can instantly see others' updates to the shared source code directories and files in real-time. ATCoPE resolves operation conflicts and ensures consistency of shared data in the face of concurrent manipulation, and provides advanced workspace awareness support.

Design Objective 3: Capability of supporting any-time collaborative programming

ATCoPE supports not only simultaneous real-time and non-real-time collaboration sessions for different projects, but also any-time collaboration sessions for the same project, which may consist of real-time and non-real-time collaboration sessions at the same time. An any-time collaboration session comes into existence as long as there are multiple programmers working in both real-time and non-real-time collaboration sessions for the same project. In an any-time collaboration session, programmers may work individually, collaborate with others in a conventional non-real-time fashion, and work in a closely-coupled real-time fashion at the same time. ATCoPE also supports real-time collaborating programmers to perform conventional non-real-time collaboration functions (e.g., *check-out*, *update* and *commit*) for the shared project and collectively resolve non-real-time collaboration conflicts in a real-time collaboration fashion. Moreover, ATCoPE allows programmers to switch among different collaboration modes and sessions flexibly according to their collaboration needs.

---

[9] http://www.microsoft.com/visualstudio

[10] http://www.eclipse.org

Design Objective 4: High performance and scalability

ATCoPE provides end-users with high local responsiveness (as responsive as single-user programming tools and environments), fast remote notification and merging for real-time collaborating programmers, and efficient bandwidth usage for communications among any-time collaborating programmers. ATCoPE also maintains good system performance as the increase of the number of collaborating programmers and the number of simultaneous active collaboration sessions for large-scale software projects.

3. SYSTEM ARCHITECTURE AND FUNCTIONAL DESIGN

3.1 ATCoPE System Architecture

To achieve the design objectives, the ATCoPE system architecture is proposed in Figure 1, and the functionalities of its key components are also specified. The ATCoPE system consists of a server and multiple clients connected by communication networks.

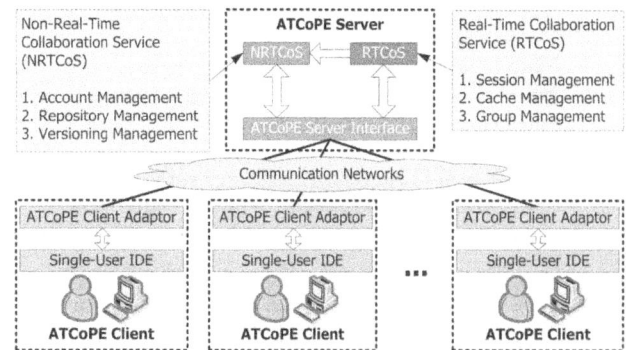

Figure 1. The ATCoPE system architecture.

The ATCoPE Server contains a *Real-Time Collaboration Service* (RTCoS) component and a *Non-Real-Time Collaboration Service* (NRTCoS) component, as well as a uniform *ATCoPE Server Interface* for any-time collaboration service (Design Objective 3). The NRTCoS component is responsible for account management, source code repository management, and versioning management, which are commonly supported by version control systems. The NRTCoS component incorporates these functionalities from existing systems (Design Objective 1). The RTCoS component is responsible for providing advanced real-time collaboration services (Design Objective 2), including real-time collaborative programming session management, project cache management, and group membership management. The RTCoS makes use of the NRTCoS for conventional account and repository management, as well as other non-real-time collaboration services (Design Objective 3).

An ATCoPE Client provides an integrated development environment (IDE) with comprehensive facilities for coding, compilation and debugging, as well as various tools (e.g., class browser). The IDE is also integrated with a version control client for supporting non-real-time collaboration. Such features are commonly supported by conventional IDE products (e.g., Eclipse), so the ATCoPE Client can incorporate existing tools and systems without reinvention (Design Objective 1). While preserving all conventional IDE functions and interface features, the ATCoPE Client also provides additional features for real-time collaborative programming. The *ATCoPE Client Adaptor* is designed to transparently convert a conventional IDE into an ATCoPE Client, without any change to the source code of the IDE, which can be achieved by following the *Transparent Adaptation* (TA) approach proposed in prior work [19]. Among various tools and facilities encapsulated in an IDE, the current design of the ATCoPE Client focuses on extending source code editing tools for supporting any-time (both real-time and non-real-time) collaboration (Design Objective 3).

3.2 Functional Design of ATCoPE

3.2.1 Logging into the ATCoPE System: Account and Repository Management

Like working with a conventional version control system such as SVN, a programmer needs a user account to use the repository, version control, and other collaboration services in the ATCoPE system. Within the ATCoPE Server, the NRTCoS component is responsible for incorporating source code repository and version control functions from existing tools, and the ATCoPE Client Adaptor is responsible for keeping the process of using user accounts to log into the ATCoPE system the same as that of using a conventional IDE with an integrated version control client. For end-users, the ATCoPE login process for both real-time and non-real-time collaboration is the same: using the same user account and interface to access the same source code repository managed by the same version control system. After logging into ATCoPE, the programmer can proceed to access and browse the source code trees granted to his/her account in any way.

3.2.2 Creating a Session: Start of Collaboration

After logging into ATCoPE, a user may select any source code file or sub-tree of files, and then issue a *check-out* command to download the selected files to the local workspace, which triggers the creation of an ATCoPE session. The difference between real-time and non-real-time collaboration sessions comes into existence when different collaboration options are chosen at the time of checking out files (see Section 5.2).

If the *"non-real-time"* option is chosen, the selected files are downloaded from the NRTCoS repository to the ATCoPE Client, without any interaction with the RTCoS component. The notion of a non-real-time session is *implicit* in the sense that no explicit session record is created in the ATCoPE Server.

If the *"real-time"* option is chosen, the selection of the files to be checked out, together with the user account authentication data, is transmitted to the RTCoS component to create a real-time session record, which includes the group membership information (initially the first user's account name and authentication data) and a cache of the source code copy being checked out. The source code copy associated to this session is then downloaded and duplicated at the client. The creation of a real-time session is transparent to the NRTCoS: the check-out process in the version control system is always the same, regardless of whether a real-time session is created or not. Each explicit real-time session managed by the RTCoS component corresponds to one implicit non-real-time session in the NRTCoS version control system, and such correspondence facilitates close integration and easy switching among real-time and non-real-time sessions (see Section 4.3).

For end-users, the creation of a real-time or non-real-time session in the APCoPE system is nearly the same, except for ticking a different option at the time of checking out files from the version control repository. What happens at the server-side is invisible to the user, but some distinctive visual clues must be provided at the ATCoPE client interface to differentiate whether the current session is real-time or non-real-time (see Section 5.2).

3.2.3 Joining a Session: Dynamic Session Membership Management

In the ATCoPE system, a user is provided with not only a conventional repository interface for browsing and checking out files to create new sessions, but also a list of existing real-time sessions available for the programmer to join (see Section 5.2). Joining a non-real-time session happens implicitly as long as the programmer checks out files from the version control repository. Differently, to join a real-time session, the user needs to request permission. In the simplistic case, a user may automatically become a new member of a selected existing real-time session if the session is open for anyone who holds a valid ATCoPE account. In addition, more sophisticated group membership management policies and strategies are possible. For example, the creator of a real-time session may give permissions to a specific group of ATCoPE users, and/or require late-comers to make explicit requests and grant permissions on a case-by-case basis. Once the permission is obtained, the user will join the real-time session under the control of a distributed join-protocol for ensuring consistency (to be discussed in Section 4.2). Upon joining, the new session member is recorded in the RTCoS component and the source code copy associated to this session is downloaded and duplicated at the ATCoPE Client of this new member. At the same time, all existing members of the real-time session are notified of the joining of the new member.

3.2.4 Working in a Session: Features of Any-Time Collaboration

In a non-real-time session, a programmer works on source code copies inside the private workspace; changes to those copies are local and invisible to the public until the local programmer manually *commits* the changes back to the version control repository. To incorporate changes made by others, a programmer has to explicitly issue an *update* operation, which merges the latest version of the shared source code copy at the version control repository with his/her local version. The *update/commit* process may involve conflict detection and conflict resolution, as conflicts may occur in the face of concurrent changes on shared files.

In a real-time session, a programmer also works on source code copies inside the local workspace, but changes to those copies become visible automatically and instantly to other collaborating programmers without manually executing *update/commit* operations. Especially, multiple programmers may jointly edit one file at the same time, thus creating an internal real-time collaborative editing session. To differentiate these real-time sessions, we use the term *real-time project session* to refer to a real-time session created when checking out files from the version control repository, and use the term *real-time file session* to refer to a real-time collaborative editing session created when multiple programmers are editing the same file inside a real-time project session.

During a real-time session, programmers may freely and concurrently perform two types of editing operations: (1) *file-level editing*: to edit the content of any source code file by inserting and deleting texts; and (2) *project-level editing*: to create, delete and rename directories and files for the shared project. The timeliness of propagating changes to other collaborators depends on the nature and need of the collaborative work, as specified below:

1) When multiple programmers are working on the same source code file in a real-time file session, changes made by one programmer are propagated to all members within the same file

session *instantly*, but to other members who are outside the file session but within the same project session *at the time of saving the file*. Conflicts caused by concurrent editing operations on the file content are automatically resolved by underlying consistency maintenance techniques such as the *Operational Transformation* (OT) [18] and *Dependency-based Automatic Locking* (DAL) [8]. The delayed propagation to those members outside the file session is reasonable as they are not working on or interested in the latest content of the file at the moment, and this helps achieve good performance and efficient use of communication bandwidth (Design Objective 4).

2) When multiple programmers are concurrently changing the shared source code copy by creating, deleting and/or renaming directories and/or files, their changes are *instantly* propagated to all members within the same project session. If concurrent editing operations target the same directory/file, operation conflicts may occur and will be automatically resolved by certain conflict resolution measures provided in the underlying system. The conflict resolution mechanisms and policies have been designed for ensuring consistency of the shared source code copy and preserving conflicting operations' effects as much as possible. For example, if two concurrent *Create* operations use the same name for the directory/file to be created, a reasonable conflict resolution result is to keep both but rename them properly, in order to preserve both *Create* operations' effects while ensuring consistency.

In addition to project-level and file-level editing operations with effects in the scope of the same real-time session, a programmer may also issue version control operations (e.g., *update*, *commit*) to merge the source code copy of the real-time session with the latest committed versions from other non-real-time collaborators in the version control repository. All interactions between a real-time session and the version control system are performed in the name of one user who created the real-time session. From the version control system's perspective, a real-time session is merely a single user, regardless of how many members are actually involved in the session. If conflicts with other non-real-time collaborators are detected and reported in processing *update* or *commit* operation, real-time collaborators may jointly resolve them: they may separately resolve conflicts in different files, or jointly resolve conflicts in the same file in a real-time file session. Such kind of close interaction among real-time and non-real-time collaborators is a unique any-time collaboration feature of the ATCoPE system.

3.2.5 *Leaving and Terminating a Session: Completion of Collaborative Work*

Upon completion of collaborative work, a programmer may leave a session at any time. Leaving a non-real-time session is implicit by simply issuing a *commit* operation to merge the local source code copy with the latest copy in the version control repository. Leaving a real-time session can be initiated by a session member under the control of a distributed leave-protocol that flushes all local changes at the leaving site to other existing sites and notifies them of the leaving event, and the corresponding session membership record will be updated in the RTCoS component. After the last session member has left a real-time session, this session will be terminated, which results in the removal of the whole session record from the RTCoS component. Before the termination of a real-time session, the source code copy in the RTCoS cache will be committed back to the version control repository, which signifies leaving the corresponding non-real-time session.

3.2.6 *Switching among Collaboration Modes and Sessions: Flexible Any-Time Collaboration*

With ATCoPE, a programmer may switch among real-time and non-real-time sessions freely. For example, a programmer may check out a collection of source code files from the version control repository and work individually in a non-real-time collaboration fashion (by using *update* and *commit* operations) for a while. At a later moment, this programmer may wish to have more closely-coupled interaction with some collaborators for solving certain problems, and s/he can simply click a button at the client interface (see Section 5.2) to create a real-time session based on the local source code copy. Internally, this will trigger the uploading of the local source code copy to the RTCoS cache and the creation of a new real-time session, which will become visible to other programmers who have currently (or later) logged into the system. Conversely, a real-time session member may quit the current real-time session and continue to work on the same project (based on his/her local source code copy) as a non-real-time collaborator.

4. TECHNICAL ISSUES AND SOLUTIONS

In this section, several major technical issues and solutions are presented for supporting the ATCoPE system as designed in previous sections.

4.1 Consistency Maintenance

To achieve responsive and unconstrained real-time collaboration in high latency communication networks like the Internet, the real-time collaborative source code editor in the ATCoPE Client has been designed with a *replicated architecture* where the shared source code copy is replicated at each collaborating site to allow local operations to be responded and executed quickly (Design Objective 4). When a programmer is editing any shared directory or file in a real-time session, editing operations issued are immediately performed on the local replica (thus achieving responsiveness), and then captured by the ATCoPE Client Adaptor and instantly propagated to remote sites for execution (thus achieving real-time notification and merging). Such kind of collaborative editing is unconstrained in the sense that programmers can freely and concurrently access and update any part of the shared programming artifacts at any time.

Under the replicated architecture, consistency maintenance becomes an essential requirement and technical challenge: after all editing operations are propagated and executed at all collaborating sites within a real-time session, the distributed replicas of the source code directories and files should be identical across all collaborating sites. As there are two types of real-time sessions (i.e., real-time project session with project-level editing operations and real-time file session with file-level editing operations), suitable consistency maintenance techniques have been devised and applied for each of them respectively, as follows.

4.1.1 *Consistency in Real-Time Project Sessions*

In a real-time project session, each project-level editing operation is immediately performed at the local replica, automatically captured by the ATCoPE Client Adaptor, and instantly propagated, via the *real-time session manager* inside the ATCoPE Server, to all other collaborating sites for remote execution. As mentioned in Section 3.2.4, concurrent editing operations may cause conflicts. One possible approach to solving this problem is to use a locking-based protocol to serialize concurrent operations. Under this approach, one site must obtain the permission token from the central coordinator before performing any project-level editing operation, and the token must be returned back to the coordinator after the operation has been done locally and executed at remote sites. This approach achieves consistency by prohibiting concurrent project-level editing operations, thus eliminating the possibility of operation conflicts. However, it is too restrictive for real-time collaborative work (which often requires unconstrained interaction), and may incur high computation and communication overhead because each project-level editing operation needs a costly global synchronization in high-latency communication networks.

To achieve high performance and scalability (Design Objective 4), an optimistic approach to concurrency control has been adopted for project-level editing operations: programmers are allowed to perform project-level editing operations without any delay, and the system automatically detects and resolves operation conflicts at remote sites. To detect and resolve conflicts among project-level editing operations, the following techniques are applied. Firstly, a scheme based on state vectors [18] is devised to time-stamp each project-level editing operation with a state vector, which is used to derive causal relationships (one necessary condition for conflicts) among operations. Secondly, a history buffer is maintained at each site to save all project-level editing operations that have been executed at the site. When a remote operation arrives and becomes causally ready for execution, operations saved in the history buffer are scanned to check whether they are concurrent with the newly arrived operation by comparing their timestamps. If an executed operation is found to be concurrent with the newly arrived one, detailed operation information (such as the operation type and the pathname of the targeted directory/file) is further examined to check whether the concurrent operations are conflicting with each other. In case that a conflict is detected, the corresponding conflict resolution strategy is applied.

4.1.2 Consistency in Real-Time File Sessions

In a real-time file session, consistency maintenance is concerned with the textual content of the shared source code file that is being collaboratively edited. After all file-level editing operations are executed at all sites within a real-time file session, the textual content of the shared source code file in each local replica should be identical. Similar to a project-level editing operation, a file-level editing operation is also immediately applied on the local replica of the shared file, automatically captured by the ATCoPE Client Adaptor, and then instantly propagated, via the ATCoPE Server, to all other collaborating sites within the same real-time file session. Concurrent file-level editing operations may also conflict with each other due to the positional shifting effects of textual editing operations, which is a well-known problem and can be resolved by using the OT technique contributed in prior work [18]. The OT technique has been invented to maintain consistency without restricting user interactions, which is able to achieve two key consistency requirements: (1) *convergence*: all replicas of the shared document must be identical after executing the same group of operations; and (2) *intention preservation*: the effect of an operation in all replicas must be the same as its effect at the local replica. With the support of other distributed computing techniques, a real-time collaborative editing system also ensures *causality preservation* to ensure that editing operations are always executed in their *cause-effect* order at all collaborating sites. Technically, the OT technique transforms parameters of concurrent operations to compensate the positional shifting effects (in the domain of plain text editing), so that their execution in different orders can produce consistent and intended results.

4.2 Join-Protocol for Dynamic Membership

ATCoPE supports dynamic membership in real-time sessions where collaborating sites can join and leave a session at any time during collaborative programming. To accommodate late-comers at any time in a reliable way, a distributed join-protocol has been designed, with the following communication messages:

- JOIN: sent from a new client to the session manager to request joining an existing real-time session.

- START: sent from the session manager to all existing clients in the real-time session to inform the start of a join-protocol procedure for accepting a new client.

- READY: sent from an existing client to the session manager to inform its readiness for entering the *quiescence* state.

- FINISH: sent from the session manager to all clients (including the new client) to inform the completion of the procedure.

Major steps of the join-protocol are listed and described below. In addition, an example is presented in Figure 2 to illustrate how the join-protocol works step-by-step in a real-time session with two existing clients for accepting a new client to join.

- When a new client attempts to join a real-time session, it sends a JOIN message to the real-time session manager of the ATCoPE Server. After that, this client is blocked (with no UI operation allowed) until the completion of the procedure.

- Upon receiving a JOIN message from a new client, the session manager broadcasts a START message to all existing clients in the real-time session.

- Upon receiving a START message sent from the session manager, a client completes all ongoing operations and sends back a READY message to the session manager. After this, the client is blocked (with no UI operation allowed), but still allows the execution of remote operations, which is required by the synchronization protocol.

- Upon receiving READY messages from all existing clients, the session manager broadcasts a FINISH message to all (existing and new) clients. At the same time, the session manager registers the new client in the session's active membership list.

- Upon receiving a FINISH message, a client is unblocked for resuming normal editing work. Particularly, the new client will also receive the latest source code copy of the project from the server, together with the FINISH message.

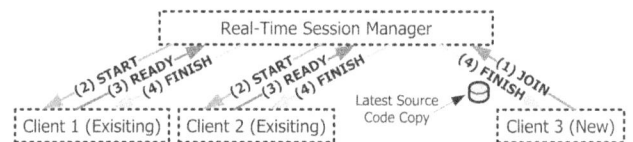

Figure 2. Join-protocol in real-time sessions.

Under the assumption that all communications between clients and the server are performed in FIFO channels (e.g., TCP connections), a session will enter the quiescent state when all clients have received the FINISH message. In a quiescent state, there is no message in transition, and all sites must have executed the same collection of operations and hence have consistent copies of source code. At the end of the join-protocol procedure, the new comer will receive the latest source code copy of the project, and all sites will resume work as if a fresh session is started. In case that multiple clients concurrently issue joining requests for the same session, they are serialized by the session manager to avoid inconsistency and complication. When a joining request arrives at the session manager, if one join-protocol procedure for the same real-time session is in progress, the coming request will be queued until the ongoing procedure is completed. However, concurrent joining for different sessions can be processed in parallel. For a leaving request from an existing client, the session manager simply broadcasts a LEAVE message to other existing clients to inform the event, removes the site from the session's active membership list, and closes the network connection with the client.

4.3 Incorporating Non-Real-Time Collaboration Service in ATCoPE

Based on the general design objectives, ATCoPE should be compatible with existing single-user programming environments and non-real-time collaboration supporting tools, and achieve such compatibility by transparently incorporating existing IDEs and version control systems. The transparent integration with existing single-user programming environments and converting them into multi-user real-time collaborative programming environments can be achieved by taking the TA approach proposed in prior work [19]. The transparent integration with non-real-time collaboration service involves multiple components inside the ATCoPE system, which collectively achieve the following objectives: (1) incorporating conventional and existing non-real-time collaboration service supporting tools for non-real-time collaborative programming sessions in ATCoPE; and (2) bridging non-real-time collaboration service and real-time collaborative programming sessions. In the following parts, we present how various ATCoPE components collaborate with each other to achieve these objectives.

As shown in Figure 3, for a non-real-time collaborative programming session, an ATCoPE Client issues version control operations (e.g., *check-out*, *update*, *commit*) in the same way as working in a conventional IDE integrated with a version control client. The ATCoPE Server Interface processes these operations by simply passing them to the NRTCoS component in the ATCoPE Server, which in turn invokes public interfaces of existing version control systems to execute these operations. At the beginning of a non-real-time session, the source code copy is checked out from the NRTCoS repository to the local workspace of the ATCoPE Client. In the face of *update/commit* operations, the source code copy is either downloaded from the NRTCoS repository to the ATCoPE Client's local workspace (by *update*), or uploaded from the local workspace to the NRTCoS repository (by *commit*). In summary, the ATCoPE client user issues version control operations by using the same process and user interface, executing operations with the same semantics, and achieving the same results as working with a conventional IDE and version control client.

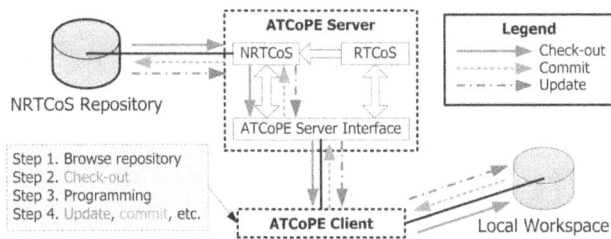

Figure 3. Incorporating non-real-time collaboration service for non-real-time collaboration sessions in ATCoPE.

As illustrated in Figure 4, to support the use of the non-real-time collaboration service from real-time collaboration sessions, each real-time session is associated with a *Non-Real-Time Client Proxy* in the RTCoS component, which bridges the non-real-time collaboration service and the real-time collaborating programmers. Inside the ATCoPE Server, each real-time session has a corresponding *session cache* for storing the latest copy of the project's source code as a shared repository for the period of the real-time session. When a real-time session is created by an ATCoPE user, the source code copy is checked out from the NRTCoS repository to the corresponding session cache for the newly created real-time session in the RTCoS. The source code copy is then downloaded from the RTCoS Session Cache to the client's local workspace via the ATCoPE Server Interface. Similarly, when a new site joins the real-time session, the latest copy of the project's source code is transmitted from the RTCoS Session Cache to the local workspace of the new client, upon completion of the join-protocol procedure as presented in Section 4.2. During a real-time session, programmers concurrently perform various editing operations on the shared source code copy, and changes are propagated to other sites instantly and saved to the RTCoS Session Cache as well.

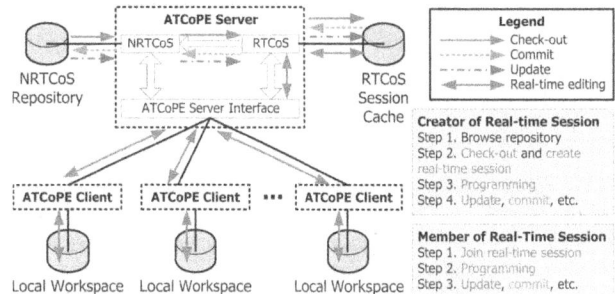

Figure 4. Bridging non-real-time collaboration service and real-time collaboration sessions in ATCoPE.

Whenever a member of the real-time session issues an *update* or *commit* operation, this operation is transmitted to the corresponding Non-Real-Time Client Proxy inside the RTCoS component, which relays these version control operations (and associated data) to the NRTCoS version control system. In processing an *update* operation, the latest copy in the NRTCoS repository is downloaded and merged with the current copy stored in the session cache, and the updates are then downloaded to all clients within the real-time session. Conversely, in processing a *commit* operation, the latest source code copy stored in the session cache is committed to the NRTCoS repository. The Non-Real-Time Client Proxy represents the real-time session's creator and acts as a single client of the NRTCoS, so the credentials of the session creator must be saved in the RTCoS session manager at the time of session creation for facilitating authentication when communicating with the NRTCoS component.

In processing non-real-time version control operations within a real-time session, the proxy must also ensure consistency of the shared source code copy among all session members. This has been achieved by using synchronization protocols to force the session to reach a quiescent and consistent state. For supporting *update* and *commit* operations in real-time collaborative programming sessions, synchronization protocols similar to the join-protocol have been devised, which simply replace the JOIN message with an UPDATE or COMMIT message. When the session reaches a quiescence state, the shared source code copy must be consistent across all sites, and this latest copy is committed to the

NRTCoS repository, or merged with the downloaded copy from the NRTCoS repository by the *update* command. In executing either *update* or *commit* operation, conflicts may be detected and reported by the NRTCoS version control system, and the resolution of those conflicts can be carried out in a real-time collaboration fashion (using ATCoPE real-time collaboration service). Moreover, in the face of concurrent version control operations issued by multiple active members in the same real-time session, they are serialized by the session manager.

5. PROTOTYPE IMPLEMENTATION AND PRELIMINARY EVALUATION

To validate the feasibility of ATCoPE as well as the functional design and technical solutions, a prototype named *ATCoEclipse* (*Any-Time Collaborative Programming with Eclipse*) has been implemented, which realizes the system architecture, techniques, and solutions derived from the research, and serves as a proof-of-concept for ATCoPE.

To achieve transparency and compatibility with existing single-user programming environments, the ATCoPE Client has been implemented as a plug-in with the popular Eclipse IDE, using the TA approach and the *Generic Collaboration Engine* (GCE) contributed in prior work [19]. To achieve compatibility with existing version control systems for non-real-time collaboration service, the SVN has been adopted for supporting conventional version control functionalities in the ATCoEclipse system.

These design decisions have been made based on the following reasons. Firstly, the Eclipse IDE is an open platform with a core runtime engine and various subsystems as plug-ins, allowing developers to add extensions easily. SVN is also a free and open source system which provides extensibility and reusability. Secondly, the Eclipse IDE contains a rich set of popular plug-ins that provides not only useful features but also programming interfaces for other plug-ins to utilize. Similarly, SVN also provides rich interfaces for supporting version control functions that can be utilized by external applications in communicating with the SVN service (e.g., sending SVN commands). Last but not least, the Eclipse IDE is widely used by a large number of users in software industry and academic communities due to its free, open-source, and extensible properties, and similarly, SVN is also a sophisticated and popular system with a wide range of users. Large popularity of Eclipse and SVN provides great opportunities for usability study and evaluation.

5.1 ATCoEclipse System Architecture

As presented in Figure 5, the ATCoEclipse system architecture is an instance of the generic ATCoPE system architecture in Figure 1, with the ATCoPE Client instantiated by the *ATCoEclipse Client*, and the ATCoPE Server instantiated by the *ATCoEclipse Server*. The ATCoEclipse system takes a client-server communication structure where multiple ATCoEclipse Clients are connected to the ATCoEclipse Server via the Internet.

At the client-side, the *ATCoEclipse Client Adaptor* transparently converts the existing single-user Eclipse source code editor into an advanced multi-user real-time collaborative source code editor. Within the ATCoEclipse server-side, the SVN Service is incorporated as the non-real-time collaboration service. The *RTCoServer* (*Real-Time Collaboration Server*) component contains various functional modules for collectively offering real-time collaboration service, and transparently incorporates the SVN Service for

supporting non-real-time collaboration functionalities in real-time collaboration sessions. The *ATCoEclipse Server Interface* provides a uniform any-time collaboration interface for processing both real-time and non-real-time collaboration requests and commands from all ATCoEclipse Clients.

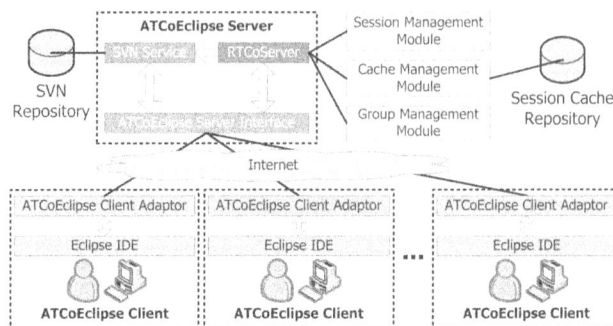

Figure 5. The ATCoEclipse system architecture.

5.2 User Interface Design of ATCoEclipse

Figure 6 presents the user interface for a programmer to initialize programming work with ATCoEclipse, which is designed according to functional specifications in Section 3.2.1, 3.2.2 and 3.2.3. In the upper-left part of the dialog box, the programmer specifies the SVN repository to access and the user account (with username and password) used in the SVN system, which is similar to the authentication process for using a conventional SVN client. Upon successful authentication (performed by the SVN Service via the ATCoEclipse Server Interface), the source code directories and files located at the specified location are retrieved and displayed as a tree at the ATCoEclipse Client, as shown in the lower-left part of Figure 6.

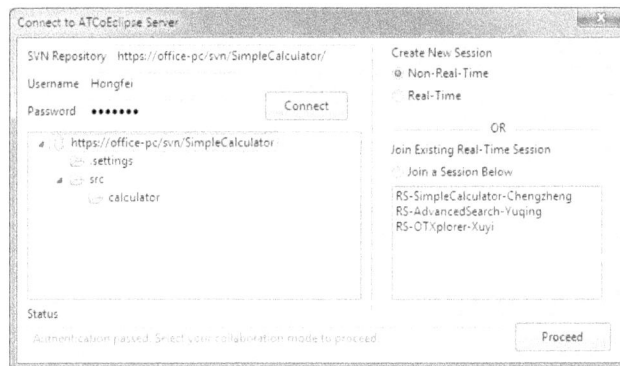

Figure 6. Initialization of programming work.

If the programmer wants to create a new collaboration session, s/he can browse this source code tree and specify a location to check out, which acts similarly as a conventional version control client integrated with single-user programming environments. After specifying the source code directories and files to check out, the programmer proceeds to choose the collaboration mode in the right panel. The programmer is provided with two options for the collaboration mode: (1) non-real-time collaboration, which will directly check out the source code copy from the SVN repository to the local workspace; and (2) real-time collaboration, which will trigger the ATCoEclipse Server to create a new session (with this user as the session owner and creator), check out source code copy from the specified location in the SVN repository to the session cache at the ATCoEclipse Server, and then transmit the source code copy to the programmer's local workspace.

Alternatively, the programmer can also join an existing real-time collaborative programming session that is available in the system. In the lower part of the right panel in Figure 6, a list is displayed to show all existing real-time sessions that are available for this programmer to join. In this figure, there are three real-time sessions that are available at the moment: (1) *RS-SimpleCalculator-Chengzheng*, which is a real-time session for the project named *SimpleCalculator* created by the programmer named *Chengzheng*; (2) *RS-AdvancedSearch-Yuqing*, which is a real-time session for a different project named *AdvancedSearch* created by another programmer named *Yuqing*; and (3) *RS-OTXplorer-Xuyi*, which is a real-time session for another project named *OTXplorer* created by a programmer named *Xuyi*. By simply choosing the collaboration mode in the right panel, the corresponding collaboration session is created or joined, leading the user to the programming work.

Figure 7 presents the main user interface of the ATCoEclipse Client when a programmer is conducting programming work in a real-time collaboration session. Similar to the single-user Eclipse IDE, ATCoEclipse's programming interface contains a *package explorer* as shown in the left panel, but additional real-time collaboration features have been embedded: when the programmer issues any operation in the package explorer to create, delete or rename a directory or file, this operation is instantly propagated and replayed at all other active sites within the same real-time session. Similarly, other session members' changes to the source code tree are also performed in this package explorer in real-time.

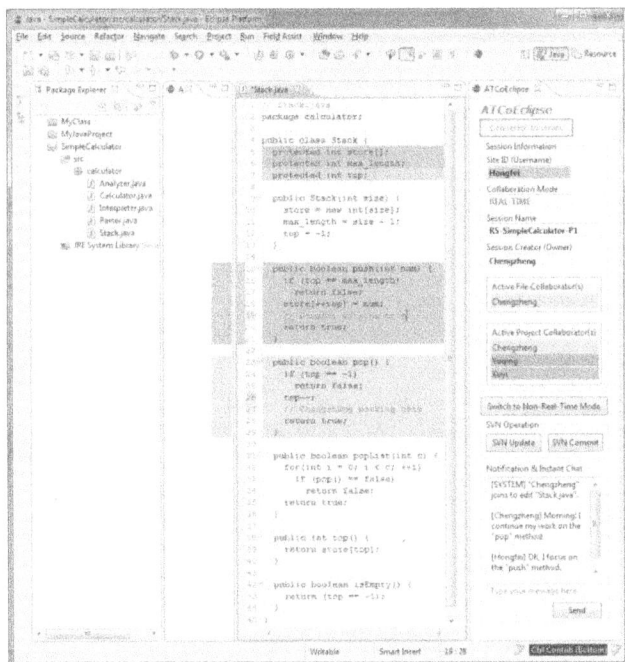

Figure 7. Main user interface of the ATCoEclipse Client.

In the middle panel, the source code editor looks almost the same as the single-user Eclipse source code editor, but many advanced real-time collaboration features have been embedded. Firstly, the local programmer's changes on the textual content of the source code file are instantly propagated to other active members in the same file session, and editing performed by other programmers in the same file session can also be noticed at this site in real-time. While programmers are concurrently editing the same source code file in a flexible and unconstrained way, consistency of the source code is maintained by underlying techniques at all times. Second-

ly, advanced collaboration awareness techniques devised in prior work [9] have been applied in the source code editor. As illustrated, workspaces of different programmers are highlighted by different background colors, so each programmer can intuitively see where and what others are doing in real-time, thus improving the communication and understanding among collaborators. In addition to workspace awareness, ATCoEclipse also incorporates novel techniques related to dependency relationships among source code regions (e.g., methods/fields of the Java class) contributed in prior work [8], which are applied to automatically derive dependency relationships among these regions (e.g., a method invokes another method, a method references a field) and highlight depended regions of programmers' working regions. For example, the local programmer (*Hongfei*) is working on the *push* method which references three fields (*int store[]*, *int max_length*, *int top*) of the class, and therefore all these regions are highlighted by the color assigned to the local user. Similarly, it can be watched that another collaborator (*Chengzheng*) is working on the *pop* method, which references one field (*int top*). To differentiate the working region and depended regions with respect to a programmer, a color bar is displayed to the left of the working region. In particular, the field *int top* is highlighted by a special color to indicate that it is currently referenced by both working regions of the two programmers, and they should pay attention to potential conflicts among their work. With these awareness features, programmers not only see where others are working, but also intuitively understand the relationships among collaborators' working regions to help avoid producing incompatible programming work.

In the right panel of the ATCoEclipse Client, important collaboration-related information is displayed, including the current collaboration mode (real-time/non-real-time), the session name, and the owner of the session. More importantly, the lists of collaborators in the same file session and the same project session are displayed respectively, which are dynamically updated when a new client joins the session or an existing active site leaves the session. A unique color is assigned to each collaborator in the lists, which is used for highlighting the working region and depended regions in the source code editor, as introduced above.

In the lower part of the right panel, the programmer may click a button to switch between real-time and non-real-time collaboration modes, thus achieving seamless transition among different collaboration modes. The version control operations (SVN *update* and SVN *commit*) are also provided for real-time collaborating programmers to enjoy close interaction with non-real-time collaborators. A notification box is placed below to deliver collaboration-related messages (e.g., who joins or leaves the session, who commits the latest source code copy to the SVN repository on behalf of the group). The notification box is also integrated with instant chatting features so that collaborating programmers can conduct real-time communication in case of need.

In summary, programmers can work with the ATCoEclipse system by using familiar functionalities and interface features that were available in the single-user Eclipse IDE, while in the meantime, enjoying novel any-time collaboration features.

5.3 Preliminary Performance Evaluation

The successful implementation of ATCoEclipse has validated the feasibility of ATCoPE. Preliminary performance evaluation has confirmed that the ATCoEclipse system achieves high performance in several aspects. Firstly, the local responsiveness of the client is as good as the single-user Eclipse IDE due to the replicated architecture for the shared source code copy. Secondly, the propagation of editing operations to remote collaborating sites has been very efficient as well because most communication messages (e.g., editing operations, join-protocol messages) are less than 1kB in size, which can reach inter-continental remote sites normally within a delay of 100ms. Thirdly, a global synchronization procedure (e.g., join-protocol) involves a maximum of three single-trip messages, which can be transmitted within a total delay of less than 300ms (100ms for each single-trip). Fourthly, transmission of the entire source code copy for a project can be costly, depending on the total size of the project, but this occurs only when a new user joins a real-time session or a real-time collaborating programmer issues a non-real-time version control operation (*update* or *commit*) on behalf of the group, which is infrequent. Last but not least, ATCoEclipse is scalable, which is able to accommodate a large number of collaborating programmers for large-scale software projects, because: (1) most of the heavy work in either real-time or non-real-time collaboration sessions can be completed at individual and separated ATCoEclipse Clients; and (2) the ATCoEclipse Server has been designed and implemented to maintain administrative information and data only for active real-time sessions, without involvement in keeping track of non-real-time sessions and users or in performing real-time work, except for relaying real-time editing operations and communication messages via the session manager.

6. CONCLUSIONS AND FUTURE WORK

In this paper, we have contributed a novel *Any-Time Collaborative Programming Environment* (ATCoPE) in seamlessly integrating and supporting both real-time and non-real-time collaborative programming. Major contributions include the ATCoPE system architecture, functional design for ATCoPE, technical solutions for realizing ATCoPE, and the design and implementation of the *ATCoEclipse* prototype system as a proof-of-concept for ATCoPE. The prototype implementation and preliminary performance evaluation have confirmed the technical feasibility of ATCoPE and its supporting techniques, and provided positive feedback on the performance and scalability of the system. This research work has initiated a new direction in the domain of collaborative software development, and laid foundations for exploration of a range of interesting issues. Our ongoing work focuses on extending the functionalities of the ATCoEclipse system for conducting usability study, which will be reported in future papers.

7. REFERENCES

[1] Allen, L., Fernandez, G., Kane, K., Leblang, D. B., Minard, D., and Posner, J. ClearCase MultiSite: Supporting Geographically-Distributed Software Development. In *Software Configuration Management: Selected Papers from ICSE SCM-4 and SCM-5 Workshops, LNCS*, 1005 (1995), 194-214.

[2] Berliner, B. CVS II: Parallelizing Software Development. In *Proc. of USENIX Winter 1990 Technical Conf.* (1990), 341-352.

[3] Blackburn, J. D., Scudder, G. D., and Van Wassenhove, L. N. Improving Speed and Productivity of Software Development: A Global Survey of Software Developers. *IEEE Trans. Softw. Eng.* 22, 12 (1996), 875-885.

[4] Blackburn, J., Scudder, G., and Van Wassenhove, L. N. Concurrent software development. *Commun. ACM* 43, 11es, Article 4 (2000).

[5] Brooks, F. P. *The Mythical Man-Month (Anniversary Ed.)*. Addison-Wesley (1995).

[6] Cockburn, A. and Williams, L. The costs and benefits of pair programming. In *Extreme Programming Examined*, Addison-Wesley (2001), 223-243.

[7] Collins-Sussman, B. The subversion project: buiding a better CVS. *Linux J.* 2002, 94 (2002), 3.

[8] Fan, H. and Sun, C. Dependency-based automatic locking for semantic conflict prevention in real-time collaborative programming. In *Proc. of ACM Symposium on Applied Computing* (2012), 737-742.

[9] Fan, H. and Sun, C. Achieving integrated consistency maintenance and awareness in real-time collaborative programming environments: the CoEclipse approach. In *Proc. of IEEE Intl. Conf. on Computer Supported Cooperative Work in Design* (2012), 94-101.

[10] Goldman, M., Little, G., and Miller, R. C. Real-time collaborative coding in a web IDE. In *Proc. of ACM Symposium on User interface Software and Technology* (2011), 155-164.

[11] Loeliger, J. *Version Control with Git: Powerful Tools and Techniques for Collaborative Software Development (1st ed.)*. O'Reilly Media (2009).

[12] Nosek, J. T. The case for collaborative programming. *Commun. ACM* 41, 3 (1998), 105-108.

[13] Perry, D., Siy, H., and Votta, L. Parallel changes in large-scale software development: an observational case study. *ACM Trans. Softw. Eng. Methodol.* 10, 3 (2001), 308-337.

[14] Pilato, C., Collins-Sussman, B., and Fitzpatrick, B. *Version Control with Subversion (2 ed.)*. O'Reilly Media (2008).

[15] Salinger, S., Oezbek, C., Beecher, K., and Schenk, J. Saros: an eclipse plug-in for distributed party programming. In*Proc. of ICSE Workshop on Cooperative and Human Aspects of Softw. Eng.* (2010), 48-55.

[16] Shen, H. and Sun., C. Flexible notification for collaborative systems. In *Proc. of ACM Conf. on CSCW* (2002), 77-86.

[17] Shen, H. and Sun, C. Recipe: a web-based environment for supporting real-time collaborative programming. In *Proc. of Intl. Conf. on Networks, Parallel and Distributed Processing* (2002), 283-288.

[18] Sun, C. and Ellis, C. Operational transformation in real-time group editors: issues, algorithms, and achievements. In *Proc. of ACM Conf. on CSCW* (1998), 59-68.

[19] Sun, C., Xia, S., Sun, D., Chen, D., Shen, H., and Cai, W. Transparent adaptation of single-user applications for multi-user real-time collaboration. *ACM Trans. Comput.-Hum. Interact.* 13, 4 (2006), 531-582.

[20] Tichy, W. F. Tools for software configuration management. In *Proc. of Intl. Workshop on Software Version and Configuration Control* (1988), 1-20.

[21] Williams, L. A. and Kessler, R. R. All I really need to know about pair programming I learned in kindergarten. *Commun. ACM* 43, 5 (2000), 108-114.

[22] Williams, L., Kessler, R. R., Cunningham, W., and Jeffries, R. Strengthening the case for pair programming. *IEEE Softw.* 17, 4 (2000), 19-25.

Decentralized Documents Authoring System for Decentralized Teamwork

Matching Architecture with Organizational Structure

Frédéric Merle*, Aurélien Bénel†, Guillaume Doyen*and Dominique Gaïti*

*ICD/ERA, †ICD/Tech-CICO, STMR (UMR CNRS), Université de Technologie de Troyes
12 rue Marie Curie, 10010 Troyes Cedex, France
{frederic.merle, aurelien.benel, guillaume.doyen, dominique.gaiti}@utt.fr

ABSTRACT

While systems for collaborative distributed works focus on enhancing distributed work group productivity, little attention has been paid to their architecture. In fact, most of these systems rely on centralized ones for both user communications and data hosting. These architectures raise issues about the administrative control, maintenance and management of the central entity. In this paper, we present a new architecture based on peer-to-peer (P2P) model driven by user relationship. In our architecture, users choose the trusted co-workers they are connected with. Thus, only the most trusted users manage to obtain a high number of connections which grant them a relative authority inside the system.

Categories and Subject Descriptors

C.2 [**Computer Communication Networks**]: Distributed Systems; H.5.3 [**Group and Organization Interfaces**]: Computer supported cooperative work

General Terms

Human Factors, Design

Keywords

P2P, Virtual Communities, Collaborative Systems

1. INTRODUCTION

Over the past twenty years, numerous new collaborative systems have been developed that greatly improve the ability of distributed groups to work together. While human-computer interaction and new features have attracted much attention over the past few years, these system architectures have not undergone much improvement. In fact, most of them are highly centralized and do not attempt to adjust themselves to group organizations. Indeed, virtual communities, like those in open source projects, are far from being as centralized as the systems they use to work together [4]. Most of these communities adapt themselves to the system architectures by granting some system administration responsibilities to the most trusted members.

Nevertheless, many biases remain due to the mismatch between system architecture and group organization. Firstly many systems are hosted by a third party (service provider or institution) which dictates its own policies to users. Such policies have to be taken into account by users and can alter group organizations. Secondly, the administration of the systems grants to its user an authority over other group members. Such authority driven by architectural considerations can lead to internal tensions inside a community. Finally, centralized architectures lack reliability. Many hazards like technical failures, service closures or changes in policies of use, can affect the system access for users. This kind of situation is even more harmful for collaborative works as most of the time, data is directly hosted inside the system's central entity.

In this paper, we present the use of the peer-to-peer (P2P) model for collaborative systems. Unlike centralized architectures or other P2P systems proposals [6], our aim is to fit the social organization to the working group level. Although, fitting the architecture of an information system to the organizational structure of a company has already been thoroughly studied [1], to the best of our knowledge nothing has yet been undertaken for smaller and more changeable structures like working groups. Thus, we use the relationships between group members to drive the topology of our architecture. To do so, users are connected to co-workers only if they trust them. Thus, the number of connections of a user reflects the trust of his co-workers. Such architecture adapts itself to the changes inside the social organization of the group that can occur. Furthermore, it has the same basic advantages as P2P systems such as scalability and fault-tolerance.

In section 2, we present a realistic scenario of a group of users who collaboratively author documents. Section 3 gives an overview of existing solutions to our scenario. Then, in section 4, we present a system using our socially driven architecture. We analyze its advantages regarding our scenario in section 5.

GROUP'12, October 27–31, 2012, Sanibel Island, Florida, USA.
Copyright 2012 ACM 978-1-4503-1486-2/12/10 ...$15.00.

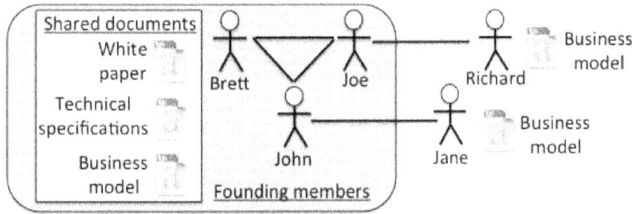

Figure 1: Social organization of the group

2. SCENARIO

We consider a group of users that collaboratively work on a set of documents with a document authoring application. For simplicity, the group has only five members and they work on three documents. Among members, three are the founding members who started the project and have access to every document and the two others are in charge of only some of the documents. Each of those remaining members was asked to help by a founding member. Moreover, only the founding member who invites a new member already knows him/her (Figure 1).

The authoring of these documents is a background task for group members and they do it in their free time. During these moments, they can have access to Internet or not. No specific workflow has been defined for group members. Thus, everyone can freely edit the documents without any control by other members. However, all users have to be able to keep track of every modification made to a document.

3. EXISTING SOLUTIONS

Different solutions are already used for collaborative document authoring, such as online word processors, file synchronization systems or revision control systems.

The most used online word processor is Google Docs.[1] In this system, every document is hosted by Google and can be authored by any authorized users with the web interface. It keeps track of every revision made to a document which allows a user to undo modifications previously made by another user. Its main advantage is to allow co-writers to synchronically edit a document. But this advantage comes with a major drawback (for users): the constant need of an Internet connection.

File synchronization systems, like Dropbox,[2] are used to synchronize files and folders on two or more different computers. These systems use centralized architecture to host the canonical version of each shared folder. Every modification to a shared folder is pushed to this canonical version and applied to every other user's folder synchronized with it. The servers of these systems are always hosted by a company which is subject to policy changes or sometimes even service closures. Furthermore, only the last revision of a folder is replicated on user computers, which means that only the last revision will be replicated. These systems have an embedded a revision control feature which can only be used from the canonical folder web interface which is hosted by the server. Thus, any recovery of older versions of files needs a connection to the server.

Revision control systems are widely used by software developers to collaboratively edit source code and documentation. Like file synchronization systems, a centralized revision control system, like Subversion,[3] uses a server to host the canonical version of the project documents. Thus, any revision control operations or modification submissions need a connection with the server. In decentralized revision control systems, like Git,[4] each user hosts a copy as well as the complete history of revision for every document of the project. Users work on their own version of a project and periodically synchronize it with other users. This synchronization can be done in P2P fashion. However, without any central server, the synchronization becomes quickly unmanageable for more than three users on the same project. Thus, these systems are mainly used with a central server. What is more, these systems are not at all user-friendly as different commands are needed to simply share or update documents. Finally, the merging tools provided with these systems are usually for plain text rather than for office documents.

None of those systems are really suitable for our scenario. They all use centralized architectures which place a heavy constraint on users. In this kind of architecture, server administrators have an overwhelming authority over users. Thus, users always have to agree to the policies of the service providers or the IT service which hosts the server. Furthermore, the service providers can close the service or remove the server for internal reorganization or strategical reasons. In addition, the founders of the group are usually given the ability to grant or revoke membership. Even if users are now accustomed to them, these computer models mimic very poorly the social organization and dynamics of a group.

4. OUR PROPOSAL

We propose to extend a decentralized revision control system with an automated decentralized synchronization feature and a user friendly interface. We chose Git as the decentralized revision control system because of its great popularity. Furthermore, it is built as a set of basic features warped together with scripts, which eases its integration. To automatize the synchronization of the user's works, we use a P2P model based on group member relationships. These systems use a virtual architecture, called 'overlay', to connect user's computers ('peers'), with each other. We use the mutual trust between users to drive the overlay construction, like in a Friend-to-Friend system [8]. Thus, our system can follow the evolution of the social organization of the user's group. Furthermore, this model allows users to collaboratively manage the group by trusting or distrusting other members. To do this, we propose an interface for user relationship management. Then, we use another abstraction of social mechanisms for document synchronization, called 'epidemics algorithm' or 'gossip protocols' [5, 2]. These algorithms broadcast information with low overheads for each peer and high guarantees about information reception for every group member as time goes by.

4.1 Overlay design driven by social organization

In this model, two peers share a connection only if their

---

[1]Google Docs, http://www.google.com/google-d-s/documents/
[2]Dropbox, http://www.dropbox.com/

[3]Apache Subversion, http://subversion.apache.org/
[4]Git, the fast version control system, http://git-scm.com/

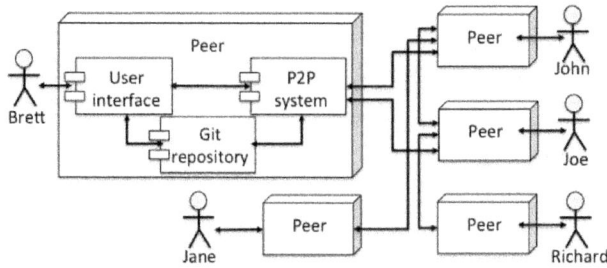

Figure 2: Deployment diagram of our application over the group define into our scenario

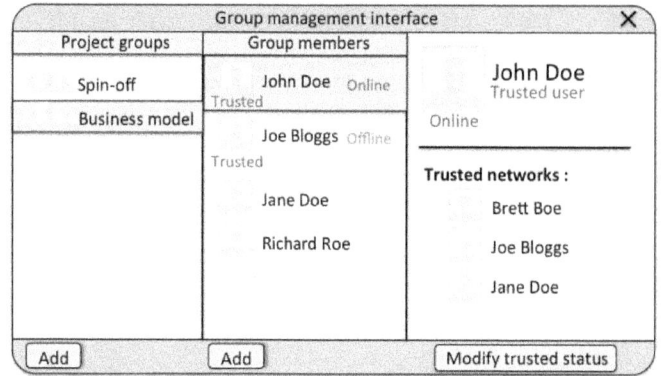

Figure 3: Brett contact management interface (mockup)

two owners agree to do so. Consequently, a user can unilaterally break a connection with another peer. Thus, the more a peer is connected with other user peers, the more the user is trusted by the other group members. If a peer does not share a connection with any other member peer, its user is evicted from the group. As a corollary, any user peer who shares a connection with another member peer is also a member of this group. Therefore, any member of the group can invite a new user inside on their own by creating a connection with his/her peer.

The data about every peer inside the system is shared by all of them. This is mandatory in order to allow users to create a new connection between their peers and another member's peer at any time. We extend this data to the list of every peer a peer is connected with. This data is translated to users into the trust relationship between them which allows any group member to evaluate the reputation of any other member inside the group. With our design, the overlay structure tends to fit in with the social organization of a group (Figure 2). Thus, mutual agreement between members can create any type of overlay structure.

Technically, to create a connection between two peers, each of them creates a new account for the other with an access to the local project repository to allow SSH connections. The peer also registers the other peer local repository as a Git remote repository. To break a connection, a peer deletes this peer account and removes its project repository from the Git remote repository list. To keep track on any group member, each peer stores two lists: the connected peers list and the peers list. The first one only refers to data about connected peers. The second list contains data about every user peer of the group.

Every part of the overlay management is controlled through a contact management interface (Figure 3). We use the address book metaphor to facilitate user adoption of the system. We enhance this kind of system with two functions. The first is group management. This feature allows a user to create a new group of users with the "add" button at the bottom of the first pane. If he does, a window will ask them for a project name and the path to the synchronized folder. A user can also invite someone from outside the group with "add" button at the bottom of the second pane. If he does, the system will ask for this user peer address in order to send it an invitation to join the group. This user is notified of the invitation through a notification interface. When this user joins the group, he automatically shares a trusted relationship with the user who invited him. The second functionality is a trust relationship management. It allows

a user to modify her relationship status with a group member. With the "modify trusted status" button, a user can change the relationship status with the group member displayed on the third pane. Every modification to the status is notified to this user through a notification interface. As the trusted relationship inside the system is bidirectional, this member become a trusted one only after he accepts the invitation. Thus, the trusted relationship reflects both mutual trust between users and their will to work together.

4.2 Synchronization process

The system synchronizes both the Git local repository and the user list of every group member peer. To achieve this synchronization, we combine two different epidemic algorithms [5] like in [2]: *rumour mongering* and *anti-entropy*.

The rumour mongering algorithm broadcasts immediately new data with a low guarantee that it reachs every peer. To enhance it, the anti-entropy algorithm periodically synchronizes the latest data known by two peers to fetch any missed rumours. This process automatically starts after a certain amount of time or when a peer returns online.

Git features are very well suited to implement these algorithms: sending new data can be carried out by a simple 'push' and the synchronization of the anti-entropy process done by a 'fetch'. Furthermore, with Git server-side 'hooks', the system can be notified of these modifications and process them. For this reason, we have choosen to use Git for the users list to manage updates. To limit the size of the user's list modification history, all modifications are made inside a 'branch' which is weekly pruned.

For the synchronization management, the user interface is divided into two parts: an icon on the system tray and another which can be found on the files and folders contextual menu. The system tray icon of the system works as a instant messenger one as it notifies the user about the state of their connection with other members and their notifications. If the system cannot find a trusted team member online, this icon is shaded. Under the icon, we have a counter which shows the number of unread notifications. By a click on this icon, the user opens a contextual menu with an access to the contact management interface as its first entry. The other entries are notifications which can be removed by ignoring them or, for invitations, by accepting them.

The contextual menu of a synchronized folder or document is extended with two entries: "Share" and "History".

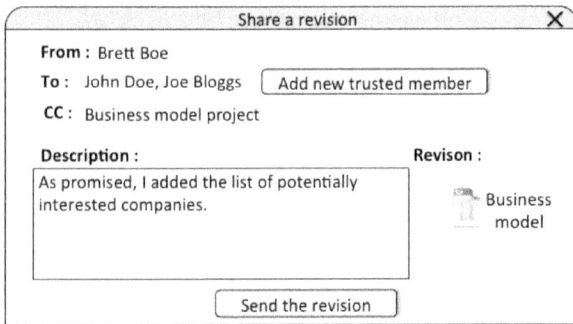

Figure 4: Share interface (mockup)

With "Share", the user pushes his revision to every member of the team. It opens an email-like interface (Figure 4) which is pre-filled with the trusted members as message recipients and all the group as a copy recipient. The choice of this kind of interface is driven by the constraints similar of committing a revision and sending an attachment by email. Any revision's commit needs a brief description of the modification as would have been made in the body of an email. Moreover, as trusted members of the group, only message recipients receive a notification of this revision. Finally, the user can add a new trusted member from this interface, as he would do if he added a new recipient for an email. Thus, this metaphor turns ordinary email practice into on of advanced revision control. "History" opens the revision history of a folder or document. The interface of this history is out of the scope of this document but could resemble a simplified version of GitX[5] or SmartGit[6] revision tree visualization.

5. ADVANTAGES OF OUR SYSTEM

Regarding the scenario that we have proposed, our system fulfils most of the requirements. Document authoring and revision control can be carried out by any member of the group during both online and offline periods. The sharing of the documents between founding members and the two remaining ones can be done by having two distinct project folders. A global one shared only between founding members and a sub-folder shared with the entire group which contains only documents for the two other members. Every modification in the organization can be made by mutual agreement between members. Thus, a founding member can be evicted from the project only if the two others agree to it. However, any of the remaining members can be evicted by the founding member who invited them to join the project. Finally, our system is fully managed by the users with no third party policies to restrict the system use. The limit of our system, compared to centralized ones, is that members work is synchronized only if two trusted members are online at the same time. However mutual online periods are very likely, e.g. during office hours, and this limit only applies to small groups.

Our model can be used for many different community organizations or applications. Indeed, our social-driven construction of the overlay is scalable and can develop the same properties as structured overlays have [3]. Thus, most of

the P2P systems previously proposed can be used with our overlay construction [6, 7]. Thus, our model is very versatile and can easily support large communities as well as a large range of features.

6. CONCLUSION

In this work, we have proposed a new kind of overlay construction for collaborative P2P systems. Our system uses social relationships between users to drive the overlay construction. Thus, it fits the social organizational structure of the group. With this overlay construction, we avoid organizational limits of centralized architectures like third party policies, or the overbearing authority of any server administrator. Furthermore, as a P2P model, our system provides higher scalability and reliability, as well as wider offline features than centralized systems. We have illustrated these advantages over existing solutions on a realistic scenario of collaborative document authoring. This work could be the first step towards a fully decentralized infrastructure for various collaborative software.

7. ACKNOWLEDGEMENT

The authors are thankful to Peter Jacobs for his comments about a preliminary version of this article.

8. REFERENCES

[1] Y. Chan and B. Reich. IT alignment: what have we learned? *Journal of Information Technology*, 22:297–315, September 2007.

[2] F. Cuenca-Acuna, C. Peery, R. Martin, and T. Nguyen. Planetp: Using gossiping to build content addressable peer-to-peer information sharing communities. In *12th IEEE International Symposium on High Performance Distributed Computing (HPDC'03)*, page 236, June 2003.

[3] M. Dell'Amico. Mapping small worlds. In *Peer-to-Peer Computing*, pages 219–228. IEEE, 2007.

[4] D. Demazière, F. Horn, and M. Zune. La dynamique de développement des 'communautés' du logiciel libre: conditions d'émergence et régulations des tensions. *Terminal, technologie de l'information, culture et société*, (97-98):71–84, 2006.

[5] A. Demers, D. Greene, C. Hauser, W. Irish, J. Larson, S. Shenker, H. Sturgis, D. Swinehart, and D. Terry. Epidemic algorithms for replicated database maintenance. In *annual ACM Symposium on Principles of distributed computing*, pages 1–12. ACM, August 1987.

[6] P. Gotthelf, A. Zunino, and M. Campo. A decentralized middleware for groupware applications. In *international conference on Groupware: design implementation, and use*. Springer-Verlag, September 2007.

[7] G. Oster, P. Urso, P. Molli, and A. Imine. Data consistency for p2p collaborative editing. In *Conference on Computer Supported Cooperative Work*. ACM, November 2006.

[8] M. Rogers and S. Bhatti. How to disappear completely: A survey of private peer-to-peer networks. In *International Workshop on Sustaining Privacy in Autonomous Collaborative Environments*. IFIP, July 2007.

---

[5]GitX, http://gitx.frim.nl/seeit.html
[6]SmartGit, http://www.syntevo.com/smartgit/features.html

Adaptive Forward Error Correction for Real-Time Groupware

Jeff Dyck, Carl Gutwin, and Dwight Makaroff
Department of Computer Science, University of Saskatchewan
110 Science Place, Saskatoon, Saskatchewan, Canada
[jeff.dyck, carl.gutwin, dwight.makaroff] @usask.ca

ABSTRACT

Real-time distributed groupware sends several kinds of messages with varying quality-of-service requirements. However, standard network protocols do not provide the flexibility needed to support these different requirements (either providing too much reliability or too little), leading to poor performance on real-world networks. To address this problem, we investigated the use of an application-level networking technique called adaptive forward error correction (AFEC) for real-time groupware. AFEC can maintain a predefined level of reliability while avoiding the overhead of packet acknowledgement or retransmission. We analysed the requirements of typical real-time groupware systems and developed an AFEC technique to meet these needs. We tested the new technique in an experiment that measured message reliability and latency using TCP, plain UDP, UDP with non-adaptive FEC, and UDP with our AFEC scheme, under several simulated network conditions. Our results show that for awareness messages that can tolerate some loss, FEC approaches keep latency at nearly the plain-UDP level while dramatically improving reliability. In addition, adaptive FEC is the only technique that can maintain a specified level of reliability and also minimize delay as network conditions change. Our study shows that groupware AFEC can be a useful tool for improving the real-world performance and usability of real-time groupware.

Categories and Subject Descriptors

H.5.3 [**Information Interfaces and Presentation**]: *CSCW*

General Terms

Performance, Design, Reliability, Human Factors.

Keywords

Synchronous groupware, latency, reliability, adaptive FEC

1. INTRODUCTION

Real-time distributed groupware often sends several different kinds of messages, each with different Quality of Service (QoS) requirements. For example, awareness messages like telepointer updates need low latency, but do not need to be completely reliable; transactional messages like object creation need reliability guarantees, but may not make strict latency demands. In addition, some message types can have different requirements depending on context, such as when telepointers are used for communicative gestures (where more messages will be needed to show smooth movement) instead of for general group awareness (where low-granularity positional information is often sufficient).

The QoS requirements of real-time groupware must be met either by infrastructural capabilities of networks or by application-level

networking techniques that are controlled by the groupware developer. The dramatic improvements to Internet availability and pervasiveness over the past several years suggest that groupware's QoS requirements can be easily met by standard protocols and techniques, but experience shows that this is not always the case.

There are two main problems. First, Internet networks are not always able to provide the quality of service that is needed for real-time interaction through groupware. Although some network connections show latencies less than 100ms with near-zero loss, there are still many settings where both delay and loss are common. For example, problems can be caused when connecting from one broadband network to another, when using wireless or cellular networks, when connecting across inter-continental links, when network traffic is heavy, or when working in rural or remote regions with less-developed infrastructure [1,3,20,22,26]. As a result, users – even in North America or Europe – may frequently experience loss rates above 5% and delays above 250ms, with higher spikes not uncommon (e.g., [1,20]). In addition, the loss and latency that users experience are higher than published network statistics (e.g., network statistics do not include delays introduced in other parts of the connection such as input controllers or display hardware, and do not count loss episodes such as packets that are out of order or too late to be useful).

Second, the network protocols that groupware developers use most commonly (TCP in particular) are poorly suited to real-time communication in real-world networks. Loss is a particular problem if groupware uses TCP, since the in-order guarantee of the protocol means that any lost packet holds up all others until retransmission completes. Many groupware messages do not need in-order delivery (e.g., telepointer messages), but need low latency, and thus interaction can suffer greatly. As a result, game developers and groupware researchers have moved to UDP-based transport for real-time groupware. UDP has many advantages for real-time communication, but also provides no reliability guarantees – and in high loss environments, this lack can be just as problematic as the limitations of TCP. Researchers have developed reliable versions of UDP (e.g., [13]) but these are not tuned to the needs of groupware – for example, they often provide 100% reliability and often force in-order delivery, when groupware messages have varying reliability and ordering requirements, and would benefit from a more flexible approach.

Forward Error Correction (FEC) [2,19,22] is a technique well known in the networking world that could provide this flexibility, and could form the basis for a groupware-centered application-level reliability scheme. FEC duplicates messages in successive network packets, such that if one is lost, the message can still be retrieved from a later packet. FEC has the advantage of providing reliability without requiring acknowledgment or retransmission (which cause the latency problems of TCP-style reliability). In addition, adaptive versions of FEC (AFEC) can provide a wide variety of reliability rates that automatically tune themselves to current network conditions [2]: in low loss situations, the adaptive technique reduces redundancy which also reduces bandwidth requirements; as loss increases, redundancy is increased until a balance between reliability and latency is met.

Adaptive Forward Error Correction is well suited to the needs of real-time groupware. However, although many researchers have studied FEC in the area of streaming media, and although it has been used in a few groupware projects (e.g., [5]), there has been no thorough analysis of the technique to establish its effects on the performance of real-time groupware.

In this paper, we carry out this investigation of forward error correction for groupware. We develop an AFEC technique designed around the reliability and latency requirements of real-time groupware, and carry out an evaluation to see the effects on groupware performance. Our study shows that the technique works very well at managing loss and latency in real-world network conditions, and is adaptable both to changes in network status and to changing demands at the application level. To make our AFEC technique widely available to groupware developers, we have built a reference implementation on top of the open-source Lidgren UDP library [14]. In this work, we provide strong evidence that AFEC is a powerful and practical technique for maintaining QoS requirements in real-time groupware; the benefits to user-level experience can substantially improve the usability of real-time collaboration at a distance.

2. BACKGROUND

Network issues for real-time systems have been studied in several domains, including distributed systems, networking, and CSCW. We review this research below, focusing on issues that are of greatest relevance to our investigation of FEC for groupware.

2.1 Quality of Service

Quality of Service (QoS) is a set of requirements for different aspects of computer networks that define performance levels for distributed systems. Many CSCW papers mention QoS and its importance (e.g. [17,18]), but there are few that discuss how to model or deliver QoS. This may be because QoS in real-time groupware is complex compared to other classes of applications, due to the wide variety of message types and the unconstrained nature of the tasks and interaction techniques [8,10].

QoS *models* include sets of QoS *characteristics* that are appropriate for a particular application type, as well as their associated QoS *parameters*. An early QoS model designed specifically for groupware is described by Mathur and Prakash [18], and includes four characteristics: latency, jitter, packet loss, and asynchrony. In the following sections, we look more closely at two of these characteristics: latency and loss. However, there are many other characteristics that could be considered for a complete QoS model of groupware, such as security, frequency, resolution, accuracy, precedence, and authenticity (which are described in the generic ISO/IEC QoS model [14]).

Managing QoS in groupware is also different from other applications because of the variable and dynamic nature of groupware sessions. Unlike systems that only transport streaming media (e.g., VoIP), groupware QoS techniques must adjust to the needs of different applications, scenarios, user preferences, and group dynamics. For example, Greenhalgh [10] describes a QoS manager for a virtual environment that allocates resources based both on application-specific settings and on a spatial awareness model to determine level of interest between participants. Although full QoS models are difficult for groupware, it is still possible to improve performance by considering individual QoS characteristics – such as delay and loss as discussed below.

2.2 Network Delay

Delay is a fact of life in real-world distributed applications because information must be transmitted across a network and processed at the other end before it can be displayed. There are two main types of delay – latency and jitter [22]. *Latency* is the time that elapses between an event and its display at another system, which results in a person's actions in the shared environment being seen after they actually occur. *Jitter* is the variation in latency due to changing network traffic conditions and processing loads; jitter reduces the smoothness of a remote user's displayed actions, such that motion (such as telepointer motion) looks halting and jerky [11].

Delays can have severe effects on collaboration – on coordination, communication, and understanding of the shared situation. Delay can make turn-taking difficult to negotiate, can hinder social protocols, and can cause inconsistencies that lead to confusion about the timing or simultaneity of key events [4,11].

There has been a large amount of research showing that network delay can negatively affects users of real-time groupware – but the effects of delay depend a great deal on the type of application, the degree of coupling between collaborators, and the temporal granularity of the interaction. For example, a study of a Pong-style game found that users did not seem to perceive latencies of less than 150ms, but that performance was affected with 500ms latency [30]; in contrast, studies of first-person shooters have found that players are sensitive to latencies below 100ms [26]. Studies of tightly-coupled coordinated interaction (where people must act based on what another person is doing) have also shown negative effects of latencies at or above 100ms [28]. Jitter has also been shown to have effects on group interaction, particularly on people's ability to predict others' movement [11]; but again, the effects of jitter are dependent on the environment and the interaction, and other studies show that these delays do not always affect users' perceptions in game environments [26].

Researchers have also considered numerous strategies for reducing or hiding network delay, such as dead-reckoning or local lag (e.g., [28]). These techniques are vitally important in an overall view of groupware QoS, but are not required for our work on reliability (although delay-compensation techniques can be integrated with the techniques proposed here).

2.3 Message Loss and Reliability

A second reality of distributed groupware is that not all messages can be successfully delivered to receivers. There are two main reasons for these delivery failures – packet loss and loss caused by out-of-order or late delivery.

Packet loss occurs whenever network packets sent by a distributed system fail to reach their destination, and is caused by a variety of problems including signal degradation, interference, congestion at routers (i.e., buffer overflows), or network errors [23]; there can even be losses induced by communication protocols themselves (e.g., some versions of the 802.11 protocol [25]).

Order-based loss occurs when a message is unusable at the receiver because it is delivered out of order, or too late. For example, telepointer messages that are delivered either late or out of order are no longer useful for showing a person's current location (although they may still be used to show traces [12]).

There are two main ways to describe loss. First, the overall loss rate (e.g., percentage of packets lost in a given time period) describes general behavior over time. Second, and more importantly for groupware, the *burst characteristics* describe the distribution of loss at the local level. Burst loss means losing more than one packet in a row, and can be described in terms of the *burst length* (the number of consecutive packets lost), and the *burst frequency* (the rate at which bursts occur) [23].

Although many networks have near-zero loss on average, there are still many settings and situations where loss can be a problem. For example, an informal five-day review of the Internet Health Report (www.internetpulse.net), which reports statistics for main North American Internet providers, showed hourly average loss rates above 2% 104 times, and above 5% 45 times (rolling hourly averages, sampled every ten minutes). Even low loss rates can be problematic if losses occur in bursts, a phenomenon that is common when traffic levels are high [1].

Losses on wireless networks (cellular networks and wireless LANs) can be much higher, up to and even higher than 20% on average for long-distance WiFi networks [20]. Overall, these situations show that techniques are needed to control the reliability of messages in distributed systems.

2.4 Techniques for Message Reliability

Reliability techniques are used to counteract ordering and loss problems that occur while sending information over the network. There are two main approaches: protocol-based reliability, and application-level techniques.

2.4.1 Protocol-based reliability

Some communications protocols (e.g., TCP/IP) build reliability into their specifications, and groupware can in some cases maintain QoS simply by selecting an appropriate protocol. However, this approach has problems in that protocols are very general tools that cannot be adequately tuned to the needs of real-time groupware.

The TCP/IP protocol shows both the value and the limitations of the infrastructural approach to reliability. TCP is simple to use for programmers, and guarantees delivery (and in-order sequencing) of messages. However, guaranteed in-order delivery does not match the QoS requirements of many types of groupware messages, and the considerable resources used for acknowledging and retransmitting lost information leads to severe performance problems when TCP is used on real-world networks [5,7].

The other network protocol used for real-time groupware is UDP/IP. Since UDP provides no reliability or ordering guarantees, custom protocols are often built on top of UDP to deliver various QoS levels [7]. Application-level protocols are discussed in the next section, but here we consider RTP, a well-established protocol that is frequently used for sending real-time voice and video information. Some researchers have used RTP for real-time groupware applications (e.g. [8]), and there are RTP payload formats for common groupware message types including text messages and telepointers. The performance of RTP for groupware has not been tested, however, and some analyses indicate that RTP is not well suited to delivering the wide range of QoS requirements exhibited by real-time groupware [24].

There is an overall trend (e.g., as seen in networked game libraries [7]) to avoid protocol-based solutions to QoS requirements. One reason is that protocols work only at the packet level, and there are many advantages to working at the level of messages instead. For example, if two message types have differing QoS requirements, these cannot be handled appropriately by a single protocol. The reliability needs of real-time groupware are most likely to be met by a message-level approach.

2.4.2 Application-level reliability

There are three main techniques for maintaining reliability levels in an application-level protocol based on UDP/IP: retransmission, path diversity, and forward error correction.

Retransmission techniques resend data that is known to be lost. There are two main ways to do this – by acknowledging all information when it arrives (ACK-based) or by requesting information when loss is detected (NACK-based) [25]. *ACK-based* error correction requires all received packets to be acknowledged; *NACK-based* techniques do not have this overhead, but require message sequence numbers in order to detect loss at the receiver. A further requirement is a continuous flow of information, since loss can only be detected after subsequent packets have arrived (it is also possible to send termination packets to indicate the end of a transmission).

Path diversity schemes sends information redundantly over two separate network routes, which can improve reliability because different network routes have uncorrelated loss patterns [16]. This technique has been shown to be successful for services such as VoIP and real-time streaming video [16]. However, current networks do not support the ability to define a network route, and so this technique is not yet feasible in most real-world situations.

Forward error correction (FEC) improves reliability by repeating information in subsequent network packets [2,19]. In the event that a packet is lost, the information can be recovered when subsequent packets arrive (see Figure 1). No retransmission is required, but additional bandwidth is used to deliver the same total amount of information. In addition, this method is only partially reliable, since burst losses that are larger than the amount of redundancy can still lead to lost information. FEC is typically parameterized with the number of repetitions used; for example, FEC-3 duplicates the previous three messages in each new packet. There are several variants of FEC that have been investigated, and the technique is used successfully in many streaming-media situations [19]; as described below, FEC is also well suited to the needs of real-time groupware.

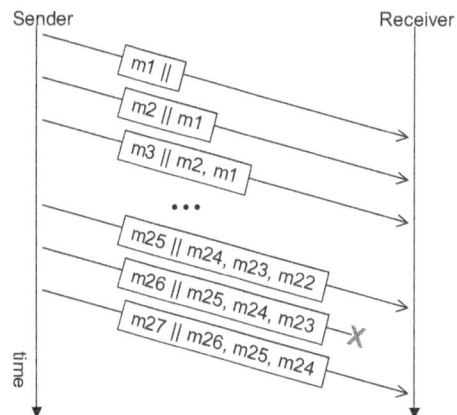

Figure 1: FEC-3 example. The last three messages are repeated in subsequent packets, allowing lost information (e.g., message 26) to be recovered without retransmission.

Adaptive FEC (AFEC) dynamically adjusts the amount of redundancy in order to meet QoS requirements while attempting to minimize the network cost of sending repeated information [2]. Adaptive FEC requires that the network conditions and the current reliability levels be monitored, and that an adaptation service continually adjust redundancy levels in response to network conditions or changing requirements.

Interleaved FEC is another variant of the basic FEC technique that disperses contiguous information among several packets by reordering portions of the messages [25]. For example, a stream that sends 20 messages per second at a packet rate of 5 packets per second (4 messages per packet) could be interleaved by sending messages 1, 5, 9, and 13 in packet 1, messages 2, 6, 10, and 14 in packet 2, and so on. In the event of a single packet loss, less contiguous information would be lost, which could result in a smoother reconstructed stream at the receiver. However, this comes at the cost of added latency, since the information cannot be reordered and played out at the receiver until all interleaved information is received.

3. AFEC FOR REAL-TIME GROUPWARE

In developing an AFEC technique for real-time groupware, we need to consider three issues: the reliability requirements of real-time groupware, the characteristics of groupware messages that could affect the design of the technique, and the specifics of the technique itself. We initially considered applying an existing AFEC technique from VoIP research, but found that there are substantial differences between groupware and the streaming-media applications that have used AFEC in the past.

3.1 Reliability requirements of groupware

Groupware applications have reliability requirements that vary depending on the type of groupware data being sent. For instance, telepointer updates do not have to be completely reliable since a small number of lost positions will not inhibit collaboration or cause shared data to be incorrect. However, adding a new object to a diagram must be a reliable operation since a lost message would make model layer data inconsistent. For this reason, we differentiate between *transactions*, which require guaranteed delivery, and *awareness messages*, which can have reliability requirements, but do not require guaranteed delivery.

Transactions occur infrequently in groupware applications compared with awareness messages. Additionally, transactions can be far less sensitive to delay, especially if awareness messages are sent to indicate that a transaction is in progress. Considering the requirement for guaranteed delivery and lower delay sensitivity, as well as the infrequency of transactions, an ACK-based protocol such as TCP seems suitable for transactions, although alternatives may be appropriate as well.

Awareness messages are sent very frequently, do not require guaranteed delivery, and require low delay. ACK-based protocols are not efficient in this situation, and plain UDP is not a suitable approach either because of unpredictable reliability, which is not acceptable for certain awareness techniques. Groupware awareness messages require efficient transmission that minimizes delay while guaranteeing a specific level of reliability.

Table 1. Message types and QoS requirements for a shared-whiteboard groupware system

Message Type	Update Rate (min..max)	Latency	Reliability
AddObject	on event	250ms	100%
DeleteObject	on event	500ms	100%
MoveObject (intermediate)	5/sec..25/sec	100ms	80%
MoveObject (final)	on event	500ms	100%
ResizeObject (intermediate)	5/sec..25/sec	100ms	80%
ResizeObject (final)	on event	500ms	100%
ModifyText (intermediate)	1/sec..5/sec	100ms	95%
ModifyText (final)	on event	500ms	100%
MoveViewport	2/sec..5/sec	250ms	80%
Telepointer	10/sec..25/sec	100ms	80%
Telepointer (during voice)	20/sec..30/sec	100ms	90%

As an example, we designed a hypothetical shared whiteboard system, and identified message types and QoS parameters for those types (see Table 1). Requirements were determined by

considering how each of the event types would be realized in the application and the effects of each of the characteristics on the user and on the application. Although these values are guided by our own intuition and experience (there is no formal approach to assigning QoS requirements for groupware), the diversity of values indicates a need for flexibility in handling reliability.

3.2 Characteristics of groupware messages

In addition to the varying reliability and latency requirements described above, real-time groupware has several characteristics that affect the design of a forward-error-correction technique.

Small and atomic messages. Groupware messages – particularly awareness messages – are small compared to the capacity of a network packet. For example, telepointer messages use 10-25 bytes when encoded efficiently [5], and other types of awareness messages (e.g., object or viewport moves) will be similar. This implies that more redundancy can be added to groupware packets, potentially allowing recovery from longer burst losses. In addition, since groupware messages often consist of state updates, event objects, or remote procedure calls, they must be sent in their complete format. This means that two techniques used in multimedia systems – sending partial data or sending a lower resolution version of the data – cannot be generally used for real-time groupware. Therefore, an encoding scheme for groupware should only include complete messages, a requirement can be met due to the small size characteristic.

Multiple message types. As seen in Table 1, several different types of groupware messages can be sent during the same session, each with different QoS requirements for packet loss, update rate, and latency. Different message types with different QoS requirements means that a groupware FEC scheme must handle the tracking and management of each message type separately. QoS performance and loss must be separately monitored for each message type, and the redundancy encoding scheme must make type-by-type decisions about which messages to include as redundant information to meet QoS requirements.

Bursty traffic. Groupware traffic is typically bursty, meaning that messages are clustered together with pauses in between. As an example, Figure 2 shows an activity trace of a shared whiteboard system [5] – in which telepointers, object manipulations, and text editing events all occur in clusters separated by inactive periods.

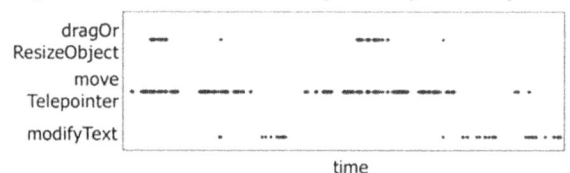

Figure 2: Occurrences of different groupware event types over time, for one user [5].

The clustering of awareness messages in groupware reflects the way that people work: telepointer motion, for example, is most often a series of moves with stops in between, rather than consistent and continuous movement. Note that we assume that awareness messages are event-driven and so are only sent out when something is happening. For a groupware FEC technique, clustering implies that when losses occur at the end of a cluster (e.g. just before a mouse move stops), messages cannot be recovered until more messages are sent. To deal with this, senders must detect the end of a message cluster and send packets containing only redundant messages until the recovery requirements are met. A similar requirement is mentioned in IETF RFC 2793 when using redundancy in text messaging applications.

Individual and contextual differences. Different people and different tasks can produce very different message patterns within the same groupware system. Different people take on different roles at different times (e.g., leader vs. worker, or active vs. passive), and people also show individual differences in the way that they work. For example, Figure 3 shows a summary of message types generated by four users carrying out a single shared task in a shared workspace [5]: two users show relatively balanced totals for four different message types, and two users differ dramatically. These dynamic differences mean that a groupware FEC technique must be able to respond to application-level and user-level changes to QoS requirements. For example, user preferences or application monitoring might determine that a user who gestures frequently to communicate should have different QoS requirements for telepointer messages.

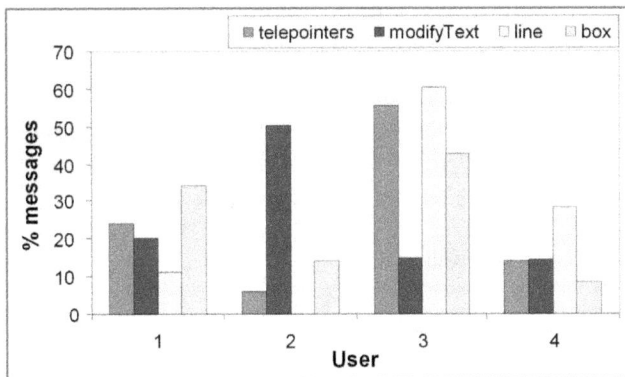

Figure 3: Message types generated by four users during a shared diagramming task [5].

3.3 The GW-AFEC Technique

We designed an AFEC technique that is tailored to meet the specific requirements of real-time groupware. The technique consists of an encoding scheme, an adaptation logic, and a code selection algorithm (which determines the number of redundant messages to be included in an outgoing packet). Our technique is based on the assumptions that messages are small, that messages must be sent in their entirety, and that the receiver knows the minimum and maximum reliability requirements for each message type. We use the term message error rate (MER) to refer to the percentage of messages that are never received. This is different from the packet error rate (PER), which is the percentage of packets lost. Note that with reliable protocols, MER is always zero and for unreliable protocols, MER is equal to PER. When using error correction, PER is greater than or equal to MER because messages contained in lost packets can be recovered.

One might ask why we would ever set a non-zero minimum for message error rate; the answer is that for information that can tolerate some loss without any problems for the users, the extra bandwidth needed to provide further reliability could be better allocated to another channel that can make better use of it (e.g., sending accompanying video at higher resolution).

The encoding scheme that we used is simple: redundant messages are included in their entirety and in their original form, rather than being distributed over several packets or sent at lower resolution. This approach works because of the small size of awareness messages. Several redundant messages can be added to each packet, allowing full recovery of lost messages, even from small

burst losses. The total number of redundant messages still varies, however, depending on the network bandwidth, the actual message size, and the message frequency.

Sending entire messages allows full recovery from a single packet. For example, adding just one redundant message allows full recovery from any single lost packet. If two packets are never lost in a row, this scheme would provide full reliability. In general, however, accommodating burst losses means that a scheme must include as many redundant messages in each packet as the maximum burst length, in order to prevent any message loss. In cases where this cannot be achieved, the number of messages lost during a burst is the number of packets lost during the burst minus the number of redundant messages in a packet.

Since it is difficult to predict loss occurrence and burst length [1], it is not feasible to determine the number of redundant messages required to meet MER requirements in advance. Although MER can be reduced significantly using a fixed amount of redundancy, non-adaptive schemes cannot guarantee reliability. An adaptive approach is required to meet MER requirements while keeping the amount of redundancy to a minimum.

The need to accommodate MER requirements for a variety of message types also makes the adaptive logic more complex. In our technique, the receiver monitors each message type separately to ensure that MER requirements are being met, and tells the sender when to add or remove redundancy. The sender uses a code selection algorithm that considers each message type separately to meet the redundancy requirements. Since there can be many participants in a groupware system, MER is monitored separately for each user by the receiver, and the redundancy requirements are tracked separately for each user by the sender.

In the next two sections we provide more details on the elements of groupware AFEC that are required in the receiver and the sender of a message (see Figure 4).

3.3.1 Receiver-side responsibilities

The receiver is responsible for monitoring MERs to ensure that they stay between the minimum and maximum values set out for each message type from each user. Incoming packets consist of one current message and some number of redundant messages, all from a single user. The messages in a packet are processed in reverse order from oldest to newest (thus, redundant messages are processed first). It is important to note that this guarantees in-order delivery, since late out-of-order packets will be discarded because the messages they contain will have been recovered already. The receiver checks for message loss using message indexes (described below); if loss has occurred, the receiver increments the loss counter for that message type. Any message that has not been seen before (including recovered and new messages) is then processed as required.

Message loss detection is performed using message indexes. The highest received index is stored for each message type, and if the index of a message exceeds this value by more than one, the number of lost messages is reported and the MER for that message type is updated. To be able to record MER correctly for each message type, we need to know what type of message was lost. Therefore, we specify type within the index using a numeric message type code that precedes the index number.

Current MER is calculated using the previous 1000 messages only, rather than all of the messages during the life of the session. This is necessary to allow the system to react to changes in network conditions and to ensure that adjustments quickly result in different behavior. Otherwise, average rates would be spread out over the life of the session, resulting in reduced responsiveness as the number of messages in the session increases. The rolling average could also be accomplished using a time-based window; however, since the message frequency is irregular, a time-based approach could result in too small of a sample size to make accurate changes to the code set size (the number of redundant messages in a packet).

The receiver is responsible for deciding when to increase or decrease the amount of redundant information being sent. If the MER exceeds the maximum MER, the code set size must be increased so that more messages can be recovered. When the MER is below the minimum, the code set size must be decreased to avoid unnecessary redundancy (since it increases traffic without benefit). These control actions are accomplished with a module that periodically checks each message type's MER. If any of the MERs are above the maximum, a negative acknowledgement (NAK) is sent to the sender immediately, telling the sender to increase the amount of redundancy for the specified message type. If a MER is below its minimum value, the receiver sends a decrease acknowledgement (DEC) message, which tells the sender to reduce the redundancy for the specified message type.

Since groupware awareness messages are often clustered, code set size is only be updated when there is significant activity. With low activity, there is a risk of overcompensation because the code selector runs in a timed thread and could update the system several times without receiving new information.

3.3.2 Sender-side responsibilities

The sender is responsible for meeting the redundancy requirements as requested by the receiver. The code selection algorithm works to ensure that the correct number of redundant messages is included in each packet as requested by the receiver. The sender keeps a history buffer of each message type and knows how many times each message has been sent. When loading messages into a packet, the encoder starts from the most recent message and moves back through the history list. Only messages whose requirements have not yet been met are included.

The sender keeps a tally of the packet size and ensures that the amount of redundancy added does not exceed the path maximum transfer unit (path MTU) for the network route. The path MTU is the largest packet size that is forwarded by a router [23]. If the path MTU is exceeded, the packet will be divided into smaller packets, which adds delay. Therefore, the path MTU must be discovered by the system and should not be exceeded. In the case that adding redundancy will exceed the path MTU, the sender sends as many messages as it can without exceeding the path MTU and sends a notification to the receiver that the QoS requirements cannot be met and should be lowered. Adjustment of requirements can be handled automatically by the application or by the user through a dialog.

Finally, since groupware messages are often strongly clustered, times in which there are no messages to be sent are detected and a few extra messages are sent from the history buffer, in order to meet redundancy requirements for the last few messages of the cluster. Without adding messages after a cluster, MER would appear to be higher for the last few messages in each burst.

It is important to note that messages recovered using FEC or AFEC arrive at the same time as the newest message, which creates a similar effect to that of network jitter. Interface-level solutions are required to deal appropriately with this late

information. One method is to use client-side buffering, which adds additional latency. Another method that is suitable for groupware is to use traces, a technique that visualizes recent movement, improving accuracy without adding latency [12].

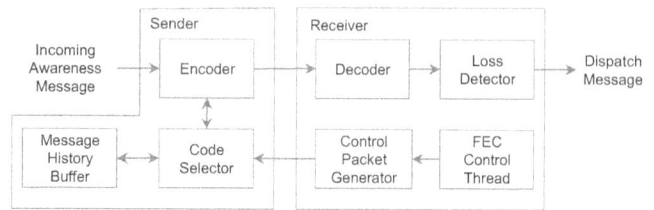

Figure 4: AFEC operation: incoming and redundant messages are combined based on the Code Selector's decisions; encoded messages are sent via UDP and decoded at the Receiver, which detects and reports loss; a timed FEC Control Thread monitors MER and adjusts the amount of redundancy.

3.3.3 Implementation

The GW-AFEC technique has been implemented both in Java and in C# using the Lidgren UDP library [15]. The system includes all of the modules shown in Figure 3, and can easily be adapted to work with many groupware architectures and event schemes. Our implementation is available at http://hci.usask.ca/gw-afec/.

4. EVALUATION OF GW-AFEC

We ran a set of experiments to see how the GW-AFEC technique would compare with TCP, plain UDP, and non-adaptive fixed-length FEC schemes under a variety of network conditions. Network conditions were simulated on a LAN using a software-based network-disabling emulator [21]. For each experiment, we measured MER and latency for each message. Our goals were to determine the following:

- How a guaranteed protocol like TCP compares with UDP-based schemes in lossy conditions;
- How FEC performance compares to plain UDP for a variety of code set sizes and bandwidth constraints;
- If and when non-adaptive FEC performs poorly;
- How AFEC compares with non-adaptive FEC;
- If and when AFEC performs poorly.

The test application was a simple telepointer application with a movement trail. We used this common awareness technique to ensure that the message patterns were similar to those found in real world groupware applications. An input message trace was recorded by moving a mouse manually in a manner that simulated natural activity with a whiteboard. This simulated the clusters of messages that happen in a groupware application. The update frequency for the telepointer was fixed at a maximum rate of 30 updates/second for all tests.

Simulations using the input trace were then run with two clients on the same machine, but with messages sent through a server on a different machine on the LAN. The network emulator ran on the server machine, simulating a variety of network conditions between the two clients. This setup enabled accurate latency measurements using the system clock on the client machine.

Loss rates, loss patterns, and amount of bandwidth were specified using the emulator to simulate different network conditions:

- *Loss rates.* We used three loss rates: 0%, 10%, and 20%.
- *Loss patterns.* Two different loss patterns were used: random and burst. The random pattern loses packets randomly based on a percentage chance of loss. We ran random loss tests at 0%, 10%, and 20% loss. For burst loss, two parameters determined the loss rate: the number of packets that would be

lost in a burst and the probability of a burst loss occurrence. Burst loss tests were run with 1-5 packets being lost with a 4% chance of starting on any packet (10% overall loss), 1-5 packets being lost with an 8% chance (20% overall), 1-10 packets being lost with a 2% chance (10% overall), and 1-10 packets being lost with a 4% chance (20% overall).

- *Bandwidth.* Each experiment was run using two levels of available bandwidth: 56Kbps and 256Kbps. Although total bandwidth will generally be higher than these levels, traffic patterns in real-world networks mean that the amount of available bandwidth is often restricted. We chose these levels as two types of resource-constrained environment.

For non-adaptive FEC, we ran tests with a variety of code set sizes (i.e., number of redundant messages) between 2 and 7. Since different code set sizes lead to different performance characteristics, we consider each as an independent technique, and will refer to them as 'FEC-n' where n is the code set size. (Note that in Figures 5 and 7, we show FEC-3, which was the best-performing of the non-adaptive techniques).

The experiments with AFEC were run with a target MER range of 5% minimum and 6% maximum. In a telepointer example, this means that we want to ensure that at least 94% of position messages arrive, but that more 95% is not needed for the type of interaction being supported. For each experiment, we measured message latency and MER.

4.1 Results

The results from our experiments are organized by the goals stated above – how different protocols perform in realistic conditions, the advantages and disadvantages of the basic FEC approach, and the behavior and performance of groupware AFEC.

4.1.1 Comparison in a realistic network situation

Our first investigation compares all protocols in terms of message latency and message error rate. Figure 5 shows average latency in a 56Kbps channel with 10% random loss for TCP, UDP, FEC-3 (i.e. FEC with code set size of 3), and groupware AFEC. Figure 7 shows MER for the same set of conditions. The most obvious result in Figure 5 is that when networks are experiencing loss, TCP's acknowledgment and retransmission policy lead to large latency. TCP latency is larger even in networks with no loss, but as loss increases, TCP quickly becomes unusable. In addition, the high variance in latency with TCP (Figure 6) makes it difficult for users to adapt to the delay.

In contrast, all of the schemes based on UDP maintain a low average latency. Differences among these three schemes can be attributed to packet size and to the resultant traffic level, since higher traffic in a limited channel generally corresponds to higher latency. UDP has the smallest packet size (equivalent to FEC-1) and therefore generates the least traffic; FEC-3 has the largest packet in this scenario, and so has slightly higher latency.

Results for message error rate (Figure 7) also show substantial differences between the protocols. Since TCP is a guaranteed reliable protocol, MER is always 0%. Since UDP provides no reliability control, its MER will always be approximately equal to the packet loss rate (here 10%). Groupware AFEC has a MER of 5%, which is within the bounds of the target MER of 5-6%. FEC-3 in this case was highly reliable – in fact too reliable, in that it used bandwidth that could have been better allocated to a different information channel (such as a video stream).

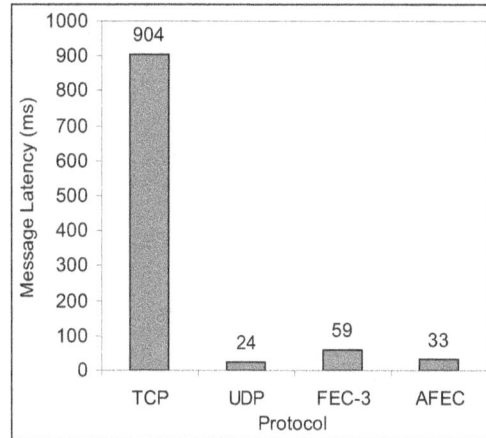

Figure 5: Average latency, by protocol, 56Kbps available bandwidth, 10% random loss.

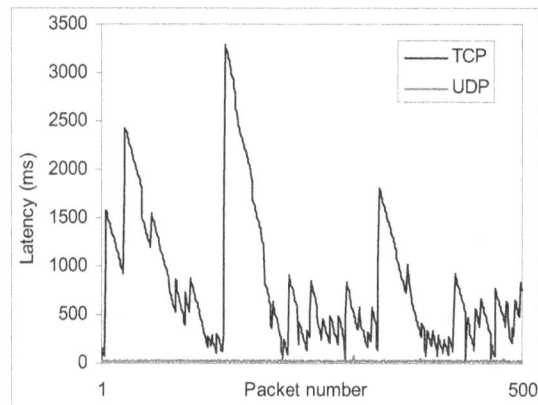

Figure 6: Typical variation in TCP and UDP latency, 56Kbps available bandwidth, 10% random loss.

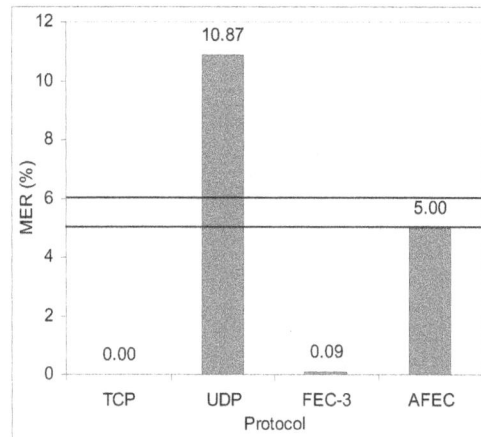

Figure 7: MER by protocol, 56Kbps available bandwidth, 10% random loss. The target bounds for MER (5%-6%) are marked with lines.

4.1.2 Performance of non-adaptive FEC

We tested non-adaptive FEC with several different code set sizes. In all tests, reliability was much higher than plain UDP, and in some experiments non-adaptive FEC showed the best performance for both MER and latency. However, these cases occurred only when the code set size happened to be an appropriate choice for the network conditions. When the code set size was not appropriate for conditions, then non-adaptive FEC showed either higher latency or an MER that was below the target range, indicating excess bandwidth usage.

One variable that greatly affected non-adaptive FEC was loss pattern. Random loss experiments resulted in very low MERs. Tests with burst loss, however, resulted in much higher MER values. The poor performance occurred because messages are lost whenever the size of the burst exceeds the code set size.

In general, although non-adaptive FEC provides an enormous improvement over plain UDP, an inappropriate choice of code set size can lead to reduced performance. This can be seen in Figure 7, where, the latency and MER of FEC with various code set sizes is compared to AFEC. Although different code set sizes lead to different performance extremes, only a few values provide a balance between latency and error rate.

4.1.3 Performance and characteristics of AFEC

The performance of AFEC was always equal to or better than that of non-adaptive FEC, as long as it was possible to meet the target MER range without exceeding the available bandwidth. AFEC shows optimal performance over time because it always moves towards the minimum code set size needed to meet the target MER range. In cases where non-adaptive FEC exceeded the reliability requirements (i.e. had a larger code set size), AFEC showed lower latency due to its smaller packet size. AFEC also selected a higher code set size to meet the target MER range in cases where FEC did not meet reliability requirements. The MER for AFEC varied between 4% and 7%, but was most often within the target range of 5% and 6%. In high burst loss conditions, AFEC was still able to meet the target MER range with low latency, as long as the available bandwidth was sufficient.

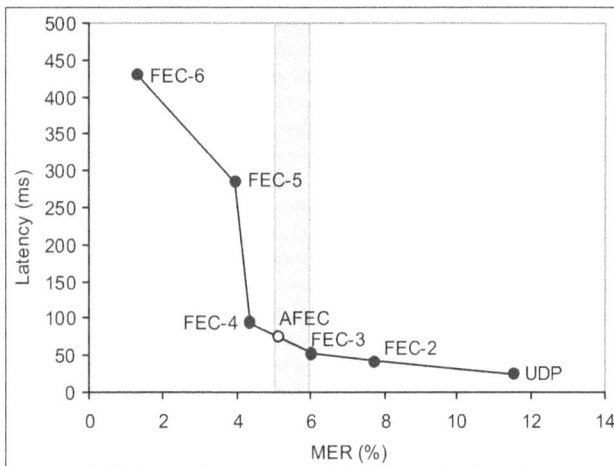

Figure 8. Average latency and MER for non-adaptive FEC with various code set sizes, and AFEC (white circle), on a 56Kbps channel with burst loss (burst size of 1-10 and 2% probability of occurrence).

Figures 9 and 10 illustrate these differences and show how AFEC works. Figure 9 shows latency of various techniques as loss increases from zero to 20%. Because AFEC varies its code set size, it can perform as fast as UDP when loss is low. As loss increases, AFEC's increasing packet size leads to higher latency; however, this is the minimum latency possible when maintaining the QoS requirements for MER.

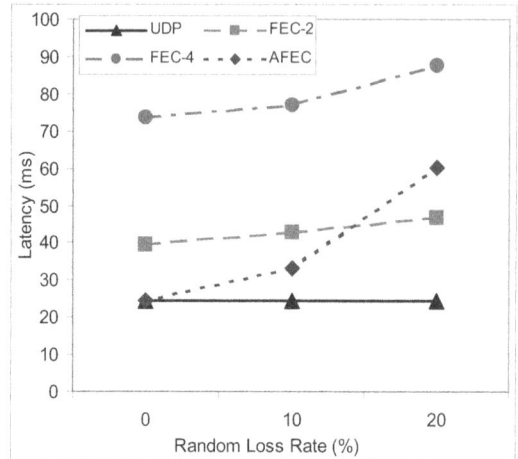

Figure 9. Average latency of different protocols at three loss rates. Note that AFEC latency increases as a result of increasing redundancy to maintain reliability.

The behaviour of AFEC is illustrated in the packet trace shown in Figure 10. At the start of the trace, AFEC has a code set size that is slightly too large, resulting in a gradual decline in MER past the specified minimum. Once below 5%, AFEC reduces code set size by one (line A in Figure 10); since this reduces packet size, latency decreases. The reduction in code set size is not enough to prevent another decline past the minimum (line B), so AFEC reduces again. This results in low latency, but also in a code set that is slightly too small for network conditions, so MER climbs rapidly. When the MER is observed outside the maximum, code set size is increased (line C); this stops the increase in MER, but does not reduce it below the maximum, so another code-set increase is made (line D), also increasing latency.

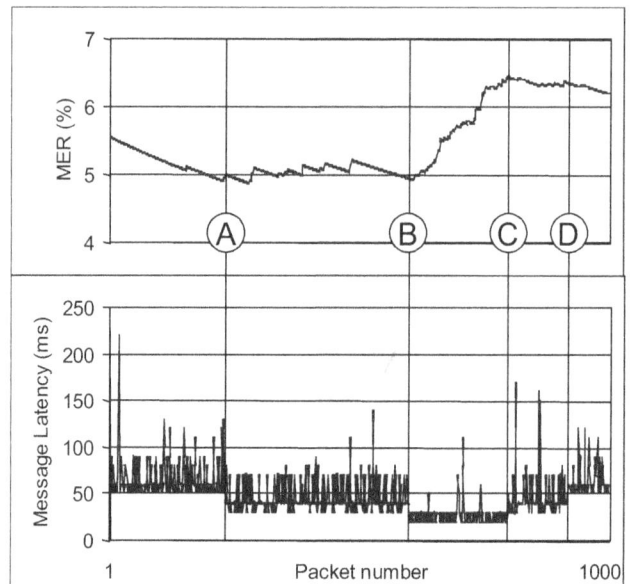

Figure 10: MER (upper) and per-message latency (lower) for 1000 AFEC packets, on a 56Kbps channel with 20% random loss. Vertical lines indicate points at which AFEC changed its code set size to stay within MER limits.

Note that the latency spikes in Figure 10 result from the latency of recovered messages, not from packet latency. Whenever messages are recovered, additional latency results from the time between the first send of the message and its eventual receipt as redundant information. Thus, message latency in AFEC is always slightly higher than packet latency.

Finally, our experiments showed certain conditions where the current AFEC technique must be paired with other techniques to be used successfully. We did not use adaptive rate control in our experiments, so certain situations involving high burst loss and low bandwidth resulted in high amounts of latency. This problem arose when AFEC attempted to increase its code set size past the bandwidth limits in order to meet MER requirements. However, when used with rate control, this problem can be avoided.

5. DISCUSSION

These experiments compared the effectiveness of TCP, UDP, FEC, and AFEC for sending real-time awareness data under a variety of network conditions. The following conclusions can be drawn from our results:

- TCP is not suitable for sending real-time interactive messages over lossy networks due to very high latency;
- FEC produces substantial reliability increases over UDP alone without adding much latency in most cases;
- Optimal code set size is impossible to determine beforehand in most cases because of unpredictable network conditions;
- AFEC can meet a predefined MER range while minimizing the amount of latency, given a fixed send rate;
- When it is not possible to meet the level of reliability without exceeding bandwidth requirements, the system must either decrease send rate, decrease MER requirements, or accept higher latency.

Our experiments reinforce earlier indications that TCP is not suitable for sending real-time interactive messages where guaranteed delivery is not required. The high amount of latency and jitter of TCP do not meet the requirements for real-time data under lossy conditions. These results help to confirm that TCP should not be used for sending real-time awareness information.

Non-adaptive FEC is simple to implement and provides large reliability benefits over plain UDP. In general, a small code set size (e.g., 2) can be used to improve reliability considerably without adding substantial latency. However, a small code set size may not always provide the desired level of reliability, so under certain conditions, larger code set sizes may be better choices. Several factors affect the amount of latency that is added, and the level of reliability attainable using FEC.

The amount of latency added by FEC depends on the available network bandwidth, message size, message frequency, number of users, and code set size. In situations where bandwidth is plentiful, large code set sizes add a trivial amount of latency. However, low available-bandwidth conditions can cause the problem described above, where code set size cannot be supported by the network. Therefore, when clients have large amounts of bandwidth, a larger code set size is a good choice, but when bandwidth is low, the code set size must be set at a level that does not exceed resources.

The level of reliability provided by FEC depends on the loss type, the loss rate, and the code set size. A larger code set size always results in the same or better reliability because it allows a longer sequence of lost messages to be recovered. Higher loss rates always result in the same or worse reliability because the frequency of losses is higher. Random losses where few packets in a row are lost result in high reliability from FEC, while longer bursts result in lower levels of reliability. Therefore, when long, frequent burst losses are occurring, a larger code set size is

desirable, but when only short bursts occur less frequently, a smaller code set size is sufficient.

The problem with non-adaptive FEC is that the application programmer must implement the code set at a fixed size, but an optimal choice depends on several unpredictable parameters: loss rate, loss pattern, and available bandwidth. If the programmer knew the network conditions beforehand, an optimal code set size could be selected. Since this is not possible, the application programmer is left with the problem of determining the optimal size. Therefore, the code set size must be selected conservatively and without certainty based on the cost-benefit analysis of reliability versus latency under unknown conditions.

AFEC improves on non-adaptive FEC by dynamically adapting its code set size to meet the MER requirements for each technique. This removes the uncertainty that results from choosing a fixed code set size for non-adaptive FEC. AFEC adjusts the code set size to the minimum that still maintains the desired MER range. In cases where non-adaptive FEC exceeds the required level of reliability, AFEC will always produce lower latency. When non-adaptive FEC does not meet the MER requirements, AFEC will automatically increase its code set size to meet the reliability requirements, as long as this does not exceed the path MTU.

The only remaining problem with AFEC is that it is sometimes not possible to meet the desired level of reliability at a certain message frequency. In these cases, either rate can be decreased or MER requirements can be lowered. The GW-AFEC module presented here does not include adaptive rate control, although this can be added in future work.

Overall, GW-AFEC is an effective technique for sending real-time interactive messages. AFEC should be considered as an addition to groupware toolkits, as it provides substantial benefits under a wide range of conditions, and because its complexity would be best abstracted away from application programmers.

6. FUTURE WORK

GW-AFEC is one of several application-level techniques that can help to improve groupware performance and usability on real-world networks. There are several future possibilities both for advances in this technique and in the general area of groupware networking. To develop better techniques for supporting real-time interaction in groupware, we need to gain a better understanding of the characteristics of groupware traffic and the QoS goals that we are trying to meet. This paper discusses a few basic characteristics of groupware traffic and important QoS characteristics. However, better knowledge of both network and QoS characteristics will facilitate development of more effective techniques that can be applied to groupware.

Once we have better knowledge of characteristics and QoS requirements, we can refine GW-AFEC and develop other techniques that take advantage of the specific characteristics and opportunities of real-time groupware. Some techniques have been considered in other work (e.g., compression [5] or latency compensation [28,29]); we are also planning to explore techniques such as adaptive concurrency policies, distributed load balancing, adaptive rate control, and receiver-driven layered multicast. The collection of networking techniques can eventually be brought together in a new real-time groupware toolkit.

7. CONCLUSION

Our experiments show that AFEC is an effective technique for sending real-time interactive messages because it can meet reliability requirements while minimizing latency under lossy conditions. AFEC works by adaptively adjusting the amount of redundancy in packets so that lost messages can be recovered without requiring retransmission. Groupware messages are generally small, which allows several redundant messages to be added to each packet. This allows AFEC to recover lost messages, even when burst losses occur.

AFEC for groupware is different from AFEC for multimedia due to several key differences between the application types. Since groupware sends many different message types with different reliability requirements, AFEC must include monitoring and tracking support for multiple message type. Irregular bursts of messages that occur in groupware can be handled by detecting breaks between bursts and sending redundant information at the end of the bursts. Groupware's small messages and payload types made it appropriate to send complete messages rather than compressed portions of historic messages.

An experiment comparing several protocols in realistic lossy network conditions shows that non-adaptive FEC improves on the reliability of UDP, but code set size must be chosen carefully. In dynamic network conditions, however, this choice is impossible to make correctly, whereas GW-AFEC is able to move towards the optimal value in most cases. Our experiments also reinforce that TCP is unsuitable for sending real-time interactive messages, especially under lossy conditions. Our results show that GW-AFEC is a useful strategy for sending interactive real-time groupware messages, and that reducing delay while providing needed reliability can substantially improve groupware usability.

8. REFERENCES

1. Bolot, J-C End-to-end packet delay and loss behavior in the Internet, *ACM SIGCOMM Computer Communication Review*, 23, 4, 1993, 289–298.

2. Bolot, J-C, Fosse-Parisis, S., Towsley, D. Adaptive FEC-Based error control for Internet Telephony, *Proc. Infocom 1999*, 1453 - 1460.

3. Chebrolu, K., Raman, B., and Sen, S., Long-distance 802.11b links: performance measurements and experience. *Proc. ACM MobiCom 2006*, 74-85.

4. Claypool, M., and Claypool, K., Latency and player actions in online games. *Comm. ACM*, 49, 11, 2006, 40-45

5. Dyck, J., and Gutwin, C., and Makaroff, D., *Using Behaviour Characteristics to Improve Groupware Performance*, Technical Report HCI-03-01, Univ. of Saskatchewan, 2003.

6. Dyck, J., Gutwin, C., Subramanian, S., and Fedak, C. High-Performance Telepointers. *Proc. CSCW 2004*, 172-181.

7. Dyck, J., Gutwin, C., Graham, N., and Pinelle, D., Beyond the LAN: Techniques for Improving Groupware Performance from Networked Games, *Proc. Group 2007*, 291-300.

8. Frécon, E., Greenhalgh, C., Stenius, M., The DiveBone - an application-level network architecture for Internet-based CVEs. *Proc. ACM VRST 1999*, 58-65.

9. Gracanin, D., Zhou, Y., and DaSilva, L. Quality of Service for Networked Virtual Environments. *IEEE Communications Magazine*, April 2004, 42-48.

10. Greenhalgh, C., Benford, S., Craven, M. Patterns of network and user activity in an inhabited television event. *Proc. ACM VRST 1999*, 35-50.

11. Gutwin, C. Effects of Network Delay on Group Work in Shared Workspaces. *Proc. ECSCW 2001*, 299-318.

12. Gutwin, C. Traces: Visualizing the Immediate Past to Support Group Interaction. *Proc. GI 2002*, 43-50.

13. IETF Network Working Group, RFC 1151, *Version 2 of the Reliable Data Protocol*, 1990, tools.ietf.org/html/rfc1151.

14. ISO/IEC. *Quality of Service: Framework*. ISO/IEC 13236, 1998. www.iso.org.

15. Lidgren UDP Library. code.google.com/p/lidgren-network-gen3/, 2011.

16. Liang, Y., Steinbach, E., Girod, B. Real-time voice communication over the internet using packet path diversity. *Proc. ACM Multimedia 2001*, 431-440.

17. Marsic, I. Real-Time Collaboration in Heterogeneous Computing Environments. *Proc. ITCC 2000*, 222-227.

18. Mathur, A., Prakash, A. *A Protocol Composition-Based Approach to QoS Control in Collaboration Systems*. Technical Report CSE-TR-27495, U. of Michigan, 1995.

19. Nafaa, A., Taleb, T., and Murphy, L., Forward Error Correction Strategies for Media Streaming over Wireless Networks, *IEEE Communications*, Dec. 2007, 72-79.

20. Sheth, A., Nedevschi, S., Patra, R., Surana, S., Subramanian, L., & Brewer, E., Packet loss characterization in Wifi-based Long Distance Networks. *IEEE INFOCOM 2007*, 312-320.

21. Shunra Software Ltd. *The Cloud WAN Emulator*, 2000.

22. Smed, J., Kaukoranta, K., and Hakonen, H. *A Review on Networking and Multiplayer Computer Games*. Technical Report 454, Turku Centre for Computer Science, 2002.

23. Peterson, L., and Davie, B., *Computer Networks*, 5th ed., Amsterdam: Morgan Kaufmann, 2011.

24. Perkins, C., Crowcroft, J., Notes on the use of RTP for shared workspace applications, *ACM SIGCOMM Computer Communication Review*, 30, 2, 35-40.

25. Perkins, C., Hodson, O., Hardman, V., A survey of packet loss recovery techniques for streaming audio, *IEEE Network*, September 1998, 40-48.

26. Quax, P., Monsieurs, P., Lamotte, W., De Vleeschauwer, D., and Degrande, N. Objective and subjective evaluation of the influence of small amounts of delay and jitter on a recent first person shooter game. *Proc. NetGames 2004*, 152-156.

27. Salyers, D., Striegel, A., and Poellabauer, C., Wireless reliability: Rethinking 802.11 packet loss, *Proc. IEEE WoWMoM 2008*, 1 – 4.

28. Savery, C, Graham, N., and Gutwin, C., The human factors of consistency maintenance in multiplayer computer games, *Proc. Group 2010*, 187-196.

29. Stuckel, D., and Gutwin, C., The effects of local lag on tightly-coupled interaction in distributed groupware, *Proc. CSCW 2008*, 447-456.

30. Vaghi, I., Greenhalgh, C., Benford, S. Coping with inconsistency due to network delays in collaborative virtual environments. *Proc. VRST 1999*, 42-49.

Authenticating Operation-based History in Collaborative Systems

Hien Thi Thu Truong
INRIA Nancy-Grand Est
615 rue du Jardin Botanique
54600 Villers-lès-Nancy,
France
hien.truong@inria.fr

Claudia-Lavinia Ignat
INRIA Nancy-Grand Est
615 rue du Jardin Botanique
54600 Villers-lès-Nancy,
France
claudia.ignat@inria.fr

Pascal Molli
University of Nantes
2 rue de la Houssinière,
BP 92208
44322 Nantes cedex 3, France
pascal.molli@acm.org

ABSTRACT

Within last years multi-synchronous collaborative editing systems became widely used. Multi-synchronous collaboration maintains multiple, simultaneous streams of activity which continually diverge and synchronized. These streams of activity are represented by means of logs of operations, i.e. user modifications. A malicious user might tamper his log of operations. At the moment of synchronization with other streams, the tampered log might generate wrong results. In this paper, we propose a solution relying on hash-chain based authenticators for authenticating logs that ensure the authenticity, the integrity of logs, and the user accountability. We present algorithms to construct authenticators and verify logs. We prove their correctness and provide theoretical and practical evaluations.

Categories and Subject Descriptors

K.6.5 [**Security and Protection**]: [Authentication]; H.5.3 [**Group and Organization Interfaces**]: [Computer-supported cooperative work]; C.2.4 [**Distributed Systems**]: [Distributed applications]

General Terms

Security

Keywords

authenticating logs, multi-synchronous collaboration, authenticators, optimistic replication, logs, operation-based history

1. INTRODUCTION

Collaboration is a key requirement of teams of individuals working together towards some common goal. In recent years collaborative editing systems such as wikis, GoogleDocs and version control systems became very popular. These systems rely on a multi-synchronous collaboration model [8, 15] that allows users to work simultaneously on shared documents following some cycles of divergence and convergence. Copies of the shared data diverge when users work in isolation and converge later when users synchronize their changes.

The mechanism, that allows replicas to diverge during a time interval ensuring that they will eventually converge at a later time, is called optimistic replication [37]. Optimistic replication can be classified into state-based and operation-based [20]. In state-based replication each site applies updates to its replica without maintaining a change log. Usually in systems adopting state-based replication such as Active Directory in Windows Server and Coda file system [38], every site sends its local state to other sites that can merge the received state with their own states. Systems that use operation-based replication such as Bayou [34], IceCube [18] and GoogleDocs keep modifications performed on a replica in a history which is then sent to other replicas. Operation-based approaches are used when the cost to transfer state is high such as in database systems or mobile systems; and when operation-semantics is important. In this work we target systems that use operation-based replication.

In operation-based replication systems users can misbehave by tampering history for their convenience. For instance, they can remove some content of the history or change the order of some operations from the history. This might be critical for some collaborative systems such as version control systems. It is vitally important to be able to retrieve and run different versions of a software. If the history can be modified, revisions do not correspond to the expected behavior of the software. Moreover, developers cannot be made responsible for the revisions for which they contributed. Furthermore, by modifying the history, a contributor may introduce security holes in the system under the name of another contributor. Therefore, there is a need to ensure integrity of the log, and in case the log was tampered, the misbehaving user should be detected.

Solutions for securing logs can be classified into two main families: non-cryptographic secure logging and cryptographic secure logging. The former approach is based on a secure logging machine such as a write-only medium (e.g CD/DVD), a tamper-resistant-hardware or a trusted hardware to prevent adversary from modifying logs [3]. However, in real-world applications deployed over large scale distributed environments, it is impractical to assume the presence of such devices. The later approach has been investigated deeply with numerously extensive research (namely, [10, 11, 4, 5, 13, 14, 25, 27, 39, 43]). These existing solutions, however, are adapted only for collaboration based on a single global stream of activity over shared data. For instance, floor control policies [10] and locking mechanisms [11] ensure a single global stream of activity by allowing a single user at a time to access objects in the shared workspace.

Multi-synchronous collaboration abandons constructing a single stream of activity out of the history of all user activities. Instead, it maintains multiple, simultaneous streams of activity, and then manages divergence between these streams. Each user maintains therefore different streams of the global history containing activity of all users. Throughout this paper we call logs standing for these different streams of activity. The main challenge that we address in this paper is how to secure logs in the multi-synchronous collaboration. To our best knowledge, no existing work addressed this issue.

In this paper, we propose a solution relying on hash-chain based authenticators for securing logs in multi-synchronous collaboration. The proposed authenticators ensure the authenticity and the integrity of the logs, i.e. any log tampering is detectable. Moreover, the proposed authenticators provide user accountability, i.e. any user can be made accountable of her misbehavior on log tampering.

The paper is structured as follows. We start with a context for our work in Section 2. We then go on by presenting in Section 3 a threat model and desirable properties our proposal tackles. We next describe in Section 4 our proposed approach based on authenticators including their definitions and examples of how they are constructed. In Section 5, we present our algorithms to construct authenticators and verify logs, and proofs of their correctness. We provide an evaluation with real collaboration histories from projects using Mercurial and an analysis showing the feasibility of our proposal in Section 6. We give an overview of related works in Section 7. In Section 8, we end the paper with some concluding remarks.

2. CONTEXT

Push-Pull-Clone (PPC) is the most general paradigm supporting multi-synchronous collaboration. Users work simultaneously on different streams of activity on the shared data. In the PPC model, users replicate shared data, modify it and redistribute modified versions of this data by using the primitives push, pull and clone. These primitives are used for managing divergence and convergence of different streams of activity. To start, users clone shared data and maintain in a local workspace this data as well as modifications done on this data. Users can then push their changes to different channels at any time they want, and other users that have granted rights may pull these changes from these channels. By using pull primitives, replicas are synchronized. In Figure 1, an instantiation of the PPC model with three users is illustrated. In this figure, *user 1* and *user 2* interact with each other by using push and pull primitives, while *user 3* performs a clone from *user 2*. The PPC collaboration model is very widely used in distributed version control systems such as Git, Mercurial and Darcs. It is a very general collaboration model without a collaboration provider where users share their data only with people whom they trust. PPC model generalizes the collaboration model with a service provider where users interact only with a server that forwards afterward the changes to the other users.

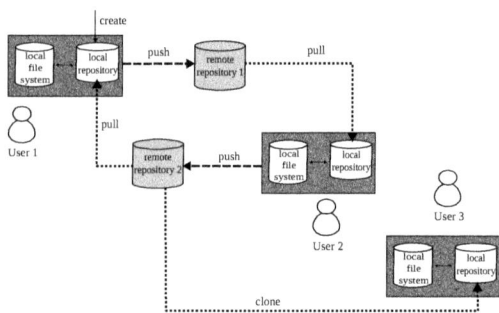

Figure 1: Push-Pull-Clone paradigm

We consider the operation-based collaboration where user changes are kept in a log that is then sent to the other users and logs are merged at synchronizations. We consider a system with a number of sites which can operate independently on replicas of shared documents. Each site keeps the shared document as a log of operations that have been performed during a collaborative process, $L = [op_1, op_2, ..., op_n]$. Each operation is parameterized depending on an application domain. A shared document can be as large as a database (i.e. Bayou) or as small as a single file. Operations can be treated at different granularities ranging from characters, lines or paragraphs in a document to deltas between revisions. A document is created at one site and replicated to other sites by means of push and clone primitives. Sites store operations in their logs in an order that is consistent with the order they were generated.

The order of addition of operations in the log is compatible with the "happened-before" relation between operations [19]. We say that op_a *happened-before* op_b, denoted as $op_a \rightarrow op_b$, if op_b was generated on some site after op_a was either generated or received by that site. The "happened-before" relation is transitive, irreflexive and antisymmetric. Two operations op_a and op_b are said concurrent if neither $op_a \rightarrow op_b$ nor $op_b \rightarrow op_a$.

Changes on the shared document made by users are propagated in weakly consistent manner from one site to another site. Users decide by means of primitives push and pull when, with whom and what data to be sent and synchronized. When a pull is performed by *user 1* from the channel where *user 2* pushed his changes, in order to minimize traffic overhead, an anti-entropy mechanism is used [6]. Only the part of the log of *user 2*, that is new to *user 1* since the last time that two users synchronized, is sent to *user 1*. The remote log from *user 2* is synchronized with the local log of *user 1*. The synchronization mechanism requires to detect the concurrency and happened-before order between changes of different sites. Also the conflicts between concurrent changes must be resolved. Replicas are consistent if their states are identical when they have applied the same set of operations. For our approach, we use the CRDT family of algorithms [36, 42] which design operations to be commutative from the start. When reconciliation is performed, operations from the remote log, that have not been previously integrated into the local log, are simply appended to the end of the local log. The log propagation mechanism uses anti-entropy which preserves happened-before order between operations. Therefore, the reconciliation mechanism ensures happened-before order between operations as well as it allows concurrent operations to appear in logs in variant orders.

We define a *partially ordered set* (poset) $H = (P, \rightarrow)$ where P is a ground set of operations and "$\rightarrow$" is the happened-before relation between two operations of P, in which "$\rightarrow$" is irreflexive and transitive. We call H as an operation-based history in our context. Given a partial order "$\rightarrow$" over a poset H, we can extend it to a total order "$<_t$" with which "$<_t$" is a linear order and for every x and y in H, if $x \rightarrow y$ then $x <_t y$. A linear extension L of H is a relation $(P, <_t)$ such that: (1) for all op_1, op_2 in P, either $op_1 <_t op_2$ or $op_2 <_t op_1$; and (2) if $op_1 \rightarrow op_2$ then $op_1 <_t op_2$. This total order preserves the order of operations from a partial order set H to the linear extensions on the same ground set P.

We call these linear extensions as individual logs observed by different sites. The Figure 2 shows an example of a history and its linear extensions.

In collaborative systems, where multiple sites collaborate on the same shared data object, we can consider that the global stream of activity of all sites is defined by a partially ordered set of operations. Each site, however, can see only operations in his workspace that it generated locally or received from other sites. The site keeps therefore an individual log as a linearization of history built on a subset of a ground set of operations. There are remaining operations

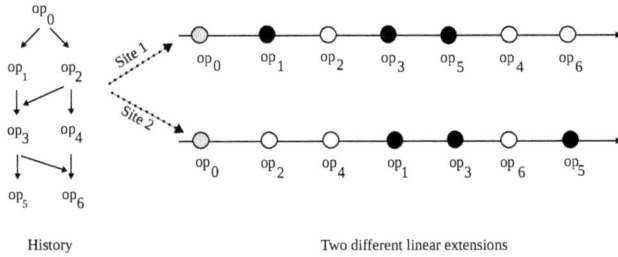

Figure 2: History and its linear extensions

of global history built on entire ground set of operations that are not visible for the site.

3. SECURITY ASPECTS

In operation-based collaborative systems, authentication of data items for collaborative workflows has gained increasing importance. Say for example, if Tom receives a document from Olivia and processes a part of it and then forwards to Pierre, the operation-based document should include the chronological log of actions that each user, Tom, Olivia and Pierre, performed on the document. The correctness of collaboration outcome is based on the trustworthiness of users who maintain the history of versions. Unfortunately, a malicious user can always introduce phony updates to forge history or alter the correct order of versions. This attack raises the threat that honest users might get forged content of shared data. Replicas with corrupted updates might never converge with other valid replicas and this is critical in replication systems. This section presents a threat model followed by desirable properties for dealing with security requirements.

3.1 Threat Model

A threat model, which models the capabilities of attackers, is necessary to analyze the threats that will be addressed by our solution.

There are two types of malicious users: insiders and outsiders. We consider in this paper an inside adversary who has full rights to access a replicated object. Such an adversary might want to alter the history including actions performed on data by authorized contributors. For example, when Tom provides a document to Olivia who can perform and contribute new updates to the document, she should not be able to modify actions that Tom performed which were recorded in log.

We assume users trust each other with their social-based relationship when they start to collaborate. However, trust it not immutable and trusted users once they gained access to the log can always misbehave. Such an active attacker can read, (over)write, delete and change order of log entries. In doing so, an attacker alters existing records or adds forged information to history.

Our work assumes only adversaries who act inside of the system. We cannot prevent outsider attacks where an adversary copies data to create a new document and claims at a later time as being an owner. This might be possible in our system if an adversary removes completely the log of operations, which corresponds to a document removal. We could deal with outsider attacks with the support of a trusted platform, however, we exclude this assumption in our collaborative system.

3.2 Desirable Properties

The following properties are addressed to authenticate operation-based history in collaborative systems.

Integrity. Adversaries are infeasible to forge a log, such as modify its entries or put new forged operations into log, without being detected. Integrity is the most important property required for securing logs in operation-based replication. Ensuring the integrity of a single document can be done easily by using cryptographic signatures or checksums. However, ensuring the integrity of a replicated document represented by a log of operations is more difficult as operations cross multi-contributors and some of them might be adversaries.

Concurrency-collision-freeness. In a history H, some operations might be concurrent, while some others might be in a happened-before relation. If L_i and L_j are different linearizations of the same history H then any authentication mechanism applied to L_i and L_j should yield the same result. The "yielding the same result" is expressed by the concurrency-collision-freeness property: the authentication mechanism holds a function f that $f(L_i) = f(L_j) \ \forall L_i, L_j \in H$. The "concurrency-collision-freeness" property should be guaranteed in authenticating logs.

In Figure 2, we give an example of a history which is linearized into two logs by two sites. The history H, which is built on the ground set of operations $P = \{op_0, op_1, op_2, op_3, op_4, op_5, op_6\}$ with "$\rightarrow$" relation, is recorded in logs, $L_1 = \{op_0, op_1, op_2, op_3, op_5, op_4, op_6\}$ and $L_2 = \{op_0, op_2, op_4, op_1, op_3, op_6, op_5\}$. They both preserve orders of all operations of the history H. In order to fulfill concurrency-collision-free property, any authentication mechanism applied to L_1 and L_2 should yield the same result. If the authentication results are different, then it means that one of the logs was tampered.

Forward-aggregated authenticity. While logs grow, log verifiers can skip verification of log entries which have been already authenticated. The authentication mechanism should allow accumulation of log verification for a time interval. Not only the integrity of individual log entries but also the integrity of the whole log stream should be preserved. This forward-aggregated authenticity property is similar to forward security and append-only property investigated in many existing works of secure log audit [1, 24, 43].

Public verifiability. This property allows any user in a collaborative system to verify the integrity of logs. Adversaries are made accountable for unauthorized actions. This property can be done by using digital signatures such as RSA or DSA signature scheme. Public verifiability is especially desirable in distributed collaborative systems where logs need to be audited by any collaborator without relying on any trusted central authority.

4. AUTHENTICATORS

In this section, we present our approach to construct authenticators $T_{@site}$ to deter users from log tampering while preserving the above mentioned properties.

When a sending site sends a document to a receiving site, it creates an authenticator for its log. The authenticator is attached to the sent document. The receiving site creates a new authenticator when it receives the document. We assume each site involved in this push-pull communication possesses a cryptographic public/private key pair that is assigned to a unique site identifier and that all users can retrieve the public key of each other. This assumption is reasonable in practice [41, 29]. The private key of the key pair is used to sign entries of log that prevent malicious sites modifying operations on behalf of other sites. Though sites can choose a public key pair on their-own, to limit Sybil attacks [7] we can require that each site possesses a digital certificate from trusted certification authority or has an offline channel (such as email) to identify the owner of public keys. In either case the certification authority plays no role in the process of authenticator creation, and it is used only during initial phase when a site joins the system. We also use cryptographic hash function with properties collision-resistant (it should be difficult to find two different messages m_1 and m_2 such that hash(m_1) = hash(m_2)) and preimage-resistant (with a given hash value h, it should be difficult to find any message m such that hash(m) = h). The collision-resistant property can be used to establish the uniqueness of logs at a certain moment when an authenticator is created.

4.1 Definitions

An authenticator is a log tamper-evident which captures a subsequence of operation(s) of a log that were generated in one updating session. An updating session at one user's site is the session between two subsequent push/pull primitives to/from other sites. For example, consider that during a working session, user U generates a log $[op_1, op_2]$ where $op_1 \rightarrow op_2$. When user U pushes his changes, he creates an authenticator for the sequence of operations in the log that their orders should not be tampered by any other user. For instance, a receiver of this log should not be able to re-order op_1 and op_2 to change the happened-before order of op_1 and op_2.

Definition 1. *An authenticator, denoted as* $T_{@site}$, *is defined as a tuple* $\langle$ID, SIG, IDE, PRE, SYN$\rangle$ *where:*

ID: *identifier of authenticator which is a tuple* < siteID, opID > *where* siteID *is the identifier of the site which creates the authenticator and* opID *is the operation identifier(s) that the authenticator is linked to;*

SIG: *the value of signature signed by the private key of the site;*

IDE: *a list of operation identifiers used to compute SIG;*

PRE, SYN: *identifiers of preceding and receiving authenticators.*

Definition 2. *The SIG of an authenticator* $T_{@site}$ *at a certain update is computed as a signature of a cumulative hash by a sender S or a receiver R, where the sender computes SIG of the most recent authenticator* $T_{m@S}$.SIG = σ_S(hash($T_{m-1@S}$.SIG $\|$ E)) *with condition that* E $\neq \varnothing$; *and the receiver computes* $T_{n@R}$ = σ_R(hash ($T_{n-1@R}$.SIG $\|$ E $\|$ $T_{m@S}$.SIG) *with the condition that there exists new update(s) from S appended to log of R, where:*

$T_{m@S}$: *the most recent authenticator committed by sender S;*

$T_{n@R}$: *the most recent authenticator committed by receiver R;*

$T_{m-1@S}$: *the preceding authenticator of* $T_{m@S}$;

$T_{n-1@R}$: *the preceding authenticator of* $T_{n@R}$;

E = $[op_{i_1}, op_{i_2}, ..., op_{i_r}]$: *subsequent changes generated after preceding authenticator;*

$\sigma_{site}(\cdot)$ *denotes the signature of* site *and* $\|$ *denotes the concatenation of arguments used in hashing, where hashing can be done using any traditional hash function such as SHA-256).*

The structure of an authenticator is illustrated in Figure 3.

When a user shares a document by sending the whole log, she creates an authenticator for log operations computed based on the preceding authenticator and new updated operations. The authenticator is signed by her private key and linked to the last operation of the log. At the receiving site, the receiver performs reconciliation and creates a new authenticator at the reception.

The authenticators of a log of operations are constructed whenever a site sends or receives a new change to/from another site. An authenticator is created in following cases:

- A site sends new changes to other sites. In this case, if a site sends a document without new changes, no new authenticator is needed.

- A site receives new changes from other sites. In this case, the receiving site will check the remote log, detect and resolve

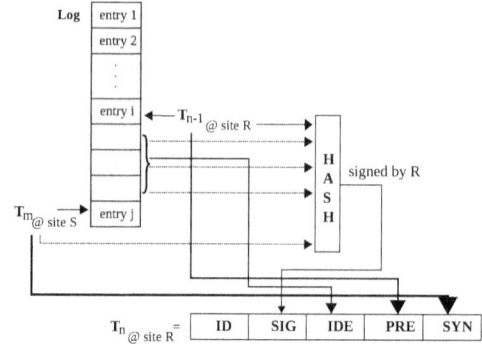

Figure 3: Structure of an authenticator.

conflicts (if there are some conflicts among operations). After these actions, if there are new changes that are added to the receiver's log, a new authenticator is created for this reception.

4.2 Example

We use the example of history in Figure 2 where two sites collaborate on a shared document having initial version $V_0|\{op_0\}$ to illustrate the construction of authenticators. We assume that the initial version of the document V_0 consisting of operation op_0 was created by some site among collaborating sites. We further assume that all collaborators agreed on this initial version and that the corresponding log of this initial version does not need to be authenticated. Each of the two sites in our example performs parallel contributions based on the initial version of the document. In the example, *site 1* creates the new version $V_1|\{op_0, op_1\}$ and *site 2* creates $V_2|\{op_0, op_2\}$ concurrently. At a later time, *site 1* reconciles with updates from *site 2* and creates the up-to-date version $V_3 \mid \{op_0, op_1, op_2, op_3\}$. In Figure 4, the two sites, *site 1* and *site 2*, will create authenticators to authenticate their logs each time they do pushing or pulling. In what follows we describe in detail how authenticators are constructed.

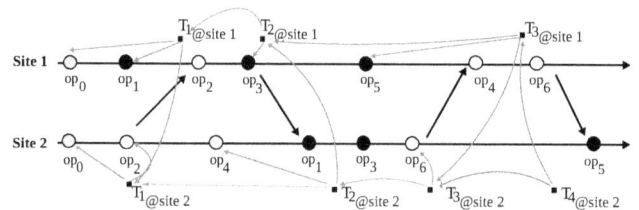

Figure 4: Example of constructing authenticators.

Firstly, when *site 2* pushes his log to *site 1*, it creates an authenticator $T_{1@site2}$ where:

$T_{1@site2}$.ID = < site2, op_2 > (linked to op_2),

$T_{1@site2}$.SIG = σ_{site2}(hash($\varnothing \| op_0 \| op_2$))

$T_{1@site2}$.IDE = $[op_0, op_2]$

$T_{1@site2}$.PRE = $\varnothing$ (no previous authenticator)

$T_{1@site2}$.SYN = $\varnothing$ (no received remote authenticator)

When *site 1* pulls changes from *site 2* and receives the log from *site 2*, it creates an authenticator $T_{1@site1}$ where:

$T_{1@site1}$.ID = < site1, $\{op_1, op_2\}$ > (linked to op_1, op_2),

$T_{1@site1}$.SIG = σ_{site1}(hash($\varnothing \| op_0 \| op_1 \| T_{1@site2}$.SIG)),

$T_{1@site1}$.IDE = $[op_0, op_1]$,

$T_{1@site1}$.PRE = $\varnothing$ (no previous authenticator),

$T_{1@site1}$.SYN = $T_{1@site2}$.ID

The two sites *site 1* and *site 2* then work concurrently and generate

134

the new changes op_3 and op_4 respectively. When *site 1* pushes his changes and *site 2* pulls those changes, two authenticators $T_{2@site1}$ and $T_{2@site2}$ are constructed. The structure of $T_{2@site1}$ is given below:

$T_{2@site1}.ID = <site1, op_3>$ (linked to op_3),

$T_{2@site1}.SIG = \sigma_{site1}(hash(T_{1@site1}.SIG \| op_3))$,

$T_{2@site1}.IDE = [op_3]$,

$T_{2@site1}.PRE = T_{1@site1}.ID$,

$T_{2@site1}.SYN = \varnothing$

Similarly, $T_{2@site2}$ is computed where:

$T_{2@site2}.ID = <site2, \{op_3, op_4\}>$ (linked to op_3, op_4),

$T_{2@site2}.SIG = \sigma_{site2}(hash(T_{1@site2}.SIG \| op_4 \| T_{2@site1}.SIG))$,

$T_{2@site2}.IDE = [op_4]$,

$T_{2@site2}.PRE = T_{1@site2}.ID$,

$T_{2@site2}.SYN = T_{2@site1}.ID$

Again, *site 1* and *site 2* contribute independently to the document, op_5 is generated by *site 1* and op_6 is generated by *site 2*. The two sites then exchange their changes with each other by pushing and pulling other changes. New authenticators are computed at each site. *site 2* computes $T_{3@site2}$ where:

$T_{3@site2}.ID = <site2, op_6>$ (linked to op_6),

$T_{3@site2}.SIG = \sigma_{site2}(hash(T_{2@site2}.SIG \| op_6))$,

$T_{3@site2}.IDE = [op_6]$,

$T_{3@site2}.PRE = T_{2@site2}.ID$,

$T_{3@site2}.SYN = \varnothing$

site 1 computes $T_{3@site1}$ where:

$T_{3@site1}.ID = <site1, \{op_5, op_6\}>$ (linked to op_5, op_6),

$T_{3@site1}.SIG = \sigma_{site1}(hash(T_{2@site1}.SIG \| op_5 \| T_{3@site2}.SIG))$,

$T_{3@site1}.IDE = [op_5]$,

$T_{3@site1}.PRE = T_{2@site1}.ID$,

$T_{3@site1}.SYN = T_{3@site2}.ID$

In the last step shown in Figure 4, *site 1* pushes his changes to *site 2* and *site 2* pulls these changes from *site 1*. Because there are no new operations since the authenticator $T_{3@site1}$ was created, no new authenticator is created by *site 1*. However, the receiving site *site 2* has to create a new authenticator since a new operation op_5 is added to the log. $T_{4@site2}$ is therefore computed where:

$T_{4@site2}.ID = <site2, \{op_5, op_6\}>$ (linked to op_5, op_6),

$T_{4@site2}.SIG = \sigma_{site2}(hash(T_{3@site2}.SIG \| \varnothing \| T_{3@site1}.SIG))$,

$T_{4@site2}.IDE = []$,

$T_{4@site2}.PRE = T_{3@site2}.ID$,

$T_{4@site2}.SYN = T_{3@site1}.ID$

We will discuss in next section the algorithms supporting the creation and verification of authenticators as well as prove that the proposed algorithms satisfy desired properties which we mentioned at the beginning of this paper.

5. ALGORITHMS

In this section we present algorithms to construct authenticators and verify logs based on authenticators. We also provide a proof of correctness of these algorithms.

5.1 Authenticators Construction

Algorithm 1 presents the algorithm for the construction of the authenticator when a sender pushes his changes. An authenticator is computed from the its preceding authenticator and the current generated operations. The algorithm takes as argument the log of the sending site S and generates as output the authenticator computed by the sender site. The condition $E \neq \varnothing$ ensures that an authenticator is created only if the sender has generated new changes; otherwise the sender sends the log without computing a new authenticator.

Algorithm 2 presents the algorithm for the construction of the authenticator when a receiver site pulls changes from a sender site. An authenticator is computed from the preceding authenticator of local log, the current operations generated by the receiver and the most recent authenticator of the remote log. The algorithm takes as arguments the two logs of sending site S and receiving site R and it generates as output the authenticator computed by the receiver site. If there are no new operations sent by the sender that have to be added to the log of the receiver, then the receiver will not compute a new authenticator. Note that in synchronizing logs, authenticators that are linked to operations must be also kept in the local workspace as they authenticate previous operations in the log.

Input: sending site S with its log L_S

Output: $T_{m@S}$

1 **begin**
2     $E \leftarrow$ list of new operations S generates after $T_{m-1@S}$;
3   **if** $E \neq \varnothing$ **then**
4        $T_{m@S}.ID \leftarrow$ <S, identifier of most recently local operation at S>;
5        $T_{m@S}.SIG \leftarrow sign(T_{m-1@S}.SIG \| E)$;
6        $T_{m@S}.IDE \leftarrow E$;
7        $T_{m@S}.PRE \leftarrow T_{m-1@S}.ID$;
8        $T_{m@S}.SYN \leftarrow \varnothing$;
9   **else**
10        $T_{m@S} \leftarrow \langle\rangle$;
11   **return** $T_{m@S}$;

Algorithm 1: Construct an authenticator for a sender

Input: sending site S, receiving site R and their logs L_S, L_R

Output: $T_{n@R}$

1 **begin**
2     $E \leftarrow$ list of new operations R generates after $T_{n-1@R}$;
3     $E_S \leftarrow$ list of new operations from L_S added to L_R;
4   **if** $E_S \neq \varnothing$ **then**
5        $T_{n@R}.ID \leftarrow$ <R, $T_{m@S}.ID.opID \cup$ identifier of most recently local operation at R>;
6        $T_{n@R}.SIG \leftarrow sign(T_{n-1@R}.SIG \| E \| T_{m@S}.SIG)$;
7        $T_{n@R}.IDE \leftarrow E$;
8        $T_{n@R}.PRE \leftarrow T_{n-1@R}.ID$;
9        $T_{n@R}.SYN \leftarrow T_{m@S}.ID$;
10   **else**
11        $T_{n@R} \leftarrow \langle\rangle$;
12   **return** $T_{n@R}$;

Algorithm 2: Construct an authenticator for a receiver

We will consider *time* and *space* complexities of algorithms to construct and verify authenticators. Note that, for the space complexity for verification of authenticators, we exclude the space complexity for maintaining the log. The algorithm to create an authenticator in Algorithms 1 or 2 is $O(1)$ in time, and $O(|\Delta|)$ in storage, where Δ is the set of operations whose identifiers are kept in $T_{@site}.IDE$. Since an authenticator is created each time a site sends or receives changes, the number of authenticators on a replicated object created by site S is the total number of interactions the site has done with other sites. Let Γ be the total number interactions of one site. Then each site needs $O(\Gamma \cdot |\Delta|_{max})$ space for all authenticators, where $|\Delta|_{max}$ is the maximum Δ of all authenticators. In synchronization, one log is updated to become the union of two logs of sites S and R, and the new log shall need $O(\Gamma_S \cdot |\Delta_S|_{max} + \Gamma_R \cdot |\Delta_R|_{max})$ space for all authenticators. We can see that the storage complexity depends on the number of interactions and the number of operations generated by two sites.

5.2 Authenticators-based Log Verification

The Algorithm 3 presents a mechanism to verify log entries based on authenticators. When a site receives a log of operations accompanied by authenticators, it verifies the log based on these authenticators corresponding to entries in the log. The main idea of verification is to check the authenticity of operations preserved by valid authenticators, including checking:

- If authenticators are valid (their signatures are correct). An authenticator is checked by verifying its digital signature using the public key of signer.

- If the log entries are corresponding to these valid authenticators. When an authenticator passes signature checking, the content and the order of operations are taken into account in the verification.

If all of these checkings pass, the log is authenticated. In contrast, a log with either operations not authenticated or authenticated by invalid authenticators is unauthorized. With any detection of the corrupted data or falsified order of changes, authenticators will be not valid and the verification algorithm returns negative result. Authenticators help users being aware of attacks and once the log is unauthorized, the site which sent tampered log is made accountable for the misbehavior.

Input: site R, log L
Output:
1 **begin**
2    $Q \leftarrow T_{n@R} \in L$;
   // Q: queue of authenticators to verify
3   verified $\leftarrow$ True;
4   **while** $Q \neq \varnothing$ **do**
5       $T \leftarrow Q.get()$;
6   check1 $\leftarrow$ T.SIG is correct;
7   check2 $\leftarrow$ order of operations in L corresponds to T.IDE list;
8   check3 $\leftarrow$ T.PRE precedes operations in T.IDE;
9   check4 $\leftarrow$ T.PRE and T.SYN precede T.ID;
10   **if** check1 & check2 & check3 & check4 **then**
11   mark operations in T.IDE as *checked*;
12   put(Q, T.PRE);
13   put(Q, T.SYN);
14   **else**
15   verified $\leftarrow$ False;
16   break;
17   **if** any operation in L is not checked **then**
18   verified $\leftarrow$ False;
19   **return** verified;

Algorithm 3: Verify a log

Let us revisit the example in the previous section (see Figure.4). Let us assume one of two sites *site 1* or *site 2*, for instance, *site 2* shares the document by sending its log to another site, say *site 3*. Then *site 3* will verify the log it receives from *site 2*. To verify log, *site 3* has to verify the validity of authenticators and log entries. If it already received one part of log before, *site 3* can skip checking every authenticator linked to that part. We now describe the worst case when *site 3* receives the log from *site 2* for the first time and therefore every authenticator needs to be checked. *site 3* performs the following steps of the log verification procedure.

It starts by checking the most recent authenticator of *site 2* $T_{4@site2}$.

- Verify $T_{4@site2}$.SIG by using *site 2*'s public key.

- Verify $T_{4@site2}$.IDE. As $T_{4@site2}$.IDE = [] then check2 and check3 can be skipped.

- Verify the order of $T_{4@site2}$.ID (linked to op_5, op_6) and $T_{4@site2}$.PRE = $T_{3@site2}$.ID (linked to op_6) by checking if the log is maintained correctly (if op_6 is logged before op_5). Similarly, the order of $T_{4@site2}$.ID and $T_{4@site2}$.SYN = $T_{3@site1}$.ID (linked to operations op_5 and op_6) is checked.

- Since $T_{4@site2}$ was constructed based on $T_{3@site2}$ and $T_{3@site1}$, these authenticators are put into a queue Q in order to be recursively verified.

If every above check passes then the authenticator $T_{4@site2}$ is said valid. For other authenticators in queue Q, the verification is performed recursively and each verification follows steps in Algorithm 3. The verification finishes when queue Q is empty. The final checking result is only positive if all checks return positive result. Otherwise, the log will be not authenticated. Note that in this example, any deletion or re-ordering of operations is detectable. For instance, if *site 2* tries to re-order operations op_2 and op_3, this attack will be detected by authenticating the authenticator $T_{2@site1}$ which is linked to op_3. We can see *site 2* cannot forge this order on behalf of *site 1* since *site 1* signed the authenticator linked to op_3. However, any re-ordering of concurrent operations will not change the verification result. The proof will be presented later.

Authenticators-based log verification has O(1) complexity in space and O(Γ) in time, where Γ is the total number of authenticators in the log. Since authenticators of a log are linked as a hash-chain in which an authenticator is linked to its preceding one, and due to the *forward-aggregated authenticity* property, it is enough to authenticate the log by checking only the most recent authenticator of a log. This verification process requires checking of all preceding authenticators. Therefore, the time complexity depends on the total number of all authenticators.

5.3 Proofs of Correctness

The algorithms, that have been presented previously for authenticators construction and logs verification, ensure the desirable properties for authenticating logs which are linearized from operation-based history.

THEOREM 1. *A log is tamper-detectable by using authenticators. A misbehaving site cannot selectively insert, delete or change the happened-before order of other sites' operations from the beginning or the middle of the log without being detected by next audit (Integrity).*

PROOF. Let M be the misbehaving site who receives a log L = [op_1, op_2, ..., op_i, op_{i+1}, op_{j-1}, op_j] from site R. Let us assume op_i and op_{i+1} were generated by R and op_{j-1} and op_j were received by R from S. Log L is accompanied with authenticators and the most recent authenticator is $T_{j@R}$ which is linked to operations (op_{i+1}, op_j). Following Definition 1 and Definition 2, $T_{j@R}$ consists of:
$T_{j@R}$.ID = <*site R*, {op_{i+1}, op_j}> (linked to operations op_{i+1}, op_j),
$T_{j@R}$.SIG = σ_{siteR}(hash($T_{i@R}$.SIG $\|$ op_i $\|$ op_{i+1} $\|$ $T_{j@S}$.SIG)),
$T_{j@R}$.IDE = [op_i, op_{i+1}],
$T_{j@R}$.PRE = $T_{i@R}$.ID,
$T_{j@R}$.SYN = $T_{j@S}$.ID
There are three cases that M can attack the log as follows.

- *Case 1 - misbehaving site M removes operations at the beginning or in the middle of the log.*

  (i) If M selectively removes any operation in range from op_i to op_j from L, i.e. op_i is removed by M but M still keeps

op_{i+1}. The authenticator $T_{j@R}$ is then either invalid (missing of op_i) or replaced by $T'_{j@R}$. However, $T'_{j@R}$ is invalid since it should be signed by R and M cannot forge R's signature on $T'_{j@R}$.

(ii) If M removes any operation before op_i, i.e. op_1 is removed, then the authenticator $T_{i@R}$ is invalid and this makes $T_{j@R}$ invalid consequently.

Therefore, if a misbehaving site removes any operation in the middle of the log, the log will not be authenticated by valid authenticators.

- *Case 2 - misbehaving site M changes the happened-before order of operations on behalf of others.*

If M changes the happened-before order of any operations from op_i to op_j then the operations list $T_{j@R}.IDE$ will be invalid. When op_{i+1} is generated by site R, op_j is generated by site S, and R receives op_j from S after generating op_i, op_{i+1}, we say op_{i+1} and op_j are concurrent and other users can change the order of op_{i+1} and op_j. In the case of changing order of concurrent operations, the authenticator $T_{j@R}$ is still valid (it passes the check of Algorithm 3 - line 7). However, if R continues to work on the document and adds new operation op_k after op_j, then commits an authenticator $T_{k@R}$, other sites cannot change the order of op_i, op_j and op_k since this misbehavior will make the authenticator $T_{k@R}$ invalid by the checking procedure in Algorithm 3 - line 8.

Therefore, if a misbehaving site changes any happened-before order, the log will not be authenticated.

- *Case 3 - misbehaving site M inserts an operation at the beginning or into the middle of log.*

We assume misbehaving site M inserts an operation op_m in the middle of existing log between op_i and op_j.

If M claims operation op_m was generated by site R then the log will be not authenticated since none of existing authenticators of site R authenticates op_m and it therefore cannot pass the verification process in Algorithm 3 - line 17, 18.

If M claims op_m was generated by himself, then it needs to commit an authenticator to authenticate op_m. In such case, op_m is considered concurrent with other operations, so it can be inserted into any position in the log L and L is still authenticated.

Therefore, a misbehaving site only can insert its own operations into its local log. The site cannot claim its insertion as operations on behalf of others because it cannot authenticate such operations.

In summary, it is impossible to forge the integrity of a log without being detected by using authenticators. $\square$

THEOREM 2. *Authenticators preserve concurrency-collision-freeness property.*

PROOF. In the proof of theorem 1, we use a log L of site R, $L_R = [op_1, op_2, ..., op_i, op_{i+1}, op_{j-1}, op_j]$. We assume operations op_i, op_{i+1} are concurrent with op_{j-1}, op_j. Thus the order between them can be interchangeable in any linearization of history. Let us consider that site S maintains a different log of same history $L_S = [op_1, op_2, ..., op_{j-1}, op_j, op_i, op_{i+1}]$. We will prove that the log verification will return the same result on checking L_S and L_R.

When sites S and R share logs with each other, we suppose that $T_{i@R}$ and $T_{j@R}$ are committed by site R before and after receiving

the log from site S; $T_{j@S}$ and $T_{i@S}$ are committed by site S before and after receiving log from site R. The log verification by checking $T_{i@S}$ and $T_{j@R}$ yields the same result regardless the order of concurrent operations. Indeed, $T_{i@S}$ and $T_{j@R}$ are valid only if they pass four checks (Algorithm 3, line 6 - 9). Consider check1 and check2 were passed, therefore they must pass check3 and check4 to be completely verified. The check3 only deals with the order of preceding authenticator against operations list IDE ($T_{i@S}$ with op_i, op_{i+1}, $T_{j@R}$ with op_{j-1}, op_j) and these orders are preserved as proved in Theorem 1. The check4 deals with the orders of preceding and synchronized authenticators with respect to the committed authenticator. Since $T_{j@R}$ is committed after $T_{i@R}$ and $T_{j@S}$ (linked to operations op_{i+1}, op_j), the check4 for $T_{j@R}$ passes. Similarly, the check4 for $T_{i@S}$ passes. Therefore, regardless the logging order of concurrent operations, the verification yields same result of checking two logs L_S and L_R. $\square$

THEOREM 3. *Authenticators are forward-aggregated.*

PROOF. This property is achieved by using hash-chain based authenticator, so that $T_{i@site}.SIG$ includes $T_{i-1@site}.SIG$ in its construction. $\square$

THEOREM 4. *Every site which is in possession of history can verify authenticators by using the public key of the site which committed them. A site which created an authenticator cannot deny having constructed it (public verifiability).*

PROOF. Non-repudiation is an important feature of digital signatures. By this property, a site that has signed authenticators cannot at a later time deny having signed them. Suppose that site S has signed an authenticator for operations $op_1, op_2, ..., op_i$ and shared them with another site. At later time, site S wants to change the history by removing op_i (e.g *insert line X*). In that case, site S should add a new operation op_j (e.g *delete line X*) instead of removing operation op_i since this will make authenticator $T_{i@S}$ invalid. Once a log has been shared with other sites, site S cannot remove its operations due to the using of non-repudiation signature for committed authenticators. Authenticators are linked to operations and replicated together with logs, therefore anyone can authenticate them. $\square$

6. EVALUATION

We are going to present a practical evaluation of our proposed algorithms to authenticate logs. As the time complexity for the creation of authenticators is not significant, we evaluated the time complexity of the algorithm for log verification based on authenticators. Verification is done when a site clones or pulls remote log and it needs to check if the remote log is shared correctly without any tampering.

We carried out experiments on real logs from projects that used Mercurial as a distributed tool for source code management. We chose randomly two projects: Hgview project [22] and one branch of OpenJDK project [31]. The project *Hgview* includes almost 700 committed patches stored in repository gathering contributions from 20 developers with 115 interactions between them. One branch of *OpenJDK* stored about 350 committed patches in repository which were created by 31 developers with 253 interactions between them. A committed patch is a sequence of operations that a user commits. It is also called a log entry. We implemented our experiments by using Python programming language.

In the histories of projects developed with Mercurial or any other distributed version control system, we are unable to know when a user pulls changes. We can only have information about push operations. We therefore considered the worst case scenario where a pull is performed at each new entry in the repository by an arbitrary user Y that had never interacted before with any other user X that contributed to the project. If previous interactions were taking place between users Y and X, an optimization could be applied.

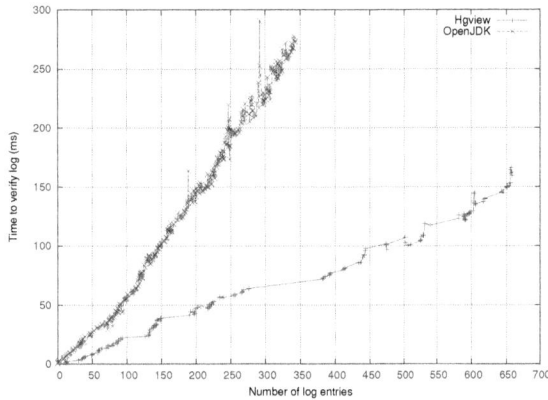

Figure 5: Time overhead to check authenticators created for Hgview and OpenJDK repositories.

In the experiment, we have first traversed the repository to extract entries and user names who contributed to the project. Then we generated for each user one RSA key pair which is later used to sign authenticators. Authenticators are created based on linearized logs of repositories. Finally, verification time is measured for the worst case scenario where a newcomer clones the repository and she has to check all authenticators created by previous contributors. The results are computed by the average values of five run times. Figure 5 presents the experimental results for the worst case behavior. In two experiments with the input data from Hgview project and OpenJDK project, the checking time grows linearly with the increasing number of authenticators. It is observed that it takes less than 50 milliseconds (ms) to verify a log if its size is less than 100 entries (this size is common for the size of all files observed in these projects). However, to check the whole repository, the verifying time depends mostly on the number of interactions between users (this means also the number of authenticators). In Figure 5, we notice that the runtime to verify log of the *Hgview* project is less than that of *OpenJDK* project even though its log size is bigger.

The main conclusion to be drawn from the results is that adding authenticators to secure logs does not create a significant time overhead for collaborative systems even for the worst case. Sites can reduce the time to verify log by skipping authenticators which are already checked when previous pulls were performed.

7. RELATED WORK

In this section, we give a review of existing securing log schemes and highlight their non suitability for securing operation-based history in multi-synchronous collaboration.

Several works introduce a trusted server to be used for verification. This approach makes the system open to a single point of failure. Peterson et al. [35] presents an approach to secure version history in a versioning file system. The approach proposed a design of a system based on generating message authentication codes MACs for versions and archiving them with a third party. A file system commits to a version history when it presents a MAC to the third party and at a later time, an auditor can verify this history. Thus it requires that the system trusts the third party that maintains MACs correctly. In the general model of multi-synchronous collaboration,

users have no need to rely on a trusted third party and therefore any user should be able to verify logs.

In a similar direction, Haeberlen et al. designed PeerReview [12] to provide accountability and fault detection for distributed systems. It guarantees the eventual detection of all Byzantine faults. Peer-Review framework contains tamper-evident logs and commitment, consistency and audit protocols. However, each node should have an identical log with others. It does not support that each node can keep different orders of operations as in operation-based multi-synchronous collaboration where users maintain different streams of activity on the shared data. The framework offers three applications of overlay multicast, network file system and peer-to-peer email, however, all of these applications do not deal with parallel modifications of data that is the case in multi-synchronous collaboration.

The integrity of audit logs has traditionally been protected through the use of one-way hash functions. There is a line of work that addresses the forward-secure stream integrity for audit logs. Ma et al. proposed a set of secure audit logging schemes and aggregate signatures [24, 23, 25]. Forward security ensures the integrity of log entries in the log stream and no selective deletion or re-ordering to stream is possible. Recently, Yavuz et al. proposed their work to secure audit log such as BAF [43] that was developed to achieve at the same time the computationally efficient log signing and the truncation-attack-resistant logging. This work could be applied only for a particular case of the multi-synchronous collaboration where all users maintain the same linearization of the collaboration history. However, it cannot be applied for the general case of the multi-synchronous collaboration where users work on different streams of activity on the shared data corresponding to different linearizations of collaboration history.

There is another line of work that relies on authenticated data structures to secure logs in distributed systems [9, 28, 27, 33]. While these approaches are computationally efficient, they do not deal with history for collaboration. Maniatis et al. introduced Timeweave [27] that uses a time entanglement mechanism to preserve the history state of distributed systems in a tamper-evident manner. However, Timeweave does not handle the information flows synchronized which is required in optimistic replication where concurrent operations appear in different orders in replicas.

Apart from above approaches, there are works that address securing logs for replication systems. Spreitzer et al. [40] uses hash chain to protect modification orders of a weakly consistent, replicated data system. Kang et al. [17, 16] proposed SHH for optimistic replication using hash values as in Merkle tree [30] for revision identifiers to protect causality of version history. It serves mainly for the purpose of securing version history construction when the log was pruned in limited storage environments such as mobile computing; and for checking distributed replicas' convergence. By ensuring decentralized ordering correctness, SHH can guarantee that all updates are not vulnerable to a decentralized ordering attack. However, SHH cannot ensure the integrity of data in the sense that it is original or forged. Using SHH the sender signature cannot be included in summary hashes since that makes them different even if the merged versions are identical, thus it makes replicas diverge. Without digital signature in summary hashes, SHH cannot protect history from attacks of unauthorized actions and it cannot provide authenticity and accountability. Similar approaches to SHH in which hashes are used as identifiers are implemented in distributed version control systems such as Git history [21] and Mercurial history [32].

Concerning securing document history, Hasan et al. [13] proposed a mechanism of preventing history forgery for a document history where a document refers to a file or database. In [13], the term "provenance" is used for the history of the ownership of items and actions performed on them. The authors present a provenance-aware system prototype that captures history of document writes at the application layer. To prevent all potential attacks on provenance chain, it requires trusted pervasive hardware infrastructure at the level where tracking is performed. However, contributions to the shared document/database are done sequentially and the approach does not deal with merging of parallel contributions to the shared document.

A different work, Mella et al. [29] proposed a framework to the document control flow in a highly distributed environment. The proposal is aimed at cooperative updates on a document flow with delegation and security policies. However, it considers one stream of update process rather than a multi-way flow of updating with reconciliation as in multi-synchronous model. Moreover, security access control policies are defined at document's attributes level that means each document atomic element is marked with a label containing a set of access control policies that apply to it. The approach described in [29] secures different XML elements, while we aim to secure patches of operations.

In the domain of database security, Mahajan et al. [26] proposed Depot to secure replicated database in the cloud. Among all issues addressed in Depot, we focus on the issues of consistency, integrity and authorization. Depot addresses these issues in the context of database where data is stored in the form of key/value and update is the main operation performed over database. We consider collaborative systems with more operations beyond update, i.e. insert, delete content to/from the shared document. Depot ensures consistency by using version vectors and version history hashes. Each update is signed by authorized node to enforce consistency and integrity. This would be too costly in a collaborative working environment where users produce a huge number of operations on the shared document. Our approach secures logs without requiring that each user signs each operation. Authenticators are created for a patch of operations each time the log is pushed/pulled to/from one user.

The state of the art of secure audit logging research was also surveyed by Accorsi [2]. Though secure audit logging was intensively investigated, we are not aware of any work that ensures secure audit logs for a collaboration history with partial order where users maintain different total ordered logs of the collaboration history corresponding to their activity streams.

8. CONCLUSION

In this paper, we introduced a technique using authenticators to face security challenges in operation-based multi-synchronous collaboration. In multi-synchronous model, users work simultaneously on different streams of activity. As the collaboration progresses, the streams of activity continually diverge and synchronize. Authenticators are used to ensure integrity and authenticity of logs of operations corresponding to different streams of activity during a collaborative process. While tamper-resistance is impossible to be ensured in multi-synchronous collaboration without a central provider, tamper-detection should be guaranteed. We presented an approach for securing logs that made misbehaving users accountable in collaborative systems without the need of a central authority. We provided proofs of correctness of our approach and analyze the complexities of our algorithms. We also conducted a set of experiments testing our proposed approach on real histories of collaboration extracted from real projects using Mercurial. The results show the feasibility of our approach that can be used to provide security, trustworthiness and accountability to distributed collaborative systems.

Acknowledgment
This work is partially funded by the ANR national research grant STREAMS (ANR-10-SEGI-010).

9. REFERENCES

[1] M. Abdalla and L. Reyzin. A new forward-secure digital signature scheme. In *Proceedings of the 6th International Conference on the Theory and Application of Cryptology and Information Security: Advances in Cryptology (ASIACRYPT'00)*, pages 116–129, London, UK, 2000. Springer-Verlag.

[2] R. Accorsi. Safe-keeping digital evidence with secure logging protocols: State of the art and challenges. In *Proceedings of the 2009 Fifth International Conference on IT Security Incident Management and IT Forensics (IMF '09)*, pages 94–110, Stuttgart, Germany, September 2009.

[3] C. N. Chong, Z. Peng, and P. H. Hartel. Secure audit logging with tamper-resistant hardware. In *Proceedings of the 18th IFIP TC11 International Conference on Information Security, Security and Privacy in the Age of Uncertainty (SEC'03)*, pages 73–84, Athens, Greece, May 2003. Kluwer Academic Publishers.

[4] S. A. Crosby and D. S. Wallach. Efficient data structures for tamper-evident logging. In *18th USENIX Security Symposium*, pages 317–334, Montreal, Canada, August 2009.

[5] D. Davis, F. Monrose, and M. K. Reiter. Time-Scoped Searching of Encrypted Audit Logs. In *Proceedings of the 6th International Conference on Information and Communications Security (ICICS'04)*, pages 532–545, Malaga, Spain, October 2004.

[6] A. Demers, D. Greene, C. Hauser, W. Irish, J. Larson, S. Shenkcr, H. Sturgis, D. Swinehart, and D. Terry. Epidemic Algorithms for Replicated Database Maintenance. In *Proceedings of the Sixth annual ACM Symposium on Principles of Distributed Computing (PODC'87)*, pages 1–12, Vancouver, British Columbia, Canada, aug 1987. ACM Press.

[7] J. R. Douceur. The sybil attack. In *Revised Papers from the First International Workshop on Peer-to-Peer Systems (IPTPS'01)*, pages 251–260, London, UK, 2002. Springer-Verlag.

[8] P. Dourish. The parting of the ways: divergence, data management and collaborative work. In *Proceedings of the fourth conference on European Conference on Computer-Supported Cooperative Work (ECSCW'95)*, pages 215–230, Norwell, MA, USA, 1995. Kluwer Academic Publishers.

[9] M. T. Goodrich, R. Tamassia, and A. Schwerin. Implementation of an authenticated dictionary with skip lists and commutative hashing. *DARPA Information Survivability Conference and Exposition,*, 2:68–82, 2001. Los Alamitos, CA, USA.

[10] S. Greenberg. Personalizable groupware: accommodating individual roles and group differences. In *Proceedings of the second conference on European Conference on Computer-Supported Cooperative Work (ECSCW'91)*, pages 17–31, Norwell, MA, USA, 1991. Kluwer Academic Publishers.

[11] S. Greenberg, M. Roseman, D. Webster, and R. Bohnet. Human and technical factors of distributed group drawing tools. *Interacting with Computers*, 4(3):364–392, 1992.

[12] A. Haeberlen, P. Kouznetsov, and P. Druschel. Peerreview: practical accountability for distributed systems. *Proceedings*

of the 21st ACM Symposium on Operating Systems Principles (SOSP'07), 41:175–188, October 2007. Stevenson, Washington, USA.

[13] R. Hasan, R. Sion, and M. Winslett. The case of the fake picasso: Preventing history forgery with secure provenance. In *7th USENIX Conference on File and Storage Technologies (FAST'09)*, pages 1–14, San Francisco, CA, USA, 2009.

[14] J. E. Holt. Logcrypt: forward security and public verification for secure audit logs. In *Proceedings of the 2006 Australasian workshops on Grid computing and e-research - Volume 54 (ACSW Frontiers '06)*, pages 203–211, Darlinghurst, Australia, 2006. Australian Computer Society, Inc.

[15] C.-L. Ignat, S. Papadopoulou, G. Oster, and M. C. Norrie. Providing Awareness in Multi-synchronous Collaboration Without Compromising Privacy. In *Proceedings of the ACM Conference on Computer-Supported Cooperative Work (CSCW'08)*, pages 659–668, San Diego, California, USA, November 2008. ACM Press.

[16] B. B. Kang. *S2D2: A Framework for Scalable and Secure Optimistic Replication*. PhD thesis, EECS Department, University of California, Berkeley, Oct 2004.

[17] B. B. Kang, R. Wilensky, and J. Kubiatowicz. The hash history approach for reconciling mutual inconsistency. In *Proceedings of the 23rd International Conference on Distributed Computing Systems (ICDCS'03)*, pages 670–677, Washington, DC, USA, 2003. IEEE Computer Society.

[18] A.-M. Kermarrec, A. Rowstron, M. Shapiro, and P. Druschel. The icecube approach to the reconciliation of divergent replicas. In *Proceedings of the twentieth annual ACM symposium on Principles of distributed computing (PODC'01)*, pages 210–218, New York, NY, USA, 2001. ACM.

[19] L. Lamport. Time, Clocks, and the Ordering of Events in a Distributed System. *Communications of the ACM*, 21(7):558–565, 1978.

[20] E. Lippe and N. van Oosterom. Operation-based merging. *Proceedings of the fifth ACM SIGSOFT symposium on Software development environments*, 17:78–87, November 1992. New York, NY, USA.

[21] J. Loeliger. Collaborating with Git. *Linux Magazine*, June 2006.

[22] Logilab.org. hgview. http://www.logilab.org/project/hgview.

[23] D. Ma. Practical forward secure sequential aggregate signatures. In *Proceedings of the 2008 ACM symposium on Information, computer and communications security (ASIACCS'08)*, pages 341–352, New York, NY, USA, 2008. ACM.

[24] D. Ma and G. Tsudik. Extended abstract: Forward-secure sequential aggregate authentication. In *IEEE Symposium on Security and Privacy*, pages 86–91, 2007.

[25] D. Ma and G. Tsudik. A new approach to secure logging. *ACM Transactions on Storage (TOS)*, 5(1):1–21, 2009.

[26] P. Mahajan, S. Setty, S. Lee, A. Clement, L. Alvisi, M. Dahlin, and M. Walfish. Depot: Cloud storage with minimal trust. *ACM Transactions on Computer Systems*, 29(4):12:1–12:38, Dec. 2011.

[27] P. Maniatis and M. Baker. Secure history preservation through timeline entanglement. In *Proceedings of the 11th USENIX Security Symposium*, pages 297–312, Berkeley, CA, USA, 2002. USENIX Association.

[28] P. Maniatis and M. Baker. Authenticated append-only skip lists. *Acta Mathematica*, 137:151–169, 2003.

[29] G. Mella, E. Ferrari, E. Bertino, and Y. Koglin. Controlled and cooperative updates of xml documents in byzantine and failure-prone distributed systems. *ACM Transactions on Information and System Security (TISSEC), Volume 9*, 9:421–460, November 2006. New York, NY, USA.

[30] R. C. Merkle. *Secrecy, authentication, and public key systems*. PhD thesis, Stanford, CA, USA, 1979. AAI8001972.

[31] OpenJDK. OpenJDK. http://openjdk.java.net.

[32] B. O'Sullivan. *Mercurial: The Definitive Guide*. O'Reilly Media, 2009.

[33] C. Papamanthou, R. Tamassia, and N. Triandopoulos. Authenticated hash tables. In *Proceedings of the 15th ACM conference on Computer and communications security (CCS'08)*, pages 437–448, New York, NY, USA, 2008. ACM.

[34] K. Petersen, M. J. Spreitzer, D. B. Terry, M. M. Theimer, and A. J. Demers. Flexible update propagation for weakly consistent replication. In *Proceedings of the sixteenth ACM symposium on Operating systems principles (SOSP'97)*, pages 288–301, New York, NY, USA, 1997. ACM.

[35] Z. N. J. Peterson, R. Burns, G. Ateniese, and S. Bono. Design and implementation of verifiable audit trails for a versioning file system. In *Proceedings of the 5th USENIX conference on File and Storage Technologies*, pages 20–20, Berkeley, CA, USA, 2007. USENIX Association.

[36] N. M. Preguiça, J. M. Marquès, M. Shapiro, and M. Letia. A commutative replicated data type for cooperative editing. In *ICDCS*, pages 395–403, 2009.

[37] Y. Saito and M. Shapiro. Optimistic replication. *ACM Computing Surveys, Volume 37*, 37:42–81, March 2005. New York, NY, USA.

[38] M. Satyanarayanan, J. J. Kistler, P. Kumar, M. E. Okasaki, E. H. Siegel, David, and C. Steere. Coda: A highly available file system for a distributed workstation environment. *IEEE Transactions on Computers*, 39:447–459, 1990.

[39] B. Schneier and J. Kelsey. Cryptographic support for secure logs on untrusted machines. In *Proceedings of the 7th conference on USENIX Security Symposium - Volume 7*, pages 4–4, Berkeley, CA, USA, 1998. USENIX Association.

[40] M. J. Spreitzer, M. M. Theimer, K. Petersen, A. J. Demers, and D. B. Terry. Dealing with server corruption in weakly consistent, replicated data systems. In *Proceedings of the 3rd annual ACM/IEEE international conference on Mobile computing and networking (MobiCom'97)*, pages 234–240, New York, NY, USA, 1997. ACM.

[41] K. Walsh and E. G. Sirer. Experience with an Object Reputation System for Peer-to-Peer Filesharing (Awarded Best Paper). In *Proceedings of the 3rd conference on Networked Systems Design & Implementation - Volume 3 (NSDI'06)*, Berkeley, CA, USA, 2006.

[42] S. Weiss, P. Urso, and P. Molli. Logoot-Undo: Distributed Collaborative Editing System on P2P Networks. *IEEE Transactions on Parallel and Distributed Systems*, 21(8):1162–1174, Aug. 2010.

[43] A. A. Yavuz and P. Ning. Baf: An efficient publicly verifiable secure audit logging scheme for distributed systems. In *Proceedings of the 2009 Annual Computer Security Applications Conference, (ACSAC'09)*, pages 219–228, Washington, DC, USA, 2009. IEEE Computer Society.

A String-Wise CRDT for Group Editing

Weihai Yu
Department of Computer Science
University of Tromsø
N-9037 Tromsø, Norway
Weihai.Yu@uit.no

ABSTRACT

Real-time group editing has been envisioned as an important application for group collaboration. Operational transformation (OT) has been the concurrency control mechanism for group editing, due to its potential for high responsiveness to local editing operations. OT algorithms are generally very sophisticated and computation intensive. Recently, commutative replicated data types (CRDT) have appeared as viable substitutes of OT. Existing OT and CRDT work suffers from serious limitations. This note presents a CRDT that addresses some of these limitations.

Categories and Subject Descriptors

C.2.4 [**Computer-Communication Networks**]: Distributed Systems—*Distributed applications*; H.5.3 [**Information Interfaces and Presentation**]: Group and Organization Interfaces—*Collaborative computing*

Keywords

Real-time collaborative editor, commutative replicated data type, selective undo

1. INTRODUCTION

A real-time group editor allows multiple users to simultaneously edit the same document from different places. Operational transformation (OT) has been established as a concurrency control mechanism for group editing [2, 7, 8, 9]. OT has the potential for high responsiveness to local operations, because local operations are done immediately on the local document before they are transformed and integrated at remote peers. However, OT algorithms are sophisticated and time consuming. Counterexamples of several published algorithms have been reported. The algorithms generally have time complexities dependent on the lengths of operation histories.

Recently, a new class of mechanisms called commutative replicated data types (CRDT) have been proposed [1, 4, 5, 6,

10, 11, 12]. Concurrent operations of a CRDT are mutually commutative, so that documents being concurrently edited are eventually kept consistent at all places. [1] reports that CRDT algorithms outperform a representative class of OT algorithms by a factor between 25 and 1000.

Currently, none of the state-of-the-art work supports all of the following desirable features:

1. Variable number of group members. For the algorithms using state vectors to detect happen-before relationships among operations, there is an upper limit of fixed maximal number of group members.

2. String-wise operations. They are the basis for other useful operations like copy-paste and find-replace. Furthermore, supporting only character-wise operations leads to significant network and runtime overhead. A large amount of small operations are propagated over the network and integrated individually. For OT algorithms whose performance are dependent on the lengths of operation histories, this also means long histories and therefor poor performance.

3. Support of operation undo. Undo is indispensable for any editor.

The table below summarizes the features supported by the current state-of-the-art research work:

Feature	[4]	[5]	[6]	[7]	[8]	[9]	[10]	[11]	[12]
1. var. mem.	✓	✓	✓				✓	✓	
2. string				✓					✓
3. undo					✓	✓	✓		

This note presents a CRDT that combines and extends the strengths of OT and CRDT approaches. The CRDT is basically a list of nodes (of sub-strings) that forms a total order, similar to the operation history in ABTU [8] that arranges operations in a total effects-relation order [3]. To support string-wise operations, additional links connect nodes belonging to the same operations. The CRDT also materializes operation dependencies (among which insertion dependencies are similar to [4]), which is in contrast to OT approaches that derive these dependencies every time an operation is integrated.

2. OVERVIEW OF APPROACH

A document is collaboratively edited by a number of peers at different sites. Every peer consists of a view, a model and three queues (Figure 1).

A peer concurrently receives local operations from the user and remote updates from other peers. Local operations take

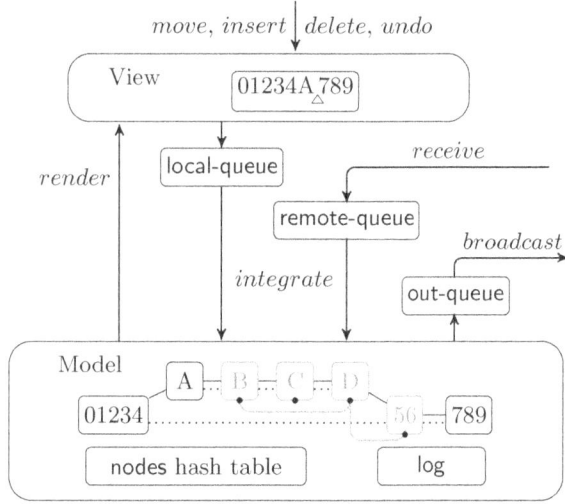

Figure 1: View, model and operations

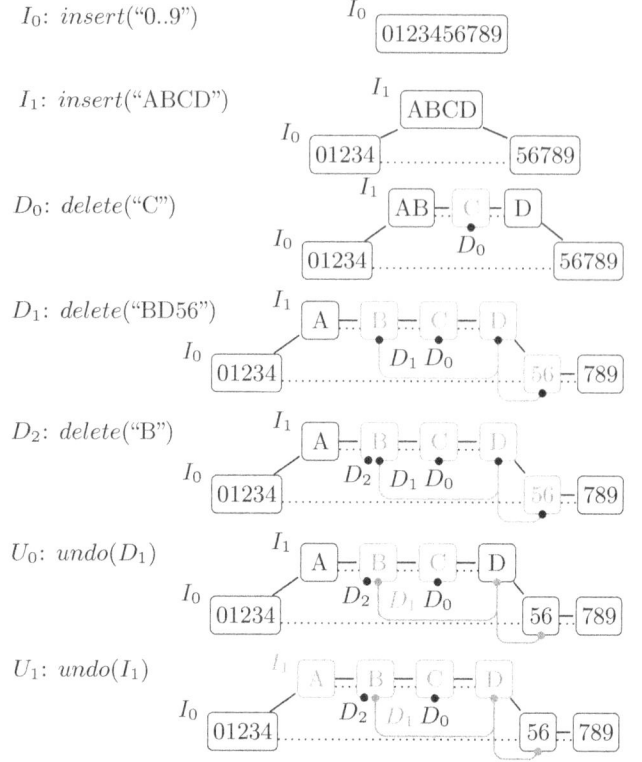

Figure 2: Examples of model updates

immediate effect in the view. Local and remote operations are first stored in *local-queue* and *remote-queue* and later be integrated in the model. Integrated local operations are first stored in *out-queue* and later broadcasted to other peers. When the model is rendered, the effects of integrated remote operations are shown in the view.

A view is a string of characters together with a current position in the string. A user at a peer can move the current position, insert or delete a sub-string at the current position, and undo an earlier executed local or remote operation.

The model is primarily a double-linked list of nodes. A node contains a sub-string, together with some additional meta-data and links for the operations on the string. A model has also a current position, corresponding to the current position in the view. When operations are integrated into the model, existing nodes are split at operation boundaries, and either new nodes are inserted or existing nodes are marked as deleted or undone. The list thus grows while the document is being edited.

Figure 2 illustrates a model list in different states. When string "0...9" is first inserted, the model has only one node. Inserting "ABCD" inserts a new node and splits the existing node. Deleting a sub-string makes the characters invisible in the view (the nodes in the figure become gray) and further splits existing nodes. Concurrent deletions D_1 and D_2 overlap at "B". When D_1 is undone, only sub-string "D56" is brought back in the view. "B" is still deleted, because D_2 remains in effect.

In addition to the list, the mode has a hash table of the nodes and a log of operations. With the hash table, a node can be accessed with its globally unique identifier in constant time. Any operation in the log can be selected and undone.

Procedure *integrate* integrates all queued local and remote operations. Procedure *render* make the effects of integrated remote operations available in the view.

3. THE MODEL CRDT

A peer has an identifier *pid* and maintains a peer update number *pun*. *pun* increments by one for every editing operation originated at the peer. An operation is uniquely identified with (pid, pun).

A *view* is a pair (str, pos) where *str* is the character string currently visible to the user and *pos* is the current position between two characters. A user may run the following operations in the view:

- $move(\delta)$ moves the current position $|\delta|$ characters. If δ is positive, the current position is moved to the right; otherwise, it is moved to the left.

- $insert(str)$ inserts string *str* at the current position and the new current position is placed at the right end of *str*.

- $delete(len)$ deletes *len* characters right to the current position.

- $undo(op)$ undoes *op*, which can be *insert*, *delete* or *undo*, and the new current position is placed at *op*.

The *model CRDT* is defined as $(nodes, curr, pos)$, where *nodes* is a hash table of nodes, *curr* is the current node and *pos* is a position in *curr*. *curr* and *pos* together refer to the current position in the model.

A node of the model contains the following elements:

- *pid*, *pun*, the identifier of the *insert* operation that created this node.

- *offset*, the distance from its left end to the left end of the original inserted string. When a node is first inserted, *offset* is 0. Splitting the node at position *pos* leads to two nodes, with *offset*s 0 and *pos* respectively.

- *str*, the character string of the node.

- *dels*, a set of *del* elements related to deletions.

- *undo*, the undo of the insertion, or *nil* if the insertion is not undone.

- *rendered*, *true* if the node has been rendered to the view.

- *l*, *r*, the left and right nodes. In Figure 2, the *l* and *r* links are illustrated with solid lines connecting nodes.

- *il*, *ir*, the left and right nodes of the same *insert* operation. In Figure 2, the *il* and *ir* links are illustrated with dotted lines.

- dep_l, dep_r, insert-dependencies, i.e., the place of the insertion at the originating peer, represented with the right end of the left node ($lpid, lpun, loffset, llen$) and the left end of the right node ($rpid, rpun, roffset$).

In the model, an *insertion* consists of the nodes chained with the *il* and *ir* links. A *deletion* consists of the nodes containing the *del* elements of the same *delete* operation. When *dels* of a node contains multiple *del* elements, the node's *str* has been deleted concurrently by multiple peers.

A *del* element has the following (sub-)elements: *pid*, *pun*, the identifier of the *delete* operation; *l*, *r*, the left and right nodes of the same *delete* operation; *undo*, *rendered*, similar to those in nodes. In Figure 2, a *del* element is depicted with a dot on the bottom edge of a node ( ). The links between the *dels* of the same *delete* operation are illustrated with lines connecting the dots ( ).

An *undo* element consists of *pid, pun, undo* and *rendered*. (*pid, pun*) is the *id* of the *undo* operation. If an undo operation itself it undone, the *undo* element refers to another *undo* element. An operation's undo elements are thus chained into a linked list. An operation is *effectively undone* if the length of the undo list is an odd number.

A node is *visible* if the insertion is not effectively undone and all *del* elements in *dels* are effectively undone.

Locally in a peer, a node can be directly referred to via its reference. So the links *l*, *r* etc. refer to nodes with their references. Node references, however, are meaningless across peer boundaries. Fortunately, a node can be uniquely identified by the identifier of the *insert(str)* operation that inserted the string *str*, together with the offset of the node's left end in *str*. In Figure 2, suppose the identifier of *insert*("0...9") is $I_0 = (0,0)$. The node with string "789" can be uniquely identified with $(0,0,7)$. We use $(pid, pun, offset)$ as the *id* of a node. Nodes are hash-indexed with their *id*s. Therefore given $(pid, pun, offset)$, a node can be obtained in constant time. In the worst case, if a local operation makes a new split at *offset*, a remote peer can start from $(pid, pun, 0)$ to find the node containing *offset* (and make a split there).

4. LOCAL OPERATIONS

The model integrates a local *insert* operation by inserting a new node into the list. If the current position is in the middle of the current node, the current node is split and the new node is inserted in between. Otherwise, the new node is to be inserted to the left or right of the current node. In this case, the new node is to be inserted between two visible nodes. When there are invisible nodes in between, a

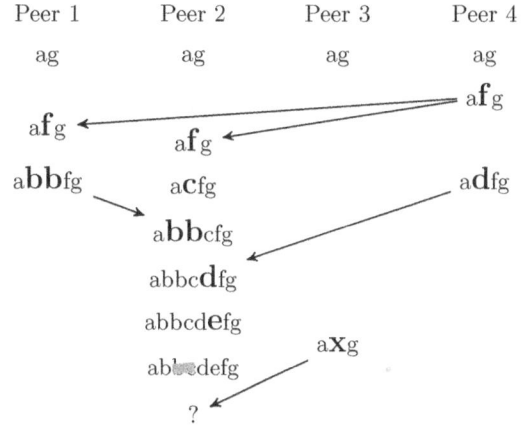

Figure 3: Example of conflicting insertions

particular order is enforced. For example, all invisible nodes are placed to the right of the new node.

After the new node is inserted in the list, the update is sent to the remote peers. The update is represented with the *id* of the insertion, the inserted string, and insertion dependencies, i.e., the place of the insertion, represented with the right end of the left node and the left end of the right node.

The model integrates a local *delete* operation by associating the *del* elements of the deletion to the corresponding nodes. Nodes at deletion boundaries may be split. Then the update for the deletion is sent to the remote peers. A deletion update consists of the *id* of the deletion, and a list of the corresponding nodes, together with the lengths of the deleted sub-string, represented with ($pid, pun, offset, str.length$).

The model integrates an *undo* by associating an *undo* element to the corresponding elements (*node* for insertion, *del* for deletion and *undo* for undo). An undo update is represented with the *id* of the *undo*, the *id* of the operation it undoes, and for *delete* and *undo*, also the *id* of the leftmost node of the operation.

5. REMOTE OPERATIONS

A remote update is ready to be integrated at a peer when all nodes and elements referenced in the update are available in the local model.

For the nodes that are concurrently inserted at the same place, a total order among these nodes must be enforced.

For two concurrent insertions that *directly conflict* at the same place, their ordering is enforced according to their *pid*. For instance, the insertion with smaller *pid* is placed to the left. Two insertions ins_1 and ins_2 *directly conflict* at a position if there does not exist a third insertion ins_3 at the same position such that ins_1 (or ins_2) is concurrent with ins_3 but ins_2 (or ins_1) insert-depends on ins_3. Figure 3 shows an example of concurrent insertions. Figure 4 shows insert-dependencies among these insertions. *insert*("x") conflicts with *insert*("d") between "a" and "g". However, *insert*("x") does not directly conflict with *insert*("d") because *insert*("d") insert-depends on *insert*("f") and *insert*("f") is concurrent with *insert*("x").

Integrating a remote insertion is handled in iterations, as

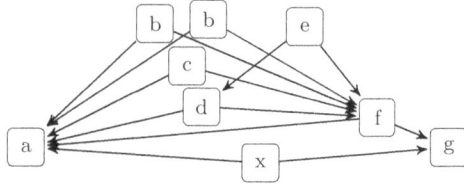

Figure 4: Insertion dependencies

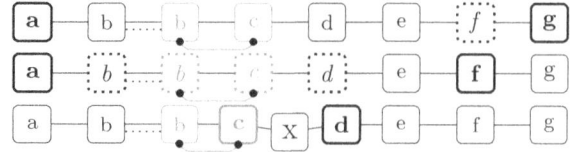

Figure 5: Ordering among conflicting insertions

illustrated in Figure 5. To insert "x" between "a" and "g" at Peer 2, we first find insertions between "a" and "g" that directly conflict with "x". In our example, this is the insertion of "f". Since insert("f") has pid 4 and insert("x") has pid 3, "x" is to be inserted to the left of "f". "x" is then to be inserted between "a" and "f" in the next iteration. The directly conflicting insertions are then insert("bb"), insert("c") and insert("d"). This process continues until there is no conflicting node between "c" and "d" where "x" is to be inserted. This process is in essence the same as in [4, 12]. Notice that deletion and node splitting have no effect with respect to the ordering of the insertions.

Integrating a remote *delete* or *undo* simply associates the corresponding *del* or *undo* elements in the model data structure. *delete* and *undo* operations are idempotent. The commutativity of *deletion* and *undo* with other operations is straightforward.

6. COMPLEXITY

The table below presents the time complexity of the different CRDT procedures.

move	$O(m)$	render	$O(r)$
local *insert*	$O(d)$	remote *insert*	$O(k^2)$
local *delete*	$O(l + d)$	remote *delete*	$O(l)$
local *undo*	$O(m + s)$	remote *undo*	$O(l)$

In the table, m is the distance of a move, i.e., the number of nodes a move traverses; r is the size of region being rendered, i.e., the number of nodes in the region; l is the size of an operation, i.e., the number of nodes that the operation involves; d is the number of invisible nodes, either between two visible nodes at the place of an insertion, or between visible nodes for deletion; k is the number of conflicting insertions; s is the span of an operation, i.e., the number of nodes between the leftmost and rightmost nodes of the operation, including the nodes of which the operation is not part of.

It can be seen that a local *undo* can be an expensive operation, because the current position must first be moved to the node of the operation to be undone and the effect of the undo must then be rendered. m and s can be considerably larger than l.

7. CONCLUSION AND ON-GOING WORK

The string-wise CRDT presented in this note advances the state of the art of group editing research by supporting unlimited dynamic group membership, string-wise operations and selective undo. We have implemented the algorithms presented in this note in Emacs Lisp, aiming at supporting group editing in a widely used open-source editor. We are currently investigating the overall performance of the approach.

8. REFERENCES

[1] M. Ahmed-Nacer, C.-L. Ignat, G. Oster, H.-G. Roh, and P. Urso. Evaluating CRDTs for real-time document editing. In M. R. B. Hardy and F. W. Tompa, editors, *ACM Symposium on Document Engineering*, pages 103–112. ACM, 2011.

[2] C. A. Ellis and S. J. Gibbs. Concurrency control in groupware systems. In J. Clifford, B. G. Lindsay, and D. Maier, editors, *SIGMOD Conference*, pages 399–407. ACM Press, 1989.

[3] D. Li and R. Li. An approach to ensuring consistency in peer-to-peer real-time group editors. *Computer Supported Cooperative Work*, 17(5-6):553–611, 2008.

[4] G. Oster, P. Urso, P. Molli, and A. Imine. Data consistency for P2P collaborative editing. In P. J. Hinds and D. Martin, editors, *CSCW*, pages 259–268. ACM, 2006.

[5] N. M. Preguiça, J. M. Marquès, M. Shapiro, and M. Letia. A commutative replicated data type for cooperative editing. In *ICDCS*, pages 395–403. IEEE Computer Society, 2009.

[6] H.-G. Roh, M. Jeon, J. Kim, and J. Lee. Replicated abstract data types: Building blocks for collaborative applications. *J. Parallel Distrib. Comput.*, 71(3):354–368, 2011.

[7] B. Shao, D. Li, and N. Gu. ABTS: A transformation-based consistency control algorithm for wide-area collaborative applications. In *CollaborateCom*, pages 1–10. IEEE, 2009.

[8] B. Shao, D. Li, and N. Gu. An algorithm for selective undo of any operation in collaborative applications. In W. G. Lutters, D. H. Sonnenwald, T. Gross, and M. Reddy, editors, *GROUP*, pages 131–140. ACM, 2010.

[9] D. Sun and C. Sun. Context-based operational transformation in distributed collaborative editing systems. *IEEE Trans. Parallel Distrib. Syst.*, 20(10):1454–1470, 2009.

[10] S. Weiss, P. Urso, and P. Molli. Logoot-undo: Distributed collaborative editing system on P2P networks. *IEEE Trans. Parallel Distrib. Syst.*, 21(8):1162–1174, 2010.

[11] Q. Wu, C. Pu, and J. E. Ferreira. A partial persistent data structure to support consistency in real-time collaborative editing. In F. Li, M. M. Moro, S. Ghandeharizadeh, J. R. Haritsa, G. Weikum, M. J. Carey, F. Casati, E. Y. Chang, I. Manolescu, S. Mehrotra, U. Dayal, and V. J. Tsotras, editors, *ICDE*, pages 776–779. IEEE, 2010.

[12] W. Yu. Constant-time operation transformation and integration for collaborative editing. In D. Georgakopoulos and J. B. D. Joshi, editors, *CollaborateCom*, pages 258–267. IEEE, 2011.

At a Different Tempo: What Goes Wrong in Online Cross-Cultural Group Chat?

Na Li[1], Mary Beth Rosson[2]
College of Information Sciences and Technology
The Pennsylvania State University
318 IST Building, University Park, 16802
[1]nzl116@psu.edu,[2]mur13@psu.edu

ABSTRACT

Cross-cultural communication has become increasingly prevalent in organizations and education systems. Such communication often takes place in a distributed fashion, and many studies have examined the impact of computer-mediated communication (CMC) on distributed cross-cultural groups. For example the literature points to cultural factors that could cause communication failures, such as individualism vs. collectivism, high context vs. low context, and power distance. We contend that language proficiency, a basic and fundamental difference between people from English speaking countries and other countries, is often neglected by researchers. Therefore, we have begun a detailed investigation of cross-cultural group chat. We chose text chat as a target technology because previous studies reported it as non-native speakers' preferred choice for CMC. Our study revealed that language proficiency played a pivotal role in cross-cultural group chat. When people conversed at different levels of proficiency, turn taking was severely disrupted, causing confusion and neglect of discussion points. We also found that some native speakers hold back ideas to accommodate the non-fluency of non-native speakers, slowing down the group process and outcomes. Working from these findings, we discuss possible designs that could assist both non-native and native speakers in cross-cultural group chat.

Categories and Subject Descriptors

H.5.3 [**Information interfaces and presentation**]: Group and organization interfaces – *Computer-supported cooperative work;* J.4 [**Computer applications**]: Social and behavioral sciences – *Sociology;* H.1.2 [**Models and principles**]: User/machine systems – *Human factors.*

General Terms

Design, Human Factors.

Keywords

Cross-cultural, group chat, language proficiency, text chat, turn taking, communication accommodation.

1. INTRODUCTION

Cross-cultural communication and collaboration has become more and more common in organizations and education systems, as multinational corporations hire local employees in their overseas branches, American companies outsource services to foreign

states, and international students take online courses at U.S. universities. As a result, cross-cultural issues in computer-mediated communication (CMC; the primary communication option for cross-cultural communication) have increasingly drawn scientific interest, exemplified by the rising number of published papers in CMC-related research venues.

A central question in this expanding body of research is how technologies shape and are shaped by cross-cultural communication. A full range of synchronous and asynchronous CMC tools have been studied, including email, discussion boards, instant messaging (IM), and audio/video conferencing tools (see [13] and [28] for examples). Most lab studies have investigated cross-cultural communication in dyads (i.e., one American and one foreigner). Wang et al. [34,35] investigated triads' communication of groups consisting either two Americans and one Chinese or two Chinese and one American, finding that both Chinese and American participants' communication styles altered due to the impact of other group members. Like Wang et al. we study cross-cultural communication in small groups, because we believe that cross-cultural communication problems are more likely to occur in multiparty situations in which participants must compete for limited resources (e.g. time, speaking turns, attentions, etc). In such settings people from particular cultures or speaking a particular language may be at an advantage/disadvantage, generating imbalanced relationships in conversations and groups.

In group communication, text chat tools have been widely adopted by non-collocated workplace users [15] and college students [17]. The use of text chat tools is especially prevalent among non-native speakers. Research in second language learning showed that in discussions and planning tasks, foreign students preferred text chat to face-to-face (FTF) communication, because text chat reduced face-threatening pressure by reducing the level of immediacy in interaction that is typically expected by interlocutors in FTF communication [6]. An interview of non-native speakers on their preference of media use also showed that non-native speakers preferred text chat tools for their reduced risk of misunderstandings caused by language problems [28].

Clark and Brennan's framework of eight conversational attributes [2] characterized how communication media support mutual understanding between interlocutors. These attributes are: copresence, visibility, audibility, contemporality, simultaneity, sequentiality, reviewability, and revisability. Although most text chat tools afford reviewability and revisability, they lack many other attributes, such as copresence, visibility, and sequentiality. Many researchers have suggested that the lack of these characteristics could cause communication problems. For example, Smith et al. [29] identified five main flaws in existing chat systems, all directly or indirectly linked to lack of interlocutor visibility. Because people are blindly "talking" to others, by the time they finish typing and send out their messages, there could be several messages submitted simultaneously by other interlocutors who are unaware of others' activity. As a result, any given utterance may not be the response to the last utterance but several utterances earlier; conversation topics are intertwined togetherl and parallel sub-conversations take place. This results in an extra cost for people to realign their conversation while it continues. Convertino et al. [5] compared the conversational process of participants finishing a map task in a CMC tool with audio support versus face-to-face communication and found that participants needed significantly more effort for grounding and conversation reorientation. Their study also showed that text-based CMC tools that offer few communication attributes require more communication management.

If text chat tools are to become more widely adopted in cross-cultural communication, then it would be beneficial to understand how their affordances affect both native and non-native speakers more fully. This understanding could provide guidance on designing/redesigning tools for cross-cultural group communication. To develop such an analysis, we conducted a mixed methods study on groups of Chinese and American students brainstorming and making decisions on a given topic in online group chat. Three types of data (surveys, chat logs, and interviews) were analyzed. This allowed us to look at situations from different perspectives, thus resulting in a comprehensive understanding of the problem.

This research complements prior studies of cross-cultural group chat. The most relevant work is that of Wang, Fussell and Setlock [34]. They conducted a lab experiment to study cultural difference and communication accommodation in online group brainstorming through either text chat or video chat. They found that Chinese participants were less talkative in general. However, in the text chat condition, Chinese and American participants were not significantly different in terms of talkativeness and responsiveness. Furthermore, they found that Chinese participants raised their responsiveness to the same level as American participants to accommodate their communication styles in cross-cultural groups. This paper expands the scope of their work by exploring participants' feelings (satisfaction/frustration) and experiences in the conversation. We found that Chinese participants were uncomfortable with the parallel conversation style in text chat, whereas American participants were not bothered by this as much. This suggests one possible reason why Chinese participants were less talkative in our study and in other related studies. We also found that some American participants accommodated their Chinese counterparts by talking less, a phenomenon not observed in the Wang study. Our findings lead to new insights for designing group chat systems that can benefit both native and non-native speakers.

2. BACKGROUND
2.1 Turn-Taking Systems in Text Chat
Systems for turn taking were first proposed by Sacks [24], who used this to describe the dynamics of spoken conversations. The turn taking action is accomplished when interlocutors exchange cues about whether they plan to hold a turn, start or end a turn, or interrupt a turn. Opportunities to talk often occur when the active speaker indicates an end of his or her turn. The next speaker may be self-selected or pre-selected by the last speaker. Under the turn taking rules, there is usually only one speaker at a time. The next speaker is expected to address the previous comment, so that his/her turn "fits into" the conversation. If it deviates from the

conversation flow, some expression denoting a topic change may be given (phrases such as 'by the way' or 'now then' can be used to indicate a new topic); if not other speakers may convey confusion, comments or rebukes (see [19] for a detailed analysis of spoken conversation). The turn taking system ensures that a conversation can carry on unambiguously and coherently.

Schegloff noted that turn taking also occurs in text-based conversations but with slightly different dynamics than in FTF conversations [25]. In most text chat systems, people receive a message immediately after the sender posts it. However, the process of producing the language is private to the poster. Before he/she posts the message, conversation partners do not know what is being written or edited; they may even not know that the person is typing. According to Clark and Brennan, text chat systems do not afford simultaneity in this sense. The lack of simultaneity generates two ramifications as pointed out by Smith et al. [29]: first, one can only begin to fit a "next" turn after the last turn has been displayed in its entirety, and second, there is a preference for short turns because one must press the return key in order to secure the floor. Even if people race for the immediate next turn so that their conversation is more coherent, other posts often arrive first, which disrupts the sequential turn-taking system.

Sometimes, a turn may connect to a prior comment several turns before; thus multiple threads can be twisted together, which could make reading and comprehending the conversation hard, especially when reviewing the chat logs later [29]. Several studies have postulated that disrupting sequential turns should generate communication confusions [10,21]. However, when examining the chat logs, researchers [12,20,23] typically find that little confusion actually arose in the chat. Participants use naming, overlapping terms, or utterance repetition to direct a comment when necessary. O'Neill and Martin [23] found that explicit disambiguation is not even used very often, because participants take it as a routine problem and can discern multiple threads very well.

One way to understand these contradictory arguments about text chat is to recognize that participants' experience of text chat may vary by situation. Voida [33] summarized five tensions between conventions of verbal and written communication in online chats and postulated that users' different interpretations of the mixed use of chat conventions may result in communication failure. In the situation of cross-cultural group chat, confusion and frustration might arise more easily, because non-native and native speakers' language proficiency and communication styles could be very different. Researchers [22] of second language learning have suggested that foreign students may feel overwhelmed and even lost in parallel and fast-flowing discussions, especially students who have slow keyboarding skills, slow reading/writing skills, or different cultural backgrounds. Little research has investigated how turn taking in text chat affects a mixed group of people consisting of non-native and native speakers, both how they are affected by the turn taking individually and how their interactions jointly shape the turn-taking system observed in cross-cultural text chat. In this paper, we tried to describe the cross-cultural communication process in order to build an understanding regarding these issues.

2.2 Language Proficiency as a Problem
In the past decade, much of the research in cross-cultural communication and collaboration has tested hypotheses regarding Hofstede's cultural dimensions [14] and Hall's high context/low con-

text culture concept [11]. These cultural factors provided explanations for cultural difference and were successfully used to interpret results in some work in the literature (see [30] and [34] for examples). However, these studies often neglect language proficiency differences between two cultures. For example, Chinese participants are typically described as "fluent or nearly fluent in English". Selection of fluent non-native speakers disguises any impact of language proficiency differences, but no one can deny language proficiency as a pervasive factor in non-native speakers' communication problems. According to Schmidt [26], the meaning of fluency does not have the same application for non-native speakers as it does for native speakers. For native speakers, fluency signifies a fluid speed in language use, and more than that a manifestation of the proficient command of the language, such as demonstrations of control over coherence, complexity and aesthetic functions of the language. For non-native speakers, it is often used as a rough synonym for global ability [18], an ability to make speech understood. In this paper, we show that lack of language proficiency affects non-native speakers, even when they are "fluent" in terms of communication success.

2.3 Communication Adaptation

If people are aware of cultural differences between them and other interlocutors, they may change their communication styles to adapt to other interlocutors. Communication accommodation theory [8] states that styles of communication may converge; speakers may shift their speech patterns toward other interlocutors so that they are more similar to each other. Anawati and Craig [1] describe a similar framework called behavior adaptation, which extends the kinds of accommodation in communication accommodation theory. Giles' communication accommodation theory only covers one aspect of accommodation behavior in cross-cultural communication – speakers may mimic other speakers' language use, so that their communication styles are similar. For example, in cross-cultural communication, a native speaker may speak slowly and keep words and sentences short to make his or her speech similar to a non-native speaker's language pattern.

Anawati and Craig used survey items and open-ended questions to investigate how team members adapt their behavior in spoken and written communication in cross-cultural virtual teams in a multinational company. They found that beyond the sorts of accommodation proposed by Giles [8], native speakers applied more strategies in cross-cultural encounters (see [1] for a complete list). For example, native speakers may list points and confirm understanding by asking questions to ensure that non-native speakers have the same level of understanding with them. They will also allow for "think time" between responses to give non-native speakers more time to digest and express ideas. These behaviors are not aimed at making speech similar but still are important strategies in cross-cultural collaborations. We also found such accommodations in our study, reinforcing the findings of Anawati and Craig. We further discussed how such accommodations affected group outcomes and design implications drawn from the analysis.

3. METHOD

We designed and conducted a mixed methods study [32] to investigate communication processes in distributed cross-cultural groups. In the literature of cross-cultural research in CSCW, researchers have been reporting contradictory results from quantitative studies. For example, Setlock et al. [27] reported that Chinese talked more in spoken conversation than in text chat, whereas Wang and Fussell [35] reported that Chinese talked less in spoken conversation than in text chat. Setlock and Fussell [28] analyzed possible reasons that could lead to these contrasting results, such as types of tasks and familiarity with certain communication tools; their interviews with 22 participants supported their analysis. Drawing from this earlier work, we expected that while we could use quantitative data to track behavioral patterns in conversations, qualitative measures would be important in explaining observed differences and understanding speakers' experiences.

3.1 Participants

We assembled five groups for study, each with two native speakers (Americans) and two non-native speakers (Chinese). After each session and set of interviews we did a preliminary coding of participants' reflections; we concluded the study after reaching the point of theoretical saturation [31], when themes were repeated in the data and no new themes were emerging.

We chose to study Chinese as the representative samples of non-native speakers because both their language and culture are very different from the western world; therefore they are likely to experience communication problems when communicating with people from the western world. We do not expect that our findings will be specific to Chinese non-native speakers, but future work will be needed to determine whether they apply to other non-native speaker populations.

The participants were undergraduate and graduate students from a large university in the Northeast United States; ages ranged from 20 to 43. There were 8 females and 12 males. Because we were not interested in gender effects, and to avoid gender-related social and communication dynamics, we ensured that all groups were of the same gender. Most of the native speakers had some experience collaborating with non-native speakers through group work (two Americans had no such experience). Some of the students had worked with non-native speakers in course projects in the past; some worked closely with non-native speakers.

3.2 Task

We adapted the task used by Freiermuth and Douglas [6], in which they studied non-native speakers' willingness to communicate in chat systems. We changed the theme of the task to a familiar topic for all of our participants. Specifically, we asked each participant to assume the role of a "Go Green" team member; they discussed how to spend $5000 to support environmental sustainability. Four participants formed a group to chat in AIM for 15 minutes. They were asked to come up to at least eight ideas and to decide on the best three. This manipulation was intended to create an intensive group discussion, so that any communication problems would be likely to emerge in 15 minutes.

3.3 Procedure

Upon arrival to the lab, each participant was led to a separate cubicle equipped with a computer. They were told that they were part of a group of four, but not informed of the other group members' nationality (e.g. non-native/native speakers). However, they may be able to infer such information from participants' screen names. After reading the consent form and the instructions, they were asked to fill out a background survey, then were given 15 minutes to chat as a group in AIM. After the task, they were asked to fill out a post-experiment survey. Finally, each of them participated in a follow-up interview separately.

Table 1. Coding scheme for online brainstorming task

Category I	Dialogue Act Codes		Category II
	Proposed solution		**Initiation**
	Questions about the problem *("Is the money for each one of the idea or all the three ideas?")*		
	Questions about solutions	**own** – the owner of the solution solicits opinions or additional information about the solution from others	
		other's – questions about other's solutions	**Response**
	Simple supportive comments *("I like that idea.")*		
	Simple critical comments *("I don't like that idea.")*		
	Acknowledgment – signals receipt of information *("yup")*		
	Supportive arguments *("I like that because ...")*		
	Critical arguments *("It's too expensive ...")*		
Elaboration	**Add information** – adds information (details, rationales, justifications, etc.) to others' solution		
	Problem clarifications – adds detail or new features to problem statement		
	Solution clarifications – adds information (details, rationales, justifications, etc.) to one's own solutions	**initiated by questions about solutions**	
		self motivated	**Initiation**
	Comments about the group process – positive, negative, or neutral comment about the interpersonal processes of the group		
	Uncodable text		

Notes: "add information", "acknowledgment" and sub-categories of "questions about solutions" and "solution clarifications" were added to the coding scheme. "Comments about the computer system" and "comments off the topic" were eliminated from the coding scheme due to rare occurrence in our data.

3.4 Survey

The post-experiment survey consisted of 10 questions adapted from Convertino's [4] work on quality and satisfaction of communication in virtual teams. (The survey can be found in [3]).

3.5 Interview Protocol

We conducted a semi-structured interview with each participant, spending approximately 30 minutes in discussion. The interview questions were guided by the three general themes below, but were open-ended enough that we could pursue new topics raised by the participant.

1. What was the most difficult thing in terms of communicating with the other group members?

2. What were the dynamics of the group's discussion?

3. What are the advantages and disadvantages of using the IM tool in this task?

Each interview was recorded and transcribed to text. Participants were interviewed in their first language. For interviews with Chinese participants, the transcriptions were translated back to English by the first author. The transcripts were then analyzed informally to discover themes related to cultural differences and communication difficulties.

3.6 Coding Scheme

We coded the chat logs in detail, so that we could carry out a quantitative analysis. We adapted a coding scheme developed for analysis of online brainstorming discussions about on-campus parking [7,16]. Table 1 shows our version of the coding scheme.

We generalized the codes in two different ways. Category I distinguishes codes that contain some form of elaboration in the expression. Category II divides codes into initiation and response roles in discussion. We first coded the chat logs according to the dialogue act codes (this includes the elaboration distinction), then reviewed them for initiation and response. This hierarchical coding strategy has enabled us to analyze the data at different levels but with consistent application of a basic set of dialogue acts. Two independent coders performed the coding task. Inter-coder reliability across the coding scheme for a sample log was satisfactory (Cohen's Kappa = 0.63).

4. DATA ANALYSIS

We found three themes from the interview transcripts – language fluency issues, impaired turn-taking system, and a slow down in group process. We used the findings from the interview data guide us to more detailed quantitative analysis when possible. Specifically, if an interesting valuable behavior or pattern was reflected from the interview data, we operationalized the behavior/pattern to consider the issue quantitatively. In the following we combine data from the surveys, interviews and chat logs to introduce and describe cross-cultural issues with respect to fluency, turn taking, and speaker accommodation.

4.1 Language Fluency

The ten non-native speakers are fluent in use of English. All have been living and studying in the U.S. for at least three years. Nine of them rated their English proficiency as advanced in the pre-experiment survey. One non-native speaker rated her English proficiency as intermediate. Advanced proficiency was defined as, "I can carry on a conversation with a native speaker of the language, although it is highly evident that I am not a native speaker of the language." Intermediate proficiency is defined as, "I can communicate with a native speaker of the language, although I find it difficult to do so; I can carry on a conversation with a native speaker of the language if (s)he speaks very slowly." Most of the non-native speakers also indicated in our interview that they could understand others' utterances without problems. Nonetheless, we learned from our interview data that language fluency affected non-native speakers negatively.

4.1.1 Slow in action

First, non-native speakers were slower in comprehending and expressing ideas, which discouraged their willingness to participate in intensive discussion. As one Chinese student said,

"Sometimes I felt like I couldn't express myself clearly. While I was thinking about how to express it, other people had been talking a lot, so I just listened to them." (Interviewee 7, Chinese)

Another Chinese student shared similar frustrations,

"Sometimes I wasn't sure how to say it in English, especially when many people were discussing, I missed the chance to speak out, after a while, I forgot it myself." (Interviewee 1, Chinese)

Although it seems that in text chat people can "begin new topics fairly much at will in a manner that would not happen in a formal face-to-face group discussion" as O'Neil said [23], this is not always the case. People still try to follow the habitual turn-taking rules from their everyday lives, because injecting new topics into the middle of discussion is thought to interrupt the group process:

"I found that several times when I was going to express my ideas, they already moved to the next topic. In this case, I would hold back my ideas, because I would slow down the discussion process. So I just followed them." (Interviewee 9, Chinese)

In such cases, when participants value group well-being and integrity more important than their fulfillment in the group, text chat may mute their voices because people are actively competing for turns and intensive short discussions can occur one by one.

This phenomenon was underscored by the speaking turns each participant had. For each person, turns was normalized as the number of turns of the person divided by the number of turns of the group, to factor out possible group differences caused by other factors. An independent sample t-test showed that non-native speakers' turns (M = 21.30, SD = 4.40) were significantly less than native speakers' turns (M = 28.50, SD = 3.34), t(18) = -4.12, p < 0.001. This result confirmed the interview data suggesting that non-native speakers were less participatory than native speakers.

4.1.2 Followers in group

Language proficiency enabled native speakers to dominate the chat in all five groups. When asked whether there was a leader in their group, everyone named one of the native speakers in their group. These individuals were able to control the conversation, such as that they "could easily move to the next topic" (Interviewee 10, Chinese) and could also respond more quickly, therefore they could easily hold the floor to talk. Some Chinese participants expressed negative feelings about being followers in the group,

"I couldn't control the conversation. The native speakers led the conversation, for example, what to discuss now, and how to discuss it. I just followed them. Because I needed some time to think

about how to express an idea, but they didn't give me the time." (Interviewee 8, Chinese)

This participant also shared her thoughts on why she wouldn't participate as actively as her American counterparts.

"If I were leading the discussion, I would think about how to express myself so that my language is not dry and rude. But if I only follow them, expressing my ideas or commenting theirs. I don't need to think as much."

This suggested that the asymmetric status in the cross-cultural groups could be related to one's proficiency of controlling a conversation. Non-native speakers do not only write or speak more slowly but also are less experienced in handling the coherence, complexity and aesthetic functions of a second language.

The post-experiment survey confirmed that non-native speakers experienced less control of the conversation. For one question participants rated whether they could control the conversation on a scale from 1 to 5 (1 = least level of control and 5 = highest). An independent sample t-test showed that non-native speakers' ratings (M = 2.60, SD = 0.84) were significantly lower than native speakers' ratings (M = 4.11, SD = 0.60), t(17) = -4.45, p < 0.001.

4.1.3 Concise in expression

Non-native speakers often produce less complicated words and shorter expressions than native speakers and we analyzed our data to determine if it was true in the group chat activity. In text chat, one cannot hold the floor for very long, so speakers must type quickly in general. As we discussed earlier, non-native speakers do not generate text as fast as native speakers, therefore they may choose to use efficient expressions, allowing them to quickly share their points. One extreme example of such efficient expression was reflected in an interview,

"I think the native speakers contributed more than us. First, they were faster. My problem was that my English wasn't fluent, so when I expressed an idea, I could only say some nouns. ... My two ideas were water and heating. I only said the two words, which were very vague, because I couldn't keep up in speed with them." (Interviewee 10, Chinese)

However, these ultra-efficient expressions were not received well by other participants. Sometimes, participants would not ask for elaborations; they expected the speaker to provide more information. If the speaker did not grab the chance to do this, his or her idea might not be picked up in the discussion. A native speaker shared what happened in his group,

"Because he (one of the non-native speakers) was not as expressive, if he didn't say much, we probably passed him by as native speakers." (Interviewee 3, American)

When we looked for confirming evidence in the chat logs, we found no significant difference in the frequency of elaborations provided by native and non-native speakers. As with analysis of turns, the likelihood of providing an elaboration was normalized as a person's number of turns coded as elaboration divided by the person's total number of the turns. However, when we examined the word count of individual's elaboration expressions, we found that native speakers were significantly more elaborative than non-native speakers, t(18) = -4.45, p < 0.001. (Note that we also normalized individual word counts by the word count of the group, to factor out possible group difference caused by other factors).

This result suggested that the problem was not a difference in non-native speakers' communication or thinking style. If they had preferred to initiate new ideas but not to develop ideas "on the table", the resulting lack of discussion might impair the outcome of the group's decision making. However, this was not the case in our study: non-native speakers allocated a similar percent of their effort in elaboration of ideas. The problem here was that non-native speakers were concise in the elaborations they offered, making their arguments easier to ignore (as the American student observed).

In sum, these examples reinforce the point we made at the beginning of this section, namely that the root of the non-native speakers' participation problems was that they were slower in using English. Our detailed analysis has shown that these language delays produced different types of problems, from perceptions of slowness, to the tendency to follow rather than lead, and to very short elaborations that were easy to pass over.

4.2 Turn-Taking

The chat logs revealed that parallel discussions were prevalent in these cross-cultural groups. Table 2 summarizes the parallel discussion episodes in the five chat logs. The numbers in the middle column refer to the index number of an idea and the parenthesis indicates that initiation or response of one idea was interleaved between responses of another idea. For example, (4 5) refers to a series of utterances during which the discussion of idea #4 and idea #5 crossed over each other.

Table 2. Summary of parallel discussions in chat logs

Group	Parallel Discussion Point	Total Number of Ideas
1	(4 5) (8 9) (11 12)	12
2	(2 3 4 5) (6 7 8 9)	9
3	(1 2 3) (5 6)	11
4	(1 2 3 4 5 6 7 8)	9
5	(1 2 3 4 5 6 7 8)	10

The table shows that a large proportion of ideas were discussed in parallel with other ideas in all group chats. Especially in group 4 and group 5, many ideas were introduced before previous ideas were finished. The participants in these discussions shared their frustrations, causing us to analyze the parallel discussions in more detail. In this, we focused particularly on how language proficiency affected this style of communication, and how native and non-native speakers coped with the associated challenges.

We found two types of disruptions in the chat logs. One case was when people initiated new ideas. People tended to express an idea in several short turns as opposed to saying it all in one turn (e.g., as you might expect in a face-to-face setting). As we discussed earlier, participants were competing for the floor by entering their ideas as fast as they could. In the chat logs, we observed a frequent pattern wherein a proposed solution was closely followed by several solution clarifications. Although this might not generate any confusion in face-to-face conversation because people could tell whether the speaker finished talking from non-verbal cues (eye contact, gestures, tones, etc), it confused interlocutors in text chat, as they don't know whether the speaker is continuously writing more elaborations or is done with the topic. One participant shared his hesitation in joining a discussion,

"It's hard to know who was taking turns speaking while preparing to speak. It's rude to take control of the conversation; it's rude to talk over someone. If there is a clear break, it's kind of hard to figure out whether you should take a pause to be, you know they are done saying something versus they are thinking over a problem." (Interviewee 17, American)

In these cross-cultural groups, people seemed to be more hesitant when taking turns because they were not familiar with the other culture's communication style, thus making it harder for them to take turns at the right time. This may be a common feeling among native speakers communicating with non-native partners. Although we did not inform participants about their group members' cultural affiliations, all of them said that they were aware of the cultural difference. Some said that they figured it out by names, and some by "the length of expressions and word choice". A native speaker reflected his feeling about hesitation of communication in their group.

"I think there's a little bit hesitation on everyone's part, because we were aware of the cultural difference." (Interviewee 3, American)

In the chat logs, we found that speakers often initiated new topics before the previous speaker finished his/hers. This caused multiple topics to be active at around the same time. Group members might be drawn to one topic and respond to it, but they might also shift from topic to topic to participate in several. One participant contrasted this to face-to-face turn-taking ,

"In face to face, usually there's only one person talking, so obviously all three other people are listening to that one person. While you are chatting, you can have four different people saying different things in the same time. Then you have to go back and read that. So it's almost like there are four separate conversations going on." (Interviewee 11, American)

Although parallel discussions were prevalent in the text chat, most native speakers seemed to have little problem with this, saying that "it's what text chat is" or "I'm used to it". This finding is consistent with related findings in the literature. In contrast, some of the non-native speakers were bothered by the intertwined, "messy" discussions. Several non-native speakers complained that ideas were neglected in the discussions. They at times attributed this to the disrupted turn-taking system, as in the following comment,

"The most difficult thing in this group discussion was that we didn't know whether others were following the last topic or the newly initiated topic. It happened a lot of times that the three of us were discussing a topic, while the fourth person threw a new topic, which was hard to follow, because we hardly noticed her idea, or even we noticed her idea, we still wanted to finished the last topic, in such case the fourth person's idea was easy to get ignored." (Interviewee 15, Chinese)

The following example illustrates a similar case, although in this case it seemed that the non-native speakers' concise way of stating her points might have interacted with the challenges of an intensive parallel discussion.

"Two of my ideas were ignored, one is growing green plants on roof tops, and the other is coating windows to cool down room temperature. I simply stated my points, but there was another discussion at the same time, so they only noticed that one instead of mine." (Interviewee 9, Chinese)

Another Chinese participant said she did not want her fellow Chinese participant's ideas to be neglected, so she shifted back to these undiscussed ideas several times during the chat. But this meant that the parallel discussion took place in the context of much later content. This sort of "long distance" disruption occurred quite often in the chat logs, as we discuss below.

A second type of disruption occurred when people responded to an idea posted by someone else. There was always some delay in these responses, simply because one can only respond to a turn after it was posted. While a response is being typed, there might be several other messages posted. So when multiple topics were present, the responses to the different topics could mix up.

Several native speakers mentioned that they missed some points in the multithread discussion, like this participant said,

"There's no immediate feedback, so like someone said something, I want to respond to that, and by the time I typed it and sent it, somebody already posted something else. So I think keeping in step with the conversation can be difficult, I kept looking back who's responding to what line. Sometimes I still respond, sometimes I just let it go." (Interviewee 14, American)

Another native speaker told us how he coped with a point that they missed earlier,

"I know a lot of times five or six messages could go all at once, while I was typing and look up the screen there were already five to six, easy to be mixed up. Like one of the ideas I completely missed, I had to go back and look over it again." (Interviewee 11, American)

The problem of delayed response occurred more often among non-native speakers because of their low competency in language proficiency, as one of the Chinese participants said,

"Our speed was much slower than them (the native speakers). They typed very fast, a lot of times they already sent several messages, while we were still typing a response to the message several lines above." (Interviewee 15, Chinese)

Sometimes the non-native speakers might be so far behind the discussion that they could even drop out of the conversation like we reported at the beginning of section 4.1. To the contrary, the native speakers seemed to be able to manage the turn-taking system although with an extra cost. We observed that native speakers had a number of coping strategies for dealing with out-of-sequence responses. They had techniques for referring to the point they wanted to comment on, for example they might quickly reiterate a point, reuse some key words, use a group member's name to direct their responses, and so on. However, non-native speakers were less likely to exhibit these strategies, perhaps because their command of the language was still rather limited.

To sum it up, multithreaded discussions and disrupted turns were common in the chat logs. Native speakers were not affected much because these patterns occur often in chat systems and they had learned coping strategies from their past experience. Non-native speakers were less competitive in such discussions, because they were generally slower in using the language. This in turn might worsen the situation: the longer they took to finish an idea (e.g., over several turns) or to respond to a previous turn would further disrupt the overall coherence of the conversation.

4.3 Communication Accommodation

Several native speakers who reported that they had closely worked with non-native speakers also indicated that they made changes in communication style to accommodate the non-native group members. In general, they slowed their speed to adopt the same tempo as the non-native speakers. For example,

"In the past when I worked with non-native speakers, there's like a reluctance I see for them to pipe up and bring up their ideas, like talk openly in a group. I don't know, maybe I worked with so many, but I tried to slow things down to make sure they have a chance to talk." (Interviewee 17, American)

Giving non-native speakers more chance to talk and more time to think was one accommodation applied by these native speakers. The following two native speakers of group 1 revealed how they implemented this in their group chat:

"I would give 20 seconds at least before I start talking. I usually tried to give a pause, everybody could think about it before I keep on typing, especially if it's a new idea, so everybody can think about it." (Interviewee 4, American)

"I think we try to give people a lot more time to express themselves. The native speakers probably would have chatted a lot more and a lot quicker, whereas the non-natives maybe took a little bit more time to make sure that they were expressing their ideas correctly and if their ideas would be accepted in the ways they were expressed." (Interviewee 3, American)

The left side of Figure 1 visualizes conversation patterns consistent with the strategy mentioned by the two native speakers from group 1. It can be contrasted to the conversation of group 3 (right side of figure), in which none of the native speakers mentioned accommodation to the non-native speakers in the chat.

To create these visualizations, we calculated the number of words expressed by each interlocutor per minute (this is analogous to calculating the density of a signal). A higher value means that the interlocutor is intensively talking during that time slot. A lower value means that the interlocutor is relatively inactive in the given time slot. We suggest that the contour of a line connecting these values depicts a "conversational rhythm" for that person. Our intuition was that if the native speakers did accommodate non-native speakers as they said in the interview, we should see a reciprocal pattern such that when non-native speakers were contributing a lot of words, native speakers would be less talkative; when non-native speakers were less talkative, native speakers would return to their normal levels of talkativeness. In our initial analysis, we found similarity within native and non-native pairs but dissimilarities across cultures. This finding is consistent with Wang and Fussell's [35] observation of sub-groups in cross-cultural groups. In their study of a mixed group of Chinese and American participants, members from the same culture were often conversationally close and the two cultural sub-groups within the group were often conversationally far away.

To compare native and non-native speakers' conversational trend, we summed the two non-native speakers' words per minute, and did the same for the two native speakers. Figure 1 (a) shows the conversational trend for group 1. We can see that when the non-native speakers were at their high points, the native speakers were often at their low points. And, whenever the non-native speakers were at their low points, the native speakers' chat density increases. We can also see exceptions to this tendency, for example around minute 10, both non-native and native speakers were engaged in the chat actively; we expect that at times it is normal and reasonable for native speakers to respond fast. However the general trend convinced us that there were communication accommodations in this group, especially in contrast to group 3.

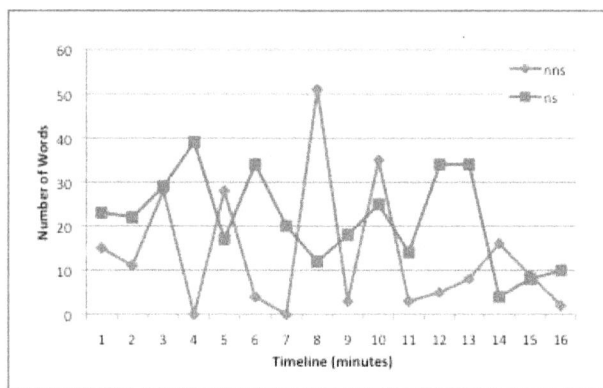

(a) Group 1.

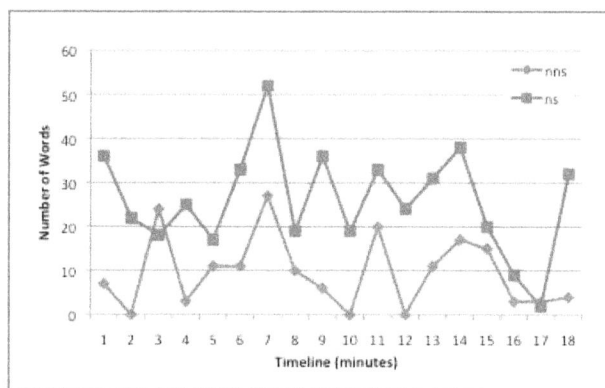

(b) Group 3.

Figure 1. Conversation trend of non-native and native speakers in group chat. Y-axis denotes the number of words in the given time slot (in our analysis is one minute), x-axis denotes the timeline in minutes. Red square trend represents the two native speakers, blue diamond represents the two non-native speakers.

No one in group 3 mentioned any accommodation to group members in their communication. In fact, two ideas from a non-native speaker ideas were neglected, which suggested that the native speakers might not have been as aware of the cultural difference, especially the non-native speakers' language limitations in the communication. Looking at Figure 1 (b), it seems that non-native speakers were in a sense "out-talked" during the discussion. In general the contours have the same shape, but the native speakers' density is almost always greater. Note that the trend of the two lines looked similar at minute 7 and minutes 11 to 15, except that the native speakers' line was much higher than the non-native speakers' line. A review of the chat log showed that the two time slots were just when the two parallel discussions happened. It's when one of the non-native speakers proposed his two solutions and the native speakers were discussing the other three solutions, they just talked passed him. It's worth noting that this non-native speaker's communication satisfaction rate (2.75) was clearly lower than other participants (mean rate was 3.95) and other non-native participants (mean rate was 4.00). This finding suggested that communication accommodation should be encouraged in cross-cultural group chat for the wellbeing of non-native speakers.

Note that despite the interview comments, it is possible that it is the *non-native* speakers who are accommodating to the *native* speakers (e.g., increasing their density when the native speakers pause to think). To better assess whether the accommodation was from the native speakers or from the non-native speakers or both, we used a technique known as the Granger causality test [9], a statistical test of the causal relationship between two time series. The test assesses whether the lagged values of time series X can improve the prediction of time series Y. If the improvement is significant, we can say that X **Granger causes** Y. This differs from a correlation test, in that the causality relationship between X and Y can be asymmetric. That is we might find that X can Granger cause Y, but Y cannot Granger cause X; or vice versa.

To carry out this analysis, we treated a single turn as the series unit; thus the entire set of turns of the conversation composed a time line. For each participant at each turn, if this person did not own the turn, we coded '0'; if this person owned the turn and had an 'initiation' dialogue act code, we coded '1'; if this person owned the turn and had a 'response' dialogue act code, we coded

'-1'. By doing so, we converted a participant's dialogue acts into a dialogue time series of 0, 1 or -1. For example, one native speaker from group 1 enacted the dialogue series for the first 5 turns in the discussion. When the Granger causality test is run on such series, an assessment is made for a specified "lag" in the two series being compared; in our series, a lag of 1 would refer to prediction of the very next turn, a lag of 2 would be the turn after next, and so on.

We first tested Granger causality between each possible combination of group members in group 1; we found that the turns of non-native speakers Granger caused those of native speakers but not vice versa; there was also no Granger causality within culture. To simplify – and to make a clearer connection to the chat density visualizations discussed earlier - we merged the series from the two non-native speakers and did the same for the native speakers. Table 3 shows the Granger causality test results of group 1, run with three different lag parameters. It clearly shows that non-native speakers' dialogue acts predicted native speakers' dialogue acts, but not vice versa. This suggested that native speakers did accommodate to non-native speakers in conversation as suggested in the interviews. We also analyzed group 3 for comparison as seen in Table 4. None of the relationships are significant for group 3, suggesting that there was no communication accommodation in this group.

Table 3. Granger causality test results (p-value) of group 1

Lag	Non-native -> Native	Native -> Non-native
1	0.17	0.41
2	**0.01**[**]	0.56
3	**0.05**[*]	0.46

Table 4. Granger causality test results (p-value) of group 3

Lag	Non-native -> Native	Native -> Non-native
1	0.71	0.32
2	0.84	0.65
3	0.90	0.58

Note that while it seems that communication accommodation for non-native speakers should enhance their positive experience in group chat, at the same time it may slow down the group process and thus may impair conversation efficiency, and perhaps even outcomes if time to communicate is restricted. This comment from a native speaker revealed that he would generally try to hold back his ideas when accommodating the non-native speakers:

"I tried not to talk when I can to give everybody a chance, even if it's quiet, I would sit this out and hang around to see whether someone else would pick it. ... I had a couple ideas but I tried to only kind of go in turn as much as possible so that everybody had a chance. I know there's always chances later, coz I had them in my head the entire time, so I knew if we had time till the end then I would go for it. But usually I tried to hold back" (Interviewee 4, American)

Given the time limits, which exist for most discussions more or less, a slow group process would produce fewer outcomes. But from the above interview, we can see that at least one native speaker may be willing to accommodate non-native speakers' speed even at a potential cost of reduced group outcomes.

Although several native speakers mentioned the strategy of accommodating to non-native speakers, only group 1 evinced a clear pattern of "holding back." This does not mean that other speakers did not accommodate, but perhaps they did so less pervasively, or perhaps one native speaker accommodated but the other did not. From the interview comments, it seems clear that this is a strategy that is learned by native speakers through experience with non-native conversation partners. It would be interesting to consider whether there are also inverse accommodations by non-native speakers; for example perhaps they would learn to "hold on" to their ideas, then to be opportunistic and jump in as soon as a native speaker pauses and gives up the floor.

5. CAVEATS AND LIMITATIONS

Because studies of cross-cultural communication have provided little detailed analysis of language proficiency and its impacts, we used mixed methods to gather as rich a dataset as possible. However we recognize that our observations come from a relatively small number of groups, and that the configural effects of a group may be very large. Extensive quantitative analyses are not appropriate for small samples such as this, so we have introduced these in only a few cases where they help to make a point suggested by the qualitative data. A more extensive study would be needed for a systematic investigation of the patterns we have described.

We also noted that many of our participants had prior experience with cross-cultural group work; this almost certainly would have affected the ways in which they communicated. Indeed the comments we shared about communication accommodation referred explicitly to prior experience of this sort. On the one hand, this makes it difficult to generalize our findings to groups with less experience. But on the other, it has allowed us in this exploratory study to observe phenomena that might be part of a more stable repertoire of cross-cultural communication practices.

6. DISCUSSION

We conducted a study of cross-cultural group chat that used a mix of qualitative and quantitative data collection and analysis. By combining across data from surveys, interviews, and chat logs, we were able to provide a detailed view of how native and non-native speakers coordinated their conversations, focusing particularly on issues of language proficiency, turn taking, and communication

accommodation. As part of this, we have shown how a time series statistical test can be used to assess relationships among different speakers or pairs of speakers. Our primary goal in this paper has been to document communication patterns and experiences, so that we and other researchers can investigate them in more detail in the future. However, we also believe that our findings have implications for the design of tools that might enhance cross-cultural group chat; we now turn to a discussion of these ideas.

One pervasive difference between native and non-native speakers was in the speed and corresponding density of communication. To some extent, this may be impossible to eliminate, as the non-native speakers are simply less fluent. Indeed, one might expect to see similar differences among native speakers who vary in some aspect of fluency (e.g., children versus adults, or skilled versus unskilled typists). However we also reported that at least some native speakers had learned accommodation strategies, and it is interesting to speculate about how such strategies might be encouraged more broadly. Perhaps a simple awareness display of group members' chat density could help individuals to notice the asymmetries; this in turn might encourage them to slow down or reduce the length of their turns – at least until time pressure causes them to shift their focus to group outcomes.

Our data showed that the turn-taking system in cross-cultural group chat was severely disrupted. The disruption was particularly problematic for the non-native speakers. The design implication is that participants need some sort of regulation or new mechanisms to repair these disruptions. For example, O'Neil and Martin [23] suggested use of an access-control rule such that when one interlocutor starts typing, others are blocked from typing. This regulation enforces the sequential turn-taking mechanism in spoken conversation, however it will significantly slow down the communication process. And it will introduce the same kind of time pressure in spoken conversation to text chat; therefore it diminishes the value of text chat being more free and flexible to interlocutors. Smith et al. [29] proposed a threaded chat design, in which a response turn is entered under an existing thread just like posting replies to a thread in forums. However, this would considerably change the natural flow of conversations in text chat. Moreover, people may not know the current topic in discussion like in every conversation. Therefore, they may more easily generate parallel discussions.

We suggest instead some mechanism for thread control that does supports turn taking while minimally affecting the natural flow of the conversation. We envision a side bar of the chat window in which users can enter responses to a turn right besides it. Users' responses can be stacked up in such a side pane, somewhat like a threaded chat. The difference is that the side bar minimizes the interruption to the flow of the conversation; it would be used only when interlocutors see a need to do so. In addition to responses, interlocutors might also note new ideas in such a side bar, especially those they hold back from the main conversation but may still want to talk about them later. We are currently exploring a design for such a mechanism and will be developing and evaluating it in the near future.

7. CONCLUSION

In this paper, we explored the communication process and participants' experience in cross-cultural group chat using IM. We identified a number of problems in this setting. We found that these communication problems were commonly caused by one fundamental problem: non-native and native speakers were conversing at different tempos. We observed that the turn-taking system in text chat was severely disrupted due to these differences in conversational tempo. Both non-native and native speakers expressed their discomfort with these problems in many ways, such as hesitation of talking, lost in parallel discussions, or simply reduced satisfaction with the group experience.

On the non-native speakers' side, we observed a greater amount of the negative experiences, stemming from their reduced language proficiency. They could not control the conversation and their ideas were at times neglected during parallel discussions. On the native speakers' side, we observed them to be less affected by the language differences and in fact at times evinced positive efforts to accommodate non-native speakers. However, we also noted that such accommodation might impair the performance outcomes of a group. Based on these findings, we analyzed how existing chat systems limit cross-cultural group chat and discussed options for future research or tool design. In our ongoing work, we are designing and evaluating an augmented IM tool aimed at assisting both native and non-native speakers in group chat.

8. ACKNOWLEDGEMENT

We thank our participants for their active participation and valuable inputs. We also want to thank Changkun Zhao for coding part of the chat logs and many inspiring discussions.

REFERENCES

[1] Anawati, D. and Craig, A. Behavioral adaptation within cross-cultural virtual teams. *IEEE T. Prof. Commun.*, 49, 1 (2006), 44-56.

[2] Clark, H. H. and Brennan, S. E. Grounding in communication. In *Perspectives on Socially Shared Cognition*, L. B. Resnick, J. M. Levine and S. D. Teasley, American Psychological Association, (1991), 127-149.

[3] Convertino, G. Survey Questions. http://cscl.ist.psu.edu/public/projects/crossculturecollab/quest.html

[4] Convertino, G., Asti, B., Zhang, Y., Rosson, M. B. and Mohammed, S. Board-based collaboration in cross-cultural pairs. In *Proc. CHI '06 extended abstracts on Human Factors in Computing Systems*, ACM, New York, NY (2006).

[5] Convertino, G., Mentis, H. M., Rosson, M. B., Slavkovic, A. and Carroll, J. M. Supporting content and process common ground in computer-supported teamwork. In *Proc. CHI '09*, ACM, New York, NY (2009).

[6] Freiermuth, M. and Jarrell, D. Willingness to communicate: can online chat help? *International Journal of Applied Linguistics*, 16, 2 (2006), 189-212.

[7] Gettys, C. F., Pliske, R. M., Manning, C. and Casey, J. T. An evaluation of human act generation performance. *Organ. Behav. Hum. Dec.*, 39, 1 (1987), 23-51.

[8] Giles, H., Coupland, J. and Coupland, N. *Contexts of Accomodation: Developments in Applied Sociolinguistics*. Cambridge University Press, 1991.

[9] Granger, C. W. J. Investigating Causal Relations by Econometric Models and Cross-spectral Methods. *Econometrica*, 37, 3 (1969), 424-438.

[10] Hale, C. *Wired Style: Principles of English Usage in the Digital Age*. Hardwired, San Francisco, 1997.

[11] Hall, E. T. *Beyond Culture*. Knopf Doubleday Publishing Group, 1976.

[12] Herring, S. C. Interactional coherence in CMC. In *Proc. HICSS '99*, IEEE Computer Society (1999).

[13] Herring, S. C. *Computer-Mediated Communication: Linguistic, Social and Cross-Cultural Perspectives*. John Benjamins Pub Co, 1996.

[14] Hofstede, G. *Cultures Consequences*. Sage Pulications, INC, 1980.

[15] Isaacs, E., Walendowski, A., Whittaker, S., Schiano, D. J. and Kamm, C. The character, functions, and styles of instant messaging in the workplace. In *Proc. CSCW '02*, ACM, New York, NY (2002).

[16] Jessup, L. M., Connolly, T. and Galegher, J. The effects of anonymity on GDSS group process with an idea-generating task. *MIS Quarterly*, 14, 3 (1990), 313-321.

[17] Johnson, G. Synchronous and Asynchronous Text-Based CMC in Educational Contexts: A Review of Recent Research. *TechTrends*, 50, 4 (2006), 46-53.

[18] Lennon, P. Investigating fluency in EFL: A quantitative approach. *Language Learning*, 40, 3 (1990), 387-417.

[19] Levinson, S. C. *Pragmatics*. Cambridge University Press, 1983.

[20] McDaniel, S. E., Olson, G. M. and Magee, J. C. Identifying and analyzing multiple threads in computer-mediated and face-to-face conversations. In *Proc. CSCW '96*, ACM, New York, NY (1996).

[21] McGrath, J. E. Time matters in groups. In *Intellectual Teamwork*, G. Jolene, E. K. Robert and E. Carmen, L. Erlbaum Associates Inc., (1990), 23-61.

[22] Mynard, J. Introducing EFL students to chat rooms. *The Internet TESL Journal*, 8, 2 (2002).

[23] O'Neill, J. and Martin, D. Text chat in action. In *Proc. GROUP '03*, ACM, New York, NY (2003).

[24] Sacks, H., Schegloff, E. and Jefferson, G. A simplest systematics for the organization of turn-taking for conversation. *Language*, 50, 4 (1974), 696-735.

[25] Schegloff, E. Discourse as an interactional achievement: Some uses of 'uh huh' and other things that come between sentences. In *Analyzing discourse: Text and talk*, D. Tannen, Georgetown University Press, Washington DC (1982), 71-93.

[26] Schmidt, R. Psychological mechanisms underlying second language fluency. *Studies in Second Language Acquisition*, 14(1992), 357-385.

[27] Setlock, L. D., Fussell, S. R. and Neuwirth, C. Taking it out of context: collaborating within and across cultures in face-to-face settings and via instant messaging. In *Proc. CSCW '04*, ACM, New York, NY (2004).

[28] Setlock, L. D. and Fussell, S. R. What's it worth to you?: the costs and affordances of CMC tools to asian and american users. In *Proc. CSCW '10*, ACM, New York, NY (2010).

[29] Smith, M., Cadiz, J. J. and Burkhalter, B. Conversation trees and threaded chats. In *Proc. CSCW '00*, ACM, New York, NY (2000).

[30] Stewart, C. O., Setlock, L. D. and Fussell, S. R. Conversational argumentation in decision making: Chinese and U.S. participants in face-to-face and instant-messaging interactions. *Discourse Processes*, 44, 2 (2007), 113-139.

[31] Strauss, A. L. and Corbin, J. M. *Basics of Qualitative Research: Techniques and Procedures for Developing Grounded Theory*. Sage Publications, Thousand Oaks, CA, 2008.

[32] Tashakkori, A. and Teddlie, C. B. *Handbook of Mixed Methods Social and Behavioral Research*. Sage Publications, 2002.

[33] Voida, A. *Exploring a technological hermeneutic: Understanding the interpretation of computer-mediated messaging systems*. Dissertation, Georgia Institute of Technology, Atlanta, 2008.

[34] Wang, H.-C., Fussell, S. F. and Setlock, L. D. Cultural difference and adaptation of communication styles in computer-mediated group brainstorming. In *Proc. CHI '09*, ACM, New York, NY (2009).

[35] Wang, H.-C. and Fussell, S. Groups in groups: conversational similarity in online multicultural multiparty brainstorming. In *Proc. CSCW '10*, ACM, New York, NY (2010).

Augmenting Classroom Participation through Public Digital Backchannels

Honglu Du, Mary Beth Rosson, John M. Carroll
College of Information Sciences & Technology
University Park, PA, USA
{hzd106, mrosson, jcarroll}@ist.psu.edu

ABSTRACT

An emerging trend in classroom technology research is the use of computer mediated communication (CMC) tools in classrooms to encourage students' in-class participation. As part of this research thread, we have been investigating the potential of *public digital backchannels* for building feelings of community among students in university courses. We designed, deployed and evaluated such a tool in a 15-week field study of two undergraduate classes. We found students found using public backchannel during the class is of little distraction, that teachers' attention to the content posted on the channel influence students' tendency to use tools of this kind. Further, we found that the relevance of the content shared is predictive of students' use of ClasCommons in the classroom; these feelings in turn are related to students' perceptions of self-efficacy, collective efficacy and course-specific social support. We also analyzed the content posted in the public backchannel and considered the benefits and drawbacks of the public digital from both students' and teachers' perspectives. We conclude with suggestions for improving the design and deployment of course-related backchannels.

Categories and Subject Descriptors

H5.3. Group and Organization Interfaces: Web-based interaction.

General Terms

Design, Experimentation.

Keywords

Backchannel, sense of community, public display.

1. INTRODUCTION

In many college classrooms, students are passive spectators. The professor arrives and gives a lecture; students learn individually by listening and taking notes. This model of teaching in classes is called the transmittal model whereby students learn by passively receiving knowledge from the teacher. However, according to social-constructivist theories of learning, knowledge cannot be simply pulled from textbooks or "poured" from teachers' heads to students' heads. Instead knowledge is constructed by engaging individual learners to actively apply prior knowledge when making sense of new information, allowing the new content to be further elaborated as knowledge embedded in their minds. Under this theoretical perspective, the knowledge construction process is influenced by the surrounding community in which a learner operates (i.e., her social context). In contrast to the transmittal model in which students are passive information recipients, the social constructivist model places students at the center of the learning process – they operate as active learners[1, 2]. Currently, active learning has been recommended as one of the seven principles for good practices in undergraduate education[3].

Many active learning techniques have focused on participation in a range of in-class activities like discussion, writing and talking. Class discussion (including discussion, debate, questioning, explaining, etc.) is often noted as a common and effective strategy for promoting active learning[3]. However, there is evidence that the typical university classroom setting includes obstacles for maximum effectiveness of active learning techniques like class-wide discussions. For example, it is common to find in university classes that (a) vocal students consume most of the scarce in-class discussion time; (b) the teacher acts as a "sage on the stage," controlling everything going on in the class; (c) some students may have negative feelings if they are called on by surprise; and (d) some students suppress their question until the end of the class.

In this paper, we present a design and empirical evaluation of a public digital backchannel discussion tool – ClassCommons – to encourage students' participation and examine students' sense of community over an extended period of time.

2. RELATED WORK

The term "backchannel" is used to describe a non-primary communication channel between speakers and listeners, through which feedback is given from listeners to speakers in unintrusive ways to show interest, attention and other reactions [4]. Examples of face-to-face backchannels are body language like eyebrow raising or brief requests for clarification (e.g., "What?") or confirmation (e.g., "Right."). Research has shown that backchannels are important for maintaining communication efficiency[5].

In classrooms, students can use backchannels to interact with the teacher in an efficient and unintrusive manner. For example students use backchannels when they nod their heads to show that they understand a topic being discussed or they shake their heads to indicate that they do not understand it, and the teacher may adjust his or her lecture based on such feedback. However as the size of audience increases, backchannels are harder to establish and the communication between the speaker and the audience loses quality. It is hard for a speaker to perceive multiple simultaneous feedbacks from different listeners; visual signals are quickly lost in a crowd [6]. As a result, speakers tend to focus only on a few audience members and their individual backchannels. In situations with a large audience (e.g., a large lecture class), it is common that just a few individuals engage actively in backchannel communications with the speaker.

In studies of computer-mediated communication, the concept of backchannel has been expanded to denote an online chat that runs in parallel to other communication activities. For example, while the instructor is giving lecture in the front, students may be using a backchannel to talk to each other at the same time using IM or an online chat room. Yardi reported an analysis of such chat logs and found evidence that the backchannel discussion supported peer-to-peer learning[7].

More generally, researchers and educators have explored a range of technology interventions that might facilitate interaction between the teachers and students in classrooms. While there are multiple researches on using backchannel to support audience participation in conferences[8], in this review, we only focus on related work in classroom settings. For instance, classroom response systems allow the teacher to present multiple choice or true/false questions; students can then respond to these with specialized handheld "voting" devices, perhaps resulting in a public display of aggregated results [9-11]. While such systems can increase class participation, they have drawbacks. First, they need special hardware, typically purchased by or provided for each student. Second, the teacher-student interaction is very structured and limited. The instructor cannot obtain a rich understanding of what students are thinking. Third, interactions occur only at the teacher's initiative. While a touted benefit of using these systems is to support students who are too shy to speak up in class, it is still the teacher who initiates the interaction. Students continue to be relatively passive actors who react to teacher-initiated issues.

Other text-based classroom technologies offer students an opportunity to engage in richer interactions with the instructor. Active Class uses PDAs for classroom communication: students can post text questions to the teacher during lectures, using a handheld device. A teaching assistant (TA) may respond to these questions during class, or the teacher may choose to address some questions. When this system was used in undergraduate computer sciences classes, the researchers found that it helped teachers get timely feedback from the students, overcame student apprehension in large classes, and enabled multiple students to ask questions at the same time[12].

Classroom Presenter extended the concept of a backchannel by allowing students to annotate a slide being discussed by the teacher; the resulting notes are publicly displayed in the classroom. A trial of this system found that it increased class participation in classes from multiple disciplines [13, 14]. The Harvard Live Question Tool allows students to submit answers to questions that are raised by the teacher; the answers are displayed publicly in the class. No formal evaluations have been conducted to study the impact of this tool, although it has been recommended by Educause as an effective way to encourage students' participation and students-teacher interaction[15].

Fragmented Social Mirrors (FSM) [6] is another tool that was investigated as a public backchannel in classrooms. Students can post messages during the lecture; they can also indicate whether the message is a question, or if they simply want the instructor to slow down. The message is projected on a separate screen in the classroom. The system was tested in 6 class sessions (3 of them used FSM and the other 3 did not use FSM) and found that FSM encouraged students' initiatives in classrooms.

The studies cited above have evaluated the effects of classroom backchannels, but only for a limited period of time (usually 1-2 class periods), leaving longer term impacts unknown. Also, it is not yet clear what factors may influence students' willingness to adopt such tools in their classes. Thirdly, although researchers have discussed the advantages of using public backchannels in classrooms, less attention has been paid to the potential problems with such technology. This study aims to fill these gaps in this field of research. The current research benefits from a long term implementation and deployment of a classroom public backchannel tool in two classes. We seek to find the answers to questions including the factors influencing students' adoption of this kind of tool, its long term impact on students' sense of community, and the benefits and drawbacks of tools of this kind in classrooms.

3. CLASSCOMMONS

The design of ClassCommons is drawn from a general design concept wherein people are offered a common interaction space to interact with one another virtually while in a shared physical environment. Thus the design requirements for ClassCommons are relatively simple: accept input from students, present students' submitted content in a controlled fashion, and manage the display of this input. The ClassCommons system accomplishes this with three basic components; there is a client device (any device with web browsing capability can be used, e.g., web-enabled mobile phones, laptops), a server and a large public display.

The goals of ClassCommons are similar to the impromptu backchannel activity studied by Yardi [7], but the tool differs in the following respect: the backchannel discussion is public, whereas in the Yardi study students simply talked to each other without any teacher involvement. In fact, ClassCommons emphasizes the public nature of the chat by integrating a large display visible to all.

Previous studies of ClassCommons found that students used ClassCommons to socialize with peers, make suggestions for course changes, share information, and seek help, facilitating feelings of community[16, 17]. The system used in this study is an improved version of the earlier prototype. Usability bugs (e.g., display readability) were addressed and new features were added, including: a) options to post emoticons, videos and photos; b) a liking function; c) threaded interaction; and d) public anonymity and private accountability (PAPA). Further, the previous studies were short term study and it was only evaluated in 2 class periods, leaving the long term impact unknown.

Any device with access to the Internet can be a client. To contribute, students log in to a posting website (Figure 1) with their university account and credentials. Students can post text messages, images and Youtube videos from the client interface. Students can choose to post with their real name or enter an alias when posting. The messages students post are shown on the public display in the front of the classroom. Students can reply to messages already posted on the client interface and can "like" individual messages.

The number after Like on Figure 2 indicates how many students have liked that message.

The messages are displayed in real time on the public display, viewable to all the students as well as the teacher in the classroom. In the current version, messages are displayed in a "First In First Out" (FIFO) fashion, namely the messages posted earlier are displayed first. The most recent message appears at the top the public display with a red new icon in the front. Whenever a new message is posted, older messages will be pushed downward. If a video or image is posted, a thumbnail of the video/image will be displayed at the right side of the display. The instructor can then decide whether to play the video or not in the class. Figure 2 shows the layout of the public display.

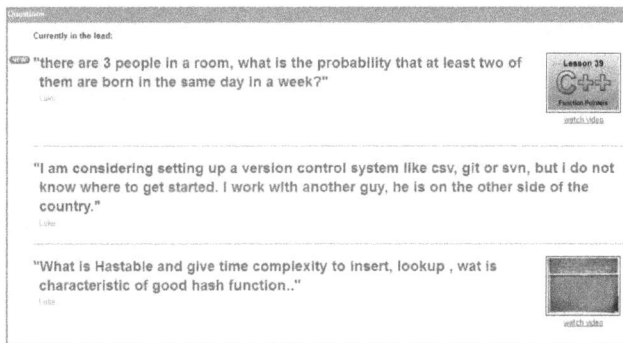

Figure 1. Client Interface of ClassCommons

Figure 2. Public display view of ClassCommons

Public Anonymity and Private Accountability (PAPA): The system implements a policy known as public anonymity and private accountability (PAPA). Students can choose whether to use their real name or enter an alias when posting a message. However if a student uses an alias, the teacher can still discover the identity of the sender. This was implemented because findings from a previous study[17] indicated that students who are shy are concerned about having their real name displayed on the public display. But on the other hand, complete anonymity could lead to more mischief. The PAPA feature allows students to choose public anonymity with respect to their classmates but still be held accountable by their teacher.

4. THE FIELD STUDY

ClassCommons was used in 2 classes for 15 weeks in the fall 2011 semester, from Aug.29th to Dec. 9th, in a large university in Northeast America. One class was about project management (PM) and had 67 students, with 16 females and 51 males. PM met twice a week on Mondays and Wednesdays for 75 minutes each time. The teacher for PM was a senior instructor teaching this course for the third time.

The second class was about human computer interaction (HCI) and had 50 students, with 7 females and 43 males. HCI met three times a week on Mondays, Wednesdays and Fridays for 50 minutes each time. The instructor of this course was a junior instructor teaching HCI for the first time.

Students in both classes were juniors and seniors, and 4 males and 1 female were members of both classes. Both classes are required courses in the undergraduate curriculum. Students were offered up to two extra credit points for participating in the study; this offer was made at the start of the semester when they were invited to complete a background survey. The amount of extra credit they received was determined by their level of participation (the number of messages posted). Students were not required to participate in the research study to gain access to ClassCommons.

We chose these courses as testbeds for ClassCommons for two reasons. One is that both courses are mid- to large-size classes where "feelings of disconnectedness are common among students" [18]. Thus we hoped that building a sense of community within students would improve the quality of students' educational experience. The second reason was more pragmatic – these two courses were taught in classrooms where every student has a laptop to use during the class, making it possible for every student to interact with ClassCommons if/when desired.

(a) PM Class   (b) HCI Class

Figure 3. ClassCommons in the 2 classes

Figure 3 shows the setup of ClassCommons in the 2 classes. The larger public display on the left is used by the teacher to project lecture slides; the second smaller public display on the right contains the content posted through ClassCommons. The public display was 5' (width) x 6' (height); pilot testing ensured that the font size used was legible from every location in the class.

The instructors chose to use different policies regarding the use of ClassCommons in their classes. The PM instructor allowed no posting of entertaining messages or any message unrelated to class content; in contrast the HCI instructor had no constraints and welcomed any content. This difference in usage protocol had consequences for how students used ClassCommons during the semester and we will report this in the result section.

5. DATA COLLECTION

We used multiple methods for data collection, including a pre-survey (before using ClassCommons), a mid-survey (about half way through the semester) and a post-survey (at the end of the semester). We also archived the ClassCommons usage logs, conducted a small set of interviews and recorded informal observations. In the pre-survey, we collected a set of background characteristics for participating students as well as initial values for perceived sense of community. We used the subsequent surveys to assess potential changes in sense of community as well as to examine students' perceptions about the system and about their course efficacy as individuals and as a class. We now describe the measures in more detail.

Pre-survey. Before ClassCommons was introduced, students were invited to complete a background survey. They were offered extra credit at this point for agreeing to serve as research participants (all students were able to use ClassCommons regardless of their participation in the evaluation process). We gathered information about participants' interests in interacting with the instructor and other students and their experiences with using social media tools like Facebook, Twitter and online discussion forums were gathered. We used 7-point Likert scales from prior research to measure personal variables, including **Extroversion**, classroom anxiety (**CAnxiety**) and public speaking apprehension (**PApprehension**) [19-21].

Because we were particularly interested in how ClassCommons might affect students' feelings of connectedness with one another, we measured *sense of community* at multiple points including prior to ClassCommons use (**PreSOC**). For this construct we adapted an existing scale of seventeen items [21, 22]. Example items were: "I feel that I am encouraged to ask questions in this class"; "I feel that I belong when I am in this class"; "I have a say about what goes on in this class"; and "I feel connected to the class", covering the four dimensions of sense of community, namely fulfillment of learning need, membership, influence and shared emotional connection[22]. We assessed scale reliability with Cronbach's alpha coefficient, which was 0.88 for the PreSOC data. According to[23], a value of over 0.5 is acceptable for a scale intended to measure a single psychological construct.

Mid-survey. At the beginning of the seventh week, students were invited to complete another survey, where we again measured sense of community (**MidSOC**). We included other measures in this survey as well but for lack of space do not report further analysis of these data.

Post-survey. At the end of the fifteenth week, students were invited to complete another online survey. Once more we assessed sense of community (**PostSOC**).

We probed reactions to the messages that had been posted: the relevance of the content (**Content Relevance**); the extent to which the student feels s/he can learn something new from the messages (**Learn New Information**); and general interest (**Interest**). These three judgments were made on a 7-point scale from 1: not at all to 7: very much. We also asked students to which degree they felt that ClassCommons was a distraction in the classroom (**Distraction**). This judgment was made on a 5-point scale from 1: Not distracting at all, to 5: very distracting. Finally, we used two open-ended questions to probe students' general feelings about ClassCommons, namely what they liked most about and least about it.

The post-survey also asked students to report how much attention they felt their instructor had paid to the messages posted on ClassCommons during the semester (**Teacher Attention;** from 1: none to 5: very much). At this point, we also gathered self-reports about **Use of ClassCommons**. We did this with three 5-point Likert scale items scale (Cronbach's alpha= 0.74). The questions were "How often did you glance at the public display for ClassCommons in the class?"; "How often did you check the ClassCommons system on your own workstation in the class?" (1: Never, 5: Very often) and "How many messages did you read?" (1: I did not read any of them, 5: I read every comment).

To investigate relationships between ClassCommons and class performance we assessed students' feelings of efficacy in the class, both for themselves and as a collective. **Self-efficacy** is the

belief that one is capable of performing in a certain manner to attain a certain set of goals[24]; it is a strong predictor of people's actual performance[25]. In this case we developed four 7-point Likert scales to assess self-efficacy in the context of the classes the students were taking (Cronbach's alpha= 0.73). Example items were: "I can have an impact on class discussions, even though I am only one member in a relatively large group of students."; "Even though I may have trouble at first, I can master the concepts that come up in this course".

Collective-efficacy is similar to self-efficacy but refers to beliefs about joint endeavors and joint outcomes[26]. It was measured using six 7-point Likert scales that we designed for this study (Cronbach's alpha= 0.90). Example items were: "OUR CLASS can ensure that all members' ideas are considered, even if one idea does not seem to fit"; "OUR CLASS can ensure that everybody gets a chance to contribute to discussions, even though we are not all comfortable speaking up".

Finally, we included a measure of **Social support** to investigate how students' class-specific social networks might relate to the other variables being assessed. Social support is defined as feeling that one is cared for by and has assistance available from other people and that one is part of a supportive social network. Students' feeling of social support was measured using six 7-point Likert scales developed for this purpose (Cronbach's alpha= 0.81). Example items were: "If I wanted to do some extra studying for a quiz, I would have a hard time finding someone to study with me"; "If I wanted to form a small reading group to study for this class, I could easily find others to join me".

Log data. All the messages students posted to the public display were logged on the server. Log data include the messages, the images, the videos and the Likes students voted.

Interviews. At the end of the semester, 10 semi-structured interviews were conducted to understand students' and teachers' (the instructors and the TAs) feelings about using ClassCommons. Six students, two instructors and two TAs were interviewed. The interviews lasted from 20 to 30 minutes. Five of the students were in both classes; one was enrolled in HCI only.

We selected the dual-enrolled students because they could provide us a rich understanding of possible differences between the two classes, including whether and how such differences might have influenced their use of ClassCommons. In addition, these 5 students used ClassCommons to different extents. Some posted more than 50 messages while others posted fewer than 10. The sixth student was selected from HCI because he used the system frequently and in many different ways.

During the student interviews, we asked about motivations for using ClassCommons, perceptions of benefits and drawbacks of ClassCommons, and the differences if any that they perceived between PM and HCI (except for the sixth student); we also asked for suggestions about how to improve ClassCommons. In the interviews with the instructors and TAs, we asked about perceived benefits and drawbacks of ClassCommons.

On-site observation. Observations were carried out during the class. One researcher was in the classroom observing students' use of this system during the whole semester.

6. RESULTS

We gathered a variety of data, much of it obtained through surveys. In some cases we repeated scales from one survey to the next. In presenting our findings, we first give an overview of measures from the pre-survey and post-survey that form the basis of the multivariate analysis reported later; we also summarize the ClassCommons usage data. We then provide a more detailed discussion of differences between the PM and HCI class, exploratory regression analyses of ClassCommons use, and a content analysis of the messages contributed by students.

6.1 Overview

ClassCommons was used in both classes from for 15 weeks. The first class session was used for familiarization with ClassCommons, so messages posted on that day are not included.

Students rated their use of social network sites like Facebook, micro-blogging like Twitter and online forums (1: never use, 2: few times a year, 3: few times a month, 4: few times a week, 5: everyday, 6: several times a day). Most students used social network sites (SNS) like Facebook often, with 76.3% of the students in PM class and 88.5% of the students in HCI class reporting that they use Facebook at least once a day. In contrast, micro-blogging is not as popular, with only about 20% of the students using a tool like Twitter every day (PM: 20.4%, HCI: 22.9%). Reported use of online forums was even more rare.

Table 1 summarizes variables measured in the pre-survey that were used in the analysis reported in Section 6.3. As the means suggest, students reported being moderately interested in having interactions with the teacher and other students (a bit higher than the neutral point of 3.0 on a 5 point scale). With respect to the personal variables, the mean values suggest that these students are somewhat extroverted (just above the mid-point of the 7-point scale), not particularly anxious about being in the classroom, and a bit apprehensive about public speaking. The two classes do not differ on these variables.

Table 1. Analysis variables measured in pre-survey

Variable	Class	Mean (S.D.)
Interest interacting with teachers	PM	3.69(0.73)
	HCI	3.77(0.65)
Interest interacting with students	PM	3.75(0.65)
	HCI	3.89(0.68)
Extroversion (index of 7 items)	PM	4.72 (0.44)
	HCI	4.68 (0.49)
Class anxiety (index of 20 items)	PM	3.26 (0.43)
	HCI	3.00 (0.40)
Public speaking apprehension (index of 6 items)	PM	4.00 (0.65)
	HCI	4.04 (0.91)

N=59 for PM; N=49 for HCI
The first two variables were assessed on a 5-point scale, the final three on a 7-point scale

Table 2 summarizes students' self-report of ClassCommons use, gathered at the end of the semester in the post-survey. The first three items in the table refer to students' ratings of the content they have been viewing on the public display over the semester (i.e., did they like using it, is the content relevant, and can they learn new things from the posts). In general these ratings were in the positive direction (collapsing across classes, each rating is significantly greater than the neutral value of 4.0, p<.001). At the same time, we can begin to see some possible differences between the two classes, with the HCI class reporting a higher value for Interest in ClassCommons than the PM class (t(92)=2.06, p<.05). A similar difference emerges in the judgments concerning how much attention the instructor paid to the system (t(91)=4.0, p<.001). Although we have no other measures of teacher involvement in ClassCommons, it seems that at least from the stu-

dent perspective there is a difference across classes. The informal notes taken by the first author while in class were also consistent with this impression.

Table 2. ClassCommons use measures from post-survey

Variable	Class	Mean (S.D.)
Interest*	PM	4.89 (1.16)
	HCI	5.38 (1.10)
Content Relevance	PM	4.66 (1.14)
	HCI	4.48 (1.24)
Learn New Information	PM	4.98 (1.09)
	HCI	5.10 (1.21)
Distraction	PM	2.13 (0.76)
	HCI	2.34 (0.98)
Teacher Attention**	PM	2.94 (1.0)
	HCI	3.75 (0.9)
Use of ClassCommons (index of 3 items)	PM	3.16 (0.63)
	HCI	3.42 (0.83)

N=53 for PM; N=41 for HCI. The first three variables were assessed on a 7-point scale, while distraction, teacher attention and system use on a 5-point scale
* difference between classes is significant, p<.05
** difference between classes is significant, p<.01

Students did not find using ClassCommons in the class was distracting (collapsing across classes, each rating is significantly greater than the mid -point value of 3.0, t(92)= -8.87, p<.001). On the 5 point scale, students felt that using ClassCommons was of little distraction to them.

We also asked more directly for ClassCommons use reports. As explained earlier, the index in the table combines students' estimated frequency (on a 5-point scale) of glancing at the public display, checking in on the system using their own machine, and reading messages. The average value is greater than the mid-point of 3.0 (t(92)=3.6, p<.001), but while there is a trend for these self-reports to be higher for the HCI class than the PM class, this difference falls sort of significance (t(91)=1.67, p<.10). Nonetheless, in combination with the contrasts of liking and teacher attention, these data suggest that system use and acceptance varied across the two classes. We will return to this point later.

Table 3 summarizes psychological variables measured in the third survey. A scan of the means suggests that perceptions of social support from other students, and both self- and collect-efficacy are moderately high but that they do not vary across classes.

Table 3. Social support and efficacy from post-survey

Variable	Class	Mean (S.D.)
Social Support (index of 6 items)	PM	5.41 (1.08)
	HCI	5.23 (0.72)
Self-efficacy (index of 4 items)	PM	5.57 (0.75)
	HCI	5.56 (0.82)
Collective-efficacy (index of 6 items)	PM	5.48 (0.86)
	HCI	5.45 (0.96)

The social support and efficacy scales were assessed using a 7-point scale

Finally, ClassCommons usage logs provided good evidence of participation, though again this appears to vary across classes. In PM, 47.8% of the students (32 of 67) in PM posted messages in the system at least once, while 84% of the students (42 out of 50) in HCI did so; a chi square test of these frequencies confirms that the pattern is significant (χ^2(1,N=117) = 16.18, p<.001). In total 641 messages were posted and 254 Likes were voted. Table 4 shows the detailed use of ClassCommons. Note that the teaching assistant in both classes contributed messages, generally in response to questions. Again the classes differed in this, with the TA contributing almost 20% of the messages for PM but just over 5% for HCI.

Table 4. The use of ClassCommons in PM and HCI

Class	Participation	Messages (Students/ TA)	Likes	Sum
PM	47.8%	84 (65/16)	95	179
HCI	84.0%	557 (527/30)	159	716

Recall that ClassCommons supports posting of photos and videos in addition to text. Across both classes, 76 images were posted, but video content was not common in students' postings; only five video clips were posted, and all of these were in HCI. Table 5 shows the details of the distribution of multi-media posts.

Table 5. Photos and videos posted in ClassCommons

Class	Photos	Videos	Sum
PM	1	0	1
HCI	75	5	80

Students in both classes made heavy use of the PAPA option (using an anonymous handle when posting), but use of this feature was more common in HCI than PM. In the HCI class, 77.9% of the messages were posted under an alias and in the PM class, 60.7% of the messages were posted under an alias ($\chi^2(1,N=592) = 10.00$, p<.05, only messages posted by students were included in this analysis). That is, students in HCI class tended to post using an alias more often than students in PM.

In general, students enjoyed using ClassCommons and the majority of students in both classes would like to use ClassCommons in other classes. In the post-survey, we asked whether they would like to use ClassCommons in future classes. 88.68% of the respondents (47 out of 53) in PM and 92.68% of the respondents (38 out of 41) in HCI indicated that they would like to do so.

6.2 Contrasting the Two Classes

One pervasive result concerning ClassCommons use is its differential impact on the two different classes: students in the HCI class used the system more and used it in more ways; they also reported that they liked it more and that their instructor paid more attention to the messages being displayed. To better understand why these differences may have emerged, we interviewed students, teachers and TAs for opinions about these differences. The fact that five of our interviewees had been in both classes was particularly useful in probing for explanations. In reviewing their comments, three themes emerged: the nature of the course topic, the amount of attention the teacher paid to the content posted on ClassCommons, and the instructors' teaching style.

The richness of the course material and the difficulty of the subject played an important role. Compared to the PM class, students in the HCI class found the course material to be more interesting and therefore more likely to evoke backchannel comments. For example, S1 (Student1) said *"I think PM, the subject is pretty dry. It is not interesting, and then human computer interaction (HCI) is a lot more interesting, a lot more fun. There is a lot more human touch to that class"*. The TA for PM commented *"It might be the material of PM is pretty straightforward. You just store the knowledge and learn. Maybe if you have a math class or something, where you have to apply what you learn to solve problems, students might use it more (to ask questions)."*

A second factor was the attention the teacher paid to the messages on ClassCommons. We reported earlier the survey finding that students in HCI reported that their instructor paid greater attention

to the backchannel than those in PM. In the interviews, students opined that their instructor's acknowledgement of ClassCommons messages encouraged them to use it more. S5 mentioned that *"I think it (the message) is more acknowledged in HCI. The professor kind of actually looked up at the public display. The questions are usually acknowledged, read and answered....(In PM class), he did not really look up at the display much"*. S4 said that *"The fact that the professor acknowledges the display encourages student to use the display. They acknowledge the posts on ClassCommons, they address the questions on ClassCommons, and it makes it more useful, more popular"*. This combination of survey and interview data emphasizes the critical role of teacher attention in adoption and use of technologies like ClassCommons.

Finally, students are more likely to use ClassCommons in classes whose instructor adopts a more personal approach to teaching. For example, S2 said that *"(instructor of HCI) is very personal the way he teaches it. Whereas PM is much more of a big class, I found that it was more impersonal."* S4 commented that *"In PM, the instructor seems stricter."* The PM teacher was quite senior relative to the HCI teacher and this may have influenced their teaching style and students' subsequent reaction to and motivation to engage with them via the backchannel. In general, though, the backchannel is intended for relatively informal exchange, so it would make sense that professors who exhibit a more informal teaching style might encourage more participation.

6.3 ClassCommons Usage Model

To gain insights into how ClassCommons affected students' classroom experiences, we carried out a series of exploratory multiple regression procedures. Given the scarcity of past related work, our goal in this was not to formulate and test hypotheses but rather to build conceptual models of inter-related factors that might be used to guide future research. To increase the power of our analysis, we used the combined data from the two classes in all regressions. Because many of the predictor variables are correlated, we used stepwise regression; in this approach multiple dependent variables are used to predict a single outcome variable, and are added to the model only when they account for variance not already accounted for by other variables[27].

6.3.1 ClassCommons Usage Model

Several student characteristics were assessed and regressed on their starting Sense of Community (PreSOC). For example we expected that students' Classroom Anxiety might negatively impact their starting Sense of Community, whereas Extroversion would show a positive relation. As expected, the regression model for PreSOC revealed a significant positive relation of Extroversion (p<.05) and a negative relation of Class Anxiety (p<.01); no other student variables provided explanatory power in the model, which accounted for 39.5% of the variance.

A number of variables might influence students' use of ClassCommons. In Section 6.2 we discussed some of the differences between classes that seemed to play a role in this, but we also wanted to explore student variables, both in terms of their personal characteristics and their beliefs about the usefulness or interest of the ClassCommons system. For instance one would expect that students who believe ClassCommons provides relevant content would find themselves using it more. To investigate this we regressed the variables from the first model (PreSOC, Extroversion, and Class Anxiety) and the four system ratings (Interest, Content Relevance, Learn New Information, Distraction, see Table 2) on the ClassCommons use index. The resulting model accounted for 36.5% of the variance and included positive relations of Interest (p<.01), Content Relevance (p<.05) and PreSoc (p<.05).

The third regression model considered the possible impact of ClassCommons use on Sense of Community. The system was designed to enhance students' feelings of community, so we expected a positive relation between use and felt community. To examine this possibility, we regressed the variables from the previous model (Interest, Content Relevance, PreSOC and PostUse) on PostSOC (in this model PreSOC is serving as a covariate, i.e. to control for individual tendencies in SOC). The resulting model accounted for 28.4% of the variance in PreSOC and included positive effects for PreSOC (p<.001) and PostUse (p<.05).

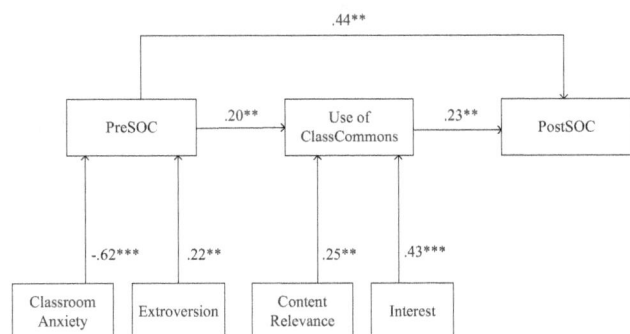

*** : sigfinicant at 99.99% level
** : sigfinicant at 99.9% level

Figure 4. Path diagram relating ClassCommons use to SOC

Figure 4 combines the results of the three regression analyses in a path diagram. In the diagram the arrows show which measures served as independent variables in each model; the numbers on the arcs report the standardized beta or regression coefficient for each predictor. The model summarizes the three overlapping models: 1) classroom anxiety and extroversion predict PreSOC; 2)PreSOC, content relevance, and student interest predict use of ClassCommons. However, personal variables like extroversion, classroom anxiety or public speaking apprehension do not predict their use of ClassCommons; they may have an influence but it is indirect through their relationship with PreSOC.

Finally, students' PostSOC is predicted by their PreSOC and their use of ClassCommons. While we acknowledge that these models are based on correlations only, this pattern of results is consistent with our expectation that use of use of ClassCommons can help students feel more sense of community.

6.3.2 Broader Impact of Sense of Community

As a secondary analysis, we also wanted to explore the broader impacts that are associated with students' sense of community. In particular, we were interested in whether and how sense of community is related to students' self-efficacy, social support and collective efficacy in the classroom. We expected that high sense of community will be positively related to students' self-efficacy, social support and collective efficacy in the classroom.

Our data confirmed this. We found that PostSOC is significantly correlated with self-efficacy (r=0.58, p<.001), collective-efficacy (r= 0.60, p<.001) and social support (r = 0.60, p<.001). As above, we cannot argue for a causal interpretation. Given the large degree of collinearity in our data, further studies will be needed to tease apart these overlapping constructs.

6.4 Sense of Community

Students' sense of community changed differently in the two classes. Table 6 reports students' sense of community in both classes along the semester. A one-way within subjects ANOVA was conducted to compare the effect of time on students' sense of community in each class. In PM, there is a significant effect of period (F (2,46) = 24.55, p < .001). Bonferroni post hoc tests revealed significant differences in the scores for PreSOC and Mid-SOC (p<.001) and for PreSOC and PostSOC (p<.001). However there was no increase from MidSOC and PreSOC: Students' sense of community increased in the first seven weeks, but stayed at the same level until the end of the semester.

For the HCI class, there was no significant effect of time at all (F (2, 23) = 2.69, p = .089). Relative to the PM class, students' sense of community started out at a high value and stayed there. One possible contributing factor for the higher initial SOC is that the size of the HCI class was smaller than PM; perhaps the smaller size helps students to feel more coherent.

Table 6. Sense of Community across classes and time

Class	PreSOC	MidSOC	PostSOC
PM	4.41(0.61)	4.86(0.68)	5.0(0.75)
HCI	4.82(0.70)	5.00(0.72)	4.79(0.75)

Based on our data, we speculate that sense of community may have an asymptotic growth trajectory in university courses. More specifically, we propose that a value of around 5.0 (on a 7-point scale) may be an asymptotic value for this construct in this context, that is when the community in question is a group of students who happen to be taking a course together. Note that in Table 6, the initial SOC value for the PM class is the only one that is not close to this value of 5.0. While individual students may experience more or less sense of community in a classroom, it may be that few of them would ever feel a sense of community intensely enough to assign scale values of 6 or 7. This does not mean that the construct is not valuable for assessing feelings of "connectedness", but it may be useful to explore an alternative to the conventional SOC scale, perhaps one that is customized for the learning communities one could expect to emerge in a 15-week class.

6.5 Content Analysis

To understand how students' have used ClassCommons, we analyzed the messages posted in each class. We used a card-sorting technique to categorize the messages. Each message was read, and assigned a descriptive label. The messages were then clustered into similar groups. We clustered the messages into nine types: social, questions, TA response, report problems, logistics, comments, share info, counter spam and random messages. Examples of each category can be found in Table 7.

Social messages refers to the small talk that usually happened at the beginning or end of class. For example, students might post a message to greet one another, or to talk about the sports and news going on campus or around the world. *Questions* are messages that contain questions about the course. *TA responses* are the messages posted by the TAs, answering students' questions or making announcements. *Report problems* are messages posted to report the problems that students found in the class.

Logistics are messages to deal with logistical issues in the class, for example locating team members. *Comments* are the messages posted by students during the lecture, commenting on the things

Table 7. Examples of the messages by type

Message Type	Example
Social	"Hi folks."; "Class is starting! IM SO EXCITED"; "have a great weekend folks!!! Stay dry, and GO STATE!!!"; "Predictions for the score on Saturday? I say 45-7."
Questions	"Anybody here able to access their u drive?"; "Unjustified claims are bad, mmmkay?"; "anyone know if we are choosing something, or making something entirely new?"
TA Response	"We suggest you find problems that apply to broader audiences."; "You can use whatever presentation technology you choose." "Grades for 4 and 5 are up (unless we didn't get your assignment)."; "Both options are acceptable. Designing something completely new, or improving an existing system."
Report Problems	"One of the problems did not match up with what was discussed in class"; "Team 3 seems to be a combination of team 8 and 9... typo?"; "it's frustrating, I can't open any documents from my desktop or drives."
Logistics	"GROUP #16 WHEN YOU'RE DONE MEET IN BACK CORNER NEAR THE CLOCK"; "TEAM 10 can we meet in the front of the room today after class?"; "Currently looking for fourth member. Must be qualified, and like puppies. Inquire within."
Comments	"awesome presentations today!"; "This design is against man law.(commenting on a design discussed in the class)"; "Can't see the stock on the left machine (commenting on 2 vending machine designs)"
Share Info	"Here's the video which goes along with the Microsoft team's blog post about Windows 8 and improvements to Windows Explorer..."; "Hey everybody! I found some cool news related to interaction design. J.D. Power and Associates recently performed a user satisfaction study for several popular smartphones. Here's the link: ...."; and Wikipedia links like http://en.wikipedia.org/wiki/Synesthesia'; "a great example of classical conditioning/pavlov's dog, http://vimeo.com/6217895"
Counter Spam	"Can you guys stop posting weird videos and pics?"
Miscellaneous	"derk-a-derrr"; "it's a tarp"

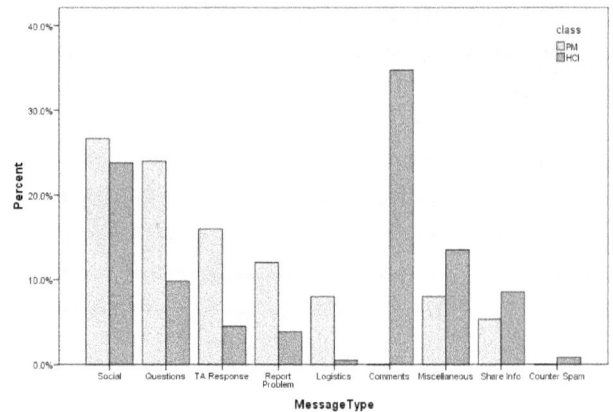

Figure 5. Content Analysis of the Messages Posted

6.6 ClassCommons Benefits and Drawbacks

To understand the tradeoffs of using ClassCommons, we asked students what they liked the most and the least about ClassCommons in the mid and post surveys. We also asked students and the teachers and the TAs similar questions during the interviews. These qualitative data helped us gain deeper insights into the benefits and drawbacks with using ClassCommons, from both the students' perspective and the teachers'.

Students felt that the benefits are that **a) they can easily ask questions and get quick responses from the TA.** For examples, students mentioned that *"What I liked best is that at any time I can post a question and get a timely response from a TA"*; *"It makes asking questions in lectures feasible without disrupting the flow of class. Often times I will not want to interrupt the professor, and hold off on asking my question, only to later forget what my question at the time was"*; *"I like the fact that I'm able to interact with others and the instructor without yelling across the room."* **b) they can interact with other students and provide peer support and learn new information from each other.** For example, students said that *"It's a great way to interact with other students during class times without being disruptive to the teacher. You can ask quick questions to other people and get a timely response"*; *"I like the ability to post a question and have it answered immediately by my peers who have the extremely unique perspective of being in the exact same position in the course"*; *"The technology and idea of it is pretty cool. I do learn things about the class from looking at the message board"*, and **c) it makes the class experience fun.** *"It was interesting to see what the other students were thinking"*; *"It is a fun and more forward approach to learning"*.

Students' only perceived downside with using ClassCommons is that the alias feature encourages people to post irrelevant content which is distracting to the class. *"The first few weeks, the messages almost always consisted of distracting and/or vulgar content, probably because submissions were anonymous. If real names were used, ClassCommons might work better in classes"*; *"Alias encourage distracting comments"* and *"People like to be anonymous in order to post stupid comments and things that don't matter, this can get annoying."*

From the teacher's perspective, the instructors felt that ClassCommons is a social media service that is more relevant to the class than Facebook. The instructor of HCI commented that *"During the class, many students spend a lot of time on Facebook, which is irrelevant to the class. I would rather like students*

that the teacher just talked about. *Share info* message are ones that were posted by students who meant to share information to the whole class. Messages of this kind usually contain a URL link to some webpage from the Internet. *Counter spam* messages were ones that were intended to stop other students from posting random messages. *Random* messages are ones that were posted during the lecture, and have nothing to do with the class. The differences between comments and share info messages are that share info messages are ones that have new information, while the comments are just messages posted by students in response to the lecture, without obvious new information inside.

Given the other differences between the two classes, it was not surprising to see differences in the types of messages posted; this can be seen in Figure 5. Students in PM made more focused use of the tool than students in HCI; they tended to use it to ask questions, report problems or for class logistics. And because students posted such questions, the TA posted more (responses) in PM than in HCI. Students in HCI often used the tool to make comments, and share information. There were also more random messages in HCI than in PM.

to spend that time on ClassCommons, which is more relevant to the class than Facebook. We can use ClassCommons to replace Facebook in classes." For the instructor of PM, he felt that the public display seems to make the class more coherent. He said that "I think this class as a whole, seems to be somehow more coherent than before. It made a community of interest around that system and that community of interest might help them. It gave them all a common thing to focus on."

The concerns the teacher had with ClassCommons were the anonymity issue and the possibility of causing embarrassments for other students. For the anonymity issue, the teachers voiced a concern similar to the students. For the embarrassment issue, the instructor of HCI mentioned that "Sometimes I will ask students to make presentations about their group project in the class. I remembered that one time when a student was presenting, he made some mistakes and some students pointed that out directly on ClassCommons. I felt that this could embarrass the student who is presenting".

6.7 Improvements

Finally, in the post survey and the interviews we asked students and the teachers for their opinions about how to improve ClassCommons. Students' feedback focused on two aspects: they wanted the instructors to improve how they use ClassCommons; and they had some detailed suggestions about improving the system. Among these two, students felt that addressing the first aspect is more urgent than the system enhancements.

Students commented that they wanted the instructor to improve the way that they used the system. More specifically, they suggested that the instructor should pay more attention to the messages posted on ClassCommons, instead of just leaving it for students to interact with other students. For example, S1 said that "The only thing I would say is to pay attention to it more... and answer the question more quickly or like pause every 30 minutes to look at it". S5 commented that: "I think if they can look at it, acknowledge the comments and answer any questions that is up there would help. Mostly, just acknowledging is the important part." S6 also suggested that "Teacher could ask questions, students respond and the teacher acknowledge them. That would be something that would be beneficial. I think it is a good way to promote engagement and excitement".

As to more detailed system level improvements, it is suggested that **a)** there should a discrete way to notify the professor when new messages are posted. S4 suggested that "Maybe there was a discrete way that the professor could be notified that something has been posted. Most of the time, the professor is lecturing, walking around the classroom, not really paying attention to the classroom display, until the end." **b)** it would be useful if users can highlight important questions on the display. For example, the instructor of PM suggested: "Please highlight the important questions on the display so that I can easily identify them and address them accordingly".

These comments reinforce our earlier discussion of the important role teachers' attention plays in encouraging students' use of the system. Students wanted the instructor to know their concerns and wanted to get the instructor's attention.

7. DISCUSSION

Our study of ClassCommons can be judged a success, given that 90% of the students would like to use ClassCommons in future classes. We feel that three of the most important lessons we have

learned from this experiences are that a) teacher's role is critical in influencing students' adoption of this tool and beyond that, the degree to which students would use this tool; b) content relevance is more important than just participation because simply trying to promote higher participation may backfire; and c) teachers need to encourage students to post using their real names.

7.1 Teachers' Use of ClassCommons

The teacher's involvement with the tool seems to have an important influence on students' willingness to use a public backchannel. The ability of a teacher to participate in a backchannel is very much influenced by what other activities are ongoing (e.g., lecturing, group supervision). Thus it may be that modifications in class pedagogy are needed to enhance the effectiveness of public backchannels in classrooms.

The original idea of ClassCommons was to provide a public backchannel for students to raise questions and receive timely feedback from the teacher or other students. Although students can certainly learn some content from other students, they seem to be more eager to get responses from the teacher than from other students. This could be because teachers' responses are more authentic and teacher can provide more expert information. However, the way the teachers conduct their classes does not meet students' needs. In both classes, the teachers spent considerable time lecturing, such that they were not able to pay much attention to the things on the public display. Although these instructors had TAs available to monitor the public backchannel and answer questions, still the students wanted to get more acknowledgements from the teacher. It is unlikely that a teacher would be willing to make radical changes in how he or she conducts a class. However, it might be that even some very simple changes in practices could better integrate the backchannel with other class activities. For example one of the students suggested "pause every 30 minutes to look at it". Other possibilities are to provide mechanisms for the students (or the TA) to gain the attention of the teacher, somewhat analogous to raising one's hand.

It is also interesting to think about the tradeoffs in teacher versus student attention. In a sense the public backchannel should be a "freeing" technology, enabling students to have their own interaction in parallel with whatever the teacher is doing. Although in this study we found an important effect of teacher attention, it would also be interesting to experiment with mechanisms for increasing students' responsiveness to each other. In fact the issue of anonymity may interact with student responsiveness – by using one's real name, one takes a public stand on a question or comment, and in time this may improve community and responsibility.

7.2 Content Quality

Content relevance was seen to be more important than simple participation. In these two classes, the teachers set different policies regarding how the students were expected to use ClassCommons. The instructor of PM did not allow students to post irrelevant contents while the instructor of HCI did not set such policy and any contents were welcome. This led to huge difference in the participation rate. A lot more messages were posted in HCI and much more percentage of the students posted in HCI than PM. However, the regression analyses suggested that content relevance played an important role in predicting use of ClassCommons and indirectly influencing sense of community in classrooms. If the public backchannel is solely left for students to post anything, it may backfire because "this can get annoying".

8. CONCLUSIONS

The 15 week field study provided us an opportunity to investigate the long term impact of public backchannel tools on students' sense of community in classrooms. It is encouraging that 90% of students were interested in using it in future classes. Based on the survey data, we modeled the ClassCommons usage pattern and found that content quality and students' interests were important factors that influence students' use of ClassCommons. Further, the use of ClassCommons is positively related to students' sense of community. The content analysis revealed how students have used the tool during the semester and the qualitative interview and students' answers to the open-ended questions enriched our understandings about the benefits and drawback of using public backchannel in classrooms.

9. ACKNOWLEDGMENTS

The authors would like to thank the teachers John Hill and Shaoke Zhang, and the students for their participation in this study.

10. REFERENCES

[1] Vygotsky, L. S. *Mind in society: The development of higher psychological processes*. Harvard University Press, Cambridge, MA, 1978.

[2] Dewey, J. *How we think*. D.C. Heath & Co, New York, 1910.

[3] Boyle, J. T. Using classroom communication systems to support interaction and discussion in large class settings. *Association for Learning Technology Journal*, 11, 3(2003), 43-57.

[4] Yngve, V. On getting a word in edgewise. In Proceedings of the Sixth Regional Meeting of the Chicago Linguistic Society (Chicago, 1970).

[5] Krauss, R. M. The role of audible and visible back-channel responses in interpersonal communication. *Journal of personality and social psychology*, 35, 7 (1977), 523-529.

[6] Bergstrom, T., Harris, A. and Karahalios, K. Encouraging initiative in the classroom with anonymous feedback. In *Proceedings of the Proceedings of the 13th IFIP TC 13 international conference on Human-computer interaction - Volume Part I* (Lisbon, Portugal, 2011). Springer-Verlag.

[7] Yardi, S. The role of the backchannel in collaborative learning environments. In *Proc. of 7th International Conference of Learning Sciences*, 2006.

[8] Harry, D., Green, J. and Donath, J. backchan.nl: integrating backchannels in physical space. In *Proc. of CHI 2009*, ACM.

[9] Dufresne, R., Gerace, W., Leonard, W., Mestre, J. and Wenk, L. Classtalk: A classroom communication system for active learning. *Journal of Computing in Higher Education*, 7, 2(1996), 3-47.

[10] Robertson, L. J. Twelve tips for using a computerised interactive audience response system. *Medical Teacher*, 22, 3(2000), 237-239.

[11] Fies, C. and Marshall, J. Classroom Response Systems: A Review of the Literature. *Journal of Science Education and Technology*, 15, 1(2006), 101-109.

[12] Ratto, M., Shapiro, R. B., Truong, T. M. and Griswold, W. The ActiveClass Project: Experiments in encouraging classroom participation. In *Proceedings of the CSCL (2003)*. Kluwer Academic Publishers.

[13] Anderson, R., Anderson, R., VanDeGrift, T., Wolfman, S. Y. and Yasuhara, K. Promoting Interaction in Large Classes with Computer-Mediated Feedback. In *Proceedings of the CSCL (2003)*. Kluwer Academic Publishers.

[14] Linnell, N., et al. Supporting classroom discussion with technology: A case study in environmental science. in *Frontiers In Education Conference - Global Engineering: Knowledge Without Borders, Opportunities Without Passports*, 2007. FIE '07. 37th Annual. 2007.

[15] EDUCAUSE 7 Things You Should Know About Live Question Tool. *EDUCAUSE* ,2011.

[16] Du, H., Rosson, M. B., Carroll, J. M. and Ganoe, C. I felt like a contributing member of the class: increasing class participation with Classcommons. *In Proceedings of the ACM 2009 international conference on supporting group work*. GROUP '09. ACM, 233-242.

[17] Du, H., Jiang, H., Rosson, M. B. and Carroll, J. M. Increasing Students In-Class Engagement through Public Commenting: An Exploratory Study. *In Proceedings of the 2010 10th IEEE International Conference on Advanced Learning Technologies* (2010). ICALT '2010, IEEE Computer Society, 373-377.

[18] Sanders, C. E., Basham, M. E. and Ansburg, P. I. Building a Sense of Community in Undergraduate Psychology Departments. *Observer*, 19, 5 (2006).

[19] Bendig, A. W. The Pittsburgh scales of social extroversion, introversion and emotionality. *The Journal of Psychology*, 53(1962), 199-209.

[20] Wrench, J. S., Richmond, V. P. and Gorham, J. *Communication, Affect, and Learning in the Classroom*. Tapestry Press, Acton, MA, 2001.

[21] Rovai, A. P. Development of an instrument to measure classroom community. *The Internet and Higher Education*, 5, 3(2002), 197-211.

[22] Peterson, N. A., Speer, P. W. and McMillan, D. W. Validation of A brief sense of community scale: Confirmation of the principal theory of sense of community. *Journal of Community Psychology*, 36, 1(2008), 61-73.

[23] Nunnally, J. C. *Psychometric Theory*. McGraw-Hill, New York, 1978.

[24] Bandura, A. Self-efficacy: Toward a unifying theory of behavioral change. *Psychological Review*, 84, 2(1977), 191-215.

[25] Bandura, A. Self-efficacy: *The exercise of control*. W.H. Freeman and Company, NY, 1977.

[26] Goddard, R. D., Hoy, W. K. and Hoy, A. W. Collective Efficacy Beliefs:Theoretical Developments, Empirical Evidence, and Future Directions. *Educational Researcher*, 33(2004), 3-13.

[27] Pedhazur, E. J. *Multiple Regression in Behavioral Research*. Harcourt Brace College Publishers, New York, 1997.

Supporting Research Collaboration through Bi-Level File Synchronization

Catherine C. Marshall, Ted Wobber, Venugopalan Ramasubramanian, Douglas B. Terry

Microsoft Research, Silicon Valley

{cathymar, wobber, rama, terry}@microsoft.com

ABSTRACT

In this paper, we describe the design and use of Cimetric, a file synchronization application that supports scholarly collaboration. The system design incorporates results of earlier studies that suggest replicating content on a user's personal devices may have different characteristics than replicating content to share it with collaborators. To realize this distinction, Cimetric performs bi-level synchronization: it synchronizes local copies of a versioned repository among collaborators' computers, while it separately synchronizes private working files between each user's personal devices. Through a year's worth of in-house use of Cimetric in a variety of configurations, we were able to investigate key file synchronization issues, including the role of cloud storage given the ability to sync between peers; the strengths and weaknesses of a bi-level design; and which aspects of the synchronization process to reveal to users.

Categories and Subject Descriptors

H5.3. [Information Systems]: Information interfaces and presentation---Group and Organization Interfaces

General Terms

Human Factors, Design

Keywords

File synchronization, cloud storage, scholarly collaboration.

INTRODUCTION

In recent years, file synchronization services have been identified as key to working across multiple devices [8, 14, 26, 27], to collaborating with colleagues [9], and to keeping files safe by replicating content in different locations [16]. Consumer-oriented products such as Groove [10], Dropbox [9], Google Drive [12], and Windows SkyDrive [35] acknowledge the varying roles of file synchronization in heterogeneous computing environments in which people access (and potentially edit) content on the device at hand, taking advantage of the available level of network connectivity.

Yet the very people who might benefit the most from file synchronization technologies have been slow to adopt them. According to a study by Dearman and Pierce [8]:

> "Our findings suggest that people do not trust automatic file synchronization, even though they employ automatic synchronization for other types of information: music, email messages, contact information, calendar data, and task lists."

We were interested in exploring the adoption and use of file synchronization technology by observing it in action. To do this, we developed and fielded an application, Cimetric, that would appeal to a local community by addressing a common activity, research collaboration and paper-writing.

In particular, we sought to address an aspect of file synchronization that has been identified in previous studies, the distinction between sharing files with oneself and sharing files with one's collaborators [11, 17, 24]. While the same general infrastructure can support both forms of sharing, the rhythm of synchronization in each case is different: authors may want to replicate incomplete drafts among their own devices while they are working on them, and share them when the writing is in a more intelligible state, ready for their collaborators' attention. They may also work with a different set of files than they share; collaborators may rely on their own datasets, analysis tools, and editors to address distinct parts of a complex task [17].

We used a topology-independent replication platform [25] as the basis for implementing Cimetric. Because the platform allows files to be synced between peers, we were able to explore the role of cloud storage in a collaboration in which some coauthors are co-located and others are distant, and some work is almost synchronous, while other work is spread out over time. Would co-located collaborators be able to take advantage of the efficiencies of peer-to-peer synchronization? What kind of feedback would be necessary for distant collaborators to know whether their local files were up-to-date and who was currently working on them? Would a design that distinguishes between syncing personal files on one's own computers and sharing files with colleagues better support collaboration or would the added complexity of a bi-level sync be a burden? Observations of Cimetric in use over time and in support of real work helped us answer these questions.

This paper begins by discussing related work, including studies of file sharing, products that are currently used by people engaged in various sorts of scholarly collaboration, and previous work on collaborative writing. We then describe Cimetric, the application we developed to reflect our understanding of scholarly collaboration and local needs. After these background elements have been laid out, we describe our observations of Cimetric in use over the course of a year for collaborative writing and other related file sharing activities. Finally, we summarize what we have learned and evaluate our efforts against our original aims.

RELATED WORK

There are three types of related work to consider: Studies of file sharing; research prototypes and products that support file synchronization; and studies of collaborative writing, particularly those in performed academic environments. The first two types of related work will be the most salient in identifying findings for our work; the third type of related work feeds into our discussion of Cimetric's design.

Studies of file sharing

Although our work can take advantage of the lessons learned by studies of general file sharing, for example, that awareness of the activities of people who are not actively collaborating may be useful to the group [21], or that there are different aspects of activities collaborators need to be aware of [33], we are the most focused on sharing that involves the co-creation of content in versioned systems. To this end, Fitzpatrick et al. describe different types of CVS events (for software developers and beyond) which need to be brought to their group's attention [11] and Yamauchi et al. discuss the role of CVS repositories in successful collaborations [36]. In general, however, we are much more narrowly focused on synchronization events.

Voida et al. [30] discuss general practices related to sharing files, identifying problems such as choice of sharing service and naming recipients; most salient to our work is their discussion of breakdowns, including several problems we anticipated such as the continued need for out-of-band notification to highlight new or changed content. This is a general problem for file syncing, and, as we discuss, we experimented with a variety of ways of surfacing changes, and documenting file location and provenance.

Although we are aware of the eventual need for introducing security mechanisms [33], we are focused most closely on the design and use of Cimetric's synchronization machinery and the feedback it offers users about its status.

File syncing systems and products

General synchronization research has been the province of the systems community (e.g, [4, 25, 26]); until recently, the results of this work have not played a role visible to users. Of particular interest is Perspective, a decentralized storage system for home use and fielded in homes [26]; one important difference, however, is that Perspective is not designed to support evolving content.

Systems work in the HCI/CSCW community has long been focused on shared online repositories (e.g. [5, 21]); needless to say, by now there are many more research systems and products. Instead of taking an approach that relies on a centralized server- or cloud-based remote repository, we are focusing on a synced local store to support sharing.

Because we are interested in real use (albeit in a local setting so it is easily observed and supported), we compare our approach with three types of products our users might consider in lieu of Cimetric: Dropbox, Google Docs, and popular distributed version control systems such as Git (and online GitHub repositories).

Dropbox is a widely adopted application that syncs local files among devices using the cloud as an intermediary that maintains file versions, which can be accessed through a Web browser. While Cimetric has some of the same functionality as Dropbox, we are interested in seeing the effect of an optional cloud store, as well as investigating an explicit distinction between working files and shared files. Finally, while Dropbox hides much of its sync mechanism (users may not be aware of how Dropbox works, conceiving of it as a literal dropbox or a cloud-only store [18]), Cimetric allows users to inspect and control many aspects of synchronization, so they can address, for example, bandwidth limitations and differences in work style.

Google Docs supports on-line synchronous editing of cloud-resident documents. Although it is a popular tool for the co-creation of content, unlike Cimetric or Dropbox, it requires always-on connected operation to support content changes, as well as the adoption of specific editors.[1]

Cimetric shares some functional aspects of source/revision control systems (e.g. CVS [7], Git [1], Mercurial [29], and Subversion [2]), including provenance-tracking, offline working sets, and asynchronous updates to shared state, although Cimetric tracks provenance on a per-file basis only and does not group edits to multiple files as a single changed version. More to the point, because it was designed for general collaboration, Cimetric omits features of revision control systems that are aimed at software development (e.g. branching, automatic merging, and exclusive locking); our prior study suggested that the complexity of a revision control system was likely to require more administrative overhead and intellectual effort than many ordinary users in our target environment would tolerate [17].[2]

Studies of collaborative writing

Although our work is not aimed at extending the scope of previous collaborative writing research [1, 23, 15, 19, 32], we rely on this research to inform our understanding of some salient local work practices and perspectives (as documented in [17]). As these studies have shown, collaborative writing is largely asynchronous (although it may become more synchronous as deadlines approach), crucially involves email for draft-passing, and is tied to the authors' normal content production tools.

CIMETRIC SYSTEM DESCRIPTION

As a result of our understanding of the intended use situation and our need to more closely observe the problems that arise from file syncing [3, 27], we developed an application called Cimetric. Cimetric is a Windows application that manages documents and other files associated with ad hoc collaborations. It serves multiple purposes: collaboration (sharing data with others); roaming (sharing data with oneself on different devices); and backup (copying data to secondary storage).

We designed Cimetric to have the following key attributes:

- Decentralized synchronization that does not rely on a single authority (such as a central server), and that can handle the demands of offline operation;

- Bi-level synchronization that distinguishes between sharing work in progress with oneself across devices, and sharing versions of these files with one's collaborators;

---

[1] Its successor, Google Drive [12], has some support for offline operation; however, unlike Cimetric, access to shared files that the user does not own requires network connectivity.

[2] In reported past experiences, version control systems were adopted by some members of a collaborative writing group, and not by others (because of their apparent overhead), thus thwarting their original purpose.

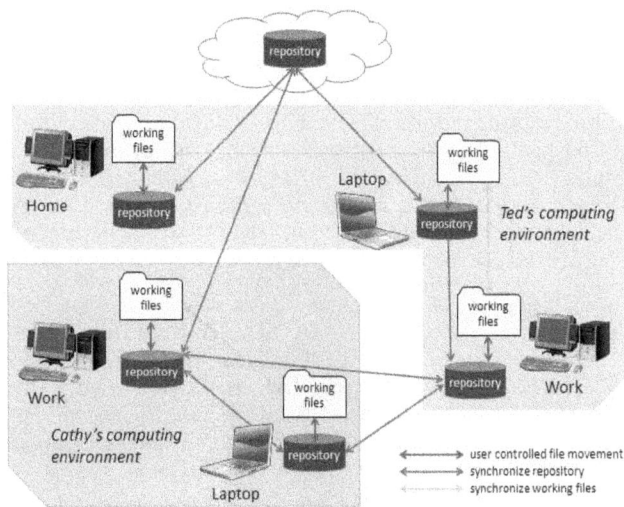

Figure 1. An example Cimetric configuration.

- User control of change integration (in other words, preventing the synchronization process from accidentally destroying local changes by overwriting them);

- Sufficient feedback to allow users to understand the system state (e.g., whether synchronization has completed when one is about to go offline);

- Lightweight mechanisms to show users what their collaborators are doing (e.g. who last wrote a file, or who is working on it now); and

- The ability to use cloud storage without relying on it.

The remainder of the section describes Cimetric's abstractions, architecture, and the feedback it offers users.

Abstractions

Cimetric is based on three central abstractions: *collaborations*, *worksets*, and *repositories*. From a user's perspective, each collaboration has two parts: (1) a *workset*, which contains a user's working files for a particular effort, and (2) a corresponding *repository*, which is the set of files that are shared among the people who are working together. A *workset* is a folder (or a folder hierarchy) in the file system which is managed by the user, and which may be replicated among the user's computers. Files in a workset are not versioned; they look and behave like normal Windows files. A *repository* is a versioned file store that is managed by Cimetric. A user controls the movement of files between workset and repository and vice-versa via a lightweight mechanism that allows users to communicate with each other about who is working on a file (or files); this mechanism also enables users to incorporate their colleagues' changes when they are ready, so their own changes are not overwritten.

From the system's perspective, a *collaboration* may be hosted at multiple client computers; the repository that stores the collaboration's constituent files is replicated in full on each computer. Worksets—i.e. a user's working files—may be replicated as well, so users can continue working seamlessly as they move from, say, a work computer to a laptop, then to a home computer. A user may be involved in multiple collaborations (possibly with different collaborators) using the same instance of the Cimetric application.

A repository instance may be hosted in the Azure cloud [6] if desired, but the cloud is not required by the application. For example, collaborators may decide to create an Azure repository instance because one person works outside the firewall. If several collaborators are on the same subnet, and are working nearly synchronously because a deadline is approaching, they may prefer to use Cimetric's peer-to-peer synchronization because it is significantly faster and lower overhead than syncing via the cloud.

Architecture

Figure 1 shows the Cimetric architecture. In this example, Ted and Cathy are working together on a paper. Ted's computing environment includes a home computer, a laptop he works on while he commutes on the train, and a computer that he uses at work. Cathy is only using two computers to work on the paper, her laptop, and a work desktop. Ted's working files (his Cimetric workset) are replicated on each of his three computers, but as Figure 1 shows, his laptop usually syncs with his home computer when he brings the laptop home, and with his work desktop when he brings the laptop back to work. Likewise, Cathy's working files are replicated on each of the computers she's using to write the paper. Both Ted and Cathy may have files replicated on their own computers that the other doesn't see; practically speaking, these files may include source content related to a particular activity each is working on alone, say creating the figures, or temporary files generated in the course of writing—for example, intermediate versions, that aren't suitable for sharing, or PDFs of references one author is reading for the purpose of filling in citations.

Each computer involved in the collaboration also has a complete local copy of the repository. Like worksets, repositories are synchronized with one another opportunistically. In Figure 1, Cathy's repositories sync with one another, and with the repository instance on Ted's work computer. The repository instance on Ted's laptop syncs with his work computer too. In this scenario, Ted and Cathy have discovered that it would be convenient to have a repository instance in the cloud because they tend to work outside of the firewall fairly frequently. Not all repository instances must sync with the one hosted in the cloud though—only Ted's home computer and laptop and Cathy's work computer sync with the cloud.

We have discussed how worksets sync with selected partners, and how repositories similarly sync with one another. How do files move between the two local stores? Users control the movement of files as they move between a workset and the corresponding local instance of the repository by using an explicit, user-initiated mechanism. Each time a user selects files from the repository and moves them to his or her workset, the mechanism overwrites the existing versions of the files; the system asks the user's permission if a newer version is being replaced by an older one. When a user moves files from a workset to a repository, new versions of the files are created in the repository instance. Older file versions can be moved from repository to workset at a user's request; they also can be inspected in place if, say, a user wants to recover specific text. The portion of the repository browser that provides access to older file versions is not prominent, however. It relies on user discovery, because we recognize that it is relatively uncommon for a user to return to an earlier file version.

Versions are visible (on demand) to users for three reasons. First, they protect a user against accidental loss. Because we are urging researchers to use the system for real, time-critical efforts, we are being conservative about potential content loss, regardless of its source (user error, system malfunction, or design infelicities).

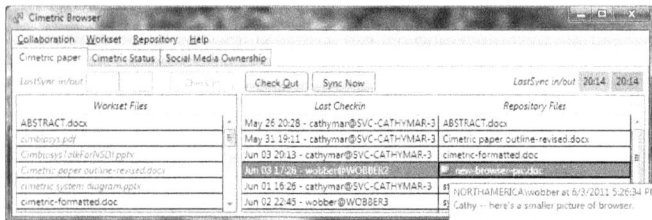

Figure 2. Cimetric Browser

Second, our system allows users to modify shared files when disconnected and, in general, to make updates asynchronously. Explicit versioning makes it possible to coordinate such modifications and to detect conflicts. Finally, system-supported versions enable us to probe the utility of specific aspects of the version abstraction from a user's perspective: will users ever retrieve content from old versions? Will they replace newer versions with older ones? Will they consult them to resolve conflicts? Will they freely overwrite their collaborators' efforts, knowing that no content is destroyed?

As Figure 1 shows, files may be checked out of or into any local repository instance, and they need not be checked into the same local repository they were checked out from. To accomplish this, workset files must carry information about their provenance at the repository of origin. At check-in time, the provenance of the workset file is compared with that of the version (or versions) in the target repository. If the former is not a superset of the latter, a conflict exists. This same mechanism allows for the detection of versions submitted simultaneously to different repositories. Since Cimetric allows simultaneous updates, the best that we can do is to show the conflicting versions to users and let them resolve the conflict after the fact.

Cimetric uses the Cimbiosys topology-independent synchronization protocol via its replication library [25]. Practically, we could have used other popular sync technologies that offer an SDK to support application development, but as we explained earlier, we were interested in exploring certain features of Cimbiosys (for example, decentralized peer-to-peer synchronization) through use. Cimbiosys uses Windows Communication Foundation (WCF), and the default mode of communications uses TCP connections and the TCP protocol. Cimbiosys guarantees *eventual consistency*. In other words, over time the replicas will converge and each will store the latest file versions; its design assumes that network connectivity will be intermittent, and that users may wish to work without cloud storage (for reasons such as privacy or performance).

It is often difficult for users to set up peer-to-peer network connections. Because we didn't want to burden users with the need to pass around complex network addresses to join collaborations, a broadcast protocol enables Cimetric instances to discover each other when they are on the same network segment; user-assigned names allow people to identify the appropriate collaboration. Thus, instances on the same network segment can establish connections with one another easily. Alternatively, there is a user interface for inserting the URL of a designated collaborator by hand (in this case, we might expect collaborators to email each other the URLs of their own instances). Finally, the cloud can be used as a central point for establishing a potential sync connection between local repository instances.

User interface

Most of the time, Cimetric does not need to be a visible part of collaborators' work; as is the case with Dropbox and other sync infrastructures, people interact with a synced folder in the file system the way they would normally, editing the files with their usual editors, and managing the files through the folder hierarchy. Cimetric can sync a user's working files in the background, keeping them up to date with a sync partner if the user works on multiple computers capable of syncing with one another. That way, it is easy for a user to switch among devices.

As an aspect of our investigation, certain aspects of Cimetric's operation are revealed through a browser, shown in Figure 2. Each browser tab corresponds to a collaboration (which may involve different people and computers). Workset files are listed on the left; repository files are listed on the right. The hierarchical structure of the workset is represented in terms of paths; in the collaboration shown in Figure 2, no subdirectories were used. Repository files show when they were last checked in (and by whom, from which computer); comments and advisory locks are shown if they exist. The advisory locks do not prevent other users from using the files—they are simply a visual indication that someone else may be modifying the same file; we expect this type of conflict to be resolved socially.

The workset file list uses visual conventions to indicate whether the user has changed the file since the last checkout, or whether there is a newer version in the repository. If both conditions are true (the user has changed the file and there is a newer version in the repository), then a user-generated conflict exists. We leave it to the user to resolve such conflicts; automatic resolution is apt to result in a merge that does not take user intent into account. Repository conflicts are likewise indicated, and are left to the collaborators to resolve. For example, if two people check in new versions of the same file, a repository conflict will result, and will require human attention.

The browser also gives the user access to the sync process. A user can initiate a manual sync and can get answers to questions such as "When did my repository and workset last sync? Where is the workset folder stored? Who is working on what file, and what are they doing?" Other functionality, hidden more deeply in the UI, allows the replication-savvy user to control parameters such as the sync interval (how often the system attempts to sync with its peers), or to turn automatic sync off and work with user-initiated sync. Logs provide an additional means of inspecting what has happened during the sync process.

As is true with some popular file synchronization services, a history mechanism allows users to inspect a file's history and retrieve older versions of it; like most version control systems (and unlike most file sync services), the versions are created explicitly when they are moved into the repository, with the idea that the versions that are shared with collaborators are more meaningful than the versions created by automatic workset syncs. Older versions may be examined or users may move them into their worksets (in which case, users are consulted to make sure that their intention was to overwrite a more recent version of the file).

Cimetric's user interface is designed to meet the expectations of its immediate audience, people who are generally familiar with synchronization concepts. If the system were to be used by a broader audience, some aspects of its functionality might be more readily accessible through visualizations (for example, of file movement during sync); others may end up being hidden from the casual user. Conversations with our user community, as well as the results of a broader study [18], indicate that synchronization has been rendered overly opaque as it stands. Changes to the user interface have been iterative, and have relied on continued feedback from the user community.

OBSERVING CIMETRIC IN USE

For Cimetric to be adopted and used locally, it needed to address a real problem and be sufficiently reliable for people to use it in the face of deadlines. Potential users needed to be assured that their data was versioned and safe. Crash recovery needed to be simple, and involve only a restart of the application. Furthermore, the application needed to be easy to use with existing material, and easy to opt out of if it didn't satisfy a group's needs.

In this section, we describe how we fielded Cimetric and what we learned from doing so. We recruited real users in our own organization; we wanted to be able to support these users and observe their collaborations closely. We knew that if Cimetric proved to be useful, the researchers who used it would pull in additional collaborators and there would be more adoption as time went on.

To recruit users, we gave talks and demos to describe Cimetric and what it might be used for; we also talked to people who were in situations that might benefit from the application (e.g. writing papers and sharing data files). To discover how the system was being used, we relied on a multi-dimensional approach: (1) we supported users (in person and via email), with an eye toward finding out what they were doing with the system; (2) we engaged in iterative design, creating frequent releases of the application with new user-driven features and bug fixes so that users felt their needs were being met; (3) users sent us feedback, both to influence system design, and to be good citizens; and (4) we interviewed users during and after they used Cimetric, using their own repositories to elicit responses. Thus our data consists of notes taken during observed use; recorded interviews; the file repositories themselves (examined with the users' permission); system logs; and accumulated email correspondence.

The observation period has lasted about a year, and has involved 9 distinct collaborative activities (summarized in Table 1). One of the collaborations, UC9, was active until recently, and two of the others, UC3 and UC5, still see intermittent activity. In all, there were 12 different users involved in the 9 collaborations; in five of the collaborations, a member of a Cimetric-based collaboration used the application for a second or third project.

Use characteristics

So far, adoption has been dominated by dyads, pairs of collaborators sharing files, although four-person and three-person collaborations used the system too. One singleton also used Cimetric to replicate his own files among multiple devices (much as he used Live Mesh, a predecessor to Windows Skydrive [35], earlier). Although we described the application to prospective users as collaborative, we felt that single-person adoption might be a viable way to encourage collaborative use when this user began new collaborative projects.

Table 1 summarizes the use cases we have been tracking in the field. Although we requested that internal users let us know when they installed the system, people in other organizations inside our company could also install it and use it without our intervention (and the existence of several mystery repositories leads us to suspect they did). Table 1 also indicates whether the collaboration

ID	Description	# of users	External collaborator	Cloud replica?
UC1	Sharing project-related files	4	No	No
UC2	Writing a paper	2	No	No
UC3	Sharing project-related files	2	Yes	Yes
UC4	Writing a paper	2	Yes	Yes
UC5	Writing a paper	4	No	Yes
UC6	Writing a paper	2	No	Yes
UC7	Developing algorithms	1	No	No
UC8	Writing a paper	3	Yes	Yes
UC9	Writing a paper	2	Yes	Yes

Table 1. Summary of observed Cimetric use

used a cloud replica, and whether an external collaborator was involved.

The uses were by-and-large successful: in 7/9 cases, the desired collaborative artifacts were created, and people did not lose their data when the system occasionally crashed (with one exceptional situation we will describe later in this section). In one case, UC3, the prospective Cimetric users switched to email, and in another case, UC9, the users switched to Dropbox when they were revising their paper; both changes were linked to cloud malfunctions.

The range of uses we observed enabled us to address key concerns about our strategy for supporting file sync and sharing, including:

- The role of the cloud;
- The efficacy of a bi-level design; and
- Which aspects of synchronization to reveal.

We have continued to encourage people to use the system now that it is stable and has been developed to the point that it is useful to different kinds of research collaborations. In the future, we would like to observe larger collaborations.

Inherent risks of synchronization

UC7 used Cimetric for four months in a configuration we did not intend; he used the system by himself to replicate files between his office computers so he would not need to store intellectual property on an outside provider's cloud (for example, Dropbox, uses Amazon's S3 cloud service). Before Cimetric, UC7 had also experimented with Microsoft's Live Mesh to sync files between his own computers. Herein lies a cautionary tale.

Dearman and Pierce warn us:

"We believe that the lack of trust in automatic file synchronization is due in part to the higher cost of failure. If a user loses an email or a calendar entry, the consequences are relatively minor, whereas losing a file that contains hours of work is much more traumatic." [6]

UC7's synced files included a subdirectory that contained a critical presentation related to his project. This subdirectory was replicated on two out of three of his office computers. Earlier he had used Live Mesh to replicate the subdirectory on all three of his office computers, as well as in the cloud. As he worked on the presentation in a last minute push before a conference, the file mysteriously vanished. He was justifiably upset: what had happened?

Figure 3 shows the drawing he created on his whiteboard to explain his model of how the sync applications interacted with one another. The "x" represents the folder that contained his lost presentation; "SkyDrive" is the Live Mesh cloud store, and 1, 2, and 3 are his computers. The left (red) box shows the folders on 1, 2, and 3 that are synced by Live Mesh, and the right (blue) box shows the folders on 1 and 2 synced by Cimetric. Interaction between the two systems' conflict resolution code apparently caused the file vanish. Naturally, the undesired delete propagated (the way it would in any replicated system). Although UC7 was subsequently able to recover a recent version of the file using a Windows 7 feature, this mishap still served as a visceral reminder of Dearman and Pierce's warning.

Because synchronization is usually fairly silent once it has been set up (i.e. in systems like Dropbox, LiveMesh, and Cimetric, the synced folder looks like a normal folder), we might expect this type of interaction between sync applications to be relatively common. It is hard for users to remember which folders have been synced, and it's easy to imagine installing sync apps on top of each other, especially if the original sync app did not perform as expected. In other words, *if one solution doesn't work, a user will probably try to solve the synchronization problem a different way, possibly without uninstalling the first solution.* Sync applications that are simultaneously applied to the same folder structure may lead to unexpected side-effects or misidentified update conflicts.

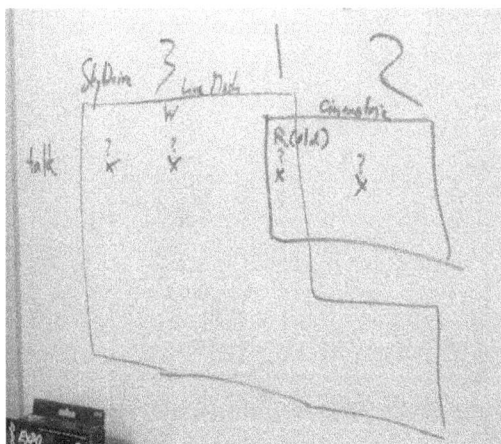

Figure 3. UC7's account of replicated system interactions

The role of the cloud

A significant proportion (6/9) of the collaborations used a *cloud replica*, a copy of the shared repository that was stored in the cloud and synchronized with other repository replicas as a peer. Using the cloud as a peer (rather than as an integral part of the synchronization architecture, as it is in many sync tools) turned out to be an effective way of incorporating the cloud without relying on it. A brief initial period of use revealed that the cloud would be necessary for three reasons:

- Some of the research collaborations involved external colleagues who worked outside the firewall, a situation that made setting up a peer-to-peer network difficult.

- Changing and unanticipated configurations made the cloud an on-demand bridge to connect sync partners that may have been peer-to-peer in the past.

- Power saving software, which is increasingly common, sometimes made the cloud necessary to ensure a path from

one PC to another, even during normal working hours (i.e. PCs were often automatically powered down if they were left unattended, even for a brief period of time).

Making the cloud optional, on the other hand, was useful for four countervailing reasons:

- When collaborators were physically proximate (working on the same subnet), peer-to-peer synchronization had better performance; syncs seemed instantaneous to users during periods of intensive semi-synchronous work.

- If the cloud wasn't working (or the connection was slow), it was still possible to sync some users' files. This situation came to pass several times during the longer-running collaborations.

- Collaborations with security concerns did not want to store data on an externally-owned cloud. In this case, the cloud was not externally-owned, but often sync tools use an external—or third party's—cloud services.

- Cloud services may incur additional costs; the cloud may be eliminated from the network when it isn't necessary. In this case, we absorbed the cost of the cloud for the prototype, but we were aware of storage and transaction costs silently accruing, and at a larger scale, these costs could have been noticeable to an organization.

Initially we fielded the system without a cloud replica, in line with the decentralized eventual consistency model assumed by the Cimbiosys platform [25]. Indeed, the system's flexible peer-to-peer topology is a distinguishing feature of the platform, one we were anxious to test. This completely decentralized strategy worked for some collaborations (and for other collaborations *some of the time*), especially for those involving co-located researchers connected to the network during overlapping time periods. In other words, people were not necessarily working on content synchronously, but their computers were connected to the network in such a way that there was an eventual path from one computer in the collaboration to another.

Without the ability to create a cloud replica, adoption was slow. Although the system provided collaborators with certain advantages (the ability to track who was working on what files, for example, and the ability to instantaneously and efficiently synchronize files among personal machines), the advantages weren't so profound that they outweighed researchers' reluctance to adopt a new technology when a deadline was in sight. Furthermore, corporate IT had steadily rolled out new automatic power saving software, so it became increasingly difficult to reach any replicas if a user was trying to sync files when her coworkers were away from their desks (including times during the day when machines powered down because people were in meetings). Without a cloud replica, one's collaborators all needed to be within the corporate firewall at least part of the time, and much collaboration in the lab (and 4/9 of the Cimetric collaborations) involved at least one academic collaborator who was always outside the firewall. The ability to span the firewall turned out to be a significant advantage in enlisting users, and was necessary off and on throughout a collaboration.

It is telling that although we began writing this paper using Cimetric in a wholly peer-to-peer fashion, by the time we were finished, we found it necessary to create a cloud replica of the repository we used to store our work. Normally we all work in the office, but one day close to the deadline, several of us ended up working from home, and our sync patterns changed abruptly; as with several of the other collaborations, we needed the optional cloud replica midstream. Interview data suggests UC2, one of two collaborations that were successfully completed without a cloud replica, would have created one if the capability were available. Instead, the dyad temporarily shifted to email, and shifted back to Cimetric when they returned to the office.

This pattern of shifting in and out of cloud-based syncing appeared in multiple collaborations as collaborators were added (or dropped out of the collaboration) and as cloud availability changed. UC8 started with a cloud replica; one collaborator was outside the firewall, and the cloud replica was necessary. During the final revision cycles, the cloud was unavailable and the external collaborator was out of the picture. Rapid revision cycles continued via a peer-to-peer connection as the remaining two collaborators worked closely.

Furthermore, it is easy to forget that there may be storage and transaction costs associated with cloud-based repositories; a peer-to-peer solution is, for all intents and purposes, free. Although storage is generally cheap, other demands—e.g., maintaining an open connection to the cloud so repositories can sync at the specified frequency—can make the costs of offering such a service conspicuous.

Evaluating the bi-level design

One of our central research questions concerned the efficacy of the bi-level design: did Cimetric's bi-level synchronization support collaboration in a useful way, or did its complexity overwhelm any potential benefits?

There are several different ways we can reflect on this question: (1) We can examine how people configured the system—did they ever use synced worksets in conjunction with synced repositories in configurations akin to Figure 1? If they didn't, did they adopt workarounds that created a bi-level configuration similar to the one the system supported? (2) Did users perceive any advantages to the system behaviors that stem from this capability, and if not why not? As part of this question, we discuss two related aspects of bi-level design: repository versioning, and controlling the scope of what is shared.

Configurations. We were aware at the outset that people might configure Cimetric in a variety of ways: e.g. one user might not sync worksets (because she writes on a docked laptop that she carries with her), while another might rely on workset synchronization (because she uses a desktop with a big screen in her office, and carries a laptop home with her). We anticipated that at least some of our users would find synced worksets useful. So at first blush, the question seems simple: did anyone (besides UC7, the singleton user we have already discussed) configure Cimetric to take advantage of workset replication?

The answer is, in fact, not simple. In principle, Cimetric users could have used workset replication more often than they did; records show that users often accessed Cimetric repositories from more than one PC. So we asked them why they didn't take advantage of this facility. Three reasons emerged: (1) the lack of a cloud-based workset replica; (2) users' need to reconfigure their computing resources on-the-fly; and (3) the complexity of configuring bi-level sync.

The first reason parallels our initial problems with repository syncing: that is, worksets weren't replicated in the cloud; they relied on peer-to-peer syncing. Thus all of the problems we

discussed in the previous subsection were true of worksets as well as repositories.

The second reason was more nuanced: we did not foresee just how often users would need to change configurations on the fly. In other words, although it was easy for new people to join a collaboration (and later, to add a cloud replica to an existing collaboration), it was more difficult for users to change a system configuration mid-collaboration. The design precluded adding a sync relationship between existing worksets or changing the way an existing sync relationship was set up.

For example, one collaborator in UC2 wanted to add another workset/repository pair when he found himself working on his laptop (which he didn't often use) in an unexpected place—a café—outside the firewall. Before a cloud-based repository replica was available (as was the case in the system's early days), this type of improvisation was completely impossible. Even so, if there wasn't already a replica in the cloud, nothing could be done to establish one in this situation short of contacting collaborators to find out if they were in a position to set one up. Finally, there was no provision for the remote worker to access his existing workset.

Thus to take full advantage of bi-level sync—and this speaks to the third point—users had to plan their work and anticipate the computers they would be using and places they would be working. In retrospect, we realize this is a lot to expect. The problem was not so much that Cimetric users did not write on multiple computers, but more that if they did, they did so in an opportunistic way. The ability to synchronize a workset with the cloud would have enabled the system to better handle these unanticipated configurations; that way, if a user found him- or herself working unexpectedly outside the firewall on a different computer, his or her working files would still be accessible (in addition to the files that had already been moved into the repository).

Workarounds. It is possible for users to set up bi-level synchronization themselves. Ironically, one of the collaborators in UC9 was unaware of Cimetric's ability to sync worksets, but he perceived a need to do so. So instead of using Cimetric to sync his workset folder (i.e. his work-in-progress), he used Dropbox to sync this folder and Cimetric to sync the repository he shared with his co-author. Thus he effectively simulated the bi-level design by using the two sync services—Cimetric and Dropbox—in tandem.

Repository versioning. While worksets were normal Windows folders, repositories were versioned; each time a user shared his or her work, a new version of the file would be created. Earlier studies documented that user communities like ours want versions to be maintained on their behalf [15, 17, 23]; popular sync and sharing applications such as Dropbox and Google Docs support for automatic versioning (with the important distinction that in those services, versions are created when files are saved, not when they are explicitly shared). Code development efforts [11] or compliance- and recovery-oriented solutions [20] also make productive use of versions. Would these results generalize to Cimetric?

Again, the answer varied with the collaboration. In some Cimetric repositories (e.g. UC1, UC2, and UC5), the co-authors maintained the same naming conventions they had in the past: collaborators passed drafts back and forth, appending their initials to indicate who had checked in the draft and renaming the file to note the version's role in the overall writing process. In others (e.g. UC9), the users let Cimetric's file versioning do a larger proportion of the provenance maintenance work for them.

For example, both authors in UC2 were asked about apparently branching versions that used naming conventions (for example, one collaborator's file, *intro.tex*, would be revised by a second collaborator, and saved as *intro-svr.tex*). One of the UC2 authors said, "*Oftentimes when I have to revise a section, I would revise it in a separate file so that if for some reason he wants to go back to the old stuff, he can do it.*" The other author in this collaboration adopted a similarly conservative approach and retained all changed text as comments in the shared file. "*You don't take away text,*" he explained. In other words, appending one's initials is a way of acknowledging the contingent nature of the changes a co-author introduces. On the other hand, UC9's collaborators, who worked together over a much longer period to create a monograph, simply overwrote one another's files, and relied on the system's versioning mechanism to keep things sorted out. In practice, none of the collaborators ever returned to old versions of their files, but the ability to do so (at least in theory) was comforting.

Controlled sharing. Bi-level design also enabled users to control the scope of what is shared. In other words, users could sync work that they had no intention of sharing (e.g., intermediate files used to produce figures, temporary files created in the process of running LaTeX, and data used to produce the results that appeared in a publication). This aspect of the bi-level design was successful; many users created files they did not share.

Revealing synchronization processes

As Cimetric development progressed, we experimented with different models of which aspects of synchronization to reveal, and which aspects could remain hidden. Certainly revealing too much was as confusing and as unhelpful as revealing too little. We kept the design of this feedback literal, with the idea that an adept designer could generalize from what we've learned, and potentially create better visualizations of portions of the sync process.

From interviews and observing use, we found that it was useful for the tool to reveal three types of information: information about file provenance; the status and progress of the sync itself; and an overview of what has changed.

Provenance. Where did a file come from? When was it last synced? Users found this information to be useful to track their own activities as well as their collaborators' work. Figure 4 shows a portion of a Cimetric browser that a user cited as useful. From this listing, he could determine not only who had last written the file, but also which computer it came from (information which might be as useful to the user who had checked the file in as it would be to his collaborators).

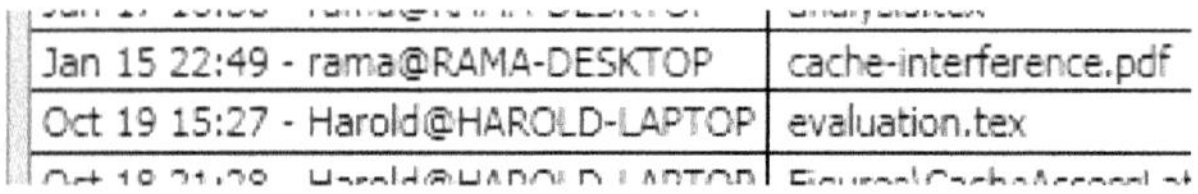

Jan 15 22:49 - rama@RAMA-DESKTOP	cache-interference.pdf
Oct 19 15:27 - Harold@HAROLD-LAPTOP	evaluation.tex

Figure 4. Snippet of file provenance information

Sync complete. When did syncing in each direction (inbound and outbound) complete? It is important that this information be unambiguous so a user can be confident that local changes have been fully propagated, and that incoming files from other computers are up-to-date. In other words, it is important to make sure the user knows that another computer was successfully contacted (sync began), and that the sync finished (sync complete). If the sync involves a cloud replica, users need to know the status of this connection that is assumed to be 'always on'.

Changes. Who has synced with the repository since the last time the user looked, and from where? What did they change, and have they added new files? This information provides useful feedback when collaborators are working at a distance (has everyone seen my changes yet? Has a specific co-author started to work on the paper yet?) and in a decentralized system, it reassures users that a remote collaborator's repository has synced with the others.

Some aspects of the sync process were visible and controllable, yet users did not seem to find them useful. For example, users were more apt to repeatedly force a sync than they were to change the sync interval to be more frequent (it was 5 minutes by default). We also found that users wanted to know when the cloud was available, and needed progress indicators for syncs that were slow to complete.

Collaborators in UC3 were sharing numerous large data files and presentations, in addition to the files directly relevant to the writing process, and the collaborators in UC9 created many smaller files as part of co-authoring a scholarly monograph over the better part of a year. These two collaborations revealed shortcomings in the initial synchronization feedback model. Specifically, both of these collaborations found it hard to tell whether their local files reflected what was in the cloud, and what had been added to the repository. For example, the collaborator who joined UC3 was not sure when the first sync was complete, or how long the sync would take. In an email, he said:

> "*After the first couple files showed up I thought the repository was somehow smaller than what [I] expected but then other files started showing up. Of course, being an impatient user, I have hit the sync button a few times so am [somewhat] unclear on whether that causes it to go retrieve additional files (via magic) or if they are being downloaded over some schedule so as to not swamp the network.*"

Thus, the person who had set up the repository had to explicitly specify how many files to expect, and roughly what was in the repository. Would it have been easy to add such an indicator to Cimetric's user interface? This is a case in which the base technology did not support such a change: the sync protocol did not surface this information. Nor could either user control the sync order: files that were more germane to current tasks might well be the last to sync. It is frustrating for both sides of a dyad to watch a series of large (but not immediately necessary) files sync while the small file necessary to make progress on the current portion of the joint effort is waiting in the wings.

CONCLUSION

Through the development of a file synchronization application, and by observing its local use for scholarly collaboration, we set out to make three types of contributions: (1) to better understand the role of a cloud store in file synchronization; (2) to build a bridge between device synchronization and file sharing; and (3) to understand which aspects of synchronization to reveal to users.

What we learned was that a confluence of factors—organizational firewalls; the power-saving mechanisms and policies that are becoming increasingly commonplace; and fluid unanticipated configurations of people and computers—made it necessary to give users the option of syncing with the cloud. Yet there are reasons to keep a cloud replica optional, rather than making it a fixed element of every session. Performance, flexibility, cost, and privacy all arose as reasons to retain the possibility of peer-to-peer syncing. For example, if users are working with highly sensitive material—e.g. code that represents significant intellectual property or data that might compromise study participant privacy—they may not want to store it on an external cloud service. Furthermore, peer-to-peer syncing was much faster than cloud-based syncing when the collaborators remained on the same subnet and were working in a semi-synchronous way as a deadline approached. Thus the topology-independent aspect of Cimetric was successful *as long as there was an option to create a cloud replica of working files or shared content.*

What of our attempt to separate device sync and file sharing? Did the bi-level design add needless complexity? Yes and no. The difficulty of understanding how to configure the system and the difficulty of changing configurations on the fly made users less likely to take advantage of bi-level syncing. Yet the work-arounds we observed (such as UC9's adoption of Dropbox to sync worksets) convinced us of two results: (1) *maintaining a distinction between the two types of syncing is useful* and (2) *worksets would have benefitted substantially from the option to sync with the cloud.*

Finally, we consider the sync information we made visible, and what we did not. In most situations, people do not examine when the last sync occurred, nor do they check the provenance of a file (where they received it from at sync time). Yet when breakdowns occurred, that information—and more (as was apparent in the feedback from UC3 and UC9)—was useful. Because we fielded the Cimetric application among technically-savvy users, it would be interesting to see whether the sync information would interpreted correctly among different user populations; some of it (when the last sync completed, who last edited a file, and from where) can be reassuring and possibly vital to interpreting what is going on.

Our investigation underscores the value of file synchronization in domains that stress the co-creation of content, just as it highlights some of the difficulties and pitfalls of sync applications. In the end, one question remains: are any of our collaborations still using Cimetric? As Grudin observed in his study of a collaborative writing tool [13], most of our collaborations did not continue using the tool after their specific activity had concluded, although several used it again when new writing tasks arose. This long-term use gives us hope that a cloud-optional approach that bridges between the rhythms of personal file sync and collaborative file sharing is a viable way to support content co-creation.

ACKNOWLEDGMENTS

We would like to thank our patient and daring users, especially those who used Cimetric in its early days.

REFERENCES

1. About Git. http://git-scm.com/about

2. Apache Subversion. http://subversion.apache.org/

3. Beck, E. & Bellotti, V. Informed Opportunism as Strategy: Supporting Coordination in Distributed Collab. Writing. *Proc. ECSCW'93* (1993), 233–248.

4. Belaramani, N., Dahlin, M., Gao, L., Nayate, A., Venkataramani, A., Yalagandula, P., & Zheng, J. PRACTI replication. *NSDI'06*, USENIX (2006), 59–72.

5. Bentley, R., Horstmann, T., & Trevor, J. The World Wide Web as enabling technology for CSCW: The case of BCSCW, *CSCW 6*, 2-3 (1997), 111-134.

6. Calder, B., Wang, J., Ogus, A., Nilakantan, N., Skjolsvold, A., McKelvie, S., Xu, Y., *et al.* Windows Azure Storage: A Highly Available Cloud Storage Service with Strong Consistency. *Proc. SOSP'11*, 143-157.

7. Cederqvist, P. *Version Management with CVS.* http://ximbiot.com/cvs/manual/

8. Dearman, D. & Pierce, J. It's on my other computer!: Computing with multiple devices. *CHI'08*, 767–776.

9. Dropbox. http://www.dropbox.com/ (retrieved 1 June 2012).

10. Farnham, S., Pedersen, E., & Kirkpatrick, R. Observation of Katrina/Rita Groove deployment. *Proc. ISCRAM'06*, 39–49.

11. Fitzpatrick, G., Marshall, P., & Phillips, A. CVS integration with notification and chat: lightweight software team collaboration. *CSCW'06*, 49-58.

12. Google Drive. https://drive.google.com/start (retrieved 1 June 2012).

13. Grudin, J. Groupware and social dynamics: Eight challenges for developers. *CACM 37,* 1 (1994), 92-105.

14. Karlson, A., Iqbal, S., Meyers, B., Ramos, G., Lee, K., & Tang, J. Mobile Taskflow in Context: A Screen Shot Study of Smartphone Usage, *CHI'10*, 2009-2018.

15. Kim, E. & Eklundh, K. How Academics Co-ordinate their Documentation Work, Royal Inst. Tech., Technical Report TRITA-NA-P9815, NADA, August 1998.

16. Kotla, R., Alvisi, L., & Dahlin, M. SafeStore: A Durable and Practical Storage System. *Proc. USENIX'07* (2007), 129-142.

17. Marshall, C.C. From Writing and Analysis to the Repository. *Proc. JCDL'08*, ACM Press (2008), 251-260.

18. Marshall, C.C. and Tang, J. That Syncing Feeling: Early user experiences with the cloud. *Proc. DIS'12*, ACM Press (2012).

19. McDonald, D., Weng, C., & Gennari, J. The multiple views of inter-organizational authoring. *Proc. CSCW'04*. ACM Press (2004), 564-573.

20. Müller, A., Rönnau, S., & Borghoff, U. A file-type sensitive, auto-versioning file system. *Proc. DocEng'10*, ACM Press (2010), 271-274.

21. Muller, M., Millen, D.R., & Feinberg, J. Patterns of usage in an enterprise file-sharing service: publicizing, discovering, and telling the news. *Proc. CHI '10*, ACM Press (2010), 763-766.

22. Noel, S., Robert, J-M. Empirical Study on Collaborative Writing: What Do Co-authors Do, Use, and Like? *Journal of CSCW 13*, 1 (2004), 63-89.

23. Posner, I. & Baecker, R. How People Write Together. In Baecker (ed.): *Readings in Groupware and CSCW*, Morgan Kaufmann (1993), 239–250.

24. Rader, E. Your, Mine and (Not) Ours: Social Influences on Group Information Respositories. *Proc CHI EA '09*, ACM Press (2009), 2095-2098.

25. Ramasubramanian, V., Rodeheffer, T., Terry, D.B., Walraed-Sullivan, M., Wobber, T., Marshall, C., & Vahdat, A. Cimbiosys: A platform for content-based partial replication. *Proc. NSDI'09*, USENIX (2009).

26. Salmon, B., Schlosser, S., Cranor, L.F., Ganger, G. Perspective: Semantic Data Management for the Home. *Proc. FAST '09*, USENIX (2009).

27. Sohn, T., Li, K., Griswold, W., Hollan, J. A Diary Study of Mobile Information Needs, *CHI '08*, ACM Press (2008), 433-442.

28. Schilit, B.N. and Sengupta. U. Device Ensembles. *IEEE Computer 37*, 12, (2004), 56–64.

29. Understanding Mercurial. http://mercurial.selenic.com/wiki/UnderstandingMercurial (retrieved 1 June 2012).

30. Voida, S., Edwards, W.K., Newman, M., Grinter, R., & Ducheneaut, N. Share and share alike: exploring the user interface affordances of file sharing. *CHI '06*, ACM Press (2006), 221-230.

31. Wang, Y., Gräther, W. & Prinz, W. Suitable notification intensity: the dynamic awareness system. *Proc. GROUP '07*, ACM Press (2007), 99-106.

32. Weng, C. & Gennari, J. Asynchronous collaborative writing through annotations. *Proc. CSCW'04*, ACM Press (2004), 578-581.

33. Whalen, T., Smetters, D., & Churchill, E. User experiences with sharing and access control. *Proc. CHI '06*, ACM Press (2006), 1517-1522.

34. Whalen, T., Toms, E., & Blustein, J. Information displays for managing shared files. In *Proc. CHiMiT'08*, ACM Press (2008).

35. Windows SkyDrive. http://windows.microsoft.com/skydrive/ (retrieved 1 June 2012).

36. Yamauchi, Y., Yokozawa, M., Shinohara, T. & Ishida, T. Collaboration with Lean Media: How Open-Source Software Succeeds Distance and Proximity. *Proc CSCW'00*, ACM Press (2000), 329-338.

Disclosure, Ambiguity and Risk Reduction in Real-Time Dating Sites

Mark J. Handel
handel@gmail.com

Irina Shklovski
IT University of Copenhagen
Copenhagen, Denmark
irsh@itu.dk

ABSTRACT

While social network capabilities are proliferating on many online services, research has focused on just a few popular social network sites. In this note, we consider a different kind of social network site, explicitly designed to support particular types of risky sexual activity among men who have sex with men (MSM). We consider the role of ambiguity built into the interface in how users manage self-disclosure and its association with articulating more friends-only or sexual connections on the site. Despite the site's explicit orientation toward risky sexual practices, we find indications that users mitigate potential public health issues through the practice of sero-sorting. We discuss how design considerations that may allow for easier entrance into a community can cause problems for long-term users, or generate potential public health issues.

Categories and Subject Descriptors

H5.m. Information interfaces and presentation (e.g., HCI): Miscellaneous.

General Terms

Human Factors

Keywords

Social networks, interface design, exponential random graphs, public health

1. INTRODUCTION

Seeking out potential dates and spending time with friends are often done together offline, yet these two activities seem to reside in separate realms online. In fact, some of the largest dating sites, such as eHarmony or match.com, are oriented toward traditional dating practices and eschew social networking functionality in favor of creating a private and personal dating experience for their members. Though there is evidence that people use social network sites for dating activities, at times alongside traditional dating sites [10], most research on social network sites focuses on topics outside of romance.

In this paper we present a study of a real-time dating site with substantial social network functionality that is designed to support an alternative dating ecology of men who have sex with men (MSM) who are primarily HIV-positive. Although the vast majority of the users of this site identify as gay, we use the more neutral MSM term here [2, 6]. Researchers have long observed that the relative anonymity of the Internet allowed people, especially those with marginalized identities, to connect with similar others [12].

Homophily [13], the tendency of people to seek out others like themselves (e.g. along race, age or education lines), is highly prevalent on dating sites [7]. There is also evidence that social network sites (SNSs) can provide more natural spaces for meeting potential dating or sexual partners, where the social network functions and context provide additional information for selecting a partner [10]. In the context of MSM and online dating, however, this ability to connect with similar others online has lead to varied consequences [2, 4]. Some MSM reported that negotiating condom use with a potential partner and revealing their HIV status was easier via a dating website or a newsgroup, thus reducing potential for abuse or sexual rejection [4]. Others described online dating through newsgroups, chat-rooms and dating sites as an easy source of partners for risky activities, such as unprotected casual sex [1]. In fact, MSM who tend to engage in high-risk sexual behaviors also tend to gravitate toward the use of the Internet for seeking out casual sex partners [11].

A logical question is whether dating and social network sites oriented toward MSM can use particular design features in their interfaces to enable negotiation of safer sex strategies even as these sites offer ways of meeting other MSM who seek to engage in high-risk sexual behavior. We discuss the role of ambiguity built into the interface of one such social network and dating site oriented toward MSM in how users manage self-disclosure as part of negotiating risky sexual practices. We consider potential public health issues involved in the use of such sites and how social network functionality and profile interface choices might be implicated in exacerbating or mitigating these issues.

1.1 Background

Thirty years into the HIV epidemic, mortality rates in the United States are going down. The development of highly active antiretroviral therapies (HAART) has improved the life expectancy and quality of life for HIV+ people. Yet new cases have been increasing in recent years, especially among younger MSM [6]. This is in part due to the re-emergence of unsafe sexual practices, including unprotected sex and the use of illegal drugs, such as methamphetamine. The success of HAART is sometimes seen as a factor in this trend by making living with HIV seem uneventful, especially for the younger MSM who do not have first-hand experiences with the horrors of the HIV epidemic of the 80s and 90s [5]. In a mixed HIV-status population, there is some evidence that sero-sorting (restricting sexual partners to those of the same HIV status) is an increasingly common sexual practice that can help reduce overall incidence of HIV [3]. This practice has been repeatedly observed on MSM online dating sites, where self-disclosure of individual HIV status in dating profiles is increasingly becoming a common practice [5].

1.2 Research context

Data reported in this paper come from a real-time online dating website, aimed at the MSM community as a place to locate partners for engagement in specific risky behaviors including drug use and unprotected sex. This site is designed and marketed for short-term sexual encounters as the primary goal. By signing up and using the site users explicitly indicate their openness to a particular type of one-time sexual encounter regardless of what other goals they might have for joining the site. The site has a mobile version, but not a mobile app. Although the site has users worldwide, it is primarily US and Canada-focused. Unusual for dating sites (even those for MSM), this site has explicit support for social network features, allowing users to publicly identify others as friends, sexual partners, and/or relationship partners. The network is reciprocal: one individual initiates the link, selecting the link type from a limited list, and the other must approve the link and the link type before it is publicly displayed. The site requires users to indicate a range of demographic information including age, race, smoking, HIV status, drug use and relationship status. Users must provide an answer for all of these demographic variables; omitting or hiding them is not an option. However, in most of these attributes, there is an option "Ask Me" presumably designed as a way to explicitly indicate the need for further negotiation among the users. "Ask me" is an ambiguous response that suggests openness to further discussion while providing users with an option to limit self-disclosure. With this site, we have a unique opportunity to explore how risk is both mitigated and exacerbated not only through choices of partners articulated on such a social network, but also through explicit design choices on a website.

2. METHODOLOGY

We gathered network data along with demographic attributes by examining the individual users' profile web pages. This was done by starting with a single seed user and following all of the connections in a breadth-first fashion until the entire network of social relationships was examined. Data collection took place over the course of three days, in August 2011. The use of semi-public information like this has been a source of concern in the past [15]. We have addressed these concerns by ensuring that this particular site's Terms of Use allowed for this kind of non-commercial data collection, by anonymizing the site itself and by presenting all of the analyses at the population not the individual level.

2.1 Analysis

The site has many small "islands" of 2-5 otherwise unconnected individuals, but the largest component of the network was a, sparsely connected network of 13,442 individuals. Because our interest was centered on health implications of such a large, demographically and geographically diverse, and interconnected group, we restricted our analysis to this single component of the network. The demographic attributes, including HIV status and social network link type were selected by the users from a drop-down list of a small number of options on their profiles. In limited cases we were not able to automatically extract these demographic attributes from the profile; these were left as missing data.

3. RESULTS

3. 1 Descriptive Statistics

We recoded to binary the following demographic user attributes: race (recoded to white (1)/ non-white (0)), relationship status (recoded to single (1)/ not single (0)), personal HIV status (recoded to positive (1)/ negative (0)), openness to an HIV+ partner (recoded to open (1)/ not open (0)), and openness to drug use (recoded to

yes (1)/no (0))[1]. Age was also extracted; in later analysis, we created a dummy variable for age indicating whether users were too young to remember life before HAART or not, using a cut-off age of 25. Finally, we also collected the number of connections on each profile, separating these connections into 'friends only' and 'sexual' connections as indicated by the users. Given this site's explicit purpose of supporting sexual interactions rather than da-

Variable Name	N w/ Answer	Mean	St. Dev	Min	Max	N w/ 'Ask Me'
Age	13391	40	9.13	17	76	N/A
White	12749	0.76	0.43	0	1	566
Single	8998	0.81	040	0	1	4081
HIV+	9610	0.68	0.47	0	1	3801
Partner HIV+	7903	0.96	0.20	0	1	5529
Drug Use	7177	0.67	0.47	0	1	6255
Friend links	13442	0.27	1.29	0	87	
Sexual links	13442	2.72	6.05	0	369	

Table 1: Descriptive statistics

ting or other types of relationships, the explicit distinction between a 'friends only' and a 'sexual' connection is important analytically. Not surprisingly, users tended to have far more sexual rather than 'friends only' connections. Descriptive statistics for each variable are presented in Table 1. We also show how many individuals chose "Ask Me" as a response for each of the variables.

3.2 Interface choices

Our first set of analyses considers the role of ambiguity in self-reporting sensitive health-related information on profiles. Using 'Ask Me' as a way to limit self-disclosure was an explicit interface design choice made by the designers of the site (for instance, other sites allow users to omit some attributes all together). We consider whether such ambiguity is associated with evidence of risky sexual behavior. Predictably, users were more reluctant to disclose sensitive information. While less than 20% of the users were unwilling to disclose their race or sexuality (the majority of our sample self-identified as gay), nearly 30% were unwilling to disclose their own HIV status, 41% were unwilling to indicate their preference for potential partner HIV status and more than 45% did not report drug use preferences.

3.3 Self-disclosure as predictors of connections

We were interested in whether selecting an ambiguous answer rather than explicitly self-reporting attributes such as HIV status or openness to drug use might be related to having more or fewer connections on the site. Specifically, we hypothesized that ambiguity may be associated with more explicitly articulated friends-only connections while openness may be related to more sexual connections. In our sample 171 individuals indicated 'Ask Me' for every attribute. Conducting analyses with and without these individuals in the dataset produced identical results thus the regressions we present include them. We used regression analysis with robust standard errors to test whether limiting self-disclosure on the profile is associated with the number of sexual or friend links [14]. In both models we controlled for the presence of the other kind of links as having friends and sexual links had a positive correlation (r=0.28, p<.0001). We found that greater ambiguity (the total number of questions answered with "Ask Me") had a significant

---

[1]Although this is displayed on-line as just "drug use," in practice, this is understood to mean methamphetamine use.

negative association with the presence of both friend (beta=-0.017, p<0.05, R^2=0.07) and sexual partner links (beta=-0.059, p<0.001, R^2=0.08). That is, greater disclosure was associated with a greater number of articulated online connections.

In order to understand which kind of self-disclosure might matter more or less, we conducted two regressions with robust standard errors, entering five dummy variables indicating if a user disclosed a piece of information or used Ask Me for race, relationship status,

	Friend links		Sexual links	
	Beta	St. err	Beta	St. err
Intercept	0.14***	0.04	2.84**	0.22
Friend links			1.25	0.71
Sexual links	0.06***	0.01		
Ask Me – Race	-0.07*	0.023	-0.14	0.20
Ask Me – Single	-0.03	0.03	-0.30*	0.13
Ask Me – HIV+	-0.02	0.03	0.20	0.12
Ask Me – Partner	0.02	0.04	-0.52***	0.13
Ask Me – Drugs	-0.04	0.02	-0.39***	0.09
	R^2=0.07		R^2=0.08	
*** p < .001	** p < .01		* p < .05	

Table 2: Predicting number of connections

HIV status, preference for sexual partner HIV status and attitude toward drug use. Thus we isolated the role of each 'Ask Me' keeping all other variables constant. Results presented in Table 2 suggest a different pattern for sexual links vs. friend links.

Results indicate that having sexual links was associated with having friends-only links but not vice-versa suggesting that users primarily pursued sexual interactions on the site. This was expected given the explicit purpose of the site. Ambiguity about information that directly pertained to potential sexual interaction such as relationship status, partner HIV status preference and attitude toward drug use were significantly associated with fewer sexual links. While we realize that the models explain under 10% of variance in the data, we feel this result is still of interest. There are no doubt many individual factors unavailable to us for analysis that are important predictors of decisions behind articulation of sexual or friend contacts. Yet these results indicate that interface choices may be implicated in such decisions as well.

3.4 Network Characteristics
The large component is estimated to be about 10% of the total users of the web site, but it had only 20,113 total edges (d = .00022). Thus the number of dyadic ties per person followed a "power law" distribution, with most users displaying few ties and exponentially fewer displaying many ties. The median individual had one connection, and the mean number of ties per person was 2.992 (Std. Dev = 6.51). However, there is a long tail with the most prolific user displaying over 400 total connections.

3.5 Homophily in Relationships
Our key question was the degree to which homophily, especially in self-reported HIV status and openness to risky behaviors predicted relationships. We tested this with exponential random graph models (ERGM), as described in [9]. ERGMs help address the dependencies in network data, which cannot be adequately addressed with traditional methods like regression analysis [8]. The estimate returned by the ERGM model is the log-odds of the attribute predicting the existence of a link; for these results this is where both sides of the link have the same value of the attribute. We stratified the sample into friends-only links and sexual connection links based

on the fact that regression analyses revealed the two are correlated but not identical. The results of the complete ERG models are shown in Table 3.

Being open to drug use predicted that both friends and sexual connections would share the sentiment. We also saw evidence for sero-sorting: openness to a partner's HIV status was a significant predictor of a sexual link, as was having the same sero-status. Further evidence of this being intentional sero-sorting is that these attributes showed few associations in the case of friend connections.

	Friend links n = 1796 edges	Sexual links n = 18317 edges
Main Model		
Drug Use	0.431 ***	0.397 ***
Partner HIV+	0.106 *	0.334 ***
HIV +	0.102	0.159 ***
Rel. Status	0.241 ***	0.127 ***
Age	.110	0.174 ***
Race	.063	0.047 **
Ask Me Model		
Total Ask Me's	-0.128 ***	-0.091 ***
*** p < .001	** p < .01	* p < .05

Table 3: Exponential Random Graph Model Results

We found that relationship status had a stronger association with a friendship than in with a sexual tie. That is, individuals in a relationship were more likely to indicate friendship with other coupled individuals. In addition, age and race were significant factors in sexual relationships, but not in friendships. These two attributes suggest that traditional categories associated with homophily were not as critical for friendships articulated on this website.

We also observed a small, yet significant result in the level of ambiguity, number of 'Ask Me' responses in the profile. For both the friend and sexual connections, greater ambiguity in a user's profile compared to a potential connection was negatively associated with the presence of the connection. People willing to self-disclose sensitive information seemed to expect or motivate the same of their connections.

4. DISCUSSION

4.1 Ambiguity as Interface Choice
Providing options for managing levels of self-disclosure in a social network profile is a logical interface design decision. While traditional dating and social network site designs focus on providing information fields for potential conversation starters, in this particular context it was precisely such starter information that could be withheld, but marked as "negotiable" actively or by default. By design, users were unable to simply skip a particular attribute. Every attribute was displayed on their profiles but some could be marked with 'Ask Me'. We found that attributes that were potentially areas of negotiation among the participants (e.g. potential partner's preferred HIV status or attitudes toward drug use) were less likely to be revealed via the profile than attributes that were not negotiable, but still sensitive (e.g. own HIV status or current relationship status). Basic information, such as sexuality or race, was most likely to be revealed perhaps because it was also implicitly communicated in the fact that the site was oriented toward gay men and in the choice of photos users posted.

SNSs in general tend to invest substantial resources into encouraging their users to disclose ever more information. Our findings illustrate that even minute design decisions such as requiring answers to particular attribute inquiries or allowing different forms of ambiguity can have differing consequences. Some demographic and personal attributes can be communicated explicitly or implicitly via a range of options, such as specified fields, photos, and expressions of approval or support. Others, such as, for example personal HIV status or preferences for sexual partner HIV status, are deeply personal and must be handled with care. The minutiae of design decisions around profile options deserves particular attention because even the smallest changes can result in substantial differences for user interactions.

4.2 Self-disclosure and "Success"

Articulations of a sexual or a friend connection on such a dating site can be construed as displays of a kind of success. Our data illustrate that greater self-disclosure was associated with higher levels of such "success", here, defined as more connections. Ambiguity was a bit of a double-edged sword. While it could provide a degree of protection in revealing sensitive personal information, potentially helping people feel more at home on this site, those who took advantage of this option consistently displayed fewer connections. Most importantly, it was ambiguity in expressing preferences for partner HIV status and drug use that appeared most strongly associated with fewer sexual links. Arguably, this kind of information is most important for speeding up a successful negotiation of a fleeting sexual encounter. Such information could likely be used as indicators for risk reduction practices (serosorting, drug use) in concert with personal HIV status. There is no one correct design for managing self-disclosure: ease of use must be balanced against complexity and community development. Critically, designers need to consider approaches that may help enculturation and easing into a new community, especially one as fraught with risks and fears such as for example becoming HIV+. For example, how might we design profile interfaces to support individuals who are in the process of adjusting to their new and possibly frightening HIV+ status and thus exploring sites that are part of this new to them community? In future work, we will consider whether the use of "ask me" is an enculturation step into an HIV+ status.

4.3 Homophily and Health Implications

Sero-sorting remains controversial as a safer sexual practice especially when it is done in lieu of condom use. Although [3] suggests it may be a viable harm reduction strategy, the risks of superinfection as well as transmission of other STDs remain. While our data suggest some sero-sorting in environments with high expectations of risky sexual activity combined with drug use, these are not large effects. Attraction, especially in the face of risk, remains difficult to understand and model.

Sero-sorting is a particularly risky choice for HIV- MSMs. In one study, over half of all HIV infections were caused by individuals who believed they were negative [4]. One real risk is that niche websites may serve to provide a false sense of confidence about potential partner's HIV status. This is an area where HCI research may be able to help: a change as simple as adding a field for last test date may alter some risks associated with using such a site. Such small design suggestions are important when considering a range of SNSs that have emerged to support niche communities engaging in risky activities.

5. ACKNOWLEDGMENTS
We'd like to thank Jed Brubaker and Ted White for valuable comments and insight. We also thank HV, SW, and B5 for comments on how they used the site.

6. REFERENCES

1. Bolding, G., Davis, M., Hart, G., Sherr, L. and Elford, J. Gay men who look for sex on the Internet: is there more HIV/STI risk with online partners? *AIDS*, 19, 9 (2005), 961-968.

2. Bolding, G., Davis, M., Hart, G., Sherr, L. and Elford, J. Where Young MSM Meet Their First Sexual Partner: The Role of the Internet. *AIDS and Behavior*, 11, 4 (2007), 522-526.

3. Cassels, S., Menza, T. W., Goodreau, S. M. and Golden, M. R. HIV serosorting as a harm reduction strategy: evidence from Seattle, Washington. *AIDS*, 23, 18 (2009), 2497-2506.

4. Davis, M., Hart, G., Bolding, G., Sherr, L. and Elford, J. Sex and the Internet: Gay men, risk reduction and serostatus. *Culture, Health & Sexuality*, 8 (2006), 161-174.

5. Elford, J., Bolding, G., Davis, M., Sherr, L. and Hart, G. Barebacking Among HIV-Positive Gay Men in London. *Sexually Transmitted Diseases*, 34, 2 (2007), 93-98.

6. Elford, J. and Hart, G. If HIV Prevention Works, Why Are Rates of High-Risk Sexual Behavior Increasing among MSM? *AIDS Education and Prevention*, 15, 4 (2003), 294-308.

7. Fiore, A. and Donath, J. S. Homophily in online dating: when do you like someone like yourself? In *Proceedings of CHI '05 extended abstracts on Human factors in computing systems* (Portland, OR, USA, 2005). ACM.

8. Goodreau, S. M. Advances in exponential random graph (p*) models applied to a large social network. *Social Networks*, 29, 2 (2007), 231-248.

9. Hunter, D. R., Handcock, M. S., Goodreau, S. M. and Morris, M. ERGM: A Package to Fit, Simulate and Diagnose Exponential-Family Models for Networks. *Journal of Statistical Software*, 24, 3 (2008).

10. Lee, A. Y. and Bruckman, A. S. Judging you by the company you keep: dating on social networking sites. In *Proceedings of the 2007 international ACM conference on Supporting group work* (Sanibel Island, Florida, 2007). ACM.

11. Light, B. Introducing Masculinity Studies to Information Systems Research: the case of Gaydar. *Eur J Inf Syst*, 16, 5 (2007), 658-665.

12. McKenna, K. and Bargh, J. A. Coming out in the age of the Internet: Identity "demarginalization" through virtual group participation. *Journal of Personality & Social Psychology*, 75, 3 (1998), 681-694.

13. McPherson, M., Smith-Lovin, L. and Cook, J. M. Birds of a Feather: Homophily in Social Networks. *Annual Review of Sociology*, 27, 1 (2001), 415-444.

14. Western, B. Concepts and suggestions for robust regression analysis. *American Journal of Political Science*, 39, 3 (1995), 786-817.

15. Zimmer, M. "But the data is already public": on the ethics of research in Facebook. *Ethics and Information Technology*, 12, 4 (2010), 313-325.

Understanding Participant Behavior Trajectories in Online Health Support Groups Using Automatic Extraction Methods

Miaomiao Wen
Language Technologies Institute
Carnegie Mellon University
5000 Forbes Avenue, Pittsburgh, PA 15213
mwen@cs.cmu.edu

Carolyn Penstein Rosé
Language Technologies Institute
Carnegie Mellon University
5000 Forbes Avenue, Pittsburgh, PA 15213
cprose@cs.cmu.edu

ABSTRACT

This paper presents an automatic analysis method that enables efficient examination of participant behavior trajectories in online communities. This method offers the opportunity to examine behavior over time at a level of granularity that has previously only been possible in small scale case study analyses, and thus complements both existing qualitative and quantitative methodologies. We provide an empirical validation of its performance. We then illustrate how this method offers insights into behavior patterns that enable avoiding faulty oversimplified assumptions about participation, such as that it follows a consistent trend over time. In particular, we use this method to investigate the connection between user behavior and distressful cancer events and demonstrate how this tool could assist in understanding participation trajectories in online medical support communities better so we are better able to design environments that meet the needs of participants.

Categories and Subject Descriptors

H.5.3 [**Group and Organization Interfaces**]: Computer supported cooperative work.

Keywords

Online support groups, Cancer trajectory, Disease event, Natural language analysis

1. INTRODUCTION

The contribution of this paper is a new automatic analysis method that enables efficient examination of participant behavior trajectories in online communities. We demonstrate how it offers the opportunity to examine behavior over time at a level of granularity that has previously only been possible in small scale case study analyses. Using this tool we are able to offer new insights into the experiences of users in

one of the largest online cancer support communities on the Internet. This insights offered by such a tool complement both existing qualitative and quantitative methodologies for studying community behavior patterns.

Online support groups provide a rich and valuable source of data related to chronic illness and the inner workings of social support. A growing number of people who suffer from chronic or life threatening diseases obtain valuable resources from online support groups, which are available anytime in the privacy of one's home [19]. These affordances of online support groups are particularly attractive in the case of stigmatizing illnesses such as AIDS, alcoholism, breast and prostate cancer, which are the topics of many popular online medical support communities [5]. In order to design such environments to maximize benefit to users, it is necessary to understand how the experiences of users of such environments unfold over time.

In this paper we seek to overcome some of the methodological limitations of current approaches to studying online support groups. Quantitative approaches to studying behavior in online communities abstract away from the details of individual users in order to reduce behavior to a small number of variables that may be related to one another statistically. Such a reduction is needed in order to understand the causal mechanisms at work. However, in order to do so in a valid way, it is important to avoid making assumptions that do not hold in practice.

Growing out of a tradition of analysis of threaded discussion forums that consist of a list of threads, each of which roughly corresponds to a topic of discussion, quantitative approaches to modeling participation in online communities typically model that participation in terms of frequency of types of contributions over time, with the idea of identifying increasing or decreasing trends and the reasons for these trends using linear modeling techniques. Our work challenges the underlying assumptions behind such approaches by demonstrating more of a periodicity in participation, centered on important cancer events. This is consistent with other work investigating the importance of key events in a patient's cancer history and their effect on behavior [20, 21].

One role for qualitative analyses of user behavior trajectories in mixed methods approaches is to offer insights that challenge overly simplistic assumptions about participation. However, even such detailed explorations are limited if they can only be conducted on a very small set of users. For example, a case study analysis of the complete posting history of one participant in an online cancer support forum has been published in prior work [26]. That analysis suggests that frequency of participation was clearly correlated with stress-inducing events. But as a case study, the generalizability of the results is limited and restricted. Mapping how the themes of posts change as patients move from diagnosis, through treatment, and towards recovery or death at a grander scale, may provide valuable insights to inform ways to tailor future psychosocial and educational interventions in online medical support communities according to a patient's cancer event trajectory [25]. However, manually extracting such a cancer trajectory is effort-consuming and time consuming. The goal of our work is to automate such an analysis so that some of the benefits can be obtained without the time and effort. Using this tool, we work to contribute deeper insights towards understanding a patient's psychosocial reactions to important cancer events as they unfold within that patient's disease progression [26].

Motivated by earlier qualitative work [26], we use automatically extracted illness trajectories, and present an analysis of data from an active online community that provides support for a statistical connection between the pattern of participation in online discussion and stress-inducing events. We demonstrate that when the users are undergoing these stressful events, they post more than 2 times as often as in non-event months. The topic of their posts also varies according to the events. We also find that almost half of the long-term users began their participation in the online support community when they were facing some kind of stressful disease event, such as chemotherapy.

In addition to the methodological contribution and analysis, our work makes a technical contribution as well. Many practical applications in Natural Language Processing either require or would greatly benefit from the use of temporal information. For instance, question-answering and summarization systems demand accurate processing of temporal information in order to be useful for answering "when" questions and creating coherent summaries by temporally ordering information. Our technical approach involves development of effective temporal expression extraction in an informal writing genre that poses significantly different challenges than generes that have more typically been the focus of work on temporal expression extraction in the past.

In the remainder of this paper, we first review related work that provides the foundation for our investigation. We then describe the online community that provides the context for our work, as well as the data we extracted from it for our analysis. We then present how we automatically generate and visualize disease trajectories from a user's complete posting history. After validation of our visualization tool, we provide an analysis that illustrates the connection between posting behavior and the generated disease trajectory. The paper concludes with discussion and future work.

2. RELATED WORK

For decades, researchers have attempted to examine the well-being of women with breast cancer as it varies over time. Most of these studies are qualitative analyses and do not examine whether disease phase, such as progression of disease or disease recurrence, influence well-being [11]. On the other side of the spectrum, in quantitative analyses, individuals are frequently grouped together for analysis in ways that gloss over individidual differences between patients, in-

cluding the specific issues they are dealing with at different times. Richer insights could be gained through analyses that consider the impact of important cancer events within a patient's trajectory.

Qualitative research studies exploring individuals' well-being across phases of disease report that distress peaks occur after diagnosis, during chemotherapy, at the conclusion of adjuvant therapy, 6 months - 1 year after mastectomy, when recurrence is diagnosed, and when the disease is declared terminal [10, 20, 21]. Researchers have constructed these cancer trajectories retrospectively from self-report questionnaires and interview data. Using such a methodology, researchers have identified distinct trajectories of mental and physical functioning over 4 years according to 363 patients' breast cancer experiences [23]. Disease trajectories for chronic illness have been defined more generally as the course of the illness over time as identified by eight disease phases: the period before the illness begins, the diagnostic period, crisis or life-threatening situation, acute illness, in which illness or complications require hospitalization, a stable phase, where illness is controlled, an unstable phase, in which illness is not controlled by a regimen, a progressive or deterioration phase, and dying [4]. This trajectory may inform the design of research about the experience of chronic illnesses such as breast cancer. Moreover, research using questionnaires and interviews do not tell us what we would see if we explored similar questions from the standpoint of what behavior looks like over time within these phases. However, these insights that are possible to glean from interviews or questionnaires are not readily accessible in the raw data traces of online communities that would allow us to go beyond self report and observe how participants respond to their cancer events in real time. The goal of pushing beyond what is possible with existing well established methodologies presents technical challenges, however. The boundaries between the phases identified here are not trivial to automatically extract from the posts.

As online support groups become more and more popular, there are more studies of online support groups [2]. Most qualitative evaluation research to date of online support groups has analyzed postings from a sample of users without relating their message content to the medical background of the patients or their disease trajectory [12, 22]. In one notable exception, researchers suggest that the pattern of online discussion group messages was clearly correlated with the stress-inducing events [26]. But as a case study, the generalizability of the results is limited and restricted. In our work, we want to do similar analysis quantitatively. We draw from prior work that offers the ability to automatically identify themes in discussion behavior in online groups. In particular, Wang and colleagues [24] have derived 20 topics from the forum posts using a technique referred to as Latent Dirichelet Allocation (LDA), which we describe later. This prior work reveals something of the distribution of topics discussed by cancer patients, but leaves open interesting questions about the topics patients talk about during specific periods related to important cancer events.

In order to construct cancer trajectories, we must associate events with points in time by extracting mentions of time points in posts. While much computational work has been done on temporal expression extraction, our own research differs from this previous work in several respects. Previous work has mainly focused on identifying the separate timepoints of each event in news text, where multiple disparate events may be described [6, 13, 17]. Newswire text is the primary genre in that work, and that genre is known to include a lot of explicit temporal expressions, which are very different from our online forum corpus. Besides specific use of temporal expressions like "MM/DD/YYYY" or "Oct. 22nd, 2001", our system resolves generic time expressions, especially indexical expressions like "tomorrow", "next Tuesday", "two weeks after my diagnosis", etc., which designate times that are dependent on the time of the post or some referential time point. What is more, we also resolve self-contained time expressions that are special to each user like "at the age of 57", "Today is my third breast cancer anniversary", and "I am six months out of Chemotherapy". As the exact date of each post is known, these expressions could be utilized to infer the illness event times. The language style in online forums is highly informal. Our automatic analysis approach also considers forum specific jargon, slang and nicknames [16].

3. CONTEXT OF RESEARCH AND DATA SET

The data for our investigation was extracted from a large, online cancer support community operated by a nonprofit organization dedicated to providing the most reliable, complete, and up-to-date information about breast cancer. This organization also provides a variety of communication platforms, including discussion boards and chat rooms for patients, family members and caregivers so that all of these stakeholder communities are able to exchange support with each other. In particular, the discussion board platform is one of the most popular and active online breast cancer support groups on the Internet. It contains more than 90,000 registered members and 66 forums organized by disease stage (e.g., Stage IV and Metastatic Breast Cancer), treatment (e.g., Chemotherapy - Before, During and After), demographic group (e.g., Women 40-60ish with Breast Cancer) or entertainment (e.g., Humor and Games). In the forums, members can ask questions, share their stories, and read posts of others about how to deal with their disease. This discussion board platform is a rich environment for studying the dynamics of online support groups. We collected all of the public posts, users, and their profiles on the discussion board platform from the forum from October 2001 to January 2011. 31,307 users had at least one post.

4. SYSTEM DESCRIPTION

We aim to automatically generate and visualize cancer event trajectories of users. Figure 1 shows the configuration of our tool "Breast Cancer Trajectory".
Area 1. User ID
Area 2. Cancer event trajectory
Area 3. Events buttons
Area 4. Monthly post frequency

Use of the tool begins by inputting a forum user's ID in area 1 in Figure 1. The whole trajectory (area 2) begins with the month of the first post of this user and ends with the month of the last post. By pressing the event buttons in area 3, the corresponding event tag will appear in area 2, unless the date of this event is not retrievable for this user. The cancer event tags, "Diag" (Diagnosis), "Chemo"

(Chemotherapy),"Rads" (Radiation therapy), "Mast" (Mastectomy), "Lump" (Lumpectomy), "Recon" (Reconstruction), "Recur" (Recurrence) and "Mets" (Metastasis) are located at the month of that event on the trajectory. When a user presses the "PostNum" button in area 3, then the bars in area 4 show the monthly posting frequency of the user. The height of the blue bar corresponds to the number of posts the user contributed to existing threads each month. The height of the pink bar corresponds to the number of thread starter posts the user initiated each month.

4.1 Automatic Cancer Trajectory Generation

Extracting cancer trajectories from a highly informal online forum is a non-trivial problem. Figure 2 shows the flow chart of event date extraction, which is the most challenging part of the process. A typical two-year frequent breast cancer forum user has 500-1000 posts, which contain 2000-5000 sentences. To reduce the search space, we first extract the sentences that may contain the temporal information of the disease events from the posts and then extract a date from these date sentences instead of directly from the complete raw posts. In Section 4.1.1, we present how we define and extract these "date sentences". The topics and contents of the messages in this forum are highly diverse. To reduce noise, we train a machine learning model to decide if the date in the date sentence is the date of the target event. Finally, we choose the most likely event date based on some intuitive rules of thumb.

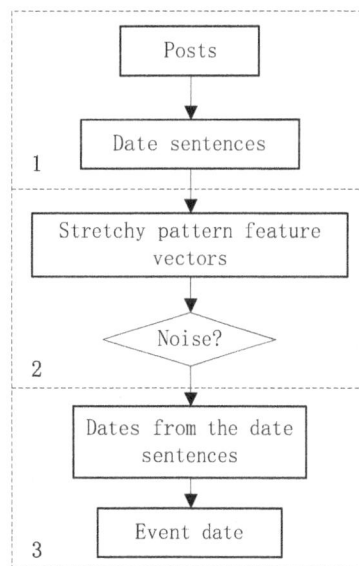

Figure 2: Event extraction flowchart.

4.1.1 Cancer Event Keywords

The cancer event is usually signaled by a set of keywords. In our experiment, we manually design an event keyword set for each cancer event. The keyword set includes the name of the event, abbreviations, aliases and other related words. For example, the Chemotherapy keyword set contains the common medical terms, such as AC (Adriamycin and Cytoxan). The Reconstruction keyword set contains the common surgery type names, such as DIEP (deep in-

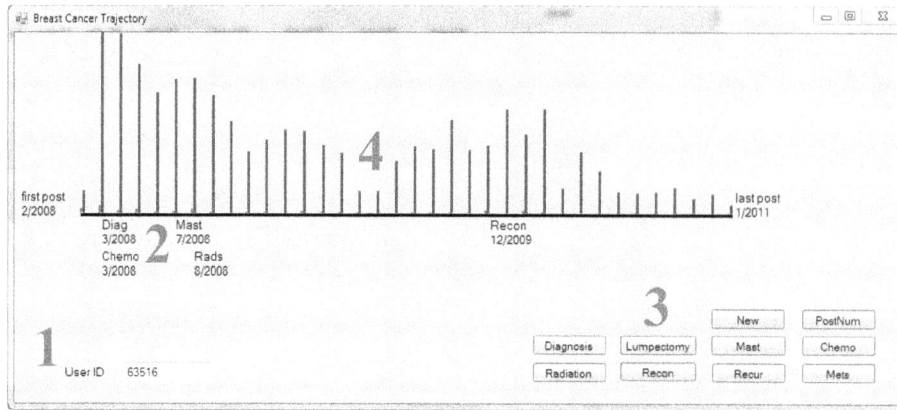

Figure 1: Automatically-generated breast cancer trajectory of an example user.

ferior epigastric perforator flap breast reconstruction). By creating an analogous keyword set, our event date extraction method could be easily adapted to other datasets.

4.1.2 Date Sentences Extraction

We define a "date sentence" as a sentence that contains at least one time expression and at least one cancer event keyword. A user frequently shares the date of her disease event in close proximity to mention of that event by posting these "date sentences". For example, if we want to detect when a user was diagnosed of breast cancer, we will extract sentences like "I was <diagnosis keyword> on <temporal expression>" from her posts. Here the keyword set, <diagnosis keyword>, is {diagnosed, dx, dx., dx'd}, where "dx", "dx." and "dx'd" are the abbreviations of "diagnosed" that are often used by the breast cancer forum users.

In our technical approach, we recognize three types of time expressions: specific expressions, generic time expressions and self-contained time expressions (As illustrated below, the items in the brackets are optional.). Specific expressions could be resolved easily. Generic time expressions usually specify the length of interval between the time of the post and the time of the event. The date of the event could be calculated by subtracting the duration from the date of the post. For example, a date sentence is "I had my first radiation three months ago." Then her first radiation is three months before the post time. The most complicated cases are self-contained time expressions. Some of them could be resolved as generic time expressions. For example, "today is my first breast cancer anniversary" means that she was diagnosed one year ago. The other cases cannot be resolved without further information about the user. For example, a lot of users use their age as time references of the events. For example, "I was diagnosed at the age of 57". We obtain the age of users from their personal profile to handle these cases. Here are some examples of each type:

- Specific expressions
  I was diagnosed on Sep(tember|(.)) ((the) 8(th)(,))
  (of) ((20)08|'08).
  I was diagnosed in (20)08|'08 Sep(tember) (8(th)).
  I was diagnosed on (0)9(/|−)((0)8)(/|−)(20)08.

- Generic time expressions

$< 2008 − 10 − 20 >$ I was diagnosed in September.
$< 2008 − 09 − 15 >$ I was diagnosed a week ago.
$< 2008 − 09 − 15 >$ I was diagnosed last week.
$< 2011 − 09 − 08 >$ Now I am three years from my diagnosis.
$< 2011 − 09 − 08 >$ I have been a three years survivor since my first diagnosis.

- Self-contained time expressions
  I was diagnosed when I was 51 ((years|yr|yrs) old).
  I was diagnosed at the age of 51.

4.1.3 Noise Reduction

The temporal expression in the date sentences may not be the modifier of the target event, the second step of our cancer trajectory generation is to build a noise reduction machine learning model. The features are designed to capture both the characteristic of noisy date sentences and the style of "true" date sentences (i.e., date sentences that tell the date of the target event that has occurred to the user herself).

There are mainly four types of noisy date sentences. In online support groups, users not only tell stories about themselves, they also share other patients' stories (see example sentence (1) below). This kind of sentence usually includes the acquaintance's name or personal pronouns. They also discuss about or share breast cancer related news or results of published studies (example (2)). This kind of sentence usually includes keywords like "study" or "research". When talking about their own illness stories, they might be just concerned but have not actually experienced the event herself, like in examples (3) and (4). Neither of these sentences' authors had metastasis at the time of the post. When a sentence includes multiple disease keywords like in example (5), we have to decide which event the date expression modifies. In example (6), the date expression "Aug 2005" modifies a Reconstruction event but not a Mastectomy event. So before we extract the date from the date sentences, we must first judge if the topic of the sentence is actually the user herself or not, and whether she had this event already or is just concerned.

(1) A friend of mine started chemotherapy this week.
(2) In a recent retrospective study by md anderson reported

Dec 2008 at San Antonio, women who had her2+ cancer with negative nodes and tumors less than 1 cm had a 5 year recurrence of 23% and distant recurrence (mets) about 15%.
(3) I already freaked out and thought this was bc mets back in march when they told me I had thyroid nodules.
(4) I was diagnosed with stage II bc without metastasis in Aug..
(5) I had my mastectomy and later had reconstruction in Aug 2005.
(6) After my mastectomy and removal of 14 nodes on April 11th, my surgeon mentioned that if i got a cut or scrape on the affected side, i should go to the er.
(7) My mets to my bones and lymph nodes were found in Feb.

Users often tell the date of their cancer events with some detailed event-related information or description. This information is more highly individualized than what N-gram features that are typical of text extraction approaches can capture. For example, in example (6), besides the disease event keyword "mastectomy" and the date expression "April 11th", the user also tells how many lymph nodes are removed, which is an important feature of the mastectomy surgery. In example (7), besides the illness event keyword "mets" (an abbreviation of "metastasis") and the temporal expression "Feb", the user also tells her the metastasis sites. To capture these detailed but important features, we adopt a recently introduced method called "stretchy pattern" features instead of the commonly-used N-gram features. These stretchy pattern features can be extracted from text using a tool called LightSIDE [14];

The intuition behind this decision is that to better capture the wide variety of flexible and informal language found in social media, we need linguistic features that have strong expressive power and can be modeled with reasonably small amounts of training data. To this end, prior work has proposed the notion of a "stretchy pattern" to model stylistic variation in sociolects [9]. A stretchy pattern is defined as a sequence of word categories, some of which may be Gaps that are able to cover some number of symbols of any type. It is the Gap categories that make the patterns flexible. We designate every word instance by its word category label. A Gap is a special category. Compared to N-gram patterns, stretchy patterns allow longer linguistic patterns to be captured, and to do so in a flexible way. Using the appropriate word categories, stretchy patterns are applied here to classify if the temporal expression in the sentence is describing the the user's target event. For sentences like example (6), numbers are replaced by a word category <Number>. For sentences like example (7), a word category <BodyPart>, which includes "liver", "lung" and "brain", etc. can appear between <event keyword> and <temporal expression>. But if $k \in$ $< event_1 keyword > \neq < event_2 keyword >$, then k should not appear between <event2 keyword> and <temporal expression>. If so, the temporal expression is more likely to be the date of $event_2$ but not $event_1$, like in example (5).

4.1.4 Rules of Thumb for Resolving Temporal Ambiguities

If there is more than one temporal expression in a sentence, then we intuitively choose the time expression that is the nearest to the event keyword. When more than one

date is extracted for an event of a user, for example, $date_i$ is extracted from N_i sentences, then we choose the date(i) with the biggest N(i). The assumption is that the more frequently the user associates the event with a date, the more probably the date is the event date.

4.2 LDA Topic Modeling

To observe how topics of a user's posts can vary with her progression of disease events, a statistical topic modeling approach is used to identify topical themes in each message. In prior work [24], cancer-related dictionaries have been constructed using Latent Dirichlet Allocation (LDA). LDA is a statistical generative model that can be used to discover latent topics in documents as well as the words associated with each topic [3]. Wang and colleagues [24] first trained an LDA model using 30,000 breast cancer messages randomly selected from the entire dataset. Then 20 latent topics were derived from this document collection. For each topic, a topic dictionary consisted of 500 words that were determined to to strongly correlate with that topic. Table 1 shows sample vocabulary for each LDA topic dictionary. A complete list is provided in the online appendix [1]. With these 20 cancer-related topic dictionaries, the topic of each post is represented as a 20-dimension topic distribution vector. Each dimension of the vector calculates the frequency of words in a message matching its corresponding dictionary. For example, in the following post,

Girls please pray for me. I am so sick.
Susan

There are 10 words in this post. 3 words, "girls", "please" and "am", belong to the "Forum Communication" topic vocabulary, so the 4th dimension is 0.3. 4 words, "girls", "I", "am" and "sick", belong to the "Emotional reaction" topic vocabulary, so the 15th dimension is 0.3. Similarly, 3 words, "girls", "please" and "pray", belong to the "Spiritual" topic vocabulary, so the 17th dimension is 0.3.

5. TOOL VALIDATION

Before describing how to use our tool to uncover new knowledge about posting behavior and cancer histories, we first validate the accuracy of our cancer trajectory extraction system in this section.

5.1 Noise Reduction

We randomly choose 100 users and manually labeled all the date sentences in their posts as the training data. We use Bayesian logistic regression as our machine learning model. The stretchy pattern features are extracted using LightSIDE [14]. In our experiment, we used 16 manually-collected word categories when extracting stretchy pattern features. For example, <I> is the first person category. <prep> is the preposition category. <doctor> category contains the words that are used to refer to doctors. We used Weka [27], a machine learning toolkit, to build the regression models. We also experimented with an SVM classifier and found logistic regression to do slightly better. The 10-fold cross validation results are shown in Table 2. The results indicate that by using the stretchy pattern features, we could reliably remove noisy date sentences.

The top 10 stretchy pattern features for Metastasis events

---

[1]http://www.cs.cmu.edu/ yichiaw/Data/CSCW2012/CSCW2012-FeatureSet.htm

Table 1: Samples of Vocabulary in LDA Topic Dictionaries

LDA Topic	Sample Vocabulary
Pre-diagnosis	Told, appointment, wait, back
Treatment plan	Clinical, risk, medicine, therapy
Forum communication	Post, read, help, thread
Adjusting to diagnosis	Understand, trying, experience
Financial concerns	Insurance, plan, company, pay
Lymphedema	Arm, pain, swelling, fluid, area
Diet	Eat, weight, food, exercise, body
Family/Friends	Daughter, sister, wife
Positive life events	Love, nice, happy, enjoy, fun
Surgery	Breast, surgeon, mastectomy
Thoughts/Feelings	Think, remember, believe
Chemo/Radiation	Chemo, radiation, treatment
Family history	Mom, children, age, young
Emotional reaction	Better, lucky, scared
Tumor Treatment	Biopsy, nodes, positive, report
Spiritual	Love, god, prayer, bless, peace
Emotional support	Hope, hug, glad, sorry, best, luck
Routine/Schedule	Today, night, sleep, work
Hair loss/Appearance	Hair, wig, grow, head
Post-surgery problems	Pain, blood, tamoxifen, symptom

Table 2: 10-fold cross validation results.

Disease event	Number of sentences	Accuracy
Diagnosis	608	0.88
Lumpectomy	238	0.75
Mastectomy	530	0.81
Chemotherapy	544	0.80
Radiation	432	0.77
Reconstruction	263	0.81
Recurrence	345	0.87
Metastasis	164	0.82

are listed below. We can see that the stretchy patterns capture the form of the date expressions well. One example sentence is illustrated below to show how the stretchy patterns capture the structure of the true date sentences.

I was diagnosed in Feb. with soft tissue mets.
$\langle$diagnosis$\rangle$ $\langle$prep$\rangle$$\langle$T$\rangle$ [GAP] $\langle$K$\rangle$
$\langle$T$\rangle$[GAP]$\langle$BodyPart$\rangle$$\langle$K$\rangle$

The top 10 Metastasis stretchy pattern features. $\langle$K$\rangle$ = $\langle$event keyword$\rangle$ = {metastasis, micrometastases, mets, metastasize, metastasises}, $\langle$T$\rangle$ = $\langle$temporal expression$\rangle$:
$\langle$K$\rangle$ $\langle$prep$\rangle$ $\langle$T$\rangle$
$\langle$BodyPart$\rangle$ $\langle$K$\rangle$ $\langle$T$\rangle$
$\langle$K$\rangle$ [GAP] $\langle$prep$\rangle$ $\langle$T$\rangle$
$\langle$T$\rangle$ [GAP] $\langle$BodyPart$\rangle$ $\langle$K$\rangle$
$\langle$BodyPart$\rangle$ $\langle$K$\rangle$ $\langle$prep$\rangle$ $\langle$T$\rangle$
$\langle$diagnosis$\rangle$ $\langle$K$\rangle$ $\langle$prep$\rangle$ $\langle$T$\rangle$
$\langle$diagnosis$\rangle$ $\langle$prep$\rangle$ $\langle$T$\rangle$ [GAP] $\langle$K$\rangle$
$\langle$BodyPart$\rangle$ $\langle$K$\rangle$ $\langle$prep$\rangle$ $\langle$T$\rangle$ $\langle$conj$\rangle$
$\langle$prep$\rangle$ $\langle$BodyPart$\rangle$ $\langle$K$\rangle$ $\langle$prep$\rangle$ $\langle$T$\rangle$
$\langle$BodyPart$\rangle$ $\langle$K$\rangle$ $\langle$prep$\rangle$ $\langle$T$\rangle$ $\langle$conj$\rangle$

5.2 Event Date Extraction

For each user, we extract the year and the month of the following breast cancer events: Diagnosis, Lumpectomy, the beginning of Chemotherapy, the beginning of Radiation Therapy, Mastectomy, breast Reconstruction, Metastasis and cancer Recurrence. Notice that not all events occur for each individual. Also some users may have multiple rounds of Chemotherapy, Reconstruction, Metastasizes and Recurrences. Among all the 31,307 users who have at least one post, 7487 users are located with at least one event date. As there is no established baseline to compare with, we randomly choose 20 long-term users, who have been active on this forum for more than 2 years [16]. Then we manually extract the event dates from their posts and profile. The results are shown in Table 3. Except for Reconstruction, we see that we are able to reliably extract the date of these disease events. There are several reasons that Reconstruction date is hard to extract. One is that as reconstruction is an purely optional surgery, it is quite common for patients to change the surgery schedule. For example, one user posted "My reconstruction is scheduled 11/08". But in her later post, she postponed the surgery date. It is hard for the classifier to distinguish between the scheduled but changed surgery dates and the actual surgery dates. Another reason is that a major kind of breast reconstruction is done at the same time with the mastectomy surgery. So these users usually will not separately state the date of their reconstruction. Instead, they will post "I had mastectomy with immediate reconstruction". In this case, it is possible to extract the reconstruction time if the user had stated their mastectomy time. But there may be no date sentences extracted for the Reconstruction event directly.

Table 3: Event date extraction evaluation results

Disease event	Total	Correctly extracted
Diagnosis	20	16
Lumpectomy	11	8
Mastectomy	12	10
Chemotherapy	14	9
Radiation	12	8
Reconstruction	8	4
Recurrence	4	3
Metastasis	4	3

6. DISEASE EVENTS AND PATTERNS OF ONLINE FORUM POSTS

In order to find the relationship between posting behavior and the cancer events, we use our tool to investigate two questions in this section. One is what prompts participation in online heath support groups? Our hypothesis is that in the important event months, the patients are more distressed and crave more interaction. So they are more likely to join the community and increase participation in the forum discussions. The other question is what are the issues of the most interest during different event months? Our hypothesis is that users will be more interested in and post messages that are related to their ongoing cancer event.

6.1 Change of Message Frequencies Across the Cancer Trajectory

The distressful events prompt cancer patients' participation in online health support forums. Firstly, during event months, we see that users initiate and follow more posts.

We first calculate the number of monthly messages across the cancer trajectory. On average, a user initiates 0.34 threads month, and posts follow-up messages on existing threads 7.83 times per month. We define the month during which at least one event happened as an "event month". In event months, a user initiates 0.84 threads per month, and posts 14.47 follow-up posts on average. The message number peaks across the post trajectories usually is a signal of the user's cancer events (See the rectangles in Figure 3). When facing these distress-inducing events, people position themselves to receive more informational and emotional support.

Secondly, a large portion of the users join this community in the same month as one of their cancer events. Among the 7487 users who are located with at least one event date, 2145 users started using the forum in an event month (Table 4). Although it would be natural to imagine that users come to the community when they are diagnosed, we found that 1123 users posted their first post when they were starting chemotherapy, which was approximately twice the number that came in their diagnosis month. Typically, they update their chemotherapy treatment frequently to a thread to connects with the other women who started chemotherapy in the same month. Such threads include "2008 October Chemo Girls" and "Starting Chemo this October". Women receiving chemotherapy have reported increased levels of psychological distress, difficulties with psychosocial function [21] and increased level of uncertainty [11] when compared with women not receiving chemotherapy. Since chemotherapy typically takes several months, the patients who participate in such threads have time to get familiar with the subcommunity of users experiencing something similar.

Table 4: Number of users who join the community when they are undergoing a certain disease event.

Disease event	Number of users
Diagnosis	509
Lumpectomy	276
Mastectomy	340
Chemotherapy	1123
Radiation	351
Reconstruction	117
Recurrence	8
Metastasis	36
Total	2145

6.2 Topics of Messages Across the Cancer Trajectory

Although prior work has pointed out that people post more when they are experiencing some of these key cancer events [26], what has not been explored is what distribution of topics people are thinking about and posting about during those times include. Investigating this question offers a portal into their coping processes during these important periods of time. In this section, we shift to looking at the message topics as they vary across the cancer trajectory. We believe that users will engage in discussion topics that are relevant to their current cancer phase. We calculate the average topic percentage vector of each disease event as the average over all a user's posts during the month of the event. From Table 5, we can see that among all the

events, the Chemotherapy event has the highest percentage on *Chemo/Radiation* topic, which validates our Chemotherapy date extraction. The Diagnosis event has the highest percentage on both *Pre-diagnosis* and *Adjusting to diagnosis* topics, which validates our Diagnosis date extraction. Both Reconstruction and Mastectomy events have high percentages on the *Surgery* topic as both these two events involve surgeries.

Our topic model analysis also provides some insights into what people are discussing about when facing these disease events. As metastasizing cancer is highly dangerous, the messages contain more Spiritual themes where people send prayers and blessings to each other during the month when Metastasis is found. The *Hair loss/appearance* topic is the most salient during the Chemotherapy month. This indicates that users are coping with the side effects of chemotherapy and adjusting to the illness during chemotherapy. For example,

Title: Hair Hair Hair - Another question
I know that there have been several threads on this, but I'm asking the question again: on average, when did your hair start growing back in after chemo?

6.3 Cancer Story Summarization and Cancer Trajectory

A majority of cancer patients find hearing and constructing illness stories useful for their own decision making [1, 8, 18, 20]. Users in the breast cancer forum search for or even directly ask for cancer stories that are similar to their own situation. Below is an example message showing this need. Currently there are few search facilities concerning illness stories on the Internet [18, 7]. Automatic cancer story summarization has tremendous potential to make cancer coping experiences accessible to patients within these online support communities, or as a biproduct of the data created within them.

Title: Boost my spirits...long term trip neg mets stories please
OK ladies.....I need a little boost here.
Most days I am doing fine with the mets Dx.
A few things still get me panicky.
One of them is the fact that almost all the long-term mets success stories I read are for hormone positive ladies.
I am a triple negative gal, and I really could use a few positive long term mets survivor stories.

Visualizing the events according to each user's cancer trajectory, as shown in Figure 3, could facilitate the summarization of the user's cancer story. In Figure 3(a), we could see that user 26326 joined this community one month before her mastectomy. She gradually got familiar with the community. She tended to post and respond to more and more posts. The number of her messages had a sharp increase when her metastasis was found (the red rectangle in Figure 3(a)). She was very frustrated and initiated a number of posts requesting both information and emotional support. Then she began chemotherapy for treating the metastasis. She posted less and less due to her worsening situation, and finally posted zero posts the month before her death. Her last message was posted by her husband after her death.

Table 5: Average topic percentage vector of disease event. The biggest percentage of each event is shown in bold. The biggest percentage of each topic is shown in italic.

LDA Topic	Avg.	Diag.	Chem.	Mets.	Reco.	Mast.	Recu.	Lump.
Pre-diagnosis	.171	*.199*	.195	.180	.191	.192	**.173**	.189
Treatment plan	.104	.124	.105	.110	.104	.104	*.144*	.114
Forum communication	.146	*.165*	.156	.158	.153	.154	.159	.152
Adjusting to diagnosis	.160	*.180*	.172	.168	.169	.172	.160	.165
Financial concerns	.113	*.117*	.114	.116	.114	.114	.117	.115
Lymphedema	.130	.137	.145	.129	.145	.146	*.153*	.138
Diet	.122	.116	*.131*	.118	.118	.120	.123	.119
Family/Friends	.147	.156	.142	*.160*	.146	.142	.135	.137
Positive life events	.119	.097	.102	.115	.107	.106	.102	.105
Surgery	.142	.167	.151	.133	***.209***	.193	.143	.159
Thoughts/Feelings	.138	.143	.140	.149	.144	.144	*.153*	.143
Chemo/Radiation	.111	.121	*.173*	.115	.118	.119	.117	.116
Family history	.154	*.170*	.164	.168	.159	.160	.153	.155
Emotional reaction	.184	.201	***.215***	.193	.199	**.200**	.172	**.190**
Tumor Treatment	.122	*.176*	.137	.128	.146	.159	.166	.167
Spiritual	.194	.195	.184	*.205*	.186	.181	.170	.174
Emotional support	.159	.159	.161	*.177*	.158	.154	.144	.145
Routine/Schedule	.161	.161	.193	.161	.171	.172	.141	.161
Hair loss/Appearance	.161	.161	*.189*	.161	.169	.167	.148	.161
Post-surgery problems	*.189*	.112	.128	.132	.115	.113	.129	.109

User 60351 in Figure 3(b) joined the community two months before diagnosis when her mammogram showed something unusual (the blue rectangle in Figure 3(c)). She began chemotherapy one month after diagnosis. Her post equency peaked in her first chemotherapy month (the red rectangle in Figure 3(b)), when she joined the March 2008 chemotherapy group and updated her situation to the board almost everyday. She had a lumpectomy but later found metastasis and soon began radiation therapy. The extracted cancer trajectory shows that she had both a mastectomy and reconstruction in June 2009, which is later than her last post (the black circle in Figure 3(b)). Actually, she planed to have mastectomy and reconstruction in June but failed to survive that far.

The death of members has a big influence on the online support group. Below is a message that shows the users' concern over the sudden death of community members. Our automatically generated cancer trajectory may potentially help monitor the death of the online support group members to anticipate where others may need additional support, and thus trigger interventions that might provide this needed support.

"I'll be lurking of course, but wanted to post because I know many of us can often just disappear, and I don't want to do that. My BFF will post when all is done."

User 64251 shown in Figure 3(c) joined the community when she was first diagnosed (the blue rectangle in Figure 3(c)), followed by immediate lumpectomy and mastectomy. Later she joined a large number of threads about breast reconstruction. After her reconstruction was finished, she posted less and less posts and finally left the community. The decreasing trend of the monthly post frequency shows how a breast cancer patient gradually adjusts to this life-altering disease.

From these three example users, we can see how our interface could assist understanding (1) the different reasons of entering the community; (2) the association between peaks of the monthly post numbers and cancer events; (3) the unusual posting behavior of each individual user.

7. CONCLUSIONS AND CURRENT WORK

In this paper, we describe how we built machine learning models to reliably extract cancer event trajectories from messages in online breast cancer support groups. We examined the relationship between disease events and post patterns. The results demonstrate that both the frequency and the topic of messages were correlated with the distress-inducing cancer events. These events prompt cancer patients to begin or increase participation in the online health support groups. Our message topic analysis shows that users engage more in threads that are related to their ongoing current cancer event. Our visualization tool, "Breast Cancer Trajectory" indicates further application in cancer story summarization.

Much previous work has studied how breast cancer patients psychologically and physically adjust to breast cancer [15, 23]. These studies are done with a restricted number of participants. In contrst, the automatically extracted cancer trajectories will allow us to study how users adjust to this illness at a large scale. As the cancer events are tightly related to information and emotional support seeking, our work is potentially useful for online support group studies such as those published in related work [24].

There are several potential directions for improving the current interface. First, it is possible to extract from the posts whether the user was alive or not at the time of posting. Second, we can represent the message topic variation across the cancer trajectory. For example, we could visualize when the user talks about death-related topics as a way of understanding better how the experience of approaching death affects participation. During different cancer treatments, the cancer patients will develop close relationship with several different doctors. There are many posts in the forum that talk about doctors. Since trust in doctor-patient relationships is an important factor in patient wellbeing, we are currently working on understanding patients' attitudes towards doctors and how they change over time in relation to important cancer events.

8. ACKNOWLEDGMENTS

We want to thank Dong Nguyen and Yi-chia Wang, who helped provide the data for this project. The research reported here was supported by National Science Foundation grant IIS-0968485.

9. REFERENCES

[1] K. Arthur. *The Illness Narratives. Suffering, Healing, and the Human Condition.* Basic Books, New York, 1988.

[2] A. Barak, M. Boniel-Nissim, and J. Suler. Fostering empowerment in online support groups. *Computers in Human Behavior*, 24(5):1867 – 1883, 2008.

[3] D. M. Blei, A. Y. Ng, and M. I. Jordan. Latent dirichlet allocation. *Journal of Machine Learning Research*, 3:993–1022, 2003.

[4] J. M. Corbin and A. Strauss. *In Chronic Illness Trajectory Framework: The Corbin and Strauss Nursing Model.* Elsevier, New York, 1992.

[5] K. P. Davison, J. W. Pennebaker, and S. S. Dickerson. Who talks? the social psychology of illness support groups. *American Psychologist*, 55(2):205 – 217, 2000.

[6] V. Eidelman. Inferring activity time in news through event modeling. In *Proc. ACL-HLT2008, Student Research Workshop*, pages 13–18, 2008.

[7] G. Eysenbach. The impact of the internet on cancer outcomes. *CA: A Cancer Journal for Clinicians*, 53(6):356–371, 2003.

[8] A. W. Frank. *The Wounded Storyteller. Body, Illness, and Ethics.* The University of Chicago Press, Ltd., London, 1995.

[9] P. Gianfortoni, D. Adamson, and C. P. Rosé. Modeling of stylistic variation in social media with stretchy patterns. In *Workshop on Modeling of Dialects and Language Varieties at EMNLP2011*, pages 49–59, 2011.

[10] M. Hanson Frost, V. J. Suman, T. A. Rummans, A. M. Dose, M. Taylor, P. Novotny, R. Johnson, and R. E. Evans. Physical, psychological and social well-being of women with breast cancer: the influence of disease phase. *Psycho-Oncology*, 9(3):221–231, 2000.

[11] B. A. Hilton. Getting back to normal: the family experience during early stage breast cancer. *Oncology Nursing Forum*, 23(4):605–614, 1996.

[12] K. Luker, K. Beaver, S. Leinster, and G. R. Owens. Information needs and sources of information for women with breast cancer: A follow-up study. *Journal of Advanced Nursing*, 23:487–495, 1996.

[13] I. Mani and G. Wilson. Robust temporal processing of news. In *Proc. of ACL-2000*, pages 69–76, 2000.

[14] E. Mayfield and C. P. Rosé. LightSIDE: Open Source Machine Learning for Text Accessible to Non-Experts. In *Invited chapter in the Handbook of Automated Essay Grading (in press)*, 2012.

[15] T. Morris, H. S. Greer, and P. White. Psychological and social adjustment to mastectomy: a two-year follow-up study. *Cancer*, 40(5):2381–2387, 1977.

[16] D. Nguyen and C. P. Rosé. Language use as a reflection of socialization in online communities. In *Workshop on Language in Social Media at ACL2011*, pages 76–85, 2011.

[17] T. Noro, T. Inui, H. Takamura, and M. Okumura. Time period identificaiton of events in text. In *Proc. COLING-ACL2006*, pages 1153–1160, 2006.

[18] R. I. Overberg, L. L. Alpay, J. Verhoef, and J. H. M. Zwetsloot-Schonk. Illness stories on the internet: what do breast cancer patients want at the end of treatment? *Psycho-Oncology*, 16(10):937–944, 2007.

[19] R. S. and C. Q. Internet community group participation: Psychosocial benefits for women with breast cancer. *Journal of Computer Mediated Communication*, 10(4), 2005.

[20] B. F. Sharf and M. L. Vanderford. *Illness narratives and the social construction of health.* Lawrence Erlbaum Associates, NJ, 2003.

[21] P. Trief and D.-S. M. Counseling needs of women with breast cancer: what the women tell us. *The Journal of Psychosocial Nursing and Mental Health Services*, 34(5):24–29, 1996.

[22] B. van der Molen. Relating information needs to the cancer experience: Themes from six cancer narratives. *European Journal of Cancer Care*, 9:48–54, 2000.

[23] S. H. Vicki, P. Snyder, and H. Seltman. Psychological and physical adjustment to breast cancer over 4 years: Identifying distinct trajectories of change. *Health Psychology*, 23(1):3–15, 2004.

[24] Y. Wang, R. Kraut, and J. Levine. To stay or leave? the relationship of emotional and informational support to commitment in online health support groups. In *ACM Conference on Computer Supported Cooperative Work*, pages 833–842, 2012.

[25] K.-Y. Wen and D. H. Gustafson. Needs assessment for cancer patients and their families. *Health and Quality of Life Outcomes*, 2(11), 2004.

[26] K.-Y. Wen, F. McTavish, G. Kreps, M. Wise, and D. Gustafson. From diagnosis to death: A case study of coping with breast cancer as seen through online discussion group messages. *Journal of Computer-Mediated Communication*, 16:331–361, 2011.

[27] I. H. Witten and E. Frank. *Data Mining: Practical Machine Learning Tools and Techniques, second edition.* Elsevier, San Francisco, 2005.

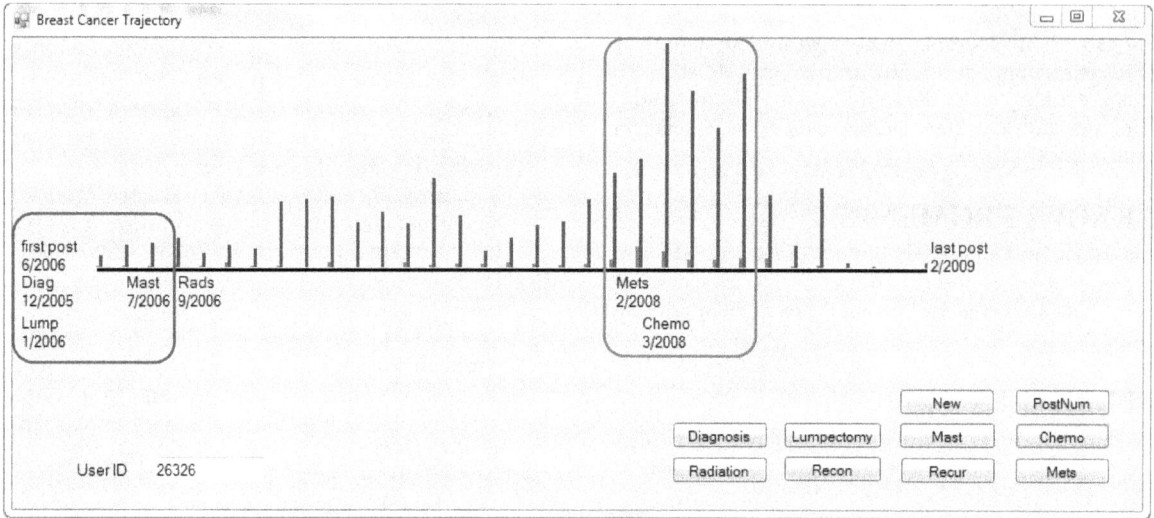

(a)

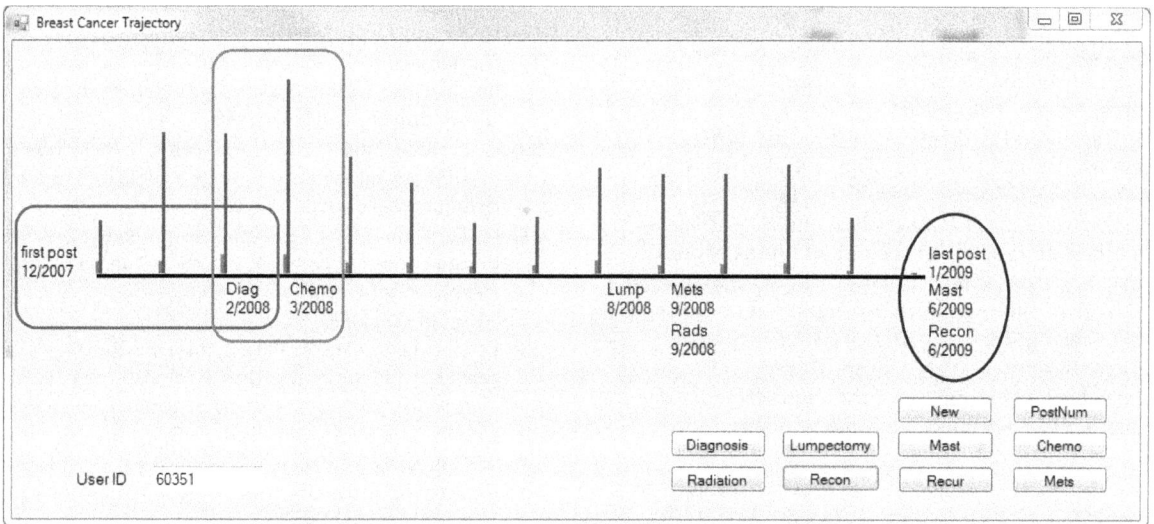

(b)

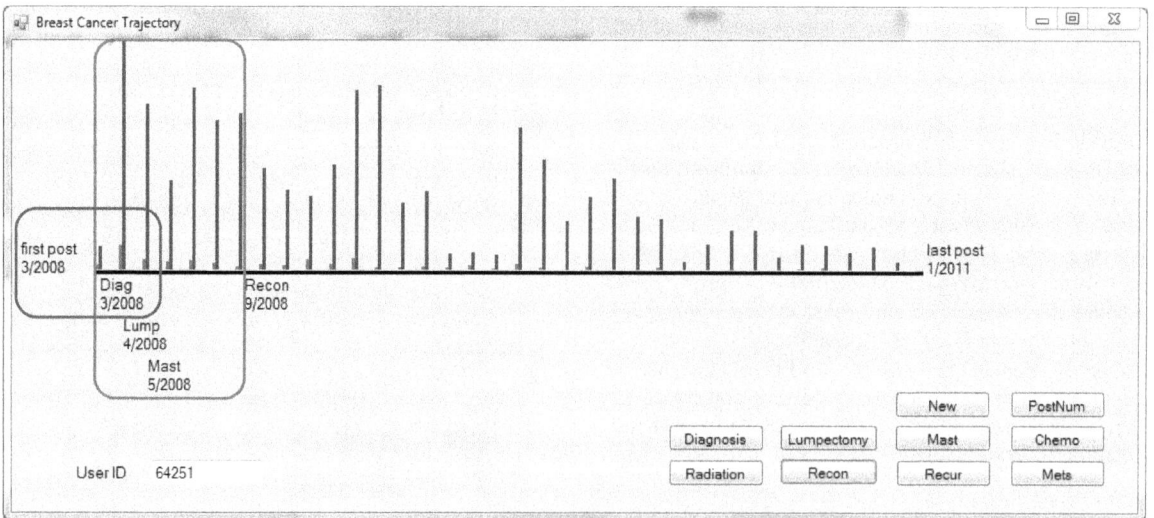

(c)

Figure 3: Automatically-generated breast cancer trajectories of three users.

Personalized Incremental Users' Engagement: Driving Contributions One Step Forward

Claudia López
University of Pittsburgh
135 North Bellefield Ave.
Pittsburgh, PA 15260, US
cal95 @ pitt.edu

Rosta Farzan
University of Pittsburgh
135 North Bellefield Ave.
Pittsburgh, PA 15260, US
rfarzan @ pitt.edu

Peter Brusilovsky
University of Pittsburgh
135 North Bellefield Ave.
Pittsburgh, PA 15260, US
peterb @ pitt.edu

ABSTRACT

Successful contributors in online communities go through a lifecycle of membership status starting from the periphery and moving to the core over time. We argue that a personalized incremental engagement strategy can mobilize a larger proportion of members through this process. This paper presents our approach to identify a progression of contributions in an online community and the design of personalized incremental engagement strategy which will drive users' contributions one step forward. The results of our field study show that the personalized incremental approach significantly boosts contributions in an online community for academic conferences.

Categories and Subject Descriptors

H.5.3. [**Group and Organization Interfaces**]: Web-based interaction

Keywords

User Studies; Social Computing and Social Navigation; Virtual Community/Community Computing; User Experience Design/Experience Design

1. INTRODUCTION

It has been observed that building sustainable online communities is a challenging task. Even the most successful examples of these communities face key challenges such as encouraging contributions, developing commitment and socializing newcomers [22]. For example, Wikipedia –with about four million articles and 16 million registered users in the English version– still faces important challenges. According to the statistics published by the WikiMedia Foundation, only .03% of Wikipedia users can be considered active contributors[1] and approximately 90% of the content in Wikipedia is created by 10% of its users [28]. Sixty percent of Wikipedia editors never edit another article after the first day of membership [29]. Beyond these successful examples, many efforts to build online communities fail and the community never reaches the critical mass necessary to become self-sustaining. For example, a third of online mailing lists are inactive over a four-month period [10]. Only 10.3% of the Open Source projects that have been created in SourceForge have more than three members [33].

Diverse research methodologies have been used to understand why users participate in online communities [37, 34, 6]; how to socialize newcomers [8, 13]; how to foster users' commitment [35, 32]; and how to leverage contribution levels [2, 23]. In particular, a number of projects focusing on increasing user engagement in online communties have been motivated by goal-setting theory [25]. This theory indicates that goal-setting strongly motivates people, especially when the goals are specific and challenging. Researchers have explored ways of increasing the motivational impact of goal-setting by combining it with other user engagement strategies. For example, adding rewards and enhancing reputation for achieving a goal can increase users' contributions in an enterprise social network site [12].

While prior research has confirmed the effectiveness of goal-setting, supplementary engagement strategies lead onto mixed results. For example, rewards and enhanced reputation increased contributions in an enterprise social network site but it also encouraged undesirable behavior such as gaming and it interfered with users' intrinsic motivation to contribute [12]. While one study reports that mentioning community or personal goals did not significantly increase the number of contributions [2], another study shows that showing community or personal goals increased the users' contribution levels [31]. We hypothesize that a plausible explanation for these mixed results can be that the effectiveness of the engagement mechanisms depends on users' characteristics, and not solely on the engagement mechanism itself. The research presented in this paper is an attempt to explore whether adapting user engagement strategies to users' characteristics increases the effectiveness of the engagement strategy.

Members of online communities can differ in a range of characteristics such as gender, age, cultural background, experience with the system, level of digital literacy, and roles in the community. All of these characteristics may be important in creating personalized engagement strategies. However, privacy and data collection burdens limit access to

---

[1]http://strategy.wikimedia.org/wiki/Wikimedia_users

many of these characteristics. The goal of our research is to identify user characteristics that could be easily acquired from most types of online communities. In a preliminary study, we explored several easy-to-acquire parameters such as users' previous experience with the system. We observed that effectiveness of user engagement messages correlates with users' status in the system. For example, newcomers were more likely to visit the site in response to an invitation to participate than current members of the site [26]. The study presented in this paper attempts to take the next step: to explore whether user status can serve as a basis for adapting engagement strategies.

In this paper, we define user status to mean the extent and the type of users' past contributions to the community. It has been recognized that members of online communities go through a lifecycle of membership status starting from the periphery and moving to the core over time [30]. For example, contributors in Wikipedia start making small edits in articles and then progressively increase the magnitude of their contributions [17]. A similar pattern was found in open source software development. New developers begin their contributions by reporting bugs and then those motivated to contribute further get more involved in the community and increase the significance of their contributions [38].

We hypothesize that strategies that encourage users to perform a task are more effective if the proposed task is an extension of previous activities. On the other hand, the strategies which ignore the users' prior status are less effective. We assess engagement with the system by measuring the users' interaction with the system including their browsing activities and contributions. To test this hypothesis, we designed a personalized goal-setting mechanism to encourage users to move one step forward in their membership status. The mechanism is based on a progression of possible actions in the community that are introduced to the users in order to engage them in new and more sophisticated tasks. We implemented this approach in an online community for academic conferences and evaluated its effectiveness in a field study. The results show that our personalized incremental engagement mechanism was significantly more effective in encouraging users to participate in the system than a non-personalized one. Particularly, personalization fostered contributions from users with who had prior experience in the community.

2. RELATED WORK

This work is focused on personalized incremental engagement messages that consider the users' current status and encourage them to progress to the next stage of participation. While we believe that this approach is innovative, it has roots in two areas - user engagement in online communities and personalized user interfaces. This section reviews the relevant work in both areas.

2.1 Encouraging contributions

Encouraging contributions to online communities has been the focus of several research studies. Two major approaches are (1) manipulating the interface of the social site to reflect a particular intervention (e.g. [7, 9, 11, 12, 19, 31]) and (2) sending direct messages to participants (e.g. [2, 8]). Each approach has advantages and drawbacks. To be effective, it is important to employ the appropriate strategy based on the characteristics of the online community.

Interface changes can be more visible and influential since every time a user is in the system they are exposed to the intervention. At the same time, the cost of making interface changes is much higher than sending messages. Moreover, users who do not login to the system are not exposed to the interface intervention at all. For sites with a small number of active users, changes in the interface might not be noticed by enough users to be effective. In those cases, sending direct messages can be more effective. Prior research has demonstrated that sending periodic reminders is effective in engaging users and boosting the overall participation in different online communities [1, 2]. It provides users with a clear and specific goal which is shown to motivate contributions [25]. Moreover, messages are effective in encouraging contributions by targeting individual users directly instead of broadcasting a request to the general audience [9]. In the current work, we have adopted direct messages as an approach to implement our personalized engagement strategy.

2.1.1 Adapting Engagement Strategies to Individual Differences

While several studies have explored the value of sending direct messages in order to motivate users' contributions, fewer works have examined how individual differences impact the effectiveness of these direct messages. Prior research suggests that users volunteer their time for many different reasons and individuals have different motivations for contributing to volunteer organizations [6, 37]. Given the personal nature of direct messages, they provide a great opportunity for adaptation. The content of messages can be adapted to individual differences to increase their effectiveness.

A recent study [7] in a movie recommender system demonstrated how individual differences modify the value of social feedback. In an experiment where users were presented with the median value of participation by the community, all the users demonstrated regression towards this central value of contributions. However, users with higher level of competitiveness demonstrated a different behavior. Competitive users who had been contributing less than the median value increased their contributions faster than the average user and those who were above the central value of contributions decreased their level of contribution slower than the average user. The authors suggest that designing a personalized engagement strategy can take advantage of these differences to achieve more effective results.

An analysis of newcomers' socialization in Wikiprojects - a group of Wikipedia editors who collaborate on managing and writing a collection of pages on a specific topic, e.g., military history - shows that newcomers who received personalized welcoming messages demonstrated higher levels of contribution and commitment to the project while those receiving standardized messages decreased their level of contribution and commitment to the group.

Personalized task routing algorithms offer another example of how personalization improves users' motivation. Wikipedia editors are significantly more likely to respond to an editing request if the request takes into account their personal interest area and ask them to edits articles related to their interest [9]. The personalized messages reduced the effort required to figure out how to contribute by suggesting tasks that were needed and matched the user interests. A similar result was achieved in the movie recommender system [19]. Messages requesting movie ratings which considered users' movie interests were more successful than those which ignored personal interests. A recent study reported that users' motivations influence their patterns of contributions in online communities. For example, users with a stronger pro-social behavior are more likely to edit resources. The authors of this paper proposed personalized interfaces designed considering the users' motivations [18].

In this work, we propose an approach to personalize engagement strategy by considering users' prior activity in the system. Our work complements prior work in personalized engagement strategies by attempting to identify easy-to-acquire users' characteristics that can guide a personalized incremental approach for user engagement.

2.2 Intelligent Help Systems and Incremental Interfaces

The problem of adapting system behavior to individual users has been extensively explored in the areas of user modeling [16], adaptive interfaces [36], and adaptive Web systems in general [4]. This area is sometimes referred to as automatic personalization as the personalization of system behavior is produced not by the user (user-driven personalization is also known as customization), but by intelligent algorithms that take into account various user features and parameters. Personalized incremental user engagement can be considered as a specific strategy in this area and it has connections to two prior research streams in this field - adaptive help systems and incremental interfaces.

Adaptive help systems [3], also known as intelligent help systems [20], attempt to provide effective assistance to a user of a sophisticated information system by considering the user's anticipated goals and level of knowledge. To provide this support, they predict users' most likely next actions based on the history of past actions. If this prediction can be done well, an adaptive help system can serve the user when they ask for help. It can also proactively help by informing the user about important (but not yet used) functionality which can improve the user's experience [16]. Prior research in the area of adaptive help introduced a number of powerful mechanisms for adaptive help. They range from relatively simple state transition diagrams and goal hierarchies [36] based on system analysis to advanced Bayesian networks [21] and social comparison models [24] based on extensive mining of user logs.

Similar ideas were explored in a related area of incremental interfaces. The concept of the incremental interface is based on Fischer's theory of user incremental learning in interactive systems [15]. Fischer argued that in complex interactive systems users learn about interface functionality incrementally, starting with a small subset of features and then progressing to more complicated subsets depending on the users tasks and needs. The idea of an incremental interface is to restrict the complicated user interface to the set of features that correspond to the users' mastery subset by hiding more advanced features. Once the user masters the current subset, new features can be enabled and introduced to the user. The incremental interface was first explored in [5] in the context of Web systems and later adapted to the context of office applications in [14, 27].

The goal of both adaptive help and incremental interfaces is to determine what is the next most probable stage of user activity in the system and to help the user in advancing

to this stage. In this work, we pursue a similar goal by personalizing incremental engagement strategies.

3. RESEARCH PLATFORM

Conference Navigator (CN) [12] is an online community designed to help conference attendees make decisions about which talks to attend. CN guides conference attendees by augmenting the conference schedule with meta-information about talks such as popularity for a particular area of interest or user-defined tags describing a talk. CN provides recommendation of relevant talks to its users and enables them to rate these recommendations to further increase the quality of the recommendations. The users can also connect to other researchers in the field through the system. Figure 1 presents an interface of CN showing the most popular talks. The talks are annotated with the number of users who scheduled this talk and whether the talk is recommended to the target user.

To assess the effect of a personalized incremental user engagement mechanism, we conducted a field study in CN during the 2011 User Modeling, Adaptation and Personalization Conference (UMAP). The conference offered CN before and during the conference. Conference attendees and authors of papers were invited to use CN few weeks before the conference began. Information about CN was displayed in the main page of the conference website and two reminders about the system were sent by email.

4. PERSONALIZED INCREMENTAL USER ENGAGEMENT

To implement our incremental user engagement strategy, first we need to identify users' characteristics that are easily acquired and which will provide meaningful basis for personalization. Second, we categorize users based on these characteristics and design a personalized engagement mechanism that takes advantage of this categorization.

4.1 Identifying Users' Characteristics to Guide Personalization

In a preliminary study, we observed that the user status in an online community can explain differences in their participation pattern in response to receiving messages encouraging contributions [26]. We observed that newcomers responded to these messages by increasing their investigation of the site while previous contributors responded to the messages by increasing their contributions.

To adapt personalized messages to a user's status, the first step is to model a conceptual progression of possible contributions to the system. Performing log analysis of users' actions in the site can inform the design of this model.

We analyzed usage behavior of 151 users from the UMAP community who logged on to the system prior to our field study. We considered users' first 100 actions and divided their actions into bins of 10 actions. Figure 2 presents the proportion of different kinds of contributions among users' actions. The results suggest a trend that users at the beginning focus their contributions on scheduling talks and over time they move to tagging talks and networking with other members. Among the first 20 actions of all users, all contributory actions are focused on scheduling. After the 50th, the users' actions shift towards tagging and networking.

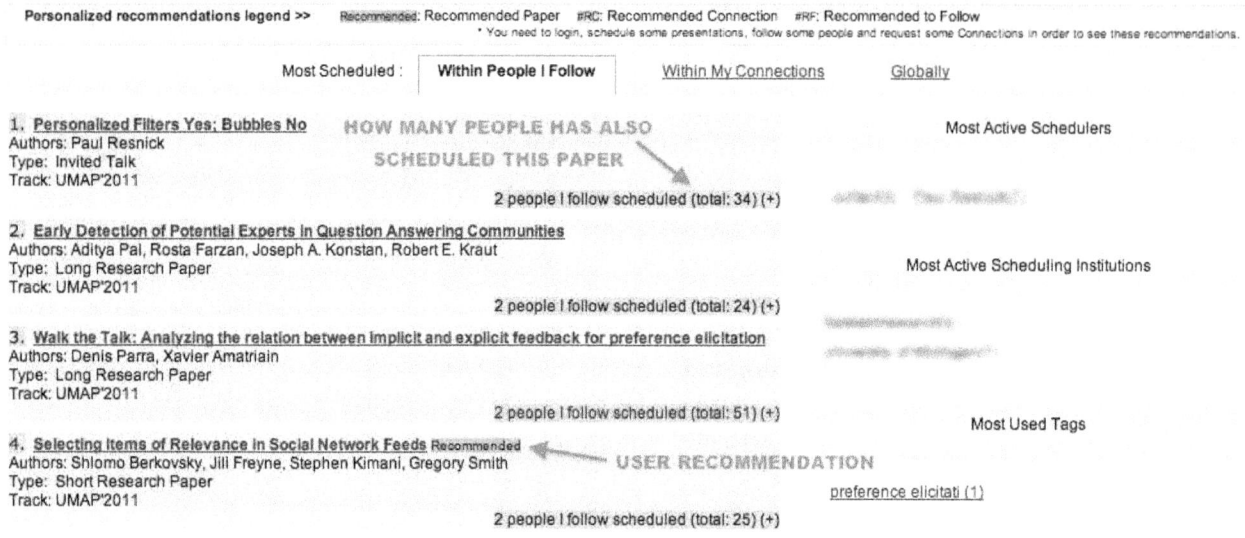

Figure 1: Research Platform: Conference Navigator

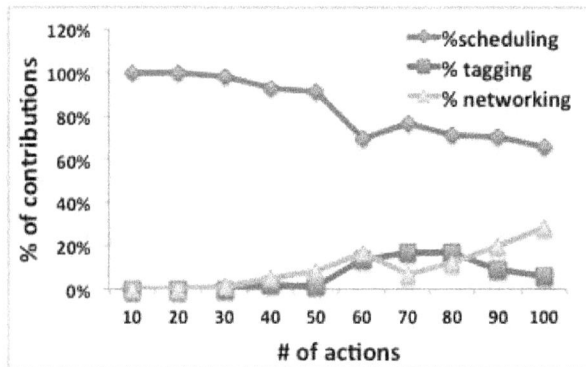

Figure 2: Logs of Conference Navigator

4.2 Design of Personalized User Engagement

The results of log analysis suggest the existence of a progression of actions. Users start contributing by scheduling papers and then they move to other contributory actions. The system's usage data is not entirely conclusive about which action is more likely to be undertaken after scheduling. The rates of tagging and networking actions are very similar over the first 100 users' actions. As the number of more advanced users is much lower, we do not have enough data to distinguish the importance of tagging versus networking.

These results match our expectations of system usage. CN was designed as a conference support system, therefore, the most basic and expected contributions of users is to schedule a talk in which they are interested. Second, they will add tags and eventually consider connecting with other conference attendees. Once a user has provided enough information to the system, CN can recommend relevant talks to the user. Afterwards, the user can rate the usefulness of these

recommendations. However, none of the users had rated their recommendations before running this field study.

Based on these observations and the expected system usage, we designed a model of users' contributions in CN as shown in Figure 3. There are four primary types of contributions (1) scheduling a paper, (2) tagging a paper, (3) networking with other users, and (4) rating system recommendations.

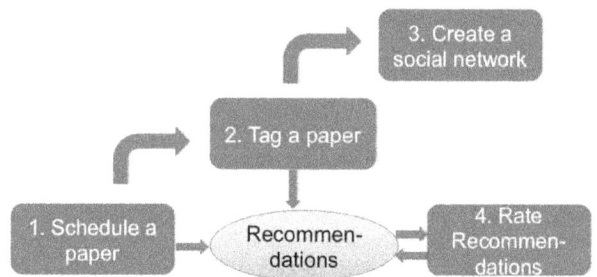

Figure 3: Progression of Contributory Actions

5. FIELD STUDY DESIGN

We designed a field study to assess the effect of personalized incremental user engagement strategies based on the progression of actions described in the previous section. We hypothesize that, in comparison with non-personalized messages, personalized incremental user engagement that takes into account current user status increases participation in the site. The increased participation will be revealed by more visits and more contributions to the site. Therefore, our hypotheses are:

- **H1a.**: Personalized incremental engagement generates *more visits to the site.*

192

- **H1b.**: Personalized incremental engagement fosters *more contributions to the site*.

We categorized CN users into three groups: Newcomers, Inactive Users and Active Contributors. We define newcomers as those who agreed to be registered in the system but never logged in, inactive users as those who have been members of the site but have not been active in either visiting the site or contributing to the site, and active contributors as those who have scheduled at least five talks.

Users in each category are randomly assigned to one of two possible conditions: non-personalized or personalized. All users in the non-personalized condition received the same message independent of being a newcomer, an inactive user, or an active contributor. The message encouraged them to contribute to the site by scheduling or tagging the talks which are the necessary action for the users to receive a better quality recommendation. Users in the personalized condition received a message adapted to their status and what they had already done in the system. Newcomers were asked to schedule a talk. Inactive users (who had not done any scheduling) were asked to schedule and those who had scheduled a few talks were asked to tag papers. Active contributors were asked to rate the quality of recommendations they received from the system. Partial samples of the personalized messages are shown in Figure 4 and Figure 5. Figure 6 illustrates part of the non-personalized message.

(...) Please, check the conference schedule and start creating your personal schedule by adding most interesting papers to it. In turn, CN can recommend you more relevant papers once you schedule at least 5 papers that you are interested in. (...)

Figure 4: Personalized Scheduling Request

(...) Since you have already scheduled a few UMAP papers, CN can immediately recommend you interesting workshop papers. The quality of content-based recommendations may not be high since you scheduled too few papers, however, you can receive some useful tag-based recommendations by adding tags to at least 5 of your favorite papers in UMAP. (...)

Figure 5: Personalized Tagging Request

(...) Scheduling or tagging at least 5 papers will help Conference Navigator to better recommend you most interesting papers at the conference and associated workshops. (...)

Figure 6: Non-Personalized Message

We designed the requested task in all the messages to focus on improving the quality of system recommendation to keep the goal the same for all of the users. We decided to avoid promoting the networking actions as an option for active contributors since networking would not have contributed to the quality of recommendations.

6. RESULTS

The study included 127 users who were UMAP 2011 attendees, authors and previous users of the system who at least visited the schedule of UMAP 2011. We compared users' participation in the site, both in terms of browsing and contributing, one week after receiving the message.

6.1 General Statistics

Table 1 presents the number of users in each group who responded to the messages by visiting or contributing to the site. Overall, 43 out of 127 users receiving the messages visited the system within the following week. Significantly larger number of users in the personalized group responded to the message (28 (43%) vs. 15 (24%), $\chi^2 = 5.053$, p = 0.025).

Table 1: Engagement Statistics for Each Group

Group	Strategy	Total	Engaged (%)
Newcomers	non-pers.	26	5 (19.2)
	pers. - scheduling	22	9 (40.9)
Inactive Users	non-pers.	12	2 (16.7)
	pers. - scheduling	8	7 (87.5)
	pers. - tagging	16	4 (25.0)
Active Contributors	non-pers.	16	8 (33.3)
	pers. - rating	19	8 (42.1)

non-pers.: non-personalized; pers.: personalized.

The general statistics on participation before and after the field study are shown in Table 2. Scheduling, tagging and rating recommendations were the actions advertised in the engagement messages. Among them, scheduling remains the most popular type of contributions which increased by 50% (378 new scheduling actions) as a result of the field study. The field study had the most significant effect on increasing tagging behavior by 146% which is partially due to little tagging activities prior to the field study. However, the field study was less successful in motivating ratings of recommendations: it resulted in only ten new ratings.

Table 2: General Statistics of Participation

	Before	New (% Increase)
Contributions	828	416 (50.24)
Scheduling	784	378 (48.21)
Tagging	15	22 (146.6)
Rating	0	10 (——-)
Networking	29	6 (20.69)
Visits to	4,004	1,749 (43.68)
Recommendations	110	184 (167.3)
Other pages	3,894	1,565 (40.19)

Table 3 reports the number of actions and contributions for each group of users. Newcomers perform the largest share of browsing actions in the system and they contribute the most along with the inactive users. Previously active contributors exhibit the least number of contributions.

6.2 Data analysis consideration

In all of the analysis, we assess the effectiveness of the engagement strategies by measuring the users' participation

Table 3: Statistics for Each Group

Group	Strategy	Actions Total	Actions Mean	Contributions Total	Contributions Mean
Newcomers	non-pers.	304	11.69	44	1.69
	pers.	562	25.55	158	7.18
Inactive Users	non-pers.	111	9.25	15	1.25
	pers.	359	14.96	160	6.67
Active Contributors	non-pers.	175	7.29	16	0.67
	pers.	238	12.53	23	1.21

non-pers.: non-personalized; pers.: personalized.

in the system. Our response variable is the count of actions, which is over-dispersed due to large number of users with no actions. Therefore, negative binomial best describes the distribution of this variable. We used negative binomial regression to predict participation in the system given our experimental condition denoted as "strategy". This variable is coded as zero for those who have received non-personalized messages and one for those who received the personalized messages. To include users' previous status in the system, we included their prior contributions in the model, denoted as "prior contributions" and we included the interaction of their status with the engagement strategy (the experimental condition).

6.3 Participation

To assess our first hypothesis, we measured users' overall participation by calculating the total number of visits to the site as well as the number of visits to the recommendations page during the week after receiving the engagement messages.

To predict the overall number of actions, we controlled for users' prior activity level by including users' prior number of actions in the model, denoted as "prior actions". The result of regression analysis is shown in Table 4 and Table 5. The model is significant, $\chi^2 = 13.821, df = 4, p < .008$. There is a main effect of the engagement strategy. Personalized messages doubled ($e^{.743} = 2.1$) the number of visits to the site compared to the non-personalized messages. There is neither a main effect of prior actions nor an effect of prior contributions. This unexpected result is probably related to the fact that a major share of new actions were performed by newcomers who had no previous actions or contributions. There is no interaction between users' status and engagement strategy.

Table 4: Predicting number of new actions

Predictor	B	S.E.	χ^2	p
Strategy(1)	.743	.211	12.400	.000
Prior actions	-.002	.0028	.568	.451
Prior contributions	.011	.0108	1.143	.285
strategy(1) × prior contributions	-.023	.0162	1.998	.158

We are particularly interested in visits to the recommendation pages because they were explicitly mentioned in all of the engagement messages. To predict the number of visits to recommendation pages, we controlled for users' prior visits to those pages. As a result, the model includes the experimental condition, the number of visits to recommen-

Table 5: Estimated means of actions

Strategy	Mean	S. E.
non-personalized	9.4379	1.27322
personalized	17.0868	2.21712

Covariates appearing in the model are fixed at the values:prior contributions=6.52; prior actions =31.5276

dations before the study (prior recommendation), the number of prior contributions and the interaction effect between number of prior contributions and the experimental condition. The model is significant, $\chi^2 = 31.469, df = 4, p < .001$. Table 6 and 7 shows the results of the regression.

Similar to overall actions, there is a main effect of the engagement strategy. Personalized messages increased number of visits to recommendation pages by 7.55 times ($e^{2.021} = 7.55$) compared to the non-personalized messages. The effects of prior visits to recommendations, previous contributions and the interaction between contributions and the engagement strategy are not significant.

Table 6: Predicting number of visits to recommendation pages

Predictor	B	S.E.	χ^2	p
strategy(1)	2.021	.4683	18.615	.000
prior recommendation	-.023	.0917	.061	.805
prior contributions	-.001	.0300	.001	.972
strategy(1) × prior contributions	-.021	.0378	.318	.573

Table 7: Estimated means of visits to recommendation pages

Strategy	Mean	S. E.
non-personalized	.1452	.17488
personalized	.9528	.05203

Covariates appearing in the model are fixed at the values:prior contributions=6.52; prior actions =31.5276

The result of our analysis supports our first hypothesis. Compared to the non-personalized engagement messages, the personalized incremental messages increases participation in the system as well as the number of visits to those specific pages mentioned in the engagement messages. For both of the dependent variables, the effect of users' prior levels of participation in the system is not significant.

6.4 Contributions

To test our second hypothesis, we measured users' contributions by calculating the total number of talks they scheduled, number of tags they added, number of recommendations they rated, and number of connections they added to their network. Again, we use negative binomial regression to model the levels of contributions with the same independent variables as described in Section 6.2. The regression model is significant, $\chi^2 = 73.731, df = 4, p < .001$. Table 8 and Table 9 details the result of the regression analysis.

Table 8: Predicting number of contributions

Predictor	B	S.E.	χ^2	p
strategy(1)	1.846	.2532	53.153	.000
prior contributions	.005	.0110	.239	.625
strategy(1) × prior contributions	-.131	.0267	24.242	.000

Similar to the participation measures, there is a main effect of the engagement strategy on number of contributions. Personalized messages increase the total number of contributions by 6.33 ($e^{1.846} = 6.33$) times compared to the non-personalized messages. Moreover, there is a significant interaction between the engagement strategy and the users' prior level of contributions. Users who contributed less previously were more likely to increase their contributions as a result of receiving the personalized messages. For every unit of increase in prior contributions, the expected number of contributions decreases by a factor of 0.87 ($e^{-.131} = .87$). The effect size of the personalized message is considerably larger than the interaction effect size, therefore the negative effect of personalization is more relevant among more active prior contributors than those who had contributed only few times.

Table 9: Estimated means of contributions

Strategy	Mean	S. E.
non-personalized	3.2212	.52984
personalized	1.1966	.20714

Covariates appearing in the model are fixed at the values: prior contributions=6.52

The results support our second hypothesis. The personalized incremental engagement messages significantly increase the number of contributions. However, these personalized messages particularly increase contributions from less active users.

7. DISCUSSION

This paper reports the results of implementing a personalized engagement method in a social system for academic conferences. Our log analysis of users' behavior in our research platform confirms findings of prior research that suggests members of online communities follow a progressive pattern of contributions. This progression can serve as a basis for personalization. Our work complements prior research on personalized user engagement by identifying users' characteristics which are easily acquired in a majority of online communities and which affect the success of incentive mechanisms.

We were successful in strengthening the effect of goal-setting by emphasizing a goal which naturally follows the current status of a user. Our results suggest that personalized messages requesting users to perform a particular kind of contributions that follows their current pattern of participation in the system can increase users' engagement wit h the system. A detailed analysis looking at the effect of personalized messages on interaction with users' prior contributions reveals that the effectiveness of personalized messages decreases as the number of prior contributions increases.

Less active users who do not have a clear idea of how to contribute will benefit from a personalized message which recommends the most appropriate kinds of contributions. Our results also suggest that active users were not influenced by our personalization mechanism as much as users with less experience. The lack of more conclusive data about activity pattern of more advanced users may have contributed to this result. From the log data, it is clear that the initial contribution is scheduling, however tagging and networking are competing to be the most likely subsequent kind of contribution and rating recommendations is not even present. It is possible that a lack of data has resulted in a weak model of what most attracts advanced users. It is also possible that experienced users may not benefit from personalization in general. Messages suggesting only one kind of contribution might contradicts their own idea of contribution. Our future research will further investigate this aspect.

An important goal for online communities is diversifying contributions from different kind of users. There are simple kinds of actions that a majority of users can contribute to the system, e.g. bookmarking a resource. On the other hand, there are actions that require more expertise with the system or more effort. Those actions usually are not performed by new users since they do not have the knowledge and they have not developed enough commitment for more effort-demanding actions. Personalized incremental engagement incentives can achieve the goal of diversification of actions by guiding the users through a sequence of action as they move through the lifecycle of membership in the system. In the current work, we have succeeded in focusing users' attention on a particular feature of the system, talk recommendation, by emphasizing that feature in the engagement messages. We were able to transfer users' effort from mostly scheduling to scheduling and tagging. However, we did not fully achieve the goal of broadening types of contributions as ratings of recommendations remained very low.

8. DESIGN IMPLICATIONS

The results of this study offer insights for the designers of online communities. Personalization is particularly important for users with little experience with the system. They are not familiar with the system and can have difficulty identifying ways to contribute to the system. Personalization reduces the cost for participation of a user uncertain of how to contribute by providing specific tasks. It provides goals that focus the users' effort on the sequence of actions suitable for their current status.

On the other hand, as the users become more familiar with the system and start finding ways they can contribute, personalization may harm their level of engagement with the system. As modeling active contributors is harder, personalization might suggest actions that may not match with the users' interest. Additionally, it may create a sense that the system does not trust in what they have identified as their role. This sense of distrust then can decrease their engagement with the system. Personalization can also interfere with the way the users are intrinsically interested to contribute to the system.

9. LIMITATIONS AND FUTURE WORK

The results of this study have to be considered in view of its limitations. First, the number of engaged users in each subgroup is small which follows the general pattern of participation inequality in online communities. Therefore, it is important to start with a bigger community of users in which the standard response rate will result in more significant participation for different experimental conditions. As in any field study, there is also a selection bias in our subjects sample. Additionally, our research platform, which is related to a physical event, may also differ from other completely virtual online communities, therefore our results may not be directly transferable to other kind of online communities. We believe that replication of our study is necessary to offer more robust results.

Second, all of the engagement messages emphasized the benefit of contributing as increasing the quality of the recommendations. This might have discouraged users who were not interested in recommendations. Particularly, this goal ignores the social features of the system and focuses the users' contributions on individual benefits. It is important to study the effect of our personalization approach on interaction with different types of goals, especially more community-oriented goals. In this case, personalized approaches can take into account the importance of different kind of goals for different group of users.

The goal of both adaptive help and incremental interfaces is quite similar to the goal of personalized incremental engagement strategies, which is to determine what is the next most probable stage of user activity in the system and to help the user to advance to this stage. This similarity makes it feasible to use selected advanced strategies of user and community modeling developed in the past in the areas of adaptive help and incremental interfaces for the purpose of personalized engagement. While our current work uses a relatively simple state-transition, we plan to explore more sophisticated technologies in our future work.

10. REFERENCES

[1] M. Abdolrasulnia, B. C. Collins, L. Casebeer, T. Wall, C. Spettell, M. N. Ray, N. W. Weissman, and J. J. Allison. Using email reminders to engage physicians in an internet-based cme intervention. *BMC Medical Education*, 4(7), 2004.

[2] G. Beenen, K. Ling, X. Wang, K. Chang, D. Frankowski, P. Resnick, and R. E. Kraut. Using social psychology to motivate contributions to online communities. In *Proceedings of the 2004 ACM conference on Computer supported cooperative work*, pages 212–221, 2004.

[3] P. Brusilovsky. *Berkshire Encyclopedia of Human-Computer Interaction*, chapter Adaptive Help Systems. Berkshire Publishing Group, 2004.

[4] P. Brusilovsky, A. Kobsa, and W. Nejdl. *The Adaptive Web: Methods and Strategies of Web Personalization* Springer-Verlag, 2007.

[5] P. Brusilovsky and E. Schwarz. User as student: Towards an adaptive interface for advanced web-based applications. In A. Jameson, C. Paris, and C. Tasso, editors, *6th International Conference on User Modeling*, pages 177–188, 1997.

[6] B. Butler, L. Sproull, S. Kiesler, and R. Kraut. Community effort in online groups: Who does the work and why. In *Leadership at a Distance: Research in Technologically-Supported Work.*, pages 171–194, 2007.

[7] Y. Chen, F. M. Harper, J. A. Konstan, and S. X. Li. Social comparisons and contributions to online communities: A field experiment on MovieLens. In *Computational Social Systems and the Internet*, 2007.

[8] B. Choi, K. Alexander, R. E. Kraut, and J. M. Levine. Socialization tactics in wikipedia and their effects. In *Proceedings of the 2010 ACM conference on Computer supported cooperative work*, pages 107–116, 2010.

[9] D. Cosley, D. Frankowski, L. Terveen, and J. Riedl. Suggestbot: using intelligent task routing to help people find work in wikipedia. In *Proceedings of the 12th international conference on Intelligent user interfaces*, pages 32–41, 2007.

[10] J. N. Cummings, B. Butler, and R. Kraut. The quality of online social relationships. *Commun. ACM*, 45:103–108, 2002.

[11] S. Drenner, S. Sen, and L. Terveen. Crafting the initial user experience to achieve community goals. In *Proceedings of the 2008 ACM conference on Recommender systems*, pages 187–194, 2008.

[12] R. Farzan, J. M. DiMicco, D. R. Millen, C. Dugan, W. Geyer, and E. A. Brownholtz. Results from deploying a participation incentive mechanism within the enterprise. In *Proceedings of the twenty-sixth annual SIGCHI conference on Human factors in computing systems*, pages 563–572, 2008.

[13] R. Farzan, R. Kraut, A. Pal, and J. Konstan. Socializing volunteers in an online community: a field experiment. In *Proceedings of the ACM 2012 conference on Computer Supported Cooperative Work*, pages 325–334, 2012.

[14] L. Findlater and J. McGrenere. A comparison of static, adaptive, and adaptable menus. In *Proceedings of the SIGCHI conference on Human factors in computing systems*, pages 89–96, 2004.

[15] G. Fischer. *Enhancing incremental learning process with knowledge-based systems*, pages 138–163. Springer-Verlag, 1988.

[16] G. Fischer. User modeling in human-computer interaction. *User Modeling and User Adapted Interaction*, 11(1-2):65–86, 2001.

[17] A. Forte and A. Bruckman. Why do people write for wikipedia? incentives to contribute to open-content publishing. group 05 workshop position paper. In *GROUP 05 Workshop: Sustaining Community: The Role and Design of Incentive Mechanisms in Online Systems*, pages 6–9, 2005.

[18] P. Fugelstad, P. Dwyer, J. Filson Moses, J. Kim, C. A. Mannino, L. Terveen, and M. Snyder. What makes users rate (share, tag, edit...)?: predicting patterns of participation in online communities. In *Proceedings of the ACM 2012 conference on Computer Supported Cooperative Work*, pages 969–978, 2012.

[19] F. M. Harper, D. Frankowski, S. Drenner, Y. Ren, S. Kiesler, L. Terveen, R. Kraut, and J. Riedl. Talk amongst yourselves: inviting users to participate in online conversations. In *Proceedings of the 12th international conference on Intelligent user interfaces*, pages 62–71, 2007.

[20] S. J. Hegner, P. Mc Kevitt, P. Norvig, and R. L. Wilensky. *Intelligent Help Systems for UNIX*. Kluwer Academic Publishers, 2001.

[21] E. Horvitz, J. Breese, D. Heckerman, D. Hovel, and K. Rommelse. The Lumiere project: Bayesian user

modeling for inferring the goals and needs of software users. In *Fourteenth Conference on Uncertainty in Artificial Intelligence*, pages 256–265, 1998.

[22] R. Kraut, M. L. Maher, J. Olson, T. W. Malone, P. Pirolli, and J. C. Thomas. Scientific foundations: A case for technology- mediated social- participation theory. *IEEE Computer*, 43:22–28, 2010.

[23] R. E. Kraut and P. Resnick. *Building Successful Online Communities: Evidence-based Social Design*, chapter Encouraging Contribution to Online Communities. Cambridge, MA: MIT Press., 2012.

[24] F. Linton, D. Joy, and H.-P. Schaefer. Building user and expert models by long-term observation of application usage. In J. Kay, editor, *7th International Conference on User Modeling*, pages 129–138, 1999.

[25] E. A. Locke and G. P. Latham. Building a practically useful theory of goal setting and task motivation. *American Psychologist*, 57(9):705–717, 2002.

[26] C. López and P. Brusilovsky. Towards adaptive recruitment and engagement mechanisms in social systems. In L. Ardissono and T. Kuflik, editors, *Advances in User Modeling*, pages 382–396. Springer Berlin / Heidelberg, 2012.

[27] J. McGrenere, R. M. Baecker, and K. S. Booth. An evaluation of a multiple interface design solution for bloated software. In *Proceedings of the SIGCHI conference on Human factors in computing systems: Changing our world, changing ourselves*, pages 164–170, 2002.

[28] F. Ortega, J. Gonzalez-Barahona, and G. Robles. On the inequality of contributions to wikipedia. In *Proceedings of the 41st Annual Hawaii International Conference on System Sciences*, pages 304–308, 2008.

[29] K. Panciera, A. Halfaker, and L. Terveen. Wikipedians are born, not made: a study of power editors on wikipedia. In *Proceedings of the ACM 2009 international conference on Supporting group work*, pages 51–60, 2009.

[30] J. Preece and B. Shneiderman. The reader-to-leader framework: Motivating technology-mediated social participation. *AIS Transactions on Human-Computer Interaction*, 1:13–32, 2009.

[31] A. M. Rashid, K. Ling, R. D. Tassone, P. Resnick, R. Kraut, and J. Riedl. Motivating participation by displaying the value of contribution. In *Proceedings of the SIGCHI conference on Human Factors in computing systems*, pages 955–958, 2006.

[32] Y. Ren, R. Kraut, S. Kiesler, and P. Resnick. *Evidence-based social design: Mining the social sciences to build online communities*, chapter Encouraging commitment in Online Communities. MIT Press., 2012.

[33] P. Resnick, J. Konstan, Y. Chen, and R. E. Kraut. *Building Successful Online Communities: Evidence-based Social Design*, chapter Starting New Online Communities. MIT Press., 2012.

[34] C. Ridings, D. Gefen, and B. Arinze. Psychological barriers: Lurker and poster motivation and behavior in online communities. *Communications of the Association for Information Systems*, 18(16), 2006.

[35] K. Sassenberg. Common bond and common identity groups on the internet: Attachment and normative behavior in on-topic and off-topic chats. *Group Dynamics*, 6(1):27 – 37, 2002.

[36] M. Schneider-Hufschmidt, T. KÃijhme, and U. Malinowski. *Adaptive user interfaces: Principles and practice*. Human Factors in Information Technology, 1993.

[37] M. M. Wasko and S. Faraj. Why should I share? examining social capital and knowledge contribution in electronic networks of practice. *MIS Quarterly*, 29(1):35–57, 2005.

[38] Y. Ye and K. Kishida. Toward an understanding of the motivation open source software developers. In *Proceedings of the 25th International Conference on Software Engineering*, pages 419–429, 2003.

Supporting Initial Trust in Distributed Idea Generation and Idea Evaluation

Jana Schumann[1], Patrick C. Shih[2], David F. Redmiles[3], Graham Horton[1]

[1]Department of Simulation and Graphics
Otto-von-Guericke-University Magdeburg
Universitätsplatz 2,
39106 Magdeburg, Germany
jana.schumann@st.ovgu.de,
graham.horton@ovgu.de

[2]College of Information Sciences
and Technology
Pennsylvania State University
University Park, PA 16802 USA
patshih@ist.psu.edu

[3]Department of Informatics
University of California,
Irvine
Irvine, CA 92697-3440 USA
redmiles@ics.uci.edu

ABSTRACT

Previous research has shown that diversity within distributed collaborative teams can lead to innovation, but trust must exist for the open expression of innovative ideas and establishment of idea credibility. Initial trust is pivotal for distributed teams where team members have never met face-to-face and have only a very limited time to accomplish a task. Our goal is to determine if knowing specific information about other team members could enhance initial trust and improve productivity and satisfaction in idea generation and idea evaluation sessions. In an experiment, we showed that cognitive and affective trust could be successfully enhanced by presenting relevant information elements, such as domain expertise and personal hobbies, and could have positive effects on the quality and quantity of ideas in idea generation sessions as well as the satisfaction of the participants with the rating result in idea evaluation sessions. However, participants receiving personal information often misconstrue this as professional competency. We also describe gender differences observed in the idea generation sessions and discuss how to better design future systems for supporting idea generation and idea evaluation activities.

Categories and Subject Descriptors

H.5.3. Group and Organization Interfaces: Collaborative computing, Computer-supported cooperative work, Synchronous Interaction.

General Terms

Design, Experimentation, Human Factors

Keywords

Trust, creativity, idea generation, idea evaluation, brainstorming, TWAN schema, distributed teams, virtual teams, globalization

1. INTRODUCTION

With the spread of globalization, there is an increased need for collaboration through distributed teams and, consequently, an increased need for technological support. Distributed teams provide some advantages over traditional teams, such as taking advantage of geographically dispersed experts without having to physically relocate them, having greater flexibility, faster responsiveness, and greater diversity of perspectives [24, 29]. However, distributed teams encounter challenges due to their distribution and communication limitations.

One major issue in distributed teamwork is trust. It is especially critical for fast-forming teams where team members have never met face-to-face. Previous studies have shown that trust forms and develops over time in traditional face-to-face teams; team members have time to assess one another based on personal interaction and shared experiences [15, 45]. Distributed team members often do not have enough time to get the needed information about other team members. It is more difficult to determine whether a person is trustworthy or not, especially if the group's formation is only temporary. Therefore, trust in distributed teams must be even higher than in traditional teams in order to successfully achieve a shared goal [17].

Open innovation is increasingly common in the workplace today. Crowd-sourcing and open-source software development platforms allow strangers to collectively contribute to an end product while remaining anonymous. In many instances, people may interact virtually once and never again. Our work aims to understand how we could enhance initial trust with different information elements about team members' backgrounds, and to see how trust can be incorporated into the design process to improve productivity and satisfaction in idea generation and idea evaluation sessions. We first review prior literature on innovation and trust, and then we delve more deeply into studies that form the basis for our approach. Then, we describe our study's goals (and hypotheses) followed by its design. Thereafter, we discuss the experimental results. Finally, we conclude with a discussion of the results, implications for design, limitations, and future research directions.

2. MOTIVATION
2.1 Understanding the Concept of Trust

Many definitions of trust have been proposed in different contexts [5, 23]. In general, trust can be considered as the *"belief that the trustee will meet the expectations of the trustor"* [43]. Relatedly, researchers have observed that trust can be defined as a belief or confidence about another party's integrity and benevolence in order to accept vulnerability [32, 39]. According to multidimensional trust research, two dimensions of trust have been identified as important to organizations: *cognitive trust* and *affective trust* [30]. Specifically, *"cognition-based trust results from deliberate assessment of each other's characteristics and the process of weighting benefits of trusting over risks, whereas affect-based trust involves one's emotional bonds and sincere concern for the well-being of the others"* [21].

Previous research [22, 23] has shown that distributed teams develop trust swiftly at the beginning of the project. Iacono considered initial trust in general, but did not differentiate between cognitive and affective trust [22]. In 2002, Kanawattanachai found that distributed teams developed a higher degree of cognitive trust than affective trust [26]. That result supports the swift trust proposition of Meyerson [31]. Meyerson claimed that cognitive trust is more important than affective trust in a temporary team [31]. He described a temporary group as an analogy to a *"one-night stand"*. This so-called *swift trust* develops within *"a finite time span, forming around a shared and relatively clear goal or purpose, and depending on tight and coordinated coupling of activity to achieve success"* [31]. Therefore, converting the individual skills and efforts of strangers into interdependent work in a short period of time poses a major challenge to distributed team collaboration.

Our work aims to aid the development of initial trust in distributed teams by building on the concept of cognitive trust and affective trust in a distributed environment. Furthermore, we want to determine whether higher initial trust influences the outcome of idea generation and idea evaluation sessions, which are both part of innovation processes.

2.2 Importance of Innovation

Innovation is a process and several models exist to describe the different phases of that process. Herstatt defines the first phase of the innovation process as a sequence of generating and evaluating ideas [18]. *Idea generation* and *idea evaluation* are the phases where initial trust is necessary because they are part of the first phase of the innovation process. Idea generation (or ideation) *"is the creative process of generation, developing, and communicating new ideas, where an idea is understood as a basic element of thought that can be either visual, concrete, or abstract"* [25]. The result of idea generation sessions are usually a large number of ideas, however a good idea does not always appear to be a good idea at first glance. Therefore, an evaluation process that aims to select a limited number of good ideas for further development is crucial for the innovation process.

Within innovation processes, two different *degrees of newness* can be distinguished. New-to-the-world ideas for products or services are called *radical innovation*, and minor adaptations of products or services are called *incremental innovation* [4]. Both kinds of innovation represent opposite ends of the newness spectrum [4]. More precisely, radical innovations are truly novel or unique technological solutions [33], the development or application of new technologies, or state-of-the-art breakthroughs in technology or product category [11]. Incremental innovations are new products involving only minor or no changes in technology and are also called simple product improvements [11]. Both degrees of newness are important for innovation processes, and we hope to identify how radical and incremental ideas are affected in teams with different levels of initial trust.

2.3 Creativity and Trust

To produce both radical and incremental innovation, creativity is necessary. Creativity is the ability to produce work that is both novel (i.e. original, unexpected) and appropriate (i.e. useful, adaptive concerning task constraints) [42]. Originality is the hallmark of creative behavior, and ideas are not considered to be creative if they are not new or unusual. Although ideas must be original in order to be called creative, they will not be implemented if they are not feasible. Hence, the usual definition of a *good* idea is an idea that is both highly original (or unusual) and highly feasible (or useful).

One way to enhance the creative process is by using so-called creativity techniques. More than 100 creativity techniques can be found in the literature [19]. In this paper, we focus on electronic brainstorming, a computerized version of the brainstorming technique introduced by Osborn [34]. Osborn defined brainstorming as *"a creative conference for producing a list of ideas - ideas which can be subsequently evaluated and further processed"*. We focused on electronic brainstorming because it is one of the most common creativity techniques. Knoll et al. [28] stated that most of the creativity techniques or idea generation techniques support an associative process with external stimuli, which are received through the five senses of the individual. Thus, brainstorming contains general rules to support a process, which is the basis for many other creativity techniques.

As previous research has shown, diversity within a team can lead to innovation in collaboration [37], but trust must exist for the open expressiveness of innovative ideas by team members. Trust has a positive characteristic leading to desirable behavior and outcomes, although negative expectations and trust can also occur during collaborations [1]. Thus, trust plays an important role in innovation, efficiency, and effectiveness of teamwork, as team members do not tend to cross-check each others' work [5, 23]. Moreover, low trust leads to an increase in faulty attributions regarding the source of disagreement in distributed teams [41]. In low trust environments, trust can be fragile and often fractures rapidly, and team members are more likely to question others' intentions [23].

In this work, the main goal of supporting trust in idea generation sessions is to increase the number of radical ideas. Idea generation sessions are about risking vulnerability by writing down unusual ideas. This social effect is called *evaluation apprehension*. It causes participants to hold back their contributions during the process because they are afraid to be criticized by someone in the group [12]. Postmes indicated that anonymity reduces this effect [36]. On the other hand, anonymity can easily lead to social loafing. Social loafing describes the tendency of participants to expend less effort when they believe that their contributions are not needed for the group success [27]. Previous laboratory experiments showed that while participants reported less perceived level of evaluation apprehension, anonymity made no impact on the creative outcomes [2, 44]. Collaros and Anderson are the first to study the effects of perceived team member expertise level on the idea generation outcome. They found that participants in a team full of experts generated ideas of lower originality and feasibility, and they report higher perceived inhibition in idea generation sessions [8].

Open exchange of information should be promoted since people are more likely to collaborate with individuals they trust [23]. The literature regarding the correlation of trust and creativity in face-to-face teams remains largely inconclusive. It was found that trust is beneficial to increase creativity in face-to-face teams [41], but more recent studies showed that there is no positive impact of trust on creativity in teams [7]. Similarly, Bidault found that higher trust does not always lead to more creativity [3]. There seems to be a level of trust that maximizes the creative output. However, no previous research has focused on studying the correlation of trust and idea generation in distributed teams.

2.4 Rating Behavior and Trust

A successful idea generation session typically results in a large quantity of ideas. An evaluation process that aims to select a limited number of good ideas is necessary for further development. An effective method for idea evaluation is necessary to make the right decision whether an idea is original, feasible, or both. If expertise information of team members is not made sufficiently transparent during an idea evaluation session, a lack of trust of other members' judgment about an idea can easily develop. A lack of commitment can increase due to mistrust. Commitment is important to form a consensus about an idea within a team. The main goal of supporting trust in *idea evaluation* sessions is to allow the team members to arrive at a consensus while maintaining a reasonable level of satisfaction. Team members have to trust each other regarding their ability to select one or several good idea from an idea pool. There exist many approaches to evaluate ideas. One well-known technique is the *SWOT analysis* that evaluates ideas based on the following objectives: Strengths, Weaknesses/Limitations, Opportunities, and Threats [13]. Approaches such as the SWOT analysis are useful for comparing the advantages and disadvantages of a specific idea.

To support trust in idea evaluation sessions, we borrow the basic idea of a recommender system in that users are presented with pre-populated ratings provided by other users. Research has shown that showing predictions during the rating process (e.g. movies) could influence the users' rating outcomes [10]. Similar approach could also work for the evaluation of ideas and result in higher member satisfaction. A large amount of literature regarding trust and decision-making considers recommender systems, e.g. in e-commerce [10], recommending and evaluating choices in a virtual community of use [20]. Recommender systems are useful when too much information is present.

Research on decision-making has focused on trust as a variable that affects decision outcomes. In 2009, Parayitam found that the perception of trustworthiness, when based on the competence of a person, enhances decision quality and commitment, whereas no effects on outcomes can be observed when it is based on relationships [35]. Rietzschel identified the strong tendency of people to select feasible and desirable ideas at the cost of originality as the main reason for their poor selection performance [38]. However, no publications could be found containing results about the correlation of trust and idea evaluation in distributed teams. To our knowledge, no studies have analyzed how different levels of trust can impact the idea evaluation session outcomes. In this work, we attempt to study the rating behaviors of participants with higher cognitive trust or higher affective trust.

3. A TEMPLATE FOR SUPPORTING INITIAL TRUST
3.1 Support of Initial Trust

The focus of this work is to find out how initial trust can be supported in a distributed team when team members only have a very limited amount of time to accomplish a task, and how trust might improve the work results in distributed teams. Therefore, the approach of the so-called *first impression* could be used. People make guesses on signs and signals they perceive, which is the seed of trust or distrust and also affect their subsequent behavior [9, 16]. Signs and signals, which appear in face-to-face interaction, might or might not appear differently in computer-mediated interaction. Since members of distributed teams often do not have a prior working history and may never meet again, oral exchanges and face-to-face interaction often do not exist [23]. To enable distributed team members to form a first impression, information about their co-workers could be offered. Research has shown that the availability of information can influence trustworthiness assessments positively [40]. However, it is not entirely clear which information elements are most supportive for the assessment of team members, especially regarding teams dealing with innovation.

One way to support distributed team members with the formation of trustworthiness is to provide opportunities for accumulating personal knowledge and task-relevant background information [21, 26]. Feng claimed that, "*developing artifacts to help people to identify others who are similar to themselves or who have similar experiences may be helpful for promoting empathic attitudes that build interpersonal trust*" [14]. Jarvenpaa and Leidner found that high-performing distributed teams exchanged *background and personal information* and were *socializing more* with other members at the very beginning of their project [23]. Therefore, we aim to determine what information to provide in the beginning of a project to support initial trust in distributed idea generation and idea evaluation sessions. Furthermore, we need to know how this information is correlated to trust.

3.2 Information Elements

Rusman introduced the TrustWorthiness ANtecedents schema (TWAN) as an approach to inform trustworthiness assessments in the initial phase of collaboration [40]. This is used for the design of measures to accelerate the formation of interpersonal trust. Her study determined the information elements that are important for assessment of trustworthiness. The schema of perceived trustworthiness of a trustee consists of five main categories: *communality, ability, benevolence, internalized norms,* and *accountability*. Each of these main categories can be split up in more detailed antecedents.

Since our work focuses on affective trust and cognitive trust, we divided the different trustworthiness antecedents into two parts with *cognitive trust* referring to the main categories of *communality, ability,* and *accountability* and *affective trust* referring to *communality, benevolence, and internalized norms*. Note that *internalized norms* are not considered in this paper because they only refer to long-term projects and therefore cannot be integrated in the approach of this paper.

Our work focuses on making impact at the start of a project, but also aims to identify how knowing different information could affect different phases of the innovation process—idea generation and idea evaluation. To refine the findings of Rusman, a set of interviews was performed to discover important information elements adapted for the intended subject pool consisting of students.

Table 1. Information Elements

Personal	#	Expertise	#
Hobbies	14	Experience (projects)	15
Gender	13	Specific skills	15
Honorary activities	12	Specialization & interests	14
Age	11	References & awards	14
Nationality	8	Degree & years in the program	12
Taste in music	7	Companies	8
Favorite TV shows	6	Department	7

Overall 15 students were asked what personal and professional information they would like to know about team members they have to work with, but have never and will never meet face-to-face. In Table 1, the summary of the results of our interviews is shown. The table lists criteria (personal information and expertise) that the students listed as important, and their frequency (#).

3.3 Relation of Information Elements to Trust

Information elements can have a direct relationship to the introduced trustworthiness antecedents [40]. Table 2 provides a summary of the information elements available before the collaboration activities occur and their relationship to TWAN as specified in [40]. These are factual information that can be used by the participants to know their teammates prior to team activities. In Table 3, the information elements derived from behavior during the collaboration according to Rusman are shown. They can be perceived by the participants passively through the collaboration process.

Table 2. Available information before collaboration

Information element	Relation with TWAN
Age	Communality, Availability, Sharing
Gender	Communality, Availability, Sharing
Nationality	Communality, Availability, Sharing
Hobbies	Communality, Availability, Sharing
Honorary activities	Communality, Availability, Willingness to help, Faith in intentions, Caring, Friendliness, Commitment, Openness, Sharing
Favorite TV shows	Communality, Availability, Openness, Sharing, Receptivity
Taste in music	Communality, Availability, Openness, Sharing, Receptivity
Companies, Experience (projects), References & awards	Communality, Self-confidence, Knowledge, Reliability
Department	Communality, Skills, Knowledge
Degree & years in the program	Communality, Reliability, Consistency, Responsibility, Persistence, Competence
Specialization & Interests	Communality, Consistency, Persistence, Competence, Knowledge
Specific skills	Communality, Knowledge, Competence, Skills

Table 3. Information derived from behavior

Information element	Relation with TWAN
Message read by addressed person	Availability, Reliability, Responsibility
Suggestion/idea	Competence, Willingness to help, Sharing, Openness, Commitment, Self-confidence, Persistence, Responsibility
Task-status overview (task, accepted by, deadline, status)	Competence, Reliability, Responsibility
Average response	Availability, Receptivity, Commitment, Consistency, Responsibility

Different information elements affect trust in different ways, so the TWAN schema was divided into affective and cognitive trust. In this construct, the information elements should support affective trust and the expertise information elements should support cognitive trust.

3.4 System Design and Implementation

Since distributed teams usually collaborate via the Internet, a web-based software tool is one possible way to implement an initial trust template for idea generation and idea evaluation sessions. The prototype consists of a client (web browser) and a server (web server with database). The idea generation session consists of two different web pages. The start page of the idea generation session consists of the following: an overview about the different steps of the session to provide an overview for the participants, the task for the session so that the participants know what to do in the next step, information about the technology used in the task in case the participants are not familiar with it, and the profiles of two other participants, depending on the condition to which the participant was randomly assigned.

The second web page of the idea generation session consists of four main parts (see Figure 1). Part (1) shows the specific task and the brainstorming rules so that the participants are reminded what they are supposed to do and how they are supposed to do it. Part (2) is a chat window that displays the contributions of the participants. Part (3) is a pre-defined input mask for the entry of the participant's contributions. Part (4) shows the profiles of the two other participants as on the start page.

Figure 1. Idea Generation Session Template

The idea evaluation session also consists of two different web pages. The start page of the idea evaluation session consists of the following: an overview about the different steps of the session to provide an overview for the participants, the task for the session so that the participants know what to do in the next step, information about the technology used in the task in case the participants are not familiar with it, and the profiles of two other participants as in the idea generation session.

The second web page of the idea evaluation session also consists of four main parts (see Figure 2). Part (1) shows the specific task so that the participants are reminded what they are supposed to do and how they are supposed to do it. Part (2) is the rating area that allows the participant to rate ideas by clicking on the stars. Part (3) shows the previously rated ideas by two other participants and the average rating of the idea, which represents the final group rating. Part (4) shows the profiles of the two other participants as on the start page.

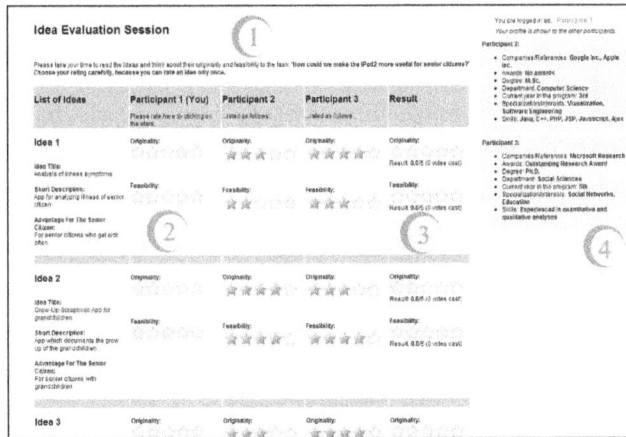

Figure 2. Idea Evaluation Session Template

4. GOALS AND EXPECTATIONS

As previously described, the goal of our experiment is to examine whether knowing specific information about collaborators might support trust in distributed idea generation and idea evaluation sessions. Moreover, we would like to determine how trust could impact the idea generation and idea evaluation sessions. Based on the information elements adapted from TWAN, we expect the following:

Hypothesis 1a: Knowing personal information of an individual leads to higher affective trust during the distributed idea generation session.

Hypothesis 1b: Knowing the expertise information of an individual leads to higher cognitive trust during the distributed idea generation session.

If this expectation is satisfied, we must further determine whether an increased trust among distributed team members could affect the contributions generated during idea generation sessions. Since higher affective trust allows team members to express themselves more freely and higher cognitive trust allows team members to focus on assessing the ideas more critically, we form the following hypothesis:

Hypothesis 2a: Higher affective trust during the distributed idea generation session leads to more radical ideas.

Hypothesis 2b: Higher cognitive trust during the distributed idea generation session leads to more incremental ideas.

Similar to the idea generation sessions, we expect to see the following as outcomes of the idea evaluation sessions:

Hypothesis 3a: Knowing personal information of an individual leads to higher affective trust during the distributed idea evaluation session.

Hypothesis 3b: Knowing that an individual is an expert in a specific field leads to higher cognitive trust during the distributed idea evaluation session.

If this expectation is satisfied, we must further determine whether an increased trust among distributed team members could affect the rating behaviors during idea evaluation sessions. Since higher affective trust allows team members to express themselves more

freely and since higher cognitive trust allows team members to focus on assessing the ideas more critically, we form the following hypotheses:

Hypothesis 4a: Higher affective trust in the distributed idea evaluation session reduces consensus formation within the group.

Hypothesis 4b: Higher cognitive trust in the distributed idea evaluation session induces consensus within the group.

To investigate the aforementioned hypotheses, a software prototype has been designed and implemented to find out if perceived trustworthiness leads to the hypothesized results. Finally, idea generation literature has traditionally used either all male or all female groups citing important gender differences. However, to our knowledge, no idea generation studies focused on detailing such gender differences, and in studies that involve mixed-gender groups, gender is obviously not carefully controlled. In this study, we control for gender groups and hope to lead to future designs that better account for gender differences.

5. EXPERIMENTAL DESIGN

5.1 Participants and Confederates

Table 4. Confederate information
(P = Personal Information; E = Expertise Information)

	Information	Confederate 1	Confederate 2
P	Age	27	25
	Gender	male	female
	Nationality	American	American
	Hobbies	playing basketball and guitar	music, photography, swimming
	Honorary activities	dean's list, athletic department honor roll	co-founder of a non-profit association
	TV shows	How I Met Your Mother, Chuck, Seinfeld	Sex and the City, The Big Bang Theory, The Simpsons
	Taste in music	rock, indie	electronic
E	Companies& References	Google Inc., Apple Inc.	Microsoft Research
	Awards	None	Outstanding Research Award
	Degree	M.Sc.	Ph.D.
	Department	Computer Science	Social Sciences
	Current year in the program	3rd	5th
	Specialization & Interests	Visualization, software engineering	social networks, education
	Skills	Java, C++, PHP, JSP, JavaScript, Ajax	experienced in quantitative and qualitative analysis

We recruited 36 participants from UCI for the experiment. 18 of them were male and 18 were female. They were between the ages of 20 and 33 years. The participant pool contained undergraduate as well as graduate students from different departments. The participants were asked to complete a short questionnaire about their background. On a 5-point Likert scale, all subjects except for one were somewhat familiar with idea generation (mean = 3.77) and idea evaluation (mean = 3.94) techniques. On a 7-point Likert scale, most of the participants reported they were comfortable working with strangers (mean = 4.80), they occasionally have online collaboration (mean = 3.77), and they tended to trust strangers slightly (mean = 3.55).

Participants worked in groups of three with two of the three being confederates (computer bots). One of the challenges in evaluating ideas in experimental studies is that groupthink tends to dictate the idea flow, and the ideas of participants are often triggered by the ideas generated by other participants in the same session. In this study, confederates were used in order to ensure consistent participant experiences across all experimental conditions. In the idea generation sessions, each confederate entered a predetermined list of ideas at specific time intervals. Each confederate had a list of ten ideas that were applicable to the given topic. Depending on the condition, different profile information of the confederates were shown to the participants. Under condition N, no profile information was shown except for the fact that two other participants are logged in. Under condition P and E, the confederates portrayed the profile information identified in Table 4.

5.2 Independent Variables

The study followed a 2 (gender) x 2 (idea generation and idea evaluation sessions) x 2 (topic A and topic B) x 3 (information element conditions N, P, and E) counterbalanced, randomly assigned, within-subjects design (see Table 5). Since there was no significant difference between topic A and topic B, we combined the results in both topic A and B in the analyses. All participants first accomplished an idea generation session and then an idea evaluation session. The ordering of the topics was counterbalanced; participants either generated ideas about topic A in the idea generation session and then evaluated ideas about topic B in the idea evaluation session or vice versa. Topic A involved ideas for using Facebook as a platform for learning in the classroom setting, and topic B involved ideas for using the iPad2 to assist the elderly. Each participant was randomly assigned to one of three information element conditions. In *condition N*, the participants did not receive any information about their team members. In *condition P*, the participants received personal information about their team members. In *condition E*, the participants received the expertise information of their team members (see Table 4).

Table 5. Study design

Idea Generation (IG) & Idea Evaluation (IE)											
Male						Female					
Topic A => Topic B			Topic B => Topic A			Topic A => Topic B			Topic B => Topic A		
N	P	E	N	P	E	N	P	E	N	P	E

5.3 Procedure

The study took place at a behavioral research lab. Each participant was asked to complete a demographic survey. A research staff member explained the research procedure and asked the participant to provide verbal consent. The subject then received a short training on the use of the system. Each subject logged into the system and generated ideas for 15 minutes with two confederates on the assigned topic. In the idea generation session, the participant was asked to provide a label, a short description, and the advantage for the target group for each idea. Each confederate entered a pre-populated list of ten ideas relevant to the assigned topic into the chat window at a time interval that was designed to emulate the natural thinking and typing speed that one

would expect to encounter in a regular idea generation meeting. This was done to ensure that all participants encountered the same ideas across different experimental conditions. After a five-minute break, the participant was asked to fill out a questionnaire about his/her personal trust level during the idea generation activity, as well as the satisfaction with the result of the idea generation session. Then the participant was given a five-minute break. In the idea evaluation session, the participant was given 15 minutes to evaluate six pre-populated ideas that are relevant to a second topic for originality and feasibility on a five-point scale. The system also showed the ratings provided by the confederates. This was done to see if knowing either personal or expertise information about their teammates could alter the participants' rating behaviors. After a five-minute break, the participants were asked to fill out a questionnaire about their personal trust level during the idea evaluation as well as their satisfaction with the result of the idea evaluation session. The entire study procedure lasted approximately 60 minutes.

5.4 Dependent Variables

5.4.1 Trust and Satisfaction

To measure affective and cognitive trust of the participants we used a questionnaire adapted from the TWAN schema [40]. The cognitive trust measure asked about communality (1 question), ability (3), and accountability (5) of the participants (Cronbach's alpha=0.93). The affective trust measure asked about communality (1 question) and benevolence (8) of the participants (Cronbach's alpha=0.87). Six additional questions were asked to measure the participants' satisfaction level (Cronbach's alpha=0.72).

5.4.2 Quality and Quantity of Ideas

We measured the quantity, diversity, and quality of the ideas generated in the idea generation session. Idea quantity is defined as the number of unique ideas. Idea diversity is measured by the number of idea clusters grouped by similarity. All ideas were clustered and rated independently by two experts for originality and feasibility on a five-point scale. The quality of an idea is defined as a combination of *originality* and *feasibility*. The inter-rater agreement coefficient was calculated as shown in previous idea generation studies, which assumed that the ratings were in agreement if the expert ratings fell within one point of each other [12, 38]. The two experts agreed on 89.3% of the originality ratings and on 90.4% of the feasibility ratings. Differences were reconciled by averaging the ratings. We further group ideas into radical ideas (high originality and high feasibility) and incremental ideas (above average originality and above average feasibility).

6. RESULTS
6.1 Idea Generation

Table 6 summarizes the results in the idea generation sessions. To test Hypothesis 1a, 1b, 2a, and 2b, MANOVA was performed. The test showed that there is no effect of gender and topic on the trust level of the participants. The F-test showed that there is a significant effect regarding the different conditions and the trust level of participants in the idea generation session (F[14,48] = 3.52, p<0.0006). Post-hoc t-tests showed that the participants in both *condition P* (t[22] = 3.96, p<0.0003) and *condition E* (t[22] = 3.46, p<0.001) developed significantly higher affective trust in the idea generation session than the control group. Participants in *condition E* also developed significantly higher affective trust than in the control group. Similarly, participants in both *condition P* (t[22] = 3.06, p<0.003) and *condition E* (t[22] = 2.73, p<0.006) developed significantly higher cognitive trust in the idea generation session than the control group. In regard to affective trust, it was shown that knowing of personal information leads to higher affective trust during the distributed idea generation session. It was surprising to observe that *knowing the expertise level also leads to higher affective trust when its primary goal is to support cognitive trust.* The same applies to cognitive trust. The results showed that *knowing both personal information and expertise level enhance affective and cognitive trust in the idea generation session.* Thus, *knowing any information (personal or expertise) could enhance trust in general.* As a result it can be said that the data supports *Hypothesis 1a and 1b—knowing expertise and personal information could lead to higher cognitive and affective trust during the idea generation sessions.*

Table 6. Idea Generation Results

	N	P	E
Quantity	4.0 (0.48)[b]	6.4 (0.56)[a]	4.3 (0.54)[b]
Diversity	3.5 (0.51)[b]	6.0 (0.48)[a]	3.9 (0.48)[b]
Incremental Ideas	1.2 (0.30)[b]	2.3 (0.43)[a]	1.1 (0.29)[b]
Radical Ideas	1.0 (0.35)[b]	1.6 (0.15)[a]	0.4 (0.15)[c]
Cognitive Trust	4.1 (0.23)[b]	5.1 (0.23)[a]	5.1 (0.18)[a]
Affective Trust	4.6 (0.19)[b]	5.5 (0.16)[a]	5.2 (0.17)[a]
Satisfaction	4.3 (0.19)[b]	4.9 (0.12)[a]	4.5 (0.17)[b]

* The results is displayed as Mean (Standard Deviation), with superscripts denoting the following statistically significant relationships: a > b > c.

The participants were also asked about their general satisfaction about the idea generation process. Post-hoc t-tests showed that participants in *condition P* felt significantly more satisfied than the participants in both *condition E* (t[22] = 1.85, p<0.04) and in the control group (t[22] = 2.55, p<0.009). This shows that *knowing more personal information about the other team members not only resulted in higher trust, but also induced higher satisfaction during the process.*

In terms of idea quantity, post-hoc t-tests showed that participants in *condition P* created more unique ideas than in the control group (t[22] = 3.29, p<0.001) and in *condition E* with a significance of (t[22] = 2.68, p<0.006). Similarly, participants in *condition P* also created significantly more diverse ideas than in *condition E* (t[22] = 3.06, p<0.002) as well as in the control group (t[22] = 3.56, p<0.0009). This shows that higher affective trust makes the participants open up more to others and that they are able to express their ideas more freely. This also confirms prior research that participants in a team full of experts reported higher perceived inhibition in idea generation sessions [8].

In terms of idea quality, post-hoc t-tests showed that participants *in condition P* tended to produce more radical ideas than in the control group (t[22] = 1.54, p<0.06) and that the participants in the control group tended to produce more radical ideas than in *condition E* (t[22] = 1.54, p<0.06). Also, participants in *condition P* created more radical ideas than in *condition E* (t[22] = 5.54, p<0.0001). For incremental ideas, post-hoc t-tests showed that participants in *condition P* created significantly more incremental ideas than the participants in *condition E* (t[22] = 2.26, p<0.01) and in the control group (t[22] = 2.07, p<0.02). The enhanced affective trust in *condition P* provides participants enough confidence to write down more interesting or unusual ideas. This result supports *Hypothesis 2a* but not *Hypothesis 2b—higher affective trust resulted in more radical ideas, but higher cognitive trust did not produce more incremental ideas.* Furthermore, it can

be claimed that knowing the expertise information of the other participants has a negative influence on producing radical ideas due to the higher perceived inhibition despite the high cognitive trust.

In regard to idea originality and feasibility, a significant effect of gender was found (F(2,147) = 3.02, p<0.04). Post-hoc t-tests showed that *female participants on average created more feasible ideas whereas male participants on average created more original ideas* (see Table 7).

Table 7. Gender Differences

	Female	Male
Originality	3.01 (0.78)[b]	3.25 (0.87)[a]
Feasibility	3.97 (0.77)[a]	3.69 (0.87)[b]

* The results is displayed as Mean (Standard Deviation), with superscripts denoting the following statistically significant relationships: a > b.

Although no prior idea generation literature focused on gender differences, existing gender in software interfaces suggested that females tend to be more risk-averse [6]. We believe that this is especially true in a distributed environment where participants do not know their remote teammates, and could lead to females proposing more feasible ideas in order to not provoke undesired responses from their teammates.

6.2 Idea Evaluation

Table 8 summarizes the results in the idea evaluation sessions. To test Hypothesis 3a, 3b, 4a, and 4b, MANOVA was performed. The test showed that there is no effect of gender and topic on the trust level of the participants.

Table 8. Idea Evaluation Results

	N	P	E
Originality	3.0 (0.12)	3.2 (0.18)	2.9 (0.19)
Feasibility	3.8 (0.15)[a]	3.9 (0.14)[a]	3.5 (0.16)[b]
Cognitive Trust	4.2 (0.21)[c]	4.8 (0.15)[b]	5.4 (0.12)[a]
Affective Trust	4.5 (0.15)[b]	5.0 (0.21)[a]	4.8 (0.18)
Satisfaction	4.6 (0.19)[b]	5.2 (0.14)[a]	5.1 (0.19)[a]

The F-test showed that there is a significant effect regarding the different conditions and the trust level of participants in the idea evaluation session (F[10,52] = 3.55, p<0.001). Post-hoc t-tests showed that only the participants in *condition P* developed significantly higher affective trust in the idea evaluation session than in the control group (t[21] = 2.07, p<0.02). As a result it can be stated that *knowing personal information leads to higher affective trust in the idea evaluation session.* For cognitive trust, Participants *in condition E* developed higher cognitive trust than in the *condition P* (t[22] = 3.03, p <0.003), and that the participants in the *condition P* developed higher cognitive trust than in the control group (t[22] = 2.32, p<0.01). It makes sense that expertise information has a much stronger influence on cognitive trust, but this also means that personal information could also be misconstrued as domain competency during the idea evaluation process. As a result it can be said that the data supports *Hypothesis 3a and 3b—knowing expertise and personal information could lead to higher cognitive and affective trust during the idea evaluation sessions.*

The participants were also asked about their general satisfaction about the idea evaluation process. Post-hoc t-test showed that participants in both *condition P* (t[22] = 2.67, p<0.006) and condition *E* (t[22] = 1.97, p<0.03) felt significantly more satisfied than the participants in the control group. This shows that information about other team members in general (both personal and expertise) could induce higher satisfaction during the idea evaluation process. This difference, in contrast with the idea generation process in which personal information is more desirable than expertise information, is perhaps due to the generative nature of the idea generation process versus the selective nature of the idea evaluation process.

Although participants seem to provide similar original ratings on the ideas presented to them in the idea evaluation sessions, no correlation was found between the ratings of the participants and those provided by the confederates. However, by comparing the average feasibility ratings of all participants in the three conditions, it was found that participants in *condition E* provided lower ratings than in *condition P* (t[22] = 1.93, p<0.03) and in the control group (t[22] = 1.68, p<0.05). This means that *knowing the expertise information of other team members, participants were led to judge more critically on the feasibility ratings*.

Our results indicate that higher affective or cognitive trust did not lead to consensus formation as there was no correlation in their rating behavior, but to better satisfaction regarding the result. Thus, the data does not support *Hypothesis 4a* and *Hypothesis 4b*—higher *cognitive and affective trust levels did not exhibit correlation with consensus formation during the idea evaluation sessions.*

7. DISCUSSION AND LIMITATIONS

The results of the experiment showed that topic and gender differences have little effect on trust in idea generation and idea evaluation sessions. There is, however, a significant effect of knowing information elements of participants' profiles on their trust level and their output. The study results showed that knowing personal information leads to higher affective trust and knowing expertise information leads to higher cognitive trust, which validated our initial hypotheses. However, what surprised us was that knowing either personal or expertise information of the team members boosted both trust levels. Although cognitive trust is, by definition a type of trust that is based on the perception of domain knowledge and task competency and affective trust is based on the perception of emotional comfort, we found that our participants were not able to clearly distinguish these two dimensions of trust. Essentially, knowing any information about others, regardless of it being personal hobbies or professional knowledge could help the team members relate to and familiarize with each other and therefore lead to higher perceptions of trust.

In terms of idea generation, although personal and expertise information are capable of enhancing the participants' perception of trust overall, the personal informational elements are much more conducive (more radical and incremental ideas) whereas the expertise information elements are detrimental to idea generation outcomes (less radical ideas and no more incremental ideas than the control group). This is consistent with the literature, as people tend to be more reserved due to evaluation apprehension when the perceived expertise level is high. In this study, we further showed that knowing personal information about the teammates could reduce that hindrance and lead to sharing more and better ideas.

Another important finding is that we found gender differences in the idea generation sessions: female participants created more feasible ideas while male participants created more original ideas in the experiment. Previous literature points to the fact that females tend to be more risk-averse in unfamiliar environments

[6]. Since this research focuses on inducing initial trust on distributed teams filled with strangers, this environment may be especially uncomfortable for female participants to openly share their ideas. Future studies should focus on information elements that will engender lively contributions from the female participants.

Similar to idea generation sessions, the study showed that knowing personal information leads to higher affective trust and knowing expertise information leads to higher cognitive trust during the idea evaluation sessions, which validated our initial hypotheses. However, there is a difference in terms of how the information elements affected the trust level across the two phases of creativity. Due to the evaluative nature of the idea evaluation task, participants are much more cognizant of the competency level that the other team members have to offer. The expertise information elements induced higher cognitive trust than both personal information and the control groups. Participants are also much more critical at assessing the feasibility of the ideas presented to them. Our results also showed that neither type of information elements led to better consensus formation.

This research has some limitations. The study was conducted with a limited pool of just 36 participants. It would be useful to perform an experiment with a larger number of participants. Computer confederates were used in order to ensure that the participants received consistent treatment across different experimental conditions. Since computer bots cannot simulate human and social behavior completely, it would be interesting to see if the results are influenced if this study is conducted with a group of real participants. Participants consisted of students, and therefore the information elements were adapted to students as well and the results may not be generalizable to professional groups. The information elements used in this study will have to be extended or replaced by other information elements that are more suitable for other settings. Furthermore, this work is based on the TWAN schema, and other researchers may have different interpretations of the proposed schema. This study lasted only about an hour. In a long-term project, the fifth category from the TWAN schema—internalized norms—could be included in the analysis. It would also be interesting to apply that approach in this paper to other distributed group work besides idea generation and idea evaluation sessions.

8. CONCLUSION AND FUTURE WORK

In this work, we determined how knowing expertise and personal information of other team members affects trust in a distributed team environment, and how trust influences idea generation and idea evaluation sessions. Our findings support previous trust research by confirming that trust influences the behavior of people in a positive manner. It also supports the two-dimensional trust research dividing trust into affective trust and cognitive trust. We provide basic research about the positive correlation of trust and distributed idea generation as well as idea evaluation. We also found indications that trust support should be carefully considered for gender groups in the innovation process, and this work can be used as a first step for further exploration and design implications.

The results of this study show that information elements can be effectively used to support initial trust building in the distributed team environment. The findings of this research can be used to support the development of templates that could provide communication support for distributed teams. Higher affective trust appears to have the ability to reduce evaluation apprehension in the idea generation sessions. Since it was shown that knowing personal information has the biggest influence on affective trust in the idea generation session, developers could incorporate this kind of information in designing interface layouts or group process enhancements for the purpose of an idea generation session. Likewise, interface and group process designers could incorporate expertise information elements to assist distributed idea evaluation sessions. Making the expertise information available could make people more critical about their own evaluation criteria. In general, providing any information is better than providing no information at all, as anything that could help the team members relate and share experiences could help team build trust and make their work more effective. Offering information increases team trust, which is a key factor to success in innovation processes.

For future work, other ways of carrying out an idea generation or idea evaluation session could be implemented. For example, a more structured technique for creating ideas could be applied instead of using brainstorming. It would also be interesting to know what information elements are needed when participants are communicating with other mediums such as video and audio chat. Another question is whether the proposed template is scalable for a bigger group. The more information is shown the higher the cognitive load is imposed upon the participants. As another future work, a potential next step could be to create a taxonomy of information elements that are suitable for different participants, tasks, and distributed settings. This knowledge could be used for supporting collaboration, and providing group process designers the possibility to better integrate the trust factor in their processes in a structured and predictable way. Additionally, further research is necessary for understanding how systems can be better designed to encourage more creative contributions from the female participants.

9. ACKNOWLEDGEMENTS

This material is based upon work supported by the National Science Foundation under Grant Nos. 1111446, 0943262, and 0808783. We thank our colleagues for their advice and feedback, especially Drs. Matthew Bietz, Gary Olson, and Filippo Lanubile, as well as the entire CRADL research group at Irvine. We also thank the anonymous reviewers for their helpful comments.

10. REFERENCES

[1] Al-Ani, B. and Redmiles, D. 2009. Supporting Trust in Distributed Teams through Continuous Coordination. *IEEE Software* 99, 1 (August 2009), 35-40.

[2] Barki, H. and Pinsonneault, A. 2001. Small Group Brainstorming and Idea Quality: Is Electronic Brainstorming the Most Effective Approach? *Small Group Research* 32, 2 (April 2001), 158-205.

[3] Bidault, F. and Castello, A. 2009. Trust and Creativity: Understanding the Role of Trust in Creativity-Oriented Joint Developments. *R&D Management* 39, 3 (June 2009), 259-270.

[4] Booz, A. 1982. *New Product Management for the 80s.* Booz, Allen, and Hamilton Inc., New York, NY.

[5] Bos, N., Olson, J., Gergle, D., Olson, G., and Wright, Z. 2002. Effects of four computer-mediated communications channels on trust development. In *Proceedings of the SIGCHI Conference on Human Factors in Computing Systems: Changing Our World, Changing Ourselves* (Minneapolis, Minnesota, USA, April 20 – 25, 2002). CHI'02. ACM, New York, NY, 135-140.

[6] Burnett, M.M., Beckwith, L., Wiedenbeck, S., Fleming, S.D., Cao, J., Park, T.H., Grigoreanu, V., and Rector, K. 2011. Gender Pluralism in Problem-Solving Software. *Interacting with Computers* 23, 5 (September 2011), 450-460.

[7] Chen, M.H., Chang, Y.C., and Hung, S.C. 2008. Social Capital and Creativity in R&D Project Teams. *R&D Management* 38, 1 (January 2008), 21-34.

[8] Collaros, P.A. and Anderson, L.R. 1969. Effect of perceived expertness upon creativity of members of brainstorming groups. *Journal of Applied Psychology 53*, 2 (April 1969), 159-163.

[9] Cooper, A., and Bott, M.W.J. 1999. Influence of Expectancies and Experience on Impression Formation. *Journal of Psychological Inquiry* 4 (1999), 21-24.

[10] Cosley, D., Lam, S. K., Albert, I., Konstan, J. A., and Riedl, J. 2003. Is seeing believing? How recommender interfaces affect users' opinions. In *Proceedings of the SIGCHI Conference on Human Factors in Computing Systems* (Fort Lauderdale, FL, USA, April 5 – 10, 2003). CHI '03. ACM, New York, NY, 585-592.

[11] Crawford, M.E. 1994. *New Products Management.* 4th Edition. Irwin Inc., Boston, MA.

[12] Diehl, M. and Stroebe, W. 1987. Productivity Loss in Brainstorming Groups: Toward the Solution of a Riddle. *Journal of Personality and Social Psychology* 53, 3 (September 1987), 497-509.

[13] Dosher, M., Benepe, O., Humphrey, A., Stewart, R., and Lie, B. 1960-1970. *The SWOT analysis method.* Stanford Research Institute, Mento Park, CA.

[14] Feng, J., Lazar, J., and Preece, J. 2004. Empathy and online interpersonal trust: a fragile relationship. *Behaviour and Information Technology* 23, 2 (March-April 2004), 97-106.

[15] Gabarro, J.J. 1990. The Development of Working Relationships. In *Intellectual Teamwork,* J., Kraut, R. E., and Egido, C. Galegher Eds. Erlbaum, Hillsdale, NY, 79-110.

[16] Good, D. 2000. Individuals, Interpersonal Relations, and Trust. In *Trust: Making and breaking cooperative relations,* by D. (ed.) Gambetta, 31-48. Blackwell, Oxford, UK.

[17] Hartman, F. 1999. Teams and team building. In *The Technology Management Handbook,* R.C. Dorf Ed. CRC Press/IEEE Press, Boca Raton, 8-12.

[18] Herstatt, C. 1999. Theorie und Praxis der fruehen Phasen des Innovationsprozesses. *Management* 68, 10 (1999), 72-81.

[19] Higgins, J.M. 1994. *101 Creative Problem Solving Techniques: The Handbook of New Ideas for Business.* New Management Publishing Company.

[20] Hill, W., Stead, L., Rosenstein, M., and Furnas, G. 1995. Recommending and evaluating choices in a virtual community of use. In *Proceedings of the SIGCHI Conference on Human Factors in Computing Systems* (Portland, Oregon, USA, April 2 – 7, 2005). CHI '05. ACM, New York, NY, 194-201.

[21] Hung, Y.C., Dennis, A.R., and Robert, L. 2004. Trust in Virtual Teams: Towards an Integrative Model of Trust Formation. In *Proceedings of the 37th Hawaii International Conference on System* Sciences (Big Island, Hawaii, January 5-8, 2004). HICSS '37. IEEE Computer Society, Washington DC.

[22] Iacono, C. and Weisband, S. 1997. Developing Trust in Virtual Teams. In *Proceedings of the 13th Hawaii International Conference on System Sciences* (Wailea, Hawaii, January 07 – 10, 1997). HICSS '37. IEEE Computer Society, Washington DC, 412-420.

[23] Jarvenpaa, S.L. and Leidner, D.E. 1999. Communication and Trust in Global Virtual Teams. *Organization Science* 10, 6 (June 1999), 791-815.

[24] Jarvenpaa, S.L., Knoll, K., and Leidner, D.E. 1998. Is anybody out there? Antecedents of trust in global virtual teams. *Journal of Management Information Systems* 14, 4 (March 1998), 29-64.

[25] Johnson, B. 2005. Design ideation: the conceptual sketch in the digital age. *Design Studies* 26, 6 (November 2005), 613-624.

[26] Kanawattanachai, P. and Yoo, Y. 2005. Dynamic nature of trust in virtual teams. *The Journal of Strategic Information Systems* 11, 3-4 (December 2002), 187-213.

[27] Karau, S.J. and Williams, J.W. 1993. Social loafing: A Meta--Analytic Review and Theoretical Integration. *Journal of Personality and Social Psychology* 65, 4 (October 1993), 681-706.

[28] Knoll, S.W. and Horton, G. 2010. Changing the Perspective: Improving Generate thinkLets for Ideation. In *Proceedings of the 43rd Hawaii International Conference on System Sciences* (Honolulu, Hawaii, January 5 – 8, 2010). HICSS '43. IEEE Computer Society Press, Los Alamitos, 1-10.

[29] Lipnack, J. and Stamps, J. 2000. *Virtual Teams: People Working Across Boundaries with Technology.* 2nd Edition. Wiley, New York, NY.

[30] McAllister, D.J. 1995. Affect- and cognition-based trust as foundations for interpersonal cooperation in organizations. *Academy of Management Journal* 38, 1 (February 1995), 24-59.

[31] Meyerson, D. Weick, K.E., and Kramer, R.M. 1996. Swift Trust and Temporary Groups. In *Trust in Organizations: Frontiers of Theory and Research,* Kramer (Eds.), R.M. and Tyler, T.R. Sage Publications, Thousand Oaks, CA, 166-195.

[32] Nooteboom, B., Berger, H., and Noorderhaven, N.G. 1997. Effects of Trust and Governance on Relational Risk. *Academy of Management Journal* 40 (1997), 308-338.

[33] Nystrom, H. 1985. Product Development Strategy: An Integration of Technology and Marketing. *Journal of Product Innovation Management* 2, 1 (March 1985), 25-33.

[34] Osborn, A. F. 1963. *Applied imagination: Principles and procedures of creative problem solving.* 3rd Revised Edition, Charles Scribner's Sons, New York, NY.

[35] Parayitam, S. and Dooley, R.S. 2009. The interplay between cognitive- and affective conflict and cognition- and affect--based trust in influencing decision outcomes. *Journal of Business Research* 62, 8 (August 2009), 789-796.

[36] Postmes, T. and Lea, M. 2000. Social processes and group decision making: anonymity in group decision support systems. *Ergonomics* 43, 8 (August 2000), 1252-1274.

[37] Pyysia☐inen, J. 2003. Building Trust in Global Inter-Organizational Software Development Projects: Problems and Practices. *International Workshop on Global Software Engineering* (May 2003), 69-74.

[38] Rietzschel, E.F., Nijstad, B.A., and Stroebe, W. 2010. The selection of creative ideas after individual idea generation: Choosing between creativity and impact. *British Journal of Psychology* 101 (February 2010), 47-68.

[39] Ross, W. and LaCroix, J. 1996. Multiple Meanings of Trust in Negotiation Theory and Research: A Literature Review and Integrative Model. *The International Journal of Conflict Management* 7, 4 (1996), 314-360.

[40] Rusman, E. 2011. *The Mind's Eye on Personal Profiles - How to inform trustworthiness assessments in virtual project teams.* Doctoral Thesis. Open Universiteit Heerlen, The Netherlands.

[41] Simons, T.L. and Peterson, R.S. 2000. Task conflict and relationship conflict in top management teams: The pivotal role of intragroup trust. *Journal of Applied Psychology* 85, 1 (February 2000), 102-111.

[42] Sternberg, R.J. (Ed.) 1988. *The nature of creativity.* Cambridge University Press, New York, NY.

[43] Trainer, E., Al-Ani, B, and Redmiles, D. 2011. Impact of Collaborative Traces on Trustworthiness. In *Proceedings of the 4th International Workshop on Cooperative and Human Aspects of Software Engineering.* (Honolulu, Hawaii, May 21, 2011). CHASE '11. ACM, New York, NY, 40-47.

[44] Valacich, J.S., Dennis, A.R., and Nunamaker, J.F. 1992. Group Size and Anonymity Effects on Computer-Mediated Idea Generation. *Small Group Research* 23, 1 (February 1992), 49-73.

[45] Wilson, J.M., Straus, S.G., and McEvily, W.J. 2006. All in due time: The development of trust in computer-mediated and face-to-face groups. *Organizational Behavior and Human Decision Processes* 99, 1 (January 2006), 16-33.

From Credit and Risk to Trust: Towards a Credit Flow Based Trust Model for Social Networks

Yuqing Mao
School of Computer
Engineering
Nanyang Technological
University
Singapore
maoy0002@e.ntu.edu.sg

Haifeng Shen
School of Computer Science,
Engineering and Mathematics
Flinders University
Adelaide, Australia
haifeng.shen@flinders.edu.au

Chengzheng Sun
School of Computer
Engineering
Nanyang Technological
University
Singapore
czsun@ntu.edu.sg

ABSTRACT

Trust management is a paramount issue in social networks. Existing models based on global reputation are simplistic as they do not support personalised measures for individual users. Models based on local trust propagation tend to be too subjective to be reliable as they do not consider a social network in its entirety. More importantly, neither model has taken the risk factor into the consideration of trust management. In this paper, we contribute a novel trust model that allows personalised measures to be naturally established on objective grounds through tracing credit flows within a social network, where the trust between a pair of users can be derived from the credit flowing from one into the other and the relative risk disparity between them. This model uses power flows in an electrical grid as a metaphor for the credit flows in a social network and is based on the hypothesis that the credit flows in a social network are similar in nature to the power flows in an electrical grid. Experiments with a real-world dataset have proved the hypothesis and the results have shown that the credit flow based trust model can derive not only personalised but also more accurate trust measures than existing models do.

Categories and Subject Descriptors

H.3.5 [**Information Storage and Retrieval**]: Online Information Services—*Data sharing, Web-based services*; K.4.3 [**Computers and Society**]: [Computer Supported Collaborative Work]

General Terms

Algorithms, Design

Keywords

social networking, trust inference, credit flow

1. INTRODUCTION

Past few years have witnessed not only the wide spread of various online social networks but also the exponential growth of virtual relationships. Online social networks take various forms pertaining to how virtual relationships between parties are established. A relationship could arise from online interaction, for example, one making comments on a video posted to YouTube by another, or from online transactions, for example, one purchasing an item from another through eBay, or from friendships inherited from the real world or encountered in the virtual world, for example, friends on Facebook.

Trust is a characteristic that lives within all of us and that fundamentally underpins a variety of activities where people share, communicate, interact, and collaborate with one another because taking the solution from someone else about a problem one is trying to solve or collaborate with someone on a joint task requires trust of that person. To some extent, supporting group work is more a matter of trust than a technology because if one did not trust the information from one's collaborators, all efforts of making the information perfect would be in vain. Recently, trust management becomes a paramount issue in online social networks as the population of social networking users receiving critical information from or making financial transactions with their virtual relations has skyrocketed. In recent years, a number of trust models have been proposed and used for trust management in a variety of social networks. Depending on whether global or local metrics are used to derive trust measures, they can basically be divided into global or local models [27].

A global model adopts a unified measure of trust for all nodes in a social network. It assigns a trust score to each node and every other node in the network trusts it in a unanimous way that is decided by the score. For example, if Alice has a higher trust score than Bob does, every other user in the network would trust Alice more than Bob. A global model can be regarded as a reputation model, where each node's reputation is calculated by global metrics that are based on the entire network structure or link analysis. For example, with the PageRank algorithm [12] or its variations [17], Alice would have a good reputation too if nodes linking to her were all reputable.

In contrast, a local model uses a personalised measure of trust for every individual node in a social network. It assigns multiple trust values to each node, one for every other node in the network, which trusts it in such a way that is decided by the corresponding trust value. For example, Alice's trust value towards Carol is 0.6, while Bob's trust value towards Carol is 0.1, indicating that Alice trusts Carol more than Bob does. To calculate the trust value for every pair of nodes in a network, trust values between directly connected nodes must be collected from users as additional input parameters and local trust metrics need to propagate these values over the network to derive the trust values between indirectly connected nodes. For example, assuming propagation of trust along a path is multiplicative, if Alice's trust towards Bob is 0.6 and Bob's trust towards Carol is 0.5, Alice's trust towards Carol may be $0.6 \times 0.5 = 0.3$.

Global trust models are suitable for social networks where explicit personal trust values for all nodes are not available, but interactions between nodes can be used to infer the overall reputation of each node. As bias is a natural property of trust, global models are simplistic and too objective because they do not support personalised measures towards the same node. While local models have addressed this issue, they tend to be too subjective to be reliable because they do not consider a social network in its entirety and it is non-trivial to collect accurate personal trust values only based on the partial network information.

More importantly, neither model has taken the risk factor, a factor that is inherently related to a user's expertise in providing information to their social networking peers and consequently essential to infer the trustworthiness of that information, into the consideration of trust management. For example, Alice happens to own high credit in a subject field but people who gave her credit are novices in that field. In contrast, Bob, who is in the same social network, owns relatively lower credit but people who gave him credit are all experts in the field. In this case, Alice may have a higher risk factor than Bob does and therefore should not necessarily be trusted more than Bob.

In this paper, we contribute a novel trust model CoreTrust (Credit Over Risk Equals Trust), which allows personalised measures to be naturally established on objective grounds through tracing credit flows within a social network, where the trust between a pair of users can be derived from the credit flowing from one into the other and the relative risk disparity between them. This model uses power flows in an electrical grid as a metaphor for the credit flows in a social network and is based on the hypothesis that the credit flows in a social network are similar in nature to the power flows in an electrical grid. Experiments with a real-world dataset have proved the hypothesis and the results have shown that this model can derive not only personalised but also more accurate trust measures than existing models do.

The rationale behind this model has three folds. First, a user's objective reputation derived from their interactions with others in a social network in its entirety is more reliable than a subjective trust value explicitly specified only based on partial network information. Second, since bias is a natural property of trust, it is simplistic to assign a uni-

versal reputation to each user and force every one else to trust them unanimously. Last, incorporation of subjective risk assessment between users based on their expertise disparity into each user's objective reputation is likely to yield personalized and more accurate trust measures.

The rest of this paper is organised as follows. First, we review existing trust models. Then we present the credit flow based trust model, including credit flow modelling, the CoreTrust model, and credit flow based trust inference. After that, we discuss the experimental evaluation of the model. Finally, we conclude the paper with a summary of major contributions and future work.

2. RELATED WORK

Social computing applications and social networking services such as *Facebook* and *Google+* have attracted a good deal of interest over the last few years. In most social computing applications or services, including recommender systems and social search systems, trust management is crucial for someone to determine the trustworthiness of anyone else with whom she/he will exchange information. Especially for those who do not personally know each other in the real world or have no prior direct interaction in the virtual world, trust inference is a critical approach to establishing new trust measures in a social network [8].

Trust models that calculate a universal measure of trust for all users in a social network are classified as global, as the objective of these models is to rank all nodes with a global reputation. For example, Kamvar et al. proposed the *EigenTrust* algorithm to calculate trust rating of each node in a network with a variation of the *PageRank* algorithm [5]. Richardson et al. described an approach that first finds all paths from a node to every other node, each of which represents an opinion of a statement, and then aggregates trust values along every path to calculate the final trust value [14]. Guha built a generic trust engine using the *TrustRank* and *DistrustRank* algorithms to capture the global trust rankings, which allows people to rate the content and the associated ratings from others [2]. Xiong and Liu presented the *PeerTrust* model, where the trustworthiness of a peer is calculated as the average feedback weighted by the rankings of the feedback contributors [22]. The PowerTrust [24] and GossipTrust [25] models proposed by Zhou and Hwang used the power-law feedback characteristics and the power of gossip respectively to disseminate feedback and reputation data from which a global trustworthiness value for each peer was derived. Liu et al. described *StereoTrust*, which attempted to derive the expected trust by aggregating stereotypes - built on the basis of existing agents' observed memberships of particular groups - that match an unknown agent's profile [9].

In contrast, trust models that calculate personalised trust values for each user are classified as local, as these models take individual bias into account by only considering partial network information. Local trust models exploit a user's personal experience and the web of trust to compute the trust value for every other user in the network. For example, Jøsang introduced the subjective logic to assess trust values based on the triplet representation of trust [4]. Similarly, based on the Dempster-Shafer theory of evidence and the explicit notion of uncertainty [18], Yu and Singh [23] developed a heuristic discounting approach that combined the local evidence with the testimonies of others evaluating the trustworthiness. Raph Levin's *Advogato* project applied the network flow in graph theory to a modified graph, which composed certificates between members to determine a member's trust level and their membership within a group [7]. Ziegler and Lausen presented the *Appleseed* algorithm for local group trust computation, which was inspired by propagation of activation over a network like neurons in psychology [26]. Golbeck proposed the *TidalTrust* model to infer trust values in continuous trust networks. When a node wants to infer the trust rating of a sink node, it first asks its trusted neighbours for the rating of that node, and then calculates a weighted average trust rating of its neighbours to the sink node [1]. Massa and Avesani developed *MoleTrust*, which predicted one's trust towards another by walking through the social network and propagating trust values along trust edges [11].

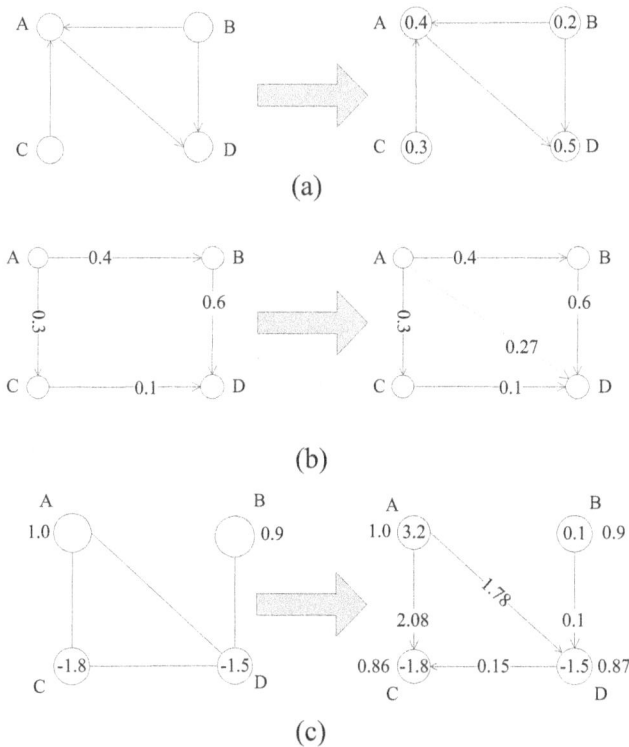

(a)

(b)

(c)

Figure 1: (a) objective trust inference; (b) subjective trust inference; (c) credit flow based trust inference

Local trust models use personalised trust measures to accommodate diverse subjective views on the same node in a social network, whereas global models use an objective reputation to approximate how much a network as a whole trusts each of its nodes. While existing models are primarily based on either global or local trust inference, in most social networks, both the subjective and objective properties of trust should be considered in order to infer personalised and more accurate trustworthiness of each node. The novelty of the CoreTrust model is to propagate trust within a social network in the form of credit flows. Suppose A, B, and C are

three nodes in a social network. A would trust B if credit flowed from A to B, e.g., when A gave credit to B through good ratings or positive comments. If C's risk factor were lower than B's, e.g., because C is an expert, whereas B is a novice in a subject field, A would probably trust C more than B. Therefore the trust is decided by the credit flow and the risk disparity between B and C. A node would be more trustworthy if more credit flowed into that node or that node had a lower risk factor.

Figure 1 compares the differences among objective, subjective, and credit flow based trust inferences. Figure 1(a) describes the acquisition of objective metrics using an algorithm similar to PageRank. A node's PageRank value, shown as a number within the node, can be obtained through voting, where a vote is a trust link from any other node to this node (the damping factor is set to 0.85). Figure 1(b) illustrates the propagation of subjective metrics using a strategy where the trust value between a pair of indirectly connected nodes can be calculated from existing trust values between directly connected nodes. In this example, the trust value from node A to node D, shown as a dashed edge, is derived from existing metrics: $0.4 \times 0.6 + 0.1 \times 0.3 = 0.27$.

Figure 1(c) depicts the inference of trust values through tracing credit flows. A node's risk factor, e.g. 1.0 for node A and 0.9 for node B (relative to A), is derived from the expertise level of that node against that of another node it is compared to. Assume node B's credit is 0.1 and credit can only flow from node A to other nodes. An expected trust inference could be that credit sourced from A is 3.2 (1.8 + 1.5 - 0.1), with 1.65 and 1.55 flowing into C and D respectively and that C's and D's risk factors (relative to A) are 0.86 and 0.87 respectively and that trust values from A to C and D are 2.08 $((1.65 + 0.15 \times 1.55/(1.55 + 0.1))/0.86)$ and 1.78 $(1.55/0.87)$ respectively.

3. CREDIT FLOW BASED TRUST MODEL

3.1 Credit Flow Modelling

It is essential for a credit flow model to be established on a solid mathematical and/or physical foundation so that it can be properly evaluated. The direction of a credit flow determines the trust relationship, e.g., if a credit flow is from user A to user B, A would trust B, but not vice versa. Risk disparity determines the credit flow direction, i.e., a credit flow is always from a user of high risk into a user of low risk. Risk factor is determined by expertise level, e.g., a user with a high expertise level would have a low risk factor. Risk factor is also relative in that a user's risk factor is relative to the risk factor of the user to be compared to. A metaphorical relationship among credit, risk, and trust would be *credit = risk × trust*, where high credit or low risk infers high trust.

Based on the requirement analysis of the expected credit flow model, we decide to use the power flow model for an electrical grid as a metaphor to present our solution because we conjecture that the credit flows in a social network are similar in nature to the power flows in an electrical grid. An electrical grid is a network of electrical components that supply, transmit and consume electrical power. All power systems have three major types of components: generator devices that supply electrical power, load devices that consume electrical power, and transmission/distribution devices that transmit electrical power from generator devices to load devices. Each power system has one or more sources of power and the sources are connected to the loads via conductors such as transmission lines. For instance, Figure 2 shows a simplistic power system consisting of 5 buses, 7 transmission lines, 2 generators, and 3 loads.

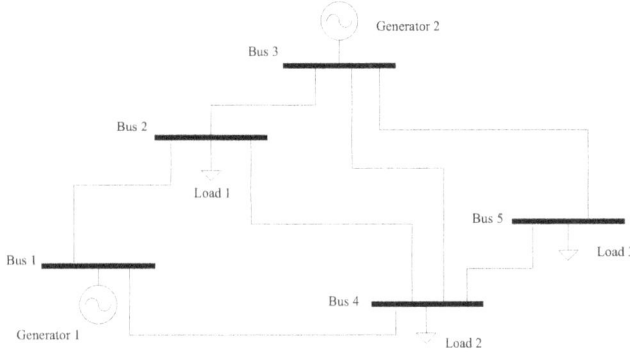

Figure 2: A simplistic power system

If a load device contains inductance or capacitance that can store electrical energy, the energy will periodically return into the power source and will flow back and forth across the conductors, generating reactive power, which is opposite to the real (or active) power provided for the load device to do useful work, e.g. lighting a bulb.

If an electrical grid's network structure and all its constituent devices' impedances and loads are known, we can use Kirchhoff's circuit law to solve all the currents in the grid with the following basic node equation:

$$I = Y_{bus}V \quad , \qquad (1)$$

where V is the vector of voltages at all nodes, I is the vector of currents injected at all node buses, and Y_{bus} is the nodal admittance of the buses in the system. However, because loads in an electrical grid are specified in terms of real and reactive powers instead of currents, we cannot directly use the node equations that rely on the voltages at all nodes and the currents injected at all node buses, but the power balance equations that are based on voltages, real powers, and reactive powers, such as:

$$P_i - jQ_i = V_i^* \sum_{k=1}^{N} (Y_{ik} \times V_k) \quad , \qquad (2)$$

where N is the total number of nodes in the grid, P_i and Q_i are per-unit real and reactive powers at node i respectively, V_i^* is the complex conjugate of the per-unit voltage at node i, V_k is the per-unit voltage at node K, and Y_{ik} is the total admittance between nodes i and k, which can be found from the nodal admittance matrix of the buses in the grid. Given a reference node, the admittance matrix is built according to the following two rules: (1) the admittance of elements connected between node k and the reference node is added to entry (k, k) of the admittance matrix, and (2) the admittance of elements connected between nodes i and k is added to entries (i, i) and (k, k) of the admittance matrix, while the negative admittance is added to entries (i, k) and (k, i) of the admittance matrix.

In reality, not all variables in a power balance equation are known; therefore such an algebraic non-linear equation needs to be transformed into a sequence of linear equations whose solutions approach the solution of the original equation. This is referred to as load flow analysis [16], which can be used to analyse the system performance in normal steady-state operation by calculating the voltage drop on each feeder, the voltage at each bus, and the power flow in each branch and feeder circuit. There are several methods for solving the nonlinear power balance equations. The *Newton-Raphson* method is widely used in load flow analysis, which is known for its convergence characteristics and speed.

Identification of the known and unknown variables from the types of buses they are associated with is the first step and also a key to solving power balance equations. The buses in an electrical grid are classified into three types: *load bus* - a bus without any generator device connected to it, *generator bus* - a bus with at least one generator device connected to it, and *slack bus* - the only bus in the grid that can provide the necessary power to maintain the power balance in the event that the real and reactive powers are not known at all buses. For the slack bus, the voltage magnitude and the phase angle are known (the voltage phase angle is normally set to zero degree). For a load bus, the real power and the reactive power are known. For a generator bus, the real power and the voltage magnitude are known.

If we metaphorise users, credit, risk, and trust in a social network into buses, power, voltage, and current respectively in an electrical grid, we can observe their similarities. For example, some users give credit to a social network; while others take credit from it as if some buses generate power; while others consume power in an electrical grid. Trust flows from users of high risk into users of low risk as if current flows from buses of high voltage into buses of low voltage. The *credit = risk × trust* relationship is metaphorical to the *power = voltage × current* relationship. Therefore, we will first model credit flows in a social network after power flows in an electrical grid, then infer the trust relationships between users in the network through credit flow analysis using the physical and mathematical principles of load flow analysis, and finally conduct a set of experiments with a real-world dataset to evaluate the credit flow based trust model against existing global and local trust models.

3.2 The CoreTrust Model

Most online communities, such as Weblogs *Blogger* and *Blogosphere*, shopping sites *eBay* and *Amazon*, social media sites *YouTube* and *Digg*, review sites *Epinions* and *Slashdot*, and peer-to-peer networks *eDonkey* and *BitTorrent*, allow members to rate the content generated by their peers. Global trust models have used the rating information to infer each node's universal reputation, but our model utilises such information to derive credit and further to trace the credit flows in order to infer personalised and accurate trust values. The credit flow model consists of four key elements: credit, risk, bias, and trust, analogous to power, voltage, phase angle, and current respectively in the power flow model.

Credit represents the confidence a user has in all other users. It can be derived from a user's ratings given to other users (i.e. the credit brought into the network by the user) or a user's ratings received from others (i.e. the credit taken out by the user). In a social network, a user's confidence may vary in different context, given a specific category, a user's credit in this category is called real credit C (analogous to the real power in an electrical grid), while their credit in other categories is called reactive credit D (analogous to the reactive power in the electrical grid). It is worth clarifying that unlike in an electrical grid, inductance or capacitance does not exist in a social network and therefore reactive credit simply means irrelevant credit as it is derived from the reviews received in categories other than the one in which the user's expertise is to be estimated. Because the total credit derived from all the reviews given and received in all categories in a social network is balanced, reactive credit balance equations are needed to derive the risk factors and infer the trust values. To simplify the model, we only consider the net credit brought into the network, i.e. the credit brought in by a user minus the credit taken out by the same user. Specifically, user u's real C_u and reactive credit D_u can be defined as:

$$C_u = \sum_{i \in Ca} \overrightarrow{R_u^i} - \sum_{j \in Ca} \overleftarrow{R_u^j} \quad \text{and} \qquad (3)$$

$$D_u = \sum_{k \notin Ca} \overrightarrow{R_u^k} - \sum_{l \notin Ca} \overleftarrow{R_u^l} \quad , \qquad (4)$$

where i and j are reviews in category Ca, k and l are reviews in categories other than Ca, $\overrightarrow{R_u^i}$ is the rating given by user u to the review i in category Ca, while $\overleftarrow{R_u^j}$ is the rating received by user u for her/his review j in category Ca, and $\overrightarrow{R_u^k}$ is the rating given by user u to the review k in categories other than Ca, while $\overleftarrow{R_u^l}$ is the rating received by user u for her/his review l in categories other than Ca.

Risk represents the possibility of incurring loss or failure when believing a user. Risk of believing someone is related to the expertise level, i.e. the level of one's expert knowledge or skill in a particular field, of the person to be believed. Generally speaking, one with a high level of expertise would have a low risk of trust. Suppose the expertise E is the degree of competency in providing accurate ratings and exhibiting high activities in an online community [6]. A user's risk factor R can be derived from their reviews on items in a category.

First, if an item i has received ratings from N users, each providing the rating R_u^i ($1 \le u \le N$) for it [1], the average rating of this item from all the N users is:

$$AR_N^i = \frac{\sum_{u=1}^N R_u^i}{N} \quad .$$

If user u has provided a rating for item i, then the average rating for item i from all other $N-1$ users excluding u is:

$$AR_{N-1}^i = \frac{\sum_{u=1}^N R_u^i - R_u^i}{N-1} \quad .$$

Next, a small difference between user u's rating and the average rating from all other users suggests user u has a high level of expertise. The rationale behind this is to trust the

[1] To be consistent with the notations used to define credit, R_u^i should be $\overrightarrow{R_u^i}$. Because we do not use the ratings a user has received for their reviews in the definition of risk, we choose this notation for the sake of simplicity.

"wisdom of crowds" [19], where large groups of cognitively and socially diverse individuals have proven superior than the elite few in solving problems, fostering innovation, or decision making. Therefore, user u's expertise of rating item i is:

$$EX_u^i = 1 - \frac{|R_u^i - AR_{N-1}^i|}{R_{Max}^i}, \quad \text{where}$$

R_{Max}^i is the maximum rating scale.

Finally, if user u has provided ratings for M items in a category, the risk of believing u is defined by the accumulated expertise of rating the M items:

$$RK_u^M \propto \frac{1}{EX_u^M} = \frac{M}{\sum_{i=1}^M EX_u^i} = \frac{M}{\sum_{i=1}^M (1 - \frac{|R_u^i - AR_{N-1}^i|}{R_{Max}^i})} \quad . \qquad (5)$$

Bias represents a user's preference in giving credit to a piece of information given by another user. For example, in the music category, if one is interested in classical music and another is interested in pop music, the bias between the two users might be up to 90 degrees. The bias between two users u_a and u_b who have reviewed N items can be defined as:

$$\beta(u_a, u_b) = \arccos(\frac{W_a \times W_b}{\|W_a\|\|W_b\|})$$

$$= \arccos(\frac{\sum_{i=1}^N (W_a^i \times W_b^i)}{\sqrt{\sum_{i=1}^N (W_a^i)^2 \times \sum_{i=1}^N (W_b^i)^2}}) \quad , \qquad (6)$$

where W_a and W_b are items reviewed by users u_a and u_b respectively, N is the total number of items reviewed by u_a or u_b, and $W_u^i = 1$ if user u reviewed item i or 0 otherwise.

Trust represents how much one user believes another in a particular subject field. It is directional and needs to be inferred from all relevant credit flows between three types of users in a social network: *source user*, *appraisal user*, and *beneficiary user*, analogous to the three types of buses respectively in an electrical grid: *slack bus*, *generator bus*, and *load bus*.

A source user's trust values towards all others need to be inferred. A source user's risk and bias are set to 1 and 0 respectively and the user's credit needs to be derived because it is unknown in the beginning how much credit the user would bring into the network, but it is assumed that the user has a good balance between real and reactive credit.

An appraisal user evaluates other users by giving them credit. It is assumed that an appraisal user's risk is known a priori. In the initial state, all credit in the network is brought in by the appraisal users. When inferring trust values for the source user, we suppose all credit is brought in by the source user and as such there is no need to calculate each appraisal user's credit, which is set to a default minimal value.

A beneficiary user receives credit from appraisal users. A beneficiary user's credit is negative as they take credit from instead of contributing credit to the network.

It is worth clarifying two points. First, users who have not been evaluated by others and who have evaluated others but have shown no expertise are excluded from our model as their credit could not be measured or verified. Second, the definitions of real and reactive credit refer to net credit, i.e. the credit brought in by a user minus the credit taken out by the same user. Therefore, an appraisal user would have positive credit, whereas a beneficiary user would have negative credit.

3.3 Credit Flow Based Trust Inference

We first formulate the credit balance equations:

$$C_i - jD_i = RK_i^* \sum_{k=1}^{N} (Y_{ik} \times RK_k) \quad , \tag{7}$$

where N is the total number of users in a social network, C_i/D_i is the net real/reactive credit given to user i, RK_i^* is the complex conjugate of users i's risk factor, RK_k is user k's risk factor, and Y_{ik} is the total admittance between user i and k, which can be found from the user admittance matrix of the network. Give a source user among all the users, the admittance matrix is built according to the following two rules: (1) the admittance of elements connected between user k and the source user is added to entry (k,k) of the admittance matrix, and (2) the admittance of elements connected between users i and k is added to entries (i,i) and (k,k) of the admittance matrix, while the negative admittance is added to entries (i,k) and (k,i) of the admittance matrix.

The rationale behind the credit balance equation is the balance between the credit brought into the network and the credit taken out of the network. All credit brought into the network is properly distributed to the users that consume it, as if in an electrical grid, where the generated power is properly distributed to all the load devices that use it. Therefore, we conjecture that credit distribution in a social network follows the rules similar to those for power distribution in an electrical grid. On the one hand, if credit is fixed, lower risk infers more trust, which is similar to an electrical grid, where lower voltage leads to stronger current if the power is fixed. On the other hand, if risk is fixed, more credit infers more trust, which is similar to an electrical grid, where high power leads to stronger current if the voltage is fixed. For example, we would trust someone we are unfamiliar with if they were acclaimed by a well-known expert (i.e., the risk of believing this expert is low) or by lots of people (i.e., this person has high credit).

Next, we formulate the credit flow equations:

$$C_i = \sum_{k=1}^{N} |RK_i| \times |RK_k| \times (G_{ik} \cos \beta_{ik} + B_{ik} \sin \beta_{ik}) \quad \text{and} \tag{8}$$

$$D_i = \sum_{k=1}^{N} |RK_i| \times |RK_k| \times (G_{ik} \cos \beta_{ik} - B_{ik} \sin \beta_{ik}) \quad , \tag{9}$$

where G_{ik} and B_{ik} are the real and imaginary parts of the admittance matrix element Y_{ik} (in Equation 7), and β_{ik} is user i's bias against user k.

We then use the Newton-Raphson method to derive each beneficiary user's risk and all credit flows within a social network. To do so, we first determine the normalised trust value between every pair of directly connected users using the following formula:

$$T_{ij} \propto \frac{RK_i - RK_j}{r} \quad ,$$

where r is user i's resistance factor against user j. Resistance is a psychological factor describing one's instinctive distrust towards a stranger. The further away user A is from user B in a social network, the higher resistance (or the weaker trust) A would place on B because trust can be diluted over a long propagation path [4]. For example, if a propagation path consists of 10 nodes and the trust value from one node towards the next in the path is all 0.9, the last node will only receive the trust value of $0.9^{10} \approx 0.35$, and for this reason, some trust models such as *MoleTrust* [11] limit the length of a propagation path using a maximum depth in search.

The resistance factor is analogous to the impedance factor associated with each transmission line in an electrical grid, which causes power loss in transmission. However, it is non-trivial to model resistance in a social network because many factors need to be considered and they are generally difficult to estimate accurately. For the sake of simplicity, the resistance factor between every pair of users is set to a constant and small value $r = 0.05 + j \times 0.2$ in the above formula, where 0.05 and 0.2 are empirical coefficients drawn from experimental data and j is the imaginary unit for irrelevant credit. Credit dilution is related to the risk difference in that a higher risk suggests more diluted credit. The two empirical coefficients also suggest that irrelevant credit is diluted faster than relevant credit.

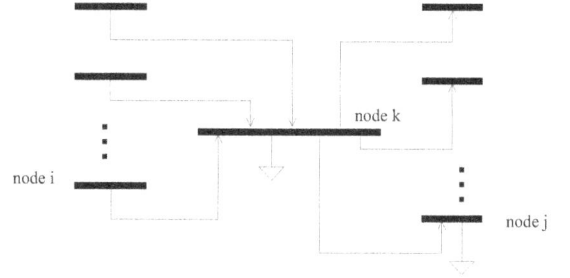

Figure 3: Example of trust propagation from node i to node j via node k

According to the Kirchhoff's circuit law, the credit flowing out of a node equals to the credit flowing into that node, and we can infer the trust value between each pair of indirectly connected users as such. It is worth clarifying that given a particular node, the outgoing credit to its neighbouring nodes may not equal to the incoming credit from its neighbouring nodes, but the outgoing credit to all reachable destination nodes must equal to the incoming credit from all source nodes because the total number of ratings given by the appraisal users must equal to the total number of ratings received by the beneficiary users. As shown in Figure 3, node i is directly connected to node k, which is also directly connected to node j. If the credit flows from node i to node k and from node k to node j are C_{ik} and C_{kj} respectively, and the total credit flowing into node k from directly connected nodes is C_k^Y, then the credit flowing from node i to node j, and the trust value from node i to node j are:

$$C_{ij} = C_{ik} \times \frac{C_{kj}}{C_k^Y - C_k} \quad \text{and} \quad T_{ij} = T_{ik} \times \frac{T_{kj}}{T_k^Y - T_k} \quad ,$$

where T_k^Y is the total trust towards node k from directly connected nodes and T_k is node k's total trust towards directly connected nodes.

If node i has M directly connected nodes and node j has N directly connected nodes, the trust value from i to j is:

$$T_{ij} = \sum_{k=1}^{M} T_{ik} \times \frac{\sum_{k=1}^{N} T_{kj}}{\sum_{k=1}^{M+N} T_k^Y - \sum_{k=1}^{M+N} T_k} \quad (10)$$

Figure 4 shows an example of inferring trust relationships in a simple social network. Suppose Alice is the source user and we have already derived Bob's, Carol's, Dave's and Eve's credits to be 0.1, -3.2, -1.6, and -2.0 respectively using the credit flow based trust inference model. We can further derive that the real credit brought into the network by Alice is 6.9. If Bob's risk is 0.95 (relative to the Alice's risk 1.0), we can also derive Carol's, Dave's and Eve's risk factors to be 0.59, 0.62, and 0.38 respectively. Finally we can infer Alice's trust value towards Carol, Dave and Eve to be 0.51, 0.26, and 0.23 respectively.

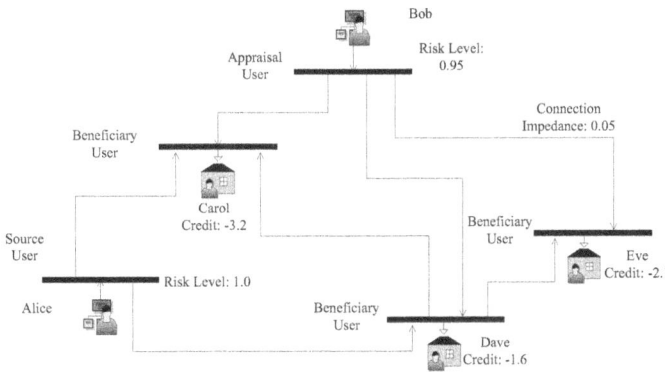

Figure 4: Example of credit flow based trust inference

In summary, the credit flow based trust inference in a social network using the credit balance equations is done through the following steps:

1. Compute each user's real and reactive credit using formulae 3 and 4.

2. Choose one source user from the social network.

3. Compute each appraisal user's risk and bias, relative to the source user whose risk and bias are set to 1 and 0 respectively, using formulae 5 and 6.

4. Build the user admittance matrix based on the topological structure of the social network and form the credit balance equations 7.

5. Solve the credit flow equations 8 and 9 using the Newton-Raphson method to derive the risk factors of all beneficiary users and infer the trust values from the source user to all directly connected users.

6. Infer the trust values from the source user to all indirectly connected users using formula 10.

7. Choose a different source user (iterate from step 2) and perform credit flow based trust inference again until all users have been considered source users.

4. EVALUATION OF THE TRUST MODEL

We have conducted a set of experiments using a real-world dataset to evaluate the CoreTrust model against existing models with objective and subjective trust metrics in order to answer the following two questions:

1. How does the credit flow based trust model compare to the global trust models in terms of accurately identifying a user's trusted peers in a social network based on the reputation ranking of all other users in the network?

2. How does the credit flow based trust model compare to the local trust models in terms of predicting a user's trust towards others in a social network based on the distributed trust propagation between users in the network?

4.1 The Epinions Dataset

Epinions is a popular online e-commerce system where users can rate or write reviews on various items such as cars, books, or music, and rate the reviews contributed by other users. We used the Epinions dataset in our experiments. The dataset, consisting of various types of user interactions and rated objects in multiple categories, combines explicit user ratings and trust values with social networking. Epinions allows users to write their own reviews or rate other users' reviews by assigning a helpfulness rating from 1 (not helpful) to 5 (most helpful). To encourage high quality reviews, the *Income Share* program is adopted to pay users according to the ratings of their reviews, where trust management is a critical issue. As such, Epinions allows a user to specify how much they trust others and the product reviews are ranked according to the web of trust for the user.

We developed a program using the techniques contributed by Richardson [15] to retrieve the trust relationships in Epinions by crawling the website. The dataset contains 28,377 users who contributed a total of 258,122 reviews on different categories of products, which received a total of 1,784,182 ratings. Due to the computational complexity, we only chose the "Video & DVD" category in our experiments as it has more reviews per product than other categories. Only users who contributed at least one review or rated at least one review are included in the dataset. A record in the dataset is either in the format of $\langle review\_id, contributor\_id \rangle$ where *review_id* is the ID of a review on a subject, e.g., a movie in the category and *contributor_id* is the ID of the user who contributed the review or in the format of $\langle review\_id, rating, evaluator\_id \rangle$ where *rating* is in the scale from 1 to 5 and *evaluator_id* is the ID of the user who gave the rating.

We then extracted the trust relationships among these users, forming a web of trust graph consisting of 6,847 vertices and 77,965 edges. The graph is stored as records of $\langle truster\_id, trustee\_id \rangle$ pair, where *truster_id* is the ID of the user making the trust statement, *trustee_id* is the ID of the user on which the trust statement was made, and the trust relationship is a directional edge from the *truster_id* vertex to the *trustee_id* vertex. In our web of trust graph, 2,879 vertices had at least one outbound and inbound edges and 4,576 vertices had at least one inbound edge.

It is worth pointing out that Epinions users can also keep a set of distrust relationships (or blacklist) by specifying users they do not trust at all, but unlike Guha's work [3], we did not exploit distrust relationships and instead only focused on the trust relationships in our experiments primarily because the amount of distrust relationships are rather small, for example in the dataset from Victor et al. [20], about 85% of the statements are labeled as trust. Nonetheless, we will investigate whether distrust relationships can be used to improve credit flow based trust model in our future work.

The dataset confirmed the similarity between a social network and an electrical grid in that they both follow the power law distribution [13] and are both small-world networks [21]. For example, we found that most users contributed very few reviews or ratings and that very few users contributed extremely many reviews or ratings. Similarly, we found that most users trusted very few others and that very few users trusted extremely many others.

4.2 Comparing with Global Trust Models

We first compare the prediction accuracy between the credit flow based model and global trust models using metrics such as Precision, Recall, and F1. Given a prediction result as the ranking of the topmost trustworthy users in a network, we define:

$$RTU = \{real\ trusted\ users\}$$

$$PTTU = \{predicted\ topmost\ trustworthy\ users\}$$

$$precision = \frac{|RTU \cap PTTU|}{|PTTU|}$$

$$recall = \frac{|RTU \cap PTTU|}{|RTU|}$$

$$F1 = \frac{2 \times precision \times recall}{precision + recall}$$

It is worth clarifying that the list of users who have been given trust statements by a user is much smaller than the list of users who are really trusted by this user, because the number of explicit trust statements in Epinions is rather small. Therefore it is difficult to exactly measure the accuracy of trust prediction because we cannot simply assert whether a user trusts or distrusts other users without referring to explicit trust statements. To overcome this difficulty, we treat the user trust statements as the ground truth and compare them with the objective reputation ranking of all users in the network by adjusting the length of topmost ranking according to each user's preference. For example, if a user made trust statements about 5 users, we can measure the prediction accuracy based on the predicted top 10 most trustworthy users. In this experiment, we compare the CoreTrust method with the following two global trust methods:

- The *Average* method, which ranks all users in such a way that is similar to the simplified eBay model. It evaluates each user according to the ratings the user has received from others.

- The *EigenTrust* method [5], which assigns a global trust rating to each user using an algorithm similar to PageRank. It aggregates users' trust information through performing a calculation approaching the eigenvector of the trust matrix over the users.

Because these methods provide a unified objective ranking of reputation for all users, but our model provides personalised ranking of trustworthiness for every individual user, we first derived unified and personalised trust values using the three methods respectively, then calculated the Precision, Recall, and F1 metrics for each user, and finally took the average of the three metrics for the entire network.

Table 1 shows the prediction accuracy of the three methods. The EigenTrust method performs slightly better than the Average method, but the CoreTrust method significantly outperforms the other two, especially in terms of the F1 metrics, where both the precision and the recall are taken into account. The Average and EigenTrust methods assign a universal trust score to each user and every other user in the network has to trust it in a unanimous way that is decided by the score. However, in the Epinions community, an individual user has different preference and expertise and may be trusted by different users differently. The CoreTrust method has taken that fact into consideration by allowing multiple trust scores to be assigned to each user, one for every source user. Therefore, its Precision, Recall, and F1 metrics are much better than those for the Average and EigenTrust methods.

Table 1: Prediction Accuracy

Methods	Precision	Recall	F1
Average	0.47	0.61	0.53
EigenTrust	0.53	0.72	0.61
CoreTrust	0.79	0.82	0.81

4.3 Comparing with Local Trust Models

We then compare the trust propagation accuracy between the credit flow based trust model and local trust models. In local trust models, explicit trust values are specified for directly connected users, while trust values for indirectly connected users need to be inferred through trust propagation. In our experiments, we use two trust networks: one is the original web of trust collected from Epinions and the other is the web of credit constructed from the credit flow based trust model. We use the subjective metrics to propagate trust over both networks and compare their results.

This evaluation is a kind of leave-one-out cross-validation, where we are given a network with all (but one) of the trust values between nodes visible, and we need to predict this single suppressed value. The original web of trust in Epinions is a collection of binary ratings, i.e., trust (1) or distrust (0). We consider two commonly used metrics for evaluating binary classifiers: the classification *accuracy* for predicting correct ratings and the *AUC* for representing the area under the receiver operating characteristic curve (ROC curve). If we define the number of trusted users and distrusted users as P positive instances and N negative instances respectively, a true positive TP occurs when both the prediction outcome and the actual value are trust, whereas a true negative TN occurs when the prediction outcome and the actual value are both distrust. Therefore, the *accuracy* is defined as:

$$ACC = \frac{TP + TN}{P + N}$$

The AUC value is calculated as an integral of ROC curve, which equals to the probability that a user who should be trusted is correctly predicted as a trusted rather than a distrusted. Therefore it outputs a probability instead of a binary decision.

In this experiment, we compare the CoreTrust method with the following two local trust methods:

- The *Direct* method, which propagates trust by direct propagation. For example, if Alice trusts Bob and Bob trusts Carol, then trust propagates from Alice to Carol.

- The *MoleTrust* method [11], which propagates trust by combining trust ratings across all paths from a source vertex to a destination vertex in a graph. Paths are searched in a typical breadth first search fashion (maximum depth is set to 2 in our experiments).

Because a trust value is binary in the web of trust but non-binary in the web of credit, a threshold is used in the web of credit to determine between trust and distrust. In the Direct method, trust is propagated as long as the inferred trust value in the web of credit is greater than the threshold. In the MoleTrust method, paths with the aggregated trust values above the threshold are selected for trust propagation. A tradeoff can be made between TP and TN by adjusting the threshold. We used a consistent predefined threshold to calculate the accuracy and AUC metrics.

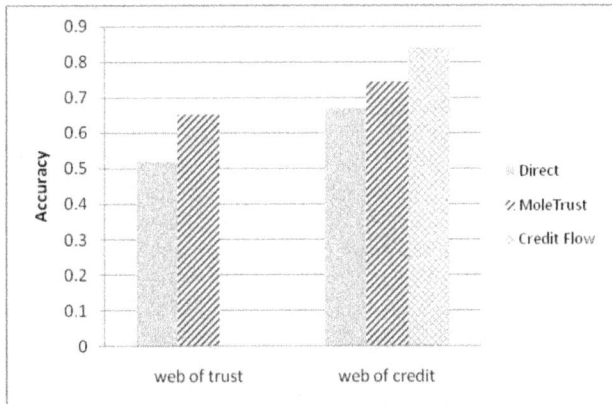

Figure 5: Accuracy evaluated on the web of trust and the web of credit

The Direct and MoleTrust methods were tested for prediction accuracy on both the Epionions web of trust and the web of credit constructed using the credit flow based trust model. Figure 5 shows that the two methods' prediction accuracy results on the web of credit are clearly better than those on the web of trust, confirming that the credit flow based trust model can construct more accurate trust connectivity from an online community with users' rating data. This may attribute to the sparse nature of the Epinions web of trust because the number of explicit trust statements made by each user in Epinions is rather small. In contrast, the web of credit is much denser because the credit flow based trust model can derive significant more trust relationships from users' rating data.

More importantly, comparing the Direct, MoleTrust, and CoreTrust methods tested on the web of credit, the CoreTrust

method clearly outperforms the other two. This is because the CoreTrust method considers both generally agreed reputation and individual users' preferences and expertise levels, while the other two methods only consider users' subjective trust statements. The performance comparison is double confirmed by the results for AUC metrics in Figure 6, which are similar to those for the accuracy metrics in Figure 5.

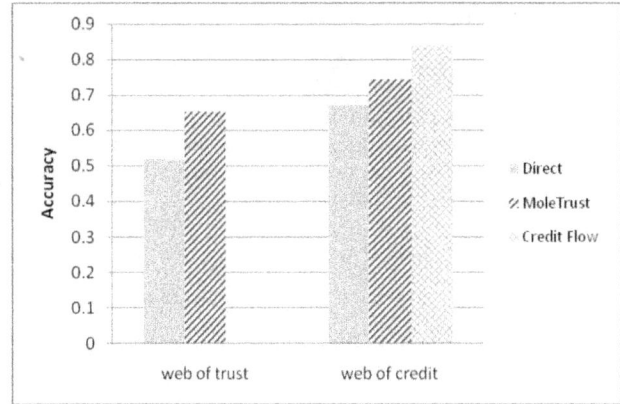

Figure 6: AUC evaluated on the web of trust and the web of credit

5. CONCLUSIONS AND FUTURE WORK

With the increasing popularity of online social networking, information exchange between virtual relations has grown drastically over the past few years. Consequently trust management in social networks becomes imperative as the information quality is closely related to the trustworthiness of the user from whom the information is received.

Existing objective trust models estimate a universal reputation for each node and do not allow others to take personalised measures towards the same node. Conversely, existing subjective trust models only rely on explicit trust statements to construct a web of trust and do not consider a social network in its entirety. In this paper, we proposed the credit flow approach to modelling and inferring trust relations in social networks. This approach can construct a web of credit from the interactions in a social network and infer trust values by making use of both generally agreed reliability and subjective individuality in the network. The experimental results on a real-world dataset show that the approach can accurately construct a web of credit and infer more accurate trust values than objective and subjective trust models do.

Although power flows in an electrical grid were used as a metaphor to model credit flows in a social network and our initial research has confirmed the hypothesis, we are conscious of their differences. For example, an appraisal user can be a beneficiary user at the same time and vice versa in a social network, but a generator bus is normally not a load bus at the same time in an electrical grid. Therefore, we need to continue polishing the credit flow based trust model by refining existing model elements and their relationships and exploring new elements that can improve the model. For example, if one is both an appraisal and beneficiary user, it will be represented as two different nodes, leading to a more complex network but allowing for more accurate trust inference. Resistance can be extended to model a user's instinctive distrust towards a stranger from mental, physical and cultural factors. We are also investigating more efficient algorithms for solving the credit balance equations, e.g., Fuzzy Logic Control, in order to reduce the computational complexity involved in our approach. We plan to showcase the credit flow based trust inference technique by applying it to a social search system [10], where participants can exchange information with their trusted peers.

6. ACKNOWLEDGMENTS

The work was partially supported by an establishment grant (36426) from Flinders University, Australia. The authors would like to thank anonymous reviews for their comments that helped improve the paper.

7. REFERENCES

[1] J. Golbeck. *Computing and Applying Trust in Web-based Social Networks*. PhD thesis, University of Maryland, 2005.

[2] R. Guha. Open rating systems. Technical report, Stanford University, 2003.

[3] R. Guha, R. Kumar, P. Raghavan, and A. Tomkins. Propagation of trust and distrust. In *Proceedings of the 13th International Conference on World Wide Web*, pages 403–412, 2004.

[4] A. Jøsang. An algebra for assessing trust in certification chains. In *Proceeedings of the Network and Distributed Systems Security Symposium*, 1999.

[5] S. D. Kamvar, M. T. Schlosser, and H. Garcia-Molina. The eigentrust algorithm for reputation management in p2p networks. In *Proceedings of the 12th international conference on World Wide Web*, pages 640–651, 2003.

[6] K. Kwon, J. Cho, and Y. Park. Multidimensional credibility model for neighbor selection in collaborative recommendation. *Expert Systems with Applications*, 36(3):7114–7122, 2009.

[7] R. Levien. *Advogato Trust Metric*. PhD thesis, UC Berkeley, 2003.

[8] G. Liu, Y. Wang, and M. Orgun. Trust inference in complex trust-oriented social networks. In *Proceedings of the 2009 International Conference on Computational Science and Engineering*, pages 996–1001, 2009.

[9] X. Liu, A. Datta, K. Rzadca, and E. Lim. Stereotrust: a group based personalized trust model. In *Proceedings of ACM International Conference on Information and Knowledge Management*, pages 7–16, 2009.

[10] Y. Mao, H. Shen, and C. Sun. Supporting exploratory information seeking by epistemology-based social search. In *Proceedings of the 15th ACM Conference on Intelligent User Interfaces (IUI'10)*, pages 36–39, 2010.

[11] P. Massa and P. Avesani. Controversial users demand local trust metrics: An experimental study on epinions.com community. In *Proceedings of the 20th National Conference on Artificial Intelligence*, pages 121–126, 2005.

[12] L. Page, S. Brin, R. Motwani, and T. Winograd. The pagerank citation ranking: bringing order to the web. Technical report, Stanford University, 1999.

[13] A. G. Phadke and J. S. Thorp. *Computer relaying for power systems*. John Wiley & Sons, 1998.

[14] M. Richardson, R. Agrawa, and P. Domingos. Trust management for the semantic web. In *Proceedings of International Semantic Web Conference*, pages 351–368, 2003.

[15] M. Richardson and P. Domingos. Mining knowledge-sharing sites for viral marketing. In *Proceedings of the 8th ACM SIGKDD International Conference on Knowledge Discovery and Data Mining*, pages 61–70, 2002.

[16] H. Saadat. *Power System Analysis, 2nd Edition*. McGraw-Hill, 2002.

[17] K. Sankaralingam, S. Sethumadhavan, and J. Browne. Distributed pagerank for p2p systems. In *Proceedings of the 12th IEEE International Symposium on High Performance Distributed Computing*, pages 58–68, 2003.

[18] G. Shafer. *A Mathematical Theory of Evidence*. Princeton University Press, 1976.

[19] J. Surowiecki. *The wisdom of crowds: why the many are smarter than the few and how collective wisdom shapes business, economies, societies and nations*. Little, Brown & Company, 2004.

[20] P. Victor, C. Cornelis, M. de Cock, and P. P. da Silva. Gradual trust and distrust in recommender systems. *Fuzzy Sets and Systems*, 160(10):1367–1382, 2009.

[21] D. J. Watts and S. H. Strogatz. Collective dynamics of 'small- world' networks. *Nature*, 393:440–442, 1998.

[22] L. Xiong and L. Liu. Peertrust: Supporting reputation-based trust for peer-to- peer electronic communities. *IEEE Transactions on Knowledge and Data Engineering*, 16(7):843–857, 2004.

[23] B. Yu and M. P. Singh. An evidential model of distributed reputation management. In *Proceedings of the International Joint Conference on Autonomous Agents and Multiagent Systems*, pages 294–301, 2002.

[24] R. Zhou and K. Hwang. Powertrust: A robust and scalable reputation system for trusted peer-to-peer computing. *IEEE Transactions on Parallel Distributed Systems*, 18(4):460–473, 2007.

[25] R. Zhou, K. Hwang, and M. Cai. Gossiptrust for fast reputation aggregation in peer-to-peer networks. *IEEE Transactions on Knowledge and Data Engineering*, 20(9):1282–1295, 2008.

[26] C.-N. Ziegler and G. Lausen. Spreading activation models for trust propagation. In *Proceedings of the IEEE International Conference on e-Technology, e-Commerce, and e-Service*, pages 83–97, 2004.

[27] C.-N. Ziegler and G. Lausen. Propagation models for trust and distrust in social networks. *Information Systems Frontiers*, 7(4-5):337–358, 2005.

Tagging Wikipedia: Collaboratively Creating a Category System

Katherine Thornton
The Information School
University of Washington
thornt@uw.edu

David W. McDonald
The Information School
University of Washington
dwmc@uw.edu

ABSTRACT

Category systems have traditionally been created by small committees of people who had authority over the system they were designing. With the rise of large-scale social media systems, category schemes are being created by groups with differing perspectives, values, and expectations for how categories will be used. Prior studies of social tagging and folksonomy focused on the application and evolution of the collective category scheme, but struggled to uncover some of the collective rationale undergirding the decision-making processes in those schemes. In this paper, we qualitatively analyze the early discussions among editors of Wikipedia about the design and creation of its category system. We highlight three themes that dominated the discussion: hierarchy, scope and navigation, and relate these themes to their more formal roots in the information science literature. We distill out four styles of collaboration with regard to category systems that apply broadly to social tagging and other folksonomies. We conclude the paper with implications for collaborative tools and category systems as applied to large-scale collaborative systems.

Categories and Subject Descriptors

H.5.3. Group and Organization Interfaces, H.5.4 Navigation

General Terms

Design, Human Factors.

Keywords

Categorization, Wikipedia, information organization.

1. INTRODUCTION

Trent was recently browsing Wikipedia and stumbled on a new page for the indie folk band Aquabats. Trent decided he would help by categorizing this page. He had never tagged in Wikipedia, but he had used del.icio.us before - how hard could this be? He looked for the category "Bands" and found it was redirected to another category. He found "Musical groups by genre" but couldn't find "Indie" or "Independent". He found "Folk" but couldn't categorize the Aquabats as "Folk rock" nor "Folk punk". He considered trying to add a new category, but a category with only one item wouldn't be all that useful. Thinking to himself that this was going to be harder than he initially thought, he gave up on the idea of helping.

Social tagging became wildly popular with the advent of del.icio.us. Suddenly, the idea of visible and shared categories became popular with developers and researchers. Researchers could study how shared category metadata was applied, how it evolved, and how individual use differed from collective use. Yet, despite the large number of studies of tags and tagging behaviors, none have considered the collective rationale behind the tagging scheme because largely the rationale had to be divined from the tags themselves. This paper specifically considers the collective effort and negotiation that generated one tagging scheme currently in use and analyzes those negotiations.

Schemes for categorization or tagging have a direct impact on how people access information and how they can collaborate. These pieces of metadata can be used to help manage processes as tags are added and removed. Further, they form a type of communication system, a set of signals that collaborators can use. A better understanding of the rationale behind a tagging scheme will inform the future development of tools to improve the quality of the scheme, how the scheme is applied, and the way it provides access.

Wikipedia is an online encyclopedia created entirely of user-generated content. Roughly two years after Wikipedia began, the community decided to create a category system to organize and tag the content of the site. The category system has changed over time, as have conceptualizations of what role it should serve in Wikipedia. This study analyzes six months of discussion about the design and implementation of the category system in Wikipedia. The analysis reveals a set of important themes that related to category systems and tagging broadly.

In the following, we outline the prior work that considers tagging practices and relate that to some of the traditional work in information science. We describe our data collection, our approach to analysis and describe four key themes that emerge from the data. We then present a set of analytic frames for thinking about how category systems enable styles of collaboration and illustrate how individuals contributing to the discussion assumed these roles at different times. We close the paper with a short discussion and implications for collaborative systems.

2. TAGGING AND WIKIPEDIA

In Wikipedia, categories are applied to pages as an internal hyperlink to a 'category' page (see Figure 1). The WikiMedia system reads those special internal links and groups together all pages that include the link. Any number of category links can be applied to a page. The category system contains traditional content categories as well as management and historical categories that are often hidden when the page is requested. The simple application of a link to a page is similar to the metadata practice of adding a tag to a piece of content.

```
[[Category:American country rock groups]]
[[Category:American country music groups]]
[[Category:American folk rock groups]]
[[Category:Grammy Award winners]]
[[Category:Musical groups established in
1966]]
```

**Figure 1. Example category links from the Wikipedia page
"Nitty Gritty Dirt Band"**

In an early analysis of tagging behavior, Golder and Huberman [5] argue that sensemaking is one purpose of tagging and that individual conflicts at the level of tag specificity makes collaborative tagging systems fuzzy and less precise. Subsequent studies by Sen et al. [12], Farooq et al. [2], and Millen et al. [10] served to illustrate the tension between individual tag choice and group tag use, quantitative techniques for considering whether a tag had information value, and the different motivations for tagging within an organization as compared to public tagging.

Our study extends what we know about tagging systems by characterizing the decisions about how a tag-based category system should operate, and how best to address these known issues through the design of the system.

The category system in Wikipedia has been considered from a number of different perspectives. Some studies follow a quantitative approach. For example, Muchnik et al. [11] tested five algorithms for automatic extraction of hierarchical relationships among Wikipedia pages against the extant category system. Kittur et al. [8] quantitatively mapped the categories used in Wikipedia into seven topical areas. This work collapsed the category system using a shortest-path-to-root approach for determining where node content would be assigned. This obscures the significant work Wikipedians have undertaken to systematize category hierarchy and encourage editors to apply category labels according to community convention. Holloway et al. [6] conducted a quantitative study of the category system from 2004 through 2007 to produce a thorough description of the category system as it stood in 2007.

As these studies show, quantitative approaches can illustrate the depth and breadth of the category system and compare the relative prevalence of topical content. But the quantitative approach cannot illustrate the collaborative rationale behind the system, and some quantitative approaches may specifically obscure the community efforts to apply category tags in a systematic manner.

Still, other studies have considered participation in Wikipedia from a qualitative perspective. Forte and Bruckman [3] outline social roles that exist in the Wikipedia community. They describe the negotiation that takes place in the wiki, and on related mailing lists between individuals who are trying to create community-wide policies. This highlights the negotiated aspects of much of the work in Wikipedia, including that around the category system. In a study of the types of work valued in the Wikipedia community, Kriplean et al. [7] point out that both category creation and category link application are types of work acknowledged and valued by the community. This work will support their argument by providing rationales for elaborating content organization advanced by the community in the early stages of the development of the category system. Analyzing discussions related to the creation and implementation of the category system, we describe strategies that the Wikipedia community employed in the attempt to make the implementation of category designations consistent throughout the site.

In the field of information science, knowledge organization (KO) theorizes, analyzes and critiques systems designed to organize information. From a KO perspective, Voss [15] described the Wikipedia category system as a thesaurus built through collaborative tagging. While Voss notes that simply adding categories to other categories facilitates the creation of hierarchy, he did not outline how different implied relationships are created, and sometimes confused, between categories when they are nested. Our analysis extends this finding by characterizing types of relationships present among super- and sub-categories in Wikipedia. There is surprisingly little evidence of the community prioritizing designs that would help users' distinguish between different types of relationships in the early discussions of the category system in Wikipedia.

3. METHODS

We collected the text of the Category talk page covering the six-month period from June 2004 through January 2005. That marked the start of the community effort to implement a category system in Wikipedia. At this point the design of the category system was completely open; changes were still being discussed and codified. We coded the data thematically in order to begin a content analysis of each section of the archived talk page. Through open coding we developed a codebook of 31 codes.

After coding the data and arranging codes into families, several themes emerged from the data. The editors who were participating in the discussions of how to design and implement the category system frequently returned to issues of hierarchy, scope, navigation and collaboration. By contrasting the editors' discussions of hierarchy with theory about constructing hierarchy in indexing languages, it is clear that many of the same conclusions reached through trial and error in Wikipedia have been described in the KO literature. The editors' discussions of how to scope the number of categories and the type of categories in the system are especially interesting when considered in the context of the recurring appeals to the community to consider extant schema for information organization as potential models. Discussions of navigation through Wikipedia via the category system reflect a very clear understanding of the category system as a navigational tool, something that no longer seems to be the case for many members of the Wikipedia community.

We then collected a second set of data (spanning January 2005-January 2007) from the same talk page and coded that data using the codebook. The primary difference between this data collection and coding process and the first round is that the number of codes relating to the purpose of the category system increased. Enough new codes relating to purpose were needed that we decided to introduce a new theme, that of 'purpose'. Our goal for collecting data from the second period was to learn how the community understood these themes as the category system was expanded and changed. We were also investigating whether new themes would emerge and how the focus of the community would shift over time. We will cover these themes in the following sections of the paper.

4. CATEGORY SYSTEM DESIGN THROUGH DISCUSSION

While working together to decide how a category system should function in Wikipedia, interested contributors shared their thoughts and debated the merit of many proposals. Several themes emerged from their discussion: hierarchy, scope, and navigation and collaboration. In terms of hierarchy, many editors felt that the best way to structure the category system would be through category tags structured into hierarchical trees, and the WikiMedia code was designed to prompt users to always place a newly- created category into the supercategory of their choice. Scoping concerns are reflected in the way editors debated the appropriate number of category tags to apply to a given page in Wikipedia. Another theme addressed the question of whether navigation was considered as one of the purposes of the category system, and how best to address user needs related to navigation. Editors were also generally concerned with how the category system would facilitate forms of collaboration. We cover each of these themes in detail.

4.1 Hierarchy in the Wikipedia Category System

The community of editors who participated in the discussions was very concerned with ensuring that hierarchy would be a feature of the category system. The fact that the community felt hierarchy to be such an important element for organization is consistent with how the KO literature describes the advantages of hierarchical structures. Svenonius [14] noted that hierarchical relationships provide excellent advantages for supporting user navigation and the ability to instrument the relevance and size of a set of results for a user query. The fact that these advantages were apparent to the editors who designed the category system in Wikipedia is evident. When looking at the categories displayed at the bottom of any page it is possible to click on any of them (they are all hyperlinks) and see related categories and all subcategories. The editors who contributed to the design of the category system shared a vision of this feature that it would allow users to more quickly understand the context of any individual article by making relationships between articles visible.

Hierarchical structures allow users to see how different concepts relate to one another in a given system. Aitchison et al. [1] defines four types of hierarchical relationships: generic, whole-part, instance, and polyhierarchical.

Generic - A generic hierarchical relationship is defined as a conceptual transitive closure. There are very few examples of this in the category system. But there are other indexing tools in Wikipedia that are organized in this way, for example, the Wikipedia page for 'List of birds'. That is, if we take the class to be 'birds', all of the pages for which links are supplied in the list are pages for birds.

Whole-part - This relationship consists of a single concept or entity as the class with parts of that concept or entity as the subclass. An example of this type of hierarchical relationship in Wikipedia would be the pages listed under the category 'States of the United States'. Other than the page 'U.S. state', the other pages under this category are all parts of the category itself.

Instance - These are general concepts or classes which have specific instantiations as a subclass. It is difficult to find examples of categories for which the subcategories are all instances of the category. This is more often achieved through lists in Wikipedia. An example of this type of hierarchical relationship in Wikipedia would be the 'List of cathedrals' page. If we take 'cathedrals' to be the class, all of the cathedrals listed on that page are instances of the class.

Polyhierarchial - This type of relationship describes cases when one term is located underneath more than one category. Many categories in Wikipedia are located in more than one parent category. Polyhierarchy is very common in the category system of Wikipedia.

Much of the discussion in the data set illustrated a failure to discriminate between these different types of hierarchy, and multiple, sometimes contrasting, assumptions of what type of hierarchy was being proposed. All four types of hierarchy are in use in the category system of Wikipedia. In an ideal hierarchical structure a consistent relation would link terms. This recommendation is not followed in the category system of Wikipedia, and is likely a source of unaddressed, perhaps unrecognized, conflict in discussions of how the categories should be managed.

Browsing through the category system in order to examine the types of relationships that exist between superclasses and subclasses, the predominant relationship is one of association. Strictly, an Associative relationship is not hierarchical. The category system of Wikipedia, although perhaps envisioned to be a hierarchical system by some in 2004, is now full of categories related to other categories by an associative relationship. This is significant because although the designers felt that they were creating a hierarchical category system, many of the relationships in the category system are not hierarchical.

The fact that the relationships between supercategories and subcategories in Wikipedia include both hierarchical relationships as well as associative relationships is due to the fact that the category system emerged from a community in which there were divergent views of what the system should look like. One of the editors who contributed to the discussions in the dataset stated:

```
So I think we need a way of distinguishing
between   a   category   where   (a)   you   are
asserting that everything in the category is
an example of the thing it is in (ie list
categories),   and   (b)   categories   where   you
are   just   providing   hierarchical   links   for
convenience. (editor 1)
```

The first type of category they describe encompasses the first three types of hierarchical relationships described by Aitchinson et al. [1], generic, whole-part and instance. The second type of category this editor describes would make use of the non-hierarchical, associative type of relationship. This editor is highlighting the need to be clear about the different types of relationships in the category system as it is being designed and created, and the differences this editor points to are elaborated in the KO literature.

Another editor provided the following example of why one page might need multiple category designations:

```
I'm thinking about some of the dog topics.
For example, dog is a member of pets; dog is
also a member of mammals; both mammals and
pets are members of animals but neither is a
subcategory of the other. Now, how about dog
agility? It needs to go under the dog sports
category,   which   needs   to   be   under   the   dog
category,   because   it's   related   to   dogs.   It
also needs to go under the sports category,
because it's a sport. It probably also needs
to go under the hobby category. But dog and
sports   do   not   at   any   higher   point   in   the
hierarchy have a common parent. (editor 2)
```

This statement is a clear articulation of the need for polyhierarchy. The editor would like there to be hierarchy, but would also like a single category to be able to belong to more than one superclass. This is an excellent example of the community working through the issues until they come to a point of recognizing what they need. The advantages and limitations of this type of hierarchical relationship are well-documented in KO, and the Wikipedia community recognized the same issues when planning out the category system.

By 2006 the many editors were aware of the disjointed state of hierarchy in the category system:

```
Welcome   to   the   chaotic   state   of
categorization on Wikipedia. As has been
discussed extensively here and elsewhere,
much of the chaos arises from two aspects:
1) there is no clear distinction between
strictly hierarchical categories (article X
is a type of/member of category Y) and
associative categories (article X is somehow
(often tangentially) related to category Y).
The related to categories can turn into
trails of free association. 2) Some editors
will inappropriately remove an article from
a parent category and instead place the
article's eponymous subcategory within the
parent category. This can lead to very
strange hierarchies. Well, and aside from
those two fundamental problems, there is
always the problem of inexperienced users
naively (mis-)applying categories. (editor
3)(period 2)
```

4.2 Scope of the Wikipedia Category System

Another theme that emerged from the discussions was the scope of the category system. The editors were very concerned about the number of category labels that would be applied to each page. One editor commented:

```
Even if each of these categories is relevant
(which can be doubted) the original page
starts to clutter up rapidly. Logically,
there is no almost limit to the extent to
which categories can be applied to any page
for the imaginative editor. (editor 4)
```

This editor was worried that categories would be assigned unevenly. Some individuals would choose to apply a large number of category labels, while others would apply few.

Some shared the concern that the number of categories applied to different articles would be widely divergent. One argument put forth was:

```
I suggest that there should be a Guideline
for categorisation by which editors (1)
exercise caution and err on the side of not
ascribing a category unless the text of the
page justifies it (2)limit the size of the
categorisation link text so that it remains
small in relation to the size of the page.
(editor 4)
```

While this editor clearly wanted to create hierarchical relationships between categories, they had observed how inconsistently these hierarchies were constructed.

Other editors felt that the work of scoping the category system of Wikipedia was such a large task that it should be modeled on existing structures for information organization. One editor brought up the challenge of making relationship types explicit and

suggested modeling the category system on the Resource Description Framework (RDF).

```
The fix is to label the arrows: describe the
relations.   This   is,   in   my   limited
understanding, what RDF does. That uses the
terms subject, predicate, and object. The
subject is the thing you're categorizing.
The object is the category you're adding it
to.   And   the   predicate   describes   the
relation.   Predicates   allow   you   to   make
semantic     inferences     programmatically.
(editor 5)
```

Other editors suggested modeling the category system on extant directories created to index the World Wide Web.

```
To minimise reinvention of wheels, consider
the category structures of Web directories
such   as   www.zeal.com,   which   have   been
painstakingly thought out over long periods.
(editor 6)
```

This editor is pointing out how much effort could be saved if the category system were modeled on an extant structure.

The design, creation, monitoring and evaluation of the category system required significant community effort. In order to create the most effective system, many discussions were based around how best to scope the category system. Members of the community expressed concern over inconsistency in the average number of categories that might get applied to a given page, made appeals to modeling the syntax of the system on RDF and suggested web directories as other potential models for the category system.

4.3 Navigation via the Category System

In the first period of data collection (June, 2004 through January, 2005) the hyperlinked category labels for each Wikipedia page were displayed at the top of each page. However, it is now the case that the category information is displayed in a box at the bottom of each page. There are many pathways to any individual page in Wikipedia. Users arrive to specific pages via a link from a results page from a search engine, from a link in the text of another page, from a link in an infobox located in the upper-left or upper-right- hand corners of many pages which typically contain pointers to a large amount of related content, from a list of links, or from the list of pages provided on the page for any category. At this time it is unclear how often the category system is used for navigation in Wikipedia. Regardless of the current reality, many of the editors who contributed to the design of the system in 2004 felt that navigation was a primary way the category system would be used.

One contributing editor articulated the following vision of navigating through the category system:

```
We have to think from the encyclopedia
user's point of view. He/she is starting at
the top level of the hierarchy with a
subject in mind, and they need to know which
blind path to go down to find an article on
that subject. It might help to think of the
problem as a game of twenty questions. The
first question we may ask is, "If they
wanted to know about Stephen King's books,
they might choose Category: Things, and have
a     choice     of     Category:Animals,
```

Category:Vegetables, Category:Minerals, Category:Ideas, etc., and go down one of those paths. My point is, Categories link only as a hierarchy; Wikipedia articles link as a network to every related article. So as long as the user reaches the article on Steven King (the person), or the articles on Steven King's books using the categories, the articles themselves link to each other. (editor 7)

This statement clearly indicates that the editor felt people would begin their search by looking at the category system from top to bottom for desired content.

Lee and Olson [9] compared the hierarchical navigation structure of Yahoo! directories with information retrieval via keyword searching in a search engine. One of the factors that they consider in their study is the location of the hierarchical browsing tool on the Yahoo! main webpage. They noted the harder it was to find the directory/ category information the less it was used.

From looking at the discussions in this dataset, it is clear that the decision to move the category box to the very bottom of each page predated community understanding of how the category system would be utilized.

Another editor presented a contrasting vision for how the category system would be used.

On the other hand, I think there's a good case to be made for a more bottom-up approach; let's take a look at how things are being categorized, and try to find the patterns in that. It's more the Wikipedia way, too. For example, I've noticed that there are a lot of categories that are non-plural, such as Category:Medicine, Category:Biology and Category:Law. In those cases, rather than being categories containing only one article (Medicine, Biology and Law, respectively) they are instead full of articles and subcategories that are about the indicated topic. (editor 8)

This editor is articulating a need for specific guidelines for term construction to facilitate vocabulary control, another example of the Wikipedia community echoing principles frequently discussed in the KO literature. This editor's comments suggest that some members of the community felt that the amount of effort that was being expended in the design of the category system could be reduced if the purpose of the category system were explicitly articulated.

4.4 Purpose of the Category System

In our initial period of data collection and coding we created several codes relating to the purpose of the category system. These codes were few in number and, in general, were used to label sections of text on the discussion page in which editors expressed desire to come to agreement on the purpose of the category system. In the second round of data collection, many editors expressed opinions about what they felt the purpose of the category system to be, thus we added more codes relating to purpose. This was such a frequently-discussed topic that we chose to add a fourth theme, that of purpose. All of the excerpts provided in this section are from the second period of data collection.

Some editors expressed that categories were tools for browsing:

Categories are intended to be an aid to browsing, rather than an general taxonomy (which would be POV and destined to fail). (editor 9)(period 2)

One editor stressed that their best use would be to support browsing, in particular, as opposed to search:

You don't need categories to find a particular article. Categories are not a search tool, they're a search-for-related-things tool. If you want to find a particular article, like Portland, Oregon, just type Portland, Oregon in the search box. (editor 10) (period 2)

Other editors raised the question of whether browsing was the primary purpose:

A question concerning the purpose of categories: Is the primary purpose of categories to: Aid the reader in finding material that may be of interest, or relevant to a particular topic? Producing a taxonomy; wherein being included in one or more categories is an indication—nay, a declaration by the Wikipedia community—that the subject of an article is an instance of the category it is included in. I seem to suspect the latter... (editor 11)(period 2)

Contrasting purposes were raised:

There seems to be a dichotomy between those who are looking to hone categories into encyclopedic taxonomies and those who are looking for a tagging system in which they can do keyword searches. The more we push at removing overcategorization, the more there is a need for a simpler tagging system. If we can answer that need, it might make everyone happier. (editor 12) (period 2)

The fact that multiple, sometimes conflicting, conceptualizations of the purpose of the category system were evident two years after the category system had been introduced is a challenge that the community frequently discussed.

5. MODES OF COLLABORATION AROUND CATEGORIES

Large-scale collaboration among editors of Wikipedia to create the category system is one of the primary differences between this system and development in the KO literature. Negotiations between editors take place around each decision that is made about the design and implementation of the system. While there are a far greater number of people contributing to the category system in Wikipedia than historically have labored over the conceptualization of a classification system such as the Dewey Decimal Classification (DDC), progress can sometimes be impeded by disagreements. In the discussions we observed several prominent themes related to collaboration. We identified four modes or styles of collaboration around the category system that were assumed by the participants:

- Collaboration with the category system - This theme describes discussion in which editors were conceptualizing the category system as an entity that facilitates navigation and or retrieval, clustering or conceptual visualization.

- Collaboration over the category system - This theme describes discussions in which editors were conceptualizing the category system as an object of work that individuals must use and manipulate. These include be debates about how categories should be applied, what types of relationships should exist and be made explicit between categories.

- Collaboration through the category system - This theme describes discussion in which the editors were conceptualizing the category system as a mechanism for communicating and interacting with others.

- Tools for category collaborations - This theme describes discussions in which editors discuss tools they are using to facilitate collaboration with, over and through the category system.

In the following we illustrate how participants in the discussions appealed to each of these styles or modes when making a case for features in the emergent category system.

5.1 Collaboration with the Category System

The theme of collaboration with the category system is applicable to discussions in which editors discussed how the category system will be engaged with by users. One contributing editor articulated the need to balance the workflow of editors who are applying categories with the needs of Wikipedia users.

```
People are creating categories from the
bottom up because that's the easiest way for
editors to work -- they put the four Beatles
together in a category then lump them
together into larger categories, because few
people want to attempt to create a list of
hundreds, or thousands, of articles. But
however it's done, we have to make it easy
for encyclopedia users to navigate from the
top downward. Vegetarianism is fine within
the discipline of Food and drink, as long as
it isn't within a subcategory that's a list
of foods or a list of drinks. (editor 7)
```

Another editor, replying directly to this comment, stated the importance of reducing the number of clicks users would be required to make in order to get to related content of interest.

```
I think we have a philosophical difference
here. You rightly talk of the importance of
top-down, and of a properly understood and
maintained hierarchy. I agree completely.
Where we disagree is that I think the wiki
can encode much more than that (without
breaking the behaviour you would like). It's
clear that this is what people are trying to
do, but only by breaking the hierarchy in
the process. I also take the view that
people are more likely to start in the
middle of the hierarchy than at the top:
they'll google their way to a Wikipedia
article, spot the categories, and jump into
the tree. Where do they go from there? From
a user's perspective, categories are
```

```
primarily a navigational tool. Frankly it
would annoy me intensely if I surfed from a
footballer to Category:Football (soccer)
players and then had to start from the top
of the hierarchy to reach Category:Football
(soccer) rather than follow a single link.
That link could go in a "Related links"
section of the Football players category
page, sure. But that's a kludge, I'm afraid,
and throws away what could be meaningful
data. I think the approach to take here is
to add the ability to have relations in the
category. It doesn't remove anything from
the system that we have now and may add
something. In the first implementation off
this, all that should change is that the
category page would have multiple lists, one
for each relationship, rather than the
single list it has now. This shouldn;t be
too hard to code up and add extra
possibilities without any downside (apart
from the implementation time). (editor 13)
```

Another contributing editor highlighted the importance of categories as a support for browsing.

```
My boosterism of functional categories has
been in support of that skimming, browsing
user. Reading the above description,
although intriguing, I must confess I have
never considered the category tree as
supporting that sort of precision data-
mining search. Wikipedia strikes me as more
of an imprecise, people-to-people exercise
in information transfer, like any
traditional encyclopedia in that sense.
(editor 14)
```

Editors were very concerned with making decisions that would ensure the design of a category system to support navigation and retrieval, clustering of related content and conceptual visualization. In this way editors were designing a category system that would itself be a partner in the collaborative process of expanding Wikipedia.

5.2 Collaboration Over the Category System

The theme of collaborating over the category system is evident when editors discussed the category system as an object of work that individuals must use and manipulate. One editor expressed a need to find a solution to sorting issues within categories:

```
Consider the situation of a Category
containing 30 articles with Sort Keys Book
01, Book 02, ..., Book 30. These would all
appear under B using the current system;
this would still hold if the threshold was
measured against the number of articles as
opposed to the number of "sort buckets". The
latter is what I want to measure. The system
which has been unilaterally adopted in
Category:Harry Potter movies will only work
for a series up to 9 items, since an article
with Sort Key 10 will appear under 1 and
screw up the sorting arrangement. I would
prefer to use the system I originally
installed, being more scalable, but am
unwilling to impose it without some
discussion. (editor 15)
```

This comment demonstrates concern for how design decisions will affect user experience and also serves as an appeal to other interested parties to help reach a majority opinion on how to mediate this issue.

Editors also discussed how the category system might help users conceptualize topics in relation to one another.

I'm not sure why "ease of maintenance" is an issue on this, or why that overcomes the great navigation and classification benefits that have previously been mentioned. Articles that define categories are not only the parents of those categories but will also logically be a member of whatever parent categories their own categories belong to. The articles should reflect this, for navigation purposes, as well as to properly classify the article. These are the two functions of categories. A reader of an article may not want to read just more topics on that article, but to see others of the same kind, and he may not even know that such a parent category exists without the article being tagged with it. Categorizing Ohio only under Category:Ohio just tells you that there are more articles about Ohio. A non-U.S. reader in particular may not assume that clicking through that may take him to other categories on other states, plus he may wonder why Ohio isn't classified as a U.S. state, if that's what the article tells him it is. Why unnecessarily increase the steps required to find what should logically be right there? Why omit classifications on the articles that are obviously the most (or all equally) important instances of that classification by virtue of their having a subcategory? (editor 16)

Concerns over how the category scheme as an object of work that individuals must use and manipulate required the editors who participated in the design and implementation of the category system to collaborate over the system design. This collaboration entailed providing scenarios with different outcomes in relation to issues of concern. It also involved explicitly soliciting the input of others before a decision would be implemented. We will discuss tools that were used to facilitate such calls for collaboration below.

5.3 Collaboration through the Category System

Collaboration through the category system is a theme that applies to discussions of how the categories themselves might serve as a mechanism for communicating and interacting with others. Feinberg [3] argued that knowledge organization tasks are vehicles for the expression of the creators' beliefs. The discussions about the Wikipedia category system expand her argument in the realm of systems in which the design has been massively collaborative. The participants must reconcile which points of view will be expressed through the organization and assignment of categories and how the resulting system affects adherence to the neutral-point-of-view policy.

Editors were concerned with how the assignation of categories might violate the neutral-point-of-view policy.

We as a group have begun in a few different places around WP to identify a potential problem with POV in categorization. It seems this is happening when a category is created that has a negative connotation and no self-evident criteria for inclusion/exclusion. (It probably could also happen with a category having an extreme positive connotation, but I haven't seen that come up yet.) I think it may be useful to understand more fully just which actual, current categories are subject to this phenomenon, so that we may draw better-grounded conclusions after inspecting a more full set of actual examples. To that end, I'm starting an alphabetical list here (feel free to chip in) of categories I think are likely to cause POV controversy. (editor 14)

This comment provides evidence that the community was aware of the potential for expression in the act of naming and applying a category. This discussion also contains a direct appeal for collaborative effort toward the end of identifying examples of categories that might be contentious.

Another example of how categories were seen to have the potential to be expressive of bias is evident in the following discussion:

I really don't like the idea of categorizing people by race, religion, or sexual orientation, so Category:Gay people should go, and Category:Jews and Judaism should be just Category:Judaism. Gay rights activists would be a proper category, however, as would Jewish religious leaders, as long as it is categorized by something someone does rather than what they supposedly are. I think categorizing people under Category:African Americans or Category:Asian Americans is highly offensive and POV. Whether someone is one or not is largely a matter of self-identification (how do you label yourself if you are multiracial?), and it is inherently POV to think that people are appropriately classified based on what race they are, as if that is a defining trait. It is much less offensive but still problematic to merely include this...information in list articles, because at least that way you're not slapping a classification on the subject of an article, saying "this is what he is". (editor 17)

5.4 Tools for Category Collaborations

As mentioned above, there were multiple points in these discussions where appeals for collaboration were explicitly made. Several tools were named that editors were using to facilitate this collaboration. On the topic of how category links are highlighted if they are created but left without being assigned to a parent category, one editor invited others to help address the problem.

If people created categories responsibly, there would never be a redlink category. A red linked category does not mean it doesn't have a parent. It means it has no description. (And if it has no description, it can't have a parent, but that's not the

point.) There are many criteria that
determine if a category "exists"...does it
have articles? Does it have a parent? Does
it have an article (description)? Only the
last of these means anything to the link
color. If you hate red categories so much,
maybe you'd like to join me in fixing them
on Category:Orphaned categories where I have
lots of them listed. (editor 18)

The function that such categories are highlighted with the color
red could also be interpreted as a tool to support collaboration
itself as it indicates to editors that the category lacks a parent, a
vital part of the category assignment process. But as well, in the
quote we see a range of ways to determine "existence" of a
category that point toward a range of technical assistance for
category creation and application.

Another way that editors collaborated was by sharing
recommendations for how to accomplish certain types of tasks.

In the meantime, one useful method I've
found is to go ahead and edit the article or
subcategory you'd like to classify. Type in
your best guess at the name of the proper
category/ies, AND the name of a larger
category that you're sure exists, which
could be a (grand)parent (i.e.
Category:Medicine or Category:Music, or
Category:Musical groups by genre, as
specific as you can get). Then use the SHOW
PREVIEW, not the Save page button. Look for
the previewed categories at the very bottom
of the page (it may be below the Preview
edit box, depending on your Preferences
settings). If your best guess is blue,
you've hit upon an existing category tree;
if red, it doesn't exist or is spelled or
worded differently. (editor 19)

This advice was a helpful work-around when the software did not
support any type of browsing of the category system other than
via an alphabetical list of all categories.

Editors also made direct reference to tools external to Wikipedia.

In Bugzilla, there is 'Bug 450: Categories
need to be structured by namespace'. To some
extent the lists are already structured by
namespace (their name sorts them together).
Contrary to the deletion log sometimes
included in categories or user pages, images
aren't just noise in the category, but
informative. As it's easy for readers and
other users to distinguish them from
articles, I'd include them. As another
example, one could quote Category:Saint
Helena. (editor 20)

This comment indicates that some editors made use of the bug-
tracking software, Bugzilla, to keep track of work that needed to
be tackled within the Wikipedia project. Another editor mentioned
Sourceforge:

RfE 964667 is probably the closest task in
sourceforge and is currently unassigned.
(editor 21)

This response was made to address a question of whether anyone
had proposed creating a visualization tool that would display all
dependent subcategories for a given category to facilitate the
accurate assignation of categories to pages.

6. DISCUSSION AND IMPLICATIONS

Tagging is a valuable and popular collaborative technology. Many
prior studies have focused on the application of tags without a
clear tie to the underlying assumptions of the users who are
applying those tags. The act of tagging, or labeling, an item as a
member of some category of things or concepts has profound
implications for the way we see or understand that item. In a
collaborative context, the ability of the members to successfully
negotiate disagreements over instances of labeling directly
influences the progress and success of the collaboration.

The content of Wikipedia is connected as a graph structure with
many pages explicitly linked to other pages using largely
associative relations. Early on participants argued for the creation
of a category system with clear hierarchical relationships. Many
discussions of hierarchy did not distinguish between different
types of hierarchical relationships, nor did they cover the
challenges users would face when trying to interact with a system
in which many different types of relationships would exist
between categories without being explicitly described.

This points to specific opportunities for category tools. While
Wikipedia has some extensions that allow for the exploration of
the category system, there is nothing that specifically visualizes
the assumed or real relationships among category nodes. A tool
that in some way displayed the relation among categories would
help regular users navigate with the category system and help
individuals who wanted to tag pages.

Members of the community were also conscious of the issue of
appropriately scoping the category system. They worried about
consistency in terms of the number of categories and supercategories that might be applied to a page. They also suggested
external models for the structure and syntax of the category
system. They recognized that models and syntax structure would
require work to create and maintain. Further, they also recognized
that they might become a barrier to entry for newcomers who
want to participate by categorizing uncategorized pages.

Scoping tools represent yet another possible technical
enhancement. A scoping tool could help users understand whether
a page might be over or under categorized. Similarity measures
between sets of category tags and the text of pages could suggest
new categories that might be applied or categories that may be
unnecessary.

The category system was initially conceived as a navigational tool
to complement traditional search. Many recommendations were
made as to how to facilitate navigation through Wikipedia using
the category system. It is unclear what role the placement of the
category tags at the bottom of articles plays in the utilization of
the system for navigation, but studies of other systems suggests
that it may have a negative impact.

Wikipedia currently relies on search as the primary navigation
system. But with all of the labor that has gone into the category
system, an obvious enhancement would be to leverage the
category system to provide users more contextual information
about the content that they are viewing. Visual snippets of the
categories relating to the page alongside their super- and subcategories could help users understand a specific article or could

be attached to internal page links to present more context about the possible target page.

There is much future work to be done in this area. In particular, while there has been work to look at the relative distribution of tags (Kittur [8]) the growth of the category system itself has not been considered. Further how the growth of the category system mirrored or has not mirrored the application of category tags would also be important to know relative to existing studies of other collaborative tagging and folksonomic systems. The approach that Spinellis and Louridas [13] employed to examine the growth of Wikipedia via links to pages that do not yet exist and are subsequently created would be a useful model to explore for a similar study of the expansion of the category system.

7. CONCLUSION

Our study has analyzed the early efforts to collaboratively create a category system for Wikipedia. Through analysis of group discussions, we saw the collective concerns for how the category system would be structured, how it would be applied, and how it could be useful for future users of Wikipedia. Our analysis unpacks some of the collective and social concerns that individuals had about the creation and use of a category system.

Our analysis extends what we know about social tagging systems and the collaborative creation of category systems. The analysis of how the category system functions to enable different styles of collaboration is important in relation to the other collaborative tagging studies. This rubric of collaboration styles should be tested in other large-scale collaborative projects where category schemes are fabricated and used.

While we know from the work of Kriplean, et al. [7] that the labor invested in maintaining and improving the category system is valued work in the Wikipedia community, the system itself seems to be underutilized. If we harness the power of the information structures built by thousands of editors to provide context for each article among related content in order to present such relationships visually to users, this would provide an alternate navigational option with the potential to support sensemaking. If we are able to display category information that would support tagging decision making, we could encourage increased participation in the expansion and refinement of the category system, especially among novice editors.

8. ACKNOWLEDGMENTS

This material is based on work supported by the National Science Foundation under Grants IIS-0811210 and IIS-1162114. The opinions, findings, conclusions or recommendations expressed are those of the author(s) and do not necessarily reflect the views of the National Science Foundation.

9. REFERENCES

[1] Aitchison, J., Gilchrist, A., and Bawden, D. "Section F structure and relationships." In *Thesaurus Construction and Use: A Practical Manual*. Chicago: Fitzroy Dearborn Publishers (2000): 49-84.

[2] Farooq, U., Kannampallil, T.G., Song, Y., Ganoe, C., Carroll, J.M. and Giels, C.L. Evaluating Tagging Behavior in Social Bookmarking Systems: Metrics and Design Heuristics. In *Proceedings of the ACM 2007 International Conference on Supporting Group Work*, (2007), 351-360.

[3] Feinberg, M. Expressive bibliography: personal collections in public space. *Knowledge Organization 38* (2) (2011).

[4] Forte, A., and Bruckman, A. Scaling Consensus: Increasing Decentralization in Wikipedia Governance. In *Proceedings of the 41st Annual Hawaii International Conference on System Sciences*, (2008).

[5] Golder, S.A. and Huberman, B.A. The Structure of Collaborative Tagging Systems. *Journal of Information Science*, **32** (2). 198-208.

[6] Holloway, T., Bozicevic, M. and Börner, K. Analyzing and visualizing the semantic coverage of Wikipedia and its authors. *Complexity*, 12 (2007), 30–40.

[7] Kriplean, T., I. Beschastnikh, and D. W. McDonald. Articulations of wikiwork: uncovering valued work in wikipedia through barnstars. In *Proceedings of the 2008 ACM conference on Computer supported cooperative work*, (2008), 47-56.

[8] Kittur, A., Chi, E. and B. Suh. What's in Wikipedia?: mapping topics and conflict using socially annotated category structure. In *Proceedings of the 27th international conference on Human factors in computing systems*, (2009), 1509-1512.

[9] Lee, H. L. and Olson, H. A. Hierarchical navigation: An exploration of Yahoo! directories. *Knowledge Organization*, **32** (1) (2005), 10-24.

[10] Millen, D.R., Feinberg, J. and Kerr, B., Dogear: Social Bookmarking in the Enterprise. In *Proceedings of the ACM Conference on Human Factors in Computing Systems*, (2006), 111-120.

[11] Muchnik, L., Itzhack, R., Solomon, S. and Louzoun, Yoram. Self-emergence of knowledge trees: Extraction of the Wikipedia hierarchies. *Physical Review E* **76**, 1 (2007), 016106.

[12] Sen, S., Lam, S.K.T., Rashid, A.M., Cosley, D., Frankowski, D., Osterhouse, J., Harper, F.M. and Riedl, J., tagging, communities, vocabulary, evolution. In *Proceedings of the 2006 ACM Conference on Computer Supported Cooperative Work*, (2006), 181- 190.

[13] Spinellis, D. and Louridas, P. The collaborative organization of knowledge. *Communications of the ACM* **51**(8), (August 2008), 68-73.

[14] Svenonius, Elaine. 2000. *The intellectual foundation of information organization*. MIT Press.

[15] Voss, J. Collaborative Thesaurus Tagging the Wikipedia Way, (2006) http://arxiv.org/abs/ cs/0-604036. Accessed Jan 21, 2011.

Twitter Zombie: Architecture for Capturing, Socially Transforming and Analyzing the Twittersphere

Alan Black
Drexel University
Philadelphia, PA
aeblack@gmail.com

Christopher Mascaro
Drexel University
Philadelphia, PA
cmascaro@gmail.com

Michael Gallagher
Drexel University
Philadelphia, PA
michael.gallagher24@g
mail.com

Sean P. Goggins
Drexel University
Philadelphia, PA
outdoors@acm.org

ABSTRACT

Social computational systems emerge in the wild on popular social networking sites like Facebook and Twitter, but there remains confusion about the relationship between social interactions and the technical traces of interaction left behind through use. Twitter interactions and social experience are particularly challenging to make sense of because of the wide range of tools used to access Twitter (text message, website, iPhone, TweetDeck and others), and the emergent set of practices for annotating message context (hashtags, reply to's and direct messaging). Further, Twitter is used as a back channel of communication in a wide range of contexts, ranging from disaster relief to watching television. Our study examines Twitter as a transport protocol that is used differently in different socio-technical contexts, and presents an analysis of how researchers might begin to approach studies of Twitter interactions with a more reflexive stance toward the application programming interfaces (APIs) Twitter provides. We conduct a careful review of existing literature examining socio-technical phenomena on Twitter, revealing a collective inconsistency in the description of data gathering and analysis methods. In this paper, we present a candidate architecture and methodological approach for examining specific parts of the Twittersphere. Our contribution begins a discussion among social media researchers on the topic of how to systematically and consistently make sense of the social phenomena that emerge through Twitter. This work supports the comparative analysis of Twitter studies and the development of social media theories.

Categories and Subject Descriptors

H.5.3 [**Group and Organization Interfaces**]: Web-based Interaction

General Terms

Algorithms, Design, Experimentation, Standardization.

Keywords

Twitter, data collection, data management, methods, social media

1. INTRODUCTION

There are recognized empirical and theoretical gaps in the application of social science theories to raw, electronic trace data like that retrievable from Twitter [23]; a record of interaction through technology does not necessarily act as a proxy for social interaction. Such gaps are further exacerbated by the opaqueness of Twitter's API for retrieving data, and different choices researchers make about how to retrieve, store and analyze data from Twitter. Each peer reviewed study of Twitter interactions, in domains ranging from disaster relief, to sports viewing, political action and celebrity engagement with fans, presents an explanation of how data is captured, analyzed and related to findings within the individual study. The explicitness of these descriptions is variable. Consequently, comparisons across Twitter studies and aggregation of findings leading to more comprehensive theories of social media interaction are difficult because of the lack of a shared view of well understood and documented methods for gathering and analyzing electronic traces from social media, including Twitter.

A few papers have attempted to build community understanding of how to select and use different Twitter application programming interfaces (APIs) for research. Zhao et al. [50] , for example, contrast the three main APIs provided by Twitter – the REST, Search and Streaming APIs – but their paper is either out of date a year after publication, or incorrect in its interpretation of Twitter's API's.

Scholarship that references, documents or contrasts different social media platform APIs, including Twitter's, face the challenge of working to reverse engineer a system whose traits may be shifting over time. What we report on today with regards to the Twitter API may not be sustained over time by the Twitter platform. The two key gaps in analysis of social media generally, and Twitter in particular, then, are 1) Each study constructs it's own approach to gathering Twitter data and 2) Attempts to explain the Twitter API through analysis are difficult to verify because the data delivered by API may be changing over time.

We see three potential ways of overcoming the challenges we identify. First, social media vendors could make the completeness of data retrieved through their API's more transparent. This is stifled by privacy and competiveness concerns. Second, individual studies of Twitter may begin to follow a standard methodology for gathering data, appropriate to the problem context, and referencing articles focused on these methodological approaches. Third, the community might consider a standard architecture for the capture of social media, which would constitute a technical architecture to ensure consistency of social science results; in a sense, using computers for what they are good at, and people for what they are best at.

Fully developed solutions to these challenges are an important, long-range goal for the social media research community. In this paper we present a modest, but integrated methodological approach and technology architecture for the standard capture, social transformation and analysis of Twitter interactions using the Search API. We contrast this API with the other two, describe the results of experiments conducted using our tools, which we call Twitter Zombie, explain our process of social transformation, and describe a pilot visualization and analysis project using this methodological approach and toolset. We conclude with a road map for methodological enhancements to social media research.

2. PRIOR TWITTER WORK

2.1 Twitter and its Affordances

Twitter research has evolved from the time when Twitter was first introduced in 2006. Early research on Twitter attempted to characterize user behavior in the technology. Java et al. [26] found that individuals used Twitter to discuss daily routines and to exchange news. At the same time, other researchers attempted to characterize user behavior on Twitter and identify specific behavior around Twitter's numerous affordances [29].

The three most common affordances in twitter are the hashtag, retweet and @-mention. Hashtags are used to highlight streams of discourse for others to attend to [24; 42] and retweets are a mechanism of forwarding another user's message in one's own Twitter stream [8]. In addition to the inclusion of hashtags and retweets, the inclusion of @-mentions (@ followed by a username) signifies a direct addressal to or highlighting of a message to someone else and may be indicative of targeted information sharing or discourse [22].

In addition to these technological affordances, researchers are able to collect the device or application that a user utilized to send a tweet. Analysis of the device activity can highlight the utilization of different technological access mechanisms for different purposes [48]. We illustrate such differences in the description of our pilot study in section five. When coupled with geographic location from the user profile, or from where the tweet originated, researchers can identify geographically specific information such as localized discourse [39] or attempt to identify the overall happiness of people in certain geographic areas [41].

Unlike other forms of social media, only 22% of Twitter relationships are reciprocal [30]. This creates an environment of "context collapse" in which a user has multiple audiences for their tweets, and the user may not be aware of who is in those audiences [33]. As a result of this asymmetric network structure, information diffusion is significantly different on Twitter than in social networking platforms that have symmetric relationships [31]. Substantial prior research utilizes the follower/following relationships to characterize user behavior on Twitter [28].

Measuring the number of followers an individual has (as in-degree influence) illustrates popularity, but does little to measure their ability to influence others [9]. Though follower/following relationships are important for understanding initial information diffusion, collecting and characterizing actual user behavior such as retweet behavior, the number of mentions and reply-to's, and the content of tweets are much better indicators of influence [3; 6]. Influence in Twitter is also shown to be the result of long-term reputation building in a network of individuals [9].

One of the more commonly used affordances in Twitter is the retweet. A retweet is the process of an individual further propagating another's message by copying it into their Twitter stream. Prior studies illustrate that 16% of tweets on a daily basis on Twitter are retweets [38]. In specific domains, such as political discourse, the percentage of retweets can be as high as 56%, depending on the topic [38]. Kwak et al. [30] found that 75% of retweets occur within the first hour of the original tweet, but that 10% of retweets occur a month later. This illustrates a different intent and purpose of retweeting and a different trajectory of information diffusion. There are many reasons that individuals retweet messages, which include: to propagate information, to illustrate that they are "present" in the conversation or in the space, and to attempt to return favors to other individuals to prop up their twitter followers [8]. In addition to these reasons, retweets are seen as a mechanism of conversation that takes on different characteristics depending on the user's network and the content of the original tweet. One study found that positive messages are more likely to be retweeted than negative messages, illustrating how content can affect information diffusion through the network through the retweet mechanism [17].

Honeycutt and Herring [22] identify the technological affordance of @, which directs a message towards someone else, as a form of addressivity [46] in Twitter. In their analysis, they found that close to 90% of the instances of @ were someone addressing another individual in a conversation and these conversations on average lasted 3-5 messages. Of the larger sample that included tweets with both @ and without, they found that those tweets with @ tended to be more interactive in their content. For example, they found that messages that employed the @-mention affordance received a response 31% of the time, which is higher than previous studies of technologically mediated communication. This number is also a conservative estimate, as it does not take into account the possibility that a reply may have been sent in another channel [49].

2.2 Applied Twitter Analysis

One of the most significant areas of research on Twitter has been the use of sentiment analysis and other modeling techniques to examine, explain, or predict offline events [2; 4]. Some research has indicated that the brevity of Twitter messages affords more reliable sentiment classifications [5]. These approaches have been applied to predicting the direction of the US Stock market [7], analyzing debate performance in a 2008 US Presidential Debate [13] understanding the outcome of 2011 Portuguese Presidential elections [14] and identifying general public opinion [1]. Further research indicates that the volume of Twitter activity may mirror box office performance, but may not be as representative of stock market activity [34]. These findings indicate possible different uses of Twitter in different social domains, and also may represent a demographic difference in user activity. Understanding sentiment on Twitter has also been used to further understand sporting events such as the Olympics [17] and Brazilian Soccer Leagues [18].

The medical community has also studied Twitter as a way to understand whether or not the public adopts certain terminology in the context of a Pandemic [10]. In this instance, the researchers were interested in whether the public used the term "swine flu" or the more medically formal term, "H1N1." Early research analyzing medical information diffusion on Twitter has also attempted to identify the mechanisms that users utilize to judge trust and validity of medical information. This research has demonstrated that the originating user and the content of the message is likely to be a significant factor in how individuals assess the validity of information. [36]. Researchers have also attempted to identify influenza outbreaks through the monitoring of Twitter for certain keywords, but have had limited success [12].

One of the greatest areas of research on Twitter is the analysis of political activity and participation in Twitter. Researchers identify partisan clusters in retweet behavior illustrative of echo chambers of ideas in information diffusion in Twitter [11]. These researchers also find examples of "content injection" that identifies users adopting partisan hashtags or keywords to broadcast material that may be counter to the ideology of the party to proliferate a message. Similar activity is also been noted in the context of the conservative hashtag #tcot (Top Conservatives on Twitter) [32]. Additionally, researchers show how multi-dimensional scaling can be used to classify users based on hashtag and @-mention usage [19].

Researchers in the U.K. found a difference in adoption of Twitter based on partisan affiliation of members of parliament (Williamson et al 2010). Additionally, many of the studies focused on the utilization of Twitter by the US Congress found that members used Twitter for self-promotion as opposed to communicating directly and specifically to citizens [16]. Analysis of political activity in Korea has found that "resource-deficient politicians" may be more likely to engage with followers and use it as a mode of connecting to citizens [28]. Research has identified similar behavior in the United in the 2010 US midterm election where the conservative minority was more effective at using social media to build support [32] and challengers tended to interact more with the public than incumbents [40].

Using hashtags to analyze political discourse on Twitter has been done across cultures as well. German researchers used politically oriented hashtags to identify 2009 election discourse [27]. During this election, German Twitter users were encouraged to use party related hashtags followed by + or – to illustrate agreement or disagreement with the message. Through this hashtag valence the researchers were better able to understand the network structure of individuals and identify "small worlds" of connected individuals had similar political viewpoints.

In addition to understanding how politicians, candidates and the public use Twitter in the political context, there has been a significant amount of work that has attempted to illustrate how social media may be able to predict elections [45; 47]. A review of this work illustrates fundamental flaws in the approaches and illustrates the lack of comparison to traditional mechanisms of prediction and analysis such as polling or historical evidence, illustrating that the incumbent wins close to 90% of the time in United States Congressional election [35]. Metaxas et al. further extend this critique by identifying that much of this "prediction" occurs after the election and may actually be worse than traditional models. When attempting to repeat experiments that "predicted" wins in electoral races, Metaxas et al. [35] were unable to reproduce the results.

The contrast between planned and unplanned events is one that has been explored in the context of crisis informatics on social media such as Twitter. Research that compared national political events and natural disasters have found that Twitter is used as a way to broadcast information out to the public and in the case of natural disasters Twitter is used as a frequent way to share links with the public [25]. Twitter has also been instrumental in understanding crisis events and natural disasters. One of the reasons that individuals use Twitter during a crisis event is to relay information from the place where the activity is happening and also to synthesize current information to proliferate it through the network of individuals [43]. Researchers have studied the use of Twitter for information diffusion and sense making related to unplanned, social and violent events like school shootings [21]. Research on the 2007 wildfires in California illustrated how social media – Twitter in particular – can be an important source of information for citizens and described how broadcast media turned to Twitter to get information about what was happening [44].

2.3 Extending our Collection Knowledge

Our survey of the existing literature that we discuss above reveals a significant variation in how individuals collect Twitter data. Currently, Twitter provides three API's to collect data, with the two most popular being the Search API and Streaming API. Our review of the literature shows that studies that look at specific affordances such as hashtags, @-mentions or other keywords contained within tweets tended to use the Search API to access data about specific events or topics [2; 8; 13; 17; 21; 30; 42], while other studies that attempt to look at longitudinal opinions of movies, politics and other domains use the Streaming API to access data [6; 19; 34]. The differences between how data is collected by these two API's may significantly alter the type of dataset collected by researchers, though these differences are not discussed in detail in empirical studies of Twitter.

In addition to lab developed access mechanisms that query the Twitter API directly, there are other tools such as NodeXL [20] that provide an interface for users to access data, and statistical libraries such as twitteR for the statistical program R [15]. In addition to these access mechanisms, Twitter also provides feeds of the Twitter stream to some organizations. These feeds are described by Twitter as a random sample of a percentage of the overall Twitter stream. We found only one explicit mention to this access mechanism in our survey of the literature and that was the Twitter "garden hose" which provides a sample of 10% of all tweets. This access was used by the individuals of the Truthy project at Indiana for a series of papers [11; 35; 37; 38]

Our review of the literature illustrates the domain breadth, affordance diversity and methodological approach differences associated with prior Twitter research. We show that social media research in general, and Twitter research specifically presents with a diverse set of approaches for gathering and analyzing socio-technical phenomena that share Twitter as a social media platform. Twitter literature to date illustrates that there is not a consistent, repeatable set of tools for collecting, analyzing and reporting on Twitter facilitated social groups. Further, different studies present and explain their methods of capture and analysis with an inconsistent level of clarity and specificity. These gaps make it difficult to draw comparisons across studies of similar phenomena in Twitter, and impair the development of broader social media theories.

3. TWITTER ZOMBIE
3.1 Twitter Data Collection Facilities

The contribution we make to address the challenges presented is a methodological approach and technical tool (Twitter Zombie) for Twitter data collection and analysis. Our Twitter Zombie system for capturing data from Twitter and the associated experiments we present provide a repeatable foundation for the community to use for social media capture verification and our pilot study illustrating our methodological approach illustrates the collection idiosyncrasies associated with certain collection parameters, and how different parameters can alter the collected datasets. If played out over time and across studies, these small differences may be significant and alter findings. Presently, as we noted, such differences are seldom surfaced in empirical studies of social phenomena on Twitter. We invite other researchers to share their experiences with their specific systems as an important methodological step in addressing the opaque nature of the Twitter API structure.

Twitter offers three primary methods for allowing software developers access to Twitter data: the Streaming API, the REST (Representational State Transfer) API and the Search API. The

Streaming API relies upon a continuously open network connection between Twitter and the receiving host and is designed to support significant volumes of data transfer. By contrast, the REST API follows a typical client-server request and response communication pattern where connections between Twitter and the requesting host are dynamically created on a per-request basis. Both APIs return data in JSON (JavaScript Object Notation) format, a compact human-readable data interchange format akin to an XML document representation, though less verbose.

Twitter Zombie utilizes the third publically available API, known as the Twitter Search API. The Search API employs a REST communications pattern and provides a mechanism to query the real-time index of tweets. The index contains tweets that are six or fewer days old and may include tweets up to nine days old. In addition to temporal limitations, the search API imposes a number of important performance constraints. First, a query request can be rejected if it is too complex, although complexity is not publically defined. Also, results from the Search API are rate limited. Unfortunately, the parameters related to these limitations are unpublished. Finally, queries submitted via the search API are limited to a maximum of the 1,500 results, which may contain less than the most recent six days of tweets depending on how prolific the user is.

Selecting an API is an important decision for researchers, but one that is often not specified in empirical work and not rationalized in the face of research questions as illustrated in our previous review of existing literature. For this application, the Search API offers a number of advantages over the REST or Streaming APIs. The Search API does not impose explicit rate limits as does the REST API. Perhaps most importantly, batch use of the Search API allows Twitter Zombie to maintain distinct result sets from each search, even when a unique tweet is returned multiple times in response to different query strings.

3.2 Twitter Zombie Architecture

We access the Search API using a software system we developed in PHP, called Twitter Zombie. Data collected by Twitter Zombie is stored in a MySQL relational database management system. Twitter Zombie is designed to gather data from Twitter by executing a series of independent search jobs on a continual basis, 24 hours a day, 7 days a week. The execution interval for each search can be controlled independently through a rudimentary job management system. Each search job can be programmed to execute once every n minutes (where n >= 1) using a run interval value. This allows us to run searches for high volume queries (those returning many tweets) more frequently than those associated with low volume result sets. High volume queries are typically run every minute or two, while some low volume search jobs are scheduled to execute only once each day (or every 1440 minutes). The search job control system also allows us to stop, restart, and change execution intervals on the fly.

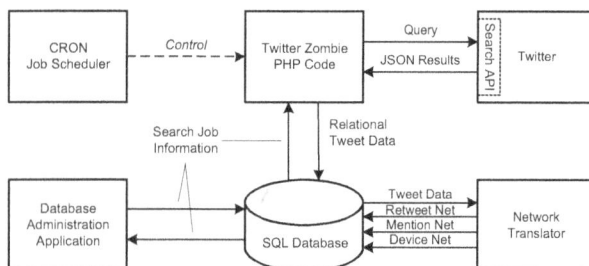

Figure 1 - Twitter Zombie System Diagram

The workflow for creating a new Twitter Zombie search job begins at Twitter's advanced search web page. This simple page provides a text input field for the user's query string as well as access to a handy pop-up reference that lists search operators along with usage examples. These operators include OR, the minus sign (-) for negation, the ampersand (@) for referencing people, the pound sign (#) for locating Twitter hash tags, "near" and "within" for geo-based searches, and others including attitudinal and temporal operators.

To develop a new search job, we begin by entering a query into the advanced search page and executing it. If no results are returned, this is generally an indication of a malformed query. If results are produced, they are inspected for face validity. This process is repeated until a suitable query is constructed and tested. At that point, the URL encoded search string is copied from our web browser's address field for later entry into the Twitter Zombie job control system. In effect, we are using Twitter facilities to help develop, pre-flight and encode our queries.

Once a new query string is successfully tested, it can be entered into Twitter Zombie's job table. This table contains one record for each search job (active or inactive). Each record represents a complete search job definition that includes a run interval value, a human readable job description, the ID of the last collected tweet for this search and the encoded query string. Storing the Twitter supplied ID of the most recently collected tweet allows Twitter Zombie to request only those tweets that have been created since the last time the search job was executed which greatly improves overall collection efficiency.

The Twitter Zombie PHP code is executed each minute by the Linux time-based job scheduler, cron. During each running of Twitter Zombie, the entire search job table is scanned to determine which queries should be executed. If a search job's run interval value indicates that it's time to execute the query, a request is made to Twitter. The Twitter Zombie control architecture can therefore be thought about as two loop constructs, one inside the other. The outer control loop responsible for repeatedly executing Twitter Zombie is managed by cron, while the inner search job loop is managed by the PHP code, which references the job table.

In addition to storing and manipulating search job control data, the MySQL database is also used to store the collected tweets and associated metadata. The database schema is optimized for insertion efficiency. This is important in the context of a system that may be called upon to handle sudden unanticipated surges in tweet volume. Unforeseeable surges are common in disaster relief scenarios or when a news story breaks that impacts a large number of Twitter users. In terms of a design tradeoff, we have chosen to optimize the efficiency of data writes at the expense of storage consumption by forgoing a more space conserving, fully normalized database schema.

Much of Twitter Zombie's utility as a research tool stems from its ability to capture the hierarchical relationships in the data returned by Twitter. The search results are run through a tool we call the "network translator" which performs post collection processing and records the results in the database. The complete tweet text and all related entities (e.g. hashtags and mentions) are stored separately. We explain this further in section 4.1, which describes our conceptualization of how to socially transform raw Twitter data to reflect interactions between people, and between people and artifacts. Preserving the data's original structure allows us to leverage the power of SQL (Structured Query Language) to perform post hoc data transformation in order to answer specific research questions.

3.3 Tweet Data

3.3.1 Character encoding and counting

Social media researchers make implicit or explicit choices about whether or not to include the full character set for non-English languages; or multi-byte languages like Arabic, Chinese or others at all. This is due to the way Twitter handles character encoding, and the subsequent handling of that encoding by common software tools. Twitter stores the text strings that comprise tweets and other data as UTF-8 encoded characters. This means that tweets may include a variety of characters not represented in the ASCII (American Standard Code for Information Interchange) encoding scheme. UTF-8 encoding allows Twitter to handle the entire Unicode character set, but this affordance comes at the cost of complexity. Because UTF-8 is a variable-width encoding scheme (where a single character may be represented by two or more bytes), visually counting characters does not necessarily reveal the number of bytes required to store a given string. This uncertainty is exacerbated by the fact that some words with accented characters can be encoded using more than one representation. In order to not disadvantage users of non-English characters, Twitter employs Unicode Normalization Form C[1] in order to compute character count. This reality has obvious implications for the Twitter Zombie database design. In order to ensure that the full text of a tweet is faithfully recorded, the field containing the tweet string must be able to store four bytes for each character for a total of 560 bytes (i.e. 140 characters * 4 bytes per Unicode code point).

In order to alleviate the need for all of our downstream analysis tools (and even some basic system utilities) to support UTF-8 encoding, Twitter Zombie is capable of performing transliteration. This process maps Unicode characters that cannot be represented in ASCII to a suitable character or character string substitute. For example the euro sign would be replaced with the string "EUR" when transliteration is enabled. In future versions of the tool, full support for UTF-8 will be developed. Our review of dozens of previous Twitter studies reveals no explicit mention of how multi-byte Tweets are handled.

3.3.2 Metadata

In addition to receiving the raw text of a tweet, Twitter provides a wealth of metadata that is captured by Twitter Zombie. This invaluable metadata includes the time and date of a tweet and the tweet language expressed as a two-letter code defined by the ISO 639-1 standard. Tweet search results also include a source field that names the application used to create each tweet. Some tweets (the vast *minority,* unfortunately) are returned with geo-location data expressed as a point in terms of longitude and latitude.

Entities such as hashtags, mentions, and URLs are returned as distinct elements within the JSON representation. Each entity is further described by metadata that identifies its exact location within the tweet text. The metadata indicates the beginning and ending character positions for each entity providing a simple mechanism to calculate entity length.

Finally, each tweet returned to Twitter Zombie carries information regarding the author (i.e. sender). A unique Twitter ID as well as a long and a short user name identifies the tweet's creator. Tweets that are directed to a particular Twitter user also contain ID and name data for the intended recipient.

3.3.3 Duplicate tweets

Twitter employs processes to remove duplicate and near-duplicate tweets from search results. The duplication detection technique relies on the MinHash algorithm. A number of signatures are computed for each tweet. These signature sequences are only four bytes in length. A tweet is considered a duplicate if it shares a set of signatures with another tweet.

3.3.4 Result quality and relevance

Twitter filters the results delivered by both the Streaming and the Search APIs in order to exclude tweets that are deemed low quality. While the filtering algorithm is unpublished, and therefore, is likely to change without warning, Twitter does provide some insight into the filtering methodology. Frequent tweets that are considered repetitious are targeted for filtering. Twitter also filters tweets from suspended accounts and tweets that fail to meet other vaguely defined standards.

When working with the search API, the result set may have also been culled based upon relevance. Twitter returns only the most relevant tweets pertaining to the query based upon unpublished criteria. The relevance filtering process is not imposed on results returned from the Streaming API.

4. Experimental Results

We performed several experiments using Twitter Zombie in order to better understand the operational characteristics of the Twitter Search API. The search terms "sports" and "sex" were chosen as they represent high tweet volume subjects, each returning hundreds of tweets per minute during most hours of the day.

Table 1 - Experimental Job Parameters

Experiment	Collection interval (min.)	API Query
1	1	q=sex
1	2	q=sex
1	3	q=sex
2	1	q=sports
2	2	q=sports
2	4	q=sports
3	1	q=sex
3	1	q=sex

In experiment number one, the same query was performed with different collection time intervals. All three search jobs were started at the same time. The graph in Figure 2 shows that the number of tweets collected each hour tracks closely across the three search jobs over a 24-hour period.

---

[1] http://unicode.org/reports/tr15/#Norm_Forms

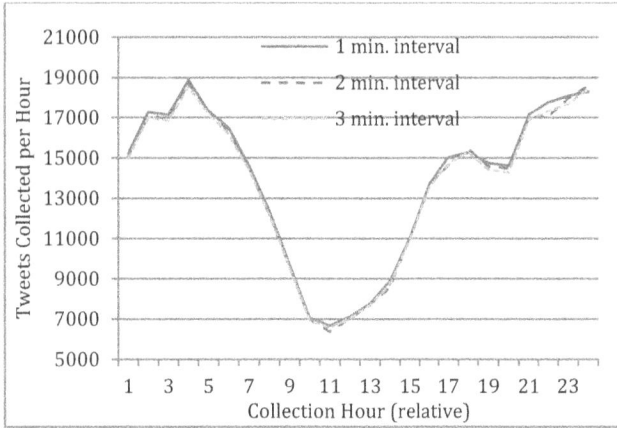

Figure 2 – Tweets per hour for q=sex at 1, 2, and 3 min. collection intervals

Despite the close agreement in hourly tweet counts, there appeared to be a slight but consistent drop-off in the number of tweets collected when using collection intervals longer than one minute (the baseline interval). Figure 3 shows the reduction in tweet counts for search jobs run at two and three minute intervals as a percentage of tweets collected with the same search performed each minute.

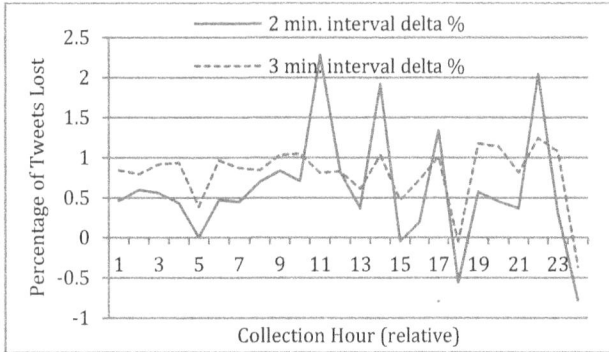

Figure 3 – Percentage drop-off for q=sex at 1, 2, and 3 min. collection intervals

As was true for experiment one, the number of tweets collected over a 24-hour period, this time using one, two and four minute collection intervals, tracked over time as shown in Figure 4.

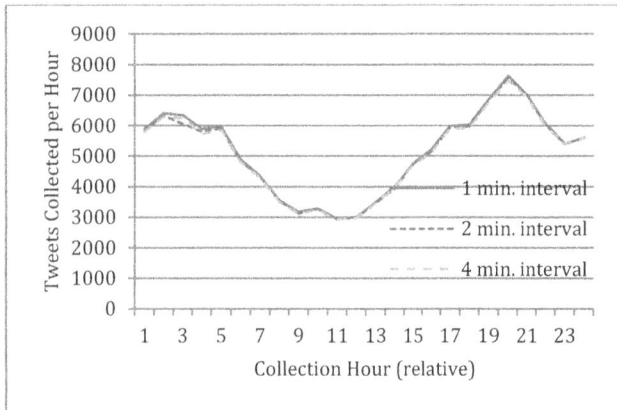

Figure 4 - Tweets per hour for q=sports at 1, 2, and 4 min. collection intervals

The pattern of recovering fewer tweets when using longer collection intervals appears again in experiment two. These results show the phenomenon more clearly than in experiment one due to the use of a longer maximum collection interval (4 min. versus 3 min. in experiment one).

While the mechanism or mechanisms responsible for reducing the number of tweets returned from Twitter when using longer collection intervals is unknown, one obvious potential source of the discrepancy is user deleted tweets. This highlights an important difference between the Search and Streaming APIs. The Streaming API provides tweet deletion messages that signal receiving software to discard previously recorded tweets. By contrast, the Search API provides no information regarding deleted tweets.

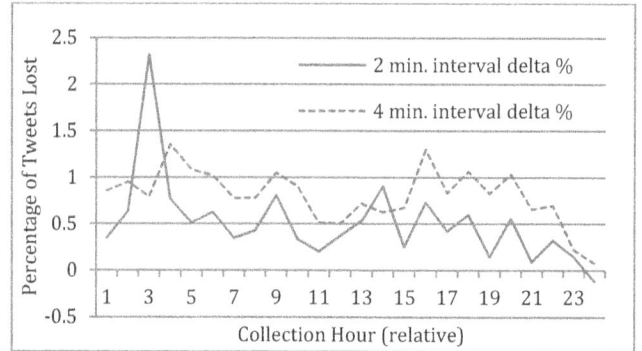

Figure 5 - Percentage drop-off for q=sports at 1, 2, and 4 min. collection intervals

Experiment three continues the effort to characterize the Twitter Search API. Twitter Zombie was used to run two identical search jobs both starting at the same time. Figure 6 shows how closely the hourly counts of returned tweets agree. The percentage differences are detailed in Figure **7**.

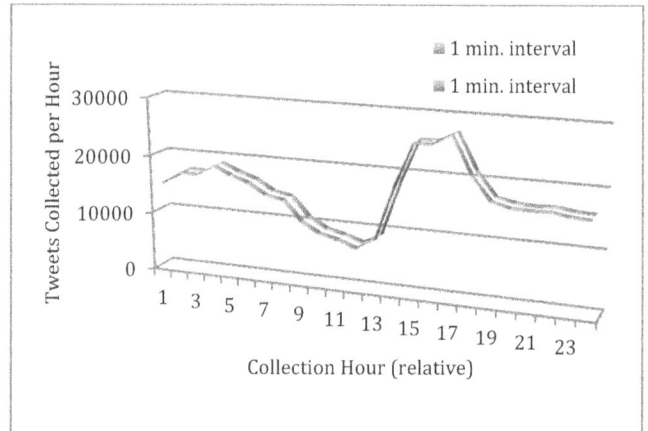

Figure 6 - Tweets per hour for q=sex at 1 min. intervals

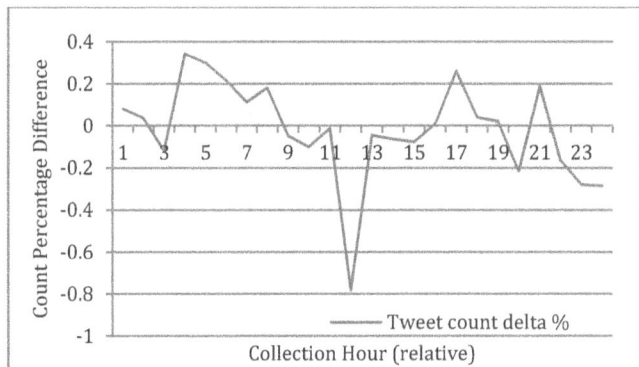

Figure 7 - Percent difference for q=sex at 1 min. and 1 min. collection intervals

4.1 Social Transformation of Tweets

We use the metadata of Tweets, described in Section 3.3.2 to transform the raw Twitter data into a representation of interactions. These social interaction representations take the form of social networks around four key affordances: one each for direct mentions, retweets, devices and hashtags. These representations surface the social structure that is implicit in tweets containing traces of these user affordances, and transform them into easily analyzable node pairs in a table. This aspect of Twitter Zombie further enables statistical analysis of Twitter metadata with relative ease. Direct mentions and retweets are stored as node pairs of individual Twitter users in the analysis tables. Device information and hashtags are stored as bipartite networks, where one node type is a person, and the other is a device type or hashtag respectively.

4.2 Analysis of Socially Transformed Tweets

Our extraction of social metadata from the tweet string enables Twitter Zombie to swiftly visualize social and device information about Twitter activity related to planned and unplanned events that emerge in the Twittersphere. To illustrate the utility of this aspect of the Twitter Zombie Architecture, we conducted a pilot study, which we describe in following section.

5. PILOT STUDY

We utilized the Twitter Zombie Collection Architecture and methodological approach to study Twitter activity around the US Republican Party Presidential Primary Debate in South Carolina on January 16th, 2012. In an effort to focus our collection efforts only on data related to that specific debate we collected Twitter messages that contained the hashtag #SCDebate. In addition to that hashtag, the debate sponsor, FOX News, encouraged individuals to tweet the candidate's name along with the hashtag #answer or #dodge when a question was asked to identify whether the public believed that the candidate was providing an answer to the question or dodging the question. In order to facilitate this activity, FOX News created a page on their website where individuals were able to use a button specifically created to facilitate the tweeting of #answer and #dodge. The following findings illustrate the presence of different types of communication networks and the adoption of specific technological applications for different purposes.

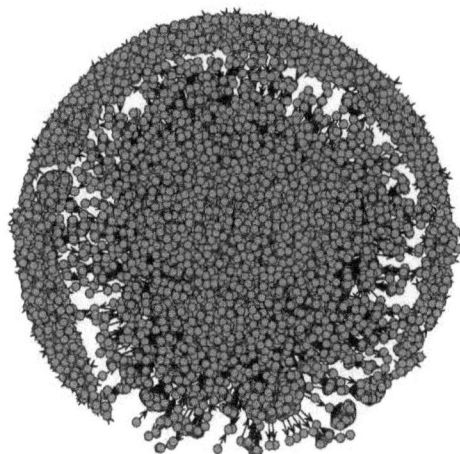

Figure 8 - Reply To Network

The methodological approach explained earlier in this article allowed us to identify several interesting characteristics of the public Twitter behavior surrounding the debate. Utilizing the #scdebate collection we are able to analyze reply-to and retweet networks to illustrate two distinctly different behaviors. Figure 2 illustrates the diffuse network of reply-to behavior in the #scdebate data. We see that there are a lot of disconnected groups of discourse indicative of an unstructured set of Tweets directed towards other individuals.

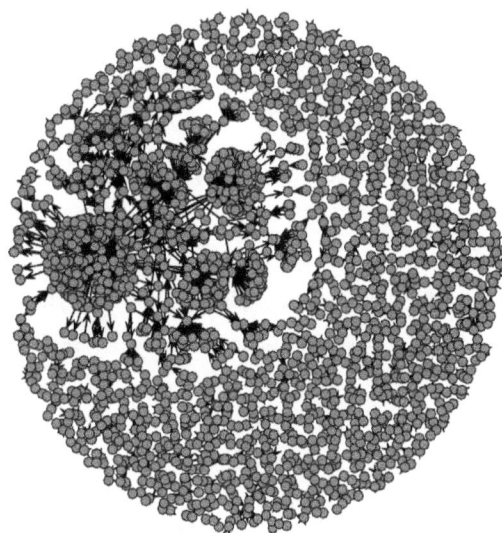

Figure 9 - Retweet Network

On the other hand, we see in the retweet network (Figure 3) that there is a significant amount of disconnected retweet behavior similar to the reply to network, but we also identify a set of clusters that illustrate concentrated retweet behavior. The most retweeted individuals are: BorowitzReport, TheFix, BretBaier and washingtonpost. These accounts all represent journalistic entities tweeting about the debate, with BretBaier being the moderator. The below distribution of devices that are used to tweet in our dataset illustrates that the "web" was the most popular mechanism for tweeting followed by Tweetdeck for the hashtag #scdebate.

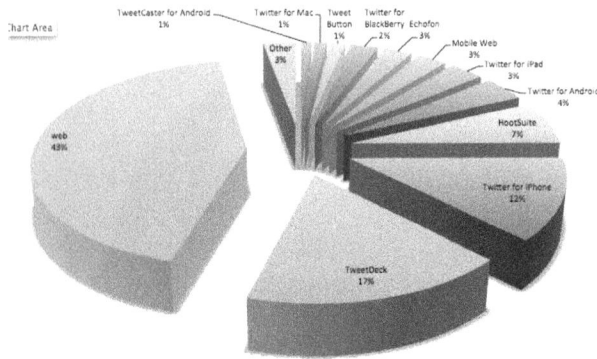

Figure 10 - #SCDebate Device Distribution

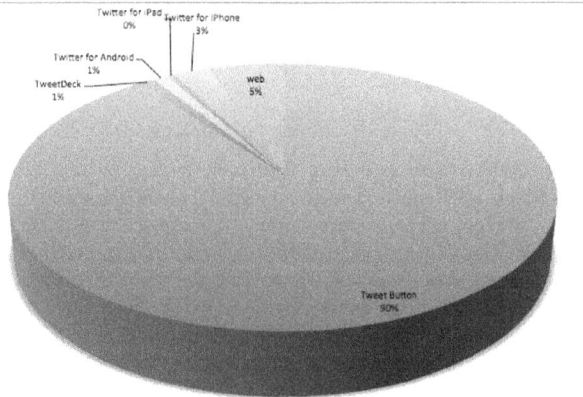

Figure 11 - #answer device distribution

In our second stage of analysis we examined the dataset of collected tweets using #answer and #dodge. The hashtags #answer and #dodge did not need to be tweeted with #scdebate indicating that there did not need to be overlap between the two datasets. The device distribution of #answer and #dodge is quite different from that of #scdebate. Figure five illustrates the device uses for the #answer button.

Figure six illustrates the device usage for the #dodge button. You can see that 90% of people answering, "answer" used the Fox News web page, while 85% of people saying "dodge" did. .

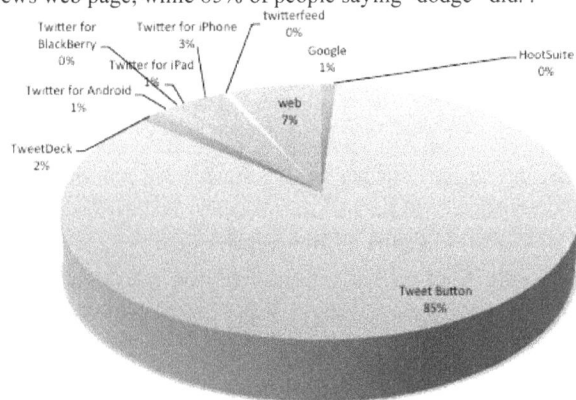

Figure 12 - #dodge device distribution

The Tweet Button on the http://www.foxnews.com website was the most dominant technique for tweeting using those hashtags. The contrast in device distribution between the dataset of #scdebate and #answer and #dodge identified two distinct areas of discourse that warranted deeper analysis of the individual activity

within each dataset to highlight the differences of the behavior related to one event using different hashtags.

Table one, below, illustrates the number of unique participants relative to the number of tweets. The lower the percentage, the higher number the number of repeat participants. Based on the statistics, individuals using #answer and #dodge posted more times than those that used #scdebate. This is indicative of the more focused purpose of the #answer and #dodge hashtags, relative to the more general discourse happening with the #scdebate hashtag. This higher level of repeat participation could also be a result of a concentrated technological mechanism to utilize those hashtags such as the Fox News website.

Table 2- Hashtags in South Carolina Debate

Hashtag	Percent of Unique Tweeters
Answer	32.63%
Dodge	29.93%
SCDebate	55.02%

We wanted to extend this line of inquiry further and understand the participation rates between the #answer and #dodge hashtags. Our findings indicate that close to 37% of the individuals posted a tweet using both #answer and #dodge. This demonstrates that some participants were interested in participating in discourse relative to candidates using both #answer and #dodge, but that close to 63% of the total participants only participated using either #Answer or #Dodge.

In an effort to identify if there were distinct discourse communities we compared the user composition of the two datasets (#scdebate versus #answer and #dodge). We treated the individuals that contributed using #scdebate as one dataset and individuals using either #answer or #dodge as the other dataset. Our analysis identified that only **13%** of the individuals that used the #SCDebate hashtag participated in the #Answer vs. #Dodge exercise.

This low percentage of participation in both the general discourse and the #Answer versus #Dodge exercise illustrates that there were two different discourse communities active on Twitter, participating in social media in relation to the January 16th debate. This distinction is illustrated by the differences in device utilization as well as the differences in user overlap across the two distinct hashtag sets.

Our pilot study illustrates the power of the Twitter Zombie toolset for providing rapid, consistent analysis of planned and unplanned events as represented through Twitter discourse. The architecture, social transformation and analysis software system developed here helps to close an important gap of consistency and transparency in social media research.

6. DISCUSSION
Twitter is participatory mass media. Our architecture and methodological approach paves the way for other researchers to examine emergent, social phenomena on Twitter. We enable this continued inquiry with a tool called Twitter Zombie, which gives social media researchers, like other social science researchers before us, a transparent framework for data gathering, analysis and reporting. As Howison et al point out [23], electronic trace data is not representative of social interaction, even though people are responsible for its creation. How people interact through a particular socio-technical milieu of tools, affordances and

practices is different in each instance. Our validation of the results of using our tool shows that differences and assumptions about data returned must be carefully and regularly examined. We do not know if our findings with relation to the Twitter API are a result of shifts in the API over time, or shortcomings in the methods of other researchers or, plausibly, us. The inability of the social media research community to speak with authority about these kinds of data completeness and quality issues is at once expected at the dawn of a research era, where we are now, but is also essential to address in order to ensure increasingly useful, valid and relevant results for society. Our demonstration of the use of the Twitter Zombie in a pilot study illustrates how powerful validated tools can be.

Some elements of research method complexity are specific to the social media platform. In the case of Twitter, the selection of API is demonstrated here to play a significant role in filtering data. For the social science researcher these choices, like decisions of methodological approaches such as survey sampling, ethnography site selection or theory for classic social science researchers, will influence the resulting findings and ensuing development of theory.

When a phenomenon is new, as social media has been for the past decade, inductive research methods are called for to define the salient constructs for future inquiry. In the case of social media research, which often includes the examination of electronic trace data, and other quantitative methods of inquiry, the road map for inductive research is ill defined from prior phenomena. We are now moving into an era where key constructs, like the socio-technical interaction, the technical interaction and others, are clearly defined by prior literature. We are also entering an era where we can look back on a decade of research on social media in general, and six years of research on Twitter, to discern the inconsistencies in our approaches. These inconsistencies, while expected as inquiry begins, are important to iron out as inquiry advances.

We do not claim to have built the ultimate, or even the penultimate data collection, transformation and analysis software system and methodological approach for Twitter research. Instead, we put forth this example as a reference for other researchers to use. The work presented here should inspire critique from over 100 researchers whose work we build on, but upon whom we also call to advance the field.

7. CONCLUSION
We make our collection, transformation and analytical processes for Twitter available for scrutiny and use by other researchers[2]. Our hope is that the social media research community, as a whole, will rise up to the challenge of building corpora of comparative studies looking at social computational phenomena across the Twittersphere. Through this approach, our findings will grow, theory will emerge and our contribution to an increasingly technologically mediated world will possibly find easier translation.

8. ACKNOWLEDGMENTS
We would like to thank Leysia Palen for her assistance in understanding the challenges associated with data collection and management in Twitter research. Thanks to Nora McDonald for providing numerous reviews of this paper's drafts. We also thank Scott Robertson and Ravi Vatripu for their insights on data collection and management in social media research.

9. REFERENCES
[1] Akcora, C. G., Bayir, M. A., Demirbas, M., and Ferhatosmanoglu, H. 2010. Identifying Breakpoints in Public Opinion. Workshop on Social Media Analytics.

[2] Bae, Y. and Lee, H. 2011. A Sentiment Analysis of Audiences on Twitter: Who is the Positive or Negative Audience of Popular Twitterers. ICHIT 2011. 732-739.

[3] Bakshy, E., Hofman, J. M., Mason, W. A., and Watts, D. J. 2011. Everyone's an Influencer: Quantifying Influence on Twitter. WSDM.

[4] Barbosa, L. and Feng, J. 2010. Robust Sentiment Detection on Twitter from Biased and Noisy Data. International Conference on Computational Linguistics. 36-44.

[5] Bermingham, A. and Smeaton, A. 2010. Classifying Sentiment in Microblogs: Is Brevity an Advantage? CIKM. 2010.

[6] Bigonha, C. A. S., Cardoso, T. N. C., Moro, M. M., Almeida, V. A. F., and Goncalves, M. A. 2010. Detecting Evangelists and Detractors on Twitter. Brazilian Symposium on Multimedia and the Web (WebMedia).

[7] Bollen, J., Mao, H., and Zeng, X. 2011. Twitter mood predicts the stock market. Journal of Computational Science. 2, 2011, 1-8.

[8] boyd, d., Golder, S., and Lotan, G. 2010. Tweet, Tweet, Retweet: Conversational Aspects of Retweeting on Twitter. Hawaii International Conference on System Sciences. 43.

[9] Cha, M., Haddadi, H., Benevenuto, F., and Gummadi, K. P. 2010. Measuring User Influence in Twitter: The Million Follower Fallacy. ICWSM. 4th.

[10] Chew, C. and Eysenbach, G. 2010. Pandemics in the Age of Twitter: Content Analysis of Tweets during the 2009 H1N1 Outbreak. PLoS One. 5, 11.

[11] Conover, M. D., Ratkiewicz, J., Francisco, M., Goncalves, B., Flammini, A., and Menczer, F. 2011. Political Polarization on Twitter. ICWSM. 5th.

[12] Culotta, A. 2010. Towards detecting influenza epidemics by analyzing Twitter messages. Workshop on Social Media Analytics. 1st.

[13] Diakopoulos, N. A. and Shamma, D. A. 2010. Characterizing Debate Performance via Aggregated Twitter Seniment. CHI.

[14] Fonseca, A. 2011. Modeling Political Opinion Dynamics Through Social media and Multi-Agent Simulation. First Doctoral Workshop for Complexity Sciences.

[15] Gentry, J. 2012. twitteR package for R.

[16] Golbeck, J., Grimes, J. M., and Rogers, A. 2010. Twitter Use by the U.S. Congress. Journal of American Society for Information Science. 61, 8, 1612-1621.

[17] Gruzd, A., Doiron, S., and Mai, P. 2011. Is Happiness Contagious Online? A Case of Twitter and the 2010 Winter Olympics. Hawaii International Conference on System Sciences. 44th.

---

[2] link included in final version (blind review omitted)

[18] Guerra, P. H. C., Veloso, A., Meira, W., and Almeida, V. 2011. From Bias to Opinion: a Transfer-Learning Approach to Real-Time Sentiment Analysis. KDD. 2011.

[19] Hanna, A., Sayre, B., Bode, L., Yang, J., and Shah, D. 2011. Mapping the Political Twitterverse: Candidates and Their Followers in the Midterms. ICWSM. 2011.

[20] Hansen, D., Schneiderman, B., and Smith, M. A. 2011 Analyzing Social Media Networks with NodeXL. Elsevier.

[21] Heverin, T. and Zach, L. 2011. Use of Microblogging for Collective Sense-Making During Violent Crises: A Study of Three Campus Shootings. Journal of American Society for Information Science. 10.1002/asi.21685.

[22] Honeycutt, C. and Herring, S. C. 2009. Beyond Microblogging: Conversation and Collaboration via Twitter. Hawaii International Conference on System Sciences. 43.

[23] Howison, J., Wiggins, A., and Crowston, K. 2012. Validity Issues in the Use of Social Network Analysis for the Study of Online Communities. Journal of the Association of Information Systems. 12, 2.

[24] Huang, J., Thornton, K. M., and Efthimiadis, E. 2010. Conversational Tagging in Twitter. HT.

[25] Hughes, A. L. and Palen, L. 2009. Twitter Adoption and Use in Mass Convergence and Emergency Events. ISCRAM. 6th.

[26] Java, A., Song, X., Finin, T., and Tseng, B. 2007. Why We Twitter: Understanding Microblogging Usage and Communities. WEBKDD/SNA-KDD Workshop.

[27] Jurgens, P., Jungherr, A., and Schoen, H. 2011. Small Worlds with a Difference: New Gatekeepers and the Filtering of Political Information on Twitter. WebSci.

[28] Kim, M. and Park, H. W. 2012. Measuring Twitter-Based political participation and deliberation in the South Korean context by using social network and Triple Helix indicators. Scientometrics. 90, 1.

[29] Krishnamurthy, B., Gill, P., and Arlitt, M. 2008. A Few Chirps about Twitter. WOSN.

[30] Kwak, H., Lee, C., Park, H., and Moon, S. 2010. What is Twitter, a Social Network or a News Media? WWW.

[31] Lerman, K. and Ghosh, R. 2010. Information Contagion: An Empirical Study of the Spread of News on Digg and Twitter Social Networks. ICWSM. 4th.

[32] Livne, A., Simmons, M. P., Adar, E., and Adamic, L. A. 2011. The Party is Over Here: Structure and Content in the 2010 Election. ICWSM. 5th.

[33] Marwick, A. E. and boyd, d. 2011. I tweet honestly, I tweet passionately: Twitter users, context collapse, and the imagined audience. New Media Society. 13.

[34] Meador, C. and Gluck, J. 2009. Analyzing the Relationship Between Tweets, Box-Office Performance and Stocks. Methods.

[35] Metaxas, P. T., Mustafaraj, E., and Gayo-Avello, D. 2011. How (Not) To Predict Elections. International Conference on Social Computing. 165-171.

[36] Murthy, D., Gross, A., and Oliveira, D. 2011. Understanding Cancer-based Networks in Twitter using Social Network Analysis. IEEE International Conference on Semantic Computing. 5th.

[37] Mustafaraj, E., Finn, S., Whitlock, C., and Metaxas, P. T. 2011. Vocal Minority versus Silent Majority: Discovering the Opinions of the Long Tail. International Conference on Social Computing.

[38] Mustafaraj, E. and Metaxas, P. T. 2011. What Edited Retweets Reveal about Online Political Discourse. Workshop on Analyzing Microtext.

[39] Naaman, M., Becker, H., and Gravano, L. 2011. Hip and Trendy: Characterizing Emerging Trends on Twitter. Journal of American Society for Information Science. 62, 5, 902-918.

[40] Pole, A. and Xenos, M. 2011. Like, Comments and Retweets: Facebooking and Tweeting on the 2010 Gubernatorial Campaign Trail. State Politics and Policy Conference. 11th.

[41] Quercia, D., Ellis, J., Capra, L., and Crowcroft, J. 2012. Tracking "Gross Community Happiness" from Tweets. CSCW.

[42] Romero, D. M., Meeder, B., and Kleinberg, J. 2011. Differences in the Mechanics of Information Diffusion Across Topics: Idioms, Political Hashtags, and Complex Contation on Twitter. WWW.

[43] Starbird, K., Palen, L., Hughes, A. L., and Vieweg, S. 2010. Chatter on The Red: What Hazards Threat Reveals about the Social Life of Microblogged Information. CSCW.

[44] Sutton, J., Palen, L., and Shklovski, I. 2008. Backchannels on the front lines: Emergent use of social media in the 2007 Southern California fire. Information Systems for Crisis Response and Management Conference.

[45] Tumasjan, A., Sprenger, T. O., Sandner, P. G., and Welpe, I. M. 2010. Predicting Elections with Twitter: What 140 Characters Reveal about Political Sentiment. ICWSM. 4th.

[46] Werry, C. C. 1996 Linguistic and interactional features of Internet Relay Chat. In Computer-mediated communication: Linguistic, social and cross-cultural perspectives, S. C. Herring,Ed John Benjamins.

[47] Williams, C. and Gulati, G. J. 2008. What is a Social Network Worth? Facebook and Vote Share in the 2008 Presidential Primaries. American Political Science Association.

[48] Wohn, D. Y. and Na, E. K. 2011. Tweeting about TV: Sharing television viewing experiences via social media message streams. First Monday. 16, 3.

[49] Zelenkauskaite, A. and Herring, S. C. 2008. Television-mediated conversation: Coherence in Italian iTV SMS Chat. Hawaii International Conference on System Sciences. 41.

[50] Zhao, S., Zhong, L., Wickramasuriya, J., and Vasudevan, V. 2011. Human as Real-Time Sensors of Social and Physical Events: A Case Study of Twitter and Sports Games. rxiv preprint arXiv:1106.4300.

Towards an Understanding of Social Inference Opportunities in Social Computing

Julia M. Mayer, Richard P. Schuler, Quentin Jones
New Jersey Institute of Technology, USA
jam45, rps22 @njit.edu and qgjones@acm.org

ABSTRACT

Social computing applications are transforming the way we make new social ties, work, learn and play, thus becoming an essential part our social fabric. As a result, people and systems routinely make inferences about people's personal information based on their disclosed personal information. Despite the significance of this phenomenon the opportunity to make social inferences about users and how this process can be managed is poorly understood. In this paper we 1) outline why social inferences are important to study in the context of social computing applications, 2) how we can model, understand and predict social inference opportunities 3) highlight the need for social inference management systems, and 4) discuss the design space and associated research challenges. Collectively, this paper provides the first systematic overview for social inference research in the area of social computing.

Categories and Subject Descriptors

H.1.2 [Information Systems]: User/Machine Systems

General Terms

Human Factors, Design, Theory

Keywords

Social inference, social computing, impression management, privacy, personalization

1. INTRODUCTION

Social computing applications connect users to each other to support interpersonal communication (e.g. Instant Messaging), social networking (e.g. Facebook) and the sharing of user-generated content (e.g. YouTube). These applications are transforming the way we make new social ties, work, learn and play, thus becoming an essential part our social fabric. Everyday use of social computing applications, such as posting on a Facebook wall, checking-in to a location, uploading a picture, or liking or sharing a website, generates an enormous amount of personal data. The richness and widespread availability of this data enables *social inferences* about user preferences, identity, location, and private user information. Such *social inferences* are an emergent form of social computing that can occur when unrevealed personal user information, e.g., identity, location, user preferences, or profile information, is correctly inferred from revealed information in combination with *background knowledge*. We define *background knowledge* as information that has not

been provided by the user or revealed by a social computing system and is available from other sources.

The following scenarios illustrate the ubiquity, versatility and the basic dynamics of social inferences in social computing:

Scenario 1: Susan met this cute guy on a party last weekend, Josh. When Josh adds her on Facebook the next day, she's excited and studies his profile. He has tons of friends, lots of cool pictures and she finds out that he likes the same music as her. She doesn't have a lot of private info on her Facebook profile because she has some privacy concerns. However, she now quickly adds some of her favorite bands to her profile, hoping he will infer that they have a similar music taste. Later that day, Josh, who also enjoyed meeting Susan, curiously looks over Susan's profile. Seeing that they have several favorite bands in common, confirms his plan of meeting her again because he infers she must have a good music taste which is important to him. He knows that one of the bands they both like will play in town soon so he invites her to come with him.

Scenario 2: Greg started using a mobile dating app. One day, his phone vibrates and says 'somebody nearby wants to meet you'. He is just having coffee at Starbucks so he looks around to see what girls are nearby with a phone in their hand. There are several, however, only one is staring right back at him. She must have observed him pulling out his phone and then scanning his surroundings. He feels uncomfortable because the girl is not really his type. He looks away, gets up and quickly leaves. He tells himself to uninstall the app later.

Scenario 3: Susan told her friend Lily that she can't help her with this class project because she needs to visit her grandma in Delaware over the weekend and she won't have internet there. However, when Lily checks Facebook she sees in the Ticker that Susan just liked a recipe at the food network's website. Since Lilly knows that Susan does not have a smartphone, she infers that Susan must be online on her desktop having lied about the grandma visit or the internet problem there because she didn't want to help her.

Scenario 4: Maggie's boyfriends just broke up with her and she is indignant. She assumes that he cheated on her but she wants to know for sure. Since he won't admit it to her she decides to try to get into his email account. She does not know his password but the system prompts her to answer two security questions that will reset the password. She can easily answer the question about her boyfriend's first pet since he posted a photo of his beloved dog on Facebook labeling it with "Charley" and she knows his mother's maiden name. After resetting his password she reads his emails finding out that he has been cheating on her for weeks.

Scenario 5: *Joe the robber is specialized in what he calls 'social media robberies'. His newest line of attack is looking at public location logs of Twitter and Foursquare users in his city and searching for people who go on vacation and inferring their home address from their check-ins. This works pretty well. Just last week he captured a lot of booty when he figured that the Smiths are gone for two weeks because they tweeted that they are excited for their vacation to Mexico and regularly checked-in to a location called "home" before.*

Scenario 6: *Greg travels a lot for work. To meet interesting people during his travels, he uses a location-based social matching system. One day he's walking down the street in Tokyo when his phone vibrates and tells him there is somebody nearby who went to the same college as him. He never entered in his matching preferences that he'd be interested in people from his college. However, the phone infers from his unusual context that now this might be interesting to Greg. Since Greg is alone in Japan, he is up for meeting another student from his US College so he starts chatting with him.*

These scenarios illustrate how the increasing use and sophistication of social computing applications and their related technologies has significantly increased the opportunities for social inferences. Motahari et al. [19] found that people often make both incorrect guesses and social inferences about other users based on their social networking profiles. However, at the same time people are very poor judges of the ability of other users and software systems to make inferences about them [22].

Unfortunately, current social computing system designs do not adequately take into account the potential for social inferences and do not provide users the tools necessary to manage them. When users of social computing applications provide or share personal information through the system (e.g. their interests, demographics, a picture, or their location), they are not informed about how their decision to reveal this information may impact potential social inferences. As a result, users of social computing applications have a limited understanding of the implications of their personal information sharing decisions.

In order to gain a solid understanding of social inferences and their impact on social computing system design we believe that extensive research into the different components of social inferences and the dynamics of social inference opportunities is necessary. Unfortunately, the underlying logic, namely that *background knowledge* when combined with *revealed user information* can lead to a *social inference opportunity* (Figure 1), has not been examined and researched systematically.

Figure 1. Underlying Logic of Social Inference Opportunities

To support the exploration of this problem we introduce a model outlining and linking the various components of social inferences. The understanding of these components and how they relate to each other will aid in effective social inference management system design and building. We pose the following questions in order to structure the discussion of our social inference model:

1. Why are social inferences important to study in the context of social computing systems?

2. How can we model, understand and predict social inference opportunities?

3. How can we design and develop social inference management systems that inform users about potential social inferences and allow them to regulate them?

Collectively, this paper provides the first holistic overview of the social inference phenomenon in social computing systems and lays out future direction for researchers.

The remainder of this paper is organized as follows. In the next section we provide an overview of the diverse aspects of social computing in which social inferences occur and explain the basic dynamics of social inferences. In section 3 we present four different social inference modeling approaches that can be used to identify social inference opportunities. Section 4 highlights the need for tools that raise awareness and allow users to control social inference opportunities. In section 5 we discuss open research challenges related with the principled design of social inference management systems. Section 6 concludes.

2. SOCIAL INFERENCES IN SOCIAL COMPUTING

Although there has been relatively little research into the social inference phenomenon in social computing systems, some other fields have explored the inference problem. The problem of inferences is well known to database researchers [8, 23, 24, 40]. A typical example comes from the database privacy literature [5]: the relation <Name, Salary> is a secret, but user *u* may request the following two queries: "List the *rank* and *salary* of all employees" and "List the *name* and *rank* of all employees." None of the queries contain the secured <Name, Salary> pair; however, an individual may utilize the known information <Rank, Salary> and <Rank, Name> to infer the private <Name, Salary> information through deductive reasoning. For example, the knowledge that Bob is a manager and all managers earn $x, can help one deduce that Bob earns $x. This problem is known as *data re-identification* [31], the process of linking datasets without explicit identifiers such as name and address to datasets with explicit identifiers through common attributes. Another example is the linkage of hospital discharge data to voter registration lists that allows sensitive medical information to be inferred [32]. Considerable work has been undertaken exploring the general inference problem as a security threat to databases [8] and as a privacy risk in data mining [23, 24, 40]. *K-anonymity* [31], a method widely used in the database and privacy domain to detect and prevent such inferences about private user information works on the principle that "data is safe to release if at least k entities share the same attributes".

However, social inferences in social computing systems are very different in nature than inference problems that typically arise in the database and data mining domains (as seen from the example scenarios above). This is because both the inferred personal user information, as well as background knowledge used to make an inference may not be stored in the application database. Some examples of inferable information are users' identity at physical appearance granularity (seeing the only person with a phone nearby - scenario 2) and users' activity and location (tweets about an upcoming vacation in Mexico - scenario 5). Furthermore, the availability of revealed user information and background knowledge is extremely dynamic in nature, especially in mobile social application, since it can be based on the user's context, such as time and location. Social inferences are also not only a privacy-risk but also have the potential to be beneficial and actively desired by the user (to impress or to receive valuable recommendations - scenario 1 and 6).

Social inference can affect very diverse aspects of social computing. Until now, inferences were only studied for certain and very limited contexts (e.g., as threat to database security). However, it is important to understand that social inferences occur across various areas of social computing and may have very different implications. Social inferences in social computing 1) can help users to manage their online impressions (*impression management*), 2) may lead to privacy invasions and loss of anonymity (*user-privacy and security),* and 3) can help to receive personalized social recommendations (*system personalization*). These three aspects of social computing affected by social inferences are illustrated in the sub-sections below.

2.1   Impression Management

According to Goffman [12], people routinely manage impressions through varying self-presentations depending on the social setting and audience. Social inferences usually occur in this context because impressions are formed both based on explicitly revealed personal information as well as unrevealed but inferred information. Similarly, users of social computing systems, particularly social networking sites (SNS), consciously or unconsciously attempt to influence the perceptions other people have about them by regulating and controlling the personal information they share [12] (see scenario 1). For example, an important part of the value proposition of business-oriented Social Networking Sites (SNS) such as LinkedIn comes from the social inferences they enable about members. Users often make inferences about other members' skills and business networks based on fairly limited user-profile information and weak-tie relationships. Social inferences about the extent of an individual's expertise made from information provided through LinkedIn could be used to find worthwhile employees.

However, while users routinely rely on social inferences made about them when presenting themselves on SNS these systems do not provide users a method to understand what others might be able to infer from their profile information. Thus, to effectively aid impression management users require methods to go beyond traditional profile management and enable them to perform what we call 'social inference management'.

2.2   User-Privacy and Security

Due to the growing ubiquity of social computing and the manner in which people use them and in turn how those systems collect and share information raise pertinent privacy and security concerns.

Social inferences can potentially lead to unwanted disclosure of personal user information, for example, a user's identity or location. This is illustrated by the following actual incident [29]. During the deployment of CampusWiki, a location-aware application that allows users to create and edit location-linked content which can be anonymous or identified, a student anonymously added unpleasant comments about a course professor. The professor was able to utilize the time-location stamps of page edits to determine that the comments were made during his class period and near the classroom. He then proceeded to monitor laptop use by students during the class in question, and was then able to determine the student responsible for the comments. The result was a confrontation, which lead to the student dropping the course. In this case a user's expected privacy was violated due to a social inference.

A simple, yet to-the-point definition of privacy is "a person's right to control access to his or her personal information" [3], i.e., the expectation that others will not know and cannot find out what they wish to keep secret. In other words, a person should have the ability to exclude others from accessing individuals' personal information and to determine when, how, and to what extent he or she will release personal information. Anonymity preservation, to be unidentifiable among a certain number of other people [22], also is an important aspect of privacy.

While privacy is well researched in the literature, there has been scant research on the social inference problem as threat to user privacy in social computing communities. Motahari et al. [20, 21, 22] investigated identity inferences in open partially anonymous computer-mediated communication (CMC) used to support interaction between partially or fully anonymous individuals and found that users were able to make social inferences about their chat partners' identity while they assumed to be anonymous. Users of social computing applications often engage in conversations (chats) where they want to stay anonymous, e.g., initial conversations on social matching / dating sites, private messages with an unknown member on Twitter, online forums, Chat roulette, or in massively multi-player online games (MMOG). Here, information disclosed during the conversation may allow for identity inferences while users still assume to be anonymous.

User-location is increasingly popular information item collected and shared via social computing applications (e.g., location-based social networks like Foursquare). Motahari et al. [22] also investigated anonymity and identity inferences in proximity-based social applications and found that disclosure of location and patterns of co-location often lead to social inferences about users' identity (see scenario 2). A study by Krumm [16] showed that the location of a user's home and his/her identity can be computed only using pseudonymous GPS data, simple algorithms and a free Web service. An official warning by the United States Military was given due to the risks posed by geotagging, adding a geographical metadata to a picture and uploading it to a social computing application [26]. This could potentially allow inferences about the exact location of a soldier by an enemy allowing for an attack. This risk can basically be extended to anyone who uploads geotagged pictures to social computing applications. A factor mediating this risk is having hundreds of 'friends' that may have never been met in person. From tagged locations like the frequently visited restaurants, the gym visited everyday and the street living in, these 'friends' (that are actually strangers) can infer routines and habits. This way, social inferences may also enable stalking. For example, a college student's SNS profile including information about residence location, class schedule, and location of last login may help a potential stalker to determine the user's whereabouts [13]. PleaseRobMe [11] is a website that aims at raising awareness about oversharing, particularly how users of location-based services make themselves vulnerable to housebreaking by checking-in to locations online (see scenario 5).

A possible consequence of identity inferences is identity theft. Making birth date, hometown, current residence, and current phone number publicly available at the same time can be used to estimate a person's social security number and exposes her to identity theft. Since a vast majority of Facebook profiles not only include birthday and hometown information, but also current phone number and residence (often used for verification purposes by financial institutions and other credit agencies), users are exposing themselves to substantial risks of identity theft. Passwords and answers to security questions may also be jeopardized as a result of a social inference. Users often select passwords that have a personal meaning for them as they are easy to remember [28, 17, 37] (e.g. name of a favorite pet, birth date, social security number) that may be able to be determined via a social inference. Furthermore, many systems insist on the use of security questions for lost or forgotten passwords intentionally based on potentially inferable personal information [28]. For example, typical security questions ask users about their home town, their mother's maiden name or their pet's name; information that is often publicly visible on social networks or through search engine results (see scenario 4). A very public and well known example of this problem is known as the "Palin Hack" [39]. During the 2008 United States presidential election campaign someone had obtained access to Sarah Palin's private email account and posted several screenshots of her emails in an online forum. The "Palin Hack" did not require any real skill, instead, the hacker simply reset Palin's password by answering the security questions on the account using her birth date, ZIP code and information about where she met her spouse - information that was easily obtained by a simple web search. This shows how answers to security questions are prone to be inferable from revealed personal information and by searching various sources for user attributes which may lead to security holes.

These diverse examples illustrate how social inferences can have significant implications on user-privacy. In order to effectively protect users' privacy in social computing, we need to understand and model social inference opportunities which in turn will allow us to build and develop social inference management systems.

2.3 System Personalization

Social inferences can also be valuable to the user for system personalization, specifically for recommendations. System personalization is usually based on explicit data such as interests or implicit data such as context of each individual user or user group [35]. With the exponential growth of available information on the Web, social inferences about user preferences can help to tackle the information overload problem by personalizing the systems appearance and behavior and recommending information that is relevant to the user.

Social computing systems often provide personalized services based on user profile information. Social inferences about user preferences that are not explicitly stated provide a sophisticated way to personalize recommendations. For example, personalized social recommendations can help users form new relationships by suggesting other individuals of interest (e.g., Facebook's and LinkedIn's "People You May Know") [35]. Social matching systems (e.g., dating sites like Match.com) typically base match recommendations on users' explicit matching-preferences and/or measures of the overall affinity between individuals.

Current personalized services often inadequately inform the user about the reasons for the personalized recommendations and do not provide adequate control over how recommendations are made. This may lead to frustrations and undesired recommendations when users do not agree with or understand the reasons for the system's personalization decisions (e.g., repeatedly being shown the hated ex-girlfriend as "people you may know"). Furthermore, this can potentially reveal information that invades users' privacy or leads to compromised security, for example when user-location is used for people recommendations and the system reveals the proximity between two users leading to an identity inference (see scenario 2).

Social inference about users' match preferences (e.g., interest in another student from the same U.S. college while traveling in Japan – scenario 6) can potentially yield to more desirable social match recommendations. Context (user location, activity, resources, etc.) is a helpful piece of information to allow for valuable social inferences in the area of mobile social matching. Mayer et al. [18] found that recommendations made based on user-context and contextual rarity of shared user attribute are more interesting to users. We need to gain a deeper understanding as to how social inferences can be used to personalize services in socially intelligent ways based on information such as user-context, as well as how users want them to be used for system personalization. Together with impression management and user-privacy, system personalization needs to be effectively managed by users by providing them with social inference management tools.

3. DYNAMICS OF SOCIAL INFERENCES

We define social inferences as inferences about personal user information (e.g. user preferences, identity, location, and profile information) that has not been explicitly revealed but can be inferred from revealed information in combination with background knowledge. The act of inferring always involves two entities: 1) an individual about whom something is inferred, i.e. the inferee, using his/her revealed personal information and 2) an inferring entity (an individual or system), i.e. the inferer, who combines this information with background knowledge to perform a social inference (see Figure 2). Figure 3 shows a more detailed version of the simple underlying logic of social inferences in Figure 1. It illustrates what different types of *background knowledge* can, when combined with *revealed user information*, lead to a *social inference opportunity*.

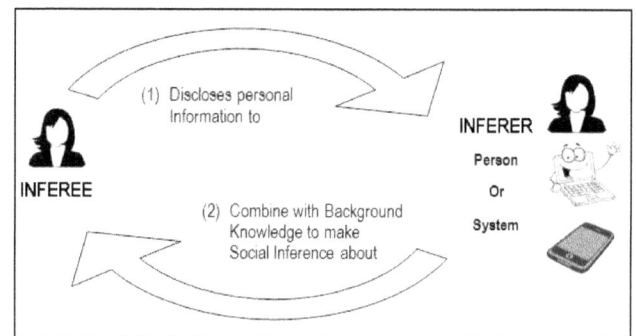

Figure 2. Dynamics of Social Inferences

Since the inferring entity can be a system or a user we differentiate between two different types of social inferences; those made by systems (*system-based social inferences*) and those made by people (*human social inferences*).

System-based social inferences can occur when a system combines its background information (implicitly collected, e.g., from internal user-profiling, web crawling, sensor data) with information explicitly disclosed by the user by applying heuristic rules. This is similar to the idea of emulating human reasoning to extend a system's knowledge base that is explored in the field of artificial intelligence and semantic web using methods like statistical inference (e.g. Bayesian inference [33]), or automated ontology construction [4]. In social computing, system-based social inferences about users' social matching preferences can be valuable for personalized social recommendations [18].

On the other hand, *human social inference* are inferences users of social computing systems can often perform when interpreting other users' revealed information. By combining personal background knowledge with what the system reveals about a user, an inferee might be able to infer unrevealed information, such as a user's nationality based on the user's name or hometown, a user's approximate age based on the graduation year, or the impression made based on personal pictures and status updates. Users can build up background knowledge in various ways over time, for example, through experience and learning, through observation, or a web search.

3.1 Revealed User Information

Revealed user information is the information a user explicitly discloses through a social computing system. This information can be static (e.g. user's demographics) or dynamic (e.g., user's location). For example, users disclose personal information, such as interests, hobbies or educational and professional information on SNS profiles like Facebook or LinkedIn. Behavioral information, such as user's activity and interactions could be revealed through status updates on Facebook or Twitter. Geotemporal information, such as a user's current location, is typically disclosed though check-ins (e.g. Foursquare, Facebook Places).

Today's social computing applications tend to promote and push users to share more and more personal information. The value of

social computing systems comes from sharing. Systems are designed in a way to get users create rich personal profiles disclosing increasing amounts of personal information and sharing it with the world.

3.2 Modeling the Social Inference Opportunity

A social inference opportunity exists if it is *logically possible* to make a social inference. We consider a social inference logically possible if unrevealed information can be deduced by analysis of a user's or system's background knowledge using the additional revealed information provided by the user.

The fact that a social inference is logically possible (a *social inference opportunity*) does not mean that a person or system will make a social inference. To calculate the probability that a social inference will actually occur, requires 1) knowing that an inference is logically possible, then 2) having a reliable estimate of (a) the number of potential inferers exposed to the revealed information, (b) the range of contexts in which the potential inferers are exposed to the revealed information and (c) the likelihood that for each '*potential inferrer-inference context*' an inference will actually be made. Clearly, it is considerably more difficult to determine the likelihood of a social inference than if a social inference opportunity exists. However, for system designers and CSCW researchers we do not believe that the initial focus of our efforts should be on assessing the social inference probability. The following analogy helps illustrate why this is the case: People routinely lock their cars in public parking even though on most occasions no individual will attempt to open the door to steal items inside. The decision to lock the doors can be based on the logical possibility of easy item theft, rather than the overall probability that somebody will walk past and try opening the car door in case it is unlocked and steal an item. Car designers do not worry about such probabilities; instead they provide drivers with the ability to know if they have controlled easy access – i.e. if they have locked the door. Similarly, we first need to provide users with an understanding of the social inference opportunities of various information sharing decisions. To achieve this end we need to be able to model the logical possibilities of social inferences.

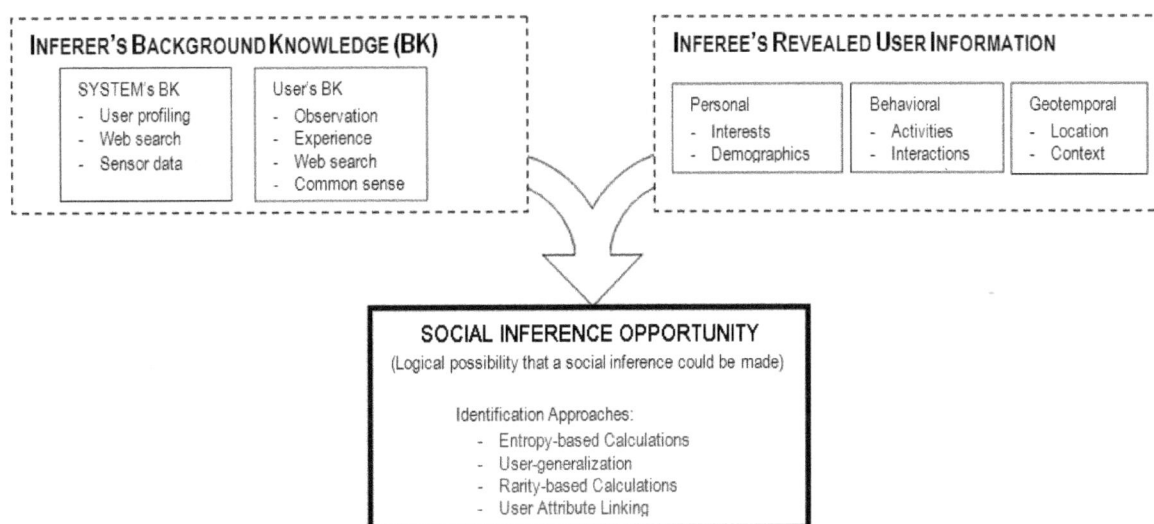

Figure 3. Modeling the Social Inference Opportunity

In following four subsections, we provide a brief overview of the approaches we are aware of for identifying social inference possibilities: 1) entropy calculations, 2) user-generalizations, 3) rarity calculations, and 4) user attribute-linking.

3.2.1   Entropy-based Calculations

The entropy approach is based on the following fact: as individuals or applications collect more information about a user, our uncertainty about other attributes, such as his/her identity, may be reduced, thus increasing the opportunity of a social inference. The following scenario from a user experiment of online chat between anonymous partners illustrates the social inference opportunity assessment framework [22].

> *Bob engages in an online chat with Alice. At the start of communication, Bob does not know anything about his chat partner. He is not told the name of the chat partner or anything else about her, so all users are equally likely to be his partner. After they start chatting, Alice's language and chat style help Bob guess her gender and that she is Hispanic. After a while, Alice reveals that she plays for the university's women's soccer team. Bob, who has prior knowledge of this soccer team, knows that it has only one Hispanic member. This allows Bob to then infer Alice's identity.*

Here, as Bob combines his background knowledge of the female Hispanic soccer players on campus with what Alice reveals, his uncertainty about his chat partner's identity decreases, thus increasing the opportunity of a social inference. This uncertainty can be measured by an *information entropy* calculation [30]. Information entropy, as used in information theory for telecommunications, is a measure of the decrease of uncertainty in a signal value at the receiver site. Here we use the fact that the more uncertain or random an event (outcome) is, the higher the *entropy* it possesses. If an event is very likely or very unlikely to happen, it will not be highly random and will have low entropy. Therefore, entropy is influenced by the probability of possible outcomes. It also depends on the number of possible events, because a greater number of possible outcomes make the result more uncertain. In our context the probability of an event is the probability that an attribute (such as a user's name) takes a specific value. As the inferrer collects more information, the number of entities that match her/his collected information decreases, resulting in fewer possible values for the attribute and lower information entropy.

The information entropy modeling approach was tested in two different areas of social computing: 1) for anonymous computer-mediated communication, through a laboratory chat experiment between unknown chat partners and 2) for proximity-based applications, through a mobile phone field study that explored patterns of co-location and anonymity of the subjects. In both studies, entropy-based inference modeling was the strongest predictor of social inference opportunities [20, 21, 22].

3.2.2   User-generalization

This approach is based on the following fact: Individuals or applications can derive general concepts from repeated experiences or observations and then apply these concepts to a certain user, allowing for a potential social inference. This is typically done by recommender systems that attempt to infer user preferences based on buying behavior and preferences of other users (e.g., someone buying several science fiction books must like other science fiction books because other users showed that same interest).

Furthermore, matchmaking systems are usually based on the concept of homophily, i.e., that people like people who are like them (similar demographics, interests, etc.). Currently, social matching systems calculate user affinities by weighting the similarities between users over a set of user attributes stored in the user profile. Standard user attributes include interests (hobbies, favorite music), social ties, demographics and personality. In order to find valuable social matches, rich user profiles are needed. The more information a system has about a user, the better it can compute social matches. Ideally, mobile social matching systems could improve matching by leveraging geo-temporal social data [18].

Generalizations about geo-temporal data can be used to make inferences about user's local context, for example, involvement in an activity based on location: Tony is at the gym, so he is probably working out [10, 15, 34]. Short-term and long-term trajectories, location logs, and geo-temporal patterns may also be used to infer user's interests from a user's frequently visited places (Susan regularly goes to the church; then she is Christian). Proximity patterns can be used to identify people who are nearby each other often but do not know each other yet [15].

3.2.3   Rarity-based Calculations

Potential social inferences can also be identified based on user attribute rarity. This is based on the following fact: the rarer an information item in the system is the more meaningful it is to the system, thus increasing the social inference opportunity. This is related to the concept of TF*IDF (term frequency-inverse document frequency) in data mining [25] which assumes that the frequency of a word in a document compared to the frequency of that word in the set of all documents is an indicator of the importance of that word.

The rarity-based approach was explored in the context of mobile social matching. Social matching systems are social recommender systems that help users to find other individuals of interest [35]. Traditional social matching systems calculate user affinities by weighting the similarities between users over a set of user attributes. Mobile social matching extends social matching to mobile devices by recommending people to people based on their current local context. It was found that in mobile social matching not only the similarity between two users is useful to determine the value of a match but also the rarity of this similarity in the user's current context [18]. *Contextual rarity* is a measure of how many other individuals have the same attribute in the user's social context. A generally common attribute can become 'contextually rare' in certain contexts. The scenario that follows illustrates this point:

> *Daniel is an undergraduate student in Information Systems at an American college. He uses a mobile social matching tool with social inference management technology. When on his campus, the system knows he is not interested in receiving recommendations to meet other students. On the other hand, during the summer Daniel goes as an exchange student to Italy. As the matching system recognizes the contextual rarity of being from his American college in Italy, the system is able to infer that a recommendation to meet another unknown exchange-*

student from his college who is in his vicinity when shopping in down-town Rome would be of value.

In the above example, the match relevance was inferred from the rarity of the particular context (it is really unusual for two students who do not know each other and are from the same American college to be in each other's vicinity in Italy). This scenario highlights how the rarity of a user attribute can lead to beneficial social inferences about users' match preferences. The prevalence of an attribute in a certain population, which might be the user's greater social environment or a particular current context, is calculated the following way: $P(a) = \frac{n_a}{N}$. The prevalence P of an attribute a equals the number of occurrences of attribute a divided by the size of the population N. Rarity is the inverse of the prevalence, i.e. attributes with a high prevalence are not rare (i.e., are common) but attributes with low prevalence are very rare. For example, rarity of being German at an American college equals the number of people at the American college divided by the number of Germans at this college.

The contextual rarity approach was tested using a personalized self-reported web survey exploring seven different affinity types (interests, needs, geographical background, educational background, distinct characteristics, places and friends) [18]. For each section respondents were instructed to enter three of their own user attributes. Then, for each attribute and the combination of all three in this section, they were asked two sets of questions: First, they had to rate the commonness of the attribute in different contexts (home, work, social circle, etc.) and second, they were asked about their level of interest in a potential match with same user attribute in different stationary, mobile, common and rare situations. The results of this survey study confirmed that people are generally more interested in matches based on rare user attributes. They also found that the relative contextual rarity can influence the desire for a social match [18].

We consider this relationship between contextual rarity and users' match preference as a social inference opportunity. Systems can potentially infer users' context-dependent match preferences using rarity calculations. However, this approach has not yet been implemented and we only have a limited understanding of the applicability and generalizability of this method to detect logical possibilities of a social inference.

3.2.4 User Attribute Linking
This approach is based on the following fact: individuals or applications can link together a number of isolated facts from various sources, thus leading to a potential social inference.

It has been shown previously that a large portion of the US population can be re-identified using a combination of 5-digit ZIP code, gender, and date of birth [32]. For example, information can be searched from several online sources. People routinely search what personal information about them or others are publicly available online, e.g. using search engines, to make potential social inferences. In addition to these easily accessible search results, there are other personal data publicly available that are not directly accessible through common search engines, e.g., intelius.com [14] to find somebody's age, zabasearch.com [38] to find an address or home phone number, or portals to public government data to find a state employee's salary [1]. Often times, inferees are not aware that this kind of information is publicly available, which could lead to potential social inference, for example about a user's password (see "Palin Hack" [39]).

User attribute linking can also be used for face re-identification by linking facial images from social networking profiles to other available facial images, e.g., from public websites. Gross and Acquisti [13] were able to correctly link facial images from Friendster profiles without explicit identifiers with images obtained from fully identified university web pages using a commercial face recognizer.

4. DESIGNING SOCIAL INFERENCE MANAGEMENT SYSTEMS
Current social computing systems do not consider social inference opportunities. They implement basic access control systems that provide users with an interface to directly control people's access to their information [7]. Social networking sides (SNS) usually provide users with profile management and privacy setting user interfaces (UIs) that allow them to manage revealed profile information. These are usually structured for the kind of data a user can enter (e.g. name, interests, contact information, demographics and a profile picture). Some social network systems (e.g., LinkedIn, Facebook) differentiate between a public profile (visible to everybody) and a private profile (visible only certain people in the social network systems, e.g. friends, contacts). For example, Facebook's privacy settings allow users to customize the visibility of each item on their profile for different friend lists, as does Google+ with the 'circles' feature. Similarly, various mobile location-aware applications such as Loopt allow users to set rules about their locatability in particular locations for particular people. Users are generally able to view how their profile is seen by other users based on the information explicitly disclosed.

However, users are often neither aware nor informed about the issue that personal information about them might be inferable. Simple access control systems and profile management UIs only allow users to see and control the information explicitly revealed about them but none of these systems consider and inform users about social inference opportunities. This shows that current simple rule-based approaches to privacy and security do not cope well with the dynamic and context-dependent nature of social inference opportunities.

Based on the highlighted issues, we propose social inference management systems that support users' awareness of social inference opportunities through UIs and visualizations and allow users to control them through management tools. These systems would ideally provide users with visualizations of social inferences opportunities in relation to:

1) Their digital self-presentation for *impression management*;

2) Resulting *privacy and security* implications of data sharing (e.g., level of anonymity in the current context);

3) Opportunities for *personalized recommendations* (e.g., inferred contextually rare match criterion used for personalized recommendation).

Unfortunately, there is a large gap in social computing research investigating system interfaces and mechanisms to manage social inferences. In order to build effective social inference management systems we believe that broad and extensive research efforts are necessary to study the social inference phenomenon across the different presented areas.

5. RESEARCH CHALLENGES

There are several research challenges associated with the principled design of social inference management systems. Based on the previous discussion we argue that current social computing system designs do not provide users with the proper methods to understand and manage social inferences. In order to transform our understanding of social inference opportunities in social computing and be able to design and build effective social inference management systems, we need to overcome research challenges in terms of:

1) Users' current understanding of inference opportunities, their risks and benefits;

2) How to model and reliably predict social inference opportunities; and

3) User-interface design alternatives and their likely effectiveness in various contexts.

We will discuss each of these challenges in more detail in the following three sub-sections.

5.1 User's Understanding of Inference Opportunities (Risks and Benefits)

In order to design social computing systems that incorporate social inference management, we first need to explore people's current understanding and perceptions of the social inference opportunities associated with the social computing applications they presently use. Research into users' awareness of social inference opportunities (to what extent people guess that systems or other users can infer private information about them), and what users perceive to be the implications of such opportunities (to what extent people perceive social inferences as negative, e.g., privacy invasion, or as beneficial, e.g., personalization), will inform us about how users currently experience social inferences in social computing systems. In particular we need to explore:

1) People's beliefs about other users' abilities to infer information about them via various apps they use as well as the various contexts of use;

2) What they want (and do not want) to be inferable about themselves from apps;

3) Their satisfaction and frustrations with personalization, recommendations and privacy settings of applications they use (e.g. adjusting the information shared based on location). How well do the applications infer needs, preferences and desires and give users control over these settings?

4) People's inferences about other users in order to identify possibly important components in our inference opportunity modeling;

5) Their preferences, from a privacy-point of view as well as from a system personalization-point of view.

Collectively, this will provide us with a better understanding of how social inferences are perceived by the broad user-community. This in turn will provide us with important insights into social inference management system design requirements.

5.2 Social Inference Opportunity Modeling

Social computing systems that incorporate social inference management must be able to effectively and efficiently model the logical possibility of social inferences. In order for systems to provide social inference based impression management, privacy and personalization we need to learn how to evaluate and compute potential social inference opportunities associated with user-information sharing in various contexts. We must also generate methods for understanding and evaluating the quality of social inference detection. To achieve this goal we need to thoroughly examine how to:

1) Quantify and model the background knowledge used by people to make social inferences in the domains of impression management, privacy and personalization;

2) Create and populate a world model that can be used to support the social inference management UIs; and

3) Assess and refine the entropy, rarity, user-generalizations, and user attribute-linking calculation techniques used to make social inferences.

To achieve this goal, profound studies examining users' ability to make inferences about others as well as to assess other users' ability to make inferences about them are necessary. Many of the social inference calculations require the accurate assessment of the probability/prevalence of an attribute occurring in a particular context; e.g., the chance of a student knowing another random student who is on campus and the chance that a student is coming from Germany and studying HCI. As a result, the world model needed will need to contain extremely detailed information. This could be achieved using commercial entities that have much of this data on hand (e.g. over 90% of current students have Facebook accounts) or using a software tool that enables the collection of rich social network data and in-depth information from a large number of individuals within short timeframes (e.g. [22]). It is important to gain knowledge of subject's social ties, to profile individual users and collect background knowledge of the social activities subjects engage in.

Based on that, research efforts need to further examine how social inferences can logically be predicted by combining revealed information with the data contained in the world model. The aim here should not be to create an ideal world model, but rather to learn about the requirements for effective modeling.

Data management and system building is another challenge that requires our attention. To model social inference opportunities, data could be pulled from the outside sources or it could be stored in massive internal databases. Furthermore, the computational models could be constructed internally or externally.

We have to explore advantages and disadvantages related to various options and create and evaluate IT artifacts that can help us gain deeper understanding about social inference opportunity modeling.

5.3 Social Inference Management User Interfaces

A third research challenge is to learn how visualizing social inferences opportunities can help users to: 1) learn about digital self-presentation for impression management; 2) estimate more accurately the privacy and security implications of data sharing; and 3) control personalization of various social software services. We need to develop theories and tools that allow for the principled design and development of social inference management systems by providing the user with the opportunity to learn about and control the social inference possibilities associated with their system use and personal data-sharing.

Basic design alternatives can include visualizations showing highlighted profile sections that could be inferred in addition to the user profile as seen by others, awareness displays [2, 6] that visualize the logical possibility of a social inference and visualizations that explain social inference opportunities to users in form of words, statistics, probabilities, etc., so users can learn and understand the process. Furthermore, different intervention mechanisms could be incorporated: Passive mechanisms could warn or alert the user about social inference opportunities when disclosing certain information without inhibiting the disclosure, while active mechanisms could blur the information, e.g. revealing the age bracket instead of date of birth or even blocking the information sharing. Automated mechanisms could allow users to set a certain required level of privacy and instruct the system to keep this level by prohibiting social inferences.

6. CONCLUSION

Social inferences are a ubiquitous yet under researched phenomenon in social computing systems. This current situation poses a serious challenge to the Group/CSCW research community since social inferences happen regularly, users and researchers lack awareness and understanding, current access control systems are far from sufficient in addressing this issue, and social inferences impact wide aspects of system use (impression management, user privacy and security, system personalization).

Therefore, the aim of this paper was to make the case for a focused effort to be made by the Group/CSCW community to understand and address these challenges. Much more remains to be done, however, our work shows that social inference opportunities can successfully be modeled and predicted, and shows that we can establish guidelines that will help designers make informed decisions when designing social computing systems that take social inference opportunities into account.

7. REFERENCES

[1] Asbury Park Press DataUniverse Portal to Public Government Data. Retrieved Nov 10, 2011. http://www.app.com/section/DATA

[2] Biskup, J. and Bonatti, P. 2004. Controlled query evaluation for enforcing confidentiality in complete information systems. *International Journal of Information Security, 3* (1), 14-27.

[3] Black, G., 2011. Publicity Rights and Image. *Oxford: Hart Publishing*, page 61-62

[4] Blaschke, C. and Valencia, A. 2002. Automatic ontology construction from the literature. *Genome Informatics Series.* 13201–213

[5] Brodsky, A., Farkas, C. and Jajodia, S. 2000. Secure databases: constraints, inference channels, and monitoring disclosures. *IEEE Transactions on Knowledge and Data Engineering, 2* (6), 900-919.

[6] Cadiz, J. J., Venolia G.D., Jancke G., Gupta A., 2002. Designing and deploying an information awareness interface. CSCW 2002: 314-323

[7] Crampton, J. and Khambhammettu, H. 2008. Delegation in role-based access control *International Journal of Information Security, 7* (2), 123-136.

[8] Cuppens, F. and Trouessin, G. 1994. Information Flow Controls vs Inference Controls: An Integrated Approach *Third European Symposium on Research in Computer Security* Springer Berlin / Heidelberg, 447-468.

[9] Dey A., Lederer S., Beckmann, C., Mankoff, J. 2003. Managing Personal Information Disclosure in Ubiquitous Computing Environments. *Technical Report CSD-03-1257.* UC Berkeley, Berkeley, CA, USA.

[10] Eagle, N., Pentland, A. 2006. Reality mining: sensing complex social systems, Personal and Ubiquitous Computing, v.10 n.4, p.255-268

[11] Fletcher, D. February 18, 2010. Please Rob Me: The Risks of Online Oversharing. Retrieved March 5, 2012. http://www.time.com/time/business/article/0,8599,1964873,00.html

[12] Goffmann E. 1059. The presentation of self in everyday life. New York, Anchor Books.

[13] Gross, R. and Acquisti, A. Information revelation and privacy in online social networks. In *Proceedings of the 2005 ACM workshop on Privacy in the electronic society* (2005). ACM, New York, NY, USA, 71-80.

[14] Intelius People Search. Retrieved Nov 10, 2011. http://www.intelius.com/

[15] Jones, Q. and Grandhi, S.A. P3 Systems: Putting the Place Back into Social Networks *IEEE Internet Computing*, 2005, 38-47.

[16] Krumm, J. 2007. Inference Attacks on Location Tracks. *Fifth International Conference on Pervasive Computing* (Toronto, Ontario, Canada, May 13- 16, 2007)

[17] Lennon, M. Oct 12, 2010. Survey Reveals How Stupid People are With Their Passwords. Retrieved Nov 10, 2011. http://www.securityweek.com/survey-reveals-how-stupid-people-are-their-passwords

[18] Mayer, J.M., Motahari, S., Schuler, R.P. and Jones, Q. 2010. Common attributes in an unusual context: predicting the desirability of a social match. In *Proceedings of the fourth ACM conference on Recommender systems*. ACM, New York, NY, USA, 337-340.

[19] Motahari, S., Manikopoulos, C., Hiltz, R. and Jones, Q. 2007. Seven privacy worries in ubiquitous social computing. In *ACM International Conference Proceeding Series; Proceedings of the 3rd symposium on Usable privacy and security*, 171-172.

[20] Motahari, S., Ziavras, S. and Jones, Q., 2009. Preventing Unwanted Social Inferences with Classification Tree Analysis. In *IEEE International Conference on Tools with Artificial Intelligence (IEEE ICTAI)*.

[21] Motahari, S., Ziavras, S., Naaman, M., Ismail, M. and Jones, Q. 2009. Social Inference Risk Modeling in Mobile and Social Applications *IEEE International Conference on Information Privacy, Security, Risk and Trust (PASSAT)*.

[22] Motahari, S., Ziavras, S., Schular, R. and Jones, Q. 2008. Identity Inference as a Privacy Risk in Computer-Mediated Communication. *IEEE Hawaii International Conference on System Sciences (HICSS-42)*, 1-10.

[23] Narayanan, A. and Shmatikov, V., 2005. Obfuscated Databases and Group Privacy. in *12th ACM conference on Computer and communications security*, 102-111.

[24] O'Leary, D.E. 1995. Some Privacy Issues in Knowledge Discovery: The OECD Personal Privacy Guidelines. *IEEE Expert: Intelligent Systems and Their Applications 10* (2), 48-52.

[25] Robertson, S. 2004. Understanding inverse document frequency: on theoretical arguments for IDF, *Journal of Documentation*. Vol. 60 Iss: 5, pp.503 – 520

[26] Rodewig, C. March 7, 2012. Geotagging poses security risks. Retrieved Macrh 10, 2012. *The Official Homepage of the United States Army.* http://www.army.mil/article/75165/Geotagging_poses_security_risks/

[27] Samarati, P. and Sweeney, L. 1998. Protecting privacy when disclosing information: k-anonymity and its enforcement through generalization and cell suppression. *Technical report, SRI International*.

[28] Schechter, S., Bernheim Brush, a. J., Egelman, S.2009. It's no secret: Measuring the security and reliability of authentication via 'secret' questions. In 30th IEEE Symposium on Security and Privacy.

[29] Schuler, R.P., Laws, N., Bajaj, S., Grandhi, S.A. and Jones, Q. 2007. Finding Your Way with CampusWiki: A Location-Aware Wiki to Support Community Building *The ACM.s Conference on Human Factors in Computing Systems CHI2007*, San Jose California, USA.

[30] Shannon, C.E. 1950. Prediction and entropy of printed English. *The Bell System Technical Journal*, *30*, 50-64.

[31] Sweeney, L. 2002. Achieving k-Anonymity Privacy Protection Using Generalization And Suppression. *International Journal on Uncertainty, Fuzziness and Knowledge-based Systems*, *10*, 571-588.

[32] Sweeney, L. 2004. Uniqueness of simple demographics in the U.S. population. *Technical report, Carnegie Mellon University, Laboratory for International Data Privacy*.

[33] Tenenbaum, J.B., Griffiths T.L., 2001. Generalization, similarity, and Bayesian inference. Behav. Brain Sci. 24: 629-40; discussion 652-791.

[34] Terry, M., Mynatt , E.D., Ryall, K., Leigh, D., 2002. Social net: using patterns of physical proximity over time to infer shared interests, *CHI '02 extended abstracts on Human factors in computing systems*, (Minneapolis, Minnesota, USA, April 20-25, 2002),.

[35] Terveen, L., and McDonald D. 2005. Social Matching: A Framework and Research Agenda. In *ACM Transactions of Computer Human Interaction*.

[36] Weiser, M. 1991. The Computer for the 21st Century. *Scientific American*.

[37] Yam, M. Jan 22, 2010. Your Top 20 Most Common Passwords. Retrieved Nov 10, 2011. http://www.tomshardware.com/news/imperva-rockyou-most-common-passwords,9486.html

[38] ZabaSearch. Free People Search and Public Information Search Engine. Retrieved Nov 10, 2011. http://www.zabasearch.com/

[39] Zetter, K.,(2008, Sept 18) Palin E-Mail Hacker Says It Was Easy. *Wired.* Retrieved March 8, 2012. http://www.wired.com/threatlevel/2008/09/palin-e-mail-ha/

[40] Zhan, J. and Matwin, S. 2006. A Crypto-Based Approach to Privacy-Preserving Collaborative DataMining *Sixth IEEE International Conference on Data Mining Workshops*, 546-550.

The Gap Between Producer Intentions and Consumer Behavior in Social Media

Emilee Rader, Alcides Velasquez,
Kayla D. Hales
Communication Arts and Sciences
Michigan State University
emilee, velasq24, haleskay @ msu.edu

Helen Kwok
Chicago, IL, USA
HK@u.northwestern.edu

ABSTRACT

It can be difficult for social media users to tell who is paying attention to what they post. As producers of content, Facebook users make assumptions about who will be part of their intended audience. However, when the same user's role shifts to that of consumer, the criteria for consumption depends on factors outside of the original producer's control. This creates a gap between producer intentions and consumer behavior; producing content that is actually consumed by one's intended audience is neither guaranteed nor easily confirmed.

Categories and Subject Descriptors

H.4.3 [**Communications Applications**]: Information browsers; H.3.5 [**Online Information Services**]: Web-based services

Keywords

social media, audience, producer, consumer, common ground

1. INTRODUCTION

In a social media system like Facebook or Twitter, it can be hard to know whether anybody from one's *intended audience*—"the people who I want to see what I post"—is paying attention. Unlike like communication technologies that support explicit turn-taking (email, IM, video), contributions to "social awareness streams" largely do **not** consist of messages exchanged between senders and recipients [3]. Social media systems also do not operate under the traditional one-to-many broadcast model (radio or TV), where *audience* means passive spectators and there is a clear distinction between the source of the content and those who are consuming. Instead, for any given piece of content contributed in social media there is a *producer* (the person who posted the content) and possibly a *consumer* (the person who attends to the content), and each user plays both roles. The existence of a consumer for an individual contribution is not a given; in fact, at a recent media event representatives from Facebook claimed that "the average news feed story from a user profile reaches just 12% of their friends"[1].

---

[1] http://techcrunch.com/2012/02/29/
facebook-post-reach-16-friends/

Our beliefs about who is listening to us in conversation affect our assumptions about aspects of the context in which a contribution takes place, such as what information we can count on having in common with a conversation partner. We tailor what we say for who we think is listening, and what we think those listeners know [5]. In addition, people expect others with whom they've interacted to have paid more attention during that interaction than they actually do [1], leading to mistaken assumptions about the amount of shared knowledge they can take advantage of when making future contributions. People also overestimate how well they communicate with people they feel close to. We assume those people are more like us than they actually are, and therefore don't work as hard to monitor their perspective and understanding as we do with people we don't know very well [4].

Reports from previous research investigating contributions and audience in social media indicate that people tend to expect their strong ties—close friend and family—to be consumers for the content they post. Lampe et al. [2] looked at changes in Facebook users' perceptions of audience between 2006 and 2008. They found that Facebook friends (hereafter referred to as FB FRIENDS) who interact with each other offline were the most common perceived audience. Stutzman and Kramer-Duffield [6] similarly found that producers' "expected audience", or the people one expects to be viewing one's Facebook profile, consist mostly of strong ties, defined as best friends and family members. However, strong ties are typically a minority of one's FB FRIENDS, and a given contribution is likely to be much more widely consumed.

Many of these studies consider production OR consumption, separately, which introduces an artificial separation of roles. In reality, social media users are both producers and consumers. Studying them separately makes it more difficult to see the connections between producer and consumer behavior that might allow us to understand the system-level dynamics at work. In this project, we set out to answer questions about what producers post, who they intend to see different types of posts, and why consumers' choose to pay attention to some posts and not others. We also compared what people told us about their production and consumption behaviors to discover ways in which consumer attention might (or might not) line up with producer intent.

2. METHOD AND PARTICIPANTS

We conducted 15 semi-structured interviews (5 men, 10 women) between May and July 2011[2]. Participants were adult users of Facebook who had at least 100 FB FRIENDS; who posted status updates

---

[2] At the time these data were collected, Facebook had not introduced "Timeline". It was also not possible to "unfollow" a post, or "unsubscribe" from a person. Finally, the "audience selector" and "tag review" for posts had not been implemented.

at least once per week, on average; and who worked in industries not directly related to social media (or the study of social media).

Recruiting took place via snowball sampling using Facebook messages and status posts, starting from FB FRIENDS of members of the research team who were asked to pass on the recruiting messages to others in their networks. Strong ties and recent colleagues of the researchers were not eligible to participate. We sampled with diversity in mind, so that participants would be able to provide data about a variety of experiences and perspectives. Participants had 182 to 1158 FB FRIENDS (M=526, Mdn= 454). Five participants were undergraduate or graduate students (P09, P12-P15) and two were university professors (P07, P08). The others were a nursing home dietician (P01), a domestic caregiver (P02), a policy researcher (P03), an Army officer (P04), a recent college graduate employed part-time (P05), an office manager (P06), a librarian (P10), and a product manager (P11).

Interviews were conducted via telephone and screen-sharing using a service called join.me, so that the interviewer could see the same information as the participants during the interview. Participants answered general questions about how they used Facebook, "friending" and "unfriending", and their recollections of inappropriate behavior on Facebook. We also asked questions about the background, context, and inferences about intentions and audience surrounding posts and comments participants had produced or consumed.

Interviews were recorded and transcribed, and the transcripts were anonymized. The transcripts were coded using an inductive approach. All members of the research team participated in open, iterative coding to develop the coding scheme, during which time the team met frequently to discuss and revise the codes. This early coding stage focused on labeling and categorizing participants' behaviors and attitudes regarding producing and consuming content on Facebook, and their interactions with other users. The final coding scheme was applied to a single transcript by all members of the research team. We met to resolve differences, and the remaining transcripts were coded by one person each. In later stages of the analysis, high-level themes emerged as connections were drawn between codes, participants, and production/consumption behaviors.

3. FINDINGS

Below we describe the types of Facebook posts our participants reported making in their role as "producers" and who was in their *intended audience*; in other words, who they said they wanted to see these posts. Then, we present reasons these same people reported for paying attention—or not—to posts contributed by their FB FRIENDS. Finally, we highlight a gap between the intentions of producers, and consumers' reported behavior.

3.1 What Producers Post

Information about their activities.

Participants reported contributing posts to make others aware of what is going on in their lives and to stay visible to people in their network. For example, P11 contributed a post to keep others updated on how he's doing: "I put [a post] on just so people would know we made it to [destination] safely... So this was in part for the people who live out there, this was in part as a shout-out to my wife for doing part of the driving, but for mostly just so people knew that we got there safely." Another participant posted a status updated for the mother of one of her child's friends, to keep her updated on what was happening during a playdate: "We had a friend over and I knew his mom was checking Facebook and I wrote that the kids were bored and I gave them a cardboard box to play with because I knew she'd get a chuckle out of it... I posted it mainly

for my other mom friends because I thought they would think it was funny" (P2). Some participants, like P3, used Facebook as a way to keep distant friends and family members up-to-date on their daily activities: "I'm out and about in [location] where I live and if something interesting happens or I'm doing something fun then I will upload photos. Part of this is that I have a lot family who are my FB FRIENDS, so like the person who commented here, that is actually my mom..."

Six participants reported instances where status posts served as an announcement of big news, such as a job change, graduation, pregnancy or birth of a child, etc. P12 stated, "But generally, if there's any significant life events like passing exams or getting into a specific University or anything, that will get lots of comments or saying like it's my birthday or whatever, that kind of thing." Most of these posts reported by our participants were positive, consisting of "good news". However, P1 mentioned that her posts about [health problems] received a lot of responses, and P7 expressed an opinion that one of her FB FRIENDS seemed to be "fishing for support" when posting "bad news". Three participants reported feeling like there were some announcements they wanted to hear about in person rather than seeing it first on Facebook or hearing it second-hand from someone who had seen it posted there. P1 put the feeling to words: "Thanks for telling me, I had to find out on Facebook."

"Found content" for others.

Other posts participants discussed producing were "found content" such as links, videos and Internet memes that they feel are interesting or entertaining, and think some of their FB FRIENDS might want to see as well. Usually participants talked about these posts both in terms of being provided for others' enjoyment or information, and also signaling their own interests to others. For example, P4, who was very well versed in current events, said that he likes to share interesting content about politics and causes that he supports. He posted about a particular upcoming event: "So, I like the fact that it is a fund raiser and people may use this in the way to support the [cause] and it's an event worth supporting. So it's kind of a double way to share what I'm doing and also let everyone know that I'm interested in that quite a bit." P5 described a time when he found something online he thought was funny and believed his FB FRIENDS would also enjoy it: "Yeah. So, I was watching a cartoon in the morning... That's one of my favorites and I know that other people like it so I posted a quote."

Start or contribute to conversations.

Three participants indicated that one purpose for some of their Facebook posts was to start an online conversation, or comment thread. In one instance, a participant discussed posting particular remarks simply because he knew it was controversial and wanted to elicit a response: "I was probably being somewhat inflammatory, making some comment about [topic] or something to get a response out of people" (P15). P6 reported that he feels Facebook is more fun when conversations are going on, and so he tries to start conversations: "Anyway, I just thought this was interesting. I'll post pictures and make a little smart ass comment frequently. But certainly, like, I'm just trying to start a conversion." One way these participants mentioned starting conversations is by tagging people they want to see a particular post. P11 described one instance where he did this: "I saw this really interesting story. So I was like, 'Wow! I wonder what [a FB FRIEND] thinks about this.' Then posted it hoping he'd follow up."

A message to someone in particular.

Participants reported that they tagged someone in a post to draw the person's attention to the post, or to let the tagged individual know that the participant was thinking of them. For example, P01 indicated posting to Facebook because she wanted to relay a message to specific people she cares about: "One of my girlfriends who I grew up with is back in town to see her sister graduate... I just want to let them know that I missed them and I'm hanging out with them [soon]." Tagging is also used conveniently when wanting to address more than one person: "Sometimes I want to post something on a few people's walls and so I'll just use it to tell them both at once, or sometimes somebody helps me think of something or see something, and so I just give credit where credit is due" (P5). P6 sometimes used tags as an indirect way of telling several people at the same time that he cares: "They're graduating and I like, I really love these guys and so I thought, 'Oh, just tag them and let them know I'm thinking of them.'"

However, in some circumstances despite the fact that a post is specific to someone, it might not include a tag: "I actually posted this and a link to [a FB FRIEND], who is a patent attorney... I wanted to get a patent attorney's take on this on this. He actually responded back pretty quickly in the comments that he'd seen this and posted this [online] a while back" (P11). In situations like this, the producer makes the assumption that even without using the tagging function, the message will reach the person it is intended for.

Make a request.

Our participants described a small number of instances in which they posted a status update that was a request of some kind, to which they wanted a response, or a call to action. These posts included things like asking a question, requesting advice, or seeking moral support. P2 posted something without explicitly asking for help, but with the expectation that some of her FB FRIENDS who are also moms would provide advice about a specific issue: "I just expected other mothers to notice and sympathize, especially the local moms. So, you know, I was hoping for some of them to give me their advice on how they get their kids to sleep." Other participants used their status updates to promote themselves or organizations or businesses that are important to them: "...this is another message about [organization] that I'm involved in. And this, I sort of treated this as partly a personal thing and partly a little bit of marketing. Like reminding people that [organization] is awesome" (P10).

3.2 Reasons for Paying Attention

Information-based judgment.

Every participant reported that they like to consume content that is related their interests. The judgment about whether to pay attention to these posts was based on the information they contained. For P03, posts from her colleagues help her keep up-to-date on issues related to her career: "I often pay attention to the things that [a FB FRIEND] posts just because it's like a professional, like, 'Oh, I should stay up on that'". The information can also be relevant to non-work interests: "[A FB FRIEND] lives in [state] where my wife is from, so I would actually look up that restaurant, see where it was and we're guessing we might go sometime. I am always looking for a new good restaurant to go to" (P04). This type of content allows participants to develop in their profession or serves as a source of information allowing them to plan or act based on what they learn.

Participants also reported using Facebook to find things out about other people. P7 used the content available on the site to learn about the lives of people with whom she is not very close, or that she might not know: "Occasionally I look up people I don't know and I just kind of... I don't know what you'd call it but I click like on someone I know's profile or a picture. If someone had commented on a friend's picture who I don't know, I click on the picture if it looks interesting. And then I tend to look at this new person's pro-

file. And from there potentially look at their photos or their friends depending on their privacy settings and just kind of profile skip..." She described her consumption of content in this way as fueled by elements of voyeurism: "You know the little snippets of people's lives....there's a certain aspect of voyeurism". P8 also reported this behavior, and described it as an interest in monitoring the environment, with a negative connotation, as if there is something strangely not right about staying informed about goings-on back home when one is out of town: "Facebook stalking. Facebook lets me know what is going on, even though I was in [another country] for two weeks or even though I am out-of-state."

Some participants stated that they have a very clear preference regarding the topic or characteristics of the posts they do NOT want to consume. For example, some disliked getting constant updates about people's activities in online games. Some reported hiding posts from FB FRIENDS that post too frequently, or whose lives are no longer of interest to them. P8 described it this way: "So if I hide them, it's because I've gone a few weeks and their posts had just been, they have a lot of posts, so they're kind of annoying. Or they take up a lot of space and they don't ever, they aren't worth my time to read them or follow links. I've got a couple of friends that are stay-at-home moms, and all they ever do is post about potty training for like months."

Person-based judgment.

Participants were interested in using Facebook to pay special attention to content posted by certain people, usually those the participant cared more about, like family, close friends, or those that are part of a specific social group to which the participant belongs. Those people are only a small subset of one's network: "I've got over a thousand friends on Facebook. But I'm of course closer to some of them than others. So, I'm going to scroll through and find the people who mean the most to me and see what their updates are" (P4). Also, sometimes participants seek out content from a particular person they are close to they have not seen posts by in some noticeably long time interval: "If I'm worried about a particular friend, I'd go to their profile, scan what they've been up to for the last couple of weeks, what they've been posting" (P8).

However, the content that demands special attention is not always from family or close friends. Sometimes, as illustrated by P05, it is related to a particular topical interest, but it is the identity of the producer—a proxy for what the post is about—that first catches the consumer's attention: "That's interesting because she is a friend of mine, and she is an accompanist of mine, and I know about this concert that she's doing."

As mentioned above from the producer side, announcements and special events are particularly salient for consumers. For example, P14 expressed interest in a post by one of her best friends who had recently completed three years in his job: "I would 'like' this because he is one of my best friends. And wish him congratulations." P07 mentioned a post in which a close friend shares the arrival of a new member to her family: "This one kind of sticks out because it's an important life announcement in one of my good friends."

Ambiguous posts occur when consumers feel like they don't have the background information to understand posts contributed by their FB FRIENDS. Some find this annoying, but most just expect not to "get" everything they see on Facebook. P03 said, "Just as I am not going to understand everything that people post, I also don't feel the need to make every post explanatory to every single person on my Facebook friend list." P14 reminds us that everyone's FB FRIENDS do not have the same background: "something which I post about [home country]... I don't expect some of my friends from [home country] or [where P14 lives now] to under-

Reasons for Producing:	Reasons for Paying Attention:			
	SIGNAL	PERSON	INFO	Intended Audience:
Share personal info		X		Friends/family who keep "up to date"; **others interested in my life***
Share content		X	X	**Anyone who finds the content interesting***
Conversation	X	X		People I want to talk to, primarily friends and family
Send a message		X		Specific friends and/or family members
Make a request	X	X		**Anyone who can help or answer the question***

Figure 1: Cells with an 'X' indicate conditions under which the producer's intended audience might choose to read the contribution. Bold text indicates situations when consumers only decide they are interested AFTER looking at a post, creating a gap between what producers can know about their audience a priori, and the actual consumers.

stand about." Participants reported skipping over or hiding ambiguous posts, assuming they were meant for somebody else: "[A FB FRIEND] posts things sometimes that I just don't know what is going on. I don't know the people he is referencing, or it just doesn't make sense to me. So, that would be one where I might hide his posts. They aren't annoying, but I never understand them."

Signal-based judgment.

Most participants looked for signals that they could use as defacto "endorsements" to help them decide which posts to pay attention to. Several explicitly stated the perception that posts with more comments and "likes" are more worthy of one's attention, given the evidence of others' interest presented via the interface. However, it was less clear from these interviews whether participants would be able to make this determination based on the post itself, and not the behavioral traces of others. In other words, more attention may make ANY post more interesting. P04, for example, stated that when he notices a lot of people have posted comments to a status update he will look at it. Furthermore, if it has no activity at all, he might not even pay attention to it: "Normally if I see someone's status update or especially an article or a repost that has no comments, I may or may not look at it. But if there are several comments on there, I am more likely to look at the status update or the comments." P15 looks not only at the amount of comments, but also at how much the post has been liked: "Because a number of my friends have liked it, it would probably draw attention."

Participants reported paying special attention to posts that contain links to videos or news when the producer frames the content via a text blurb. This helps consumers know what the producer thinks about the content: "So, the posts that generate the most comments I think are the ones with a link. It's like here's a link. Here's what I think about it. What do you think?" (P6). Some participants also mentioned that they use 'who posted the content' as an endorsement as well: "Yeah. I usually don't click on videos. I don't really care enough unless it's someone I know and like a lot of people indicated that it's worth watching" (P7). P15 took this a step farther, stating: "The blurbs make them stand out more. Also the vast majority of them have a little blurb. It's rare for me to... I think it's rude for people to post things without explaining at least briefly why they're posting them."

4. DISCUSSION

Sometimes when producers contribute status updates on Facebook, they feel like they have a pretty good idea who they are talk-

ing to. But there are other times when they put stuff out there for "anyone who might find it interesting". Producers know there are consumers paying attention, partially, we think, because *they themselves* are consumers, and partially because they receive responses to their own posts. However, there are some posts (in bold, in the table to the left) for which the producer simply cannot know in advance who is going to pay attention—because that is only determined by consumers after the post has already been made, as they are deciding whether or not they are interested. This is the gap we alluded to earlier in the paper, which makes it impossible for producers to personalize and direct these posts to particular consumers. Instead, producers must guess who might be interested, and adapt their behavior on the next post based on whatever response they receive to the current one. Only a few of our participants seemed somewhat aware of this indirect feedback loop.

This research highlights the fact that there are cases in social media when direct feedback on one's contributions is difficult to come by, and that these instances primarily occur when producers contribute to share information or ask questions, and consumers do not have a close relationship with the producer. The resulting gap—the indirect feedback loop—affects the dynamics of the system as a whole; imagine if Facebook solely consisted of directed messages in the form of tagged posts that were meant for specific people, with whom shared context was assumed. Reading the posts of FB FRIENDS might become even more voyeuristic and creepy than some of our participants reported feeling like it already is. Or, we might find much less content we feel like we can connect with—because it is all tailored for specific people, not a general audience—and tune out just like people say they do now for posts for which they assume they are not the intended audience.

We chose Facebook as the platform for this research because many, many people visit regularly and contribute posts about wide-ranging topics, for a variety of different audiences. Similar features to the News Feed are available in systems like LinkedIn, Google+, and Twitter; however, the amount and character of participation varies across these sites. We do not suggest that our findings generalize directly to these other systems; rather, we hypothesize that the indirect feedback loop we describe here interacts differently with the specific participation dynamics and system capabilities in each case. Future work will examine the specific mechanisms by which the indirect feedback loop takes place, and its effect on the character and content of producers' contributions.

5. REFERENCES

[1] T. Gilovich, V. H. Medvec, and K. Savitsky. The Spotlight Effect in Social Judgment: An Egocentric Bias in Estimates of the Salience of One's Own Actions and Appearance. *J PERS SOC PSYCHOL*, 78(2):211–222, 2000.

[2] C. Lampe, N. Ellison, and C. Steinfield. Changes in Use and Perception of Facebook. In *CSCW 2008*, 2008.

[3] M. Naaman, J. Boase, and C.-H. Lai. Is it Really About Me? Message Content in Social Awareness Streams. In *CSCW 2010*, pages 189–192, 2010.

[4] K. Savitsky, B. Keysar, N. Epley, T. Carter, and A. Swanson. The closeness-communication bias: Increased egocentrism among friends versus strangers. *J EXP SOC PSYCHOL*, 47(1):269–273, Jan. 2011.

[5] M. Schober and H. Clark. Understanding by addressees and overhearers. *COGNITIVE PSYCHOL*, 21(2):211–232, 1989.

[6] F. Stutzman and J. Kramer-Duffield. Friends only: examining a privacy-enhancing behavior in facebook. In *CHI 2010*, 2010.

Supporting Artifact-Mediated Discourses Through a Recursive Annotation Tool

Federico Cabitza
University of Milano-Bicocca
Viale Sarca 336, 20126
Milan, Italy
cabitza@disco.unimib.it

Carla Simone
University of Milano-Bicocca
Viale Sarca 336, 20126
Milan, Italy
simone@disco.unimib.it

Marco P. Locatelli
University of Milano-Bicocca
Viale Sarca 336, 20126
Milan, Italy
locatelli@disco.unimib.it

ABSTRACT

This paper focuses on tight communities and specifically on the distributed, mediated discourses that their members articulate around documents and inscribed material artifacts. The paper presents a prototype-based design experience toward the definition of a collaborative annotation tool that is endowed with *discourse oriented* functionalities whose main characteristics have emerged from case studies we undertook in the healthcare and agricultural domains. In latter domain an initial prototype was proposed and progressively tuned to help users propose modifications to an institutional document through the expression of comments gathered *around* and *about* a common artifact, and then build a representative summary of the opinions emerging within the community as a result of this distributed discussion. In light of the reported case study, we discuss a new perspective on this class of annotating applications and the related functionalities that could realize a new simplified model of discourse and foster its adoption in distributed settings and communities of practice.

Categories and Subject Descriptors

H.5.3 [**Group and Organization**]: Computer-supported cooperative work

General Terms

Design, Human Factors

Keywords

Annotation Systems

1. INTRODUCTION

One of the main contributions of CSCW to the HCI field has been to have recognized and comprehensively studied the central role of *artifacts-in-use* in human collaboration. A number of studies (e.g., [1, 26, 3, 24]) have shed light on the multiple ways artifacts mediate interaction and support cooperation in terms of both activity articulation, awareness promotion and knowledge sharing in specific settings. When such a mediation occurs through paper based artifacts, it is common to observe that actors exploit various kinds of annotations to enrich their documents with additional, often informal and highly situated information (e.g. [11, 30, 14]) that can serve all of the purposes mentioned above, as well as be easily related to the irreducible need for users to appropriate the available means for ad-hoc and even unanticipated purposes [2, 29, 4].

Nowadays powerful and relatively cheap devices are available that are endowed with multimedia, touch-sensitive interfaces; this could facilitate the digitization of coordinative artifacts that closely mimic the affordances and flexibility that traditional artifacts exhibit when they are used in cooperative settings. Then it is natural to think of a digital and sound counterpart of paper based annotations that could exploit the increasing versatility and flexibility that characterize some commercial *apps* for handheld devices (e.g., iAnnotate PDF, GoodNotes for iPad, DioMemo and Handrite for Android Tablets).

When cooperation occurs in a distributed setting, the initial, almost stigmergic, coordinative purposes of annotations [10] are increasingly complemented by their use as a support of indirect discourse by the actors that access shared artifacts and annotate them [13]. In other words, the coordinative, reflective and communicative roles of annotations in artifacts-in-use become increasingly intertwined and therefore call for a unified and coherent support.

When technology is called to support discourse an immediate question arises: to which degree should the technology impose a sort of model or structure to situated communication? This issue is as old (and controversial) as the Coordinator [31], g-IBIS [12] and all the technologies these inspired to some extent and of which it would be difficult (if not plethoric) to give an exhaustive account here. We believe that answering this question cannot happen in a vacuum or by adopting any pondered reflection over the nature of discourse in general terms and from contrasting standpoints (e.g. Searle and Habermas) [27].

Rather, our point is that addressing how to support discourse, and therefore the continuous emergence and reconciliation of multiple interpretations of shared contents, has to be situated in the context of the setting where specific discourses take place and unfold. In this light, we can distinguish between situations where cooperating actors gather in *loose* communities: in this case, the links between community members are weak, since members can come to interact for the first time or because their previous interactions did not build a recognizable common background [19]; and situations where actors constitute a *tight* community, whose members are mutually acquainted with each other since they either share previous experiences or rely on sufficiently understood and agreed-upon notions and conventions [8].

It is reasonable to believe that a loose community is likely to need a support that proposes some sort of ordered discussions so that the process does not diverge in an unproductive way: this situation is referred to, e.g., in terms of "large-scale argumentation" in [18] and in terms of "contested collective intelligence" in [13]. In both cases the proposed technology offers predefined categories to structure discourse with different degrees of prescriptiveness.

Conversely, a tight community would benefit from a support that exploits the (mainly social) mechanisms the community naturally adopts to make discussion among its members productive. These mechanisms tap into the conventions and mutual understanding the community has developed in its evolution. The present paper focuses on tight communities and, as anticipated, on their discourses situated around *inscribed material artifacts* (typically documents). This scenario covers a set of situations that make the conception of a specific support both interesting and challenging at the same time.

Examples of documents *around* which discourses (e.g., to discuss the contents, propose amendments, judge their quality, take some decision, reconcile diverging interpretations) can unfold encompass: sets of policies to be checked against coherence and applicability; new business processes or medical protocols; sets of guidelines aimed at guaranteeing high quality of outcome and efficiency; project proposals and project drafts; also drafts of scientific papers, and so on. It is evident that these situations and the related artifacts that are made object of discussion differ from each other; nevertheless they also share common features if we assume that those artifacts tend to be the stratified and agreed upon expression of a quite tight community: e.g., common background, common goals and above all common practices to get access and relate to the shared artifact.

In the past year, we have been involved in two research projects with the aim to support collaboration between the stakeholders involved: in the first project these were agricultural growers belonging to a regional association that were supposed to exchange experiences and knowledge and to articulate tasks to, among other aims, make technical policies coherent with their practice and their practices compliant with those technical policies. In the second project, the actors involved were doctors and patients involved in a distributed care program. Although different with respect to many aspects, in both cases annotating shared artifacts was one of the relevant practices we observed. The first outcomes of our investigation in the healthcare domain are being reported in [4]. In this paper we briefly report those findings that from this latter investigation regard annotations; and we will present and discuss the findings elicited from the field study in the agricultural domain in some more details since these led to the development of a prototype that fulfills the requirements extracted from both settings.

From these two empirical researches, we then derived a set of indications that we outline in the next section; in light of these requirements we are currently developing an an-

notation tool called RAT (Recursive Annotation Tool) that serves as sand-box for testing the feasibility of functionalities to be proposed, and possibly engineered, in future projects[1]

2. FROM THE EMPIRICAL FIELDS

The common element observed in both the field studies mentioned above was that the texts[2] that were made object of annotation and discussion were not to change during the process of their progressive annotation. Even when the final goal of the discussion was the improvement and related modification of the documents' content, as in the agricultural case, this activity was framed within an ordered practice where at some time the content is "locked" (or "freezed") to allow actors to discuss it. This behavior actually recurs in many cases: more than an aspect that is pursued because it can simplify the technology of annotation involved (since this can also do without serious functionalities of version control), this is rather a natural condition to allow for distributed and asynchronous discussion, and any situation where the "ground cannot be cut from under the participants' feet" (to borrow an expression used by an interviewee). This practice can be decomposed in a set of steps like the following ones: a first step where the discussion is carried on, almost unmoderated, and the annotations are created by the community around and about a common object; then a second step where the committed/appointed people are supposed to order and make sense of the annotations produced that far; and then a third step, where changes that derive from the annotated standpoints are selected, approved and finally executed. Possibly this simplified and very lightweight workflow is repeated to further refine the content at each iteration, until a satisfactory formulation has been reached: this collaborative process is reminiscent of the so called "pulsar" model, proposed by Holt years ago [16].

To support this specific collaborative process, researchers would be called to address a twofold aim: first, to define a collaborative annotation system that suitably supports collective discourse and collaborative sense-making; second, how to support the activity of building a meaningful and representative summary of the collected opinions and that possibly facilitates the modification of the document content. This research agenda shares most of the requirements identified in [13] and in this vein we tried to interpret the requirements collected from the two field studies at hand.

In the next two sections we will present the main points elicited in the distributed healthcare case and we will describe the context of the project in the agricultural domain. In this latter domain an initial solution was developed and experimented with selected key users. Both experiences triggered the conception of a set of more sophisticated *discourse oriented* functionalities that we will outline in Section 3 when describing a new tool addressing the indications drawn from the field. The concluding remarks reported in Section 5 will position the proposed annotation tool into a more com-

---

[1]A preliminary version of this paper was presented at the "Collective Intelligence as Community Discourse and Action" Workshop held in conjunction with the ACM CSCW 2012 Conference in Seattle, WA, USA.
[2]We choose this term purposely to indicate, as in the semiotics tradition, any assemblage of signs, words and images that have been constructed and are interpreted with reference to a set of local, sometimes even only tacit, notions and conventions.

prehensive research agenda, and will hint to the next steps of our research in this field.

2.1 The distributed care case

During our interactions with practitioners in the healthcare domain we proposed them the idea of providing patients and caregivers with a flexible and general-purpose tool by which to annotate the texts they exchange during the care process, e.g., reports, prescriptions, schedules, emails with requests for clarifications and the like. This idea was grounded on their needs that emerged from the discussion and that were increasingly engrossed by the tenets of the so called "narrative medicine" [9]. According to this approach, the relationship between a patient and her doctor is not the one between comrades that "fight the battle against disease" [21]; it is rather the one coming out of a process of progressive mutual understanding, viewpoints sharing and personal relationship development between patient and doctor toward the recovery and well-being of the former.

This mutual understanding is aimed at, on the one hand, making a health problem explicit as this is perceived and expressed by a patient in her own idiosyncratic terms; and, on the other hand, at understanding what should be done that fits the socio-psico-physical characteristics of the patient to solve her problem and have her fine again. As such, the interviewees claimed that the structured and positivist way of describing illnesses and patients, e.g., in the structured charts and forms of an electronic medical record, could straightjacket and curb their hermeneutic and situated task of understanding the patient's complaints and, the other way round, of making their indications be appropriated by the patient and followed actually.

Thus, a tool by which to annotate the flow of electronic messages and their attachments that we were told are usually exchanged between doctors and their patients after the first visit was recognized being of great value: it would help a doctor extract, "isolate", relevant data from the textual accounts a patient makes of her condition while, in doing so, preserving the original context where these data make sense to both; and, on the other hand, such a tool would enable mutual commenting: doctors would comment passages of their patients' accounts; patients, in their turn, would comment passages from their doctors' reports and prescriptions, as a way to facilitate sense making and clarification.

Thus, the availability of an annotation functionality of electronic patients' accounts and doctors' reports, both in terms of semantic tagging and free-text commenting, was envisioned as a way to unleash the full potential of the unstructured content of these documents and to reach a grounded understanding between the actors involved beyond the unavoidable rigidities and constraints of any "universal" or standard model of illness and medical intervention that would be imposed upon their interactions.

2.2 The growers association case

At the same time of these encounters in the healthcare domain, we have also been involved in a project, called Misura124, whose aim was the design of technological solutions for a heterogeneous community of fruit and vegetables producers that recognized themselves under a so called GOA, or Growers Organizations Association. In this project, one of the tasks that was very soon recognized as most valuable to support was the management of comments and proposals of amendment that were expressed by production experts regarding the so called Technical Policies (TP). These are official documents that are issued by either a Regional authority or an institutional body to regulate various aspects of agricultural practice for a given kind of produce of the land. TP documents are issued every year to include the best practices gathered so far from the territory and present clear indications that mandatorily specify how crops must be treated in the next campaign. For their nature, the drafting of TPs requires the tight collaboration of heterogeneous professionals and experts from organizations of growers to pre-validate and, in some cases, ameliorate these indications before their official issuing.

The Regional authorities collect the feedback from the qualified organizations to which these experts belong since it is acknowledged that professionals at the grassroots level own a very valuable practical knowledge about the effects of the strict application of the guidelines on the quality of the produced fruits and vegetable. The process of discussing the guidelines reported in a TP, detecting areas of improvement and amendment and reaching a consensus about those proposals of change to submit to the Regional authority involves a scattered community of experts as well as people that work for a GOA within a smaller area, in our project the Lombardy Region. Regional rules state that the annual TP document that is issued by each region can be amended by the GOA operating in this region. This rule in turn implies that the GOA is supposed to collect proposals for amendment from all the affiliated growers. This task has been told us to be a very difficult and time consuming activity. Indeed, each grower assigns an *agricultural consultant* (AC) to propose the amendments: these consultants are the experts that are usually called to help growers in applying the best practices reported in the TPs; moreover a GOA's employee acts as *coordinator*: she receives all the proposals for amendment and is responsible for editing the final amendment lists that must be sent back to the pertinent regional authority. The amendment collection is a complex negotiation process due to two main factors: a) a limited set of amendments can be sent back to the regional authority, otherwise they are not really considered; b) amendments may conflict, and often do, with each other.

In our observational study we saw that this task was carried out in a fragmented way that can be outlined as follows: 1) the coordinator sends the TPs to each AC by email, with a spreadsheet in attachment to collect the amendment proposals; 2) each AC collects her own amendments and sends the edited spreadsheet back to the coordinator; 3) then the coordinator produces a unified spreadsheet of the amendments and identifies the most important and controversial points from this exchange of multiple emails; 4) the coordinator and the ACs meet all together to reach consensus on the various standpoints, prioritize the elements to amend and define the final list: this usually happens three/four times before they all come up with a final version of the amendment list. Step 3 is the most frustrating for the coordinator because usually not all the ACs send their spreadsheet on time, and she has to solicit them by email several times; in addition, sometimes ACs do not fill in the spreadsheet as they are supposed to. Thus making order out of the magmatic material collected that far was perceived (and probably was) an awkward task.

In order to address the shortcomings of the current TP

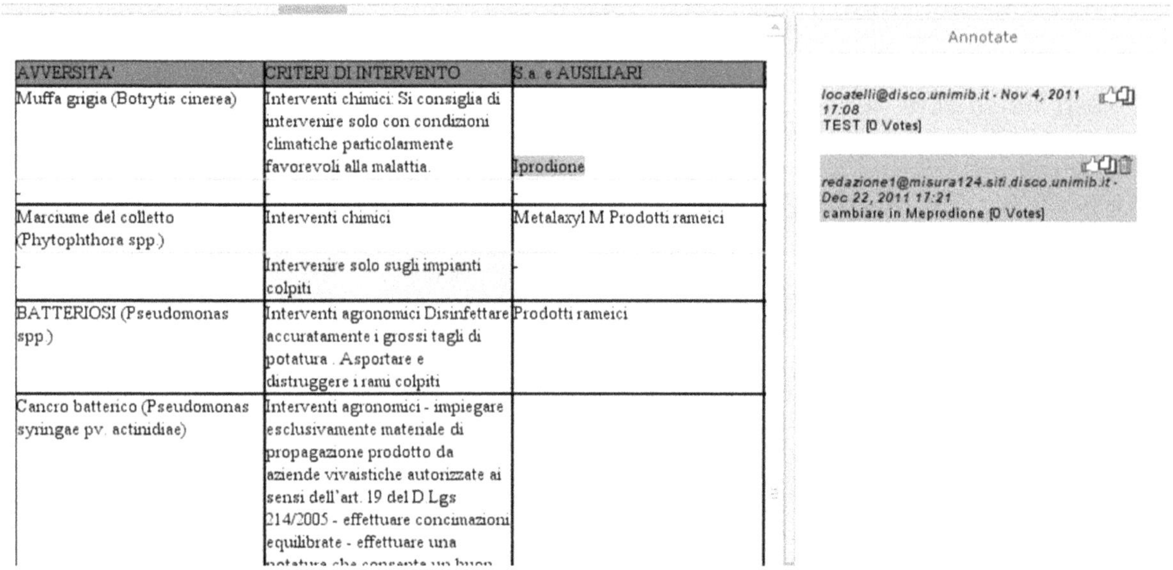

Figure 1: A screenshot of the Technical Policy prototype. Two amendments referring to the same part of the document (highlighted) are displayed.

amendment process, we deployed a prototypical service, the "Technical Policy Service" (TPS). In so doing, we immediately realized that the consolidated practices regarding the process of TP amendment led to a flat resistance to the new support, although all ACs complained about the old process. Moreover, since readiness to adopt and use ICT proficiently was generally low, many ACs expressed concerns about the introduction of "a too complex tool".

Then, we decided to split the digitization process in two steps. First, we proposed a basic online service that was aimed at overcoming the above mentioned fragmentation by offering a unique place where the technical policy documents could be shared among the ACs and the coordinator, and where amendments can be attached close to the pertinent text in terms of textual annotations (the list of amendments on the right in Figure 1). Amendments were added by highlighting a part of the document (the text in gray on the left in Figure 1) and by filling in a new amendment form that is displayed in a separated panel of the graphical interface when the user clicks on the Annotate button. Second, we planned to deal with richer functionalities more focused on discourse and negotiation once the ACs had become more accustomed to the interaction practices induced by this new virtual "place".

Moreover, the TPS was intended to be part of a more comprehensive platform supporting various kinds of interactions among the GOA's members and their staff. For this reason, the ACs and the coordinator were invited to use a standard Forum to exchange opinions on the contents of TPs at hand and on how to amend them. This opportunity notwithstanding, interacting with the coordinator and some of the ACs during the development and adjusting of the TP service made us understand that there were some essential *discourse elements* that users wanted to be *directly* connected with the annotations. To this aim, we made some specific controls available in the annotation area according to the user profile (see the rightmost side of the annotation header in Figure 1). By clicking on the "sheets" icon

within an existing amendment, both the ACs and the coordinator were then endowed with the capability to add a further amendment referring to the same target within the TP. This sort of shortcut to the creation of alternative amendments to the same point in the TP was aimed at a twofold aim: first, to oppose an amendment through the constructive proposal of an alternative way to amend the same passage; second, to promote awareness of an existing correlation between multiple amendments so as to facilitate their interpretation, post-hoc analysis and, hence, collaborative discussion. Conversely, by clicking on the "thumb-up" icon, both the ACs and the coordinator could express their support or approval to an existing amendment, without the need to add any other and redundant annotation confirming the points stated therein. Moreover, users could delete their own amendments by means of the "trash" icon, unless these had already been "voted for" by some other user. This regarded the tacit convention that "not yet approved comments" were to be considered as *provisional* both for their authors and for the other ACs. This constraint was not purposely implemented for the coordinator, who could delete any amendment irrespectively of their approval state: this addressed the tacit convention by which only the coordinator could "prune" the TP of amendments, as it usually happened as a result of a discussion (either in the forum or face-to-face) that had led to an agreement in this sense. In addition, one more control was meant for the coordinator only, to support the other typical way she contributed to the discussion. She could see all the annotations endowed with an additional "tick" icon (see Figure 2), by which an amendment would be officially approved and taken for consideration for the final draft: this formal approval would prevent the annotation be deleted or modified even by its author as, in some way, it implies a sort of "promotion" to the status of representative amendment of the community, which should be not disputed any more as some consensus has been already reached. Also in this case, making this information

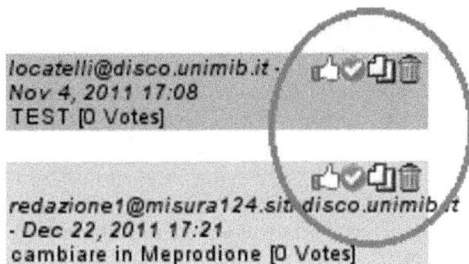

Figure 2: Two examples of annotations and the coordinator controls (top right).

available was considered helpful to move the discussion on and begin tackling more controversial points.

The TPS was then a first tool that we put in the users' hands to alleviate the drawbacks we observed in the practice of TP amending. From its initial use we saw that annotating and simultaneously sharing annotations allowed all users involved to get a fast picture of what was "hot" at any given time, i.e., what was argued and debated, and not to overlap in their contributions. In doing so, the actual negotiation process could start earlier and be kept more focused than it was to be because all the contributors had all the necessary information "ready to hand".

Making amendments available online and close to the TP that was under discussion was perceived as a clear advantage that allowed the stakeholders involved to reduce the need to organize time-consuming and expensive colocated meetings to only those where to discuss the most important and delicate issues that were deemed impossible to resolve in an asynchronous and distributed manner. On the other hand, the semantic information that the iconic controls allowed users to attach to their annotations enabled additional capabilities aimed at supporting the coordinator in the fourth and perhaps more chaotic step of the drafting process, when amendments had to be selected and consolidated. Information available about how many people "voted for" an amendment, on how many amendments were created for the same targets, and the like allowed the coordinator to export a prioritized list of amendments as a spreadsheet that she could process according to internal conventions and Regional policies and then send back to the Regional authority. Here again, a tacit convention allows the coordinator to have the final word on all the controversies that may have outlived the related debates, as it usually happens when the deadline imposed by the regional authority approaches: the coordinator (as representative of the GOA) is the only interface of the interactions with the Regional authority and she has to respond to any possible clarification request. However, the coordinator uses this power sparingly: amending TPs is only one of the many occasions in which the GOA representative is called to collaborate with the ACs and keeping mutual trust is the basis of this sometimes complex interaction.

The timing of the project did not allow a systematic validation of the TPS described above. However, during the meetings we organized to review the functionalities and to train the ACs "on the job" by simulating full drafting cycles on existing TPs, end-users showed a progressively clearer appreciation for having a virtual "place" where to share amendments; on the other hand, they were not fully persuaded that the overall platform could "actually" support the related dis-

cussions and therefore reduce the number and nature of their face-to-face meetings. They blamed the fact that the Forum was not completely integrated with the annotation service: thus we started a set of brief talks with the coordinator and some of the ACs that expressed their willingness to help us further refine our service along the "discourse" dimension of their cooperative task. In these talks, we realized that adding new functionalities to this aim had to be done carefully: the risk at stake is to unduly increase the complexity of the tool to adopt and, first and foremost, to break those tacit conventions that permeate their long run experience of interaction, e.g., by imposing a model of discussion that could be perceived as artificial or unrealistic: even the very simple discourse model introduced by the TPS was disregarded by some ACs.

3. A NEW PERSPECTIVE AND TOOL

The case of the Technical Policy and the feedback that we received from the users of the TPS prototype show a point that is central in our proposal. We saw ACs and the coordinator propose amendments and discuss them with both textual annotations (i.e., side notes, comments) and semantic ones: these latter were de facto associated with the "thumbup" icon to back up an amendment, and with the "sheets" icon that was used to propose a better alternative. But we also saw users discuss about these judgments in subsequent and correlated comments; likewise, users told us they would appreciate to "vote for a vote" or explicitly contest an amendment with a thumb-down icon, and the like. In short, comments and tags would be used almost interchangeably.

This sheds light on the shortcoming that is inherent in any tool by which users can annotate a content (e.g., [20]): the structured model of discourse that they adopt and enact to make order out of chaotic annotations. These models usually disregard the fact that natural language is inherently recursive and hence distinguish (at least) between target documents and annotations. On the contrary, we observed practices of "annotation annotating" that could call for a different perspective (see Figure 3), where any text can be object of an annotation and this, in its turn, can be made the target of some other text. Moreover in many cases these models also propose a more or less prescriptive ontology to characterize annotations and their targets to make them machine processable. Yet, users are often wary of these ontologies since annotations are heavily context dependent, both in respect to the community of users that share them and to the contingent situation where they make some sense to the users.

These considerations led to the development of RAT, i.e., a Recursive Annotating Tool by which users can add an informal layer with respect to "content", and yet be able to discuss and characterize it as it were just but content, since it also is strictly situated, contextualized and bounded to the discourses that users make around and about an electronic resource. The main goal of this tool is to address those advanced requirements like reply-threading and bottom-up taxonomy development that have difficulty in breaking forth the prototypes that have been proposed so far only within the Academia (such as Annotea, MADCOW, Debora) and "are difficult to communicate to users and even more difficult to integrate into an easy-to-use tool interface" [15].

In RAT, an annotation is just a *text* that is anchored to another *text* and is given to the interpretation of either

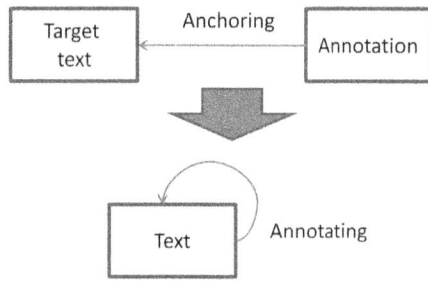

Figure 3: A new perspective on digital annotation.

users, machines or both level. Moreover, targets can be nested within each other: for instance, a document can be made target of (one or more) annotations, as well as any of its parts. In doing so, an annotation can "stand for" an N-ary relation between targets (see the tag 'redundant' in Figure 4).

In this view the aspect of annotations of being a content is important and it intentionally overrides any strong (i.e., ontological) distinction between *textual* annotations, i.e., comments by which humans discuss over some content; and *semantic* annotations, i.e., tags and labels that are attached to content to enable some sort of machine interoperability. This intentionally flat model leaves room for customization in terms of a particular "use" of the semantic tags the tool allows to attach to electronic resources as it does not rely on any predefined domain model to either *adopt at* or *adapt to* a particular setting.

Only once annotations have been created, and bound to each other in a flat web of references (see Figure 4) with relationships that are semantically "neutral" (i.e., void of any predefined meaning), they can either be associated to specific application behaviors, or left to the interpretation of human actors that attach them to their documents and share them to communicate[3].

The purposely flat model of RAT and its high configurability make it (at least in principle) a system that is able to emulate (in conjuction with specific application companions that would tap in its semantic tags) the functionalities of any other domain-specific or task-oriented annotation platform, like g-IBIS, Cohere, CACHE, Collaboratorium and Debategraph (see in [13]). This is because RAT differs from any tool that allows (either explicitly or surreptitiously) to instantiate and apply formal ontologies on content and conversations: rather, its aim is to allow users to made their intended meanings more explicit and shared; this, in turn, can facilitate human users in understanding each other or enable the automatic filtering, ordering and rearrangement of annotations so as to enable discussion, sense making and consensus building, on the one hand; and spur argumentation, the reconciliation of potential misunderstandings and the emergence of minority standpoints, on the other hand.

---

[3]The reader could notice that also hyperlinks challenge a too strict distinction between textual and semantic annotations: indeed hyperlinks can be written by actors on-the-go in an ad-hoc manner to refer their interlocutors to an external resource. But yet they are also associated to a specific application behavior, like launching a browser instance to get access to a Web resource or trying to dispatch a message to a receiver in case of mailto URIs.

4. RAT AT WORK

RAT is mainly aimed at supporting two human behaviors: first, RAT enables the progressive nesting and intertwining of human "discourses within discourses", that is, coping with the intrinsically magmatic and multi-topic nature of human conversations and allowing their unfolding in terms of threads. See for instance in Figure 4 the comment Z is intended as a reply to what said in comment Y (a semantic annotation clarifies that) and this, in its turn, is a reply to comment X. Yet, comment Y is also intended to address a circumscribed passage in comment X (highlighted in Figure 4), with comment Z and K, which challenges a vote against X, intended to be connected in a single thread of discussion. In short, comments X, Y and K can be seen as one single discussion about the same passage in the document, where comments Z is also applied to another passage.

Second, RAT supports the bottom-up specification and clarification of concepts, and the creation of links. Semantic annotations can be attached for the sake of (self-)clarity, to ask for and propose further specifications as well as to allow the system to re-arrange comments and their annotated portions so that single topics, standpoints and points could be presented more orderly and discussed in a more efficient way (cf. phase four of the TP amending process). Possible semantic tags can be, e.g., 'this is a summarization', 'this is a reformulation', 'this is against', 'this is in favour', if these labels are found to support users' needs to "typify" content. For example, users can use semantic annotations to attach concepts to (any) content that either specialize or generalize each others (e.g., the label 'seeds' and 'plants' in Figure 4). Potential ambiguities or contradictions between mutually referring nodes would not be considered breaches in the ontological model (which is not provided at all) but rather opportunities to discuss shortcomings in human utterance and to resolve or suspend them for the task's aims.

The model-flatness of RAT is reflected also in terms of a simplified interaction with it. To this aim, the RAT interface offers just a small floating circular switch that user can set in only one of three possible states: namely "off", "target mode" and "annotation mode". Thus, the typical use case unfolds as follows:

1. The user activates the "target mode"; if the switch is turned off at any time, target(s) selected so far are discarded. In this mode, one of the following cases can occur:

   (a) the user selects portions of text to annotate. To this aim, she can select arbitrary long passages of a textual document. These portions of text can be multiple and even not mutually close (in this case, selected by holding down the Control key); in any case, the system considers each portion as a single target.

   (b) the user selects any of the annotations or targets that have been previously created (the system affords the latter ones in terms of highlighted passages);

   (c) the user selects one or more items from the list of the targets that had been created previously. The targets are reported so that the first 50 characters of the sentence can be read to facilitate the user in understanding the context, as well as the relative

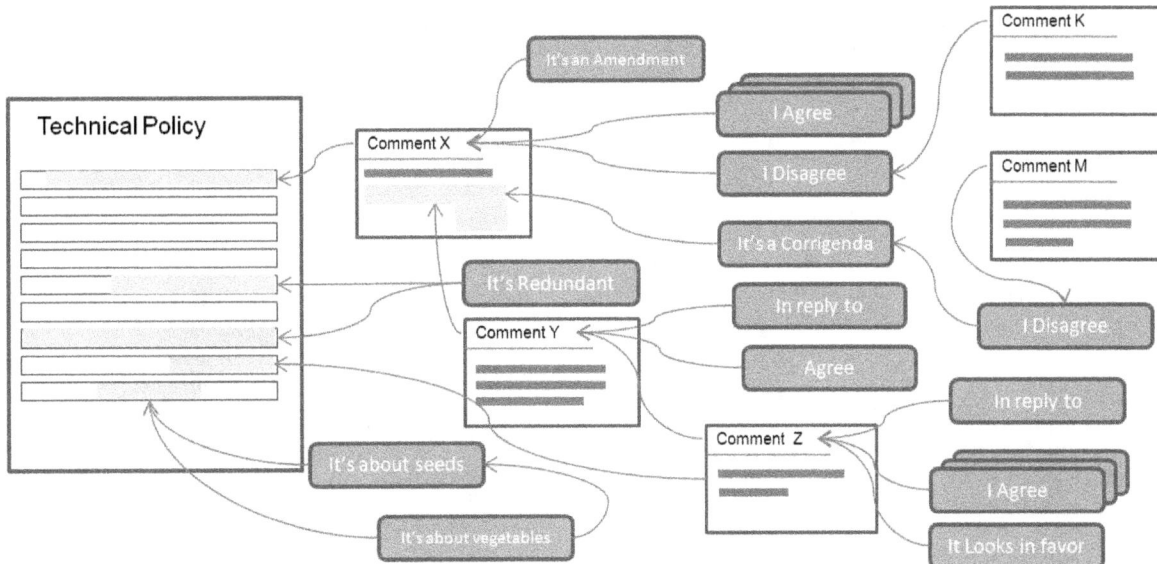

Figure 4: An abstract view of how textual and semantic annotations (rendered as comments and stickers respectively) can enrich each other.

position in the text (page, row, column of the first word of the target).

2. the user activates the "annotation mode". The system takes in the target(s) identified in the former phase. At this point, the system presents a box where the user can write some richly formatted text. When the user types in a special character (like the hash tag in Twitter) the system recognizes that a semantic annotation is being written; in this case, it provides suggestions according to what is being typed and the items available within a predefined list of tags (if any). In so doing, the system presents in different ways what is taken from a predefined, public list (usually an institutional classification scheme); and what comes from a private, user-built list, if the user has got rights to build her own list. When she is done, the user can either save the annotation or discard it. In either cases, the system deactivates the "annotation mode".

From the technical point of view, RAT is conceived as a plug-in for the most common Office Automation suites and web based WYSIWYG editor controls to endow these tools with advanced and yet general-purpose annotation capabilities. These prototypical plug-ins (one for MS Word 2010 and one for a web browser) are conceived to store annotations (and their context) into a remote server, where the Graph DBMS OrientDB[4] is used to guarantee persistence of the Directed Acyclic Graph structure of the RAT annotations.

From the TP case we collected the precise requirement to have the system display the annotation of a multimedia target as close to the target as possible. If the annotation pertains to multiple targets and these are in the same page, the annotation must be displayed as much in between as possible; otherwise the system should display the annotation as close to the first target as possible. Thus, the main problems at stake with the development of RAT regard two

aspects on which we are currently working: first, the extension that makes RAT process also non-textual elements (at first in web pages) within a document, such as images and arbitrary lines (what we call "scribbles" to hint at the typical handwritten side notes of paper-based documents), and create annotations by letting users anchor them to any part of these document elements. Second, at the GUI level to improve the current straightforward interface: how to display meaningful shortcut commands; how to display multiple comments and labels close to their targets, especially when there are many of them accumulated over time; how to render semantic annotations in terms of visual clues (e.g., colors, font formatting) in a clean and clear way; how to allow users switch between a page layout of the annotated artifact (i.e., the usual way where comments are attached to the document in the side margin) and an alternative visualization of content and comments that results from filters enabled by the semantic annotations so that these complementary ways to display content is neither disorientating nor overloading. These problems are only partly technological ones, but they rather regard how users of a specific setting (with their typical skills, needs and expectations) can exploit the fruits of the additional effort of annotating the shared content. This point is specifically addressed in the next section.

4.1 RAT configuration and the TP case

As said previously, RAT is just an annotating tool. Yet, for users to find annotating of some value and this additional effort worth of being paid, it is important to define what to do with the annotations produced; i.e., what kind of functionalities the system must provide especially in regard to the semantic annotations. This is what we call the design of the functionalities enabled by RAT, a task that can be seen as its customization to a specific application case. Moreover, RAT can look "simple" in its conception and reference model but this essentiality does not make it necessarily "easy" to use; or clear to the user what advantage there is for her

---

[4]http://code.google.com/p/orient/

259

in annotating things. Thus, in order to make annotation user-friendly and convenient in a collaborative setting, RAT is intended to employ visual shortcuts and icons that aggregate the targeting and annotating functionalities at GUI level in a more contextualized manner.

Generally speaking, the customizations that are necessary to make RAT more suitable to address the specific needs of a cooperative setting regard the definition of:

1. predefined (and eventually extendible) lists of semantic items (in terms of predefined labels or tags) by which users can annotate documents, comments and tags themselves;

2. specific iconic shortcut controls that can simplify the selection of specific targets (e.g., some document structure) or commit specific types of annotations (e.g., semantic tag to "vote for" an existing comment, as in the TP case) on the basis of some local convention;

3. a three-dimensional permission table that specifies what actions are allowed to what role with respect to what portion of the document (this table can be obviously left "full" if everyone can perform any kind action on the entire document).

4. a set of rules by which annotations and their anchored content can be rearranged in some manner to facilitate retrieval, summarization, discussion and reconciliation of diverse standpoints.

In Figure 5 we indicate in a tabular form the main interventions of customization of RAT that we discussed with the users involved in the Technical Policy case described in Section 2. In particular, the list of semantic annotations reported in such table had been drawn on the basis of the qualitative research performed at the specific setting via a series of interviews with the coordinator and a number of key agronomists, and observations of the meetings where amendments were collaboratively discussed.

Provided the usual magmatic way in which points to discuss could emerge and be referred in extempore comments, semantic annotations would enable the tool to make order out of them and present meaningful threads of discussion in a structured way and in a Forum-like manner, while leaving users free to express their points as they feel. The proposal of support that is enabled by semantic annotation is intended to be provided in two different phases of the TP amendment process. On the one hand, in the phase of collaborative commenting/amending of a document and according to the adopted convention, automatic rearrangement of comments and interventions would make the tool display them as close as possible to the pertinent targets: "corrigenda" first, top valued or agreed upon first, associated to their explanations and related discussions (to possibly extract from not necessarily sequential interventions)[5]. On the other hand, before and during the final co-located meeting (be it virtual or face-to-face), the rearrangement could be exploited when the final report has to be generated by reporting highly agreed proposals at the top, for their

---

[5]Indeed, this approach raised a discussion about the possibility to have available private annotation spaces flanking the shared one. However, this opportunity would require a deeper investigation of the underlying integration policies and was discarded.

easy consolidation, while highly controversial points could be endowed with the pertinent threads of discussion. In so doing, RAT is customized to address the main problems that actors used to face in the TP amending process: mainly to reach an acceptable consensus within the community of experts on what amendments to provide the Regional authority with for the final drafting of the policy document. In this case, the functionality to comment either paragraphs of the TP document (possibly by proposing punctual corrigenda of its parts) or previous comments in some sort of discussion thread is aimed at surrogating some of the debates that, without such support, would have required extensive and expensive co-located meetings before the final and resolving one, whose output is the TP enriched with a well-contextualized and clear set of proposals of amendment. In short, the intended use of RAT considers that users are always left free to annotate their own comments or portions of comments: the more they do it, the better chances that their interventions could be reported in a contextualized way in the right place in the report and be referred to the right targets and points so as to improve their visibility during the meeting and the chances their point could be really understood and taken in consideration.

The important thing to remind is that RAT does not necessarily impose an annotation schema. Users would be able to annotate the TP freely: we expect in real cases to observe conventions and good practices emerge about how to make a proper target with respect to the content to amend. These conventions are purposely left external with respect to the application, as it would be difficult to embed them and probably useless. For instance, in the TP case annotation by user-defined keywords was deliberately prevented, not to create unnecessary "noise" on the shared virtual space.

5. CONCLUSIONS AND FUTURE WORK

Our empirical investigations showed that various forms of annotation are used to support cooperation in situations where asynchronous interaction occurs with the mediation of a shared inscribed artifact. Annotations in this case play the twofold role of conveying additional content that enriches the target document, and of supporting either implicit or explicit steps of the discourses going on "around and about" this content.

The core idea to recursively associate an additional content to any kind of document element is however not enough to support the richness of the collective conversation the annotation tool is called to support; yet it is the main precondition. The additional content that is conveyed by and through the annotations enables a reorganization of the content according to specific and highly situated needs: these needs are expressed in terms of rules that let various discourses emerge and that produce "thematic threads" from those mutually nested annotations by requiring users the limited effort to semantically annotate some of those annotations. RAT attempts to achieve this flexibility by combining nowadays widespread habits of Web 2.0 users: tagging, commenting, creating links and connections between the available textual resources.

The development of an annotation tool is then part of a broader research agenda that can be briefly summarized in terms of reaching the goal to convey various types of awareness promoting information (what we called API in [7]) through affordances that can be partially conveyed by the

Target type	Enabled/Promoted Action by RAT	Additional Notes
A whole document	To Write a comment (and possibly to associate a unique label to this comment to characterize it and make it machine-processable).	
Part of a document (either a policy paragraph or some text selected explicitly by the user). In doing so, the system attaches the annotation "target" to this selection.	1. To Write a comment (and possibly to associate a unique label to this comment to characterize it and make it machine-processable) 2. To Annotate by choosing an item from these: - "expunge this" - "need to be expanded" - "not clear" - "wrong" (a social convention should require to add a comment that could explain what is wrong)	When the user double-clicks on a target, she gets the list of annotations associated with that target and can add her own one. Also, users can gets a list of current targets and select from this list the target to refer to with a new annotation. This would limit the case in which multiple targets are created in a spurious way to indicate the same "thing".
Part of a comment (selected explicitly by the user). In doing so, the system attaches the annotation "target" to this selection.	1. To Write another comment in reply (the system annotates the latter comment automatically as "reply of x"). 2. To Annotate by choosing an item from these lists: 2.a) - "verbatim corrigenda" (conventional meaning: this is the text intended to literally substitute the target). - "in reply to" (the user should then select a second target from those already tagged as "target") 2.b) - "I Agree" - "I disagree"	1. is allowable only to others than the writer of the target comment. 2.a is allowable only to the writer of the target comment. 2.b is allowable only to others than the writer of the target comment.
A whole comment, "X" (whose target can be either a portion of the document or a comment).	1. To Write another comment ("Y") in reply. (the system annotates Y automatically as "reply to target X"). 2. To Annotate X by choosing one from: 2.a) - "Amendment" (This is the label to mean that comment X is aimed at proposing a substitution in the X's target; comment X should contain a "verbatim corrigenda"). - "Addition" (this is the label to mean that comment X is aimed at proposing an addition to insert in the targetted point by X). 2.b) - "In favour" - "Against" (of the X's target) 2.c) - "Looks in favour" - "Looks against" (of the X's target) 2.d) - "I Agree" - "I disagree" (with X).	1. is allowable only to others than the writer of the target comment. 2.a is allowable only to the writer of the target comment. In doing so, she characterizes it. 2.b is allowable only to the writer of the target comment. 2.c is allowable only to others than the writer of the target comment. 2.d is allowable only to others than the writer of the target comment.

Figure 5: The list of RAT customizations for the TP case.

system but more importantly interpreted by the users through pertinent policies and conventions [8] and their computational counterparts, i.e., setting-specific rules [6, 5]. Annotations are one of the main means to achieve this goal, as they are grounded on long-established practices of appropriation and use of habitual artifacts.

The idea leading this research agenda is to build a conceptually unified framework where supports of Cooperative Work and Knowledge Management are available and coherent with each other [7], and to integrate specialized functionalities defined to address the (ever evolving) needs of specific settings on the basis of empirical studies.

Another extension under consideration regards to allow the anchoring of an annotation to an arbitrary number of targets belonging to two or more different electronic documents: this would allow to draw relationships across a whole document management system and would contribute to create an electronic "web of artifacts" as the domain of distributed care, among other domains, impose to consider. Here the challenge is the combination of simplicity of usage, clarity of presentation and richness of added value for the users who are willing to pay the effort of annotating their

resources. Related to this need, but with different aims, it is the management of private places of annotation that should complement what is shared and put into "common (information) spaces" [25]: here the challenge is even more demanding since the main problem to be solved is the integration of different and possibly conflicting meanings associated to the chosen labels [22], a situation that recalls the collaborative dynamics occurring across communities of practice and the concept of boundary object [28]: indeed, a tool that makes no distinction between free-text and semantic annotations could address that seeming (but yet extremely fruitful) contradiction of an artifact that is "weakly constructed in common use, and [...] strongly structured in individual-site use", as the former type of annotation would support common use and discussion, while the latter type would enable a reorganization of content according to some individual site structure or model.

The scenario targeted by this research agenda requires to consider the "structures" [23, 17] that are progressively consolidated within a community during its evolution and to build technological supports that are *malleable* enough to adapt to their continuous development: here is where the main challenge lies, irrespective of the setting at hand.

6. REFERENCES

[1] S. Bødker and K. H. Madsen. Methods & tools: context: an active choice in usability work. *Interactions*, 5(4):17–25, July 1998.

[2] S. Bringay, C. Barry, and J. Charlet. Annotations: A functionality to support cooperation, coordination and awareness in the electronic medical record. In *COOP'06: Proceedings of the 7th International Conference on the Design of Cooperative Systems*, France, Provence, 2006.

[3] F. Cabitza. "Remain faithful to the earth!": Reporting experiences of Artifact-Centered design in healthcare. *Computer Supported Cooperative Work (CSCW)*, 20(4):231—263, 2011.

[4] F. Cabitza, G. Colombo, and C. Simone. Leveraging underspecification in knowledge artifacts to foster collaborative activities in professional communities. *International Journal of Human - Computer Studies*, forthcoming, 2012.

[5] F. Cabitza, S. Corna, I. Gesso, and C. Simone. WOAD, a platform to deploy flexible EPRs in full control of End-Users. In *EICS4Med* 2011: Pisa, Italy, June 2011.

[6] F. Cabitza and I. Gesso. Web of active documents: an architecture for flexible electronic patient records. In *Communications in Computer and Information Science*, volume 127, pages 44-56. Springer

[7] F. Cabitza and C. Simone. Affording mechanisms: an integrated view of coordination and knowledge management. *Computer Supported Cooperative Work (CSCW)*, forthcoming, 2011.

[8] F. Cabitza, C. Simone, and M. Sarini. Leveraging coordinative conventions to promote collaboration awareness. *Computer Supported Cooperative Work (CSCW)*, 18(4):301—330, 2009.

[9] R. Charon. *Narrative Medicine: Honoring the Stories of Illness*. Oxford University Press, 2008.

[10] L. R. Christensen. The logic of practices of stigmergy. page 559. ACM Press, 2008.

[11] E. F. Churchill, J. Trevor, S. Bly, L. Nelson, and D. Cubranic. Anchored conversations: Chatting in the context of a document. In *CHI 2000. The Hague, Netherland, pp. 454-461*, 2000.

[12] J. Conklin and M. Begemann. gIBIS: a hypertext tool for argumentation. *ACM Transactions on Office Information Systems*, 4(6):303–331, 1988.

[13] A. De Liddo, A. Sándor, and S. Buckingham Shum. Contested collective intelligence: Rationale, technologies, and a Human-Machine annotation study. *Computer Supported Cooperative Work (CSCW)*, 21(4-5): 417-448, 2011.

[14] S. Guibert, F. A. Darses, and J. Boujut. Using annotations in a collective and Face-to-Face design situation. In *ECSCW 2009*, pages 191–206, 2009.

[15] B. Haslhofer, W. Jochum, R. King, C. Sadilek, and K. Schellner. The LEMO annotation framework: weaving multimedia annotations with the web. *International Journal on Digital Libraries*, 10(1):15–32, 2009.

[16] A. Holt. *Organized activity and its support by computer*. Kluwer Academic Publishers, 1997.

[17] M. R. Jones. Giddens's structuration theory and information systems research. *MIS Quarterly*, 32(1):127-157, Mar. 2008.

[18] M. Klein. The MIT collaboratorium: Enabling effective Large-Scale deliberation for complex problems. *SSRN Electronic Journal*, 2008.

[19] T. Koschmann and C. D. Le Baron. Reconsidering common ground: examining clark's contribution theory in the OR. In *ECSCW '03*, pages 81—98, Norwell, MA, USA, 2003

[20] T. Kriplean, M. Toomin, J. Morgan, A. Borning, and A. J. Ko. Is this what you meant? promoting listening on the web with reflect. In *CHI 2012*, May 5-10, 2012, Austin, Texas, USA, 2012.

[21] B. E. Lewis. Narrative medicine and healthcare reform. *Journal of Medical Humanities*, 32(1):9–20, Oct. 2010.

[22] G. Mark, V. Gonzalez, M. Sarini, and C. Simone. Supporting articulation with the reconciler. In *CHI 2002 Extended Abstracts*, pages 814–815, 2002.

[23] W. J. Orlikowski. Using technology and constituting structures: A practice lens for studying technology in organizations. *Organization Science*, 11(4):404–428, July 2000.

[24] V. Pipek, V. Wulf, and A. Johri. Bridging artifacts and actors: Expertise sharing in organizational ecosystems. *Computer Supported Cooperative Work (CSCW)*, 21(2-3):261–282, 2012.

[25] K. Schmidt and L. Bannon. Taking CSCW seriously: Supporting articulation work. *Computer Supported Cooperative Work (CSCW)*, 1(1-2):7–40, 1992.

[26] K. Schmidt and I. Wagner. Ordering systems: Coordinative practices and artifacts in architectural design and planning. *Computer Supported Cooperative Work (CSCW)*, 13(5-6):349–408, 2004.

[27] M. Schoop. An introduction to the language-action perspective. *ACM SIGGROUP Bulletin*, 22(2), 2001.

[28] S. L. Star and J. R. Griesemer. Institutional ecology, 'Translations' and boundary objects: Amateurs and professionals in berkeley's museum of vertebrate zoology, 1907-39. *Social Studies of Science*, 19:387–420, 1989.

[29] G. Stevens, V. Pipek, and V. Wulf. Appropriation infrastructure: Supporting the design of usages. In V. Pipek, M. B. Rosson, B. Ruyter, and V. Wulf, editors, *End-User Development*, volume 5435, pages 50–69. Springer Berlin Heidelberg, Berlin, Heidelberg, 2009.

[30] C. Weng and J. H. Gennari. Asynchronous collaborative writing through annotations. In *CSCW '04*, pages 578–581, New York, NY, USA, 2004. ACM.

[31] T. Winograd. A Language/Action perspective on the design of cooperative work. *Human-Computer Interaction*, 3(1):3–30, 1988.

Discovering Habits of Effective Online Support Group Chatrooms

Elijah Mayfield and
Miaomiao Wen
Carnegie Mellon University
Pittsburgh, PA 15213
{emayfiel, mwen}
@cs.cmu.edu

Mitch Golant
The Cancer Support
Community
Washington, DC
mitch@cancersupport
community.org

Carolyn Penstein Rosé
Carnegie Mellon University
Pittsburgh, PA 15213
cprose@cs.cmu.edu

ABSTRACT

For users of online support groups, prior research has suggested that a positive social environment is a key enabler of coping. Typically, demonstrating such claims about social interaction would be approached through the lens of sentiment analysis. In this work, we argue instead for a multifaceted view of emotional state, which incorporates both a static view of emotion (sentiment) with a dynamic view based on the behaviors present in a text. We codify this dynamic view through data annotations marking information sharing, sentiment, and coping efficacy. Through machine learning analysis of these annotations, we demonstrate that while sentiment predicts a user's stress at the beginning of a chat, dynamic views of efficacy are stronger indicators of stress reduction.

Categories and Subject Descriptors

I.2.7 [**Artificial Intelligence**]: Natural Language Processing—*Discourse*;

Keywords

discourse analysis; efficacy; sentiment analysis; social media; synchronous chat; group dynamics; information exchange

1. INTRODUCTION

The Internet provides invaluable resources for adults who suffer from chronic or life threatening diseases. Beyond the physical hardships associated with many of these conditions, patients suffer from intense emotions like fear, anger, and sadness, which lead to the experience of stress. Online support groups have the tremendous potential to make social support experiences accessible to patients with limited social circles or even physical mobility [41]. Nevertheless, while the positive effects of face-to-face support groups have been studied extensively, the inner workings of online support

groups are much less well worked out. For example, facilitation in face-to-face support groups is well studied [1], but online, the role of a facilitator is still unclear. Additionally, most prior work studying online support groups has focused on asynchronous communication, for example on maintaining group membership [52] or meeting needs of caregivers [49]. Our work focuses instead on sychronous chat.

In this paper we present operationalizations that are valuable for monitoring and understanding the stress of each participant in an online support group context. Improving automated analysis in this context has potential benefits for facilitators, both in real-time, as interfaces can be designed to support facilitation through this style of analysis, and after the fact, as a source of insight for training, reanalysis, and summarization. The computer-supported collaborative work (CSCW) community has provided inroads to both of these applications. In real-time, triggered interventions in an online conversational setting can greatly benefit from a deeper understanding of communication processes [23, 24]. Interface designs supporting group discussions, especially for facilitators, have also been shown to be effective in chatroom contexts for learning [47] and project meetings [11]. After the fact, social network analysis has used graphs between participants to study group problem solving dynamics [46] or for performing structural analysis of group social networks [14, 42]

We focus in this work on post hoc analysis of chat, in particular on two aspects of group interactions. From a linguistic standpoint, the text of a chatroom discussion can be viewed through the lens of sequences of interaction; a higher-level view of the group dynamics of a chat may focus on the linking of participants together through network analysis of this linguistic connection between users. Second, from a psychological standpoint, we study the emotions and coping strategies of participants in online chat, at a level that allows us to understand the potential shortfalls of coarse-grained sentiment analysis. In order to make the best use of the data that is available to developers of groupware systems, a deep understanding of the processes behind both linguistic and psychological aspects of chat is required.

Chatrooms elicit a complex structure of multiparty conversation, and understanding this structure is of particular importance for sociolinguistic research. In particular, the disentangling of threads of conversation, and the flow of information and emotional support between speakers, lends insight into how groups communicate. Understanding how to represent threading has been a problem in the CSCW community for many years [45]. Often, CSCW researchers have followed the conversation analysis framework and the notion of adjacency pairs from Schegloff [43]. One study has directly applied this framework to the context of online support groups [35], identifying the structure of interactions between facilitators and patients.

In prior work attempting to understand the emotion of speakers, identifying the coping strategies and the social connections being made between speakers has typically been formulated as a sentiment analysis problem, where speakers' opinions are labelled as either positive or negative. This formulation has been used to understand group discussions in numerous contexts, such as political blog posts [39] or visualizations of computer-mediated communication [32]. In these works, emotion or sentiment is treated as a property of the language employed in the text. Language then reflects the emotional state of the one who has uttered that text.

In contrast, our work aligns with a more complex view of emotion, in which text reflects not just the bias of the one who has uttered the text, but also of their assumed audience. This view has been largely explored in sociolinguistic literature, both in the context of fiction writing [7] and publication within academic communities [19]. Work in this tradition expects a text not only to display the projected image of the author but also that of the assumed audience. In our work, we explore an additional factor, namely, the contrast between the reflection of the participant's emotional state and the reflection of how that emotional state is changing through participation in the interaction of a chatroom. Automating this style of analysis has led to more complex modelling of bias detection [33] or contentiousness of viewpoints in news articles [40].

To further researchers' understanding of these processes, we demonstrate this contrast in the context of online support groups through an empirical analysis of chatroom behavior, both at the level of basic information flow, and at the level of framing the coping experience itself. We demonstrate that the features that predict emotional state are different from the features that predict changes in emotional state over the duration of the conversation. This analysis argues against the idea that emotion is a property of text, and argues instead for a slightly more nuanced view. By this understanding, conversational strategies operate on emotions, and thus emotion and processing emotion may be operationalized as distinct social processes that are encoded in language in distinct ways. To motivate the annotation of our transcripts used by the machine learning models, and explanatory theory from the social cognitive processing model [25] as well as social cognitive theory [3].

In the remainder of the paper we review related work related to theories of coping and work related to analysis of emotion in text. We then describe the data used in our analysis, how the data provides opportunities to contribute to the literature on support groups as well as basic research on conversation. Next we discuss the operationalization of the reliable annotation schemes we have developed, and our annotation effort. Then we present regression models that show the impact of these annotations both on the level of language use, as well as higher-level annotations, for analyzing both entrance stress and shift in stress of a participant over the course of a chat. We conclude with a discussion of the limitations of this work and plans for continued research.

2. PRIOR WORK

Our work draws from and contributes to several bodies of literature. First, it draws from the extensive literature on coping, from which we primarily draw from the Social Cognitive Processing model and Social Cognitive Theory. Among other things, this literature promotes disclosure of negative affect in support group interactions. We also examine our data from a linguistic point of view, understanding the nature of discourse and discursive processes for sharing information. Finally, the language technologies community has shown great promise in simpler views of sentiment and emotion recognition, which contributes to the notions of stress and coping that we are interested in. Because we wish to facilitate automated analysis in later stages of our research, we also take into account work from this field.

2.1 Social Psychology Theories of Coping

The coping literature provides us with lenses through which we can view conversational behavior in our chat corpus from the perspective of pscyhological processes that have already been identified in the social psychology literature. One such lens is the Social Cognitive Processing model [25], which places a great emphasis on disclosure, positive social settings, and disinhibition. A model that provides a complementary perspective, investigating the constructs of coping efficacy and empowerment, is that of Social Cognitive Theory [3]. We review both here.

The social cognitive processing model defines the coping process as one of intense emotional encounters that provide opportunities for confronting and then integrating traumatic experiences in ones psyche, which is referred to as "adaptation" [25]. In this paradigm, cancer is a traumatic life event that shifts a person's core beliefs about themselves. In this model, stress is caused by a discrepancy between a person's mental model of themselves, formed over a lifetime, and the "new normal" that emerges after being diagnosed. Observed events do not match a person's preconceptions. Reducing stress therefore requires either *assimilation*, where events are reappraised to fit preconceptions, or *accommodation*, changing preconceptions to fit new information.

These notions can be easily associated with conversational practices. For example, patients who share a great deal of information about themselves, especially through narrative and contemplation, should be expected to reduce stress. A major factor impeding this information sharing, however, is social constraint. Unsupportive social environments, where sharing information is met with unexpected responses or suppression of discussion, are likely to impede the cognitive processing that leads to stress reduction. On the other hand, positive responses and empathetic responses are more likely to foster an environment that encourages emotional expression and validation. This is particularly important in expressing primary negative affect– fear, anger and sadness. Social constraint on disclosure of these emotions leads to increased anxiety, suppressing anger increases the likelihood of hostility, and suppression sadness increasing the likelihood of depression [12].

The issue of social constraint becomes even more important in a chatroom-based online setting, where the only form of support is via a text-based exchange. Walther and others have underscored the "self-disclosure miracle" associated with online support groups: the only method of connection is by sharing about yourself [50]. However, social cues for cohesively handling multiple "threads" of conversation are more limited in a text-only context [6]. Tone is also difficult due to the lack of both verbal and non-verbal cues, such as body language, and participants overestimate their ability to convey tone [22]. Therefore, informational and emotional exchanges with others who understand your experiences is believed to enhance social cognitive processing.

In our qualitative explorations of the chat data, we noticed that one distinguishing characteristic of participants was the extent to which they framed their hardships as fixable or un-fixable. In some cases, this characteristic distinguished individuals who participated in the same interaction, but came out with differential effects on reported distress. In particular, we observed participants who engaged in discussion about their issues framed as fixable and came out reporting a reduction in distress, and in the same interaction observed participants who engaged in discussions in which issues were framed as unfixable, and who came out reporting increased levels of distress. One goal of the analysis we report in this paper was to investigate whether this pattern is stable across the corpus, or only idiosyncratic. In our investigation of the coping literature, we found evidence from questionnaire based research that beliefs in ones ability to cope with hardship is associated with positive tangible effects on well-being [37]. The general concept of Self-efficacy, which is defined as people's belief in their ability to effect change in a particular context, has its roots in Social Cognitive Theory [3]. The more specific relevant construct within the coping literature is the concept of coping efficacy, which can be defined as a person's belief that they have the ability to impact their own well-being, as it pertains to their experience with their illness, either physically or emotionally. Drawing from our observations related to framing, we expect to find evidence of coping efficacy in an operationalization of the framing of hardships in the online discussions [48].

2.2 Information Authority in Discourse

The Negotiation framework, as formulated by the systemic functional linguistics (SFL) community, places a special emphasis on how speakers function in a discourse as sources or recipients of information or action. We use a formulation rooted in the sociolinguistic literature [26]. This work highlights the moves that are made in a dialogue as they reflect the authoritativeness with which those moves were made, and gives structure to exchanges back and forth between participants. We are interested in this framework because of its descriptiveness for social interactions, which makes it easy to track shifts in positioning and the sources of information over time.

We use a formulation of Negotiation which has previously shown to be reliable and automatable for coding using machine learning [31]. The key insight from these codes (defined in section 4.1) is a notion of the source of information, resulting in a metric of authority and ownership over information. This definition of authority, based in the Negotiation framework, has been shown in prior work to have meaningful relationships with constructs that are important to analysis of group interactions. In a learning setting, measurements of authoritativeness using this definition have correlated with learning gains [18] and self efficacy [17]. In task-based dialogue with two speakers, per-line annotation of authority has assisted in predicting task success [29] and in identifying differences in practices across cultures [28].

To our knowledge, however, the work we present here is the first study of authoritativeness's impact in a purely social setting.

For our purposes, this framework also provides an important advantage over analysis using adjacency pairs from conversation analysis. While initiation-response pairs give structure to a dialogue, they do not give a clearly-defined unit of analysis for emotion or higher-level concepts, such as efficacy. Indeed, for long sequences of information exchange, the complex structure of adjacency pairs rapidly becomes unreliable between human annotators. The Negotiation framework, by contrast, focuses heavily on a relatively flat notion of sequences, emphasizing the exchange of information between speakers. This makes this framework ideal for defining a unit of analysis above an individual utterance.

2.3 Automated Analysis of Emotion in Text

In the past decade, there has been a consistent stream of work in the language technologies community related to the analysis of emotions in text using machine learning and text mining techniques. A thorough review of this literature is beyond the scope of this paper, thus we restrict ourselves to mentioning a few representative publications. Some of the most famous early work demonstrated that machine learning models for classifying sentiment of product reviews and movie reviews outperformed rule based models [38]. Other work has focused on how transitory emotions are expressed within an ongoing text or discourse [20]. A series of investigations have sought features that are effective predictors of sentiment. The greatest improvements in performance have been achieved with features that insightfully capture the essence of the linguistic constructions used to express sentiment [53, 21]. Other recent work investigates how to achieve greater generality in trained models for sentiment analysis [8].

Our current work is not concerned with automatic detection of sentiment. Rather, what we explore is the conceptualization of the relationship between emotion and text. In particular, below we discuss how we distinguish expression of general outlook from the more specific expressions of ones conception of their own coping efficacy or that of others. This paper demonstrates the value of these more nuanced operationalizations of emotion in text, which provides motivation for our planned future work in which we adapt and extent techniques from the area of sentiment analysis to the problem of predicting these three more specific constructs.

3. DATA COLLECTION

Our data comes from the Cancer Support Community[1]. Participants were recruited and provided with a wide range of support services such as educational services, physician lectures, and exercise programs. Each conversation took place in the context of a weekly meeting in a real-time chat an online chatroom over the course of one hour, with up to 6 participants in addition to a professional therapist facilitating the discussion. Facilitators were explicitly asked to avoid developing 'therapeutic relationships' with online group members and to instead use their comments to promote the development of social support among members and to focus group discussion. Group members were also en-

---

[1]www.cancersupportcommunity.org

K2				C	[M], fast question, did your son have a biopsy?
K2				C	or does that happen when he comes home
	K1			V	i have 3 dogs.
	K1			V	2 are new puppies so they keep me happy.
	K1			V	man's best friend
	f			S	:-D
	o			C	and women
	K2			J	what kind of dogs????
		K1		C	[D], I keep seeing that you are typing and then it stops
		K2		C	how are you doing this week
	K1			V	i feel ery surrounded by women lol.
	K1			V	the puppies are a maltese/yorkie mix and the full grown is a pomaranian/yorkie.
K1				M	No, he did not have a biopsy.
K1				M	The surgeon that he saw examined him and said that by feel, he did not think the lump was cancerous, and he should just wait until he got home and saw a surgeon to see what he suggested.
f				C	that has to be very hard
			o	M	A question, however– [J], you would probably know.
			K2	M	He was told that they could not just do a needle biopsy, that he would have to remove the whole lump in order to tell if it was malignant.
		o		D	Yes.
			K1	D	I was waiting for [M] to answer.
			K1	J	That sounds odd to me

Table 1: An example excerpt with Negotiation labels and threading structure annotated.

couraged to interact using an asynchronous discussion board during the week; those posts are not studied in this paper.

This corpus provides the opportunity to study support groups from a fresh angle. Studies of online support groups have mostly focused on bulletin boards or forums [4]. In our work, on the other hand, we study chatrooms, which allow for a synchronous discussion that is not supported by forum discussions. Previous work has described facilitators' perceptions of differences between F2F and online support groups [36]. Limitations of the medium are the primary concern, including difficulty pacing the discussion and creating cohesion within the group.

In addition to contributing to the literature on online support, our collected corpus allows us to investigate issues related to a distinct flavor of group discussions than what has been the object of study within the language technologies community. Freely available benchmark corpora are more limited in scope than our corpus along a variety of dimensions. For example, the well known Switchboard corpus contains telephone conversations, but is limited to two speakers, and each conversation averages only six minutes in length [13]. Aoki et al. [2] studied floor-taking in small-group sociable talk, and had large groups of up to ten speakers, but studied only seven one-hour conversations. These studies involved spoken language interactions, and therefore do not directly address the question of group participation in a chatroom setting. In online synchronous interactions, [10], studying IRC chatroom thread disentanglement, performed their experiments on a corpus of one conversation held over two hours, totalling 1,500 utterances, while [44] collected approximately 1,600 utterances in the context of classroom-based text message threads.

By contrast, our conversations are held between many speakers, in a chatroom setting, and persist over a total of one hour each. Our corpus consists of 21 such conversations totalling 9,365 lines of chat. In addition, our unla-

belled data, which may be useful for future work, has over 2,000 such conversations spanning hundreds of users over the course of five years. Therefore our study, though larger than any known previous work on chatroom dynamics at this fine-grained level of analysis, has massive room for growth in our future work.

What makes our corpus particularly valuable for addressing our question about how language processes encode evidence of reflecting stress and processing stress is the inclusion of a per-user, per-conversation self-reported measure of distress. Upon entering and exiting the chatroom, participants were asked to mark their level of distress on a scale from 0 to 10, with non-response left available as an option. In assembling our corpus of 21 conversations, we selected only those with a high response rate on distress indicators. Thus, in no conversations that we sampled did more than one speaker provide a non-response to the distress measure. To the extent that we are successful in learning which features of conversational interactions encode the process of reflecting stress or processing stress, these features will have the potential to offer insight into these processes even in the absence of these external metrics.

4. ANNOTATION

Our analysis uses two levels of data annotation. These conversations were annotated for information sharing and authority with the Negotiation framework [26], a sociolinguistic framework descring these factors in conversation. These annotations are made per-line. Next, we group the turns into threads, using the structure from the turn-level Negotiation coding as an intermediary. Finally, we annotate coping efficacy and sentiment at the level of threads. In this section we describe each of these annotation schemes in detail.

4.1 Information Sharing

The Negotiation coding scheme attempts to code information exchange on a turn-by turn basis. To this end, we use the following annotations:

- Utterances containing new information are marked as **K1**, as the speaker is the "primary knower." These utterances can be either opinions, retelling of narrative or other contextualized information, or general knowledge about the world, for instance about medicine or hospital procedures.

- Utterances requesting information are marked **K2**, or "secondary knower," when the speaker is signalling that they want information from another speaker in the dialogue.

- Social feedback moves are labelled **f**, when there is clear sentiment attached but no new content. This can include emoticons, as well as fixed expressions such as "good luck" or social niceties, such as thanking or friendly banter.

- Moves which directly subvert or contradict a previous move are labelled **ch**, for challenge. These lines are more than just disagreement, which is labelled a K1 - instead, a challenge move rejects a premise from a previous turn.

- All other moves are labelled **o**. This includes for example typo correction, delaying or attention grabbing moves, or moves for tracking of the conversation (such as naming the target of an upcoming move).

There are multiple advantages to using the Negotiation framework to annotate information exchange. First, it has well-defined notions of what does or does not count as information exchange, meaning that inter-annotator reliability is achievable at a high level. Second, there is a notion of *sequences*, with internal constraints on ordering of labels based on observed attributes of language use. For instance, a **K2** move should not follow a **K1** move in the same sequence, and a speaker should not give a **K1** move in response to their own **K2**. A full treatment of these constraints is given in [31]. In that work, this layer of structure was built into machine learning models to enhance the accuracy of those systems for automated coding.

One final attribute that we can define based on Negotiation labels is the *authoritativeness* of a speaker. This construct refers not to the control over a discourse directly, but rather to the source of information in a discourse. Using Negotiation labels, we can define authoritativeness as a continuous variable, assigned per speaker, based on their ratio of information sharing to requesting:

$$Auth(S) = \frac{\# K1}{\# K1 + \# K2} \qquad (1)$$

This framework is not specifically dedicated to the domain of chatrooms nor does it have any codes related specifically to cancer ,support groups, or even the medical domain. This is advantageous for the prospect of future work using these annotations. In the language technologies community, automatic coding of information exchange, including the Negotiation framework, has rapidly been advancing. This is likely to benefit our work more quickly if the models built for other domains can be easily transferred to our data. Therefore, we do not attempt to refine these categories for a topic-specific set of codes.

4.2 Defining Threads

Earlier in this paper we discussed the notion of threads as a series of sequences, potentially entangled, that are based on a shared topic. In this section, we elaborate on their definition and describe ways in which we have annotated thread-level behavior.

It is easy to observe that social talk, especially that with multiple participants, often diverges into separate simultaneous conversations, which we term threads. These behaviors have been studied quantitatively before through the lens of conversation analysis [2], inspired by social science, or through discourse coherence [10], a more information theoretic approach. Others have framed the problem as a topic detection [5] or information retrieval [44] task. We attempt to capture aspects of each of these approaches in our annotation. Humans can navigate these conversations with ease, even in unfamiliar environments. Threading is occasionally discussed explicitly in our chatroom data, e.g.:

> **S:** I know you said you have some trouble with all the jumping around that happens online.
> **S:** Are you okay with it now? Have you gotten used to it? I know it's a little more so with more folks?
> **M:** Yes, it's better now.
> **M:** I just post a response and don't worry so much about being out of sequence.
> **S:** [M], good!
> **B:** that's the only way to do it [M] we all just try the best we can.
> **B:** it helps to direct your answer to the person who made a statement that you are replying to.

For our annotation, we begin with Negotiation sequences as our unit of analysis. These sequences, based on constraints, are useful as a stepping stone to defining threads. We group sequences based on their topic using intuitive judgements, along with heuristic rules - for instance, connecting sequences based on anaphora or coreference to entities in a previous sequence.

4.3 Thread-Level Annotations

For each of these threads, we wish to assign each user participating in those threads an annotation describing their attitude, especially as it relates to coping efficacy. We use the following annotation schemes:

4.3.1 Sentiment

We mark each user as expressing positive (1), neutral (2), or negative (3) sentiment. Positive sentiment includes affect as well as many social supportive moves or expressions of hope, while negative sentiment can include uncertainty or worry in addition to affect. All annotation of sentiment was performed manually and holistically based on the entire content of a user's contribution to a thread, rather than relying on keyword-based or machine learning approaches, which are vulnerable to sparsity of evidence in the highly contextual chat domain our data is drawn from.

4.3.2 Coping Efficacy

In this work we define efficacy specifically as it relates to coping with illness, and perform annotation on each thread in two passes. First we identify whether a person expressed any content related to their belief in the ability to effect change or well-being. This is the *efficacy identification* task. Then, for those cases where expressions of efficacy were identified, we assign a grade for positive (1), conflicted (2), or negative (3) efficacy; this is the *rating* task. Because of the nature of these groups, we assume that mentioning efficacy without an explicit marker of affect is positive. Therefore, our middle variable represents cases where explicit indicators of both positive and negative efficacy were present in the same span. Importantly, we measure both *self-efficacy*, a person's belief about their own ability to effect change, and *other-efficacy*, the encouragement or support given to others that they can effect change in their own lives.

To illustrate by example, negative efficacy often takes the form of doubt or uncertainty, in both other- and self-efficacy:

> **B:** how the hell can I say yes when I don't know how I'll be in April or even if I'll be in April

Positive efficacy, on the other hand, is often characterized by certainty, confidence, or, especially in the case of other-efficacy, advocacy for plans of action:

> **I:** It's about taking control of your life and not allowing cancer to take control of you.
> **I:** And enjoying life, too!

While the examples so far have matched positive efficacy with positive sentiment, the two annotations are not always correlated. In the case of negative efficacy, we see that the feeling is often softened with positive sentiment, while positive efficacy is often tempered or restrained by the real problems faced in difficult situations:

> **D:** just an incurable cancer eating away at my bones, it could be worse!

> **A:** I have your encouragement, which after a day like today, is priceless.
> **A:** even if my attitude is in the cellar at the moment.

4.3.3 Thread Ownership

To tie the notion of information sharing into our annotation of threads, we define thread *ownership*. This term is meant to define the user who holds the floor in a thread, sharing the most information on the topic of that thread. We assign ownership based on the user that gives the most **K1** moves in a thread. All lines and sequences in that thread are designated as "owned" by the user, as they are related to the topic they are sharing information on.

This construct allows us to not only measure amount of information shared, but also the response of other group members to that information. For instance, without this notion, it would be difficult to assign **f** moves to a particular user for calculating positive social feedback. With the notion of thread ownership we make the simplifying assumption that all **f** moves in a thread are directed at the thread owner. Conceptually, we use this as a proxy measure of the amount

Annotation	Reliability
Negotiation	$\kappa = 0.70$
Thread Segmentation	$f = 0.75$
Self-Efficacy Identification	$\kappa = 0.73$
Self-Efficacy Grading	$r = 0.72$
Other-Efficacy Identification	$\kappa = 0.77$
Other-Efficacy Grading	$r = 0.75$
Sentiment	$r = 0.68$

Table 2: Inter-annotator agreement across multiple layers of annotation.

of social feedback an individual member receives over the course of a chat.

4.4 Inter-annotator Reliability

Fundamentally, the analysis we present here relies on hand-coded data. Our annotations span multiple levels and we ensured that each level was reliable. Therefore, for each annotation scheme, we iteratively developed a coding manual while testing the inter-rater reliability between two annotators. During these evaluations, neither annotator was aware of the others' annotations. Once we established a coding manual that achieved high reliability, all data for a particular scheme was annotated by a single annotator. For efficacy, because many threads contain no efficacy indicators, each annotator completed two conversations, instead of one, to gather enough data points for a meaningful kappa between annotators.

Our annotations are not all performed at the same level and cannot be evaluated identically. For Negotiation coding, each possible label per line is independent, so we can use the standard kappa metric. For graded thread-level annotations, we wish to account for "near-miss" labels. Efficacy must first be annotated as either present or not present; for this evaluation we use kappa agreement. Sentiment and efficacy (when identified as present) both can be annotated in a range from 1-3. To measure the agreement between annotators we use correlation coefficient. For thread disentanglement within a chat, the standard evaluation metric is the micro-averaged f-score [10], and we use the measures from prior work to compute this f-score. All evaluations of agreement are presented in Table 2 and all are high.

5. PREDICTION EXPERIMENTS

The previous section defined two levels of annotations. The first (the Negotiation framework) is primarily linguistic in nature, and is annotated on a turn-by-turn level. The second (sentiment and efficacy) is primarily social and based on a holistic evaluation of behavior, rather than particular linguistic indicators. In this section, we turn to the question of how these dimensions interact with self-reported stress levels.

We wish to test two aspects of stress prediction. First, how well can a model discern a person's overall stress level, based on their behavior in a chat? Second, can a model detect the impact that the chat will have on stress level? What elements of chat behavior result in lowered stress self-reporting on exit? This value ranges from 0 to 10, though in the sampling of the data set used in this work, no user recorded a value higher than 8.

5.1 Prediction with Thread-Level Annotations

To refine our understanding of social cognitive processing, coping efficacy, and their relation, we test the amount of variance explained with our thread level annotations. We first calculate the average self-efficacy, average other-efficacy, and average sentiment of each participant. For a given speaker S, we calculate their sentiment, self-, and other-efficacy scores $Eff(S)$ as the weighted average over the threads in which they expressed a non-zero score.

We evaluate the impact of our measurements using two metrics. The first is the amount of variance in stress (either entrance or shift) that is explained by this variable in a regression. For this we measure both the impact of a feature alone (a regression with one factor) and the impact of incrementally adding that feature to a multiple regression. In each table listed below, we list features in the order they were added to this multiple regression, so that we can list a third value, showing the improvement in the model's r^2 by adding that feature. The second measurement that we use to evaluate a model is quadratic loss, also known as mean squared error, based on the model's fitted value for a data point and that data point's actual value.

$$Eff(S) = \sum_{t \in T} \frac{\#\ S\ lines\ in\ t}{\#\ S\ lines\ total} \times Eff(S,t) \qquad (2)$$

This provides three variables representing the sentiment, self-efficacy, and other-efficacy of each speaker. We demonstrate their explanatory power in two models: entrance stress and shift in stress over the course of a conversation. For these analyses, we exclude speakers who were facilitators; we also do not include speakers who did not express any positive or negative self- or other-efficacy over the course of an entire conversation. This results in $n = 68$ total data points across 21 conversations.

First, we perform a multiple regression predicting the entrance stress level of users. The results of this regression are given in table 3. This essentially means we are measuring the impact that incoming stress has on the behavior that is subsequently observed. We see that sentiment is predictive of entrance stress levels, while efficacy measures have essentially no impact. This is consistent with the commonly-assumed static view of sentiment.

Annotation Variable	Variance Explained			MSE
	Alone	**Cum.**	**Gain**	
Sentiment	.2763	.2763	-	2.436
Self-Efficacy	.0517	.2774	.0011	2.432
Other-Efficacy	.0000	.2886	.0112	2.394

Table 3: Variance in entrance stress explained by each thread-level measure of language affect.

Next, we perform a multiple regression predicting exit stress. Entrance stress is included as a variable in the regression, essentially meaning that our variables are predicting the residual impact of the conversation. The results of this multiple regression are shown in table 4. This regression indicates that entrance stress is the most important factor in determining exit stress.

The key finding from this regression is that while sentiment is useful in predicting the incoming stress of a user, the predictive power of sentiment analysis for shifts in stress

Annotation Variable	Variance Explained			MSE
	Alone	**Cum.**	**Gain**	
Entrance Stress	.5101	.5101	-	1.166
Self-Efficacy	.1193	.5454	.0353	1.082
Other-Efficacy	.0479	.5836	.0382	0.991
Sentiment	.1955	.5854	.0018	0.987

Table 4: Variance in residual exit stress explained by each measure, indicating the impact of efficacy on coping during a conversation.

due to chat is then limited. Instead, indicators of efficacy show the strongest predictiveness. Between other- and self-efficacy, over 7% of variance is explained over the baseline. Interestingly, self-efficacy and other-efficacy are not significantly correlated. This suggests that there are distinct motivations behind expressing high coping self-efficacy and encouraging high efficacy among others.

5.2 Prediction from Language Behaviors

At a high level, we have now shown the impact of sentiment and efficacy behaviors. Sentiment is highly correlated with entrance stress levels, but is not predictive of shift in stress over the course of a conversation. Contrastingly, entrance stress has no bearing on efficacy, but the levels of efficacy expressed in a conversation indicate the degree of stress reduction upon exiting. We now reanalyze those behaviors through the lens of language behaviors at the turn level. Again, we study both entrance stress and shift in stress. Our goal is to test whether convergent evidence for these behaviors exists on the level of information sharing.

We perform a machine learning regression experiment. We developed multiple indicators of linguistic behavior and use them as a feature space to predict the entrance stress of participants. Feature selection and regression were performed using the LightSIDE machine learning toolkit [30]. From our large set of linguistic features, we perform correlation-based feature subset selection [16] to find a small number of predictive, uncorrelated features. Linear regression is performed using the M5P algorithm [51]. Experiments were performed using leave-one-out cross-validation, where for each fold a regression model is trained on 20 conversations and evaluated on the final, held-out conversation.

To evaluate performance of our model, rather than discussing specific weights on the final regression model, we instead show coverage of different features across folds. Because each fold is trained separately, feature selection will give different results. In the tables below we list only the features that occurred in at least 4 of the 21 folds. Again, we first attempt to predict entrance stress; we then attempt to predict the residual shift in exit stress after taking entrance stress into account. For the first task of predicting entrance stress, the most frequently selected features are shown in table 5.

Our model for predicting change in stress must be conditioned on the entrance stress of a speaker. Therefore, to perform machine learning on shift, we attempt to predict the residual change in stress after performing a regression based on entrance stress. Because users with an entrance stress level of 0 essentially always remain at 0, we exclude those cases from our training set. This results in a total of

Feature	Folds	High Stress
% K2 Lines	20	Fewer K2 lines
# Owned Sequences	20	More ownership
Authoritativeness	4	Less authority
# Seqs with **f** Responses	4	More feedback
Average r^2 (cross-validation): 0.217		

Table 5: Variance in entrance stress explained by utterance-level language annotations.

Feature	Folds	Stress Reduction
# Owned Sequences	20	More ownership
% K2 Lines	11	Fewer K2 lines
Authoritativeness	10	Less authority
% ch lines	9	Fewer ch lines
Average r^2 (cross-validation): 0.138		

Table 6: Variance in exit stress residual explained by utterance-level language annotations.

$n = 49$ users for this experiment. The results of this machine learning experiment are given in table 6.

The results of these models are in line with the higher-level constructs from our first set of experiments. Language behaviors account for over 20% of variance in entrance stress, similar in scale to the performance of sentiment annotation. Meanwhile, after accounting for entrance stress, language behaviors as we have represented them account for an additional 13.8% of variance in the residual shift.

Qualitatively, we find that the features which are used by the model align with our findings from section 5.1. The most important indicators of an individual's stress are related to information sharing. In most folds, the feature indicating the percent of K2 moves, along with sequence ownership, are the strongest (or only) predictors. Users with high incoming stress tend to request less information from others, as a percentage of their time, and share much more information, in absolute terms. Both insights are valuable. The first suggests that users experiencing high stress do not take on the facilitative, conversation-leading role that would be indicated by a high percentage of K2 moves. Instead, their contributions are more focused on either sharing their own information, or taking on a less engaged role in the discussion, primarily providing feedback to others. Next, the inclusion of ownership rather than K1 count alone suggests the group process behavior of "rallying around" stressed individuals. On a further group process level, we see empirical evidence of feedback moves being used more frequently for stressed individuals. More social feedback from others is indicative that the user came in with a high stress level.

The Authoritativeness feature plays a curious role, as it at first glance is weighted counter to our hypotheses on information sharing. However, this is a peculiarity in the regression - when authoritativeness is selected as a feature, the initial intercept of the regression is much higher, indicating very high stress; but the weighting for the % K2 lines feature is also higher. This suggests two alternative models. In one, predicted stress is assumed to be very high, and is drastically lowered by behaviors eliciting information from others. In the other, predicted stress is affected primarily through thread ownership, which indicates information sharing, and the impact of information requests is less drastic.

Both models fit the social cognitive processing hypotheses emphasizing information sharing.

We observe similar features selected by the stress reduction model compared to the entrance model. This is expected, as users entering with high stress inherently have more room for stress reduction. The two features used most frequently for predicting entrance stress continue to appear in this context. The weighting, however, tends to give less weight towards information requests and more towards ownership. An interpretation of this model is that while speakers with high entry stress do not tend to ask for information from others, it is not this lack of questioning that leads to stress reduction. Rather, the lack of questioning is an artifact of the high entry stress, and it is the process of sharing information that is most highly indicative of stress reduction.

Social feedback from other speakers is not included in the stress reduction model, while it is occasionally included in the entry stress prediction model. This suggests that while users may respond strongly to negative sentiment and high entrance stress by giving support, it is less necessary to have explicit support, and more important merely to have an environment conducive to sharing and disclosure. In contrast, a factor that appears in the stress reduction model that does not appear in entrance stress involves **ch** moves. These moves are rare in our corpus. When they do appear, it is usually on topics unrelated to their illness. This suggests that these support groups do avoid direct challenges in supportive contexts; such negative moves occur only outside of the context of illness, aligning with theory from social cognitive processing on reducing social constraints and allowing disclosure.

6. CONCLUSIONS

This work presents an empirical study of the emotional and social functions of online support group chatrooms. Emotional states are a fluid attribute and do not fit well into a single numeric value, especially when discussing coping with a serious illness. To this end, this work highlights multiple views of emotional affect. We measure both self-reported entrance and exit scores, as well as annotating at a thread level language use and behavior that indicates authority, information exchange, sentiment, coping self-efficacy, and belief in the coping efficacy of others.

The picture that emerges illustrates the complexity of language. The stress of a user upon entering a chatroom can assuredly be predicted using sentiment analysis techniques on their language. However, we find that there is little added value from sentiment analysis when predicting improvement in stress over the course of a conversation.

Instead, we find utility in constructs from the social sciences related to information sharing and efficacy. In a machine learning paradigm we used regression models to demonstrate that coping efficacy is more explanatory than sentiment. We also find that information sharing, which is closely backed by the social cognitive processing model of coping, is predictive of stress reduction. In particular, after disentangling conversation into distinct threads, we find that "ownership" of a topic - sharing your own narrative or beliefs - is linked to stress reduction. These findings have important implications on the future direction of automated analysis of text, where sentiment classification continues to improve in performance at breakneck speed, with less attention being paid to more complex models of human emotion.

6.1 Future Work

These experiments were conducted on 21 conversations and nearly 10,000 lines of chat, one of the larger corpora to have ever been analyzed at this granularity. However, this is a fraction of the data available to us. Thousands of conversations within the Cancer Support Community have not been annotated or analyzed. Furthermore, our most recent work has shown that the information exchange annotations and thread structure within this dataset can be reliably annotated [27]. Automation of thread-level sentiment or efficacy annotation presents a promising direction for future work; results in related areas such as email conversations [15] and dialogue systems [9] have been effective. Thus it is likely that an ensemble of methods will allow us to annotate our entire corpus along all dimensions described in this paper.

This large-scale annotation will allow us to study many questions about the interactions of users in online support groups. Longitudinal studies of support groups have been performed in the context of discussion boards, e.g. for language adoption [34] and membership attrition [52], but studying the change in language use in synchronous communication is much sparser. In this work we have also limited ourselves to the text contributions of members; however, we have valuable information in the form of social network data, and work in social network analysis between group members may lend further insight into the group practices which are most effective for stress reduction. Automatic annotation of very large data sources, augmented by the insights gained in this paper and proven methods for group interaction analysis, will lead to a much deeper understanding of support group communication habits.

Acknowledgements

The research reported here was supported by National Science Foundation grant IIS-0968485.

7. REFERENCES

[1] Cancer support groups: A guide for facilitators. *American Cancer Society*, 2005.

[2] P. M. Aoki, M. H. Szymanski, L. Plurkowski, J. D. Thornton, A. Woodruff, and W. Yi. Where is the "party" in "multi-party"? analyzing the structure of small-group sociable talk. In *Proceedings of the Internation Conference on Computer Supported Collaborative Work*, 2006.

[3] A. Bandura. *Self-Efficacy: The Exercise of Control.* 1997.

[4] A. Barak, M. Boniel-Nissim, and J. Suler. Fostering empowerment in online support groups. In *Computers in Human Behavior*, 2008.

[5] E. Bingham, A. Kaban, and M. Girolami. Topic identification in dynamical text by complexity pursuit. In *Neural Processing Letters*, 2003.

[6] S. D. Black, J. A. Levin, H. Mehan, and C. N. Quinn. Real and non-real time interaction: unraveling multiple threads of discourse. In *Discourse Process*, 1983.

[7] W. C. Booth. *The Rhetoric of Fiction.* 1983.

[8] H. I. Daumé. Frustratingly easy domain adaptation. In *Proceedings of the Association for Computational Linguistics*, 2007.

[9] J. Drummond and D. Litman. Examining the impacts of dialogue content and system automation on affect models in a spoken tutorial dialogue system. In *Proceedings of the ACL Special Interest Group on Discourse and Dialogue*, 2011.

[10] M. Elsner and E. Charniak. Disentangling chat. *Computational Linguistics*, 2010.

[11] W. Geyer, H. Richter, L. Fuchs, T. Frauenhofer, S. Daijavad, and S. Poltrock. A team collaboration space supporting capture and access of virtual meetings. In *Proceedings of the International Conference on Supporting Group Work*, 2001.

[12] J. Giese-Davis, A. Conrad, B. Nouriani, and D. Spiegel. Exploring emotion-regulation and autonomic physiology in metastatic breast cancer patients: Repression, suppression, and restraint of hostility. *Personality and Individual Differences*, 2008.

[13] J. Godfrey, E. Holliman, and J. McDaniel. Switchboard: telephone speech corpus for research and development. In *Proceedings of the International Conference on Acoustics, Speech, and Signal Processing*, 1992.

[14] S. P. Goggins, K. Galyen, and J. Laffey. Network analysis of trace data for the support of group work: Activity patterns in a completely online course. In *Proceedings of the ACM Conference on Supporting Group Work*, 2010.

[15] G. Groh and J. Hauffa. Characterizing social relations via nlp-based sentiment analysis. In *Proceedings of the International Conference on Weblogs and Social Media*, 2011.

[16] M. Hall and L. A. Smith. Practical feature subset selection for machine learning. In *Australian Computer Science Conference*, 1998.

[17] I. Howley, D. Adamson, G. Dyke, E. Mayfield, J. Beuth, and C. P. Rosé. Group composition and intelligent dialogue tutors for impacting students academic self-efficacy. In *Proceedings of Intelligent Tutoring Systems*, 2012.

[18] I. Howley, E. Mayfield, and C. P. Rosé. Missing something? authority in collaborative learning. In *Proceedings of Computer Supported Collaborative Learning*, 2011.

[19] K. Hyland. *Disciplinary Discourses: Social Interactions in Academic Writing.* 2004.

[20] D. Inkpen, F. Keshtkar, and D. Ghazi. Analysis and generation of emotion in texts, in knowledge engineering: Principle and technique. In *Proceedings of the International Conference on Knowledge Engineering Principles and Techniques*, 2000.

[21] M. Joshi and C. P. Rosé. Generalizing dependency features for opinion mining. In *Proceedings of the Association for Computational Linguistics*, 2009.

[22] J. Kruger, N. Epley, J. Parker, and Z. Ng. Egocentrism over e-mail: Can we communicate as well as we think? In *Journal of Personal and Social Psychology*, 2005.

[23] R. Kumar and C. P. Rosé. Architecture for building conversational agents that support collaborative learning. In *IEEE Transactions on Learning*, 2011.

[24] R. Kumar, C. P. Rosé, Y.-C. Wang, M. Joshi, and A. Robinson. Tutorial dialogue as adaptive collaborative learning support. In *Proceedings of Artificial Intelligence in Education*, 2007.

[25] S. J. Lepore. A social-cognitive processing model of emotional adjustment to cancer. In *Psychosocial intervention and cancer: An introduction*, 2001.

[26] J. Martin and D. Rose. *Working with Discourse: Meaning Beyond the Clause*. Continuum, 2003.

[27] E. Mayfield, D. Adamson, and C. P. Rosé. Hierarchical conversation structure prediction in multi-party chat. In *Proceedings of SIGDIAL Meeting on Discourse and Dialogue*, 2012.

[28] E. Mayfield, D. Adamson, A. I. Rudnicky, and C. P. Rosé. Computational representations of discourse practices across populations in task-based dialogue. In *Proceedings of the International Conference on Intercultural Collaboration*, 2012.

[29] E. Mayfield, M. Garbus, D. Adamson, and C. P. Rosé. Data-driven interaction patterns: Authority and information sharing in dialogue. In *Proceedings of AAAI Fall Symposium on Building Common Ground with Intelligent Agents*, 2011.

[30] E. Mayfield and C. P. Rosé. An interactive tool for supporting error analysis for text mining. In *NAACL Demonstration Session*, 2010.

[31] E. Mayfield and C. P. Rosé. Recognizing authority in dialogue with an integer linear programming constrained model. In *Proceedings of Association for Computational Linguistics*, 2011.

[32] J. McIntire, O. I. Osesina, and M. Craft. Development of visualizations for social network analysis of chatroom text. In *Proceedings of the International Conference on Collaboration Technologies and Systems*, 2011.

[33] D. Nguyen, E. Mayfield, and C. P. Rosé. An analysis of perspective in interactive settings. In *Workshop on Social Media Analysis at the ACM Conference on Knowledge Discovery & Data Mining*, 2010.

[34] D. Nguyen and C. P. Rosé. Language use as a reflection of socialization in online communities. In *Workshop on Language in Social Media at ACL*, 2011.

[35] K. Ogura, T. Kusumi, and A. Miura. Analysis of community development using chat logs: A virtual support group of cancer patients. In *Proceedings of the IEEE Symposium on Universal Communication*, 2008.

[36] J. E. Owen, E. O. Bantum, and M. Golant. Benefits and challenges experienced by professional facilitators of online support groups for cancer survivors. In *Psycho-Oncology*, 2008.

[37] E. M. Ozer and A. Bandura. Mechanisms governing empowerment effects: A self-efficacy analysis. In *Journal of Personality and Social Psychology*, 1990.

[38] B. Pang and L. Lee. A sentimental education: Sentiment analysis using subjectivity summarization based on minimum cuts. In *Proceedings of the Association for Computational Linguistics*, 2004.

[39] S. Park, M. Ko, J. Kim, Y. Liu, and J. Song. The politics of comments: predicting political orientation of news stories with commenters' sentiment patterns. In *Proceedings of the International Conference on Computer-Supported Collaborative Work*, 2011.

[40] S. Park, K. S. Lee, and J. Song. Contrasting opposing views of news articles on contentious issues. In *Proceedings of the Association for Computational Linguistics*, 2011.

[41] S. Rodgers and Q. Chen. Internet community group participation: Psychosocial benefits for women with breast cancer. In *Journal of Computer Mediated Communication*, 2005.

[42] D. Rosen, V. Miagkikh, and D. Suthers. Social and semantic network analysis of chat logs. In *In Proceedings of the International Conference on Learning Analytics and Knowledge*, 2011.

[43] E. Schegloff. *Sequence organization in interaction: A primer in conversation analysis*. Cambridge University Press, 2007.

[44] D. Shen, Q. Yang, J.-T. Sun, and Z. Chen. Thread detection in dynamic text message streams. In *Proceedings of SIGIR*, 2006.

[45] M. Smith, J. J. Cadiz, and B. Burkhalter. Conversation trees and threaded chats. In *Proceedings of the International Conference on Computer-Supported Collaborative Work*, 2000.

[46] G. Stahl. How a virtual math team structured its problem solving. In *In Proceedings of the Conference on Computer-Supported Collaborative Learning*, 2011.

[47] G. Stahl, J. X. Ou, M. Cakir, S. Weimar, and S. Goggins. Multi-user support for virtual geogebra teams. In *Proceedings of the North American Conference on Geogebra*, 2010.

[48] D. Tannen. *Framing in Discourse*. 1993.

[49] M. Tixier, G. Gaglio, and M. Lewkowicz. Translating social support practices into online services for family caregivers. In *Proceedings of the ACM Conference on Supporting Group Work*, 2009.

[50] J. Walther and S. Boyd. Attraction to computer-mediated social support. 2002.

[51] Y. Wang and I. H. Witten. Induction of model trees for predicting continuous classes. In *Proceedings of the European Conference on Machine Learning*, 1997.

[52] Y.-C. Wang, R. Kraut, and J. M. Levine. To stay or leave? the relationship of emotional and informational support to commitment in online health support groups. In *Proceedings of the International Conference on Computer-Supported Collaborative Work*, 2012.

[53] J. Wiebe, T. Wilson, R. Bruce, M. Bell, and M. Martin. Learning subjective language. In *Computational Linguistics*, 2004.

The Role of Narratives in Collaborative Information Seeking

Arvind Karunakaran
Massachusetts Institute of Technology
100 Main Street, #E62-383, Cambridge, MA-02139
arvindk@mit.edu

Madhu Reddy
Pennsylvania State University,
321J, IST Building, University Park, PA-16802
mreddy@ist.psu.edu

ABSTRACT

There has been a growing interest within the CSCW community to understand how actors in organizations collaboratively seek information. This focus had led to the emergence of the research area of collaborative information seeking (CIS). Despite an increasing number of conceptual as well as technical studies related to CIS, many fundamental questions still remain unanswered. For example, researchers within this space have argued that CIS goes beyond two or more individuals posing "question and answers" to each other in their attempt to seek the needed information. If CIS is not just about "question and answers", then what does it exactly constitute? We propose that one way to answer these questions is to conceptualize CIS as being constituted through, and orchestrated via, "narratives". In this research note, we elaborate upon the notion of "narratives", and talk about the potential usefulness of such a conceptualization for furthering CIS research and advancing CSCW scholarship.

Categories and Subject Descriptors

H.3.3 [**Information storage and Retrieval**]: Information Search and Retrieval – search process.

Keywords

Collaborative work, Collaborative Information Seeking, CIS, Narratives, Theory.

1. INTRODUCTION

Modern organizations are becoming more collaborative [8, 14]. With the increasing level of interdependence among actors, activities, and artifacts [9, 20], the lines between individual and collaborative tasks are becoming blurrier. Furthermore, organizations are becoming information-intensive, but at the same time, information is becoming more and more fragmented and distributed across multiple actors, artifacts, and systems [15]. Consequently, collaborative information seeking (CIS) has become an increasingly important part of organizational work [27]. Over the past decade, it has also emerged as a distinct stream of research within CSCW [7, 8, 14-16, 18].

CIS can be defined as the activity in which "two or more individuals work together to seek needed information in order to satisfy a goal". It may involve a variety of systems, people, and channels in order to address the information need for the task-at-hand. CIS researchers have conducted a number of conceptual as well as technical studies in trying to explicate what the concept really mean, the triggers and activities that underlie the concept, [8, 14-16], and how these, in turn, could inform the design of information retrieval (IR) systems [7, 18].

In spite of a growing number of conceptual and technical studies concerning CIS, fundamental questions still remain unanswered. For example, researchers have argued that CIS is not just about two or more people posing questions and answers to each other in their attempt to look for specific information [15]. Instead, they have posited that CIS is much more complex – involving the ongoing interweavement of actors, artifacts and activities – than the simple process of questions and answers [8, 14, 16]. If CIS is not just about "Q&A", what does it exactly constitute? What are the underlying mechanisms and practices that underscore CIS? We propose an analytical lens for investigating these issues. We argue that CIS is *constituted through and orchestrated via narratives*. Understanding how these narratives are created, shared and put to use in 'real time' would, in turn, help us uncover the fundamental mechanisms that drives CIS.

In this research note, we first elaborate upon our perspective concerning the role played by narratives in constituting and orchestrating CIS. We then demonstrate the utility of our perspective by providing illustrative examples from field studies of collaborative work that we have conducted in the past. We conclude by discussing the implications of the "narratives" perspective for CIS research.

2. NARRATIVES – WHAT ARE THEY AND HOW DO THEY MATTER

Often, the terms 'narrative' and 'story' are used interchangeably. Though they have many commonalities (for e.g. chronological order), there are also some differences. Stories are *"...instantiations, particular exemplars, of the grand conception"* [5] which respond to the question: "and then what happened?'' Narratives, on the other hand, focus on that grand conception itself by implicitly dealing with questions such as "what is it all about?" or "what does all of this mean?"[5] In this sense, stories are only a subset of a narrative.

Narratives could be thought of as descriptions that provide "a holistic account of a set of events and contain a mixture of beliefs, intentions, actions, and contextual details that are temporally ordered, and have an implied "plot" that connects them in terms of causality" (p.327) [1] In simple terms, narratives are *"set of events and the contextual details surrounding their occurrence"* (p.108) [2] that is meaningfully synthesized by a *plot*. This plot temporally orders the set of interrelated incidents into the past, the present and the future, and places them within a larger socio-historic context. This temporal ordering, however, is not a mere act of sequencing [4, 17]. Rather, it shows how humans actually go about doing things in the world, and how they make sense of the world [1, 2].

A functional event is said to be the building block of a narrative [13]. A functional event consists of "two actants connected by some action, so they are similar in structure to a simple sentence: ''subject–verb–object.'' [13]. For example, statements such as "I click on the 'FirstNetED' icon to get to the patient record quickly" or "I text John Smith from the DB support team whenever I face any connectivity issues" could be considered as functional events. A collection of such functional events [13] that are ordered temporally in the form of stories lead to what we call as a "narrative".

2.1 Why are "Narratives" important?

Most social information in our everyday life is transmitted in the form of narratives. Indeed, research within organizational studies suggests how most of our organizational realities are transmitted via narratives [20]. These studies have shown how narratives provide a way for people to share their occupational knowledge with one another [3, 17] and create a common ground for promoting coordinated action [2, 9]. Information is said to have encoded in human memory as narratives, and consequently, people have a natural predisposition to record, share, and retrieve information in the form of narratives [6].

Why is this important for CIS research, specifically, and CSCW generally? First, as Weick [20] has argued, narratives enable and empower organizational actors with powerful means for making sense of their everyday work contexts. They provide a mechanism for people to share contextual information with one another [4, 9, 11] that could otherwise not be shared in the form of abstract propositions. Since people who belong to different professions within an organization neither have the common vocabulary to facilitate easier communication and information sharing, nor the shared mental models to promote common ground and understanding, it becomes extremely difficult for information to be sought, understood, interpreted and disseminated across disparate epistemic boundaries. However, through the usage of plots, narratives offers a "point of view" of an actor towards handling a specific event or a situation [1]. This point of view, as illustred by Orr [11] and Bobrow and Whalen [3] in their respective studies, goes beyond being mere *descriptions* of the situation to becoming active *reenactments* of the situation [20]. That is, this plot help the seeker of information to see and visualize (in the present) how that event (of the past) unfolded in real-time, and how it could in turn be used to address information needs and demands (of the future). These, in turn, helps information to be sought and shared across different occupational boundaries. This simultaneous explication of the past, present, and the future provides narratives with the generative power that neither the simple information-seeking and sharing workflows nor the formalized business rules used by IR systems offer. Narratives, in other words, help actors to actively structure their temporality. It shapes the *attention in the present by evoking memories of the past and expectations of the future* [17].

Second, if we could think of actors as having a predisposition to store and categorize information in memory in the form of narratives, then narratives do indeed become the mechanism through which they also seek and share this information. In other words, people not just seek information using the *help* of narratives; instead, the very act of information seeking happens *through* narratives. In short, narratives become the platform through which CIS is orchestrated. Through narratives, actors not only continually throw question and answers at each other but also contextualize, de-contextualize and re-contextualize the situation in order to attend to the task-in-hand [9]. In doing so, they evoke past memories and experiences, contrast it with the current situation in order to find out how similar or different those situations are from the current situation, and take the needed action to resolve the information needs of that situation. That is, narratives not only *reflect* but also *enact* the patterns of actions

and interactions that unfold among actors, artifacts and activities within an organization.

This duality of narratives to promote sensemaking as well as to generate action [2, 4] enables and empowers actors-on-the-ground to not only make sense of the problem or the situation but also to instigate appropriate actions in order to seek the needed information. This conceptualization would let us capture and understand how things actually "get done" within organizations. All of these would indeed help us understand what goes constitutes CIS beyond just Q&A.

Third, when actors evoke a narrative, it automatically and simultaneously implicates "the physical artifacts (e.g., equipment, databases and documents), work processes (e.g., analytic techniques and standard operating procedures), and people (e.g., expertise, power and political clout)" [2] that are involved in a past situation. In other words, narratives not only tell us *which* people to talk to or *what* tools to use while seeking a particular information but also about *how* to contact those people and *how* to use and appropriate those tools [13]. Since tools, technologies, and artifacts are part and parcel of CIS, these narratives could be potentially very useful for actors on the field to address the information needs of the specific situation.

By focusing on narratives, researchers could understand the mechanisms that underlie CIS i.e. what constitutes CIS, how CIS is orchestrated, the tools and technologies it implicates and more. Also, since narratives play a dual function in being a device for sensemaking and a vehicle for generating action, adopting a "narratives" perspective could let CSCW researchers embrace (and in some ways, even transcend) both the "cognitivist" and the "interactional" perspectives for the study of collaborative socio-technical work.

3. AN ILLUSTRATION

We now illustrate the utility of our "narratives" perspective using examples from two field studies in the healthcare domain that we had conducted in the past [12, 19].

Consider vignette A given below (See Table 1) that portrays an episode of CIS within a multidisciplinary patient care team in a hospital emergency department [12]. From this vignette, we could see how information is collaboratively sought, interpreted, and made sense of via a trajectory of narratives. It starts with the registration associate's narrative about how she feels sorry for the patient in room 20 who is 8-weeks pregnant and was hit by a car. This information was made into a narrative by charge nurse 1. CN1 constructed that narrative through *infusing the information* (that the RA gave) *with meaning* (i.e. if adequate action is not taken, it would result in the death of the baby). This was done through building upon her past experiences and memories, which was then shared with the charge nurse 2. It is important to note that these past memories and experiences themselves are not "merely" transferred as-is to another person (i.e. charge nurse 2) as abstract data points in a propositional form. Rather, they were packaged and shared via narratives. For instance, when the CN1 remembers the case of a former patient who was "7 months pregnant when brought to the emergency department and the baby had been lost because no one realized that the patient was pregnant", she is not just transferring some past information to CN2. Neither is she providing an answer to a question that was posed. Instead, she is evoking a narrative of the past through weaving a plot that then gets re-contextualized and re-applied to the problem-at-hand by CN2 [20]. Through this plot, temporality is structured. Past, present, and future are re-ordered to cater to the problem-at-hand i.e. attention in the present is shaped by evoking memories of the past and expectations of the future [17]. Although some wrong information is passed in the process (i.e. 8 months instead of 8 weeks pregnant), this is not merely "a case of miscommunication of information" [12]. Instead, it is about making the *meaning* underlying the information more sticky and salient (i.e. death of the baby, criticality of the patient, need to take quick action etc.)

1:40pm: Registration associate (RA) tells me that she feels sorry for the patient in room 20 who is 8-weeks pregnant and was hit by a car. The next shift's charge nurse (CN2), arrives and the current charge nurse (CN1) tells CN2 information about each patient by going through FirstNet, a patient record system.

CN1 tells CN2 that the patient in room 20 was hit by a car and is 8 months pregnant. CN1 remembers the case of a former patient who was 7 months pregnant when brought to the emergency department and the baby had been lost because no one realized that the patient was pregnant.

5:00pm: CN2 is talking to the attending physician (AP) about her patients. She specifically tells AP that she is worried that the patient in room 20 who is 8 months pregnant.

AP (surprised): "How pregnant?"

CN2: "8 months. I've been told baby is ok."

AP is still concerned, so he and CN2 pull up the patient's record in FirstNet and discuss various aspects of her case. They don't verify the pregnancy information. They miss that the record says 8-weeks pregnant. They discuss how the patient should be treated given the advanced stage of pregnancy.

Table 1. Vignette A from a Field Study of a Hospital Emergency Department [12]

In this way, collaborative information seeking happens through a process of narrative co-construction, where the plot gets continually re-worked and re-contextualized by both the parties involved. The people engaged in the information seeking act, thus, are not mere senders and receivers of information. Instead, they both are active co-constructors of the narrative. They use the narrative to make sense of the evolving situation as well as to take action to cater to the problem-at-hand. (It is, however, important to note that the actions that are generated by narratives might not always lead to positive outcomes. Narratives structure the reality for organizational actors, rendering some information significant and other, non-significant. Hence, narratives should not be thought of as a form of panacea for organizational actors to successfully complete their tasks).

Consider another example of vignette B (see Table 2) from a different field study of an IT support team within a hospital [19]. Here, the IT support staffs are collaboratively seeking information regarding issues about folder permissions to a particular set of users. Unlike vignette A, it is not the narratives of the past that gets evoked, interpreted, re-contextualized, and put to use to cater to the task-at-hand in the present. Instead, it is the *present* itself that gets narrated. The ad-hoc team "talks through" the present about what permissions should and should not be given to users. They narrate the tacit theories and hypotheses that they believe in to each other. Each of the members of the ad-hoc team had partial information on how to resolve the issue. But it is through weaving an ongoing narrative that they were able to collectively seek, synthesize and evaluate the needed information "on-the-fly". In this process, they were not only able to diagnose/make sense of what the problem was, but also were able to take the needed actions during the very process of narrating that problem.

Jim, a CSC representative, cannot resolve a client issue in the time allotted; therefore, he creates a HEAT ticket and assigns it to Richard on the Clinical Software Services team. Richard is able to determine the cause of the problem immediately.

However, Richard does not have the knowledge to determine exactly how to resolve the issue. Therefore, Richard pulls together an ad-hoc team of experts to tackle the problem. Richard calls a meeting to discuss the problem.

On his computer, Richard shows the team the current permissions settings for the scan folders. They talk through what permissions should and should not be given to users based on a previous system configuration.

The team discusses if the scanning groups should be broken down more granularly. After the team members share their particular knowledge on the subject, Matt says, "Why don't we take the global group and give them read/write/modify? I could have sworn modify allows for deleting of files."

Richard suggests that they test Matt's hypothesis. Richard edits the share permissions and then suggests that they do a preliminary test where Chris attempts to get access to the scan folder now that the "Everyone" group has been removed from share permissions.

Richard and Matt walk over to Chris's desk to have him test his access. Chris's access to the scan folder is denied. This proves that removing the "Everyone" group from the share permissions seems to have worked. The meeting is adjourned.

Table 2. Vignette B from a field study of IT support team within a hospital [19]

Both these vignettes illustrate how narratives orchestrate as well as constitute CIS. Vignette A showed how narratives of the past are re-contextualized and re-applied to the problem-at-hand. Vignette B showed how the problem-at-hand in itself could be constituted through narratives. In both these cases, narratives acted not only as a device for sensemaking, but also as a vehicle for generating action.

4. DISCUSSION AND IMPLICATIONS

Narratives enable us to capture and understand the interdependence between, technology and organization, on the one hand, and information and collaboration, on the other. It enables us to see how actors, artifacts and activities are entangled with one another, and helps us to capture the complex interaction patterns that unfold at the nexus of technology, information, and collaboration [8, 11, 14]. In doing this, narratives have the potential to address a long-standing debate (concerning processes and practices, plans and situated actions) that has been widely discussed within CSCW [11, 14, 19] and Organizational studies [3, 13].

To elaborate, current business processes and technologies to support those processes are built on top of what is called as propositional knowledge [1, 2]. This knowledge is based on "if-then" rules (If situation X, on condition Y, do Z), deployed using 'request-response' systems that sequentially seek and retrieve information via database queries [14]. These propositions are, in turn, represented as business rules, visualized as workflow diagrams and formalized across the organization in the form of process charts and handbooks. Although these business processes could be useful in some situations, one problem with them is that they tend to simplify, abstract, or even ignore the actual "practices" that underlie them [3]. Essentially, this problem could be said to occur due to the tension between simplicity and complexity, between parsimony and richness. Processes and workflows are simplified abstractions, while practices are complex elaborations. Representing and formalizing *processes* into simplified workflows, on the one hand, could reduce the cognitive load of actors who only care about finishing the task-at-hand, but at the same time, it could also lead to other problems because important contextual and socio-historic information are lost. On the other hand, representing and elaborating *practices*, is extremely difficult and putting them to use is an arduous task.

We posit narratives as mechanisms that could provide us the much needed middle-path between the "process-centric" and the "practice-centric" viewpoints. People, when presented with narratives, will have the <u>implicit</u> ability to a) construct propositions from them, and, b) elaborate practices from them. However, we have very few mechanisms and systems in place that could store, categorize, retrieve narratives, and help actors in constructing, interpreting, and using them as a part and parcel of everyday work activities. Consequently, organizations tend to lose these powerful narratives as soon as people quit the organization. So far, the design of IR systems has only focused on how to codify, represent, formalize and implement 'propositions'. Therefore, the research challenge for us is to not only understand how people construct, interpret, sensemake, and use narratives as a part and parcel of their everyday work [10], but also to explicate how these narratives act as the underlying platform for orchestration of CIS (as well as for other collaborative activities). The insights gained from these have the potential to advance not only the CIS research but also impact the broader CSCW research.

Acknowledgements

This work was supported by funding from NSF grant #084497.

5. REFERENCES

1. Bartel, C. and Garud, R. Narrative knowledge in action: Adaptive abduction as a mechanism for knowledge creation and exchange in organizations. *The Blackwell Handbook of Organizational Learning and Knowledge Management.* 2003, 324 - 342.

2. Bartel, C. and Garud, R. The role of narratives in sustaining organizational innovation. *Organization Science*, 2009, *20* (1). 107-117.

3. Bobrow, D.G. and Whalen, J. 2002. Community knowledge sharing in practice: the Eureka story. *Reflections*, *4* (2). 47-59.

4. Bruner, J. The narrative construction of reality. *Critical inquiry*, 1991, *18* (1). 1-21.

5. Feldman, M.S., Sköldberg, K., Brown, R.N. and Horner, D. Making sense of stories: a rhetorical approach to narrative analysis. *Journal of Public Administration Research and Theory*, 2004, *14* (2). 147.

6. Fiske, S.T. and Taylor, S.E. *Social cognition.* Addison-Wesley Pub. Co., Reading, Mass., 1984.

7. Golovchinsky, G., Adcock, J., Pickens, J., Qvarfordt, P. and Back, M., Cerchiamo: a collaborative exploratory search tool. *In proceedings of the* CSCW' 08, San Diego, CA, USA.

8. Gorman, P., Ash, J., Lavelle, M., Lyman, J., Delcambre, L., Maier, D., Weaver, M. and Bowers, S. Bundles in the Wild: Managing Information to Solve Problems and Maintain Situation Awareness. *Library Trends*, 2000, *49* (2). 266-289.

9. Lutters, W.G. and Ackerman, S.M. 2002. Achieving safety: a field study of boundary objects in aircraft technical support. ACM Conference on Computer Supported Cooperative Work. CSCW '02.

10. Mønsted, T., Reddy, M. and Bansler, J. (2011). The Use of Narratives in Medical Work: A Field Study of Physician-Patient Consultations. In Proc. of European Conference on Computer Supported Cooperative Work (ECSCW'11). Aarhus, Denmark. September 24-28, 2011.

11. Orr, J.E. *Talking about Machines: An Ethnography of a Modern Job.* Cornell University Press, Ithaca, NY, 1996.

12. Paul, S. and Reddy, M., Understanding together: sensemaking in collaborative information seeking. *In proceedings of the 2010 ACM conference on Computer supported cooperative work*, CSCW' 10, 321-330.

13. Pentland, B.T. and Feldman, M.S. Narrative networks: Patterns of technology and organization. *Organization Science*, 2007, *18* (5). 781-795.

14. Reddy, M. and Dourish, P., A Finger on the Pulse: Temporal Rhythms and Information Seeking in Medical Care. in *In Proc. of ACM Conf. on Computer Supported Cooperative Work (CSCW'02)*, New Orleans, LA, 2002, 344-353.

15. Reddy, M. and Jansen, J. A Model for Understanding Collaborative Information Behavior in Context: A Study of Two Healthcare Teams. *Information Processing and Management*, 2008, *44* (1). 256-273.

16. Reddy, M., Jansen. B.J., and Krishnappa, R. (2008). The Role of Communication in Collaborative Information Searching. *In Proc of American Society of Information Sciences and Technology (ASIST'08)*. Columbus, OH. Oct. 24-29, 2008.

17. Ricoeur, P. *Time and narrative.* University Of Chicago Press, 1990.

18. Shah, C. Coagmento - A Collaborative Information Seeking, Synthesis, and Sense-making Framework *CSCW'10*, Savannah, GA, 2010.

19. Spence, P.R. and Reddy, M. Beyond Expertise Seeking: A Field Study of the Informal Knowledge Practices of Healthcare IT Teams. *Journal of Computer Supported Collaborative Work,* 2011.

20. Weick, K. *Sensemaking in Organizations.* Sage Publications, Inc., Thousand Oaks, CA, 1995.

Qualitative Data Collection Technologies:
A Comparison of Instant Messaging, Email, and Phone

Jill Dimond, Casey Fiesler, Betsy DiSalvo, Jon Pelc, Amy Bruckman
School of Interactive Computing & GVU Center
Georgia Institute of Technology
85 5th St NW
Atlanta, GA 30332 USA
{jill.dimond, casey.fiesler, edisalvo3, jpelc3, amy.bruckman}@gatech.edu

ABSTRACT

With the growing body of qualitative research on HCI and social computing, it is natural that researchers may choose to conduct that research in a mediated fashion—over telephone or computer networks. In this paper we compare three different qualitative data collection technologies: phone, instant message (IM), and email. We use quantitative analysis techniques to examine the differences between the methods specifically concerning word count and qualitative codes. We find that there are differences between the methods, and that each technology has affordances that impact the data. Although phone interviews contain four times as many words on average as email and IM, we were surprised to discover that there is no significant difference in number of unique qualitative codes expressed between phone and IM.

Categories and Subject Descriptors

H5.m. Information interfaces and presentation (e.g., HCI): Miscellaneous.

General Terms

Human Factors

Keywords

Qualitative research, Methods, Data collection, Internet studies.

1. INTRODUCTION

Qualitative interviewing is an invaluable tool for understanding human behavior. If quantitative metrics can give us immediate access to *what* people do and with *whom*, qualitative methods can help us understand *why*. As researchers increasingly turn attention to people's behavior online, an intriguing methodological question arises: Should we use online media to conduct those interviews? Qualitative interviewing is a technique that has its roots in several disciplines, especially anthropology [2], psychology

[12], and sociology [9]. Traditionally, interviews are conducted face-to-face. However, when we study online communities and social computing environments, our participants may be distributed around the globe where face-to-face interviews are often impractical. Fortunately, multiple communication media provide convenient alternatives, including telephone (synchronous), instant message (semi-synchronous), and email (asynchronous).

In a social computing class at the Georgia Institute of Technology, the course project is to research an online community, including conducting interviews with members. To emphasize that interviews over the phone result in more data than if conducted with instant message (IM), the instructor Amy Bruckman took a transcribed copy of a sample phone interview and an online interview (conducted by the same student, about the same online site), and laid them on the floor side by side. The differences were striking. The transcript obtained via instant messaging crossed the desk, but the phone transcript crossed the room. This theatrical demonstration makes the point well, but on further reflection led us to wonder: Does a longer transcript actually make the phone the best interview method? More specifically, which of these methods is more practical, and how does the choice of interaction medium affect the quality of data? In order to answer these questions, we first reviewed prior work that examines the effect of the technological medium on the collection of qualitative data. We then conducted forty-eight interviews divided across three interview media (phone, instant message, and email) and compared the quality and quantity of data obtained.

2. RELATED WORK

As other researchers have pointed out, interviews are in fact a cornerstone of human-computer interaction research, serving both as one of the more valuable and more challenging methods [16]. The issue of the impact of medium on collected data is not a new one, and has been taken up previously in the context of face-to-face versus phone interviews [1] in the area of psychology, as well as face-to-face versus phone versus postal mail [14] in the field of public health. In this methods literature, there are a few reasons that researchers cite for using online interviews (IM or email) rather than face-to-face interviews. Some of these are logistical: (1) difficulty of in-person meetings due to distance, time, and/or cost [10,15]; (2) difficulty of transcription due to time constraints [16]; and (3) the convenience of automatic transcription [3,10]. Other reasons relate to the context of the study itself. Voida cites the possibility of metadata when a study is *about* a technology that could be used also as an interview medium, such as IM [16], and Crichton points out that online techniques may "honor the field" in which participants are engaged—the online environment [3]. Interestingly, while many researchers cite the advantages of IM interviews in terms of the infeasibility or cost prohibitive nature of travel as compared to face-to-face interviews, they often do not mention phone interviews as an alternative [3,10,15,16]. As noted above, it is possible that face-to-face is considered the "default" interview method for most researchers even with respect to studying behavior online, and therefore this would be the baseline to compare alternative media. However, it is also true that phone interviews mitigate the same distance-related issues. There has also been research taking up reflective comparisons between all four of these interview techniques—face-to-face versus phone versus email versus IM. Kazmer and Xie's methods paper presents the relative advantages and drawbacks of each technique within the specific context of Internet-based research [7]. Their discussion is based on observations collected during their own research on other topics, and focuses primarily on functional effects (such as scheduling, logistics, and data management) and methodological effects (such as probing and affective data). They provide examples of where one medium may be superior (such as email interviews being easier to schedule, or phone interviews having more conversational flow), and conclude that qualitative interviews can be successful in any medium, particularly when researchers give attention to practical issues involved.

These comparison studies that have touched on logistical differences do not always address the issue of quality of data in depth. In a review of other studies that use email interviewing in particular as a technique, Meho suggests that the quality of data gained through online research is much the same as traditional methods, evidenced by similar results from research that conducted both types of interviews [11]. In one comparison of email versus face-to-face techniques, Curasi designed a study to compare the methods by collecting interviews using both and comparing the resulting data [4]. She compared the datasets for response rate, response speed, and depth of information (though it is unclear from discussed methods how depth was judged). With respect to quality of data, Curasi concluded that quality may be dependent more on the identity of the interviewer/interviewee than the data collection method. Motivated by our own experiences and related work we ask: In what ways does the technology medium (phone, IM, or email) affect the data collected in qualitative interviews? Because you cannot conduct an interview without talking about something, we took this as

an opportunity to extend our work studying video game play practices. The following are our two hypotheses:

H1. *Word Count*: The phone method will have the highest word count over IM and email.

H2: *Qualitative Codes*: The phone method will have the highest number of unique qualitative codes, over IM and email.

Qualitative analysis methods like grounded theory, thematic analysis, and discourse analysis generate codes and themes from the data. To understand the quality of data produced, we chose to compare the number of qualitative codes generated, as well as the number of words generated.

3. METHOD
In order to investigate different interviewing methods, we piggy-backed onto an actual study examining video game play practices. We used an ongoing research project by Betsy DiSalvo that explores cultural aspects of these practices. Game play practices are the strategies and ways in which people approach playing digital games.

3.1 Recruitment
We recruited participants by emailing game email lists such as women in gaming, college game email lists, Latinos in gaming, as well as our own gaming social networks. We then used snowball sampling, where we asked participants if they knew of anyone who would be interested in participating. This constitutes a convenience sample. Participants did not receive any compensation for their participation.

3.2 Data Collection Methods
We used three different kinds of data collection technologies: phone, IM, and email. We developed a structured interview guide that could be used both in an email format and as questions read or typed. We asked the following questions:

- Do you have a favorite type of game? Tell me about what types you like and why. Tell me about your favorite video games. Which ones do you like best and why?
- Tell me about the platforms you play on. Do you play console games? What console? Handheld? Computer/PC games? Phones games?
- When do you usually play during each week? For how long?
- Tell me about the people you play games with. Do you like to play video games alone or with others in the same room with you? Do you like to play with others online with you? Why?
- Tell me about what you consider "cheating" is in video games. Do you ever cheat? Under what circumstances?
- Tell me about your experiences modifying (modding) a game.

Participants were randomly assigned to phone, IM, or email as part of the consent form. Participants did not know in advance that we were researching different interview mediums, to minimize any selection bias. In order to minimize potential bias introduced by the personal style of a particular interviewer, we had four researchers each conduct 12 interviews (four phone, four IM, and four email) for a total of 48 interviews. For the email interview, the interview text was sent, and then participants typed in their responses and sent it back. For the IM interviews, we used whatever chat client the participant chose, including GChat, Skype, and AIM. We tried to stick to the interview guide; however, as is appropriate for qualitative interviewing [13], we did ask some probing questions if we felt that the response did not completely answer the question. We used this approach with the phone and IM interviews, which were conducted through Skype and recorded. The median length of the phone and IM interviews was 25 minutes.

3.3 Qualitative Coding Method

We are interested in the number of unique ideas or codes that each method generates. By unique ideas, we mean relevant codes, or the generation of labels that associate a concept with the data, as used in qualitative methods such as grounded theory. Grounded theory is a common data analysis method for qualitative data across HCI and social computing methodologies [5]. Specifically, we approached coding the data with an inductive, open coding approach or "Glaserian" approach [5,6]. We hypothesized that the phone method would produce the highest number of unique codes that were relevant to the topic of inquiry. In order to evaluate this, we first transcribed the phone interviews. We then had two researchers code the interviews, where the unit of analysis was one sentence. Concepts that represented the codes did span sentences and reoccurred throughout the interview. As a result, coders used the sentence to mark the first time a unique idea was introduced. We only coded for concepts that were relevant to the topic of inquiry. Table 1 illustrates examples of how we coded the interviews. Each sentence was entered into a spreadsheet line, where we then identified how many new codes appeared in the corresponding column. Codes represent concepts such as the type of game they like to play, the reason why they like to play, what cheating is, the first mention of a gaming genre, and various points in their life when they have had different gaming habits. First, two researchers did a test run through one interview together. Then, the researchers independently coded a subsequent interview where they achieved a 79% inter-rater reliability using Cohen's Kappa [8]. They talked over the differences, set some additional rules, and coded another interview independently and achieved 87% reliability. They then discarded the two test interviews and divided the rest of the interviews and coded them independently.

4. RESULTS
4.1 Qualitative Coding

First, we tested for equality of variances to determine what statistical test we can use. Using Levene's test, we found p=0.529, and thus failed to reject the null hypothesis of equal variances which allows us to run an ANOVA. We ran an omnibus ANOVA which showed that there was a significant difference (we use significance at p<0.05)

between the groups, F(2,45) = 7.513, p=0.0016. Post hoc comparisons using the Tukey HSD test indicated that the mean score for the email condition (M=18.73, SD=8.84) was significantly different from phone (M=33.2, SD=12.07), at p=0.001. Email was not significantly different from IM (M=24.0, SD=9.72) at (p=0.06) and IM was not significantly different from phone (p=0.267). A post hoc power analysis using GPower indicates that we have an effect size of 0.51 that gives us a power of 0.92. This means that email produces a lower number of unique codes compared to phone. However, we cannot make any claims with respect IM.

Table 1. Example of IM Interview Coding

IM Interview I = Interviewer, P= Participant		Unique Codes
I	Could you tell me about what you consider cheating is in video games?	
P	Hm. Well, definitely code exploits that weren't put in by the game developers I would call cheating; most things automated seem like cheating to me as well, like gold farming bots in WoW and AimBots in games like counterstrike and team fortress classic/other FPS's.	2
I	What about single player games?	
P	Well, here it is somewhat abstractly: I think when developers make a game, they intend for you to go about things in a particular way, sometimes in a particular order, in order to experience the game as they intended it.	1
	Kind of like how an artist intends something with his art. Anything that subverts that is cheating.	1

4.2 Word Count

Again, when we first ran Levene's test to compare the variances among groups, we found a significant difference in variances (p=0.0038). This means we cannot assume equal variances and must use a non-parametric test, Kruskal-Wallis. Using this test, we find a significant effect of the method on word count F(2,45) = 19.347 (p=8.7e-6). Post hoc comparisons using the Tukey HSD test indicated that the mean score for the Phone condition (M = 2339.875, SD=2396) was significantly different from both IM (M = 660.250, SD=233.47) and email (M = 473.563, SD=523.71). There was no significant difference between IM and email. A post-hoc power analysis indicates that for word count, we have an effect size of .51 that gives us a power of .88. Phone had a significantly higher word count than IM or email, but there was no difference between IM and email.

Table 2. Median Scores for Phone, IM, & Email

	Phone	IM	Email
Word Count	2339.88	660.25	473.56
Qual Codes	33.2	24.0	18.73

In summary,
We accept **H1**. *Word Count*: The phone method will have the highest word count over IM and email.
We reject **H2**: *Qualitative Coding*: The phone method will have the most unique number of qualitative coded concepts, over IM and email.

5. DISCUSSION

The dramatic demonstration of spreading a phone interview transcript across the classroom was intended to prove a point: Phone is better. However, through our more systematic investigation of the issue, we find that the reality is more complicated. Our findings verify that the transcripts used in class were not a fluke—phone interviews are significantly longer than IM or email. However, our coding of transcripts shows that phone interviews do not contain substantially more unique ideas than IM. How could this be possible? Looking at our data, it's clear that the phone transcripts contain more repetition. Speaking out loud, people use more words to say the same thing. Although our data here indicate that email interviews provide less detailed and rich data than phone, email interviews also require less effort for both the researcher and subject. The issue is not which mode is better, but which is better for which kind of study. For a study where responses do not need to go into great depth and it is not necessary to follow up on users responses with questions eliciting more depth, email has substantial practical advantages. Those advantages make it possible to gather many more responses with the same amount of researcher effort. In appropriate situations, this may improve the quality of the total pool of data collected, if many short responses are desired over fewer in-depth responses.

6. LIMITATIONS

One limitation that may affect the generalizability of this study is the context that we studied: game-playing practices. Game players may be more comfortable with digital mediums, and may be fine using different mediums such as IM. Our subjects were also relatively well educated because we recruited many of our participants from college emails lists. The participants' level of education may affect which modality is preferable.

7. CONCLUSION

Despite our data showing only minor differences between IM and phone interview methods, our research team have a strong subjective impression that we still prefer phone interviews—we feel we get better data that way. One explanation is that this impression is an illusion. An alternative explanation is that our analysis here has omitted key factors that explain the preference. We will continue to explore this issue in future work. Based on these findings, we intend to allow students in future offerings of the social computing class to conduct IM interviews if they wish.

Many members of online communities are more comfortable doing interviews online, and the convenience of not needing to transcribe interview tapes is non-trivial. One hour of interview tape can take up to eight hours to transcribe [13], depending on the typist's skill and complexity of the discourse. Transcribing audio files also may put the typist at risk for repetitive strain injury (RSI). If an IM interview is of comparable quality, then it can appropriately be used in more situations.

8. REFERENCES

1. Aziz, M. and Kenford, S. Comparability of telephone and face-to-face interviews in assessing patients with posttraumatic stress disorder. *J. of Psychiatric Practice 10*, 5 (2004), 307–13.

2. Bernard, H.R. *Research methods in anthropology: Qualitative and quantitative approaches*. Altamira, 2006.

3. Crichton, S. and Kinash, S. Virtual Ethnography⍰: Interactive Interviewing Online as Method. *Canadian J. of Learning and Technology 29*, 2 (2003).

4. Curasi, C. A critical exploration of face-to-face interviewing vs. computer-mediated interviewing. *J. of the Market Research Society 43*, 4 (2001), 361-376.

5. Furniss, D., Blandford, A., et al. Confessions from a grounded theory PhD: experiences and lessons learnt. *CHI*, ACM (2011), 113–122.

6. Glaser, B.G. and Strauss, A.L. *The discovery of grounded theory: Strategies for qual research*. Aldine Trans., 1967.

7. Kazmer, M. and Xie, B. Qualitative Interviewing in Internet Studies: Playing with the media, playing with the method. *Information, Communication & Society 11*, 2 (2008), 257–278.

8. Krippendorff, K. *Content analysis: an introduction to its methodology*. SAGE, 2004.

9. Kvale, S. and Brinkmann, S. *InterViews: learning the craft of qualitative research interviewing*. SAGE, 2008.

10. Mahony, M.O. Update In-depth interviewing by Instant Messaging. *Social Research Update*, 53 (2008), 1–4.

11. Meho, L.I. E-mail interviewing in qualitative research: A methodological discussion: Research Articles. *J. of the American Society for Information Science & Technology 57*, (2006), 1284–1295.

12. Potter, J. and Hepburn, A. Qualitative interviews in psychology: problems and possibilities. *Qualitative research in Psychology 2*, 4 (2005), 281–307.

13. Seidman, I. *Interviewing as Qualitative Research*. Teachers College Pr, 2006.

14. Siemiatycki, J. A comparison of mail, telephone, and home interview strategies for household health surveys. *American J. of Public Health 69*, 3 (1979), 238–45.

15. Stieger, S. and Göritz, A.S. Using IM for Internet-based interviews. *Cyberpsych & Behavior 9*, 5 (2006), 552–9.

16. Voida, A., Mynatt, E.D.,et al. Interviewing over instant messaging. *CHI 2004*, ACM Press (2004), 1344–1347.

Workflow Transparency in a Microtask Marketplace

Peter Kinnaird
HCI Institute
Carnegie Mellon University
Pittsburgh, PA 15213

kinnaird@cs.cmu.edu

Laura Dabbish
HCI Institute and Heinz College
Carnegie Mellon University
Pittsburgh, PA 15213

dabbish@cmu.edu

Sara Kiesler
HCI Institute
Carnegie Mellon University
Pittsburgh, PA 15213

kiesler@cs.cmu.edu

ABSTRACT

Interdependent tasks in Mechanical Turk (MTurk) can be managed efficiently with a workflow, a sequence of tasks through which work passes to its completion. We ask if workers should be informed about the workflow, which we call workflow transparency. Transparency could motivate workers or induce social loafing. We describe three experiments to determine the effects of workflow transparency in MTurk. We compared a text description of the workflow, a visualization of the workflow, and the combination of text and visualization with a control condition giving no workflow information. Workflow transparency marginally increased volunteerism on a charity identification task (experiment 1) and significantly increased volunteerism and quality on a business identification task (experiment 2). Results were weaker with a less experienced worker sample (experiment 3). We suggest further research on the design of workflow information to increase workers' motivation.

Categories and Subject Descriptors

H5.m. Information interfaces and presentation (e.g., HCI): Miscellaneous.

General Terms

Human Factors

Keywords

Crowdsourcing, workflow, visualization, CSCW, task motivation, productivity, entitativity

1. INTRODUCTION

Employers and researchers are increasingly using microtask platforms such as Amazon's Mechanical Turk (MTurk), Mobile Works, Short Task, or Serv.io to accomplish work that can be separated into portions and distributed to a number of people. Typically, these workers complete brief tasks online such as identifying photos or transcribing text from photos or recordings for piecework pay. This work is a form of crowdsourcing that can sum to significant productive labor.

Fully leveraging these systems remains challenging. Quality can suffer when workers have a fleeting relationship with the employer and low pay [2, 13, 20]. Piecework is associated in some people's minds with sweatshops, undermining motivation [7]. MTurk amplifies these threats to motivation through specific design decisions such as automatic task approval, the absence of a

strong reputation management system, and impersonal persistent identifiers. Even simple jobs can employ dozens or hundreds of interchangeable, anonymous workers for a single task, apparently reducing their felt accountability for contributions, task meaningfulness, and perceived instrumentality of effort. Decades of research on groups shows that lack of contribution identifiability and interchangeability significantly reduce trust and motivation and increase free riding [5], social loafing (reductions in individual effort that sometimes occur in group settings) [11], and propensity to withhold effort [4, 12].

Employers can minimize the result of poor worker motivation with carefully designed workflows featuring high task redundancy and internal checks to account for low worker quality. Some schemes address work quality through complex incentive designs including threats of nonpayment for poor or incomplete work (e.g. [17, 19]). MTurk's best practices guide suggests asking multiple workers to complete each HIT.

We wondered if greater transparency might increase worker motivation in MTurk. The majority of work on MTurk requires the coordination of many workers; there are often anywhere from 3-7000 HITs available in a collection of tasks. This situation creates the option of forming the collection of workers into a group. Groups can be more motivating than collections of individuals because group identity enlists loyalty and social feelings among people [16]. We speculated that increasing the transparency of the workflow, that is, the apparent connectivity of tasks and workers, might increase worker motivation. We hoped to increase workers' perceived instrumentality by providing them with a big picture of the work to which they contribute in the crowdsourced setting and information about their role in this work. We accomplished this goal by providing workers with workflow information, that is, information about the division of labor, the overall sequencing of tasks, and where the worker fits in the workflow. Theories of collective effort suggest that this information might enhance worker motivation by increasing their perceived accountability and instrumentality. Further, one could argue that workflow transparency should be provided to workers to accord with the ACM's Code of Ethics sections 1.2 and 1.3.

Nonetheless, the effects of workflow information must be carefully tested because this information could potentially backfire and create harm by revealing to workers that they are only a minute piece of a larger process. Another question is how workflow information should be presented, for example, in a simple text description or through a visual representation that would enable capturing the workflow at a glance.

We conducted three experiments to examine the influence of workflow information on worker motivation. The results suggest that providing workflow information can cause greater volunteerism and higher quality work but that positive effects may be limited to particular combinations of tasks and worker populations.

2. HYPOTHESES

Almost all crowdsourced tasks present the worker with information only about their own small task even when it is embedded within a larger workflow and may be interdependent with others' work. For example, workers may be asked to transcribe part of a conversation that will be combined with other transcriptions, proof read, then corrected. Workers typically do not know how many other workers have already contributed to the task, how many will come after them, or even that they are working with others towards a common goal. In MTurk, however, workers are often implicitly working with others through one coordination scheme or another since HITs are commonly replicated or strung together in workflows [1, 14, 15]. In addition to social and institutional isolation, tasks are typically not challenging. Many crowdsourced tasks are repetitive or boring, forcing employers to motivate the work entirely from pay [19].

Numerous studies have shown that suggesting to workers that they are redundant will reduce their effort and motivation [4, 6, 8, 10, 11, 18], the de facto context in MTurk. Research on job design suggests that providing employees with information about the importance of their work to the organization can change the amount of effort they expend on their tasks. In a test of these ideas, Hackman and Oldham [6] found that task identity and task significance enriched work, and influenced employees' internal motivations to perform their jobs effectively. Given the implicit use of workflows in MTurk a priori, it is unclear what effect showing workers their role in a workflow might have on their motivation. We formulate two hypotheses that the motivational effects of seeing work as a contribution to a larger goal will outweigh the inducement of social loafing behaviors.

H1: Workers with workflow information will complete more work more accurately than those without workflow information.

Workflows can be explained in text or they can be visualized as flow charts, trees, or as directed acyclic graphs. Gestalt theory suggests a number of perceptual features of visualizations which may improve entitativity resulting in higher motivation. For example, objects that are close together are perceptually grouped together. Likewise, similar visual elements become perceived groups. Visual elements that are connected or continuous tend to be grouped together, and symmetrically arranged objects are more likely to be perceived as a whole [3, 21]. Therefore, we anticipate that the effects of workflow transparency will be greater for visualization conditions than for the text condition.

H2: Workers with graphical visualizations of workflow information will complete more work more accurately than those provided with text information about the workflow.

3. METHOD

To test our hypotheses about the impact of a transparent workflow, we conducted two between-subjects experiments on

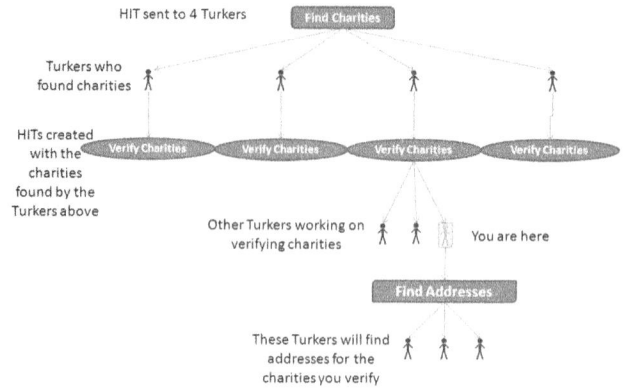

Figure 1. The workflow visualization as shown to Turkers.

Mechanical Turk and then replicated these studies with a third experiment. We limited participation to the United States to reduce the impact of language understanding on the results. Workers could participate in just one of the experiments. Participants were paid 10 cents for completing a HIT (worker task). All experiments employed the same procedure (see below). After participants accepted the HIT and completed the minimum required work they were able to advance to a brief survey.

3.1 Tasks and Independent Variables

In experiment 1, participants were presented with a list of 20 charities of which half were fictional (e.g. "Citizens for Animal Projection"). The worker's task was to check the correctness of the charities' names. In the second experiment, we replicated the task but in this case participants were given 20 businesses, half of which were fictional (e.g. "Duff Beer"). In both experiments, workers had to check on the validity of at least three of the listed organizations. The third experiment replicated the first two with random assignment to business or charity task.

Participants in all experiments were randomly placed into one of four conditions: no workflow information (control) condition, text-only description of the workflow, tree visualization of the workflow (see Figure 1), or both the text and the tree. The third experiment used a 2 x 4 design incorporating random task assignment in addition to random workflow condition assignment. In the text workflow condition, the text said:

You are working with a group of other Turkers to help identify real charities [businesses]. Your job is to determine whether the charities [businesses] listed below are real or not. Other Turkers have built up this list, but we need you to verify that they are real. Once you've verified the charities [businesses], other Turkers will be asked to find their addresses and phone numbers.

3.2 Dependent Measures

Participants were instructed that were only required to work on three charities [businesses] to receive pay. Thus any work beyond three items represents volunteer work. We used volunteerism

Table 1. Results of experiment 1: The effect of workflow information worker motivation in a charity validation task.

Dependent Measures	Control Mean (SE)	Text Mean (SE)	Vis Mean (SE)	Text & Vis Mean (SE)	Planned Contrast (Workflow vs. None)
Number of items completed	9.33 (0.88)	11.93 (0.88)	11.60 (0.91)	10.41 (0.93)	F [1, 284]=3.7, p=.05
Accuracy	0.81 (0.02)	0.80 (0.02)	0.80 (0.02)	0.80 (0.02)	n.s.
Net contribution	5.31 (0.61)	6.47 (0.61)	6.43 (0.64)	5.56 (0.64)	n.s.
Entitativity	3.07 (0.13)	3.26 (0.14)	3.29 (0.14)	3.27 (0.14)	n.s.

Table 2. Results of experiment 2: The effect of workflow information worker motivation in a business validation task.

Dependent Measures	Control Mean (SE)	Text Mean (SE)	Vis Mean (SE)	Text & Vis Mean (SE)	Planned Contrast (Workflow vs. None)
Number of items completed	6.31 (2.07)	11.38 (1.87)	11.24 (1.81)	12.92 (2.07)	F [1,55] = 5.5, p < .02
Accuracy	0.56 (0.06)	0.67 (0.06)	0.71 (0.06)	0.77 (0.06)	F [1,55] = 4.1, p < .04
Net contribution	1.38 (1.17)	4.50 (1.05)	4.06 (1.03)	5.85 (1.17)	F [1,55] = 6.6, p < .01
Entitativity	2.84 (0.28)	3.42 (0.24)	3.82 (0.24)	3.67 (0.25)	F [1,50] = 6.6, p < .01

(total number of items completed) and quality of work (accuracy rate) as behavioral measures of worker motivation. We also created a measure of net contribution which is calculated as the sum of correct responses minus the sum of incorrect responses. Large positive values for net contribution indicate a strong worker contribution to the overall subtask of which they are a part. Negative values mean that they have harmed the overall process more than they have helped it. This measure is, arguably, the most important for employers primarily concerned with productivity.

We adapted an entitativity questionnaire from Postmes et al. [9] to measure how much workers felt part of a larger group. This perception has been associated with lower social loafing [9, 11]. Items were presented on 5-point Likert scales. Two additional questions measured pertained to Turker tenure (number of prior HITs the workers had completed duration of activity on MTurk). In experiment 3 we introduced a manipulation check to ensure that workers were aware that they were only required to complete 3 items. 74% of workers passed the check.

4. RESULTS

4.1 Experiment 1: Charity Identification

The charity task had a 22% dropout rate, that is, workers signed up but did no work, leaving 288 participants. These workers were evenly spread across conditions (p = 0.31). We observed generally high output and quality, suggesting that the task was intrinsically interesting or easy. Despite our requiring participants to complete only three items to receive pay, more of them completed all 20 items (n = 100) than completed the minimum required (n = 75). The mean net contribution was 5.92 items and overall accuracy mean was 80.26% correct items.

H1 predicted that the presence of workflow information would improve the worker's motivation, operationalized as total items completed, item accuracy, and net contribution. To test H1, we ran an ANOVA across all conditions and then ran a planned contrast comparing the control condition to the other conditions. Participants completed marginally significantly more work in the workflow conditions as compared to the control condition (see Table 1). There were neither differences in accuracy, entitativity, or perceived task importance between the workflow conditions and control condition, nor between the text information and the visualization conditions. H2, therefore, was not supported

4.2 Experiment 2: Business Identification

In experiment 2, the method was the same but participants were asked to identify whether business listed were real or fake business. We again observed a 22% dropout rate with zero items completed with no significant differences across conditions, leaving 59 participants. However, once workers began, the task appears to have been less attractive or possibly more difficult than the charity validation task used in experiment 1. Overall net contributions mean was just 3.98 (SD = 4.4) versus 5.92 in

experiment 1, and mean accuracy mean was just 67% versus more than 80% in experiment 1.

In H1 we predicted that the presence of workflow information would improve workers' motivation. In this study, participants completed significantly more work, more accurate work, higher net contribution, and perceived significantly greater entitativity in the presence of workflow information. These results also are shown in Table 2.

4.3 Experiment 3: Putting It All Together

In experiment 3, participants (N = 267) were randomly assigned to workflow information condition and to either the charity or business task. The dropout rate for experiment 3 was not significantly different from the first 2 experiments. However, Turkers in experiment 3 were significantly less experienced in MTurk as compared with Turkers in experiments 1 and 2, as measured by HITs completed (mean = 308 [SD = 373] vs. mean = 452, [SD = 428], p < .004) and days using MTurk (mean = 225 days [SD = 435] vs. mean = 290 days [SD = 442], p < .0001). We think this phenomenon occurred because we did not allow the more frequent users of MTurk, who would have participated in the first experiments, participate in experiment 3. As a result, a larger proportion of Turkers in experiment 3 were relative newcomers. In general, the results were in the same direction as experiments 1 and 2 but they were not statistically significant overall. However, we were able to demonstrate with our random assignment of charity vs. business tasks that the charities task was indeed more motivating (or less difficult) than the business task. Turkers in the charities task were more accurate than those in the businesses condition by about 13% (p < .0003) and their net contribution was about 58% higher (p < .0003).

The comparatively low experience level of this sample prompted us to examine statistical interactions between condition, task type, and experience. In doing so, we could determine whether workflow transparency and task assignment varied with worker experience. We found that more experienced workers perceived greater entitativity on the charities task but less entitativity on the businesses task relative to less experienced workers (p < .03). More experienced workers also completed significantly more items (p < .02) and made a higher net contribution (p < .01) to the charities task (p < .02) than the business task.

The findings above suggest that the effects found in experiments 1 and 2 may hold only for more experienced workers. Perhaps workflow information simply confuses newcomers. The three-way interaction (p < .05) of workflow information, task, and worker experience allows us to examine this possibility. We found a significant interaction for overall accuracy (p < .007) and net contribution (p < .05). Workflow information improved accuracy (p < .01) and contributions (but not significantly) for experienced workers given the business task, replicating experiment 2. However, workflow information only helped inexperienced workers on the charities task (p < .01).

5. DISCUSSION

In all 3 experiments, workers who completed more than 3 items were volunteering for additional work. The tasks elicited a surprising amount of voluntary work regardless of condition.

The first experiment we conducted provided just marginal support for our hypothesis that workflow information will increase motivation (H1) and no support for our hypothesis that this information would have a stronger influence on motivation when presented visually (H2). A limitation of this experiment is that we might have experienced an important ceiling effect. With 31% of participants performing at 100% accuracy, the likelihood that a manipulation would significantly increase accuracy was low.

The second experiment used the same setup as the first but showed much stronger results. The move from the charity to business identification task apparently reduced workers' intrinsic interest in the task, or perhaps checking the existences of businesses was harder than checking charities. We found that workflow information increased the number of items completed, accuracy, the entitativity (group feeling), and net contribution (productivity) improved by 248% (mean of three visualization conditions against the control).

Finally, experiment 3 highlighted the importance of Turkers' relative experience. Workflow visualizations lead to significantly greater work in a number of scenarios, but, in one scenario, actually reduced the number of items completed by inexperienced workers in the business task. Perhaps inexperienced workers were confused by the task or visualization, while more experienced workers felt like part of a team or group and thus motivated to contribute to a larger goal.

We did not find a difference between a text description of the workflow and the graphical visualization. Thus we cannot say whether a different graphical design would be more effective or whether visualizations are not necessary to impart workflow information.

6. IMPLICATIONS FOR DESIGN

These results demonstrate the effectiveness of including workflow information when designing the presentation of some crowdsourced tasks. We also contribute evidence that MTurk workers with varying levels of experience respond differently to experimental manipulations. Future work will examine alternative positioning of the worker in the workflow, interactive and real-time visualizations which might depict information about other workers' contributions, and alternative visualization paradigms.

7. ACKNOWLEDGMENTS

This work was supported by a National Science Foundation grant, CNS-1040801 and the Center for the Future of Work at Carnegie Mellon University's Heinz College

8. REFERENCES

[1] Bernstein, M.S. et al. 2010. Soylent: a word processor with a crowd inside. *UIST* (2010), 313–322.

[2] Downs, J.S. et al. 2010. Are Your Participants Gaming the System ? Screening Mechanical Turk Workers. *Science*. (2010), 2399-2402.

[3] Fekete, J.-D. et al. 2008. Information Visualization. A. Kerren et al., eds. *Springer-Verlag*. 1-18.

[4] George, J.M. 1992. Extrinsic and Intrinsic Origins of Perceived Social Loafing in Organizations. *The Academy of Management Journal*. 35, 1 (Mar. 1992), 191-202.

[5] Granovetter, M.S. 2005. The Impact of Social Structure on Economic Outcomes. *J.Econ.Persp.*19,1(2005),33-50.

[6] Hackman, J.R. and Oldham, G.R. 1976. Motivation through the design of work: test of a theory. *Org. Behav. and Hum. Perf.* 16, 2 (1976), 250-279.

[7] Harris, M. 2008. Email from America. *Sunday Times*.

[8] Huberman, B.A. et al. 2009. Crowdsourcing, attention and productivity . *J.of Info.Sci.* 35,6(Dec. 2009),758-765.

[9] Jans, L. et al. 2011. The induction of shared identity: The positive role of individual distinctiveness for groups. *Pers. soc. psych. bulletin*. 37, 8 (2011), 1130-1141.

[10] Jones, G.R. 1984. Task Visibility, Free Riding, and Shirking: Explaining the Effect of Structure and Technology on Employee Behavior. *Academy of Management Review*. 9, 4 (Oct. 1984), 684-695.

[11] Karau, S.J. and Williams, K.D. 1993. Social Loafing : A Meta-Analytic Review and Theoretical Integration. *J. of Pers. and Soc.Psych.*. 65, 4 (1993), 681-706.

[12] Kidwell, R.E. and Bennett, N. 1993. Employee propensity to withhold effort: A conceptual model to intersect three avenues of research. *Acad. of Mgmt* 1993.

[13] Kittur, A. et al. 2008. Crowdsourcing user studies with Mechanical Turk. *CHI 08*. 08, April 5-10 (2008), 453.

[14] Kittur, A. et al. 2011. CrowdForge : Crowdsourcing Complex Work. *HCI* (2011), 1801-1806.

[15] Kulkarni, A. et al. 2012. Collaboratively crowdsourcing workflows with turkomatic. *CSCW* 2012.

[16] Lakens, D. 2010. Movement synchrony and perceived entitativity. *J. of Exp.Soc.Psych.* 46, 5 (2010), 701-708.

[17] Mason, W. and Watts, D.J. 2010. Financial incentives and the "performance of crowds." *ACM SIGKDD Explorations Newsletter*. 11, 2 (2010), 100.

[18] Roland E. Kidwell, J. and Bennett, N. 1993. Employee Propensity to Withhold Effort: A Conceptual Model to Intersect Three Avenues of Research. *The Academy of Management Review*. 18, 3 (Jul. 1993), 429-456.

[19] Shaw, A.D. et al. 2011. Designing Incentives for Inexpert Human Raters. *CSCW*. 2011.

[20] Snow, R. et al. 2008. Cheap and Fast — But is it Good ? Evaluating Non-Expert Annotations for Natural Language Tasks. *Emp.Meth.in Nat Lang.Proc.* 2008.

[21] Ware, C. 2000. *Information visualization: perception for design*. Morgan Kaufmann Publishers Inc.

From Consumer to Community: Factors of Influence in the Purchasing Decision Making Process

Barbara Gligorijevic
Queensland University of Technology
Brisbane, Australia
barbara.gligorijevic@qut.edu.au

ABSTRACT[1]

The impacts of online collaboration and networking among consumers on social media (SM) websites which are featuring user generated content in a form of product reviews, ratings and recommendations (PRRR) as an emerging information source is the focus of this research. The proliferation of websites where consumers are able to post the PRRR and share them with other consumers has altered the marketing environment in which companies, marketers and advertisers operate. This cross-sectional study explored consumers' attitudes and behaviour toward various information sources (IS), used in the information search phase of the purchasing decision-making process. The study was conducted among 300 international consumers. The results were showing that personal and public IS were far more reliable than commercial. The findings indicate that traditional marketing tools are no longer viable in the SM milieu.

Categories and Subject Descriptors

J.4 [**Computer Applications**]: Social and Behavioural Sciences; K.4.4 [**Computing Milieux**]: Electronic commerce.

Author keywords

Social media, Information Sources, User generated content, Product reviews, ratings and recommendations, Word of mouth.

1. INTRODUCTION

Consumers are extensively using various information sources (IS) to become informed about products or services when contemplating a purchase. IS are categorised as personal, commercial and public (Hollensen, 2003), they have different importance and power to influence consumers' opinions throughout the purchasing decision making process. Due to SM expansion and proliferation of websites supporting social networking activities, the number of IS (Kuruzovich et al., 2008) has considerably increased. While many companies have already included, or are considering inclusion of SM into their marketing mix, marketers are struggling to evaluate the impact of SM and online networking that are enabling consumers to post product reviews online, where they can be read by other potential customers. Consumers' practices to look beyond commercial IS have significantly extended in to the online environment, where they are able to search for information, ask questions and have products evaluated and rated through social networking practices

on websites that feature product reviews (Gligorijevic and Bruns, 2009). The manufacturing companies, retailers, service providers and marketing professionals are using various communication channels when competing for the attention of their potential customers. It is important to understand how social customers use IS, and what perceived reliability and influence they have on the purchasing decision making process (PDMP). This consumer behaviour study examines how reliable consumers perceive various IS, utilize them and collaborate in SM and networking websites.

2. LITERATURE REVIEW

Marketing as a discipline has been under a lot of pressure to deliver new profitable models of advertising in the environment of computer mediated communication. Lately it has been verified by marketing analysts (Ramsey, 2008; Edelman, 2010; Bughin et al., 2008) that advertising is experiencing a very strong migration from mass media to Internet and SM due to lower cost, better profiling and targeting of consumers, accessibility to market niches, and higher return on investment (ROI). Many corporations are becoming aware of advantages of SM while cutting their marketing budgets and investing further into the new web strategies or business models. According to McKenna (2002) today's marketing is a derivate of "twentieth-century mass-production mentality, and it has become something of a pseudopsychological propaganda machine" (p.5) being very static and completely relying on the broadcasting model. Technological innovations are the "agent of economic and social change" (p.7) powerful tools in the hands of consumers allowing them to manage broadcasted commercial messages. The "awakening" process among marketing professionals is changing the paradigm of advertising assuming that broadcasted messages are 'absorbed' and responded to accordingly. The market place is becoming crowded by advertising messages, while for consumers the increase of access capability is only inducing the level of 'noise'. The amplified presence of promotional messages in the market place is inevitably leading to higher level of advertising blindness among consumers. However, consumers highly value the recommendation through the WOM, and it is becoming an "incredibly powerful medium" (Bulter, 2008). Recommendations about products and services from first hand users are often regarded as important IS, and even more appreciated when coming from a friend (Marsden, 2006). PRRR websites are becoming increasingly popular as a new tool in WOM (WOM) marketing campaigns.

3. RESEARCH QUESTIONS

This cross-sectional study was conducted online, surveying consumers about their use of PRRR in their information search phase of the purchasing decision-making process. The following research questions were developed for this study:

- How reliable consumers perceive various IS when considering a purchase?

---

[1] *This research was carried out as part of the activities of, and funded by, Smart Services Cooperative Research Centre (CRC) through the Australian Government's CRC programme (Department of Innovation, Industry, Science and Research).*

- What is the consumers' attitude toward the WOM information both offline and online versus the commercial information?

4. METHODOLOGY

The quantitative study among 300 consumers was carried out from September 2011 until March 2012. The study was conducted online, utilising the structured questionnaire, with respondents from Australia (40 percent) and 30 other countries (60 percent), 52.1 percent males and 47.8 percent females respondents, and age groups up to 25 years 18.6 percent, 26 to 35 years 38.5 percent, 36 to 45 years 27.7 percent, 46 to 55 years 8.6 percent and 56 years and above 6.5 percent. The sample was recruited among international consumers invited to participate through e-mailing lists, forums and online ads on Facebook. The respondents were asked to evaluate the reliability of IS in offline and online environment in twelve categories. The listed IS were: retailers or shop assistants, manufacturers, advertising or infomercials, magazines or news stories, online retailers, automated recommendations, detailed user generated product reviews, friends and family (WOM from someone they know), short users' product recommendations, professional or experts product reviews, product ratings by users, discussion forums.

5. FINDINGS AND DISCUSSION

Consumers reported that during or while considering a purchase they regarded their friends and family (F&F) or a WOM from someone they know to be the most reliable source of information 79.2 percent. Followed by professional blogs and expert product reviews (PR) 74 percent, detailed user generated product reviews (UGPR) 73.6 percent, short product recommendations from users 63.1 percent, product information from manufacturers 63.3 percent, discussion forums 55.8 percent, product ratings by users (stars; +, -) 50.4 percent, retailers or shop assistants' advice 44.3, information from online retailers 41.5 percent, magazine or news stories 41.2 percent, automated recommendations based on purchasing patterns 23.3 percent, and advertising or infomercials 18.9 percent. Least reliable IS were considered to be advertising or infomercials 42.6 percent, automated recommendations based on purchasing patterns 37.9 percent, retailers or shop assistants' advice 25.5 percent, product ratings by users (stars; +, -) 20.2 percent, information from online retailers 21.4 percent, discussion forums 18.7 percent, magazine and news stories 16.6 percent, product information from manufacturers 12 percent, professional blogs and expert PR 11 percent, short product recommendations from users 10.4 percent, detailed UG PR 9.3 percent, and F&F 6.4 percent. Respondents considered F&F and experts or professionals that deliver PR and other fellow consumers posting PR to be trustworthy IS. Manufacturers product related information were rated considerably high as reliable, contrary to advertising or infomercials considered as very unreliable indicating that advertising messages are seen to be created by advertisers and not as an integral part of the marketing communication for companies and brands. Further user created content, in a form of PRRR, discussions in forums are noticeably highly evaluated as reliable – considerably more than automated product recommendations based on purchasing patterns of other consumers or retailers or shop assistants' advice. This signifies the trust levels toward reliability of information to be notably higher among fellow consumers than toward the recommendations coming from commercial IS. Additionally, these results signify that consumers perceive private, commercial and public IS as very different. While private IS in the form of WOM from someone they know had the strongest influence on their purchasing decisions as the most reliable, the least reliable advertisements and infomercials that communicate commercial information.

Research outcomes stipulate that customers don't conform to retailers' suggestions as strongly as to recommendations from other customers in a form of electronic WOM through UG PRRR or discussions in online forums demonstrating that these SM spaces are becoming crucially important for companies and brands when designing a marketing strategy. Hence WOM information is very influential in the PDMP among current or potential customers and as such should be carefully managed by marketers in the SM space.

6. CONCLUSIONS

The results of the study show that WOM is the dominant form of information in both offline and online environments and is the most influential through personal IS (F&F) and public sources (PRRR posted online by other consumers). While commercial IS (advertising and infomercials) are the least influential on consumers in their PDMP. The perception of reliability of IS among survey respondents when searching for information about products is showing consumers' strong preference toward their personal contacts - F&F or WOM from someone they know. Whereas the online public IS (UG PRRR, and additionally professional blogs or expert PR) were reported to be highly regarded by consumers as reliable and therefore influential, retailers and shop assistants were considerably less reliable and therefore their influence was not dominant in the PDMP. Hence the marketing strategies that strongly rely on advertising online or offline, or advertising at the 'point of sales' will have less impact than brand presence in WOM communication. Further we concluded that consumers' attitudes toward the WOM information are very positive contrary to product information coming from commercial sources. This sentiment was explicitly depicted in survey results, labelling advertising and infomercials and automated recommendations based on purchasing patterns as the least reliable categories followed by information from retailers (offline and online). The consumers have changed their shopping practices from searching online commercial or retailing websites to looking for information from friends, family and peers or by posting PRRR and collaborating in SM spaces. This behavioural change is a strong sign for marketers, suggesting that altering online marketing strategies - from advertising to conversational or WOM marketing may lead to better marketing outcomes.

7. REFERENCES

[1] Bughin, J., Shenkan Guggenheim, A., and Singer, M. 2008. How poor metrics undermine digital marketing. *McKinsley Quarterly*.

[2] Bulter, D. 2008.*The WOM Manual, Volume II*. Boston, Butman Company and Print Matters.

[3] Edelman, D. 2010. Four ways to get more value from digital marketing. *McKinsey Quarterly*. (2010. March).

[4] Gligorijevic, B. and Bruns, A.2010. *Ratings and Recommendations Websites in the Travel and Tourism Industry*. New Media Services Report, Smart Services CRC.

[5] Hollensen, S. 2003. *Marketing Management a Relationship Approach*. Harlow, Prentice Hal.

[6] Kuruzovich, J., Ritu Agarwal, S.V., Gosain, S., and Weitzman, S. 2008. Marketspace or Market place? Online Information Search and Channel Outcomes in Auto Retailing. *Information Systems Research*, vol.19, no.2, 182-201.

[7] Marsden, P. 2006. Introduction and Summary. *In*: Kirby, J. and Marsden, P. (eds) *Connected marketing; The Viral Buzz and WOM Revolution*. Amsterdam, Butterworth-Heinemann an imprint of Elsevier.

[8] McKenna, R. 2002. *Total access: giving customers what they want in an Anytime, Anywhere World*. Boston, Harvard B S P.

[9] Ramsey, G. 2008. *Seven strategies for surviving the Downturn*. eMarketer.

Social Technologies and Knowledge Sharing within and across Organizations

Mohammad Hossein Jarrahi
Syracuse University
School of Information Studies
Syracuse NY 13244, USA
+1 315 443-5504

mhjarrah@syr.edu

ABSTRACT

This doctoral research empirically investigates the role of various social technologies in informal knowledge sharing practices within and across organizations. Social technologies include both (a) traditional social technologies (e.g., email, phone and instant messengers) and (b) emerging social networking technologies commonly known as social media such as blogs, wikis, major public social networking sites (i.e., Facebook, Twitter and LinkedIn), and enterprise social networking technologies employed behind a firewall. Building from sociomateriality research, I study how these social technologies, as a suite of tools, are used in combination. The primary outcome of this research is a more complete conceptualization of the role and value of various social technologies for knowledge sharing in organizational contexts, which still remains understudied within the CSCW arena.

General Terms

Management, Human Factors

Keywords

Social technologies, Social media, Sociomateriality, Knowledge sharing, Informal ties.

1. INTRODUCTION

This research is motivated by the confluence of two broad phenomena: the importance of informal knowledge-sharing in organizations and the rapid rise in both the number of and users of social technologies. Organizations have long benefited from traditional social technologies such as phone and email, so there is an expectation that they are also likely to benefit from newer social technologies. The emergence of social media has encouraged new possibilities for organizational knowledge sharing. Recent studies have made it clear that social media uses offer opportunities for collaboration and social exchange, and are well positioned to augment and extend interpersonal social ties [7; 10].

Social technologies are increasingly pervasive in our personal life and are becoming ever more common aspects of corporate life. The push towards growth in social technologies usage has come from outside formal organizations, and much of the early use of these platforms was by young people and students. As a result, most research on the uses of social technologies focuses on non-

organizational or explicitly social contexts, with a particular emphasis on teens and student's uses [e.g., 2; 6]. To date, few CSCW or organizational studies have investigated the adoption of these social tools in the workplace. Examples are studies of wikis [e.g., 4], blogs [e.g., 5], corporate social networking sites [e.g., 11] and public social networking sites such as LinkedIn and Facebook [e.g., 10]. These studies of organizational impacts of social technologies, however, have primarily focused on a single tool in isolation. While they offer insight into organizational implications of a specific tool, they tend not to investigate how these technologies are used in combination.

With the advent of diverse sets of information and communication technologies (ICTs), people increasingly draw on a suite of technologies, rather than a single tool [12]. Empirical evidence shows that in most organizations today people interact with multiple ICTs, and the interactions among people and tools and among tools themselves cannot be examined in isolation [1]. In this context, social technologies work in concert, rather than alone, to meet different communication and knowledge sharing needs. Addressing this gap in the CSCW research, this work seeks to raise our understanding of the role of social technologies as a suite of tools. In doing so, it explores how organizational members interact with different social technologies at their disposal. To this end, the primary research question is:

- How do knowledge workers use social technologies as a whole (or in combination) to support their informal knowledge practices?

2. THEORETICAL FOUNDATION

To understand the relationships between social technologies and knowledge-sharing practices, I build from the sociomateriality research that offers up a unique view on technological affordances. Central to this view is the thesis that technological affordances, what technologies achieve in practice, can only be understood by focusing on their material performance which is always enacted by humans in practice [9].

Sociomaterilaity view treats knowledge and practice as mutually constitutive. Following this focus on social practices, the unit of analysis for this study is knowledge practices. This focus enables us to explore "effective loop of insight, problem identification, leaning, and knowledge production." [3, p. 202].

3. METHODS

This exploratory effort is a field-based study focusing on the ways in which knowledge workers use social technologies to advance their work. The main source of data is interviews. Informants for this study were selected based on the similarity of their work context and their ability and willingness to provide key information. To date, the interview informants are a purposive sample of 54 people who hold knowledge-intensive roles in a few large management consulting firms in the US. These organizational settings are considered extreme contexts as archetypes of knowledge-intensive environments which allow a better understanding of the use of social technologies in informal knowledge sharing and are better positioned for theory building effort. This is a form of theoretical sampling in which we choose cases which are likely to replicate or extend the emergent theory.

Through the interviews, the role and value of social technologies for organizational knowledge sharing were examined by focusing on the ways they may augment or extend organizational members' access to various sources of knowledge. I supplement these with secondary data collection that includes trace data of social technologies uses and relevant organizational and personal documents. The system level analysis allows me to observe the way informants employ public social technologies such as Twitter and LinkedIn in their knowledge practices. I particularly look at the user's postings and activities on these websites. The analysis of personal and organizational documents also offers an understanding about the way consulting firms regulate the use of social technologies, and relevant rules and policies.

In moving forward, I will begin a set of micro-studies to better understand daily practices of consultants and their uses of social technologies. To do this, I will shadow several participants by spending multiple hours observing them do their work. My observations will focus on their knowledge sharing activities and the use of social technologies in their work.

Data analysis is ongoing and inductive as I look for interesting concepts, leads, and issues. As these themes take shape, it will also be informed by concepts from sociomateriality research, providing me with a basis for capturing the informal knowledge practice enabled by the use of social technologies.

4. PRELIMINARY FINDINGS

Findings to date highlight five knowledge practices: (1) expertise locating, (2) expert locating, (3) reaching out, (4) socializing and (5) horizon broadening. Each practice is identified based on an underlying knowledge problem, and supported by multiple social technologies. In this way, for conducting each knowledge practice, people commonly have multiple technological options; therefore the affordances of each social technology for different knowledge practices are meaningful only in relation to other options.

Two significant dimensions of the relationships among the social technologies are *competition* and *interoperability*. The social technologies compete with one another for relevance as organizational members constantly evaluate their functional capabilities and perceive one more effective in supporting interactions. In addition, while various social technologies are often articulated as independent and discrete technologies, the interoperability of these tools in day-to-day practices makes such distinctions less meaningful. In the face of certain knowledge problems, people may take advantage of the differing capacities of various social technologies. These combinatory uses could be concurrent or sequential, meaning that knowledge workers may pair technologies simultaneously and sequentially.

5. CONTRIBUTIONS

My dissertation will make two contributions. First, findings provide holistic understanding of roles and uses of social technologies in supporting informal knowledge sharing within and across organizations. This study advances our conceptual insight regarding the affordances of different social technologies as a suite, delineating how their uses are enacted relative to other technological options. Second, this work advances the current conceptual status of ICTs relative to interpersonal social networks. Within the CSCW domain, most studies have traditionally focused on the group level analysis. This work contributes to the CSCW scholarship as it focuses on personal networks. Several researchers have highlighted the importance of the assemblage of people found through personal networks and informal practices in studies of collaborative technologies [e.g, 8].

6. REFERENCES

[1] Bélanger, F. and Watson-Manheim, M.B., 2006. Virtual teams and multiple media: Structuring media use to attain strategic goals. *Group Decision and Negotiation 15*, 4, 299-321.

[2] boyd, d., 2008. Taken Out of Context: American Teen Sociality in Networked Publics University of California-Berkeley.

[3] Brown, J. and Duguid, P., 2001. Knowledge and organization: A social-practice perspective. *Organization Science 12*, 2, 198-213.

[4] DeLuca, D., Gasson, S., and Kock, N., 2006. Adaptations that virtual teams make so that complex tasks can be performed using simple e-collaboration technologies. *International Journal of e-Collaboration 2*, 3, 65-91.

[5] Efimova, L. and Grudin, J., 2007. Crossing boundaries: A case study of employee blogging. In *Proceedings of the HICSS* (2007), 86-86.

[6] Hewitt, A. and Forte, A., 2006. Crossing boundaries: Identity management and student/faculty relationships on the Facebook. *Poster presented at CSCW*.

[7] McAfee, A., 2006. ENTERPRISE 2.0. *MIT Sloan management review 47*, 3, 21.

[8] Nardi, B., Whittaker, S., and Schwarz, H., 2002. NetWORKers and their activity in intensional networks. *Computer Supported Cooperative Work (CSCW) 11*, 1, 205-242.

[9] Orlikowski, W.J. and Scott, S.V., 2008. Sociomateriality: Challenging the Separation of Technology, Work and Organization. *The Academy of Management Annals 2*, 1, 433-474.

[10] Skeels, M.M. and Grudin, J., 2009. When social networks cross boundaries: a case study of workplace use of facebook and linkedin. In *Proceedings of the GROUP '09*, ACM, 95-104.

[11] Steinfield, C., DiMicco, J.M., Ellison, N.B., and Lampe, C., 2009. Bowling online: social networking and social capital within the organization. In *Proceedings of the The fourth international conference on Communities and technologies* (2009), ACM, 245-254.

[12] Turner, T., Qvarfordt, P., Biehl, J.T., Golovchinsky, G., and Back, M., 2010. Exploring the workplace communication ecology. In *Proceedings of the CHI* (2010), 841-850.

Communication Breakdowns in Global Software Development Teams: Is Knowledge Creation the Answer?

Rasmus Eskild Jensen
IT-University of Copenhagen
Rued Langgaardsvej 7
+45 2721 2331
raej@itu.dk

ABSTRACT
The aim of this research is to understand collaborative work practices in global software development companies with a special emphasis on knowledge creation in global software development (GSD) teams. The research is based on a work place study of a Danish software company working with a Philippine offshore department. So far I have found that miscommunication and misunderstandings between the Danish and the Philippine developers in the project are partly grounded in different social worlds. Next step is to investigate the role of knowledge creation and describe in further detail how these misunderstandings occur in the everyday work practice.

Categories and Subject Descriptors
H.1.2 [**User/machine information**]: Human factors, human information processing.

General Terms
Human Factors

Keywords
Global software development (GSD), work practice, work place study

1. INTRODUCTION
My research is situated within the field of Computer supported cooperative work (CSCW) and the initial research question was *"How can we understand the complications of knowledge creation in collaborative work practices of global software development?"* This research question is described in fairly broad terms to allow an inductive research approach where the data material can shape my research.

This study is part of an overall research project called "GSD - Next Generation Technology for Global Software Development". The project seeks to develop next generation technologies – infrastructure, tools, and methods – that bridge geographical, temporal, and cultural differences in Global Software Development.

1.1 Relevance for the CSCW
The research is relevant for the field of CSCW because it aims at describing specific cooperative practices in GSD and identify interesting areas of research in order to develop guidelines and new designs to alleviate the cost and effort involved in coordinating the work, which have recently been described by other researchers[1, 2]. This research is based on a work place

study that seek to investigate and observe the world as it is and try to understand how and why people act in the world [3]. I specifically try to comprehend the significance of knowledge creation and sharing in GSD. The importance of these concepts has previously been discussed in the CSCW literature [4-7].

2. PROJECT DESCRIPTION
GlobalSoft is a Danish company with approximately 1700 employees in different departments around the world. The majority of the employees are located in Denmark, but they also have locations in India, China and the Philippines. I have followed a specific project in GlobalSoft that started in December 2010 and will continue at least until the end of June 2012. The client of the project is the Danish government and the product will affect a large part of the public sector as well as private companies in Denmark

2.1 Data Collection
The research began in November 2010 where my colleagues and I held 14 semi-structured interviews lasting an average of 50 minutes with employees at different organizational levels (see Table 1), and as such we had the opportunity to compare the perspectives of the corporate vice president with the perspectives of the IT-developers. Analyzing the data material we coded and categorized the interview material in order to establish a systematic overview of the data.

Table 1. Data sources of preliminary research

Job function	Number of Interviews
Cooperate Vice President	1
Vice President	1
Director	1
Manager	3
Team Leader	2
Advanced Project Manager	1
Senior Project Manager	2
Project Manager	1
It-architect	1
Developer	1

Based on this preliminary study, I am now engaged in a work place study conducted in GlobalSoft that so far consists of 41 field observations; interviews, video recordings, documents and internal communication in the project. I have studied the work practices in both Denmark and in the Philippines and I have spent the time almost equally on both sides. The complexity of the project is immense and it has taken a long time to comprehend the basics of what is going on in this particular project.

3. INITIAL FINDINGS

Our recent research [8] describes how differences in social worlds [9] between geographically distributed developers become salient in their everyday interactions. We focused on communication breakdowns that occurred in the collaboration between the Danes and the Philippines. The challenge arises from the fact that GlobalSoft primarily have Danish clients from both the private and public sector. The initial negotiations of the scope and specific requirements of the project are handled by the Danish side of GlobalSoft together with the client with little or no involvement from the outsourcing partners. When the initial scope of the project is defined, the project is spilt into different tasks where some or all of the tasks are send to the Philippine outsourcing department.

Our initial data analysis suggests that taken-for-granted knowledge and context based information is not easily conveyed across geographical distance. We argue that misinterpretations and misunderstandings often is a result of differences in social worlds. A Danish project manager in the GSD Company illustrates the current situation:

Advanced Project Manager: *"We tell them that there is something called retirement wage and a retirement age and it will begin at the age of 62 or something like that and then we have the public pension age starting at the age of 64"*

Interviewer*: "Is it not just 62 and 64 that are the central numbers?"*

Advanced Project Manager: *"Yes, it is "just". Would you...you are welcome. That is this issue with words such as "just" and "simply" and in combination it is even worse. It requires a firm understanding."* Advanced Project Manager

The advanced project manager in the above quote is talking about how complex it is to communicate specific details in the project. In this case we talk about Danish pension systems and how it is not just about the numbers, but that it requires a more firm understanding of the context in order to avoid misunderstandings and misinterpretation. By analysing both interviews and observations we identified two types of situations where social worlds become salient in the everyday interactions between developers working at different geographical locations: 1) the divergence of concept and meaning and 2) the convergence of concept but divergence of meaning. We have argued that these situations are grounded in social worlds and pose a challenge to work practices in the form of miscommunications and misinterpretations of shared tasks in GSD. These results have been presented to the project team and they more or less agree with these initial findings.

4. FINAL REMARKS

My next step is to describe in further detail how these misunderstandings occur and conceptualize new processes or tools to facilitate knowledge creation instead of the current paradigm of knowledge transfer that seems to exist in the company. The notion of knowledge creation draws on the idea that knowledge is not a thing that can be transferred between individuals. Orlikowski (2002) proposes *"that knowing is not a static embedded capability or stable disposition of actors, but rather an ongoing social accomplishment constituted and reconstituted as actors engage the world in practice"* (p. 249). Instead knowledge is created in situ between people in the work practices. I will start this work by looking specifically at the people who "bridges" knowledge and information across the two locations. I would like to emphasize three questions of interest that hopefully can drive my research forward. Firstly, how can we describe the notion of knowledge? Secondly, how is knowledge created in GSD teams? Lastly, how can knowledge be shared to minimize the risk of misunderstandings and miscommunication in GSD teams? I hope to discuss these areas of interest at the Doctoral Colloquium, as it will help me in my future research.

5. ACKNOWLEDGMENTS

This research has been funded by the Danish Agency for Science, Technology and Innovation under the project "Next Generation Technology for Global Software Development", #10-092313.

I would like to thank my supervisor Associate Professor Pernille Bjørn and Postdoctoral Lars Rune Christensen for their help and support.

6. REFERENCES

[1] Boden, A., Nett, B. and Volker, W. Trust and Social Capital: Revisiting an Offshore Failure Story of a Small German Software Company. *In Proceedings of the ECSCW.* (Vienna, Austria, 2009).

[2] Herbsleb, J., Paulish, D. and Bass, M. Global Software Development at Siemens: Experience from Nine Projects. *In Proceedings of the ICSE* (St. Louis, Missouri, USA, 2005).

[3] Randall, D., Harper, R. and Rouncefield, M. *Fieldwork for Design: Theory and Practice.* Springer, London, 2007.

[4] Avram, G., Bannon, L., Bowers, J., Sheehan, A. and Sullivan, D. K. Bridging, Patching and Keeping the Work Flowing: Defect Resolution in Distributed Software Development. *Computer Supported Cooperative Work (CSCW)*, 18, 5-6 2009), 477-507.

[5] Orlikowski, W. Knowing in Practice: Enacting a Collective Capability in Distributed Organizing. *Organisation Science*, 13, 3 (May - June 2002), 24.

[6] Cramton, C. The Mutual Knowledge Problem and Its Consequences for Dispersed Collaboration. *Organisation Science*, 12, 3 (Maj - June 2001), 25.

[7] Bannon, L. and Kuutti, K. Shifting Perspectives on Organizational Memory: From Storage to Active Remembering. *Proceedings of the HICSS* (Hawaii, USA, 1996).

[8] Jensen, R. E. and Bjørn, P. Divergence and Convergence in Global Software Development: Cultural Complexities as Social Worlds. *In Proceedings of the COOP* (Marseilles, France, 2012).

[9] Bjørn, P. and Ngwenyama, O. Virtual Team Collaboration: Building Shared Meaning, Resolving Breakdowns and Creating Translucence. *Info Systems*, 192009), 26

Language Proficiency Matters in Group Chat – Supporting Cross-Cultural Communication Processes

Na Li
College of Information Sciences and Technology
The Pennsylvania State University
nzl116@ist.psu.edu

ABSTRACT

Cross-cultural group chat is an important communication method in organizational and educational settings. Studies have shown that communication problems exist persistently due to non-native and native speakers' unmatched levels of language proficiency. Realizing the profound problem and increasing need for better communication from the real world, in my dissertation I am studying the communication processes associated of cross-cultural group chat and explore possible tools to assist both non-native and native speakers to communicate better.

Categories and Subject Descriptors

H.5.3 [**Information interfaces and presentation**]: Group and organization interfaces – *Computer-supported cooperative work;*

General Terms: Design, Human Factors.

Keywords: Cross-cultural, group chat, language proficiency.

1. INTRODUCTION

Cross-cultural communication is taking place everywhere as the world is getting flat. Research conducted across many disciplines (e.g. education, psycholinguistics, sociology, HCI and CSCW) shows that language proficiency plays an important role in communication. Non-native speakers have been suffering from communication problems caused by language proficiency issues both in face-to-face (FTF) communication and distributed online communication [2,5].

Building upon past studies, my research interests in cross-cultural communication focus on non-native speakers' problems in text-based computer-mediated communication (CMC). Comparison studies show that text-based CMC is beneficial to non-native speakers. It requires less immediacy in response than is often the case in FTF communication, and allows more equality through increases in social distance (e.g., more anonymity). However, studies also show that non-native speakers experience frustration in text-based CMC, frustration that is directly linked to language proficiency issues [3]. To help non-native speakers communicate with better quality and experience, I propose a novel tool for text-based communication. The tool offers an additional channel for responding to missed points, indexing important ideas, and addressing different understandings; by so doing, I hope to enable more natural and coherent communication between native and non-native speakers. In particular, I expect the tool to promote non-native speakers' participation and positive attitudes in cross-cultural communication. Furthermore, I expect that at least part of this effect will be due to an increase in native speakers' awareness of – and accommodation to – the mismatches in communication between them and their non-native counterparts.

2. INSTANT ANNOTATION

Although researchers from different multiple disciplines have recognized communication problems in cross-cultural group chats, there is a scarcity in the literature specifying these users' needs and requirements for those chat systems, as evidenced by the small number of tools aimed specifically at cross-cultural communication. Given the difficulties that non-native speakers experience when using existing communication methods, I have begun to explore the needs and requirements of mixed groups of non-native and native speakers, with the design research goal of developing and evaluating new ways to assist them so that they can better communicate with each other.

Several earlier works have noted that non-native speakers are frustrated by the parallel discussion and rapid turn-taking typical of online chat [1,3]; these issues do not seem to be a problem for native speakers. In light of this literature, I have synthesized two streams of design research - threaded chat and collaborative annotation - and envisioned an enhancement to group chat called Instant Annotation (IA). Presently, IA is a conceptual design in which participants use a parallel channel to annotate or otherwise comment on an ongoing discussion. Figure 1 shows a snap shot of my initial IA prototype, currently under development and iterative refinement. I expect that IA will assist information retention and conversation management in cross-cultural communication.

3. RESEARCH QUESTIONS

RQ1. What are the differences between non-native and native speakers' reading and writing capacity in group text chat?

Research has shown that native speakers' reading comprehension and writing skills are superior to non-native speakers in traditional reading and writing tasks [4,7]. Recently, Specker [6] compared non-native and native speakers' reading speed in reading scrolling texts. Results showed that native speakers are still faster than non-native speakers. However, little work has been done to investigate such contrasts for situations involving dynamic information contexts, such as synchronous chats.

RQ2. If there are differences, how does it impact the group and members of the group?

If there are differences in terms of language proficiency, how does it affect members' experience in online group work; how does it affect their performance; and eventually how does it affect group outcomes? Many factors affect non-native speakers in group chats, including communication anxiety and low self-confidence about language skills or other relevant background knowledge [1]. Other factors such as power inequity, intimacy level, and gender may also affect an individual's feeling [1]; however these factors are not the focus of this study, so I plan to control them in my experiments. Another possible source of frustration may arise from the native speakers, rather than the non-

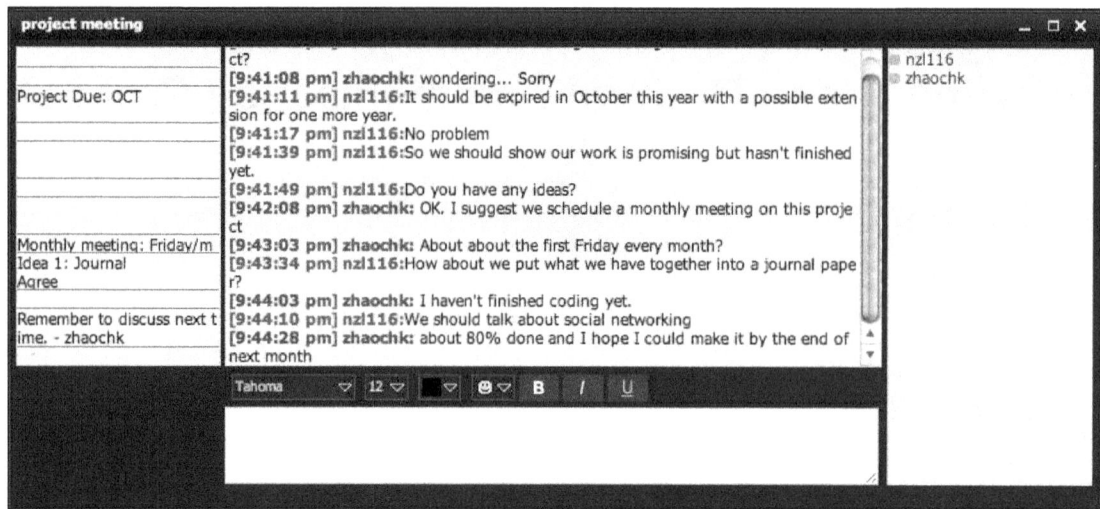

Figure 1. A conceptual design – Instant Annotation

native speakers. Native speakers may implicitly construct a discussion sub-group upon recognition of similar background, understandings and communication style; if so, non-native speakers may feel excluded. Furthermore, native speakers may even ignore non-native speakers' opinions due to insufficient attention to or communication with participants who they view as outsiders. Another important question is whether frustration will lead to low participation. Participation plays an important role in any group work; therefore examining whether non-native speakers participate at a high level, and if not how to enhance participation are among the core pursuits of my study. Finally, I want to explore the consequences of any low participation on group outcomes.

RQ3. Will a chat client featuring IA help reducing the above problems?

Does Instant Annotation increase non-native speakers' participation? Does Instant Annotation improve the communication experience of non-native speakers? Does Instant Annotation improve group outcomes? To investigate RQ3, I will use methodology that is similar to that used for RQ2. Participants will use a text-based chat for a group discussion, and similar measures of performance and experience will be collected. However in this study, some groups will work with a custom chat client that features IA, while others will use the same client but without IA support.

4. COMPLETED RESEARCH
4.1 Study 1 – Problem Identification

This study addressed RQ1 and RQ2, drawing design implications for the detailed design and implementation of an IA-enhanced chat tool. I conducted an experiment (using a brainstorming task) to investigate non-native and native speakers' communication processes in group text chat, as well as probing their experiences in a survey and follow-up interview. The results showed that language proficiency did affect non-native speakers' participation and performance. More interestingly, I found that native speakers' performance was also impacted because they sometimes reserved their ideas to give non-native speakers more chance to speak, which resulted in production loss in the brainstorming task. The major problem I found in this study was that unmatched levels of language proficiency impaired the turn-taking system in online chat, resulted in mismatched conversations and parallel sub-

conversations, which in turn discouraged non-native speakers' participation due to the high workload to repair the conversations.

4.2 Scenario-based Design and Evaluation

My current work focuses on RQ3. I have prototyped a text chat system featuring IA. I will be designing and working from several different scenarios of users interacting over the system. The scenarios will address different possible use cases of IA, drawing from users' reflections obtained in study 1. I will use confederates to enact these scenarios and recruit native and non-native speakers to chat with them. Each participant will finish two chat sessions, one that uses the IA space and one without. Results from the two conditions will be compared to find out whether the IA design is useful (whether problems found in study 1 can be reduced) and in what use cases it is particularly useful or problematic. Based on the findings of this study, I will create a task in which IA is most useful and ask naturalistic groups (i.e., no confederates) to complete the task. I will assess design features, users' satisfaction, and performance and group outcomes in this summative evaluation.

5. REFERENCES

[1] Freiermuth, M. and Jarrell, D. Willingness to communicate: can online chat help? *International Journal of Applied Linguistics*, 16, 2 (2006), 189-212.

[2] Gonzalez, D. Teaching and learning through chat: a taxonomy of educational chat for EFL/ESL. *Teaching English with Technology*, 3, 4 (2003), 57-69.

[3] Hara, N. and Kling, R. Students' frustrations with a Web-based distance education course. *First Monday*, 4, 12 (1999).

[4] McCutchen, D. A capacity theory of writing: Working memory in composition. *Educational Psychology Review*, 8, 3 (1996), 299-325.

[5] Neeley, T., Hinds, P. J. and Cramton, C. Walking through jelly: Language proficiency, emotions, and disrupted collaboration in global work. *SSRN eLibrary*(2009).

[6] Specker, E. *L1/L2 eye movement reading of closed captioning: A multimodal analysis of multimodal use*. The University of Arizona, 2008.

[7] Steffensen, M. S., Joag-Dev, C. and Anderson, R. C. A Cross-cultural perspective on reading comprehension. *Reading Research Quarterly*, 15, 1 (1979), 10-29.

Impression Formation in Online Collaborative Communities

Jennifer Marlow
Human-Computer Interaction Institute
Carnegie Mellon University
5000 Forbes Ave. Pittsburgh PA

jmarlow@cs.cmu.edu

ABSTRACT

In online collaborative communities such as open source software development, people often encounter unknown others who they must work with in the absence of any previous interaction or formal organizational relationship. These settings are increasingly supported by social networking systems that provide detailed information about individuals' activities and behaviors. My research focuses on understanding how individuals form impressions of others in work environments supported by social media, and how these impressions influence collaborative outcomes.

Categories and subject descriptors

H5 [**Information Interfaces and Presentation**]: Miscellaneous

Author keywords

Impression formation, open source development, peer production

1. INTRODUCTION

In peer production and other collaborative communities, participants may be located all over the world and often must interact with individuals they have not previously met and with whom they do not share a common organizational context. As social network functionalities (like interest networks and activity feeds) are tied with online work environments in these communities, participants are exposed to more and more cues and traces about these new colleagues' work activities and communication interactions. However, it is unclear how these traces influence the impressions they form about these collaborators, and how viewing these traces influences work outcomes.

In online interactions, people form impressions about each other based on limited information. These impressions shape the way they interact and relate to each other. Negative or inaccurate first impressions may be hard to change and can lead to undesirable outcomes such as relational conflict and delays. While much work has been done on interpersonal impression formation in settings such as online dating and friendship formation, less is known about how people form impressions of others in an online work setting.

My work extends what is known about impression formation and online interpersonal interactions in other domains to a complex and large-scale distributed work context where social media support lightweight ways of sharing information about others' behaviors and actions. Drawing from social science theories relating to social cognition and subjective distance in distributed teams, I consider how increasingly detailed behavior traces influence impression formation. My research brings literature and theory on social cognition together with advances in social technology design to understand and support impression formation in a complex distributed work context.

GROUP'12, October 27–31, 2012, Sanibel Island, Florida, USA.
ACM 978-1-4503-1486-2/12/10.

2. PSYCHOLOGICAL DISTANCE

Individuals involved in large-scale peer production communities such as open source software development often initially lack detailed information about each other's contexts, personalities, and expertise. This lack of cues may lead to a greater feeling of psychological distance from their collaborators [1] and can negatively affect satisfaction with relationships, learning from distant colleagues, and desire to work together again [3]. Wilson et al. [1] propose that organizational, task, individual, and social factors may all influence perceived distance among distributed team members. In my research, I focus specifically on the influence of social factors on impression formation, attitudes, and behaviors towards remote colleagues. I focus particularly on the early stages of impression formation in order to see how initial impressions are shaped by social technology design before direct interactions occur, and how these initial impressions affect subsequent working behaviors.

3. INFLUENCING IMPRESSIONS

The uncertainty reduction theory of impression formation suggests that individuals form impressions of others, whether meeting face to face or in a computer mediated context, to help reduce uncertainty about how someone will behave in the future and to decide whether or not to pursue further interactions. Providing different types of information about a person or their context could theoretically influence the relationship in different ways. For example, information about an individual's personality, interests, or context could lead to feelings of interpersonal closeness, while information about their work behaviors could influence impressions of expertise or skill. Thus far, I have focused specifically the impact of viewing traces of work and interaction history, which, in the absence of synchronous communication, may help distant collaborators to form more detailed impressions of each other, reduce psychological distance and improve the collaboration process.

3.1 Providing traces of work history

An important aspect of person perception in distributed work is impressions of teammates' skills, abilities and personalities. Psychological distance also affects the impression formation process by influencing how perceivers construe behavioral information about another person [2]. In many distributed work settings, team members initially do not have sufficient personal knowledge of each other's past behavior to accurately assess their abilities. Instead, they view people as members of a category rather than assessing their individual behaviors [1]. While this can be an efficient way of processing information, it can backfire if the initial impression is negative or inaccurate.

Increasingly, online peer production communities like GitHub are incorporating social media functionalities that let users view the actions and interactions of unknown developers. By providing more concrete information about individuals' expertise and past behaviors, it may be possible to reduce psychological distance and help people form more accurate impressions of each other. However, we do not yet understand how, when, or why users form impressions of each other in workspaces instrumented with social media functionality and how these impressions influence the work that is done.

To investigate these questions, I have conducted a qualitative study of impression formation in GitHub. This study involved interviews with a number of GitHub project owners asking them about 1) when they have consulted the profiles of unknown others contributing code to projects they own on the site, 2) what cues they have attended to on these profiles and 3) what impressions they have formed about these contributors based on these cues. To understand the influence of impressions on the work process, I have examined a series of case studies around specific code-based interactions mentioned by interviewees, looking at the role of profile-based impressions on outcomes such as code acceptance and relational conflict.

3.2 Using profiles for impression formation

With respect to scenarios in which developers were likely to consult other members' profiles, three main motivations emerged from the interviews. These included discovery and exploration of new people and projects (independent of any direct interaction with the person,) forming expectations about the skills of people submitting pull requests (code contributions) to the owner's project, and informing interactions with these contributors.

The second research question focused on which cues people attended to on GitHub profiles and on how they used these cues to form impressions about others. We found that profile cues such as amount of activity, type of projects, type of contributions, and specific aspects of coding style were used to assess a user's general coding abilities and specific areas of expertise. Traces of previous discussions with others on the site were sometimes used to get a feel for what a person would be like to interact with.

Overall, the results indicate that users in this setting seek out additional information about each other to explore the project space, inform interactions around contributed code, and understand the potential future value of a new contributor to their project. They form impressions of other users' expertise based on their history of activity across projects, and successful collaborations with key high status projects in the community.

3.3 Impact of impressions on collaborative work processes

The interviews also asked people to identify recent cases in which they had received a pull request (request to commit code to a project) from a contributor with whom they were not familiar and who they had never worked with before. This process is important because it is the primary way open source projects attract new contributors and extend their code base. Interviewees described what happened in the pull request process and their interactions with the submitter (including whether or not they viewed that person's profile.)

We focused on the following key outcomes associated with a pull request interaction in light of the previous work on software development and project success: whether the contribution was accepted, how long the exchange took, and whether conflict arose in the process. Based on the pull request case studies, we found that profile information was not necessarily useful in cases where the value and benefit of the code contribution was evident. However, when the code was problematic and not immediately acceptable, some developers used the contributors' profiles to

form quick impressions of their abilities and attitudes, which then helped them to form a cost-benefit analysis guiding further interaction.

For example, the cost of working with someone to fix their code so that it could be accepted (which could be high in cases where contributors were newcomers or novices) was weighed against the potential benefits of helping to mentor a new project member who could contribute in the future, or the risks of being annoyed by time consuming arguments with a novice about why their contribution was not acceptable. Cues leading to the formation of negative impressions of expertise when the contributor was a novice could be diminished by other cues indicating they were worthy of mentoring. However, one obstacle preventing many project owners working on large projects from attending to profile cues is that the process requires time and effort.

4. FUTURE WORK

Thus far, I have gained a better understanding of factors that influence the impression formation process for open source software developers based on the cues and activity traces that are provided in the GitHub environment. In the future, I plan to examine the impression formation process in other large-scale collaborative and creative environments to see how the process is similar and different in varied contexts that provide different types of behavior and activity traces. I will then use these findings to inform and evaluate interventions designed to improve the impression formation process (e.g., by investigating new ways of presenting information about other users' relevant attributes, such as work history, expertise, and interaction style.)

For example, the interviews with GitHub users have provided implications for the design of better summaries of individuals' activity and skills that can be more effective in allowing project owners to quickly and effectively assess new contributors prior to interacting with them. These summaries may also be supplemented by more information about a person's work history and/or details regarding their location (a topic investigated in [1].)

Overall, I am interested in theoretically and empirically informing the design of simple, lightweight asynchronous interventions to help people learn about each other more efficiently and accurately, thereby reducing psychological distance and improving both task-related and social outcomes in large scale collaborative environments.

5. REFERENCES

[1] Marlow, J., & Dabbish, L. 2011. Photo sharing in diverse distributed teams. *Proc. CSCW 2011*, 317–320.

[2] McCarthy, R. J., & Skowronski, J. J. 2011. You're getting warmer: Level of construal affects the impact of central traits on impression formation. *Journal of Experimental Social Psychology*, 1304-1307.

[3] O'Leary, M. B., Wilson, J. M., & Metiu, A. 2011. Beyond Being There: The Symbolic Role of Communication and Identification in the Emergence of Perceived Proximity in Geographically Dispersed Work. *Post-Print*.

[4] Robert, L. P., Denis, A. R., & Hung, Y. I. N. 2009. Individual swift trust and knowledge-based trust in face-to-face and virtual team members. *Journal of Management Information Systems*, 26(2), 241–279.

[5] Wilson, J. M., Boyer, O. L., et al. 2008. Perceived proximity in virtual work: Explaining the paradox of far-but-close. *Organization Studies*, 29(7), 979-1002.

A Framework and Future Direction for Studying Productive Applications of Social Media / Social Networking Sites

Andrew J. Roback
Illinois Institute of Technology
3301 S. Dearborn Ave.
Chicago, IL 60622
773-383-1299
aroback@hawk.iit.edu

ABSTRACT

I am researching how non-governmental organizations (NGOs) utilize social media and social networking sites (SM/SNS) in their efforts to organize, inform, and serve the communities they operate in as well as how they use these technologies to communicate and disseminate information. This study will gather data on persons posting on behalf of NGOs and examine SM/SNS data with the goal of developing a framework for both future research and contextual application of SM/SNS as a mediating artifact by NGOs. Many previous studies have addressed similar issues, but those studies are limited in context (e.g. one large software manufacturer) and they typically use only one type of research method. I will address this issue by aggregating a large data set and employing mixed methods to improve the generalizability of my findings and present a replicable framework for future studies of organizational use of SM/SNS.

Categories and Subject Descriptors

H.4.m [**Information Systems Applications**]: Miscellaneous

General Terms

Human Factors

Keywords

Social media, social networking sites, theoretical framework, models, Technology-Mediated Social Participation, Activity Theory, non-governmental organizations.

1. RESEARCH DESCRIPTION

Last year I began researching studies on the behavior of individuals on social media and social networking sites (SM/SNS) in an effort to come up with new ideas of how people use these sites to facilitate productivity and interpersonal communication and collaboration. After conducting a large literature review of studies investigating productivity-related applications of SM/SNS, I discovered that a general trend in these types of studies was to perform a contextual investigation using one type of research method; for example, collecting survey data from users of a social media application hosted on the intranet of a large software manufacturing company. While these studies had interesting insights, they were typically wholly dependent on context and had limited generalizability as a result of the pool of research participants to whom the researchers had access.

Another major issue in the study of productivity and SM/SNS is the lack of a robust body of "empirically based theoretical knowledge" [3] and a theoretical framework in which to locate research on users of SM/SNS. Researchers of technology-mediated social participation (TMSP) lament the lack of broadly applicable theories of human behavior on SM/SNS [14], and have pushed for the development and application of new theories that transcend contextual approaches [13]. Though a comprehensive theory is likely unattainable, research with generalizable results could positively impact our understanding and application of SM/SNS to address real world problems such as climate change and disaster relief by providing a framework for the contextual application of SM/SNS technology. As part of my contribution to this field, I developed a three-part framework of approaches to studying SM/SNS in enterprise environments consisting of the following categories: *user-, data-,* and *theory-centered studies.* I will briefly elaborate on the classification scheme I have developed, which will clarify why a mixed-method, large dataset approach is important to research in this area.

User-centered studies (e.g. [1, 9, 11, 17, 18]) employ qualitative research methods such as surveys, interviews, discourse analysis, and focus groups to describe users' attitudes and perceived behaviors. These studies are inductive in that they directly relate varied user feedback obtained through qualitative methods to specific activity on an SNS.

Data-centered studies (e.g. [4, 6, 7, 8, 12]) deduce user perceptions and preferences from large amounts of tracking data and server logs; these studies are less common and require system information, which raises issues of access and privacy. Data-centered studies are common among large computing companies (e.g. HP, IBM) who build their own SM/SNS application and have access to usage data and a large pool of consenting users.

A major difference between user- and data-centered studies is the distinction between motivation and participation. The feelings experienced by the user when using SM/SNS and the reasons that they use SM/SNS comprise user *motivation.* This is different from user *participation,* which is the act of contributing goods to SM/SNS. On an action level [16], I subscribe to the definition that a *motive* is a "[factor] that increase[s] the probability that an individual will make a contribution," where a *contribution* is "the effort that is given by individual volunteers to create the collective good" [5]. User-centered studies investigate motivation, which is fitting since they utilize qualitative measurements that are geared toward learning about user perceptions. Data-centered studies investigate participation, which is fitting since they measure actual user contributions on a site and do not rely on user-reported usage, which can be erroneous.

Finally, *theory-centered studies* (e.g. [2, 3, 5, 13, 15]) construct theoretical frameworks and models for describing user behavior in SM/SNS. Theory-centered studies review the history of SM/SNS, aggregate user- and data-centered case studies, and incorporate social science theory (e.g. social capital theory, social cognitive theory, etc.) into explanations of user behavior.

User-centered studies that employ qualitative methods are often limited by user perception, which may be different than actual usage patterns. Data-centered studies accurately describe actual usage patterns, but are typically limited to (corporate) networks where researchers have unlimited access to user contributions. Theory-centered studies are useful in attempting to explain human behavior, but lack empirical evidence (or rely on past case studies) and are (in some cases) restricted to the application of a single social science theory to a small dataset.[1]

It is well known that non-governmental organizations (NGOs) have a large social media presence. My research agenda is to aggregate a large set of social media data from NGOs and study how they use this technology in their efforts to organize, inform, and serve the communities they operate in as well as how they use these technologies to communicate and disseminate information. I plan to utilize methods such as content analysis (through the use of a text classifier), social network analysis, and possibly (if the scope of the project permits) a survey of persons responsible for posting content at NGOs. Through the lens of activity theory, I plan to investigate how NGOs use SM/SNS as a "mediating artifact" [16, 10] to achieve their organization-level goals. In future research, I plan to conduct an ethnographic case study to increase the robustness of my findings.

My goal with this research is to develop a picture of how organizations leverage SM/SNS for productive ends. My contribution to studies of user behavior on SM/SNS will be the development of a model of user behavior that takes into account previous research and helps illuminate context-specific observations, and a framework that locates and guides future research in this area.

2. REFERENCES

[1] Binder, J., Howes, A., and Sutcliffe, A. 2009. The Problem of Conflicting Social Spheres: Effects of Network Structure on Experienced Tension in Social Network Sites. In *Proceedings of CHI 2009* (Boston, MA, USA., April 4-9, 2009). CHI 2009. ACM, New York, NY, USA, 965-974. DOI= http://doi.acm.org/10.1145/1518701.1518849

[2] boyd, D., and Ellison, N. 2007. Social network sites: Definition, history, and scholarship. *Journal of Computer-Mediated Communication*, 13, 1, 210-230.

[3] Brandtzaeg, P. and Heim, J. 2011. A typology of social networking sites users. *International Journal of Web Based Communities*, 7, 1, 28-51.

[4] Brzozowski, M., Sandholm, T., and Hogg, T. 2009. Effects of Feedback and Peer Pressure on Contributions to Enterprise Social Media. In *Proceedings of the ACM 2009 international conference on*

Supporting group work (GROUP '09). ACM, New York, NY, USA, 61-70. DOI= http://doi.acm.org/10.1145/1531674.1531684

[5] Crowston, K. and Fagnot, I. 2008. The motivational arc of massive virtual collaboration. In *Proceedings of the IFIP WG 9.5 Working Conference on Virtuality and Society: Massive Virtual Communities*, Luneberg, Germany.

[6] DiMicco, J., Millen, D., Geyer, W., Dugan, C., Brownholtz, B., and Muller, M. 2008. Motivations for Social Networking at Work. In *Proceedings of the 2008 ACM conference on Computer supported cooperative work* (CSCW '08). ACM, New York, NY, USA, 711-720. DOI= http://doi.acm.org/10.1145/1460563.1460674

[7] Farzan, R., DiMicco, J., and Brownholtz, B. 2009. Spreading the Honey: A System for Maintaining an Online Community. In *Proceedings of the ACM 2009 international conference on Supporting group work* (GROUP '09). ACM, New York, NY, USA, 31-40. DOI= http://doi.acm.org/10.1145/1531674.1531680

[8] Geyer, W., Dugan, C., DiMicco, J., Millen, D., Brownholtz, B., and Muller, M. 2008. Use and Reuse of Shared Lists as a Social Content Type. In *Proceedings of the twenty-sixth annual SIGCHI conference on Human factors in computing systems* (CHI '08). ACM, New York, NY, USA, 1545-1554. DOI= http://doi.acm.org/10.1145/1357054.1357296

[9] Kane, G. 2011. A Multimethod Study of Information Quality in Wiki Collaboration. *ACM Trans. Manage. Inf. Syst.* 2, 1, Article 4 (March 2011), 16 pages. DOI= http://doi.acm.org/10.1145/1929916.1929920

[10] Kaptelinin, V. and Nardi, B. 2006. *Acting with Technology: Activity Theory and Interaction Design*. MIT Press, Cambridge, MA.

[11] Lampe, C., Ellison, N., and Steinfield, C. 2008. Changes in Use and Perception of Facebook. In *Proceedings of the 2008 ACM conference on Computer supported cooperative work* (CSCW '08). ACM, New York, NY, USA, 721-730. DOI= http://doi.acm.org/10.1145/1460563.1460675

[12] Muller, M., Shami, N., Millen, D., and Feinberg, J. 2010. We are all Lurkers: Consuming Behaviors among Authors and Readers in an Enterprise File-Sharing Service. In *Proceedings of the 16th ACM international conference on Supporting group work* (GROUP '10). ACM, New York, NY, USA, 201-210. DOI= http://doi.acm.org/10.1145/1880071.1880106

[13] Preece, J., and Shneiderman 2009. The Reader-to-Leader Framework: Motivating Technology-Mediated Social Participation. *AIS Transactions on Human-Computer Interaction*, 1,1, pp. 13-32.

[14] Shneiderman, B. 2011. Technology-Mediated Social Participation: The Next 25 Years of HCI Challenges. Keynote address at HCI International 2011, July 9-14, Orlando, FL, USA.

[15] Smith, M., Barash, V., Getoor, L., and Lauw, H. 2008. Leveraging Social Context for Searching Social Media. In *Proceedings of the 2008 ACM workshop on Search in social media* (SSM '08). ACM, New York, NY, USA, 91-94. DOI= http://doi.acm.org/10.1145/1458583.1458602

[16] Spinuzzi, C. 2003. *Tracing Genres through Organizations: A Sociocultural Approach to Information Design*. MIT Press, Cambridge, MA.

[17] Zhang, J., Qu, Y., Cody, J., and Wu, Y. 2010. A Case Study of Micro-blogging in the Enterprise: Use, Value, and Related Issues. In *Proceedings of the 28th international conference on Human factors in computing systems* (CHI '10). ACM, New York, NY, USA, 123-132. DOI= http://doi.acm.org/10.1145/1753326.1753346

[18] Zhang, Z. 2010. Feeling the Sense of Community in Social Network Usage. *IEEE Transactions on Engineering Management*, 57, 2, p. 225-239.

---

[1] Some studies employ mixed methods (e.g. data log analysis *and* interview), which presents a challenge to this categorization scheme. I propose a three dimensional framework for locating research in user behavior on social networking sites (user, data, and theory), with each dimension present in each study to a greater or lesser (or minimal) extent.

Learning Landscapes: Physical Space and Digital Technology in Museum Collaboration and Learning

Rolf Steier
InterMedia, University of Oslo
P.O. Box 1161, Blindern
0318 Oslo, Norway
+47 90692626
rolf.steier@intermedia.uio.no

ABSTRACT

The goal of this research project is to understand the relationship between spatial-technological features of interactive museum exhibits, and youth visitors' meaning making experiences and interactions. Through collaboration with the National Gallery of Norway, I led the design and installation of an interactive project room connected to the artist Edvard Munch. A sociocultural perspective on meaning making frames both the design and research of this project room. The study explores the interactions of small groups of teenaged museum visitors as they engage with the interactive stations in this project room and across their entire visit. This short paper introduces the research project, describes the data collection and analysis methods, and concludes with the current status and future directions of the project.

Categories and Subject Descriptors

K.3.1 [**Computer uses in Education**]: Collaborative learning

Keywords

informal learning, museum, collaboration, multitouch table, interactive exhibits, digital media, space

BACKGROUND

Museums have, in recent years, become a setting for innovative digital media that are embedded in contexts of public space and learning. Exhibits and activities in these museums have reflected a shift in conceptions of digital media interactions from that of a solitary user in front of a computer screen to include a broad range of interactions that incorporate mobility, gesture, and collaboration. Accordingly, the relationship between these media and the physical spaces in which they are embedded becomes much more significant. In contexts of learning, this shift becomes especially relevant because of new possibilities for social interaction and engagement with content.

More specifically, mobile phones, digital screens, touch displays, interactive walls and tables are all technologies being enthusiastically explored by museums as features to enhance visitor experiences, engagement, and learning with exhibits. These tools' physical relationship and place in the contexts and environments of the museum become just as significant as the virtual context within the technology. The tools both exist in the space and help mediate the spaces and content of the museum. Designing effective museum interactions depends on understanding the learning implications of space-technology relationships.

In this paper, I introduce the development and findings of a research project about the design and installation of a 'digital project room' into an art museum. Munch & Multimodality is about exploring the use of digital resources in the National Gallery in Oslo to engage young people with the work of the artist Edvard Munch, and with art in general. Working with the National Museum of Art, Architecture and Design, we have designed and installed a project room on the floor of the National Gallery that was open to the public for a period of 8 weeks between November 2011 and January 2012. This project room included various digital tools, resources, and activities with the goal of engaging visitors with Edvard Munch through social interaction and with attention to movement between the space of the room, and works of the gallery. (See Figure 1)

Figure 1 - Photograph of the installed project room.

The overarching research questions guiding this project include:

1) What are the implications for learning of the spatial-technological features of museum exhibits?

2) How does learning occur in these exhibits?

3) How can this knowledge inform the design of richer learning experiences in interactive museum exhibits?

METHODS

The methods for this research, as well as the entire project design, are grounded in a sociocultural perspective on meaning making. Accordingly, an emphasis on talk and social interaction as well as mediating tools and resources frame this research (Wertsch, 1998).

This research project has also been developed and framed as a 'design experiment' (Brown 1992, Krange & Ludvigsen 2009), whereby the goal is to design an educational activity, technology, or setting and then simultaneously research aspects of this innovation in situ. Design experiments lend themselves quite well to exploring the complexities of such a museum context and allow for a fluid relationship between the design features and research goals (Hall & Bannon, 2005).

I recruited teenaged visitors to visit the museum in small groups of 2-4 in an out of school context. In addition, I collected data on the general public that happened to visit this project room on their own. Drawing on previous research on investigating museum visitor experiences and interactions (vom Lehn et al, 2001; Gjedde & Ingemann 2008), I have incorporated a variety of data collection methods. These include: video and audio recordings of the space, as well as "walk-videos" (Gjedde & Ingemann 2008) captured through camera glasses worn by visitors. I supplemented video and audio data with: data logs from the interactive stations, interviews, and field notes.

The video recordings will be analyzed using methods from interaction analysis (Derry, et al., 2010; Hall, 2000; Jordan & Henderson, 1995).

FUTURE DIRECTIONS

To date, I have collected, reviewed, and broadly sorted video data of target visitors' trips to the interactive stations in the project room and the rest of the museum.

Next, interactions in front of these individual stations will first be interpreted before situating them in the contexts of the broader museum visits. The goal is to contribute to a better understanding of learning in the settings of technology supported museum interactions. Through both research and design, this research project will explore the role of physical space in these new museum experiences. The findings will allow us to understand and create rich social learning interactions in museums. Furthermore, as museum boundaries become more blurred, and as digital technologies become more embedded in our everyday lives, this research will contribute to learning experiences in all varieties of public spaces.

REFERENCES

1) Brown, A. L. (1992). Design Experiments: Theoretical and Methodological Challenges in creating Complex Interventions in Classroom Settings. The Journal of the Learning Sciences, 2(2), 141-178.

2) Derry, S. J., Pea, R. D., Barron, B., Engle, R., Erickson, F., Goldman, R., et al. (2010). Conducting Video Research in the Learning Sciences: Guidance on Selection, Analysis, Technology, and Ethics. *Journal of the Learning Sciences, 19*(1), 3–53.

3) Gjedde, Lisa and Ingemann, Bruno (2008) Researching Experiences – Exploring Processual and Experimental Methods in Cultural Analysis, Newcastle: Cambridge Scholars Publishing.

4) Hall, R. (2000). Video Recording as Theory. In D. Lesh & A. Kelley (Eds.), *Handbook of Research Design in Mathematics and Science Education* (pp. 647–664). Mahweh: Lawrence Erlbaum.

5) Hall, T., & Bannon, L. (2005). Co-operative design of children's interaction in museums: A case study in the Hunt Museum. CoDesign: International Journal of CoCreation in Design and the Arts, 1(3), 187-218.

6) Jordan, B. & Henderson, A. (1995). Interaction Analysis. *The Journal of the Learning Sciences, 4*(1), 39–103.

7) Krange, Ingeborg & Ludvigsen, Sten Runar (2009). The historical and situated nature design experiments - Implications for data analysis. Journal of Computer Assisted Learning.

8) vom Lehn, D., Heath, C. and J. Hindmarsh (2001) Exhibiting Interaction: Conduct and Collaboration in Museums and Galleries. Symbolic Interaction, 24, 2, 189-216.

9) Wertsch, J. (1998). Mind as Action. New York: Oxford University Press.

Scenario-Based Design of a Digital Reminiscing System for the Elderly

Elizabeth Thiry
College of Information Sciences and Technology
Pennsylvania State University
University Park, PA 16802 USA
exn152@psu.edu

ABSTRACT

There has recently been interest within the HCI community concerning both current practices and digital tools for reminiscing. Several systems have been developed to trigger and / or capture reminiscence content, however very little is known about the overall process of reminiscing or been developed for an older healthy population. For my dissertation I have investigated when and how elderly individuals reminisce and am developing a prototype system that can enhance and maintain records of their reminiscing.

Categories and Subject Descriptors

H5.m. Information interfaces and presentation (e.g., HCI): Miscellaneous.

General Terms

Design, Human Factors

Keywords

Reminiscing, Elderly, Usability, Scenario Based Design

1. Motivation

The desire and practices for reminiscing ("the act or process of recalling the past [1]") can be traced back to early civilizations where community elders were responsible for knowing and sharing the history of their community [2, 3]. However times have changed and the oral tradition of reminiscing has faded into an occasional telling of stories that are heard on special occasions.

HCI research in the area of reminiscing has investigated ways to trigger and elicit memories [4-6]. For example, Pensieve is a reminiscing system that prompts users with photos or status that they have previously posted to social networks [7]. Palaver Tree Online [8] was a system through which children and elders collaborated on the creation of oral histories. Adtep, Kay and Quigley [9] developed a table top digital photo sharing system. Other systems have been developed to allow individuals to document their entire life [10] as well as being prompted to reminisce based on old posts to social networking sites [7].

There has recently been interest within the HCI community concerning both current practices and digital tools for reminiscing [11]. The focus of this research can be viewed as responding to this call with two complementary research elements: an interest in the human-computer interaction (HCI) needs and preferences for

elderly individuals and a design research interest in digital tools for supporting reminiscing.

2. Research Goals and Methods

The dissertation project is directed towards the elderly with the goal of creating a digital reminiscing system for this target population. The research is being conducted within the framework of scenario-based design (SBD) [12]. The SBD methodology was selected not only because scenarios are an effective representation for human-centered design [13], but also because stories are a simple method for illustrating and discussing usage possibilities with elderly individuals. A co-product of the SBD process is design rationale that analyzes and documents hypothesized consequences of central design features; thus for this dissertation project, I intend to develop not just a novel software design but also a body of design rationale that connects the system's design to existing literature and to empirical data gathered as part of the project. As an instance of SBD, the process is divided into three phases of development.

Phase 1 – Requirements Analysis - *"How do elders currently reminisce?"* Before developing a system to support digital reminiscing, I needed to understand how elderly people currently reminisce, whether in a physical setting (e.g., scrapbooks, oral storytelling) or using digital tools of some sort (e.g., digital photos shared via email). Specifically, I wondered what memories they are they sharing: as well as with whom, why, when, where and how the sharing is done. In parallel I wanted to explore design preferences and requirements for a digital reminiscing system. To answer these questions I interviewed fourteen older adults (65 years of age and older) within the local community.

A number of preliminary themes of how older adults are currently reminiscing have emerged from the initial analysis of the data. Such as:

- Older adults do not feel that they have anything to share or that anyone is interested.

- Reminiscing happens both spontaneously as well as during planned events.

- The reminiscing stories they share take different forms depending on the audience.

- Reminiscing takes many different forms (oral, memoirs, scrapbook, newspaper articles, books, family trees, and so on)

In addition to the general themes in the interviews, I have begun to envision characteristics of the software system that will be design to enhance the reminiscing process for older adults.

GROUP'12, October 27–31, 2012, Sanibel Island, Florida, USA.
ACM 978-1-4503-1486-2/12/10.

- Triggers - By triggering older adults to reminisce (as I did during the interviews) we may remove their concern that they have nothing to share.

- Minimalistic - They prefer simpler communication channels like email and text documents, where they can understand what they are doing and do not have the feeling that they are missing something or putting something much online that might jeopardize their privacy or safety.

- Physicality of Reminiscence Artifact - Older adults still rely heavily on paper. Even when they type or create content on a computer they do not enjoy a sense of completion until it is printed out so that they can see and hold it.

- Collaborative – Reminiscing is not a solitary process. Oral stories are told to a specific audience. Artifacts (scrapbooks) are shared after they are complete. Therefore the system needs to provide a way to share as well.

- Cross generational - The desire to share information about one's community or more generally about historic events was prominent within our population of interviewees, particularly when the audience included individuals from younger generations.

For more information on the preliminary finds see [14]. I am currently coding the interviews by theme, starting with the themes already identified but also keeping an open eye for any other themes that may emerge. Once the interviews have been coded the results will be used to create a number of personas that depict current reminiscing.

Phase 2 – Design – *"What features of a reminiscing tool can replicate, expand upon, and enhance reminiscing?"* The personas created in phase 1 will then be used to develop problem scenarios dealing with the different design requirements that emerge. These documents will be used in a participatory design session, with the outcome being a prototype digital reminiscing system.

Phase 3 – Evaluation – "What are the benefits and drawbacks of using this system for reminiscing?" This phase involves a mix of lab studies and fieldwork, and will articulate the system's strengths and weaknesses.

3. Expected Contributions

I anticipate that the system will change reminiscing practices of the elderly who participate in the study. In particular, I will produce findings that address the research questions proposed earlier. The contributions of this research will include:

- Empirical knowledge of reminiscing motivations and practices and associated design implications.

- The design and evaluation of a system to support digital reminiscing.

- The benefits and drawbacks of using the system for reminiscing across multiple domains.

4. REFERENCES

[1] Butler, R.N., The Life Review: An Interpretation of Reminiscence in the Aged. Psychiatry, 1963. 26(1): p. 65.

[2] Butler, R.N., *Foreword: The Life Review*, in *The Art and Science of Reminiscing: Theory, Research, Methods, and Applications*, J.D. Webster and B.K. Haight, Editors. 1995, Taylor & Francis: Washington, D.C. p. xvii-xxi.

[3] Cruikshank, J., *Life Histories and Life Stories*, in *Life Lived Like a Story: Life Stories of Three Yukon Native Elders*, J. Cruikshank, Editor 1990, University of Nebraska Press: Lincoln. p. 1-20.

[4] Carroll, J.M., *The Blacksburg Electronic Village: A Study in Community Computing*, in *Digital Cities III*, P. van den Besselaar and S. Koizumi, Editors. 2005, Springer Berlin / Heidelberg. p. 43-65.

[5] Hofmeester, K., et al., A modern role for the village elders, in CHI '99 extended abstracts on Human factors in computing systems, ACM: Pittsburgh, Pennsylvania, United States. p. 43-44.

[6] Gaver, W. and A. Dunne, Projected realities: conceptual design for cultural effect, in Proceedings of the SIGCHI conference on Human factors in computing systems: the CHI is the limit 1999, ACM: Pittsburgh, Pennsylvania, United States. p. 600-607.

[7] Cosley, D., et al., Using technologies to support reminiscence, in Proceedings of the 23rd British HCI Group Annual Conference on People and Computers: Celebrating People and Technology 2009, British Computer Society: Cambridge, United Kingdom. p. 480-484.

[8] Ellis, J.B. and A.S. Bruckman, Designing palaver tree online: supporting social roles in a community of oral history, in Proceedings of the SIGCHI conference on Human factors in computing systems 2001, ACM: Seattle, Washington, United States. p. 474-481.

[9] Apted, T., J. Kay, and A. Quigley, Tabletop sharing of digital photographs for the elderly, in Proceedings of the SIGCHI conference on Human Factors in computing systems 2006, ACM: Montral, Qubec, Canada. p. 781-790.

[10] Sellen, A.J., et al., Do life-logging technologies support memory for the past?: an experimental study using sensecam, in Proceedings of the SIGCHI conference on Human factors in computing systems 2007, ACM: San Jose, California, United States. p. 81-90.

[11] Cosley, D., et al., Bridging practices, theories, and technologies to support reminiscence, in Proceedings of the 2011 annual conference extended abstracts on Human factors in computing systems 2011, ACM: Vancouver, BC, Canada. p. 57-60.

[12] Rosson, M.B. and J.M. Carroll, Usability Engineering: Scenario-Based Development of Human- Computer Interaction 2002, New York, NY: Morgan Kaufman.

[13] Rosson, M.B. and J.M. Carroll, Scenario-Based Design, in Handbook of Human-Computer Interaction 3rd Edition, J. Jacko, Editor In Press.

[14] Thiry, E. and M.B. Rosson, Unearthing the family gems: design requirements for a digital reminiscing system for older adults, in Proceedings of the 2012 ACM annual conference extended abstracts on Human Factors in Computing Systems Extended Abstracts, ACM: Austin, Texas, United States. p. 1715-1720.

Collaborating with Others Trying to do the Same Thing: Coordination in an Educational Improvement Network

Peter Samuelson Wardrip
University of Pittsburgh
Learning Research and Development
Center (LRDC) / Learning Sciences
and Policy
Psw9@pitt.edu

ABSTRACT

The use of networks to support and scale school reform initiatives and educational programs are becoming more and more prevalent. Through an initiative of the Carnegie Foundation for the Advancement of Teaching (CFAT), an emerging organizational form known as a Networked Improvement Community (NIC), offers an infrastructure for implementing and improving educational innovations. Fundamental to the work of this network is the collaboration of multiple actors and teams at multiple sites. Yet, this collaboration across time and space does not just happen. It requires coordination mechanisms to guide the actions of those involved in collaboration. This research seeks to build an initial conceptual framework to study how the joint work on an educational reform happens in a distributed or networked organizational environment. A NIC is a case of one such environment.

Categories and Subject Descriptors

H.5.3 Groups & Organization Interfaces— computer-supported cooperative work

General Terms

Management, Theory

Keywords

Coordination, Organizational Network, Learning

1. INTRODUCTION

The use of networks to support and scale school reform initiatives and educational programs are becoming more and more prevalent. There are networks to support out of school learning (e.g. Hive Learning Network), there are networks to support government-funded program implementations (e.g. Promise Neighborhoods) and networks to support teachers (e.g. National Writing Project), to name a few. In short, a network represents an emerging organizational form to develop, implement and potentially scale educational programs and innovations.

There are a variety of reasons why networks present an opportunity upon which new programs can capitalize. For example, networks enable groups of organizations to take on problems that are bigger than a single organization could tackle [9]. Moreover, the network enables the sharing of novel information [12], the utilizing of expertise that is not present in one's organization [11] as well as sharing resources [6], a network

presents an opportunity for organizations and individuals to join forces to build their collective capacity to take on ambitious goals. However, networks of distributed work are not without their challenges [13]. Some of these challenges are inherent to a network's distributed and interdisciplinary nature. For example, it matters if the work is tightly coupled or loosely coupled; that is, is the work able to be partitioned into pieces for team members to work on it separately, if the workers have common ground and past experiences together, and if the technological skills of the workers and the infrastructure of the work place support distributed work [10]. And often network practices can put pressure on already established local practices [7].

Therefore, considering these affordances and barriers to the work of a distributed network and the need for network members to collaborate, understanding the mechanisms that support networked work is crucial for educational improvement networks to be effective. There are a lot of conditions that contribute to how distributed joint work unfolds or doesn't in an educational improvement network. One way to understand this work is to understand the extent to which the work is coordinated. To further understanding in this regard, I seek to build an initial framework to understand the mechanisms that support this collaborative work in an educational improvement network. In this brief paper, I will highlight the network I am investigating, highlight the theoretical perspectives that are informing this work and the contribution I hope to make through this work.

2. A CASE OF A NETWORKED IMPROVEMENT COMMUNITY (NIC)

This research is taking place within the context of a Networked Improvement Community (NIC). A NIC is a distributed group of diverse organizations and / or individuals that is "collectively engaged in improving an agreed-upon set either of individual capabilities, or of collective group capabilities"... "for dealing with complex, urgent problems." [4]. What makes a NIC unique is that it is intended to address a common problem to the community as well as improve the community's ability to address the problem [5]. As an innovation is designed in a NIC, it is tested out in multiple sites. What is learned from these implementations is fed back into the design for another iteration. The NIC simultaneously learns about implementation of an innovation, those implementing the innovation and the conditions under which the innovation can be supported.

The Carnegie Foundation for the Advancement of Teaching (CFAT) has recently initiated an education NIC called Quantway. They conceive of NICs as simultaneously design communities and learning communities with a "diverse colleagueship" focusing on a common problem. Quantway "aims to turn around the alarming failure rate of community college students in developmental mathematics." To this end, Quantway consists of community college teams, research teams, software design teams, curriculum design teams, as well as CFAT program staff, all working to encourage success in community college mathematics and develop quantitatively literate citizens.

3. THEORETICAL BACKGROUND

Working from the definition of coordination as "managing dependencies between activities." [7], there are three strands of research that are informing this work: the notion of coordination as a dynamic activity, coordination theory and coordination mechanisms. These strands of research provide a starting point to understand coordination within an educational improvement network.

The study of groups of people who carry out work within teams and / or organizations requires a nuanced view of organizing, rather than the organization [2]. Coordination in these groups and organizations is not reduced to a set of static structures, but rather it is an ongoing and dynamic activity that unfolds when work is accomplished [3]. And it is not just the work that is coordinated, but also other factors as well such as technology, that impact the social dynamics of organizing [1].

While coordination is a dynamic process in organizations, coordination theory was developed to understand and manage organizational processes [8]. Identifying these processes provides substantial leverage for redesigning processes for organizational improvement. Furthermore, categorizing the processes by their interdependencies suggests the ways that the processes can be managed. In short, coordination theory is an ongoing attempt to build a body of "theories about how coordination can occur in diverse kinds of systems" [8].

Finally, coordination of work processes is a multi-layered activity that calls upon more than rules of interactions. There are other coordination mechanisms. For example, a coordinative protocol constitutes the set of rules and conventions that govern the interaction. A coordinative artifact is the protocol in symbolic form and thus objectified (Schmidt & Simone, 1996). Together, the coordinative artifact and protocol provide guidance to the collaborative process.

As this research is ongoing, this theoretical background guides the work of investigating how joint work unfolds in Quantway. This includes identifying the work practices of the network, categorizing these work practices by their dependencies and then inquiring into the mechanisms and enactments that coordinate these dependencies.

4. CONTRIBUTION

This research aims to a contribution to the field of education and the learning sciences. First, this works seeks to introduce and extend established work on coordination to the field of education. This may be important as networks become a organizational and policy strategy for new initiatives. For example, as networks become more prominent as an organizational form to facilitate school reform and improvement, those initiating these networks will need developed understanding of what mechanisms to support coordinated work. More to the direct spirit of this work, these initiatives will need to acknowledge the interdependencies

that exist in the work of the network and consider how those interdependencies might be coordinated. This research aims to provide some preliminary insights in this regard.

5. ACKNOWLEDGMENTS
Thanks to Louis Gomez and Jennifer Russell, my co-advisors, my other committee members: Mary Kay Stein and Lauren Resnick and Jon Dolle from the Carnegie Foundation.

6. REFERENCES
[1] Bailey, D. E.; Leonardi, P. M.; Chong, J. Minding the gaps: Technology interdependence and coordination in knowledge work". *Organization Science*, 21 (3), 2010, 713–730.

[2] Barley, S.R., & Kunda, G. Bringing work back in. *Organization Science*, 12, 2001, 76–95.

[3] Bechky, B.A. Gaffers, gofers and grips: Role-based coordination in temporary organizations. *Organization Science*, 17(1), 2006, 3-21.

[4] Bryk, A. S., Gomez, L. M., & Grunow, A. Getting ideas into action: Building networked improvement communities in education. In M. Hallinan (Ed.), *Frontiers in Sociology of Education*. New York, NY: Springer. 2011.

[5] Engelbart, D. *Toward High-Performance Organizations: A Strategic Role for Groupware*. Proceedings of Groupware '92, August 1992.

[6] Goldsmith, S. & W. D. Eggers. *Governing by network; The new shape of the public sector*. Washington, DC: Brookings Institutions Press. 2004

[7] Haythornthwaite, C., K. J. Lunsford, G. C. Bowker, & B. Bruce. Challenges for research and practice in distributed, interdisciplinary, collaboration. In C. Hine, (Ed.), *New Infrastructures for Science Knowledge Production*. Hershey, PA: Idea Group, 2006.

[8] Malone, T.W. & Crowston, K. The interdisciplinary study of coordination. *ACM Computing Surveys*, 26(1), 1994, 87-117.

[9] Mandell, M. P. Community collaborations: Working through network structures. *Policy Studies Review*, 16: 1999, 42-64.

[10] Olson, J. S., & Olson, G. M. Bridging Distance: Empirical Studies of Distributed   Teams, in Dennis Galletta and Ping Zhang, (eds.) *Human-Computer Interaction in Management Information Systems: Volume II: Applications.* M. E. Sharpe, Inc. 2006

[11] Podolny, J. M. and K. L. Page. Network forms of organization. *Annual Review of Sociology*, 24: 1998, 57-76.

[12] Powell, W.W., White, D.R., Koput, K.W., & Owen-Smith, J. Network dynamics and field evolution: The growth of interorganizational collaboration in the life sciences. American Journal of Sociology, 110(4), 2005, 1132-1206.

[13] Ribes, David and Bowker, Geoffrey C. (2008) 'Organizing for Multidisciplinary

[14] Schmidt, K. &, Simone, C. Coordination mechanisms: Towards a conceptual   foundation of CSCW systems design. *Computer Supported Cooperative Work*. 5(2-3), 1996, 155-2

Better Understanding of Human Decision Making Can Inform the Design of Sociotechnical Systems that Foster and Support Behavior Modification

Jason Zietz
University of Colorado Boulder
430 UCB
Boulder, CO 80309
jason.zietz@colorado.edu

ABSTRACT

Behavior modification is the process of identifying and changing an undesirable behavior to a more desirable one. As computational devices and the data they produce become more ubiquitous, sociotechnical systems utilizing these devices become more viable as tools to support behavior modification endeavors. These systems can be accessed at the moments people need them, supplying the right support and guidance on a personalized basis. As behaviors are based on decisions, sociotechnical systems supporting behavior modification that incorporate our understanding of human decision making are likely to be more efficacious than those that do not. These systems can also utilize our knowledge of motivation to further improve their users' likelihood of success. My dissertation research examines how our understanding of human decision making and motivation can be used to better determine how sociotechnical systems can be built that encourage and support people in their behavior modification efforts.

Categories and Subject Descriptors

H.1.2 [**Models and Principles**]: User/Machine Systems – Human information processing, software psychology

General Terms

Design, Experimentation, Human Factors.

Keywords

Judgment and Decision Making, Sociotechnical Systems, Behavior Modification, Motivation

1. INTRODUCTION

If we always did what was best for us and never exhibited undesirable behaviors, there would be no need for behavior modification. Sometimes we do not know what is best for us and it isn't until we learn otherwise that our undesirable habits are long-established and difficult to break. Other times we know what choices are best for us in the long-term but choose those that satisfy proximal hedonistic desires instead, despite the problems these decisions will cause us in the future. Unfortunately, changing our behavior is difficult, and thus people fail in their endeavors to break bad habits and instead fall back into old ways of doing things, despite the knowledge of their deleterious

behavior. Fortunately, we have learned much and continue to learn more about how and why people make decisions. Concurrently, sociotechnical systems have continued to grow in both utility and accessibility. Utilized together, sociotechnical systems that leverage our understanding of human decision making can be effective tools that foster and support behavior modification.

2. THEORETICAL BACKGROUND

Sociotechnical systems are well-suited to support individuals in their behavior modification endeavors. They are persistent (Fogg 2002) and do not forget, they provide anonymity and can be ubiquitous, and they leverage the fact that humans are innately social and obtain considerable value from social interaction (Porter 2008).

Usually for behavior modification to occur, a person must say yes: first to the decision to change their behavior and subsequently to the behavior change until the new behavior becomes practice. With this in mind, systems designed for behavior change should help individuals make the decision to change their behavior and then provide continual motivation to perform the activities that the new behavior is comprised of.

There are a number of methods that can be used to get a person to say yes to doing an activity. Nudges guide people's decisions towards predictable outcomes without restricting or appreciably modifying the economic incentives of choices (Thaler 2008). Nudges have been shown to have short-term efficacy, but their long-term effects are unclear. Because we currently cannot speak to the long-term efficacy of nudges, it is important that we develop and run experiments that validate or invalidate their ability to modify behavior on large time scales. As part of my dissertation research, I intend to pursue this area of inquiry; if nudges are only effective ephemerally and show no long-term behavior modification results, their usefulness is rather limited.

Social proof, social norms, public commitment, peer pressure, and competition are methods that utilize a person's social environment in order to increase the likelihood that they will decide to change their behavior. We have begun to explore how these methods can be utilized to influence a person's environmental decisions. For example, it is now technologically feasible for consumers to access their real-time electricity usage via smart grid technologies. We are designing a sociotechnical system that provides an individual with their personal energy consumption and allows them to compare it to the average consumption of their neighbors (social norm) as well as the neighbor with the lowest consumption (social proof).

Once an individual has decided to change their behavior, their levels of intrinsic and extrinsic motivations dictate how likely they are to continue exhibiting the new behavior. We believe that an individual is most likely to be successful in changing their behavior over extended time frames when they are intrinsically motivated rather than extrinsically motivated. For example, individuals who are trying to reduce their electricity consumption will be more likely to be successful when they are motivated by desires to help fight pollution and reduce their carbon footprint as opposed to being motivated by prizes. In a recent "energy competition" that awarded a large prize to the household that reduced their electricity usage the most, competitors reduced their usage (sometimes substantially) during the competition but reverted to original levels (or higher) when the competition ended. (Details can be found here: http://www.fastcoexist.com/1679632/energy-battle-students-show-how-games-can-cut-electric-bills.) As part of my dissertation research, I am exploring how we can better help individuals find personal reasons to want to change their behavior, and then utilize those reasons in order to be successful in these endeavors.

3. CURRENT RESEARCH

I am currently running an experiment that examines methods that can be used to foster and support pro-environmental behavior change. In this study, I am exploring how environmental awareness coupled with emotional reactions affect an individual's likelihood to take a pro-environmental action. Our energy usage behaviors are likely long established due to the existing energy infrastructure that we have interacted with for decades which have only reported our electricity usage in monthly increments via the nebulous unit kilowatt-hour (kWh). We do not believe that continuing to report electricity usage in kWh and dollars alone will help consumers understand how their usage actually impacts the environment. Alternative representations of electricity usage such as pounds of coal or CO_2, however, can help achieve this. We believe that these alternative representations can serve two purposes. First, they help better establish meaning to electricity usage: people cannot visualize what a kWh looks like, but they can imagine what 100 pounds of coal looks like. Second, emotions have been shown to play a role in environmental decision making (Vining 1987), and we hypothesize that the alternative representations have the potential to elicit an emotional reaction in consumers due to their availability and vividness. For instance, recalling a lump of coal likely conjures a negative reaction – coal looks sooty and dirty, and people can likely remember hearing about a coal mining accident. Supplementing the alternative representations with information about how the tangible objects relate to electricity (e.g., only 30% of the energy yielded from burning coal is available for electricity production (http://en.wikipedia.org/wiki/Coal)), can further strengthen these emotions.

In the study, subjects in the control group are provided with a description of what a kWh is and then asked to rate their emotional response to this description on a scale of 0-5 for happiness, sadness, fear, disgust, surprise, and anger. Subjects in the experimental groups are shown a picture of one of three alternative representations of energy use: coal, carbon dioxide, or US dollars and asked to rate their emotional response as in the control group. Next the subjects are supplied with information about the average US household's monthly electricity usage using the representation utilized in the previous step, kWh for the control group and coal, carbon dioxide, or dollars in the experimental groups. As in the previous step, the subjects are then asked to describe their emotional response to this information.

In a subsequent study, subjects will be supplied with information about the average US household's monthly electricity usage as above, but rather than asking them to describe their emotional response, respondents will instead be asked if they would be willing to commit to reducing their electricity bill by 5% in the coming month. I believe that the representations of energy use that elicit the strongest emotional reactions as found in the first study will be most likely to cause shifts toward more pro-environmental behaviors in consumers such as agreeing to try and reduce one's electric bill. The insights yielded from these experiments will be used in the design of the sociotechnical system designed to assist consumers in their energy saving endeavors described above.

4. FUTURE DIRECTIONS

Subsequent research to the work described above could explore how reported emotions change when respondents are aware of the responses of others like them. For example, will a person say they are more disgusted by a picture of coal if they know that someone like them was disgusted by the picture than if they weren't supplied with this information? In other words, can social influencers like social norms and social proof "override" a person's emotional response? And if so, are these effects long-lasting or only present when the influencers are present? Answering questions such as these can help us better understand how people make decisions, and this understanding can assist us in constructing effective sociotechnical systems designed to support behavior change.

5. REFERENCES AND CITATIONS

Fogg, B. J. (2002). Persuasive Technology: Using Computers to Change What We Think and Do (Interactive Technologies), Morgan Kaufmann.

Porter, J. (2008). Designing for the Social Web. Berkeley, CA, New Riders.

Thaler, R. H., Sunstein, C. R. (2008). Nudge: Improving Decisions About Health, Wealth and Happiness Newhaven, Yale University Press.

Vining, J. (1987). "Environmental Decisions: The Interaction of Emotions, Information, and Decision Context." Journal of Environmental Psychology 7: 13-30.

Group Dynamics Findings from Coordination in Problem Solving and Decision Making Meetings

Flaviu Roman
Ecole Polytechnique Fédérale
de Lausanne (EPFL)
Lausanne, Switzerland
flaviu.roman@epfl.ch

Himanshu Verma
Ecole Polytechnique Fédérale
de Lausanne (EPFL)
Lausanne, Switzerland
h.verma@epfl.ch

Patrick Jermann
Ecole Polytechnique Fédérale
de Lausanne (EPFL)
Lausanne, Switzerland
patrick.jermann@epfl.ch

Pierre Dillenbourg
Ecole Polytechnique Fédérale
de Lausanne (EPFL)
Lausanne, Switzerland
pierre.dillenbourg@epfl.ch

ABSTRACT

We present the results of group dynamics and their effect on success in problem solving / decision making meetings. We use a novel multiple input environment for collaboration and data collection, and a hidden profile task given to groups, whose goals are to find the correct solution. We observe that groups elect 0, 1 or 2 leaders, and the best results are obtained by the groups with a single leader. Prior acquaintance (familiarity), does not show any effect on the success or on the group strategies. Groups with a single leader tend to be more successful, and leaders expressed their authority verbally rather than by through the collaborative system.

Keywords

Group Evolution, Human Computer Interaction, CSCW, Collaboration

Categories and Subject Descriptors

D.5.3 [**Group and Organization Interfaces**]: Computer supported cooperative work

General Terms

Experimentation, Human FactorsExperimentation, Human Factors

1. INTRODUCTION

The success of problem solving and decision making in meetings is highly influenced by the way group dynamics emerge. We make use of a shared multiple-input system

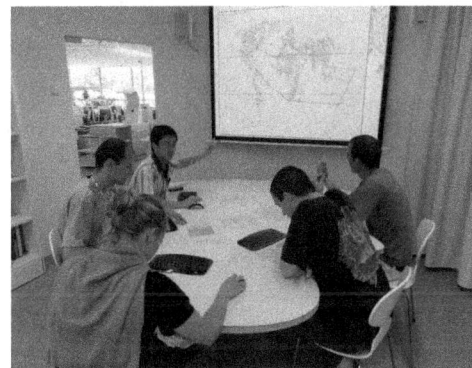

Figure 1: Wall Display, Meeting Table, Keyboards and Mice.

(using either multiple keyboards and mice or multiple pen) with a single display screen as an SDG (single display groupware), and a hidden profile task designed by Stasser [4], to evaluate how groups collaborate and how their internal dynamics are created, and to observe the impact of these on the performance of the groups. Several authors have evaluated similar settings. Rienks and Zhang [3] are looking into participation levels, Matthews and Whittaker [2] are looking at teams from the individual's perspective. Kelly and Fisher [1] are analyzing structures that emerge from collaborations in teams.

2. SETUP

The setup includes a front projected display and a meeting table placed in front of it (Figure 1).

The meeting table has a wave like shape (Figure 2) designed to facilitate positioning for both face-to-face interaction and the public display visibility. The system is equipped either with a wireless mouse and keyboard (Figure 1), or with a digital pen and paper (PP, Figure 2). The public display as well as the input devices are connected to a single computer.

Figure 2: Meeting table in the Pen and Paper setup.

3. USER STUDY

We conducted a user study recruiting 66 participants who formed groups of 3 (2 teams) and 4 (15 teams) people. The hidden profile task required the participants to play the role of detectives in identifying a perpetrator, by combining information from investigation transcripts and records that were distributed as booklets (one per participant). The information in the booklets contained parts that were common (replicated on all booklets), but also parts that were available only on individual booklets. To solve the task, the participants needed to collaborate in order to successfully merge information from all booklets. The task time was capped to two hours, but we recorded the actual duration for each team. Groups were successful if they correctly identified the perpetrator.

During the study, we had three types of information collection: logs of system use by participant; a wizard-of-oz observer attending the meeting (in the background), counting the number of utterances (separated on task-related or coordination-related), and the number of gestures (to the screen and to the material); and the participants filling in a pre-test questionnaire with prior information, and preferences and a post-test questionnaire with their perception about the task, social aspects, coordination, etc.

We collected and grouped the data into individual and group results, and used statistics (ANOVA, Kruskal-Wallis and Linear Regression) to evaluate the relations between certain factors, using the R environment. Leadership was assessed by the observers, and we categorized it into groups with 0, 1, and 2 leaders. Familiarity of the group was considered negative if at most 2 (of 4) people knew each other previously, and positive if at least 3 people knew each other, but in the vast majority of the cases, they either didn't know anyone at all, or everyone knew everyone. Some individual ranked features were evaluated at the group level by computing the mean of the individual values for people in that group.

4. RESULTS

4.1 Results about Groups

First, we did not find any impact of the group familiarity on performance or other elements measured, including success ($H[2] = 0.457$, $p = .499$). However, the perceived level of consensus was higher in successful groups compared to unsuccessful groups ($H[2] = 6.583$, $p = .01$). Another measure that had a relation with success was the gestures towards the board, in the sense that successful groups did less gestures ($H[2] = 4.3012$, $p = .038$). An explanation for such a result could be that the large number of gestures were caused by confusion, which also lead to poor performance. On the other hand, in those the groups where individuals felt they participated more, they also felt that their contributions were taken into account more ($F[2,17] = 24.46$, $p < .001$).

In terms of leadership, 73% of groups with one leader were successful, whereas only 16% of groups with 0 or 2 leaders were successful ($H[3] = 5.2391$, $p = 0.073$).

4.2 Results about Individuals

We found that leaders did not do significantly more operations on the shared screen ($F[2, 17] = 0.007494$, $p = .932$). On the other hand, leaders had significantly more total utterances than non-leaders ($H[2] = 5.5761$, $p = .018$). Therefore we conclude that leadership was expressed through verbal communication, and not through monopoly over the shared space.

Another finding was that participants who made more gestures towards the display also had more organizational utterances ($F[2, 66] = 12.27$, $p < .001$). This supports the hypothesis that more gestures were made in the presence of more confusion, and participants tried to over-organize to reduce this confusion.

5. FUTURE AND CONCLUSIONS

We presented findings about leadership, success and familiarity of groups performing a hidden profile task. Leadership is certainly an important aspect that requires more fine-tuned research, because it can prove instrumental in explaining certain patterns and in predicting the success of the groups. We plan to analyze different other ways of defining leadership, including defining formulas for leadership based on contribution and adjusting the thresholds for such measurements towards optimal values.

6. REFERENCES

[1] Kelly, J. W., Fisher, D., and Smith, M. Friends, foes, and fringe: norms and structure in political discussion networks. In *Proceedings of the 2006 international conference on Digital government research*, dg.o '06, ACM (New York, NY, USA, 2006), 412–417.

[2] Matthews, T., Whittaker, S., Moran, T., Helsley, S., and Judge, T. Productive interrelationships between collaborative groups ease the challenges of dynamic and multi-teaming. *Computer Supported Cooperative Work (CSCW) 1* (2012), 1–26.

[3] Rienks, R., Zhang, D., Gatica-Perez, D., and Post, W. Detection and application of influence rankings in small group meetings. In *Proceedings of the 8th international conference on Multimodal interfaces*, ICMI '06, ACM (New York, NY, USA, 2006), 257–264.

[4] Stasser, G., and Stewart, D. Discovery of hidden profiles by decision-making groups: Solving a problem versus making a judgment. *Journal of Personality and Social Psychology 63*, 3 (1992), 426–434.

Tweet Recall: Examining Real-time Civic Discourse on Twitter

Christopher M. Mascaro
Drexel University
iSchool
cmascaro@gmail.com

Alan Black
Drexel University
iSchool
aeblack@gmail.com

Sean Goggins
Drexel University
iSchool
outdoors@acm.org

ABSTRACT

We present a preliminary analysis of #widebate, a hashtag to identify discourse related to two debates in the June 2012, Wisconsin Gubernatorial recall election. Our analysis identifies the differences in discourse between the two debates. We find that only 14% of individuals participate in discourse surrounding both of the debates. Further, we identify differences in the way that the most active individuals in the discourse utilize syntactical features. Our findings contribute to the limited literature examining technologically-mediated discourse related to political debates.

Categories and Subject Descriptors

J.4 [Social and Behavioral Sciences]: Sociology

Keywords

Twitter, political discourse, social media, elections, civic engagement

1. INTRODUCTION

Civic debate has been one of the foundations of society throughout history. Electoral debates in the United States have evolved significantly over time and allow citizens to learn about candidates leading to more informed decisions [4]. Until the introduction of the Internet, analysis of citizen discourse related to debates relied on questionnaires, surveys and focus groups [5].

Twitter allows for examination of the public's response to electoral debates in near real-time. Research that has examined Twitter in the context of electoral debates has focused on identifying topics of the debate [3] and the individuals and content of the debate [7; 8]. Much of this research has been situated in larger discourses that examine Twitter as a back channel to live TV discourse [2]. Although previous research has examined electoral debates in an attempt to identify topical content, no prior research examines the participants in the discourse outside the context of analysis of mentions in the tweet text [7]. Understanding how individuals contribute to the discourse is important in understanding how technology facilitates civic engagement.

2. CONTEXT AND DATASET

Wisconsin Governor Scott Walker was elected in November 2010, but faced a recall election on June 5, 2012. Governor Walker won the recall election by a 53%-46% margin. In the two weeks before the election, Governor Walker debated his opponent

(Milwaukee Mayor Tom Barrett) twice, May 25 and May 31. The hashtag #widebate was used to mark discourse pertaining to the debates on Twitter.

We used the TwitterZombie architecture to query the Twitter SEARCH API every minute for tweets with the hashtag #widebate from May 21st – June 12th [1]. In total, 26,107 tweets were collected. These tweets were divided into two datasets to examine the difference between the two debates. Tweets that occurred up until May 29th at 12:00am were deemed to be associated with the May 25th debate (n=10,958), while all of the tweets following that time were deemed to be associated with the May 31st debate (n=15,149). All analysis was done using custom-built R scripts based on previous work by the authors [6].

3. FINDINGS

In total, 6,012 unique individuals contributed to the discourse using the #widebate hashtag, with 3,125 participating in the first debate and 3,780 participating in the second debate. Table 1 illustrates the syntactical feature utilization for the two debates.

Table 1: Syntactical feature utilization by all users

	Tweet Count	Links	Mentions	@Reply	Retweets
First Debate	10,958	21.30%	70.12%	5.18%	57.28%
Second Debate	15,149	22.77%	65.77%	4.31%	53.11%

We identified 893 individuals (14.9%) that participated in both of the debates. We coded these individuals who participated in both debates as: singletons (tweeted once in each debate), moderate (tweeted once in one debate and more than once in the other) or active (tweeted more than once in each debate). Table 2 illustrates the categorical distribution of the individuals that participated in both debates. A small percentage (13%) of individuals participating in both debates only participated in each dataset once, while almost 50% of the individuals did so multiple times.

Table 2: Individuals who participated in Two Debates

Category	Participants	Percentage
Singleton	116	13%
Moderate	333	37.4%
Active	444	49.7%

3.1 Examining the Active Citizen

To further understand the most prolific individuals in the two debates, we examine the top 10 contributors the two debates. There were only three individuals that were in the top 10 in both debates, illustrating diversity in participants in the debate discourse. Table 3 and 4 denote the description, number of tweets in the dataset and the number of total tweets from when the account was first created through June 25th, 2012 in the two debates. Individuals that participated in more than one debate are noted with *.

Table 3: Top 10 "Active" Individuals in First Debate

User Description	First Debate	Total Tweets
Conservative Citizen/Blogger	115	124,253
Conservative Citizen	104	3,596
Women's Rights Advocate	78	61,555
Education Advocacy Org *	72	9,307
Conservative Citizen *	61	14,903
Conservative Citizen	61	2,385
Conservative Citizen	58	13,365
Liberal Citizen *	57	23,677
Conservative Organizer	54	13,991
Progressive Political Blogger	54	292,825

We see that these individuals were not only active in the debate, but were heavy Twitter users. The number of tweets from each of the individuals ranged from 2,385 -292,825 as of June 25, 2012 (mean = 36,277, median = 14,447). These high numbers indicate that these individuals have sustained Twitter accounts and are familiar with the syntactical features of the technology.

Table 4: Top 10 "Active" Individual in Second Debate

User Description	Second Debate	Total Tweets
Conservative Citizen	109	9,632
Family Advocacy Org	104	5,398
Education Advocacy Org *	90	9,307
Conservative Citizen *	89	14,903
Liberal Citizen	87	11,456
Liberal Citizen	82	21,684
Liberal Citizen	80	43,574
Conservative Citizen	74	10,069
Liberal Citizen/Guest Blogger for Liberal Blogs	71	15,986
Liberal Citizen *	68	23,677

Table 5 illustrates the breakdown of the syntactical feature utilization of the active users. The percentages represent the total usage of all of the 17 active members that we identified in Tables 3 and 4 from above. What is of most interest is that the most active users appear to use Twitter differently than the overall population in the two debates. We see that active participants use links much less than the overall population and also use mentions and retweets less.

Table 5: "Active" user syntactical breakdown

	Tweet Count	Links	Mentions	@Reply	Retweets
First Debate	698	14.76%	65.76%	5.44%	55.87%
Second Debate	941	12.22%	51.01%	7.12%	37.41%

Looking at the change from the first to the second debate, the most significant change is the decrease in mentions and retweets along with the increase in @Reply's, illustrating conversational behavior by the most active members of the dataset. Analysis of the tweets in the second debate illustrates that the tweets are significant contributions to the discourse. Each of the tweets

averaged 15.5 words. This length coupled with the limited use of links or retweets and a preliminary analysis of the comments demonstrates that the individuals are providing substantive commentary.

4. CONCLUSION AND FUTURE WORK

This poster is an analysis of the use of one hashtag in two distinct, yet related, events in a short time period. We see that only 14% of the total participants participated in both debates. Examining the most active individuals highlights some very interesting findings.

First, analysis of the individual profiles indicates that none of the individuals who are the most active belong to a traditional media organization. This indicates that the most active individuals in the debates are citizens that are civically engaged. Second, we see that frequent contributors use Twitter's syntactical features differently and these patterns change between the two debates. Third, we see that the most active individuals are ideologically diverse based on their profiles and comments.

Our work contributes to the growing body of literature on backchannel communication. The local nature of the broadcast coupled with the national interest of the overall election provides an interesting context for examining discourse in a medium such as Twitter. This analysis helps to illustrate that social media tools may be vehicles for technologically mediated civic engagement, but further analysis is required to understand how and to what extent.

5. REFERENCES

[1] Black, A., Mascaro, C., Gallagher, M., and Goggins, S. 2012. TwitterZombie: Architecture for Capturing, Socially Transforming and Analyzing the Twittersphere. ACM Group, October 27-31, 2012, Sanibel Island, FL.

[2] Doughty, M., Rowland, D., and Lawson, S. 2011. Co-viewing Live TV with Digital Backchannel Streams. EuroITV.

[3] Hu, Y., John, A., Seligmann, D. D., and Wang, F. 2012. What Were the Tweets About? Topical Associations between Public Events and Twitter Feeds. ICWSM. 6th, 154-161.

[4] Jamieson, K. H. and Birdsell, D. S. 1990 Presidential Debates: The Challenge of Creating an Informed Electorate. Oxford University Press, USA.

[5] Lanoue, D. J. and Schrott, P. R. 1989. Voters' Reactions to Televised Presidential Debates: Measurements of the Source and Magnitude of Opinion Change. Political Psychology. 10, 2, 275-285.

[6] Mascaro, C. and Goggins, S. 2012. Twitter as Virtual Town Square: Citizen Engagement During a Nationally Televised Republican Primary Debate. 2012 American Political Science Association Annual Meeting. August 30-September 2, 2012, New Orleans, LA.

[7] Shamma, D. A., Kennedy, L., and Churchill, E. F. 2009. Tweet the debates: understanding community annotation of uncollected sources. Proceedings of the first SIGMM workshop on Social media. 3-10.

[8] Shamma, D. A., Kennedy, L., and Churchill, E. F. 2010. Conversational Shadows: Describing Live Media Events Using Short Messages. Proceedings of the 4th ICWSM.

Readers' Motivations to Participate in Hyperlocal News Content Creation

Heli Väätäjä
Tampere University of Technology
Korkeakoulunkatu 6
33720 Tampere, Finland
heli.vaataja@tut.fi

ABSTRACT

Readers are increasingly participating to news content creation by submitting user-generated content (UGC). We studied the participation motivations of active readers who send photo content to a hyperlocal news publisher. The first results based on an online questionnaire indicate that fun, the opportunity to get a monetary reward and informing others of local issues are the strongest motivators. In addition, participation to the news making activity and self-expression are important motivations. Those who intentionally planned and searched for topics to report with photos, reported more often the opportunity for extra income and development as a photographer as participation motivations than those, who captured photos when a good topic came about.

Categories and Subject Descriptors

H.5.3 [**Group and Organization Interfaces**]: Computer-supported cooperative work

Keywords

Motivation, crowdsourcing, news, photo, content, UGC, participation, participatory journalism, hyperlocal.

1. INTRODUCTION

User-generated content (UGC) by readers is gaining increasing importance in news publishing [9], especially within hyperlocal news. However, little is known about the motivations of the readers to participate in this activity. Understanding the participation motivations helps the news organizations in management and development of their collaboration with the readers [2], who are valuable and irreplaceable in the hyperlocal news production and news co-creation.

Prior research in fields involving citizens as collaborators, innovators, or UGC creators [1][3][4][5][6][7][10] describes both intrinsic and extrinsic motivations [8] to participate in the community and activity. For example, Brabham [3] reports that the strongest motivations to participate to the online photo agency iStockphoto are the desire to make money, develop individual skills and to have fun. In our earlier study in which nine readers who had sent photos to the Finnish hyperlocal news publisher were interviewed, we found that the monetary reward, sharing one's photos with others as well as informing the wider public about local issues were important motivations to participate [10][11].

This paper presents first results on the participation motivations of 39 active readers, who submit photo content to a hyperlocal news content provider in Helsinki metropolitan area in Finland.

We aim to answer the following research question based on an online questionnaire:

What motivates readers to contribute to hyperlocal news that are published by a news organization?

2. Methods

We studied the readers' motivations to send photos to the hyperlocal news publisher (Sanoma Kaupunkilehdet) which operates in the metropolitan Helsinki area (Finland). Organization publishes two print tabloids, one weekly (Vartti) and one on weekdays (Metro), as well as online news daily (Omakaupunki.fi). Organization uses readers' photo content as a central form of tip-offs for reporting hyperlocal news. The received readers' photos are published in an online gallery. The most newsworthy photos are used by the journalists as themes to report on, even within 10-15 minutes in online news from receiving the reader's photo [11]. Monetary incentives (varying from two movie tickets to 100 euros) are paid for photos that are selected to be published in the printed news tabloids [10].

2.1 Setup of the study

Jointly with the news organization we carried out a two-month field trial on mobile crowdsourcing. In the trial participants were sent mobile assignments weekly as text messages (SMS) to their mobile phones. Study included as research themes the experiences and development needs related to the crowdsourcing activity, and the participants' background and motivations to participate in the news making activity as submitters of readers' photo content.

Results presented in this paper are based on closed-ended questions on the participation motivations of the first online questionnaire. It was conducted after the first half of the trial (one month). We exclude here the motivations to participate to the crowdsourcing trial. The further results on participation motivations from sentence completions, the second questionnaire after the trial and interview results from 20 interviews will be presented in the future.

2.2 Participants

Participants were recruited to the two-month field trial on mobile crowdsourcing by the news organization. The project manager at the news organization contacted 90 most active readers, who had submitted photos and had been compensated for their published photos within the last half a year. 61 of the contacted persons agreed to participate in the trial.

After the first month, all participants were sent by email a link to the first online questionnaire and asked to fill in the questionnaire. 39 participants responded the questionnaire (18 females, 21 males) on a voluntary basis. Respondents were compensated with two movie tickets (value 17 euros).

The respondents' average age was 46 years (SD= 17.7, min=15, max=75, Md=48, q_1=32, q_3=61). Most respondents (37/39) had participated to news making by sending readers' photos from one to five years (min=1, max=23, Md=3, q_1=2, q_3=3). All respondents except one (38/39) reported capturing readers' photos for this news organization when a good topic comes about ("snappers"). Fourteen (14/39) respondents – including the one missing from the previous group of "snappers" - reported that they intentionally planned and searched for topics ("hunters").

2.3 Questionnaire

After the first half of the trial (after one month) the participants were sent by email a link to the first online questionnaire. As one of the questions in the questionnaire, we asked the respondents to select their most important motivations to submit photos to the news organization. Participants were allowed to select multiple items from a list of eight items and as a ninth item "other", with an open field to describe their other motivation(s). The eight items were created based on findings in our earlier study [10], and earlier literature on sharing photos online [7][3], online open innovation communities [1], idea contests [6], and open source software development [5], for example.

The results presented in this paper were analyzed by descriptive statistics and with crosstabulations for gender and content creation style based results.

3. Results

We first discuss the results of the whole sample and then discuss the gender and content creation style based differences.

The most important reported motivations to participate were fun (84.6%) and the opportunity to get a monetary reward (84.6%) (Table 1). The third top motivation is informing others of local issues (74.4%). These three strongest motivations are followed by participation to the news making activity (48.7%), and self-expression (46.2%). The sixth motivation is the opportunity for extra income (38.5%). These results indicate that both intrinsic and extrinsic motivations have an important role for the active readers who participate in the news content creation.

Table 1. Motivations (as pecentages) to submit photos to the studied news organization.

Items	Female (18)	Male (21)	Total (39)
Fun	88.9	81.0	**84.6**
Self-Expression	50.0	42.9	**46.2**
Informing others of local issues	72.2	76.2	**74.4**
Participation to the news making activity	38.9	57.1	**48.7**
Development as a photographer	33.3	38.1	35.9
Benefit for work experience or for professional development	11.1	9.5	10.3
Opportunity to get a monetary reward	88.9	81.0	**84.6**
Opportunity for extra income	22.2	52.4	38.5
Other	11.1	23.8	17.9

The greatest gender based differences can be found for "participating to the news making activity" and for "opportunity for extra income". The percentages for the gender based difference between these motivations are shown in Table 1 as grey cells. Male respondents report these more often as important motivations to participate. It should be noted, that the type of method used for the selection of most important motivations in this study may affect the self-reports by respondents.

Does the content creation style affect the reported motivations? We analyzed the reported motivations based on the type of the content creator's activity. We compared the respondents who reported to intentionally plan and search for topics ("hunter", N=14) to those that only captured photos when a good topic came by ("snapper only", N=25) (Table 2). Those, that intentionally planned and searched for topics more frequently reported as an important motivation the "opportunity for extra income" (64.3% vs. 24.0%), "development as a photographer" (50.0% vs. 28.0%) as well as "benefit for work experience or for professional development" (21.4% vs. 4.0%). Results seem to indicate that there is a difference between these two groups of content creators in their participation motivations.

Table 2. Motivations (as percentages) to submit photos to the studied news organization based on the type of the content creator.

Items	Snapper only (S) (N=25)	Hunter (H) (N=14)	Difference (H%-S%)
Fun	88.0	78.6	-9.4
Self-Expression	44.0	50.0	+6.0
Informing others of local issues	72.0	78.6	+6.6
Participation to the news making activity	44.0	57.1	+13.1
Development as a photographer	28.0	50.0	**+22.0**
Benefit for work experience or for professional development	4.0	21.4	**+17.4**
Opportunity to get a monetary reward	80.0	92.9	+12.9
Opportunity for extra income	24.0	64.3	**+40.3**
Other	12.0	28.6	+16.6

The difference in the two types of content creator groups poses further questions such as: how important is each of these groups in terms of the hyperlocal news production and how the different groups should be taken into account when developing the collaboration further. These issues will be reported elsewhere as well as studied further in the same context.

4. Conclusions

We studied the motivations of readers to participate in creation of user-generated content, in form of readers' photos, to hyperlocal news. Based on 39 responses to an online questionnaire from active readers we found that both intrinsic and extrinsic motivations exist for participation. The activity and participation seems to be fun and engaging in itself. Furthermore, it offers a possibility to inform others of local issues and enables self-expression. In addition, the opportunity to get a monetary reward and even the opportunity for extra income are important motivations. When comparing the content creators' motivations based on how they come across their photo topics (content creation style), we found that there is a clear difference in motivations between two groups. Those, who plan and search the photo topics (hunters) report more often the opportunity for extra income as a motivation compared to those who capture photos when a good topic comes about (snappers).

5. ACKNOWLEDGMENTS

Special thanks to Tuukka Muhonen and the editorial staff of Sanoma Kaupunkilehdet for the co-operation in the study and Petteri Lehtinen for assistance. This research was carried out within the Next Media SHOK programe of TIVIT funded by Tekes and the Finnish Doctoral Programme in User-Centered Information Technology (UCIT).

6. REFERENCES

[1] Antikainen, M., Väätäjä, H. 2010. Rewarding in open innovation communities - How to motivate members. *Int. Journal of Entrepreneurship and Innovation Managament (IJEIM)*, 11, 4, 440-456.

[2] Banks, J., Deuze, M. 2009. Co-creative labour, *International Journal of Cultural Studies*, *12*, 5, 419-431.

[3] Brabham, D.C. 2008. Moving the crowd with iStockphoto: The composition of the crowd and motivations for participation in a crowdsourcing application, First Monday [Online], 13, 6.

[4] Buehner, T. and Julie, J. 2011. Exposing the digital newshound: A study of the values, influences, and characteristics of creators of citizen-journalistic photographic content. Paper presented to the 2011 Midwinter conference of the Association for Education in Journalism and Mass Communication.

[5] Lakhani, K, Wolf, R. 2005. Why hackers do what they do: Understanding motivation and effort in free/open source software projects. *Perspectives on Free and open source sortware* (Eds. Feller et al.), MIT Press, 3-22.

[6] Leimeister, J.M., Huber, M. and Krcmar, H. 2009. Leveraging crowdsourcing: Activation-supporting components of IT-based ideas competition. *Journal of Management Information Systems*, *26*, 1, 197-224.

[7] Nov, O., Naaman, M. and Ye, C. 2010. Analysis of participation in an online-photo-sharing community: A multidimensional perspective. *J of the Am Society for Information Systems and Technology*, *61*, 3, 1-12.

[8] Ryan, R. and Deci, E. 2000. Intrinsic and extrinsic motivations: Classic definitions and new directions, *Contemporary Educational Psychology*, *25*, 54-67.

[9] Singer, J.B., Hermida, A., Domingo, D,. Heinonen, A., Paulussen, S., Quandt, T., Reich, Z., Vujnovic, M. 2011. *Participatory journalism: Guarding open gates at online newspapers*, Wiley-Blackwell.

[10] Väätäjä, H., Vainio, T., Sirkkunen, E., and Salo, K. 2011. Crowdsourced news reporting: supporting news content creation with mobile phones. *Proc. MobileHCI '11*, ACM Press, 435-444.

[11] Väätäjä, H., Vainio, T., and Sirkkunen, E. 2012. Location-based crowdsourcing of hyperlocal news - Dimensions of participation preferences. *Proc. GROUP 2012*, ACM.

Knowledge Transferability in Partially Distributed Conceptual Design Teams

Yoon Suk Lee
Grado Department of Industrial &
Systems Engineering,
Virginia Tech
Blacksburg, VA
yoonlee@vt.edu

Marie C. Paretti
Department of Engineering
Education
Virginia Tech
Blacksburg, VA
mparetti@vt.edu

Brian M. Kleiner
Grado Department of Industrial &
Systems Engineering,
Virginia Tech
Blacksburg, VA
bkleiner@vt.edu

ABSTRACT

In this paper, we aim to identify different types of knowledge that needs to be conveyed during a conceptual design task. We hypothesize that different types of knowledge has different transferability in a partially distributed team setting, and thus influences team members' communication behaviors. The impacts due to different transferability of design knowledge are discussed.

Author Keywords

Design knowledge; knowledge transferability; partially distributed team; conceptual design; computer-mediated communication.

ACM Classification Keywords

H.5.3. Information interfaces and presentation: Group and Organization Interfaces.

General Terms

Human Factors; Design; Experimentation.

INTRODUCTION

Is it always beneficial to have a video channel for distant communication? Many theories in the field of computer-mediated communication, such as media richness and social presence theories support the notion that increasing communication bandwidth will enhance communication experience and performance. Despite the wide usage of those theories [8], the empirical studies yielded inconclusive results [1, 7]. One of the reasons may be due to different tasks utilized in the experiments, as different types of task may require different types of communication technology. The task-media fit theory [9] highlights the match between communication technologies and tasks, based on the task taxonomy [2]. However, the predictive accuracy of the task-media fit theory resulted a limited support [3]. In contrast, we hypothesize that communication technology must be selected based on knowledge types associated with a task. A task may consist of many different types of knowledge, and the transferability of those different types of knowledge may differ based on the communication technology. The transferability can be defined as the amount of effort required to successfully convey knowledge to distant partners.

In this paper, we examined partially distributed conceptual design teams. Partially distributed team can be defined as a team that consists of two or more sub-teams that are geographically distributed [6]. It is one of the most frequently utilized formation in nowadays organizations, yet very little empirical research exists [4]. In such setting, communication becomes more complicated because of the co-existence of face-to-face and technology-mediated communications. Communication in conceptual design is also complex, due to the ambiguity of the task. The ambiguity is attributed to the open-ended and ill-defined problem and solution spaces [5]. Different types of design knowledge are required, and there are many phases as well as sub-tasks within a conceptual design process.

In this regard, the study objectives are (i) to identify different types of knowledge that are communicated during conceptual design task, and (ii) to examine the transferability of different types of knowledge within and across sub-groups.

EXPERIMENT

Participants

Participants were drawn from a large mid-Atlantic land-grant university. A total of 16 (8 females and 8 males, mean age=21.6, SD=1.2) junior or senior undergraduate students were recruited to form four four-person groups. There was no restriction in participants' majors to simulate a multidisciplinary team, yet at least one engineering student was included in each team. Each group was divided into two dyad sub-groups to simulate a partially distributed team. Each sub-group was separated in two different rooms and collaborated on a conceptual design task. Upon completion of the experiment, a monetary compensation of $20 was awarded to each participant. The research protocol was approved by the university's internal review board.

Wheelchair Design Task

Each group had to design an add-on device to an existing hand or arm-powered wheelchair so that it allows paraplegic users to traverse standard roadside curbs without any assistance. Groups were instructed to follow three distinct design phases, which were initiation, concept generation, and concept evaluation. This was to identify the different types knowledge associated in each design phase. Each team was required to submit one design solution, which included a detailed conceptual sketch, and a description of a use case scenario. The design task lasted approximately 2.5~3 hours, and the entire session was video recorded. During the design task, a video conferencing tool was used. Participants were able to see and hear each another. A shared whiteboard was available that allowed participants to simultaneously sketch or type. In addition, participants were also able to use paper and pen to sketch or write.

Individual Semi-structured Interview

The purposes of individual semi-structured interview were to understand the communication difficulties as well as reasons behind participant's communicative actions during the design task. The questions were developed based on video analysis of the design sessions. The first few questions focused on participant's general communication experience, while the remaining questions focused on specific of communication difficulties occurred during the task. A total of 14 out of 16 participants participated the individual semi-structured interview, which lasted about 30-50 minutes each. The interview sessions were audio recorded and transcribed.

RESULTS

A total of six types of knowledge were identified as described in Table 1. The subsequent sections aim to define, explain, and provide examples with interview excerpts regarding each type of design knowledge.

Function

Design function refers to the objective of a design solution or components of the design. The overall design function is usually discussed in the beginning of a design session. However, the design knowledge of function also refers to the purpose of each component of a design. For instance, team 2 designed a ski-like ramp that requires simple assembly of the inner and outer rods to the ramp before using it. As illustrated in figure 1, the storage sack attached at the back of the seat has its purpose of storing the inner and outer rods. Therefore, storing can be considered as the functionality of the storage sack. Based on the observation of video recordings and interview, participants did not experience much difficulty in transferring the design knowledge of function, and more frequent inter communication between two sub-groups was observed.

Types of Knowledge in Design

Function	Teleology of a design or components of the design.
Structure	Shape, weight, physical location, constituting element, and the relationships of design components.
Behavior	Movement of a design or components of the design.
Procedure	A series of associated movements of a design or design components in relation to user actions.
Concept (mechanism)	Theoretical principles.
Value	Individual perception of the quality of a design.

Table 1. Types of knowledge in design.

Structure

Design structure refers to the structural components and properties of a design solution. This is the "thing" that is developed, synthesized, and evaluated to achieve the design objective. Structural components are the constituting parts that are integrated to complete the design. As illustrated in figure 1, there are seven components that work accordingly to achieve the design objective. Each component has different shape, size, and weight, as well as property. For instance, there are triangular shaped rubber grip attached at the bottom end of the ramp. Because of the property of rubber as well as its triangular shape, it serves its own purpose of preventing the ramp from sliding.

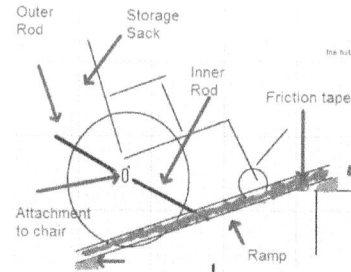

Figure 1. Conceptual sketch of team 2 design.

In most cases, participants did not have much difficulty in explaining or understanding the shape, weight, and parts suggested by other members. Yet, they frequently had difficulty when pointing out the exact location of an attachment of a part. For instance, members in group 4 spent extensive amount of time clarifying the lever attachment (figure 3-a) as described in the interview excerpt below.

"P19: Well, for me I couldn't understand because the way I saw it was the lever was attached to the chair... But the problem I was having was like, is it attached to the chair or is it attached to the wheel, and if it's attached to... if it's attached to the wheel that won't help you at all."

In such case, participants showed a tendency of explaining only to their co-located partner. They reported that because it was difficult to convey the information to their distant partners, they wanted to practice or get verification of their explanation from their co-located partner before explaining to their distant partners.

Behavior

Design behavior refers to the movement of a design or components of the design. In concept design phase, a design does not usually have a physical form. Therefore, engineers or designers must go through a mental simulation of the behaviors associated with each component. In general, participants reported that they had the most difficulty in explaining the behavioral aspect of a design. In group 1, P8 who had an idea of hand controlled ramp, tried to explain her idea by actually showing the movement of the ramp in accordance with the wheelchair, to her distant partners over the webcam (figure 2).

"P8: Yeah. I mean I feel like I awkwardly rolled my chair back and showed them what I was trying to say... and tried to show them like physically, visually I tried to use the drawings, try to explain it so I used the three major ways to tell someone..."

Figure 2. Participant 8 trying to explain the behavior of hand controlled ramp idea by physical demonstration.

P8 used her chair to describe the wheelchair movement, and two pens to describe the ramp movement. Similar incident occurred in team 4. P17 came up with a lever idea, yet his partners were all confused of how it would actually work. All of the members in team 4 pointed out that explaining or understanding the lever idea was the most difficult problem during the task.

"P17: The lever... I feel like maybe I wasn't able to convey the concept of the lever... but the lever is where we got stuck up big time and we wasted like a whole hour on that."

After a long discussion regarding the movement of a lever, P20 used a wheelie example to assure whether he accurately understood the idea. P20 demonstrated a jerking backwards motion while pulling his hands towards himself to simulate the lever and wheelchair movement (figure 3-b). P20 later responded in the interview that he intended to describe that the back wheels are stationary, the lever can be moved back and forth (figure 3-a), and as a consequence, the wheelchair tilts backwards.

As seen in the examples above, behavioral explanation of a design is difficult and requires longer time and more effort to convey, especially to distant partners. It frequently requires physical demonstration of an expected behavior of a design, and adequate example that has a similar behavioral characteristic. Similar to what occurred in conveying the design knowledge of structure, participants inclined to communicate only to their co-located partner for similar reasons. Participants also reported that small and low screen resolution aggravated the communication across sub-groups.

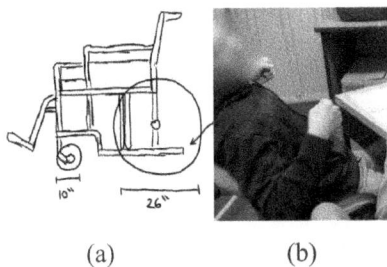

(a)　　　　　　　　(b)

Figure 3. (a) Conceptual sketch of team 4 design, (b) P20 jerking backwards to simulate wheelie motion.

Procedure

Design procedure refers to a series of associated movements of a design or a design component in relation to user actions. The distinction between behavioral and procedural knowledge in design is that user actions or behaviors are included. Thus, it is an integration of design behaviors as a consequence of user actions. Additionally, procedural knowledge describes more integral movement of the overall design, whereas behavioral knowledge only focuses on a behavior of one structure. Therefore, the communication of procedural knowledge usually occurs after each

structure and its corresponding behavior are determined in concept generation phase. Figure 4 is an example of procedural knowledge produced by team 3.

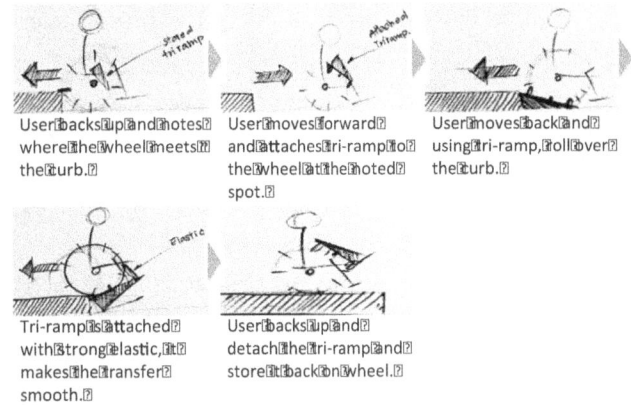

User backs up and notes where the wheel meets the curb.　　User moves forward and attaches tri-ramp to the wheel at the noted spot.　　User moves back and using tri-ramp, roll over the curb.

Tri-ramp is attached with strong elastic, it makes the transfer smooth.　　User backs up and detach the tri-ramp and store it back on wheel.

Figure 4. A use case scenario produced by team 3.

In most cases, diagrams and verbal descriptions were used to externalize or communicate procedural knowledge. Participants seemed to have less difficulty because the constituting behaviors of structures were already discussed and determined. The use of electronic shared drawing space that allows participants to watch the drawing process of their distant partners may promote better communication of the procedural knowledge.

Concept

Design concept refers to a theoretical principle or mechanism that engineers or designers apply to their design. In case of the wheelchair design brief, one way of interpreting the design objective in terms of design concept would be 'lift the wheelchair with minimum amount of force.' Team 3 applied a lever mechanism so that the paraplegic users can effectively apply their upper extremity force to tilt the wheelchair. Other teams used different types of ramps so that the users can apply their upper extremity force gradually to move the wheelchair up the curb.

Communicating design concepts required less visual communication or physical demonstration. Participants generally understood the essence of the concept that was brought up by their partners. However, there were few non-engineering majors who reported that they had difficulty in understanding the concepts. In such cases, their co-located partners usually provided an additional explanation regarding the concept.

Value

Design value refers to an individual perception of the quality of a design. Most of the discussions regarding design values occurred in concept evaluation phase. Although participants reported that they had less difficulty in communicating their opinions regarding different design values (e.g., safety, aesthetics, ergonomics, production, and cost), many conflicting situations were observed. For instance, P12, a human nutrition, foods, and exercise major claimed to have an extensive experience of taking care of paraplegic patients, emphasized the safety aspect of their design. However, P9 who is an industrial design major emphasized more on the simplicity and aesthetics aspect of the design. It took quite a while to resolve the discussion between safety and aesthetics, yet again no participant reported difficulty of sharing opinions regarding design values.

DISCUSSION

Design Knowledge in Design Phases

Different types of knowledge are communicated in different design phases. This does not mean that certain type of design knowledge never occurred in a specific design phase, since design is an iterative process in nature. However, based on our observation, certain types of knowledge dominated in each design phase. In initiation phase, participants mostly communicated the design knowledge of function. In concept generation, the design knowledge of structure and behavior were mostly discussed followed by the design knowledge of concept and procedure. In concept evaluation, values were the most actively discussed.

All of the participants pointed out that communication in concept generation was the most difficult compared to other design phases.

"P14: It's definitely the concept generation. It's hard to explain what we were talking about, what each of our ideas were, unless it was very simplistic."

One of the major reasons of such difficulty was due to the difficulty of transferring the design knowledge of structure and behavior in concept generation phase. Unlike other types of design knowledge, structure and behavioral description require visual information, such as illustration, body movement, hand gestures, as well as any objects that a speaker intends to use to describe her idea.

Knowledge Transferability & Communication Behavior

Different types of design knowledge require varying amount of communication efforts for successful transfer. More importantly, knowledge transferability changes people's communicative behavior. When a type of knowledge was difficult to transfer, participants naturally communicated only to their co-located partner. This may create information silo between two sub-groups, and may further transpire to in-group dynamics.

FUTURE WORK

Based on the identified design knowledge, we aim to demonstrate the transferability of these design knowledge in different communication settings. A combination of a fully immersive tele-presence system, laptops, and mobile devices will be utilized to further investigate the relationship between communication technology and knowledge types associated with a task.

ACKNOWLEDGMENTS

We thank all the participants.

REFERENCES

1. Kraut, R., Fussell, S., & Siegel, J. (2003). Visual information as a conversational resource in collaborative physical tasks. *Human-computer interaction, 18*(1), 13-49.
2. McGrath, J. (1984). *Groups: Interaction and performance* (Vol. 14): Prentice-Hall Englewood Cliffs, NJ.
3. Mennecke, B., Valacich, J., & Wheeler, B. (2000). The effects of media and task on user performance: A test of the task-media fit hypothesis. *Group Decision and Negotiation, 9*(6), 507-529.
4. O'Leary, M. B., & Cummings, J. N. (2007). The spatial, temporal, and configurational characteristics of geographic dispersion in teams. *MIS quarterly, 31(3)*, 433-452.
5. Pahl, G. (2007). *Engineering design: a systematic approach:* Springer V erlag.
6. Plotnick, L.; Hiltz, S.R.; Ocker, R.J.; , "Media Choices over Time in Partially Distributed Teams," System Science (HICSS), 2012 45th Hawaii International Conference on , vol., no., pp.483-492, 4-7 Jan. 2012.
7. Reid, F., & Reed, S. (2007). Conversational grounding and visual access in collaborative design. *CoDesign, 3*(2), 111-122.
8. Topi, H., Valacich, J. S., & Rao, M. T. (2002). The effects of personality and media differences on the performance of dyads addressing a cognitive conflict task. *Small Group Research, 33*(6), 667.
9. Zigurs, I., Buckland, B., Connolly, J., & Wilson, E. (1999). A test of task-technology fit theory for group support systems. *ACM SIGMIS Database, 30*(3-4), 50.

Elastic Collaboration Support: From Workflow-Based to Emergent Collaboration

Jordan Janeiro
Delft University of Technology
Systems Engineering Section
Jaffalaan 5, Delft, The
Netherlands
J.Janeiro@tudelft.nl

Stephan Lukosch
Delft University of Technology
Systems Engineering Section
Jaffalaan 5, Delft, The
Netherlands
S.G.Lukosch@tudelft.nl

Frances M.T. Brazier
Delft University of Technology
Systems Engineering Section
Jaffalaan 5, Delft, The
Netherlands
F.M.Brazier@tudelft.nl

ABSTRACT

This paper addresses the challenges of providing customized collaboration support to teams of experts. Current groupware systems only provide support for workflow-based collaboration,
avoiding new forms of collaboration such as emergent collaboration. Therefore this paper proposes a elastic collaboration approach and its implementation in a groupware system.

Categories and Subject Descriptors

H.5.3 [**Information Interfaces and Presentation**]: Group and Organization Interfaces - Computer-Supported Cooperative Work.

General Terms

Design, Human Factors

Keywords

elastic collaboration; emergent collaboration; workflow-based collaboration; adaptive systems

1. INTRODUCTION

The goal of this paper is to introduce the concept of elastic collaboration support and its implementation in groupware systems.

Elastic collaboration support represents a flexible type of collaboration, customized to users. The collaboration support is elastic because comprises a continuum of collaboration support, ranging from traditional workflow-based collaboration to new emerging forms of collaboration.

The term *elastic collaboration* is based on the dictionary entry[1] for elastic. According to one of the entry descriptions, this term refers to something that is *"capable of ready change*

---

[1]http://www.merriam-webster.com/dictionary/elastic

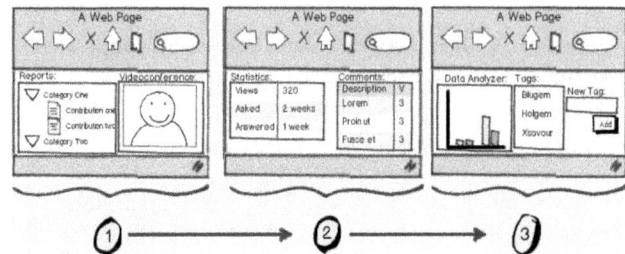

Figure 1: Collaboration components arranged according to a workflow layout.

or easy expansion or contraction: not rigid or constricted". This description reflects the concept of elastic collaboration because the type of collaboration is ready to rapidly change within the continuum of collaboration: from workflow-based to emergent collaboration and the other way around.

In this paper, the next two sections describe the workflow-based collaboration and the emergent collaboration. The section three describes the elastic collaboration, a new approach that customizes collaboration support. Finally, the section four describes the elastic collaboration applied to a machine diagnosis scenario.

2. WORKFLOW-BASED COLLABORATION

Workflow management systems represent a class of systems that separates the process logic from application functionalities [1]. Applying this class of systems to collaboration implies describing a process as a collaborative workflow, which represents a sequence of collaborative activities to accomplish a task. Each activity is supported by an application functionality [6] [4]. The goal of these systems is to transfer the coordination task of the team to the system. The idea is that collaboration experts model their expertise as a collaborative workflow, such as described by Kolfschoten [7], which is interpreted and provided by a system to a team.

A groupware system that supports workflow-based collaboration is illustrated in the Figure 1. In this Figure, a workflow contains three steps, each of them representing at least one collaboration technique. In turn, each collaboration technique represents at least one collaboration component. In this approach, the system controls the execution of

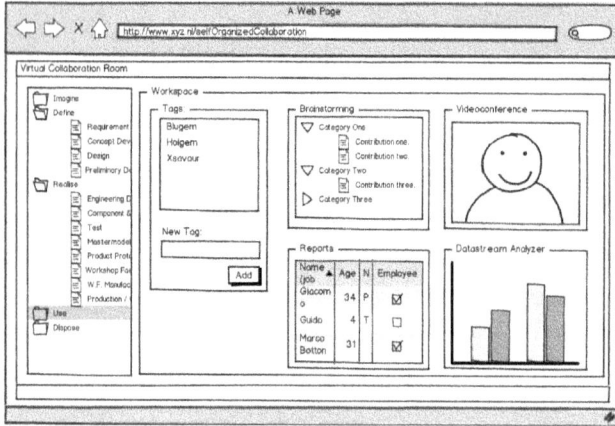

Figure 2: Collaboration components arranged according to a dashboard layout.

the workflow and presents to the team the components that should be used at a certain point in time.

The advantage in this approach is that a team does not need to manage its coordination. A system assumes its coordination role and provides the team the suitable collaboration components for every step of the workflow. However this approach lacks flexibility for the team, especially for experienced engineers. Engineers are often experienced in their intrinsic tasks, such as machine diagnosis. Due to this fact, it is unlikely that they need guidance and coordination from the system.

3. EMERGENT COLLABORATION

In emergent collaboration, users coordinate themselves to accomplish a certain task instead of the system. Whereas in the previous approach the workflow is designed in advance, in emergent collaboration, interaction between users is not pre-defined.

Emergent collaboration is a similar concept such as, self-organizing distributed software systems, defined by Serugendo [2]. The authors observe that self-organization of a software is a process in which a system adapts its internal structure, according to the changes in its goals and the environment, without an explicit external control, enabling the system to develop an emergent behaviour.

A groupware system provides collaboration components as displayed in the Figure 2 to support emergent collaboration.

Dashboards are software platforms that integrate user interfaces of various systems, presenting and organizing information for easy interpretation [3]. In the context of this paper, a dashboard displays and executes various applications (collaboration components) simultaneously. This approach is associated to emergent collaboration because users are in control of collaboration and they can choose the set of components that suit them better.

The advantage of this approach is the flexibility of the team to decide on preferred collaboration components and on their coordination to accomplish the goals of, for example, a machine diagnosis process. A system intervenes as little as possible during collaboration: assuming the role of an *observer*, learning from team behaviour.

4. ELASTIC COLLABORATION

This paper proposes the combination of both collaboration types, calling it *Elastic Collaboration*. In this approach, participants of a team may shift from one type of collaboration to the other as in a continuum of collaboration.

A groupware system that implements elastic collaboration is called as a *elastic groupware system*. These systems support workflow-based layout, the dashboard layout and the smooth transition between both collaboration types. During collaboration, participants of the team use various collaboration components that generate data, independent of the collaboration type. A transition between these implies the change of layouts and components. However, the transition should keep the state of collaboration components and the data generated by them during a collaboration type.

Another characteristic of elastic groupware system is the ability to recognize collaboration transitions. These systems constantly monitor a team to recognize their collaboration needs and propose an appropriate form of collaboration. To this purpose, the system controls the activities of users during collaboration. The main decision upon a collaboration type depends on the skills and experience of team members. Each team participant is characterized by a *set of skills* and an *experience degree*. Depending on the configuration of team skills, team experience, number of participants and time, a system can recommend a collaboration type and adapt itself to it. For example, a system recommends a workflow-based collaboration for a team in which the majority are novice engineers and face a short deadline for a machine diagnosis problem. As most of the engineers are not experienced in machine diagnosis and they have a time constraint, they need the support of the system to coordinate the collaboration.

5. MACHINE DIAGNOSIS SCENARIO

Engineers often perform maintenance activities, diagnosing machines used by the construction industry to increase their availability. These machines, e.g. wheel loaders, are connected through a remote infrastructure that monitors their performance data. If the machine issues degrading signals, a diagnosis team is allocated to investigate it and a deadline is set to avoid a machine breakdown. This situation forces engineers, from different specializations (e.g. mechanical engineering, stress engineering and fluid engineering) to collaborate, formulating a diagnosis and preparing action plans [5]. This situation is illustrated in Figure 3.

Workflow-based support is the current collaboration form to support the team, represented by the bottom part of the Figure 3. Whenever the remote infrastructure detects a machine degrading signal, it triggers the elastic groupware system. This system, in turn, configure itself to the workflow-based profile. It assumes the coordination task, selects a collaborative diagnosis process, which fits the breakdown deadline, and guides the team of experts through the process. This type of collaboration may not be suitable for a team that in their majority are experienced engineers. As these engineers are experienced in diagnosis processes and the use of collaboration components, it is likely that they can coordinate themselves and do not need this type of system support. Therefore, the elastic groupware system recommends the emergent collaboration support, represented by the top part of the Figure 3. The system reconfigures itself, in a adaptation process, stopping the workflow-based sup-

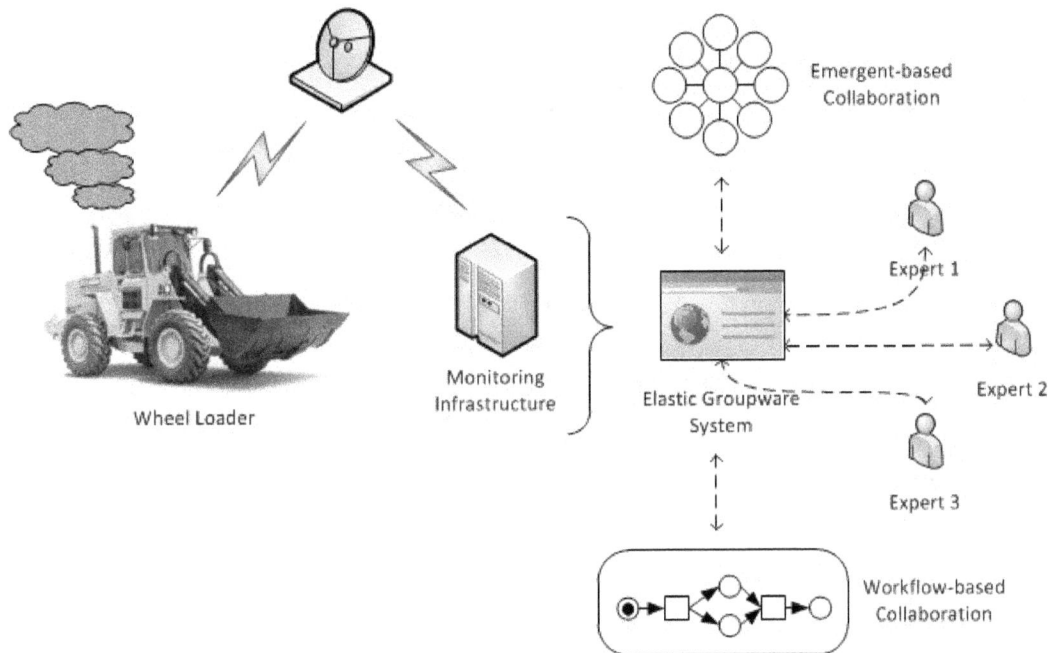

Figure 3: Applying an elastic groupware system to a machine diagnosis scenario.

port and making the most suitable components involved in diagnosis processes available to the team. As the team is not coordinated by the system, they do not receive guidance on the usage of collaboration components. However, the team relies on their experience to define a strategy, using components, to formulate a diagnosis.

Elastic collaboration support is promising because it customizes collaboration support to the specific needs of team constellations rather than forcing a team to follow a specific collaboration type. However, this approach also introduces challenges in collaboration, such as the accurate recognition of situations that demand intervention and the acceptance of users in considering the interventions.

6. ACKNOWLEDGMENTS

This work has been partially supported by the FP7 EU Large-scale Integrating Project SMART VORTEX (Scalable Semantic Product Data Stream Management for Collaboration and Decision Making in Engineering) co-financed by the European Union. For more details, visit http://www.smartvortex.eu/

7. REFERENCES

[1] A. L. Delbecq and A. H. Van de Ven. A group process model for problem identification and program planning. *The Journal of Applied Behavioral Science*, 7(4):466–492, 1971.

[2] G. Di Marzo Serugendo, M.-P. Gleizes, and A. Karageorgos. Self-organization in multi-agent systems. *Knowl. Eng. Rev.*, 20(2):165–189, June 2005.

[3] W. W. Eckerson. *Performance Dashboards Measuring, Monitoring, and Managing Your Business*. John Wiley Sons, 2006.

[4] C. A. Ellis, P. Barthelmess, J. Chen, and J. Wainer. *Person-to-Person Processes: Computer-Supported Collaborative Work*, pages 37–60. John Wiley Sons, Inc., 2005.

[5] J. Janeiro, S. W. Knoll, S. G. Lukosch, G. L. Kolfschoten, and F. M. T. Brazier. Designing collaboration support for dynamic environments. In *Proceedings of the International Conference on Group Decision and Negotiation (GDN)*, 2012.

[6] S. Knoll, M. Horning, and G. Horton. Applying a thinklet- and thinxel-based group process modeling language: A prototype of a universal group support system. In *System Sciences, 2009. HICSS '09. 42nd Hawaii International Conference on*, pages 1 –10, jan. 2009.

[7] G. L. Kolfschoten and G.-J. De Vreede. The collaboration engineering approach for designing collaboration processes. In *Proceedings of the 13th international conference on Groupware: design implementation, and use*, CRIWG07, pages 95–110, Berlin, Heidelberg, 2007. Springer-Verlag.

GROUP Workshop Proposal
Collaboration in Managing Computer Systems

Kirstie Hawkey
Dalhousie University
6050 University Avenue
Halifax, NS B3H 1W5

hawkey@cs.dal.ca

Eben M. Haber
IBM Research
650 Harry Road
San Jose, CA 95120

ehaber@us.ibm.com

ABSTRACT
Collaboration is critical to the management of modern computer systems. At every scale, making computers work is a collective task, from enterprise systems where teams of disparate specialists work together to understand, manage, and maintain vast complex IT infrastructures, all the way down to individuals seeking online, family, and co-worker help on how to keep their personal computers running. Since 2007, the CHIMIT symposium has served as a venue for research on all aspects of HCI and the management of information technology. CHIMIT sits at the intersection of several research communities, and to better draw in people from these communities, we plan to hold a series of workshops emphasizing various aspects of HCI and IT management. For GROUP, we propose a one-day workshop examining the collaborative aspects of configuring, managing, and troubleshooting computer systems at all scales.

Categories and Subject Descriptors
H.5 [**Information Interfaces and Presentation**]: H.5.3 Group and Organizational Interfaces.

General Terms
Human Factors, Management.

Keywords
HCI, IT Management, CHIMIT.

1. INTRODUCTION
Computer systems exist to achieve human goals, such as communication, creativity, and information retrieval. We define computer management as those tasks that divert us from our goals: configuration, installation, troubleshooting, etc. Enterprises must maintain large numbers of people whose entire job is management, and it seems that all of us spend more time than we'd like keeping our computers running.

Collaboration is critical to the management of computer systems. This is true at every scale, whether it is our parents asking us for help when "the internet isn't working," ourselves searching for

the meaning of obscure error messages online, or the teams of specialized enterprise administrators who must work closely together to monitor, understand, and maintain the large IT infrastructures that keep modern society going. User studies of enterprise administrators [1] and IT security practitioners [8] have shown that they engage in an incredible amount of collaboration, and that it is imperfectly supported by existing tools. Users also engage in collaborative practices when managing their home networks [6].

Since 2007, the ACM CHIMIT symposium has served as a venue for research in all areas relevant to HCI and the management of information technology. Yet CHIMIT sits at the crossroads of several different communities, including CSCW, HCI, and information visualization. In order to reach out to these communities, the CHIMIT organizers are proposing a series of workshops at other conferences to bring domain experts together with the problems of computer management. The first of these proposals is a one-day workshop at GROUP, focusing on collaboration in computer management. Over the years CHIMIT published several papers related to this space (e.g., [2-5,7,9-11]), yet much of this research describes the challenges of collaboration without exploring solutions, especially in the area of systems to improve collaboration over the complex tasks and information involved in computer management.

2. WORKSHOP GOALS
This workshop's goal is to bring together researchers, designers, and practitioners who study or have experience in collaboration and computer management. Our goal is lively discussion and exploration of how the latest collaboration research could be applied to reduce the effort of keeping computers working.

Topics for submissions include, but are not limited to:

- **Tools and techniques** for improved collaboration, including social networking for sharing complex system information and awareness.

- **User studies** of real-world collaboration in computer management.

- **Experience reports** by practitioners and researchers.

- **Computer supported cooperative work** – in enterprise IT, how do those who manage an organization's IT interact with the users they support, their technical community, and other stakeholders?

- **Knowledge Repositories** – how can shared knowledge improve computer management?

- **Processes and practices** – examples of best practices and improved processes for collaboration in IT management.

One possible workshop outcome is to write a paper describing the state of the art of collaboration tools and research for the domain of computer management. Participants would frame this paper during the workshop, and complete it following GROUP for submission to a suitable venue (e.g., ACM Interactions), and/or publication on CHIMIT's web site (http://chimit.acm.org). If sufficient novel and interesting work is submitted, it might be developed for eventual submission to an appropriate journal special issue or published under the auspices of CHIMIT.

3. WORKSHOP PARTICIPANTS

In order to foster maximum interaction, the number of participants will be limited to between 15 and 20 people. Participants will be selected based on refereed position papers. Those with a general interest in the area will be asked for up to 2 pages (regular CHI format) describing their background and potential contributions. Those with specific research contributions, either proposed or completed, may have up to 5 pages (regular CHI format). Our strategy for recruiting will include e-mail to all the usual mailing lists, as well as contacting past attendees of the CHIMIT symposium.

4. WORKSHOP ORGANIZATION

This workshop will be one-day. The schedule will be dependent on the number and type of contributions, but will include time for the organizers to frame the problem space, participants to describe their positions, and everybody to discuss how to synthesize these positions into coherent work going forward. Audio/visual equipment should include a projector to help people share their ideas.

- Position papers due: 2 weeks before notification deadline (not yet determined – early September?)

- Notification of acceptance: 2 weeks before early registration deadline (not yet announced – mid-September?)

- Workshop: October 27 or 28

5. Organizers

Kirstie Hawkey is on the Faculty of Computer Science at Dalhousie University. During her post doctoral research at The University of British Columbia, she worked on the HOT Admin project, which investigated the human, organizational, and technological aspects of IT security work. In addition, she has served on the program committee and as program chair and general chair (2011/2012) for ACM CHIMIT.

Eben M. Haber is a research staff member at IBM's Almaden Research Center. He spent much of the last decade studying enterprise IT administration, including undertaking field studies, developing prototype tools, and designing new features for middleware management products. He has filled organizational and program committee roles for ACM CHIMIT 2008-2011 (including general chair in 2009), and is a co-author on the forthcoming Oxford University Press book, "Taming Information Technology: Lessons from Studies of System Administrators."

6. REFERENCES

[1] Rob Barrett, Eser Kandogan, Paul P. Maglio, Eben M. Haber, Leila A. Takayama, and Madhu Prabaker. 2004. Field studies of computer system administrators: analysis of system management tools and practices. In *Proc. of the 2004 ACM conf. on Computer supported cooperative work* (CSCW '04).

[2] C. Travis Bowles and Min Wu. 2010. Transparent collaboration: letting users simulate another user's world. In *Proc. of the 4th Symp. on Computer Human Interaction for the Management of Information Technology* (CHiMiT '10).

[3] Jeffrey Calcaterra, John Bailey, and Kenya Freeman Oduor. 2008. Multiple people and components: considerations for designing multi-user middleware. In *Proc. of the 2nd ACM Symp. on Computer Human Interaction for Management of Information Technology* (CHiMiT '08).

[4] Cleidson R. B. de Souza, Claudio S. Pinhanez, and Victor F. Cavalcante. 2011. Information needs of system administrators in information technology service factories. In *Proc. of the 5th ACM Symp. on Computer Human Interaction for Management of Information Technology* (CHiMiT '11).

[5] John C. Mace, Simon Parkin, and Aad van Moorsel. 2010. A collaborative ontology development tool for information security managers. In *Proc. of the 4th Symp. on Computer Human Interaction for the Management of Information Technology* (CHiMiT '10).

[6] Erika S. Poole, Marshini Chetty, Tom Morgan, Rebecca E. Grinter, and W. Keith Edwards. 2009. Computer help at home: methods and motivations for informal technical support. In *Proc. of the 27th international conf. on Human factors in computing systems* (CHI '09). 739-748.

[7] Nicole F. Velasquez and Suzanne P. Weisband. 2009. System administrators as broker technicians. In *Proc. of the 5th ACM Symp. on Computer Human Interaction for the Management of Information Technology* (CHiMiT '09).

[8] Rodrigo Werlinger, Kirstie Hawkey, David Botta, and Konstantin Beznosov. 2009. Security practitioners in context: Their activities and interactions with other stakeholders within organizations. *Int. J. Hum.-Comput. Stud.* 67, 7 (July 2009), 584-606.

[9] Kevin F. White, David Gurzick, and Wayne G. Lutters. 2009. Wiki anxiety: impediments to implementing wikis for IT support groups. In *Proc. of the 5th ACM Symp. on Computer Human Interaction for the Management of Information Technology* (CHiMiT '09).

[10] Kevin F. White, Wayne G. Lutters, and Anita H. Komlodi. 2008. Towards virtualizing the helpdesk: assessing the relevance of knowledge across distance. In *Proc. of the 2nd ACM Symp. on Computer Human Interaction for Management of Information Technology* (CHiMiT '08).

[11] Min Wu and C. Travis Bowles. 2010. Principles for applying social navigation to collaborative systems. In *Proc. of the 4th ACM Symp. on Computer Human Interaction for the Management of Information Technology* (CHiMiT '10).

CSCL@Work revisited – beyond CSCL and CSCW?
Are There Key Design Principles for Computer Supported
Collaborative Learning at the Workplace?

Sean P. Goggins
Drexel University
College of Information Science &
Technology, USA

outdoors@acm.org

Isa Jahnke
Umeå University
Interactive Media and Learning
Applied Educational Science, Sweden

isa.jahnke@edusci.umu.se

Volker Wulf
University of Siegen
Computer Science
Germany

volker.wulf@uni-siegen.de

ABSTRACT

We propose an interdisciplinary workshop to explore key design principles of collaborative learning in the workplace. The workshop's theme is, simply "CSCL at the workplace". Our first workshop at ACM Group 2010, and the resulting book, raise an important set of issues and potentials for research, but does not solve the thorny and controversial issues. This workshop will be focused on for making progress on the identified issues. The ACM Group conference remains an ideal venue for a workshop on this topic because the North American and European communities who participate in Group include leading members of the international CSCL and CSCW communities. The proposed workshop will be a full day. It will open with a situating presentation by the organizers and, participant questions and proposed solutions aimed at the issues we have raised and begun to recognize, and focus working groups on the resolution of those issues in work to follow the conference. To participate in the workshop, discussants will be asked for a position paper of up to 2 pages in standard ACM format. Our edited book will be made available to participants in advance, and selected authors who will be present will provide overviews of their work and perspective in an interleaved way with the more action oriented working sessions.

Categories and Subject Descriptors

H5.3. [Group and Organization Interfaces] Computer supported cooperative work.

General Terms

Design, Economics, Human Factors, Theory

Keywords

CSCL, CSCW, collaboration, cooperation, workplace learning

1. INTRODUCTION

In 2010, we conducted a first workshop on the topic CSCL@Work. Because of its great success and the effects on the CSCL and CSCW community (Goggins, Jahnke, Wulf, 2012), we propose a follow-up workshop focused on exploring key design principles of computer supported collaborative learning in work

settings. What we already started needs further action to foster a community of interests, to bring together researchers with a natural affinity toward the ACM GROUP conference to share examples of CSCL@Work and subsequently fill a significant gap in the literature, through a journal special issue.

The motivation of the topic can be best described with words by John Seely Brown:

> "In a world of constant change where many of our skills have a half-life measured in a few years and many of our institutions are experiencing creative destruction at a daunting pace, we need to find ways to merge the best insights from formal education, where the goal is to learn what is already known, with those of organizational and workplace learning, where at least one of the main goals is to create new knowledge" (John Seely Brown, 2012).

To build a bridge between learning *what is known* and learning *that creates new knowledge* is of crucial importance for both the computer supported collaborative learning community and the computer supported collaborative work community (dePaula & Fischer, 2005). Such a "culture of participation" (Fischer 2011) is also needed for researchers, consultants and designers of CSCL@Work to foster learning@work concepts.

Learning at the workplace often focuses on learning such as the primary activity. But CSCL@Work also considers the fact that learning means to provide employees with timely access to information for conducting everyday work while respecting business goals; learning in these cases is a secondary activity and work is the primary activity (Mørch & Skaanes, 2010).

We distinguish CSCL@Work from prior research of CSCL, CSCW and knowledge management. Prior work is focused on computer supported collaborative learning, much of it investigating the application of computer support for learning in the context of traditional educational institutions, like public schools, private schools, colleges and tutoring organizations. Exciting new theories of how knowledge is constructed by groups (Stahl, 2006), how teachers contribute to collaborative learning and the application of socio-technical scripts is emerging from workplace studies [Bodker & Christiansen, 2006; Crabtree et al., 2006, Turner et al. 2006].

A number of existing works provide empirical research on collaborative work practices [Davenport, 2005; Lave & Wenger, 1991], the sharing of information at work [Brown & Duguid, 2000], and the development of communities of practice in workplace settings [Wenger, 1998]. Others examine the munificent variation of information and communication technology use in the work place, including studies of informal social networks, formal information distribution and other socio-technical combinations found in work settings [Hinds & Weisband, 2003].

Empirical research on cooperative work practices (Lave & Wenger, 1991; Davenport, 2005), the sharing of information at work (Brown & Duguid, 2000), and the development of communities of practice in workplace settings (Wenger, 1998) show how knowledge can be shared in communities of practice when that knowledge is known inside of an organizational context. But problems related to the distribution of knowledge holders and their knowledge remains unsolved (dePaula & Fischer, 2005). Prior, well-known findings like these rely on the premise that knowledge within an organization's walls can be actively diffused across the organization (Gibson & Cohen, 2003); then proceed to describe various models explaining how that occurs. Those knowledge management approaches are premised on a certain degree of environmental stability inside a company. The notion, that you can "store knowledge", implies it is likely to be useful for some period of time sufficient to justify the effort of capturing it.

The workshop aims to fill a void between existing discourse in CSCW, knowledge management and CSCL, and will open with a short presentation by the organizers, characterizing the emerging application of collaborative learning theories and practices to workplace learning. CSCL and CSCW research each make distinct and important contributions to the construction of collaborative workplace learning, first identified by Billet (2002). From a first workshop in 2010 at ACM Group, we could collect first design principles, such as

- Making Technology-embraced learning at the workplace visible
- Enabling Technology-embraced learning at work across established traditional workplace boundaries
- Fostering collaborative reflection that incorporate feedback and different learning loops from diverse sources of Social Media

Guiding questions for the workshop are:

- Are there any key design principles for CSCL@Work? (see figure 1)
- What are the theoretical and methodological implications of the (empirical) cases presented, and where do they take this emerging research space?

There are significant implications for this approach for both researchers and practitioners. Researchers will need to consider how CSCL@Work is designed for and studied. Practitioners will be compelled to rethink how workplace training is conducted, and how more collaborative learning strategies could contribute to higher performance, faster transfer of technology from research and development to product and changes to other significant output measures.

Our workshop aims to continue want we began in 2010, the process of identifying and describing the different manifestations of collaborative learning at work.

A description of the three patterns of CSCL at work that we have observed is warranted here. First, there is the use of collaborative learning to bring new employees into existing teams. This is distinct from the legitimate peripheral participation observed by Lave & Wenger (1991) and later described by Wenger as communities of practice (Wenger, 1998). In the case of CSCL at work, collaborative learning to bring new employees into a team includes tutoring, layered introduction to information resources of the team, progressive granting of access rights to the tools the team relies on and ultimately the full rights and privileges of a team member. There is a mutual recognition on the part of the new person on the team that this training is a component of doing complex work that spans multiple socio-technical systems. Software developers, engineers and scientists are among those who progress through this type of CSCL at work. Second, we have noticed a pattern of CSCL at work used to accelerate technology transfer from research universities to industrial practice. Organizer Jahnke has observed these phenomena with teams in the field of material science on her current project, Telemetric Online-Learning at Production Engineering. Organizer Goggins has observed these phenomena in computer science and engineering technology transfer. Third, CSCL at work is used as a formal device for sustaining competitive advantage in fast changing, high technology industries. Engineering, research and technology service firms are especially likely to utilize computer-mediated training that goes beyond textbooks, recorded PowerPoint lectures and prepared material. In contrast with traditional workplace learning, focused on task oriented, practice oriented or regulatory compliance objectives, CSCL at work recognizes that the nature of innovation is interwoven to the seam that binds work and learning together. In some respects, this is the tradition of university education: The integration of learning and research. In proposing this workshop, we argue that this intersection is now prevalent at work, and this prevalence should be recognized through research.

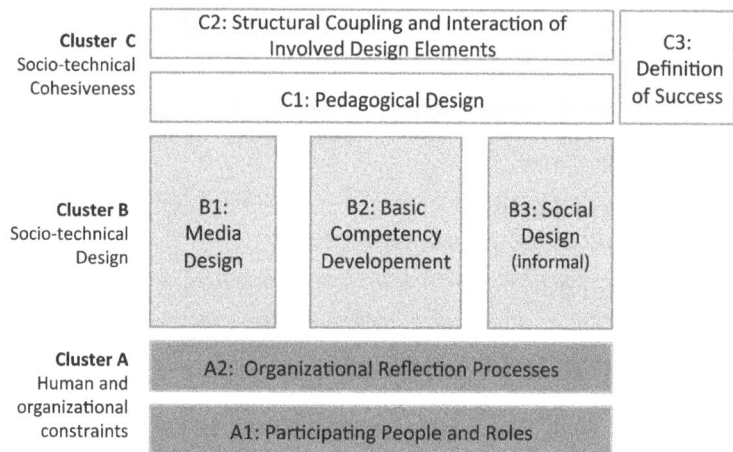

Figure 1. Possible design dimensions (derived from 8 empirical cases)

The line between collaborative work as research and collaborative learning is blurred. Our experience is that this is especially common when researchers, engineers or designers contribute to CSCL efforts aimed at those who apply their inventions.

2. SOCIAL SIGNIFICANCE OF WORKSHOP

Global economic upheaval framed by socially disconnected financial management practices, financial information obfuscation, volatile commodity prices, and an increasing need for energy define the grand social setting for this workshop. It is a time of unique peril and opportunity that will draw upon diverse research communities for solutions. In this context, learning is no longer an activity that is separate from work. Learning at work is also about more than acquiring new information to perform a task, but about developing new knowledge to help a firm, an organization or a government improve its services in socially measurable as well as economically measurable ways.

3. GOALS OF THE WORKSHOP

Three goals motivate the proposal for this workshop:

1) To identify and discuss key design principles (social, technical, sociotechnical, didactical/pedagogical design) of CSCL@Work, presented by the organizers and discussants.

2) To identify theoretical and methodological commonalities and contrasts across the represented disciplines relative to CSCL@Work.

3) To continue with cultivating a community who share an interest in exploring collaborative learning in the workplace.

4. WORKSHOP AGENDA & PROCESS

The workshop will commence with a brief introduction by the organizers. The remainder of the agenda follows a trajectory of *idea generation* and *integration* protocols; *input by different experts (I)* and *working sessions (WS)*:

Table 1: Workshop Agenda

Duration	Topic
15 mins	**Opening at 9:00am;** Presentation by Organizers to frame the purpose of the day, goals of the workshop and our hopes for research into CSCL at Work
30 mins	(WS1) Issues and Questions to Raise During the Day (Related to CSCL@Work) *[Just Collection, Method: Postcards-Symbols]* *possible clusters:* • Theoretical approaches (what exists, what is needed) • Methodology (data collection techniques, design techniques) • Research design (what kind of experiments, what kind of field studies, etc.) • Technologies (groupware, CSCL tools, social media, E-learning, etc.) • Contexts for the studies (what kind of workplaces are we talking about etc.) • Other important cross cutting themes for CSCL@ Work
30 mins	(I1) John Seely Brown – Workshop keynote *(said "strongly possible")*
30 mins	(WS2) How would you modify or add to your "postcard" based on the talk? *(Brainstorming, Collecting and Clustering Method: Metaplan-CardsRequest)*

	Coffee Break (10:45-11:00am)
15 mins	(I2) Gerhard Fischer A conceptual framework – revisited (confirmed)
15 mins	(I3) Gerry Stahl: Theories of Collaborative Cognition: Foundations for CSCL and CSCW together (confirmed)
15 mins	(I4) Anders Mørch: eLearning at Work (confirmed)
30 mins	(WS3) What can we learn from the talks? How would you modify or add to your "postcard" based on the talk? *(Collecting and Clustering; Method: Metaplan-CardsRequest)*
	Lunch (12:15-1:30pm)
15 mins	(I5) Rob Procter: Technologies of Participation (confirmed)
15 mins	(I6) Markus Rohde & Volker Wulf: CSCL@Networking - Regional Learning in Software Industries (*said "maybe"*), or/and (I6) Thomas Herrmann & team: Collaborative reflections (*said "maybe"*)
30 mins	(WS4) Sssessment of the the collected issues to bundle and confirm clusters *(Method: Metaplan-PointsRequest)*
	Coffee break (2:30-2:45pm)
90 mins	(WS5) Focused small group interactions addressing a set of themes identified on the index cards, e.g.: • Theoretical approaches (what exists, what is needed) • Methodology (data collection techniques, design techniques) & Research design (what kind of experiments, what kind of field studies, etc.) • Technologies (groupware, CSCL tools, social media, E-learning, etc.) • Contexts for the studies (what kind of workplaces are we talking about etc.) & Other important cross cutting themes for CSCL@ Work *(Method: 3-4 tables WorldCoffeeTables, groups circulate)*
	Coffee break (4:00-4:15pm)
60 mins	Presentation of Summaries by Small Groups to the larger group
30 mins	Organization and Discussion of Next Steps (e.g., publication, community cultivation)
End	5:45pm

At this workshop we already have 8 experts who agreed their coming (see below "program committee"). In addition, the workshop will be announced through a call for workshop participation where the possible participants need to show their motivations, why they want to attend. We plan for not more than 20 people.

The workshop will create an own workshop website called www.csclatwork.org and create a call for workshop participation. The program committee will decide.

5. PROGRAM COMMITTEE

Members who agree to attend the workshop:

John S. Brown (said "*strongly possible*")

Thomas Herrmann, Germany (confirmed)

Gerhard Fischer, USA (confirmed)

Sean Goggins, USA (confirmed)

Isa Jahnke, Sweden (confirmed)

Anders Mørch, Norway (confirmed)

Gerry Stahl, USA (confirmed)

Rob Procter, UK (confirmed)

Wolfgang Prinz (*said "maybe"*)

Stephanie Teasley (*???*)

Volker Wulf, Germany (confirmed)

6. REFERENCES

[1] Billett, S. (2002). Critiquing workplace learning discourses: participation and continuity at work. *Studies in the Education of Adults*, *34*(1), 56-67. Retrieved from http://www.ingentaconnect.com/content/niace/stea/2002/00 000034/00000001/art00005

[1] Bødker, S. and Christiansen, E. (2006). Computer Support for Social Awareness in Flexible Work. Computer Supported Cooperative Work. 15, 1-28.

[2] Brown, J. S. and Duguid, P. (2000). The Social Life of Information. Harvard Business School Press.

[3] Crabtree, A., O'Neill, J., Tolmie, P., Colmbino, T., and Grasso, A. (2006). The Practical Indispensability of Articulation Work to Immediate and Remote Help Giving. CSCW 2006. 219-228.

[4] dePaula, R., & Fischer, G. (2005). Knowledge Management: Why Learning from the Past is not Enough! In J. Davis, E. Subrahmanian, & A. Westerberg (Eds.), Knowledge Management: Organizational and Technological Dimensions, Physica Verlag, Heidelberg, pp. 21-54. Davenport, T. H. 2005 Thinking for a Living. Harvard Business School Press Boston.

[5] Fischer, G. (2011). Understanding, fostering, and supporting cultures of participation. ACM Interactions.

[6] Goggins, S., Jahnke, I., & Wulf, V. (2012). CSCL@Work. New York: Springer (in preparation)

[7] Hinds, P. and Weisband, S. (2003). Knoweldge Sharing and Shared Understanding in Virtual Teams. Creating Conditions for Effective Virtual Teams.

[8] Lave, J. and Wegner, E. (1991). Situated Learning: Legitimate Peripheral Participation. Cambridge University Press.

[9] Mørch, A.I. & Skaanes, M.A. (2010). Design and Use of an Integrated Work and Learning System: Information Seeking as Critical Function. In Ludvigsen, S. Lund, A., Rasmussen, I. and Säljö, R. (eds.). Learning Across Sites: New Tools, Infrastructures and Practices. London, UK: Routledge, pp. 138-155

[10] Stahl, G. (2006). Group Cognition: Computer Support for Building Collaborative Knowledge. MIT Press.

[11] Turner, W., Bowker, G. C., Gasser, L., and Zacklad, M. (2006). Information Infrastructures for Distributed Collective Practices. Computer Supported Cooperative Work. 15, 93-110.

[12] Wenger, E. (1998). Communities of Practice: Learning, Meaning and Identity. Cambridge University Press.

Moving Beyond Talking Heads to Shared Experiences: The Future of Personal Video Communication

Carman Neustaedter & Erick Oduor
Simon Fraser University
102 – 13450 102nd Avenue
Surrey, BC, Canada

[cneustae, eoduor]@sfu.ca

Gina Venolia
Microsoft Research
1 Microsoft Way
Redmond, WA, USA

ginav@microsoft.com

Tejinder K. Judge
Google Inc.
1600 Amphitheater Parkway
Mountain View, CA, USA

tkjudge@google.com

ABSTRACT

This workshop explores the future of personal video communications where systems and designs move beyond supporting conversations to a new design paradigm consisting of shared activities and experiences between distance-separated family and friends.

Categories and Subject Descriptors

H.5.3 [**Information interfaces and presentation**]: Group and Organization Interfaces - Computer Supported Cooperative Work;

General Terms

Design, Human Factors

Keywords

Families; video communication; video chat; shared experiences

1. INTRODUCTION

The use of video communication systems has rapidly proliferated over the last several years for personal and family communication given the availability of free video chat software such as Skype or Google Chat [1][5][8]. With this has come a design paradigm for video communication dominated by "talking heads." By this we mean that the common usage of video chat systems is often thought of as two people talking where each sees the other's face and not much more. Yet video chat systems of the future are likely to be much more than this where they begin to connect people in new and interesting ways to support the sharing of everyday experiences. Imagine, for example, video systems that allow family and close friends to participate in holiday meals, attend significant events (weddings, births, memorials), cook together, watch a movie together, etc. These experiences may involve more than two people and many different kinds of devices, including mobile devices that move along with activities on the go. The future is ripe for exploration.

Research has begun to explore such opportunities. Studies of existing video chat systems like Skype have shown that family members often share or view activities rather than just converse while they are connected [1][5][8]. For example, grandparents might watch their grandchildren play over Skype [1][5]. Long-

distance partners have even been found to leave video chat systems going over extended periods of time to create a shared sense of intimacy [12].

New video communication systems have also been designed to directly support the sharing of everyday activities. For example, the Family Window [6] and Family Portals [7] are media spaces designed for the home where always-on video (displayed in a digital frame) connects two or more households. Family members can see each other and even participate in shared activities over distance such as meals, get-togethers, and children's activities [6][7]. A mobile family media space called Peek-A-Boo extends this experience to mobile devices [13]. Similar in nature, the Share Table is a media space that allows children in divorced families to interact and play games with their remote parents [16].

Nokia Research has designed a number of video-based prototypes that extend the ways in which grandparents and grandchildren can connect and share reading activities over distance. For example, Family Story Play is a physical book with an embedded video chat display for distance-reading [14]. Story Visit extends this experience to the web to again support connected reading [15]. People In Books places the video feeds of children and remote grandparents within a storybook to create an additional level of immersion [2].

Microsoft Research has also explored new paradigms for video-based communications focused on connecting children for rich, social play. Video PlayDate allowed children to participate in free play over distance using a variety of display options (e.g., large displays, table displays, laptops) [17]. Building on this idea, PixIO allows children to share physical and digital objects on any surface over distance [3]. This allows them to engage in additional play activities, now involving toys and other items. VideoPlay moves beyond playing to allow children to asynchronously share video messages with their friends [4].

These systems are certainly only the beginning. Moreover, they represent only part of the continued efforts that researchers and designers are taking to explore new paradigms for personal video communications that go beyond talking heads. We plan to discuss these explorations and more as a part of this workshop.

2. OBJECTIVE

The objective of this workshop is to bring together researchers, designers, and practitioners who are studying or designing personal video communications technologies. We want to explore the future of such technologies as they move beyond the current design paradigm of "talking heads." We want to build community around this topical area, brainstorm what the next generation of video communication tools might look like and encompass, and understand the value in moving the field to video communication systems that allow people to share everyday experiences over distance. We also expect the workshop to lead to an article for Interactions magazine or Communications of the ACM, or, potentially, a special journal issue.

This workshop is also meant to build on past workshops organized by one or more of the members of the current organizational team. Past workshops included a "Designing for Families" workshop at CSCW 2008 [9], a Special Interest Group workshop at CHI 2009 [10], and a workshop at GROUP 2010 on "Connecting Families" [11].

3. INTENDED PARTICIPANTS

Intended workshop participants include academics, industrial researchers, designers, software developers and other practitioners who actively work in the area of video-mediated communication in the domestic realm. Suggested topics within this space include, but are not limited to:

- connecting grandparents and grandchildren
- supporting long distance relationships
- connecting traveling parents with their family
- virtually hanging out with friends
- infrastructure and technological issues with video communication
- mobile-based video communication
- various cultural uses of video communication systems

We see this workshop as an opportunity to develop the research community on personal video communications across academic and industrial players. We also seek participation by representatives from the major industrial players in this space beyond the workshop organizers. This includes additional representatives from Cisco, Apple, Nokia, Microsoft, Google, etc.

4. WORKSHOP DESCRIPTION

Workshop participants will be selected based on refereed submissions. We will solicit two to four page position papers (CHI archival format) and expect to accept 15-20 participants. Authors will be asked to direct their paper at describing their area of research as it relates to video-mediated communication along with the future direction they see research in this space taking. We also ask that authors include short biographies for each of the position paper's authors. We expect that only one author for each paper will participate in the workshop, though we may be able to accommodate a small number of special requests for multiple authors to attend.

The workshop will be a full day with the following tentative workshop schedule:

1. Introduction: Workshop organizers will introduce themselves and present the workshop goals and schedules to attendees.

2. Early Morning Session: Attendees will participate in a "speed dating"-like activity where they will pair up with other workshop participants to describe their research. After approximately two to three minutes, participants will rotate to a new workshop participant and describe their research again. Once complete, participants will have briefly met with and discussed their research with the majority of attendees.

2. Late Morning Session: Attendees will break into pairs and participate in an ideation activity to explore the future of personal video communications. The exact details of this activity will be planned closer to the workshop; however, the following details provide a sample of such an activity:

First, pairs of participants will have approximately 15 minutes to decide on a series of short questions that they would like to ask people about the future of video communications. These will focus on exploring what "beyond talking heads" might mean for "everyday people." Second, they will leave the workshop venue and go through either the resort or local community where they will solicit feedback to their questions. After a designated time duration, participants will return to the workshop venue.

3. Lunch: Attendees will join the group for a common lunch such that they can informally socialize with other workshop participants about their research.

4. Early Afternoon Session: Attendees will break into subgroups and discuss the responses that they received from their ideation activity in the morning session. This will be used to generate discussion points for the final session.

5. Late Afternoon Session: Attendees will come together and the organizers will lead a discussion around the themes that were identified in the preceding discussions. They will also discuss possibilities for follow-on work and collaborations.

5. ORGANIZER BIOGRAPHIES

Carman Neustaedter is an Assistant Professor in the School of Interactive Arts + Technology at Simon Fraser University, Canada. His research is in design, human-computer interaction, and domestic computing. Here he focuses on the design and use of technologies for connecting people who are separated by distance or time. This includes design for promoting family connectedness, support for workplace collaboration, and bringing people together through pervasive games. A large portion of his research over the last several years has focused on video-based communication for families. To learn more about his research group, the Connections Lab, visit http://clab.iat.sfu.ca

Erick Oduor is a PhD student in the School of Interactive Arts + Technology at Simon Fraser University, Canada. He is investigating the idea of using technology in rural developing country settings such as Kenya that are faced with limited technological infrastructure. However, mobile phone usage in Kenyan communities is widespread and provides an avenue for families that are located in the village with an opportunity to connect with remotely located relatives who live in large cities away from the village. Erick is interested in the design and integration of video applications with mobile phones to support the design of a village media space.

Gina Venolia is a senior researcher with Microsoft Research in the neXus group. Her research focuses on understanding how knowledge flows among people and building systems to make it flow more freely. Her current projects focus on real-time and asynchronous video communication.

Tejinder Judge is a User Experience Researcher at Google. Her research focuses on understanding communication needs and practices in social contexts such as family gatherings. She also designs social technologies based on these communication needs and practices. She currently conducts research on Google+. She received her PhD at Virginia Tech where her dissertation focused on the design and evaluation of domestic media spaces for connecting families across distance.

6. REFERENCES

[1] Ames, M.G., Go, J., Kaye, J.J. and Spasojevic, M., Making love in the network closet: the benefits and work of family videochat. *Proc. CSCW*, ACM (2010).

[2] Follmer, S., Ballagas, R., Raffle, H., & Ishii, H. People in Books: Using a FlashCam to Become Part of an Interactive Book for Connected Reading, *Proc. CSCW,* ACM Press (2012).

[3] Inkpen, K. Kids & Video: Playing with Friends at a Distance, *in Connecting Families: The Impact of New Communication Technologies on Domestic Life, Neustaedter, C., Harrison, S., and Sellen, A. (eds.),* Springer (2012).

[4] Inkpen, K., Du, H., Hoff, A., Johns, P. and Roseway, A. Video Kids: Augmenting close friendships with asynchronous video conversations in VideoPal, *Proc. CHI,* ACM Press (2012).

[5] Judge, T.K. and Neustaedter, C., Sharing Conversation and Sharing Life: Video Conferencing in the Home. *Proc. CHI,* ACM Press (2010), 655-658.

[6] Judge, T.K., Neustaedter, C. and Kurtz, A., The Family Window: The Design and Evaluation of a Domestic Media Space. *Proc. CHI,* ACM Press (2010).

[7] Judge, T.K., Neustaedter, C., Harrison, S., and Blose, A. Family Portals: Connecting Families Through a Multifamily Media Space, *Proc. CHI,* ACM Press (2011).

[8] Kirk, D.S., Sellen, A. and Cao, X., Home video communication: mediating 'closeness'. *Proc. CSCW,* ACM Press (2010).

[9] Neustaedter, C., Brush, A.J., and McDonald, D., Designing for Families, *Extended Proc. CSCW,* ACM Press (2008).

[10] Neustaedter, C., Yarosh, S., and Brush, A.J., Designing for Families, *Extended Proc. CHI,* ACM Press (2009).

[11] Neustaedter, C., Judge, T., Harrison, S., Sellen, A., and Cao, X., Connecting Families: New Technologies, Family Communication, and the Impact on Domestic Spaces, *Workshop in the Proceedings of the ACM Group Conference* (GROUP), ACM Press (2010).

[12] Neustaedter, C. and Greenberg, S. Intimacy in Long-Distance Relationships over Video Chat, *Proc. CHI,* ACM Press (2012).

[13] Neustaedter, C., and Judge, T.K. Peek-A-Boo: The Design of a Mobile Family Media Space, *Video Proceedings of the International Conference on Ubiquitous Computing* (Ubicomp), Springer (2010).

[14] Raffle, H., Ballagas, R., Revelle, G., Horii, H., Follmer, S., Go, J., Reardon, E., Mori, K., Kaye, J. and Spasojevic, M., Family story play: reading with young children (and Elmo) over a distance. *Proc. CHI,* ACM Press (2010).

[15] Raffle, H., Revelle, G., Mori, K., Ballagas, R., Buza, K., Horii, H., Kaye, J.J., Cook, K., Freed, N., Go, J., & Spasojevic, M. Hello, is grandma there? let's read! StoryVisit: family video chat and connected e-books, *Proc. CHI,* ACM Press (2011).

[16] Yarosh, S., Cuzzort, S., Mueller, H. and Abowd, G.D., Developing a media space for remote synchronous parent-child interaction. *Proc. IDC,* ACM Press (2009).

[17] Yarosh, S., Inkpen, K.M. and Brush A.J. Video Playdate: Toward free play across distance, *Proc. CHI,* ACM Press (2010).

Author Index

www.ingramcontent.com/pod-product-compliance
Lightning Source LLC
Chambersburg PA
CBHW080916220326
41598CB00034B/5592